Updated Second Edition

THE DISNEYLAND® ENCYCLOPEDIA

THE **UN**OFFICIAL, AUTHORIZED, AND PRECEDENTED HISTORY OF EVERY LAND, ATTRACTION, RESTAURANT, SHOP, AND MAJOR EVENT IN THE ORIGINAL MAGIC KINGDOM®

SANTA MONICA PRESS

Published by: Santa Monica Press LLC

P.O. Box 850
Solana Beach, CA 92075
1-800-784-9553
www.santamonicapress.com
books@santamonicapress.com

Printed in the United States

Santa Monica Press books are available at special quantity discounts when purchased in bulk by corporations, organizations, or groups. Please call our Special Sales department at 1-800-784-9553.

ISBN-13 978-1-59580-068-8

Library of Congress Cataloging-in-Publication Data

Strodder, Chris
  The Disneyland encyclopedia : the unofficial, unauthorized, and unprecedented history of every land, attraction, restaurant, shop and major event in the original magic kingdom / by Chris Strodder ; illustrations by Tristan Tang. — 2nd ed.
     p. cm.
  Includes index.
  ISBN 978-1-59580-068-8
  1. Disneyland (Calif.)—Encyclopedias. I. Title.
  GV1853.3.C2S87 2012
  791.06'879496—dc23
                                    2011049064

Cover and interior design and production by Future Studio

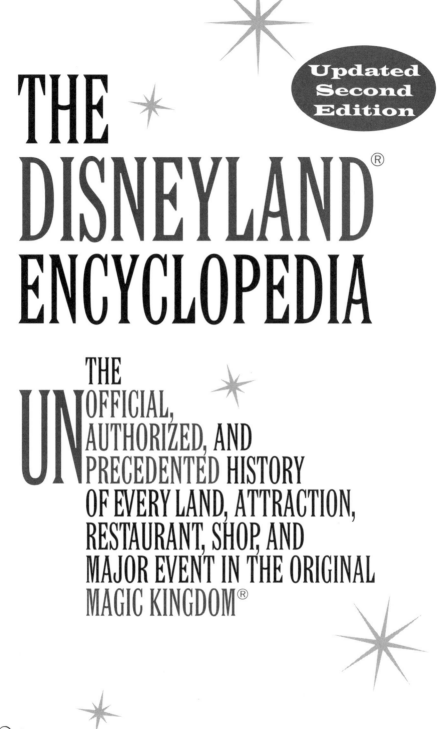

Updated Second Edition

THE DISNEYLAND® ENCYCLOPEDIA

UN THE OFFICIAL, AUTHORIZED, AND PRECEDENTED HISTORY OF EVERY LAND, ATTRACTION, RESTAURANT, SHOP, AND MAJOR EVENT IN THE ORIGINAL MAGIC KINGDOM®

SANTA
MONICA
PRESS

CHRIS STRODDER
ILLUSTRATED MAPS BY TRISTAN TANG

Contents

Introduction
to the Second Edition

"It seems to me that we have a lot of story yet to tell."
—Walt Disney

If you like receiving e-mail, write a book about Disneyland and put your contact information inside. That's what I did with the 2008 edition of this encyclopedia. The many nice comments and polite questions I received proved what Walt Disney announced at Disneyland when it opened on July 17, 1955: "Disneyland is your land."

These words are still displayed at the Town Square flagpole, and guests really take the sentiment to heart. And why shouldn't they? All Disneyland visitors are made to feel special, like the park was made just for them. They aren't merely observers, riders, or customers—they're invited guests who are being celebrated. Consequently, guests are not afraid to express their convictions about what makes *their* park great, or what currently disappoints them, or what they miss.

One common theme: "Don't the prices seem outrageous?" Pecuniary questions are as old as Disneyland itself. *MAD* magazine's December 1956 issue included a parody called "Walt Dizzy Presents Dizzyland" that reduced the *Disneyland* TV series (and the park's "Frontrearland," "Fantasticland," etc.) to a single theme: "Moneyland." Disneyland's high prices are tough to justify. According to the national average wage index used to calculate Social Security, from 1955 to 2010 the average American salary increased by a factor of 12.6 (from $3,300 a year to $41,700 a year). During those same 55 years, Disneyland's single adult admission charge increased by a factor of 76 (from $1 to $76, which rose to $80 in 2011).

Outrageous, yes; prohibitive, no. Much of the admission price does go back to improving the park. Besides, there's no place quite like Disneyland ("There will only be one Disneyland," Walt Disney said*), and millions of people (disgruntled as they may be) continue to pony up the admission fee every year—me included, for the past 40 years.

I first began taking informal Disneyland notes as a kid in the '60s, collecting everything I could find about the park. Like most impressionable kids making their first pilgrimage to a park on the scale of the Magic Kingdom, I was overcome with sensations on my first visit. There was simply too much to comprehend, too many sights and sounds to take in. Dazzled and dizzy, I came away with a swirl of over-lapping memories, a T-shirt splattered like a Jackson Pollock painting, and my first Disneyland souvenir book. As soon as we got home I read everything I could find about the park in our Northern California libraries, and I began to keep my eyes peeled for all the Disneyland-related TV specials I could tune in to on our old rabbit-eared black-and-white TV. I was just a kid, but my encyclopedia research had already begun, though I didn't know it at the time.

As a UCLA student and Los Angeles resident thereafter, I made many more visits to

---

*Bob Thomas, *Walt Disney: An American Original* (Disney Editions, 1994).

Disneyland, acquired many more maps, books, and souvenirs, and tried to keep track of detailed changes in the park. That last part was a daunting, perhaps impossible task. Not only was the park huge, it was also a moving target. Ambitiously evolving and growing, Disneyland seemed to be constantly turning its present into the past: restaurants would come and go, stores would jump from one side of Main Street to the other, new attractions would appear, and old attractions would get subtle refinements. Many of the books I read included promotional photos of the big changes, but none of them tracked the smaller tweaks or showed precise locations of everything in the park. I wanted more.

So, in the 1990s and 2000s I began doing serious research on the park's history. As I generated lists and text, I organized my material as alphabetical encyclopedia entries—unlike all the other books on Disneyland, which are typically arranged chronologically or geographically. I then made countless more park visits to photograph/measure/pace off/time with a stopwatch/etc. The result is not a travel guide with information about local motels, but a scholarly history book crafted from decades of research and firsthand experience.

Happily, Disneyland doesn't ignore its past—the park embraces it. From major art exhibits to minor architectural details, history is everywhere at Disneyland if you know what to look for. Not only is the search for understanding at Disneyland fun, it's also rewarding. As Hemingway wrote about Paris in *A Moveable Feast*, Disneyland "was always worth it and you received return for whatever you brought to it." Like Paris, the more erudition you bring to Disneyland, the more you'll get out of it.

As for what's ahead in these pages, you'll see that my point isn't to glorify Walt Disney and his Disneyland. While much of the text praises the park, it also identifies lots of miscues and mishaps and mistakes. Nor is the point merely to list historical dates and facts; dates and facts may be knowledge, but they aren't wisdom. Instead, I've tried to explain how each element of the park's history—every land, store, restaurant, attraction, and special event—is unique, how it's meaningful, and why it was created the way it was. These backstories, I think you'll see, are often just as fascinating as the attractions, stores, and restaurants themselves.

I've also included a couple dozen profiles of the park's prime movers. Some of the names are famous, some not so much, but all made mighty contributions to the overall Disneyland experience. Many were Imagineers, a hybridized term that merges imagination with engineering to describe those artists, architects, and designers who work creatively on the park and its attractions. Almost every one is a "Disney Legend," a title the Walt Disney Company has been using since 1987 to recognize key contributors to the Disney legacy. From the company's long list of movie stars, animators, songwriters, engineers, executives, and other honorees, I've selected those who

did significant work at Disneyland, either behind or before the scenes. For extended profiles of all the Disney Legends, visit http://legends.disney.go.com/legends/index.

Most of the photos in this book are brand new. As with the 2008 edition, I took all of the 350 or so photos during regular park hours and with no special access or photographic privileges. The marvelous maps are the work of Tristan Tang, who created the maps for the 2008 edition. That's also her 1959-style Monorail that loops across the front cover. I'm still thanking my lucky stars that she so generously agreed to enhance this book with her remarkable talents. I can't imagine a better collaborator.

Finally, I should mention that while I'm obviously a Disneyland fan, I've never been a Disneyland employee. As with every book I've written, this encyclopedia was completed while I held down a separate full-time job. In no way was that job, or any job I've ever had, related to the Walt Disney Company. I always paid my own way into Disneyland, and I did my own research. No foundation grants, no research assistants, no ghostwriters. I do remain indebted to the reference librarians who scoured libraries across the country to find the obscure, often out-of-print books and old photographs that I constantly requested. I'm also grateful to publisher Jeffrey Goldman at Santa Monica Press for his faith in my ideas and his team's ability to execute them beautifully.

While researching and writing this book, I sometimes felt as dazzled and dizzy as I did when I first walked down Main Street lo those many years ago. There's still so much to see, so much to do, and so much to know that taking all of Disneyland in and capturing it all on paper sometimes seemed impossible. But, as Walt Disney once said, "It's kind of fun to do the impossible." He was right.

Chris Strodder
Mill Valley, CA

Through the Turnstiles

"A land of dreams so various, so beautiful, so new."
—**Matthew Arnold,** *Dover Beach*, 1867

Here at the beginning, just as you're about to pass through this book's metaphorical turnstiles, I thought I'd try to explain why so many people have passed through the park's actual turnstiles.

When I say Disneyland is popular, I don't just mean it's a nice destination many people have enjoyed over the years. Over a half-*billion* people have stepped into Disneyland's entrance tunnels since 1955. Many of them have done so repeatedly, despite famously high prices and potentially long lines. No other entertainment or sports venue in the world has played to 30,000–40,000 paying customers virtually every day of the year for half a century. Except for a couple of sudden closures, that's over 20,000 consecutive days of attendance approaching a full Fenway Park in Boston (on some days, Disneyland attendance has soared to above 80,000). Sure, sports stadiums and concert halls can draw 30,000–40,000 people or more pretty regularly, but none have done it daily, rain or shine, for five straight decades.

Furthermore, while Walt Disney never courted scholars and intellectuals, many of them have recognized Disneyland for the unique creation it is. Kevin Starr, "California's premier historian," according to the *New Yorker* magazine, has called Disneyland

"one of the great wonders of the Modern World." Author Christopher Finch has described the park as "the Versailles of the 20th century" and "the ultimate American pleasure ground, a kind of permanent Fourth of July celebration."

Even people who aren't fans of Disneyland have to concede how important the park has been to American culture. Imagine if Walt Disney had never built his original Magic Kingdom. The scenarios unfold like George Bailey's tangled connections in *It's a Wonderful Life*. The city of Anaheim, deprived of its biggest employer and most famous landmark, probably would've grown up as an undistinguished bedroom community instead of one the state's 10 biggest cities complete with a busy convention center, a modern sports stadium, and sports teams including the Angels, the Mighty Ducks, and (formerly) the Rams.

Pre-Disneyland, Anaheim's population was around 14,000, with fewer than 100 motel and hotel rooms in the whole city. In 2011, Anaheim had 300,000 residents and over 20,000 motel and hotel rooms (the Disneyland Resort hotels alone had over 2,200). Minus its top tourist draw, Orange County may not have built its new commercial airport in the mid-'60s. Without the Disneyland formula of cleanliness, service, innovation, and family-oriented fun to draw upon, the country's scattered independent amusement parks may have continued to languish with total combined revenues in the millions, instead of flourishing into the corporate-run industry that was generating revenues in the billions just 15 years after Disneyland opened. Without Disneyland to learn from, Walt Disney himself wouldn't have considered launching the immense Walt Disney World in Florida, and today there wouldn't be Disney parks scattered across the planet. No *Pirates of the Caribbean* movies selling over a billion dollars in tickets, since those movies were based on a Disneyland attraction. No Grad Nite memories for millions of high schoolers, no submarine experience of any kind for most people, and no maddeningly catchy "It's a Small World" theme song for the collective unconscious.

So why is the park so popular?

Singularity is one enormous reason. Disneyland really is unique. It's the only Disney park that opened during Walt Disney's lifetime, and the only one he himself visited. Today, the Disneyland name is unquestionably one of the most recognized in the world, and it's become common shorthand whenever someone is describing a place that's wonderful.

That singularity was even more conspicuous in Disneyland's first few decades, back before the proliferation of Universal Studios, Six Flags, and other Disney parks. Pre-Disneyland, amusement parks were often tacky, dirty, seedy places jammed with cheap rides and random games. When an old park even had a "theme," it was either on a small scale (various Santa's Village-type parks, for instance) or it was incompletely and inconsistently developed. Disneyland's special harmony, encompassing its landscaping and architecture and music and signage and costumes, was magnificently unusual for the industry, and magnificently appealing to the public.

For a long time, the things Disneyland offered really couldn't be found elsewhere. To name just one example, Disneyland has routinely offered transportation systems unavailable to most people once they are outside the property. Roller coasters and little cars and carousels can be found all over the country, but not

Disneyland's submarines and monorails and PeopleMovers. Even a simple amble down the park's Main Street, U.S.A. is special—thousands of towns still have Main Streets, but pedestrians have rarely been able to walk slowly down the middle of them (at least during the day), and they've never been able to count on a stupendous parade showing up every single afternoon.

A sense of intimacy accounts for much of the park's charm. Compared to some other theme parks that sprawl over mammoth geographies and soar to towering heights, Disneyland is relatively compact, making it more manageable, more "embraceable." The brilliant wagon wheel design of Disneyland's Hub puts paths to all the lands, where vastly different experiences and moods await, just a few paces from

60 Disneyland Debuts

1955	July 17:	Opening Day for special guests and a TV audience, one day before the public is admitted
	July 18:	Circarama theater
	July 22:	Rocket to the Moon
	July 31:	Casey Jr. Circus Train
	August 16:	Dumbo the Flying Elephant
	August 29:	Pirate Ship Restaurant
	October 11:	A-B-C ticket books
1956	March 24:	Astro-Jets
	June 16:	Tom Sawyer Island; Storybook Land Canal Boats
	June 23:	Skyway to Fantasyland/Tomorrowland
	July 2:	Mine Train
	July 4:	Indian War Canoes
1957	April 29:	Sleeping Beauty Castle Walk-Through
	June 12:	House of the Future
1958	June 14:	Alice in Wonderland; Sailing Ship *Columbia*
	December 31:	New Year's Eve Party
1959	June 14:	Matterhorn Bobsleds; Monorail; Submarine Voyage
1960	May 28:	Nature's Wonderland
1961	June 15:	Grad Nite
	August 6:	Flying Saucers
1962	November 18:	Swiss Family Treehouse
1963	June 23:	Enchanted Tiki Room
1965	July 18:	Great Moments with Mr. Lincoln
1966	May 28:	It's a Small World
	July 24:	New Orleans Square
1967	March 18:	Pirates of the Caribbean; Blue Bayou

each other. Guests in the 1960s could go from tree house to plastic house in only 10 minutes; in any decade, an exotic jungle, a space rocket, and a storybook village have always been just a serendipitous stroll away. Walt Disney's shrewd hub-and-spoke layout has been copied and expanded in other parks and civic centers, but the Disneyland design is still definitive.

Every land in Disneyland adds a different dimension to the park's overall appeal. I'm not the first writer to identify Main Street, Frontierland, and Critter Country (formerly Bear Country) as expressions of Walt Disney's nostalgia—and everybody's nostalgia, really—for simpler times. "I love the nostalgic, myself," Disney once said. "I hope we never lose some of the things of the past."

	July 2:	PeopleMover; Carousel of Progress; Tomorrowland Terrace; Rocket Jets
	August 5:	Adventure Thru Inner Space
1969	August 9:	The Haunted Mansion
1972	March 24:	Bear Country
	June 17:	Main Street Electrical Parade
1977	May 4:	Space Mountain
1979	September 2:	Big Thunder Mountain Railroad
1983	May 25:	Remodeled Fantasyland
1986	September 18:	*Captain EO*
1987	January 9:	Star Tours
	July 11:	Disney Gallery
1989	July 17:	Splash Mountain
1992	May 13:	Fantasmic!
1993	January 24:	Mickey's Toontown
1994	January 26:	Roger Rabbit's Car Toon Spin
1995	March 3:	Indiana Jones Adventure
1998	May 22:	Rocket Rods; Astro-Orbitor; *Honey, I Shrunk the Audience*
1999	June 19:	Tarzan's Treehouse
	November 19:	FASTPASS tickets
2003	April 11:	The Many Adventures of Winnie the Pooh
2005	March 17:	Buzz Lightyear Astro Blasters
2006	September 29:	Halloween Time
2007	June 11:	Finding Nemo Submarine Voyage
2011	June 3:	Star Tours: The Adventures Continue

Disney's affection for a calmer era was especially poignant during the early 1950s, when the park was being planned and built. This was a disturbing time, encumbered with new apprehensions. The years preceding Disneyland's opening were marked by such enigmatic topics as the 1950–53 Korean conflict, McCarthyism and the Red Scare, the Cold War, an assassination attempt on President Truman, a recession, the accelerated production of hydrogen bombs, and escalating distress over UFOs, organized crime, juvenile delinquency, and rock 'n' roll. It was an age of anxiety; by 1957, one third of all prescriptions in America were being written for the tranquilizer Miltown.

Other areas of the park bring their own positive themes to the overall experience. Fantasyland celebrates childhood stories and dreams; high-tech Tomorrowland hums with exuberant optimism for the future; Adventureland finds its fun in the exotic; and Mickey's Toontown is a punster's paradise. Beloved Disney movies and TV shows come to life nearly everywhere you look, and the beauty of nature either saturates or punctuates every corner of the park. It's a cliché to say it, but there's truly something for everyone within the park's perimeter.

Once visitors enter that perimeter, they often feel like they've stepped into some timeless, trouble-free realm. Surrounded by its protective berm, Disneyland sometimes seems like an enchanted island in an urban sea. This sense of separation from real life and its mundane problems and ineffable threats probably contributes as much to Disneyland's ongoing popularity as any other factor. For many people, to be in Disneyland is to be free—free to play, to explore, to imagine, to remember, to forget. In letters written in 1922, D. H. Lawrence expressed something similar about another such isolated realm: "Australia is like an open door with the blue beyond.

You just walk out of the world and into Australia." So, too, in busy Anaheim: visitors walk out of the world, pass through Disneyland's turnstiles, and enter a blue beyond of boundless imagination. There they find what Lawrence did Down Under: "The great weight of the spirit that lies so heavily . . . doesn't exist here. You feel a little like a child that has no real cares."

Every visitor can probably add his or her own additional explanation for Disneyland's popularity. Its cleanliness. Its friendly employees. Its joyful family spirit. Its safe, efficient fusion of celebration, patriotism, optimism, and education with visceral thrills and entertainment. The way it successfully "hides the wires" to sustain its enthralling illusions (at Disneyland, *not* seeing is believing). The countless surprises of its endless evolution. And more—always more—because there are as many reasons for the park's success as there are people giddily walking through it wearing mouse ears. Since 1955, over 500 million have come, not just to a park, but to a kingdom. And they found there, not mere amusements, but magic.

In ways personal and profound, Disneyland dreams can and do come true. And why wouldn't they? As Walt Disney confidently and correctly declared on the 10th anniversary episode of his TV show: "Anything is possible in Disneyland."

Notes on the Text

Some things to understand about this book before you begin:

First off, know that this book focuses exclusively on Disneyland in Anaheim. Occasional references are made to Disney California Adventure (also in Anaheim), Walt Disney World in Florida, and Disney parks outside the U.S., but this book does not attempt to explicate anything in those other locations.

Regarding this encyclopedia's 544 main entries, here's a heads-up about the headings—some of the entries list multiple names, separated by "aka" ("also known as"). Two examples are the entries for the park's Circle D Corral and Plaza Inn, which are listed as "Pony Farm, aka Circle D Corral," and "Red Wagon Inn, aka Plaza Inn," respectively. As any guest who's made repeat visits would know, Disneyland often changes the names of it attractions, stores, restaurants, and services over the decades (when you come to an entry with multiple names in the headings, the reasons for the name changes are explained in the text). In this encyclopedia, most headings present the names in chronological order, with "aka" denoting subsequent (and sometimes concurrent) names. A few of the attraction headings, however, start with the common, well-known name of the attraction that technically was not the original name. For example, you'll find the text for the Autopia alphabetized with the "A" entries, not in the "T" section where its actual original name—Tomorrowland Autopia—would have placed it. Likewise, the Monorail is in "M," not in "D" despite its actual original name, Disneyland-Alweg Monorail. Hopefully this arrangement will make it easier for readers to skip around and find specific entries they're looking for. When in doubt, consult the index, where all the names, current and past, get their own listings and page references.

Next, in each of this encyclopedia's alphabetized main entries, the descriptive text includes terms that appear in **bold**. This means there's a main entry for that term elsewhere in the encyclopedia.

To make the text more readable, the official names of some entities have been simplified. A brief alphabetical listing of some of these names includes Academy Award®, Disneyland Park®, Disney's Animal Kingdom®, Disney California Adventure Park®, and Walt Disney World Resort®. Instead of these formal names, I've used the abbreviated or colloquial forms commonly understood by the general public. For most of the book I've also used the shorter name Main Street instead of the longer Main Street, U.S.A.

When you read the text, note that most encyclopedia entries are marked on one of the maps (the entries for people, films, artifacts, and some of the park-wide events are not marked on maps). These map positions are indicated with a letter (for the map) and a number (for the spot on the map). A = the Adventureland map, Fa = Fantasyland, Fr = Frontierland, TS = Town Square, and so on. In other books, including some of those published by Disney itself, Main Street often includes everything from the turnstiles up to the Sleeping Beauty Castle drawbridge. To help readers better envision where things are, I've divided this large area into three separate parts—rectangular Town Square, slender Main

Street, and circular Hub, each with its own map.

When I couldn't pinpoint an exact date, I occasionally resorted to less precise times, like "Ca. 1992" or "summer 1967." Better to be general and right than specific and wrong.

James Joyce called errors "the portals of discovery." I think of them the same way. So, should you run across something in the text you think is incorrect, or you see a fact you want to question, or you notice a possible "portal of discovery," please do two things: first, forgive my mistake (and it is my mistake, nobody else's); and second, let me know what you found by politely writing to me via www.encycoolpedia.com. I'll reply with interest and gratitude.

—C.S.

Park
(Map P)

14 BEAR COUNTRY/ CRITTER COUNTRY

15 FRO

13

12 NEW ORLEANS SQUARE

11 ADVENTUR

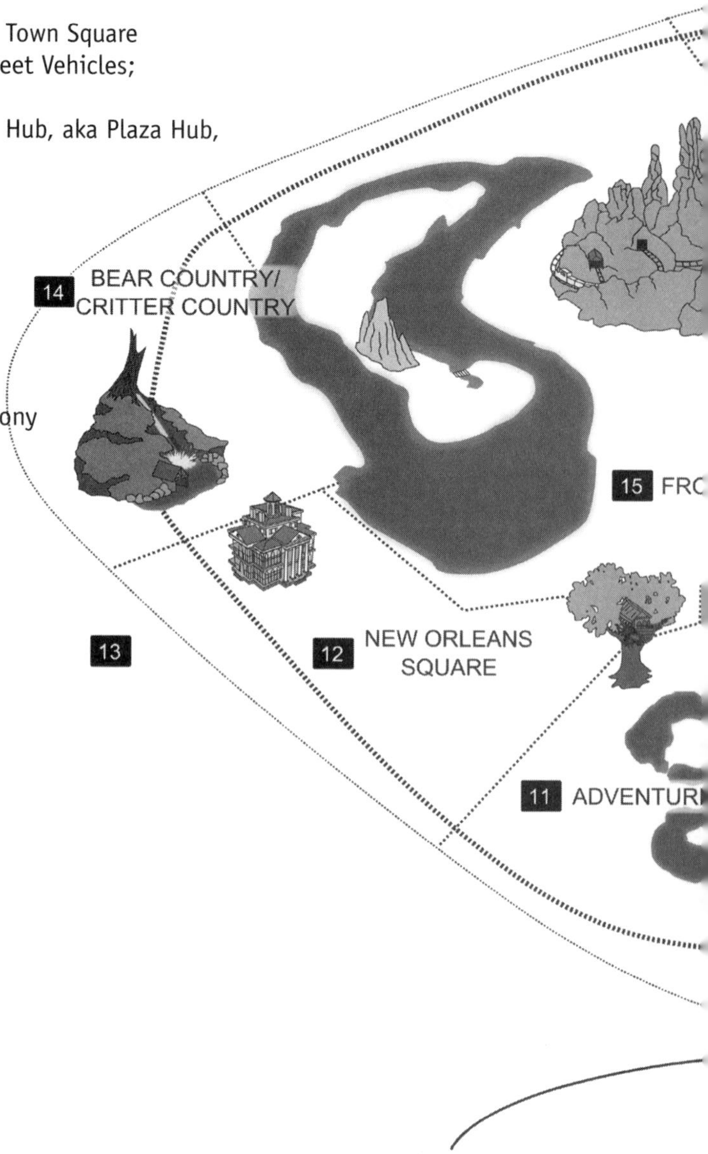

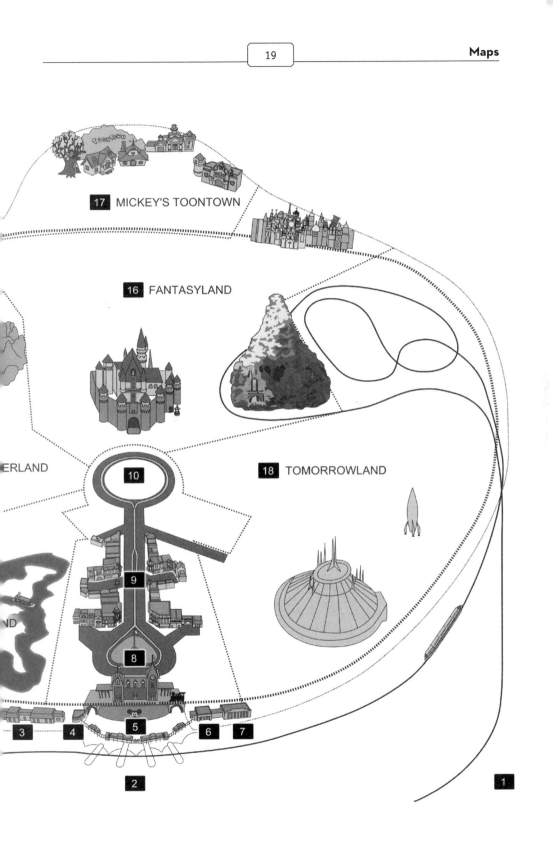

17 MICKEY'S TOONTOWN

16 FANTASYLAND

ERLAND

18 TOMORROWLAND

10

ND

9

8

3   4   5   6   7

2

1

Town Square
(Map TS)

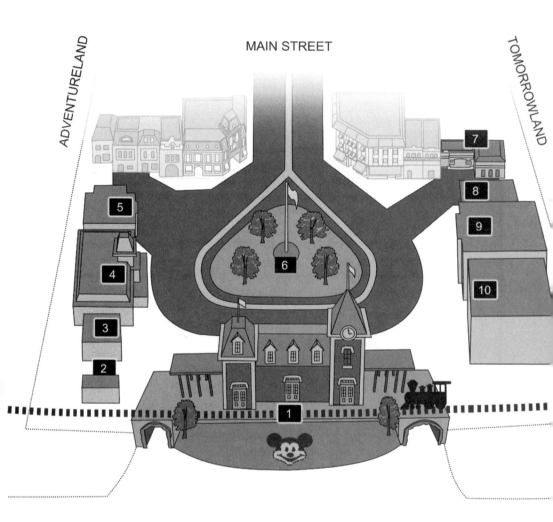

ADVENTURELAND

MAIN STREET

TOMORROWLAND

TS-1:   Santa Fe & Disneyland Railroad, aka Disneyland Railroad

TS-2:   Tour Guides

TS-3:   Police Station

TS-4:   City Hall; First Aid and Lost Children; Guest Relations; Tour Guides

TS-5:   Apartments; Fire Department, aka Fire Station

TS-6:   Flagpole

TS-7:   Dalmatian Celebration; American Egg House; Hills Bros. Coffee House and
        Coffee Garden; International Street; Liberty Street; Maxwell House Coffee
        Shop; Town Square Café

TS-8:   Jimmy Starr's Show Business Souvenirs; Mad Hatter of Main Street;
        Wonderland Music, aka Main Street Music

TS-9:   Babes in Toyland Exhibit; *Disneyland: The First 50 Magical Years*;
        Great Moments with Mr. Lincoln; Lost and Found; Mickey Mouse Club
        Headquarters, aka Mickey Mouse Club Shop; Opera House; The Walt Disney
        Story, aka The Walt Disney Story, Featuring Great Moments with Mr. Lincoln

TS-10: Bank of America, aka Bank of Main Street, aka Annual Pass Center,
        aka Annual Passport Processing Center; Disney Gallery; Town Square Realty

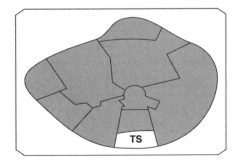

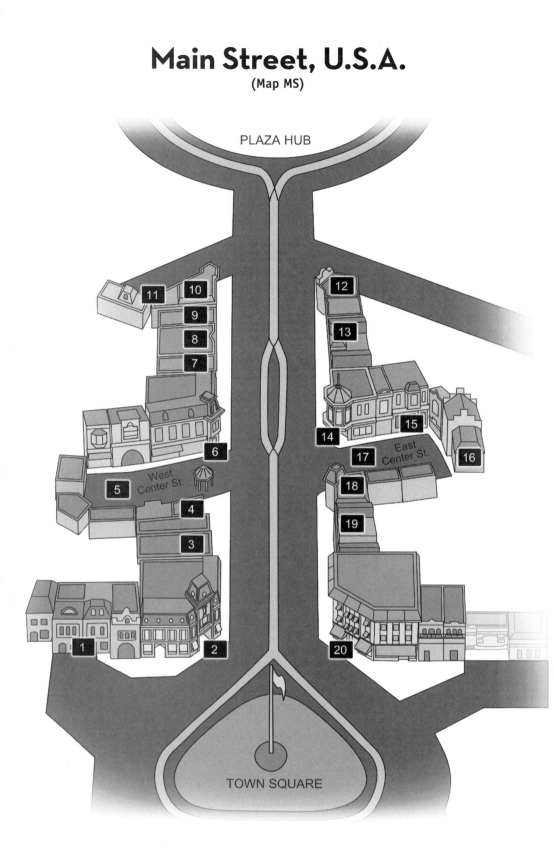

Main Street, U.S.A.
(Map MS)

MS-1:   Carriage Place Clothing Co.; Locker Area, aka Main Street Lockers &
        Storage; Lost and Found

MS-2:   Emporium, aka Disneyland Emporium

MS-3:   Candle Shop; Crystal Arcade; Glass Blower; Jemrock Shop, aka Jemrocks and
        Gem Shop; Story Book Shop, aka Western Printing Book Shop

MS-4:   Disneyana; Fortuosity Shop; Hurricane Lamp Shop; New Century Watches &
        Clocks, aka New Century Timepieces and New Century Jewelry;
        Upjohn Pharmacy

MS-5:   Carnation Café; Flower Mart, aka Flower Market

MS-6:   Blue Ribbon Bakery; Carnation Ice Cream Parlor; Puffin Bakery, aka Puffin
        Bake Shop; Sunkist Citrus House

MS-7:   Gibson Girl Ice Cream Parlor; Sunny-View Farms Jams & Jellies

MS-8:   Main Street Shooting Gallery; Penny Arcade

MS-9:   Candy Palace, aka Candy Palace and Candy Kitchen

MS-10: Refreshment Corner, aka Coke Corner, aka Coca-Cola Refreshment Corner

MS-11: Cole of California Swimsuits; Mad Hatter of Main Street

MS-12: Carefree Corner; Main Street Photo Supply Co.

MS-13: Blue Bird Shoes for Children; China Closet; Crystal Arts; Ellen's Gift Shop;
        Grandma's Baby Shop; Intimate Apparel, aka Corset Shop; Kodak Camera
        Center, aka GAF Photo Salon, aka Polaroid Camera Center; Ruggles China
        and Glass Shop; Silhouette Studio; Watches & Clocks, aka Timex Shop;
        Wonderland Music, aka Main Street Music

MS-14: Card Corner; Disney Clothiers, Ltd.; Gibson Greeting Cards; Hallmark Card
        Shop

MS-15: Coin Shop, aka Stamp and Coin Shop; Pen Shop

MS-16: Locker Area, aka Main Street Lockers & Storage; Lost and Found;
        Main Street Cone Shop

MS-17: Chinatown; Flower Mart, aka Flower Market; Main Street Fruit Cart

MS-18: Market House

MS-19: Disneyana; Fine Tobacco; Jewelry Shop, aka Rings & Things; Main Street
        Cinema; Main Street Magic Shop; Patented Pastimes, aka Great American
        Pastimes; 20th Century Music Company; Yale & Towne Lock Shop

MS-20: Disneyland Presents a Preview of Coming Attractions, aka Disneyland
        Showcase; Disney Showcase; The Legacy of Walt Disney; Wurlitzer Music
        Hall

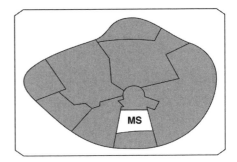

Hub
(Map H)

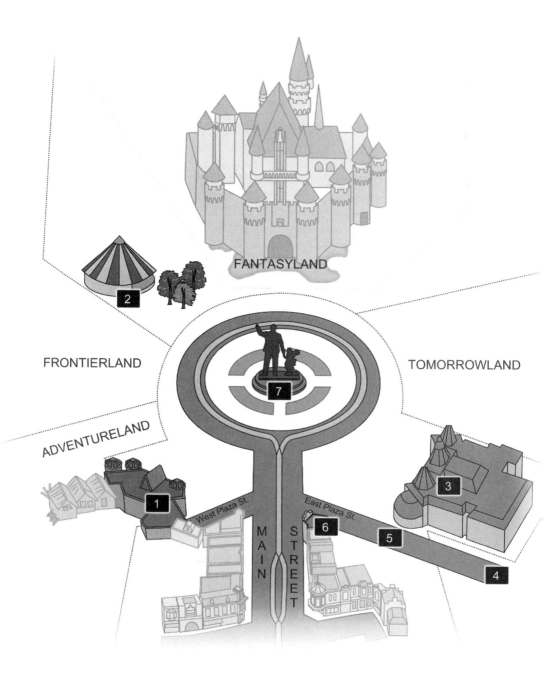

FANTASYLAND

FRONTIERLAND

TOMORROWLAND

ADVENTURELAND

West Plaza St.

East Plaza St.

M A I N   S T R E E T

1 2 3 4 5 6 7

H-1:   Disney Vacation Club Information Desk; Jolly Holiday Bakery Café; Pin
       Trading Stations; Plaza Pavilion, aka Stouffer's in Disneyland Plaza Pavillion
H-2:   Bandstand; Date Nite; Fantasy Faire; Plaza Gardens, aka Carnation Plaza
       Gardens
H-3:   Red Wagon Inn, aka Plaza Inn
H-4:   Edison Square; First Aid and Lost Children
H-5:   Little Red Wagon
H-6:   Baby Station, aka Baby Center, aka Baby Care Center
H-7:   *Partners*

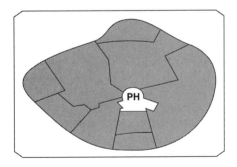

Adventureland

(Map A)

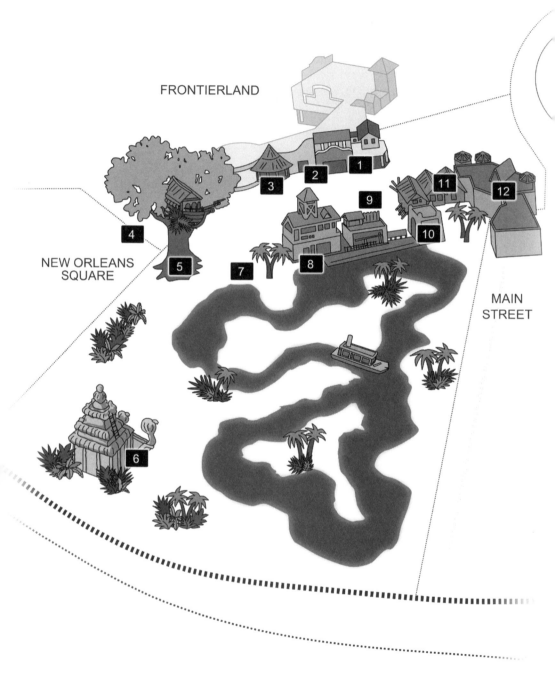

FRONTIERLAND

NEW ORLEANS
SQUARE

MAIN
STREET

A-1:   Adventureland Bazaar

A-2:   Big Game Safari Shooting Gallery; Indiana Jones Adventure Outpost; Safari Outpost; South Seas Traders

A-3:   Bengal Barbecue; Sunkist, I Presume; Tropical Cantina, aka Adventureland Cantina, aka Cantina

A-4:   Magnolia Park

A-5:   Swiss Family Treehouse; Tarzan's Treehouse

A-6:   Indiana Jones Adventure

A-7:   Indy Fruit Cart

A-8:   Jungle Cruise

A-9:   Tiki Tropical Traders, aka Tropical Imports

A-10: Aladdin's Oasis

A-11: Enchanted Tiki Room; Tiki Juice Bar

A-12: Tahitian Terrace, aka Stouffer's in Disneyland Tahitian Terrace

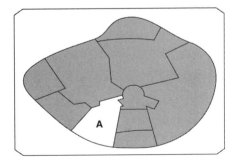

New Orleans Square

(Map NOS)

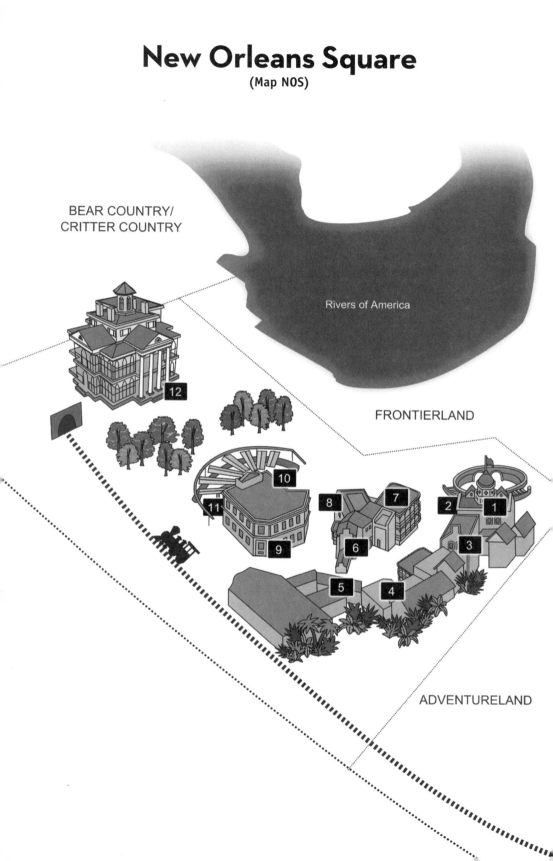

BEAR COUNTRY/
CRITTER COUNTRY

Rivers of America

FRONTIERLAND

ADVENTURELAND

NOS-1:   Apartments; Disney Gallery; Pirates of the Caribbean

NOS-2:   Royal Street Veranda

NOS-3:   Bookstand; Le Bat en Rouge; Le Gourmet, aka Le Gourmet Shop; One-of-a-Kind Shop; Pieces of Eight; Pirate's Arcade Museum; Port Royal

NOS-4:   Blue Bayou; Club 33

NOS-5:   Chocolate Collection, aka Chocolat Rue Royale; La Boutique de Noël; La Boutique d'Or; Le Forgeron; Le Bat en Rouge; Le Gourmet, aka Le Gourmet Shop; L'Ornement Magique; Port d'Orleans; Portrait Artists

NOS-6:   Cristal d'Orleans; Laffite's Silver Shop; Portrait Artists

NOS-7:   Candy Cart; Creole Café, aka Café Orleans; Royal Street Sweets

NOS-8:   La Petite Patisserie

NOS-9:   Jewel of Orléans; La Mascarade d'Orléans; Le Chapeau; Marché aux Fleurs, Sacs et Mode; Mlle. Antoinette's Parfumerie

NOS-10: Disney Vacation Club Information Desk; French Market; Parasol Cart

NOS-11: Mint Julep Bar

NOS-12: The Haunted Mansion; New Orleans Square Lemonade Stand; Omnimover

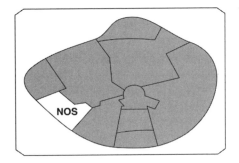

Frontierland
(Map Fr)

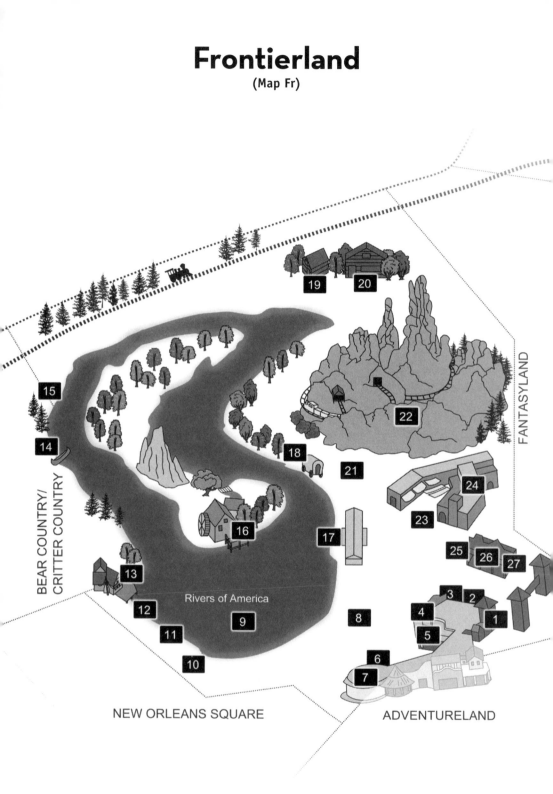

Fr-1:   Bone Carving Shop; Davy Crockett Arcade, aka Davy Crockett Frontier Arcade; Davy Crockett Frontier Museum; Davy Crockett's Pioneer Mercantile, aka Pioneer Mercantile; Frontierland Miniature Museum; Leather Shop; Reel-Ride

Fr-2:   Bonanza Outfitters; Pendleton Woolen Mills Dry Goods Store

Fr-3:   Silver Spur Supplies

Fr-4:   American Rifle Exhibit and Frontier Gun Shop; Golden Horseshoe

Fr-5:   Oaks Tavern; Stage Door Café

Fr-6:   Don DeFore's Silver Banjo Barbecue; Malt Shop and Cone Shop; Wheelhouse and Delta Banjo

Fr-7:   Aunt Jemima's Pancake House, aka Aunt Jemima's Kitchen; Magnolia Tree Terrace; River Belle Terrace

Fr-8:   Petrified Tree

Fr-9:   Rivers of America

Fr-10: Chicken Plantation, aka Plantation House, aka Chicken Shack

Fr-11: Rafts to Tom Sawyer Island

Fr-12: Mike Fink Keel Boats

Fr-13: Fowler's Harbor, aka Fowler's Landing

Fr-14: Indian War Canoes, aka Davy Crockett's Explorer Canoes

Fr-15: Indian Trading Post; Indian Village

Fr-16: Dixieland at Disneyland; Fantasmic!; Tom Sawyer Island, aka Pirate's Lair on Tom Sawyer Island

Fr-17: *Mark Twain* Riverboat; Sailing Ship *Columbia*; Ship to Shore Marketplace

Fr-18: Disney Vacation Club Information Desk; Westward Ho Conestoga Wagon Fries

Fr-19: Big Thunder Ranch, aka Festivals of Fools, aka Little Patch of Heaven

Fr-20: Big Thunder Barbecue, aka Festival of Foods, aka Celebration Roundup and Barbecue; Santa's Reindeer Round-Up

Fr-21: Big Thunder Mountain Railroad; Conestoga Wagons; Mine Train, aka Rainbow Caverns Mine Train, aka Western Mine Train Through Nature's Wonderland; Mule Pack, aka Rainbow Ridge Mule Pack, aka Pack Mules Through Nature's Wonderland; Stage Coach

Fr-22: Discovery Bay; Nature's Wonderland; Painted Desert, aka Rainbow Desert

Fr-23: El Zocalo, aka El Zocalo Park

Fr-24: Casa de Fritos, aka Casa Mexicana; Mineral Hall; Rancho del Zocalo Restaurante

Fr-25: Marshal's Office; Miniature Horse Corral

Fr-26: Frontierland Shooting Gallery, aka Frontierland Shootin' Arcade, aka Frontierland Shooting Exposition

Fr-27: Calico Kate's Pantry Shop; Frontier Trading Post; Westward Ho Trading Co.

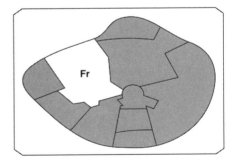

Bear Country/Critter Country
(Map B/C)

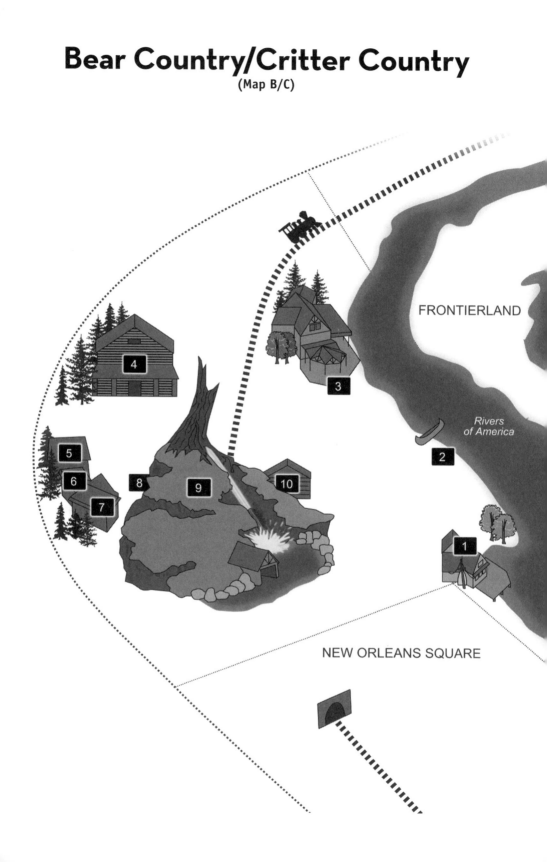

FRONTIERLAND

Rivers of America

NEW ORLEANS SQUARE

B/C-1:   Harbour Galley
B/C-2:   Critter Country Fruit Cart
B/C-3:   Golden Bear Lodge, aka Hungry Bear Restaurant
B/C-4:   Country Bear Jamboree, aka Country Bear Playhouse; The Many Adventures
         of Winnie the Pooh
B/C-5:   Brer Bar; Mile Long Bar; Pooh Corner
B/C-6:   Teddi Barra's Swingin' Arcade; Ursus H. Bear's Wilderness Outpost
B/C-7:   Crocodile Mercantile
B/C-8:   Professor Barnaby Owl's Photographic Art Studio
B/C-9:   Splash Mountain
B/C-10: Briar Patch; Critter Country Plush

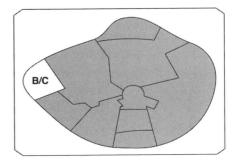

Fantasyland
(Map Fa)

MICKEY'S TOONTOWN

FRONTIERLAND

TOMORROWLAND

Fa-1: Snow White Wishing Well and Grotto
Fa-2: Fireworks; Sleeping Beauty Castle; Sleeping Beauty Castle Walk-Through
Fa-3: Arts and Crafts Shop; Castle Arts; Castle Christmas Shop; Clock Shop;
       Enchanted Chamber; 50th Anniversary Shop; Princess Boutique; Tinker Bell
       & Friends
Fa-4: Castle Candy Kitchen, aka Castle Candy Shoppe; Heraldry Shoppe, aka Castle
       Heraldry; Names Unraveled; Three Fairies Magic Crystals
Fa-5: Carrousel Candies; King Arthur Carrousel; Sword in the Stone Ceremony
Fa-6: Duck Bumps; King Arthur Carrousel; Mad Hatter's Mad Tea Party; Peter Pan
       Crocodile Aquarium

Fa-7: Tinker Bell Toy Shoppe, aka Once Upon a Time . . . the Disney Princess Shoppe; Bibbidi Bobbidi Boutique

Fa-8: Snow White Adventures, aka Snow White's Scary Adventures

Fa-9: Fantasy Faire Gifts, aka Fantasy Shop, aka Fantasy Emporium, aka Fantasy Gift Faire; Geppetto's Arts & Crafts, aka Geppetto's Toys & Gifts, aka Geppetto's Holiday Workshop; Geppetto's Candy Shoppe; Mickey Mouse Club Theater, aka Fantasyland Theater; Names Unraveled; Pinocchio's Daring Journey; Tangled; Welch's Grape Juice Stand

Fa-10: Character Foods, aka Character Food Facilities; Stromboli's Wagon; Village Inn, aka Village Haus

Fa-11: Dumbo the Flying Elephant

Fa-12: Skyway to Fantasyland and Skyway to Tomorrowland

Fa-13: Casey Jr. Circus Train

Fa-14: Dumbo the Flying Elephant; Pirate Ship Restaurant, aka Chicken of the Sea Pirate Ship and Restaurant, aka Captain Hook's Galley; Skull Rock and Pirate's Cove, aka Skull Rock Cove

Fa-15: Canal Boats of the World; Rock Candy Mountain, aka Candy Mountain; Storybook Land Canal Boats

Fa-16: Fantasy Faire Gifts, aka Fantasy Shop, aka Fantasy Emporium, aka Fantasy Gift Faire; Midget Autopia

Fa-17: Enchanted Cottage Sweets & Treats; Troubadour Tavern; Yumz, aka Louie's, aka Meeko's, aka Fantasyland Theater Snacks, aka Troubadour Treats

Fa-18: Princess Fantasy Faire; Videopolis, aka Fantasyland Theater

Fa-19: Baloo's Dressing Room

Fa-20: It's a Small World Toy Shop

Fa-21: It's a Small World; The Magic, the Memories, and You!; Topiary Garden

Fa-22: Disney Afternoon Avenue; Edelweiss Snacks, Fantasyland Autopia; Garden of the Gods; Keller's Jungle Killers; Le Petit Chalet; Lilliputian Land; Mickey Mouse Club Circus; Motor Boat Cruise, aka Motor Boat Cruise to Gummi Glen

Fa-23: Fairytale Arts; Fantasia Gardens; Junior Autopia; Names Unraveled

Fa-24: Matterhorn Bobsleds; Matterhorn Mountain; Peter Pan Crocodile Aquarium

Fa-25: Mad Hatter's Mad Tea Party

Fa-26: Alice in Wonderland

Fa-27: Character Foods, aka Character Food Facilities; Mad Hatter of Fantasyland

Fa-28: Mr. Toad's Wild Ride

Fa-29: Peter Pan Flight, aka Peter Pan's Flight

Fa-30: Briar Rose Cottage; Disney Villains; Heraldry Shoppe, aka Castle Heraldry; Knight Shop; Merlin's Magic Shop; Mickey's Christmas Chalet; Quasimodo's Attic, aka Sanctuary of Quasimodo; Villains Lair

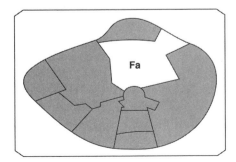

Mickey's Toontown
(Map MT)

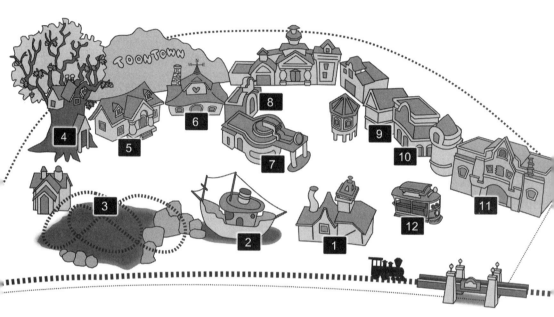

FANTASYLAND

MT-1: Goofy's Bounce House, aka Goofy's Playhouse
MT-2: Donald's Boat, aka *Miss Daisy*
MT-3: Gadget's Go Coaster
MT-4: Chip 'n Dale Tree House
MT-5: Mickey's House
MT-6: Minnie's House
MT-7: Goofy's Gas Station; Toon Up Treats
MT-8: Clarabelle's Frozen Yogurt; Daisy's Diner; Pluto's Dog House
MT-9: Toontown Five & Dime
MT-10: Gag Factory
MT-11: Roger Rabbit's Car Toon Spin
MT-12: Disney Vacation Club Information Desk; Jolly Trolley

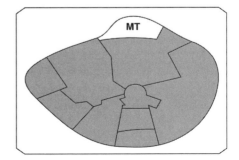

Tomorrowland
(Map T)

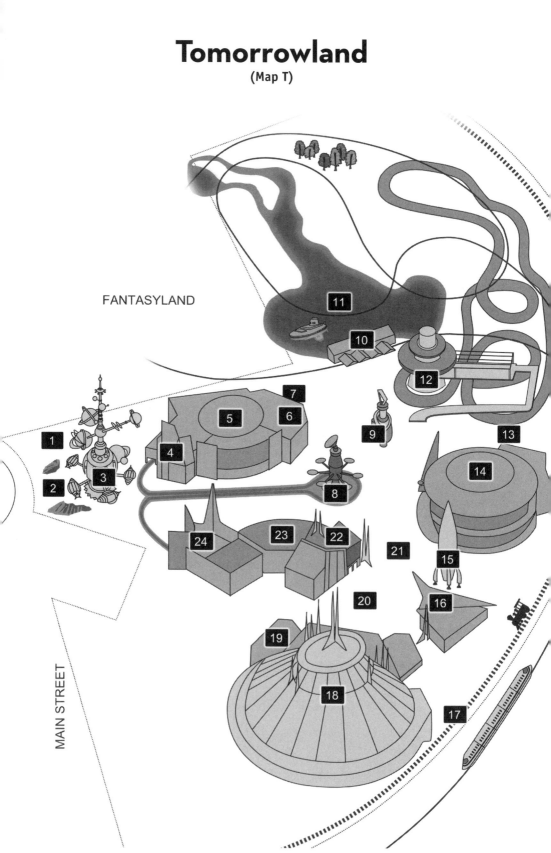

FANTASYLAND

MAIN STREET

T-1:   Alpine Gardens; House of the Future; King Triton Gardens, aka Triton Gardens; Pixie Hollow; Pixie Hollow Gift Cart

T-2:   Avenue of the Flags

T-3:   Astro-Orbitor; Clock of the World, aka World Clock

T-4:   Buzz Lightyear Astro Blasters; Omnimover

T-5:   American Space Experience; Art of Animation; Bell Telephone Systems Phone Exhibits; Circarama, aka Circle-Vision, aka Circle-Vision 360, aka World Premiere Circle-Vision; Corridor of Murals; Space Station X-1, aka Satellite View of America

T-6:   Art Corner; Little Green Men Store Command; Our Future in Colors, aka Color Gallery; Premiere Shop; World Beneath Us Exhibit

T-7:   Yacht Club, aka Yacht Bar

T-8:   Astro-Jets, aka Tomorrowland Jets; Court of Honor; Disney Vacation Club Information Desk; Lunching Pad; Observatron; PeopleMover; Radio Disney Broadcast Booth; Rocket Jets; Rocket Rods; Space Bar; Tomorrowlanding

T-9:   Club Buzz; Tomorrowland Terrace

T-10: Autopia Winner's Circle; Monorail, aka Disneyland-Alweg Monorail, aka Disneyland Monorail; Phantom Boats; Submarine Voyage, aka Finding Nemo Submarine Voyage; Viewliner; Yacht Club, aka Yacht Bar

T-11: Mermaids

T-12: Autopia, aka Tomorrowland Autopia, aka Autopia, Presented by Chevron

T-13: Autopia Winner's Circle; Mad Hatter of Tomorrowland, aka Mod Hatter, Hatmosphere; Skyway to Fantasyland and Skyway to Tomorrowland

T-14: America Sings; Carousel of Progress; Innoventions; Space Bar

T-15: Moonliner; Spirit of Refreshment

T-16: Flight to the Moon; Mission to Mars; Redd Rockett's Pizza Port; Rocket to the Moon; Toy Story Funhouse; Space Place

T-17: Grand Canyon Diorama; Primeval World Diorama

T-18: Adventures in Science; Flying Saucers; Space Mountain, aka Rockin' Space Mountain

T-19: *Captain EO*, aka *Captain EO* Tribute; *Honey, I Shrunk the Audience*; Magic Eye Theater; Starcade; Tomorrowland Stage, aka Space Stage

T-20: Cosmic Waves; Hobbyland

T-21: Flight Circle, aka Thimble Drome Flight Circle

T-22: Bathroom of Tomorrow; Character Shop; Fun Fotos; Mad Hatter of Tomorrowland, aka Mod Hatter, Hatmosphere; Star Trader

T-23: American Dairy Association Exhibit, aka Dairy Bar; Corridor of Murals; Fashions and Fabrics Through the Ages; New York World's Fair Exhibit; 20,000 Leagues Under the Sea Exhibit

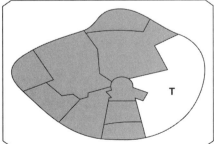

T-24: Adventure Thru Inner Space; Hall of Aluminum Fame; Hall of Chemistry; Omnimover; Star Tours

Adventureland

MAP: Park, P-11

DATES: July 17, 1955–ongoing

Guests are so used to seeing Adventureland on the left side of the **Hub**, they might be surprised to find out that Adventureland moved around in the early plans for Disneyland. One of the first color overhead illustrations of the park, drawn by **Marvin Davis** two years before **Opening Day**, placed Adventureland on the east side of the Hub, making it the first land on the lower *right* side as guests walked north from **Main Street** toward **Sleeping Beauty Castle**. Adventureland ended up, of course, as the first land to the lower *left* from the Hub (the lower-right area became part of **Tomorrowland** and is now the **Space Mountain** site).

Early on, what also changed was the name of the area. One cartographer would label it Adventureland; another would use True-Life Adventureland, in reference to the popular *True-Life* nature documentaries Disney Studios started releasing in 1949. The exotic settings of these short films—especially *The African Lion*, which was in production as Disneyland was being designed—helped inspire the themes and textures of Adventureland, as did numerous Hollywood classics and great literary tales of exploration. Ultimately, however, the setting was generalized, with no one specific place pinpointed and no particular era identified. Adventureland was and is an amalgamation of African, Asian, and Polynesian influences that's more cinematic than real, more mysterious than overt.

Even though the Adventureland location, name, and source material varied, key Adventureland elements— a winding river with a boat ride, rows of stores, and restaurants themed to remote locales—were always shown on the early maps. Artists like **Harper Goff** tried their best to pre-conceive everything, but in truth many of Adventureland's details were made up on the spot during construction. The result is a wonderfully evocative meeting place between outposts of civilization and untamed nature. From the Hub, the

Disneyland's Opening Day Attractions
(July 17, 1955)

Adventureland
Jungle Cruise*

Fantasyland
Canal Boats of the World
King Arthur Carrousel*
Mad Hatter's Mad Tea Party*
Mr. Toad's Wild Ride*
Peter Pan Flight*
Snow White Adventures*

Frontierland
Golden Horseshoe Revue
Mark Twain Riverboat*
Mule Pack
Stage Coach

Main Street
Main Street Cinema*
Main Street Vehicles*
Santa Fe & Disneyland Railroad*

Tomorrowland
Autopia*
Hall of Chemistry
Space Station X-1

*Still in operation.

main Adventureland entrance is across a small pond (the same one that spreads beneath the **Frontierland** entrance) and through a tall bamboo gate topped by elephant tusks. The "street" ahead gently curves for about 300 feet toward **New Orleans Square**, with a two-story row of thatched shops and restaurants lining the right-hand side, and more shops and the landmark **Jungle Cruise** attraction on the left.

Massive in its scale and significance, the Jungle Cruise was Adventureland's only major attraction until the **Tahitian Terrace**, **Swiss Family Treehouse**, and **Big Game Safari Shooting Gallery** were added in 1962, to be followed a year later by the **Enchanted Tiki Room** and in 1995 by **Indiana Jones Adventure**. Because of the three-decade development gap between the Tiki Room and Indiana Jones, Adventureland is one of the park's least modified sections.

Though in its infancy it may have had fewer attractions than the other lands, Adventureland has never lacked for verdant abundance. According to Disneyland's **souvenir books**, Adventureland was intended to be a "wonderland of nature's own design." As such, it has always been the most densely planted of the lands, blending thousands of transplanted trees and bushes with old-growth trees saved from the original orchards the park was built on. Even the tiki-style **trash cans** look like they belong in the jungle. Attentive guests will notice that the resplendent natural images are supplemented with the sounds of chattering monkeys and chirping birds (all natural-sounding, but all prerecorded).

In 1955 an Adventureland plaque celebrating the spirit of "romance," "mystery," "tropical rivers," and "the eerie sounds of the jungle" was created but never installed. No matter—so exciting was Adventureland's concept, so detailed was its execution, and so universal is its appeal that it's doubtful any guests have ever needed to have the area explained to them.

Adventureland Bazaar

MAP: Adventureland, A-1

DATES: July 17, 1955–ongoing

A prime location has helped make the Adventureland Bazaar a perennial shopping favorite since **Opening Day.** This big store occupies the first right-hand building inside the **Adventureland** entrance, a high-traffic spot across from the **Enchanted Tiki Room.** Covering approximately 2,800 square feet, the Bazaar operates on the

first floor of a two-story structure that has always sported variations on adventure-themed décor, including an arched entryway, thatched awnings, and weathered paint. Disney Legend **Rolly Crump** was one of the artists instrumental in creating an appealing exterior that hasn't changed much over the years.

Inside, change has come frequently. So many different shops selling unique imported merchandise have moved in and out that the Bazaar has sometimes been closer to a Bizarre. In its first decades, the building was subdivided into individual businesses that offered non-Disney items from around the world. At various times these interior shops, plus several small huts outside, included the Curio Hut (island-themed gifts), Here & There Imports, Far East Imports, Guatemalan Weavers, the Hawaiian Shop, India Magic Carpet, the Island Trade Store, the Mexican Mart, and Lee Brothers (imported Chinese gifts). The diversity of merchandise was fascinating; back then, the park's **souvenir books** often boasted about the Bazaar's "colorful wares imported from exotic lands," "items from India," "carvings from a Kenyan tribe in Africa," "tropical ceramics," and other "rarities."

In 1994 the store was temporarily closed for a major **Adventureland** remodel that brought extensive changes to the nearby **Jungle Cruise** line area. The individual shops inside the Bazaar were absorbed into one all-encompassing store. Today, the store is filled with more Disney toys than imported novelties. One unusual addition is Aladdin's Other Lamp, a display along the back wall that dispenses "the wisdom of the genie" for a few coins and a quick rub.

Adventures in Science

MAP: Tomorrowland, T-18

DATES: Never built

Page 26 of Disneyland's 1958 **souvenir book** displayed a spellbinding painting of a coming **Tomorrowland** attraction called Adventures in Science. In the painting, guests queued up under a large sloping roof and gazed through tall picture windows upon a tantalizing alien night. Outside were sharp lunar-like mountains and a large crater, with what looked like a domed observatory and giant protruding telescope standing off to the side. An immense ringed planet filled the distant sky, small moons hovered over the horizon, and stars spangled the blackness beyond. The view was more than tantalizing or beautiful—it was breathtaking, and it dramatically evoked the inspiring future that Tomorrowland represented.

That same year, the park's poster-size Fun Map marked a huge parcel of Tomorrowland real estate for the coming Adventures in Science attraction. Had the attraction been built, the location would have been approximately where **Space Mountain** was built in 1977. Adventures in Science would have begun with a Powercade, a long covering that curved from the open Tomorrowland walkway and back toward a two- or three-story white building. Under the Powercade covering, all manners of strange-looking futuristic gizmos were to be exhibited. A walk along the length of the Powercade would have brought guests into the Adventures in Science building and onto some sort of transport for a trip through the universe and/or a tour of scientific discoveries through the centuries. Concept sketches, included in the **John Hench** book *Designing Disney*, showed guests in small rocket-like pods gliding past immense colliding planets and other galactic wonders.

Alas, by 1961 no Adventures in Science attraction was being shown in the souvenir books. In 1966 planning was already underway for a scientific tour that really would materialize a year later, albeit on a different site—**Adventure Thru Inner Space**.

Adventure Thru Inner Space

MAP: Tomorrowland, T-24

DATES: August 5, 1967–September 2, 1985

Adventure Thru Inner Space was a groundbreaking new attraction when it auspiciously debuted in 1967 as a key part of **Tomorrowland's** extensive remodel. From 1955 to 1966, the Inner Space building had housed, among other things, Monsanto's static **Hall of Chemistry** display, a walk-through exhibit that showed off the wonders of chemical engineering. Identically sponsored and similarly science-influenced, Adventure Thru Inner Space was also intended to show chemical wonders, but these were to be viewed from a unique vantage point—inside the atom.

Entered from the main walkway just inside the entrance to Tomorrowland, the Inner Space line area was a bustle of activity choreographed by **cast members** wearing futuristic yellow and black jumpsuits and white boots. The winding **queue** took guests past TV-size display terminals that previewed the amazing sights to come. Guests also watched riders up ahead step into Atomobiles, blue cocoon-shaped pods that slid inside the 37-foot-long Mighty Microscope (in early 1967, Magic Microscope was one of the names considered for the whole attraction; Micro-World was another). This huge microscope "shrank" the Atomobiles and aimed them (eight-inch-tall replicas, actually) through a glass tube at a colorful, illuminated snowflake. All of this was witnessed not only by queuing guests, but also by curious passengers on the **People-Mover**, since its track traveled right through the back of the room, up by the ceiling.

Once they were out of view of the line area, "miniaturized" Atomobile riders listened as a scientist, who had already undertaken this journey, informed them that they were now hearing "suspended . . . thought waves" of his experience. To create the illusion that the Atomobiles were continuing to shrink "beyond the limits of normal magnification-cation-cation" (according to the narrator), the approaching snowflakes grew bigger and bigger, until finally the Atomobiles actually entered them. More shrinking took Atomobiles into the domain of the water molecule, and finally into one of the molecule's oxygen atoms, where speedy electrons whipped by on all sides and a glowing red nucleus pulsed.

Before the Atomobiles entered the dangerous realm of the nucleus, they were gradually enlarged back to normal size—but not before more drama ensued. The original snowflakes melted, bringing unexpected motion to the Atomobiles and the surrounding molecules. The final return to normal size was monitored under the watchful blue eye of a scientist peering at riders through a giant microscope. Guests exited into a hallway of Monsanto and Disneyland displays, among them a delicate floor-to-ceiling sculpture of oil beads spiraling down thin wires.

When it was introduced in 1967, Adventure Thru Inner Space was one of Disneyland's most advanced attractions. Working closely with Monsanto engineers, Disney's own **Claude Coats** designed much of the journey, which lasted about six minutes and covered some 700 feet of displays. **Paul Frees**, who later spoke the baritone "ghost host" lines for the **Haunted Mansion**, voiced the narrating scientist; **X Atencio**, writer of the **Pirates of the Caribbean** and Haunted Mansion ride scripts, also wrote Frees's Inner Space monologue. **Richard and Robert Sherman**, veterans of many other Disney attractions (**It's a Small World**) and movies (*Mary Poppins*), created the exhilarating "Miracles from Molecules" exit song, while **Buddy Baker** ("Grim Grinning Ghosts") penned the background music. **John Hench** drew up some of the initial concept sketches, which showed guests riding past sofa-size protozoa inside an enlarged water droplet.

Thanks to Monsanto's support, Inner Space was a completely free attraction, requiring no A–E ticket for entry; however, children had to use a special coupon from inside the **ticket books**, thus limiting the number of times they could ride unsupervised by parents. On December 15, 1972, the coupon system was abandoned, as was the free admission. From then on, a C ticket opened up the atom.

As exciting as the concept, sets, and effects were, the real breakthrough of Adventure Thru Inner Space was the Atomobile itself—it was the first Disneyland iteration of the innovative **Omnimover** ride system. In addition to efficiently conveying over 3,000 riders per hour through the attraction and cueing visual and sonic effects, the partially enclosed Atomobiles gave riders a sense of privacy and made Inner Space a prime rendezvous spot for amorous encounters. Even worse, the privacy seemed to provoke some riders into leaning out and damaging the sets. Hoping to curtail any in-the-dark intimacies or vandalism, supervisors installed closed-circuit TV cameras and sped up the Atomobiles to help limit opportunities for misbehavior.

In 1985, with its sets aging and its audience disappearing, Adventure Thru Inner Space closed to make way for the new **Star Tours** attraction that would debut two years later. In tribute to the wonders of Inner Space, Star Tours, for a time, incorporated one of the small Atomobile replicas into its line-area exhibits. A miniature Mighty Microscope was also visible in the hangar scene of the original Star Tours film, and on the **Buzz Lightyear** building across the way, snowflakes and molecules on an exterior mural reminded viewers of Tomorrowland's past glories.

Aladdin's Oasis

MAP: Adventureland, A-10

DATES: July 1, 1993–ongoing

Three months after the 31-year-old **Tahitian Terrace** in **Adventureland** closed, Aladdin's Oasis opened. While its location between the **Enchanted Tiki Room** and the **Jungle Cruise** was the same as its predecessor's, the architecture of the 300-square-foot building had drastically changed. Instead of Polynesian stylings, the new façade featured exotic elements of *The Arabian Nights*, in keeping with the theme of *Aladdin*, Disney's 1992 hit movie. Aladdin's Oasis guests enjoyed delicacies of the Middle East (shish kebabs, tabbouleh, chutney, etc.) and watched an Arabian-themed show featuring belly dancing, magic, and even a lamp and genie inspired by the movie.

In its debut year, Aladdin's Oasis wasn't open every day. After two years, the Arabian show wasn't open at all, and the Oasis was solely a table-service restaurant. Days of operation came with less frequency in 1996, and the building was often given over to private parties. Later that year the restaurant aspect of Aladdin's Oasis vanished, to be replaced in early '97 by a new stage show called *Aladdin and Jasmine's StoryTale Adventures*. The 25-minute presentation featured **cast members** dressed as *Aladdin* characters who retold (with the audience's help) tales from the Arabian Nights. This show went on hiatus in 2006 and closed permanently in 2008. Though the building still has a sign identifying it as Aladdin's Oasis, in recent years it's been referred to as Aladdin and Jasmine at Aladdin's Oasis, a prosaic meet-and-greet area where guests can mingle with costumed characters. Excitement briefly returned with a stunt show called *Secrets of the Stone Tiger*, which promoted the latest Indiana Jones movie in the summer of 2008.

Albright, Milt
(1916–)

Born in 1916, this Missourian joined Disney Studios in 1947 as a junior accountant. After getting to know **Walt Disney** personally, and after designing an unused-but-impressive car for the **Autopia** attraction planned for Tomorrowland, Albright was transferred to the nascent park and made manager of accounting. In this role, one of his duties was to write and deliver paychecks to Disneyland brass, including Walt Disney himself.

Early in his park career Albright invented and ran the **Holidayland** picnic area in the late '50s, making him "the only manager of a land at Disneyland that failed," according to his own description on the 2007 *Disneyland Secrets, Stories & Magic* DVD. Later, while overseeing the Group Sales department, he founded two long-time staples of Disneyland history: the **Magic Kingdom Club** for neighboring businesses and frequent visitors (Albright was also listed as the editor of the club's quarterly magazine) and **Grad Nite** for celebrating teens. Albright eventually headed the Special Projects and Guest Communications departments and mentored many up-and-coming Disney executives before retiring in 1992. When Milt Albright was named a Disney Legend 13 years later, he was acknowledged as being Disneyland's first-ever employee.

Alice in Wonderland

MAP: Fantasyland, Fa-26

DATES: June 14, 1958–ongoing

Themed to a popular Disney animated movie (just like **Peter Pan Flight** and many other attractions), Alice in Wonderland is one of the park's long-standing "dark rides," an industry term for indoor rides with guided vehicles. Alice in Wonderland places its guests inside a colorful caterpillar-styled car and drops them into the bizarre world of Lewis Carroll's famous Victorian novel. The attraction was originally conceived of as a series of walk-through displays, ideally to be ready for 1955's **Opening Day.** Among the walk-through scenes were some tilting stairs to climb and a slide to ride down.

Unfortunately, time and money were too tight for Imagineers to make the mid-July deadline, and Alice in Wonderland wasn't ready until mid-June 1958. By then its location had been moved from the western **Fantasyland** row that held **Snow White Adventures** to the east side of **Sleeping Beauty Castle**, opposite **Matterhorn Mountain** (today **Pinocchio's Daring Journey** fills the site Alice originally would've occupied). Alice in Wonderland shares part of its building with **Mr. Toad's Wild Ride**, and during the 700-foot trip through Wonderland the caterpillar cars actually climb up to the second floor above the Mr. Toad layout. Alice required a D ticket for admission in the late '50s and a C in the '60s, but in 1971 it needed only a B ticket.

Twenty-five years after opening, Alice in Wonderland was late in arriving once again—when the rest of Fantasyland temporarily shut down for a massive renovation in time for a 1983 unveiling, Alice closed on September 6, 1982 and didn't reopen until April 14, 1984. Pre- and post-renovation, the attraction has always been unique when compared to other Fantasyland dark rides in that it takes guests outside its building—in this case, for a gentle glide across the tops of oversize plants. Guests are then lowered from the second to the ground floor, into a surprise "un-birthday" celebration finale that was added in 1984. Because of the outdoor stretch of track and the possibility of slippery situations, Alice in Wonderland often closes when there's rain.

Inside the attraction, the displays include familiar Carroll characters—the White Rabbit, Cheshire Cat, Mad Hatter, etc.—and incorporate the surreal styles, kaleidoscopic colors, and buoyant music from the 1951 Disney movie. Kathryn Beaumont, who voiced the movie's Alice character, reprised her vocals for the attraction and even updated them in 1984. Among the major changes that resulted from the 1984 renovation were the removal of the topsy-turvy Upside Down Room and the addition of about a minute of ride time, making it a more impressive four-minute attraction.

Disney Legend **Claude Coats**, who worked on the *Alice in Wonderland* film, is credited as the attraction's main designer in its original iteration. The Imagineer who spearheaded the **Big Thunder Mountain Railroad** in the '70s, Tony Baxter, was in charge of bringing eye-popping new effects to the '84 renovation.

Alice in Wonderland, with its large butterflies, flowers, and mushrooms out front, has long presented an inviting view to guests riding on the nearby **Monorail** and **Matterhorn Bobsleds**. Attentive pedestrians will note one more nifty design element outside the attraction: recessed White Rabbit and Cheshire Cat statues, mounted in the walls along the walkway. But there's one facet of the attraction that nobody can see because it was never realized—a proposed Alice in Wonderland Toy Shop that would have presented its wares within a Wonderland-style interior.

All-American College Band

DATES: June 14, 1971–ongoing (seasonal)

Disneyland's All-American College Band was born in 1971 as a part-time work experience program for local collegiate musicians. Dressed in snappy uniforms, and now including players from all across the country, the band still appears throughout the summer, often providing the music for each afternoon's **Town Square** flag retreat and adding performances for special events throughout the park (such as Disneyland's 45th birthday celebration in 2000).

By now over 2,500 members have graduated from the band. Of the musical directors, the longest-tenured has been Dr. Art Bartner, the USC band director who began leading Disneyland's band in the late 1970s and continued for the next 28 summers. In 2005 Disneyland threw a reunion for its All-American alumni and welcomed back over 150 members for a unique afternoon performance in front of **Sleeping Beauty Castle**.

Alpine Gardens

MAP: Tomorrowland, T-1

DATES: December 1967–August 25, 1995

When the all-plastic **House of the Future** was demolished in 1967, the all-natural gardens surrounding it were retained. Rather than install another high-profile attraction in the area, Disney designers decided to save the space as a serene, largely undeveloped rest area.

Conveniently located just to the left of the main **Tomorrowland** gates, the Alpine Gardens offered pedestrians a quiet, convenient stop halfway between Tomorrowland and **Fantasyland**. The appearance of a souvenir stand detracted from, but didn't ruin, the bucolic effect. The "alpine" in the name referred to the view of **Matterhorn Mountain**, which towered only 150 feet away to the northeast (although views of **Sleeping Beauty Castle** to the northwest were just as impressive). After closing in mid-1995, the area reopened in early 1996 as **King Triton Gardens** with new landscaping and graceful new fountains.

American Dairy Association Exhibit,
aka Dairy Bar

MAP: Tomorrowland, T-23

DATES: January 21, 1956–September 1, 1958

Six months after Disneyland opened, the American Dairy Association brought some of its trade show displays into **Tomorrowland**. The building, second on the right just inside the Tomorrowland entrance, already housed the walk-through **20,000 Leagues Under the Sea Exhibit**. **Souvenir books** from the '50s described the ADA location as a not-so-tantalizing presentation of "future techniques in production and distribution of dairy products." Among other things, the room included big plastic cows watching televisions while being milked; the large, sleek gauges and containers of modern milking machines; and a model of a milkman making a delivery in some kind of small jet-powered flying vehicle.

An interior barn-shaped Dairy Bar offered guests a folksy place to sit at tables and drink obligatory glasses of cold milk in front of a sign that proclaimed milk as "nature's most nearly perfect food." Many people referred to the entire exhibit as the Dairy Bar, but Disneyland's souvenir books listed the exhibit and the Dairy Bar as two separate entities (even though they shared the same sponsor and one naturally led to the other).

In 1958 the ADA was o-u-t when a Tomorrowland remodel preempted the site for **Fun Fotos** displays. All the buildings along this row of Tomorrowland would later undergo massive changes—within a decade, the walk-through exhibits were replaced by major attractions and stores, most notably **Adventure Thru Inner Space** and the **Character Shop**.

American Egg House

MAP: Town Square, TS-7

DATES: July 14, 1978–September 30, 1983

The American Egg House is unusual because, to this day, it is one of the only Disneyland attractions, shops, or restaurants to be replaced by the same eatery it had replaced only five years earlier.

In 1976, the **Town Square Café** took over for the **Hills Bros. Coffee House and Coffee Garden** on **Main Street**. After two years as the Town Square Café, the American Egg House moved in and quickly became known as a great breakfast spot by virtue of its prime location between the prominent **Opera House** block and the beginning of **Main Street**. For many guests, it was the first eatery visible when they walked into Disneyland each morning. The Egg House also had the ideal morning menu; sponsorship by the American Egg Board led to many egg-themed menu items, naturally.

At the end of September 1983, the American Egg House cracked its last shell and the Town Square Café returned the next day for a nine-year run.

American Rifle Exhibit and Frontier Gun Shop

MAP: Frontierland, Fr-4

DATES: 1956–ca. 1986

Actual weapons, in Disneyland? Yessir, and they were right at home in **Frontierland**—where staged "shoot-outs" once took place between lawmen and villains, the **Tom Sawyer Island** fort contained realistic rifles, and the **Opening Day** celebration featured 16 Frontierland dancers cavorting with guns while singing about Davy Crockett's rifle, "Ol' Betsy." In this land, the **Sailing Ship *Columbia*** still blasts its cannon, and a shooting gallery has been operating since 1957. With all its firearms, a more fitting name for Frontierland might be Gun-tierland.

The park's 1956 **souvenir book** listed an American Rifle Exhibit in Frontierland, and the '57 book listed the exhibit and a Frontier Gun Shop, both located in the **Davy Crockett Arcade** building. The glass cases of the exhibit displayed antique weapons from American history, including various muskets, Kentucky rifles, and Colt pistols. The small Gun Shop sold replicas of those weapons—many of them, it's safe to speculate, to spirited, rifle-ready kids wearing the Crockett-style coonskin caps made popular by the gun-totin' Fess Parker on the hit *Disneyland* **TV series**. Some sundries, such as film and inexpensive gifts, were also available.

The rifle exhibit lasted for three decades, but in 1987 the whole Crockett Arcade, including the rifles, was remodeled and transformed into a large retail store called **Pioneer Mercantile**. In keeping with tradition, modern Frontierland stores such as **Bonanza Outfitters** still display individual rifles.

American Space Experience

MAP: Tomorrowland, T-5

DATES: May 22, 1998–October 26, 2003

While other **Tomorrowland** exhibits have pointed to the future, the American Space Experience celebrated the recent past, specifically the last 40 years of NASA's achievements in outer space. Opened in 1998 along with new attractions in the remodeled Tomorrowland, this educational walk-through exhibit shared with **Rocket Rods** the large building just inside the Tomorrowland entrance that had formerly housed the **Circarama** theater.

Because the space exhibit was sponsored by NASA, displays included an actual moon rock, Hubble Space Telescope photos, an Apollo spacesuit, and a live TV feed that showed NASA launches. A scale that revealed weights on other planets, models of future rockets, and a look at a bizarre space age material called aerogel were among the other displays that made this a fun and fascinating destination. In 2002 the exhibit added mock-ups of the Mars *Odyssey* spacecraft and one of the rovers soon to explore the red planet. A year after the mock-ups arrived, the Space Experience lost its space to a new **FASTPASS** area for **Buzz Lightyear Astro Blasters**.

America on Parade

DATES: June 14, 1975–September 6, 1976

In the mid-'70s, the proud patriotism already displayed throughout Disneyland, especially in such vivid attractions as **America Sings** and **Great Moments with Mr. Lincoln**, blossomed into a memorable bicentennial spectacular. A week after debuting in Walt Disney World, America on Parade began rolling through Disneyland on June 14, 1975. For the next 15 months, an immense daily cavalcade of American popular music, oversize characters, floats shaped like red, white, and blue hot air balloons, displays of iconic moments from American history, and a marching band celebrated the nation's 200th birthday. Mickey, Goofy, and Donald portrayed the three "Spirit of '76" musicians, and an April 3, 1976 TV special showed off all the pageantry. According to *Disneyland: The First Thirty Years*, 25 million people watched the 1,200 performances. After the finale on September 6, 1976, the **Main Street Electrical Parade**, which had been suspended for the duration of America on Parade, returned for another long run.

America Sings

MAP: Tomorrowland, T-14

DATES: June 29, 1974–April 10, 1988

Located in the back corner of **Tomorrowland** near the **Autopia**, the circular two-story Carousel Theater opened in the summer of 1967 as a three-quarter-acre cornerstone of the area's dramatic remodel. The innovative **Carousel of Progress** was the building's first attraction. When its six-year spin ended in 1973 so it could move to Walt Disney World, the building was revitalized with a lively new attraction, this one arriving just in time for the bicentennial festivities that would peak in 1976.

Though it revolved in the opposite direction, America Sings utilized the same rotating-theater format the Carousel of Progress had used to slowly wheel the audience around a stationary hub. Whereas the Carousel of Progress had presented mini-plays with dialogue, America Sings was more like a six-part Carousel of Music. A group of 114 **Audio-Animatronic** characters—the largest Disneyland assembly ever, at the time—saluted America's musical heritage with a 24-minute show that included a prologue, four lighthearted musical medleys, and an epilogue.

Overseeing the proceedings was a patriotic pair of Audio-Animatronic birds, an eagle named Sam and an owl named Ollie. A simple rendition of "Yankee Doodle Dandy" kicked off the show, followed by performances of more than three dozen classic American songs from, among others, a swamp of bullfrogs, a wailing possum, gospel-singing foxes, a chorus line of high-kicking birds, an Old West bird quartet known as the Frontier Four, barbershop geese, grim vultures, storks on old-fashioned bicycles, and a long-haired, modern rock band featuring a crane on lead guitar who invited the audience to join in for the rousing "Joy to the World" finale. Classic American costumes—cowboy hats, Gay '90s dresses, Jazz Age suits, etc.—and gentle humor boosted the feel-good tunes.

Some of the characters' voices probably sounded familiar to guests. Sam was performed by amiable folk singer Burl Ives, and the pig who belted out "Bill Bailey, Won't You Please Come Home" was vocalized by **Betty Taylor**, the singer who starred as Slue-Foot Sue over in the **Golden Horseshoe** in **Frontierland**. Many of the charming anthropomorphic animals were first drawn up by Disney Legend **Marc Davis**, whose illustrations in the '60s had added comic flair to **Pirates of the Caribbean** and the **Haunted Mansion**.

The whole production was popular enough to be released as a Disneyland Records soundtrack LP with 39 songs. However, once the bicentennial events had passed, so had the audiences for America Sings. With attendance in the Carousel Theater dwindling, the admission ticket was downgraded from an E to a D, and in 1988 the last song was finally sung. Offices occupied the building until **Innoventions** opened in 1992. However, although the America Sings attraction disappeared, its characters didn't. Most of the musical animals joined the zip-a-dee-doo-dah critters inside **Splash Mountain**, and the armatures of a couple of the geese were transformed into high-tech droids for the **Star Tours** line area.

Anderson, Ken
(1909–1993)

Like many of the Disney Legends who helped create Disneyland, Ken Anderson worked on Disney's animated films before he started designing park attractions. Born in 1909 in Seattle, Washington, Anderson had been studying architecture and art when he was hired by

Walt Disney in 1934 to work first on the *Silly Symphonies* cartoons and then on *Snow White and the Seven Dwarfs* (he's credited as the artist who, among other things, added Dopey's wiggling ears).

After contributing story ideas, art, and layouts to many more animated classics of the 1940s and '50s, Anderson sketched out the scenes of Norman Rockwell-style Americana that would have formed the miniature Disneylandia sets Walt Disney wanted to take on tour (when the tour idea proved to be unworkable, the park concept coalesced). In the early '50s, Anderson joined the core Disneyland design team and became a major contributor to the attractions in **Fantasyland**, especially **Snow White Adventures**, **Peter Pan Flight**, **Storybook Land Canal Boats**, and **Mr. Toad's Wild Ride**. Elsewhere in the park, Anderson worked on the **20,000 Leagues Under the Sea Exhibit** and later the **Haunted Mansion**, among other attractions.

To other Imagineers, Anderson was more than just a brilliant artist. The book *Walt Disney Imagineering*, written by Anderson's peers, calls him "the first Imagineer" because, years before Disneyland opened, he had tried to develop a nine-inch-tall "dancing man"—the earliest attempt at a Disney **Audio-Animatronics** figure.

Ken Anderson was named a Disney Legend in 1991; two years later he died of a stroke in La Cañada-Flintridge, California.

Apartments

MAP: Town Square, TS-5; New Orleans Square, NOS-1

DATES: July 1955–ongoing; ca. 1970–1987

To give **Walt Disney** and his family their own secluded nook at Disneyland, Disney had a private apartment built above the **Fire Department** on **Town Square**. This apartment wasn't merely a VIP rest stop—it was an actual residence, a place where Disney and his family could stay overnight inside the park, for days at a time if necessary. Appropriately enough for this corner of Disneyland, the posh apartment was decorated like something out of the early 1900s. **Emile Kuri**, who decorated the sets for dozens of live-action Disney movies, brought in white columns, patterned wallpaper, red drapes, antique Victorian furniture, a Victrola phonograph that actually worked, and even an old-fashioned candlestick phone (a big, squat TV was one of the few conspicuous concessions to modern times). The apartment was

small, though, just 500 square feet with a changing room, a cozy front room where the couches unfolded into beds, a bathroom, and a tiny kitchen area with a grill, refrigerator, and sink. An outside lounge area stretching toward **City Hall** was decorated with white statues, plants, and wicker chairs.

From his front windows, Disney could look out on the bustling activity of Town Square, with the **Santa Fe & Disneyland Railroad** train station to his right, the **Opera House** straight across, and the **Emporium** to his left. The public wasn't allowed inside, of course, and in fact the fire pole in the **Fire Department** below was blocked off to prevent anyone from shimmying up into the apartment (it's said that Disney himself used to slide down the pole occasionally). Also, so that the residents upstairs wouldn't be disturbed by people ringing the fire bell downstairs, the outer doors to the Fire Department were usually closed when the apartment was occupied.

No mention of the apartment was made in the park's early **souvenir books**, and no photos of the apartment were released until an exclusive shot of the Disney family relaxing in the main room ran in the August 1963 issue of *National Geographic* (the magazine dubbed the apartment "Disney's supersecret hideaway"). One of the few times the general public has seen anyone in the apartment was **Opening Day**, when the TV broadcast of the festivities showed some people watching from the front window. Today, Disney's relatives occasionally use the apartment, and it's sometimes included as a stop on special tours. As a tribute to Disney, a lamp, visible from Town Square, is always lit in the front window.

In the '60s Disney decided that he needed another private apartment at the other end of the park for both himself and his brother, **Roy Disney**. This bigger residence is located above the **Pirates of the Caribbean** entrance in **New Orleans Square**, with bedrooms for grandchildren and a balcony that connected to the private dining rooms at **Club 33**.

Disney died before the second apartment was completed. It was used as offices for the Disneyland staff until 1987, when the whole space was converted into the **Disney Gallery**, with lavish décor to suggest what the finished apartment would have looked like. On the balcony outside the gallery's front door was an ornate iron railing with the initials of the apartment's intended occupants—WD and RD—woven into the design. In late 2007 the rooms were remodeled into a 2,600-square-foot Disneyland Dream Suite for the 2008 Disney Dreams Giveaway. The new guest quarters include a patio with "fireflies," a living room with French Provincial décor, two master bedrooms, two bathrooms, an electric train, a full-size carousel horse, vintage toys, and unique audio and visual effects.

Aramaki, Hideo
(1915–2005)

In the 1960s and '70s, guests who enjoyed fine meals in Disneyland had Hideo Aramaki to thank. He was the man in charge of the food at the park for almost two decades.
Born in Hawaii in 1915, Aramaki was of Japanese descent but since childhood had
been nicknamed "Indian." A semi-professional baseball player in the 1930s, he began
working in restaurant kitchens across the country in the '40s and moved to Southern
California to run a Hawaiian-themed restaurant in the '50s.

In 1964 Aramaki was hired as the chef of the **Tahitian Terrace** in **Adventureland.**
Even though he had no formal culinary training, he was so successful that by 1967 he
was the executive chef overseeing all of Disneyland's restaurants, standardizing the
food quality, and training the park's chefs—as well as personally preparing special
meals for visiting dignitaries. After performing some of these same duties at Walt
Disney World, Hideo Aramaki retired in 1985. He was named a Disney Legend in 2005,
the same year he died, at age 90.

Art Corner

MAP: Tomorrowland, T-6

DATES: October 1, 1955–September 6, 1966

During the summer of 1955, a temporary art show operated at the north end of **Main
Street** under some canopies and a red-on-blue banner that read, "Disney Artists Exhibit." That October, the exhibit relocated into a corner building about 200 feet inside
Tomorrowland. The boxy Art Corner adjoined the round **Satellite View of America**
building and stuck out toward the **Astro-Jets** some 50 feet away. To help make the
gallery fit in with futuristic Tomorrowland, the Art Corner's exterior was painted with
colorful modern art motifs.

Inside was a French-themed setting for art supplies, Disney artwork (including thousands of inexpensive—and now rare—animation cels), and many Disneyland
postcards, among them sets that depicted Disney characters frolicking in the Art
Corner itself. Animators were on hand to draw quick portraits of guests for only
$1.50, and for convenience the shop offered framing, mailing services, and even a
mail-order catalog.

Because of the comprehensive remodel that closed many attractions throughout
Tomorrowland in 1966, the art departed from the corner site, and a year later the
building reemerged as part of the larger **Tomorrowland Terrace.** Though the attraction poster for the Art Corner listed only one location (the one in Tomorrowland),
the park's **souvenir books** of the 1950s and '60s listed another Art Corner selling
"pictures and art supplies" in **Fantasyland**; early maps pinpointed it as a small establishment northwest of the **Mickey Mouse Club Theater**, an area that later became
the **Village Inn** (now the **Village Haus**) restaurant.

Art of Animation

MAP: Tomorrowland, T-5

DATES: May 28, 1960–September 5, 1966

Like the **Art Corner**, the Art of Animation seemed slightly out of place in space-age **Tomorrowland**—both establishments basically celebrated the past, not the future. The Art of Animation sat in the big building next to the **Circarama** theater. Previously, the **Satellite View of America** had spun in this large, round space; however, by the end of the '50s, the novelty of looking at Earth from high altitude had worn off and audiences had disappeared. So did the attraction, in February of 1960.

Its replacement that spring, the Art of Animation, was an exhibit promoting Disney's own movies and requiring a B ticket from the park's **ticket book**. It was basically the same as several other Art of Animation exhibits that had already been touring the world to build excitement for *Sleeping Beauty*, the 1959 movie that was, at the time, Disney Studios' most expensive production ever. The large **attraction poster** for the Art of Animation acknowledged the other touring exhibits, its burnt-orange background decorated with sketches of three Disney characters and text that touted the attraction as the International Exhibit Direct from London–Paris–Tokyo.

The inside perimeter of the Art of Animation exhibit was lined with displays showing how animated movies were made. The center of the room was given over to arrangements of plastic chairs, potted plants, and ashtrays, enabling guests to sit, reflect, and smoke inside the exhibit. In the fall of '66, the Art of Animation vanished when the adjacent theater building expanded to become **World Premiere Circle-Vision** for 1967's "new Tomorrowland."

Arts and Crafts Shop

MAP: Fantasyland, Fa-3

DATES: Ca. 1958–ca. 1963; ca. 1970–1982

In the late 1950s, this intimate shop was located just inside the entrance to **Sleeping Beauty Castle**, on the left-hand side. The **Clock Shop** replaced the Arts and Crafts Shop around 1963, but by the beginning of the '70s the Arts and Crafts Shop had returned. This reappearance was one of the few times a closed Disneyland business reopened with the same name, in the same location (for other attractions, shops, and eateries that accomplished this trick, see the Gone/Not Gone sidebar on page 294).

Delicate, expensive gifts were sold in the Arts and Crafts Shop, including ornate imported clocks and handblown glass sculptures. Around 1982, with Fantasyland undergoing a major remodel, the shop closed for good; a year later a new glass shop, **Castle Arts**, opened in its place. The old arts-and-crafts theme lived on, however, because another new store, **Geppetto's Arts & Crafts**, also debuted in '83, its location about 200 feet north, near **Pinocchio's Daring Journey**.

Astro-Jets, aka Tomorrowland Jets

MAP: Tomorrowland, T-8

DATES: March 24, 1956–September 5, 1966

The basic Astro-Jet idea wasn't invented by Disney designers. Rides with similar vehicles that whirled around a central pivot were already working in East Coast amusement parks before Disneyland even opened. The Disneyland spin on the spinners was to upgrade the theme with better detailing. Disney artist **John Hench** drew up a concept for a whirling rocket attraction in 1955, dubbing it the Saturn Patrol Ride Rocket. The Astro-Jets, however, didn't debut until 1956, making this Disneyland's first major addition after **Opening Day**.

> **Names of the Astro-Jets**
>
> 1. *Altair*
> 2. *Antares*
> 3. *Arcturus*
> 4. *Canopus*
> 5. *Capella*
> 6. *Castor*
> 7. *Procyon*
> 8. *Regulus*
> 9. *Rigel*
> 10. *Sirius*
> 11. *Spica*
> 12. *Vega*

For the next four decades, some variation of the Astro-Jets stood in the heart of **Tomorrowland** about 50 feet west of today's **Innoventions** building. From 1956 to 1964 the attraction was known as the Astro-Jets, a dozen stubby cylinders with thin wings, a headlight on the nose, and open cockpits barely big enough for two adults. Named after bright Milky Way stars, the jets were white with either red or blue trim and seemed more like contemporary Air Force aircraft than futuristic "astro" craft (indeed, honorary Air Force personnel were on hand when the attraction opened). Each jet was mounted on an arm extending 20 feet from an axial column that looked like an air-traffic control tower. Guests paid their C, and later B, tickets from their Disneyland **ticket books** and entered the jets at ground level. Once the whirling began, pilots controlled their altitude with a lever inside each cockpit, raising the jets up to a height of around 36 feet.

On August 7, 1964, the name Tomorrowland Jets supplanted Astro-Jets to avoid any unintentional association with American Airlines, which had started painting the words Astro-Jet on the side of its airliners. Two years later, the countdown to a much bigger change began. On September 5, 1966, the Tomorrowland Jets closed for a renaming/remodeling and reopened in mid-'67 as the dramatic new **Rocket Jets** in a dramatic new location.

Astro-Orbitor

MAP: Tomorrowland, T-3

DATES: May 22, 1998–ongoing

Variations of a whirling-jet attraction began operating in Disneyland in 1956. For 1998's new Astro-Orbitor, stylings came from both Disneyland Paris, where it had originated as the Orbitron Machine Volantes (Orbitron Flying Machine), and Walt Disney World, where it had opened in 1994 as the Astro-Orbiter (with an "-er" suffix). When the latest "new **Tomorrowland**" was planned for Disneyland in the mid-'90s, designers

basically recreated the Parisian and Floridian attractions—one of the few times a Disney design emigrated from east to west, instead of the reverse.

Compared to the uncomplicated **Astro-Jets** and sleek **Rocket Jets** that had orbited in Tomorrowland for four decades, the new Astro-Orbitor is a complex conglomeration of moving spheres and fanciful spaceships inspired, as Disneyland's own publications have noted, by the works of Leonardo da Vinci. The color scheme is no longer stark and achromatic—vintage gold and brass tones, punctuated by strong blues, create the impression that this is an intricate mechanical whirligig built in some earlier century (or if not built, at least imagined in one of Jules Verne's 19th-century novels).

Not only is the look drastically different, the new location is, too. The Astro-Orbitor stands about 250 feet away from the site previously occupied by the Astro-Jets, deep inside Tomorrowland. Today, the 64-foot-tall Astro-Orbitor anchors Tomorrowland as the first attraction at the land's entrance. This new spot is just in front of the **PeopleMover** tracks and about 50 feet outside Tomorrowland's metallic gates. At night, its gleaming lights and shining metal transform the Astro-Orbitor into a kind of animated lighthouse that guides guests into the future.

As with previous iterations of Disneyland's whirling-jets concept, there are 12 vehicles, the altitude of each vehicle is controlled by the pilot via an inboard handle, and the ride-time is about 90 seconds. One curiosity never explained is the spelling: the "-or" suffix has been said to be the result of a typo in original plans, or perhaps it was intended to be a quick way to differentiate the Florida and Anaheim attractions. The hyphen in the name appears irregularly in Disneyland's own literature.

Atencio, Francis Xavier
(1920–)

From classic movies to classic rides, Francis Xavier Atencio's Disney career has paralleled Disney history from the 1930s to the '80s. Born in Colorado in 1920, Atencio came to Los Angeles in 1937 and began studying at a local art institute. A year later he was hired as a Disney animator, and soon after that he was working on *Fantasia*. Known simply as "X" around the company, he served in World War II and then returned to Disney to work on some of the studio's most popular productions, including several Oscar-winning shorts and acclaimed features like *The Parent Trap* and *Mary Poppins*.

In the '60s, Atencio began working on Disneyland projects throughout the park.

The August 1963 issue of *National Geographic* showed him programming an **Audio-Animatronics** bird for the **Enchanted Tiki Room**. He also contributed to the **Grand Canyon** and **Primeval World** dioramas, wrote the scripts for **Adventure Thru Inner Space** and **Pirates of the Caribbean**, and penned the pirates' legendary "Yo Ho (A Pirate's Life for Me)" lyrics (Atencio even performed the creepy voice for the talking pirate skull that prefaces the first waterfall). At the end of

the decade, Atencio thrilled audiences with his work on the **Haunted Mansion**. Once again, he wrote the narrator's script and the lyrics of the main theme song ("Grim Grinning Ghosts"). The cemetery outside the mansion honored Atencio's contributions with an honorary tombstone that reads: "Requiescat Francis Xavier: No Time Off for Good Behavior RIP."

When Disney expanded its theme parks to Florida, Atencio was right alongside, assisting on such major attractions as **Space Mountain** and EPCOT. He even helped with Tokyo Disneyland in the early '80s before finally retiring in 1984. A dozen years later, X Atencio was named a Disney Legend.

Attraction Posters

MAP: Park, P-5

DATES: Ca. 1955–ongoing

Beautiful posters have adorned the Disneyland **entrance** since the mid-1950s. Most guests have seen the 16 posters inside the two main tunnels that lead from the turnstiles to **Town Square**, but the posters haven't always been there. In the '50s they were placed along the low metal fence that surrounds the Mickey Mouse flower bed in front of the **Main Street** train station; additional posters have also appeared elsewhere in the park, such as along the **Avenue of the Flags**, on the walls of the **Plaza Gardens**, and inside **Redd Rockett's Pizza Port**.

Wherever they've been placed over the years, the posters have offered tantalizing glimpses of the park's highlights. The large size of the posters—three feet wide by four and a half feet tall—means they can be seen from a distance, drawing guests toward them like moths to a thrilling flame. The posters contain bold artwork that captures the spirit of the attractions at the expense of literal renderings. Thus the Jungle River poster magnifies an elephant into a trumpeting goliath towering over the foliage, the **Skyway to Tomorrowland** poster raises its buckets hundreds of feet aloft, and the **Flying Saucers** poster shows saucers that actually work.

The simple designs make the posters easy to understand—a key requirement considering most of the viewers are distracted and on the move. Stenciled by hand, the posters usually present blocky shapes and strong colors instead of intricate details

55 Attraction Poster Subjects

Sail with the wildest crew that ever sacked the Spanish Main

Adventureland
Enchanted Tiki Room
Indiana Jones
   Adventure
Jungle River/Jungle
   Cruise
Swiss Family Treehouse
Tarzan's Treehouse

Critter Country
Country Bear Jamboree
Splash Mountain
The Many Adventures
   of Winnie the Pooh

Fantasyland
Alice in Wonderland
Dumbo the Flying Elephant
It's a Small World
Mad Hatter's Mad Tea Party
Magical Fireworks
Matterhorn Bobsleds
Mickey Mouse Club 3-D Theater
Mr. Toad's Wild Ride
Peter Pan's Flight
Pinocchio's Daring Journey
Remember . . . Dreams Come
   True Fireworks
Snow White's Scary Adventures
Storybook Land Canal Boats

Frontierland
Big Thunder Mountain Railroad
Casa de Fritos
Golden Horseshoe Revue
Mark Twain Riverboat
Nature's Wonderland/Rainbow
   Caverns
Sailing Ship *Columbia*
Stage Coach/Mine Train/Mule Pack
Tom Sawyer Island

Hub, Main Street, Town Square
Great Moments with
   Mr. Lincoln
Primeval World
Red Wagon Inn
Santa Fe &
   Disneyland
   Railroad

New Orleans Square
The Haunted Mansion
Pirates of the
   Caribbean

Tomorrowland
Adventure Thru Inner Space
American Journeys
America the Beautiful
Art Corner
Art of Animation
Astro-Jets
Autopia
Captain EO Tribute
Carousel of Progress
Flying Saucers
Monorail
PeopleMover
Rocket Jets
Rocket to the Moon
Skyway to Fantasyland
Space Mountain
Space Station X-1
Star Tours
Submarine Voyage/Finding Nemo
   Submarine Voyage
20,000 Leagues Under the Sea
   Exhibit

and subtle shading. Not always, though—the later **Jungle Cruise**, **Big Thunder Mountain Railroad**, and **Country Bear Jamboree** posters are all wonderfully ornate. Whenever guests are shown in the images, they're typically either small silhouettes (their diminutive size contrasting the immensity of something else on the poster) or flat, cartoony caricatures complimenting, not distracting from, the main subject. No signatures appear on any of the posters, but several poster artists have been identified over the years, including Bjorn Aronson, **Mary Blair**, **Claude Coats**, **Rolly Crump**, Paul Hartley, and **John Hench**.

While the posters have usually advertised major attractions and exhibits, they have also promoted restaurants and businesses occasionally. **Casa de Fritos**, the **Red Wagon Inn**, the **Art Corner**, the **Art of Animation**, and the **Disneyland Hotel** have all had their own posters. Some of the attractions have had two separate posters: the Jungle Cruise, **PeopleMover**, **Star Tours**, and the **Enchanted Tiki Room** are among those that appear in multiple versions. Original posters mounted on fabric are collectors' items that sell for thousands of dollars. Relatively inexpensive productions have been sold in and out of the park for years in various formats and sizes; Disneyland's own Art on Demand service has offered customized presentations.

Audio-Animatronics

DATES: 1960–ongoing

Much has been written about Disneyland's innovative Audio-Animatronics. Even as scholarly a commentator as the medievalist Umberto Eco has surrendered to the "miraculous efficacy" of the park's A-A figures. They enabled Walt Disney to construct "a fantasy world more real than reality," Eco wrote in *Travels in Hyperreality*, with "perfect imitation" that has "reached its apex." It took years of focused effort for **Walt Disney** to attain that apex.

The seed for what would later blossom into **Great Moments with Mr. Lincoln** was planted on vacations Walt Disney took in the 1940s. During trips to New Orleans and Europe, Disney was fascinated by small mechanical birds and toys, which he brought home and studied. Inspired to try to make something similar, Disney began dreaming of a traveling exhibit with miniature sets and small mechanical figures. In '51 he even had several employees, notably **Ken Anderson** and **Roger Broggie**, create a small mechanical man who executed pre-recorded dance moves (film footage of the long-limbed song-and-dance man Buddy Ebsen helped the engineers work out the steps). Once Disneyland was on the drawing boards, early plans called for talking Chinese characters and animals in an unrealized **Chinatown** area off **Main Street**.

The first appearance in the park of early Audio-Animatronic figures came in 1960 in **Nature's Wonderland**, the **Frontierland** acreage toured by mules and mine trains. Hundreds of mechanical birds, reptiles, bears, and other wilderness animals made repeated motions that, while simple compared to later figures, seemed completely realistic from a distance. In 1963, the **Enchanted Tiki Room** brought Audio-Animatronics up-close and center stage with its cast of tropical birds and tiki sculptures that performed a complex show filled with dialogue, song, and movement all choreographed by a primitive (by today's standards) computer the size of a closet. It was in those years that Disney Legend **Bill Cottrell** coined the trademarked term Audio-Animatronics, a portmanteau word that Walt Disney eagerly appropriated as a descriptive name for the ambitious electro-mechanical figures his design team was steadily producing.

If audiences were delighted by the tiki show, they were startled by the next developments in Audio-Animatronics, first unveiled at the 1964–1965 New York World's Fair. In Queens, **It's a Small World** immediately charmed audiences with its singing children; towering dinosaurs squared off in an exhibit that later became Disneyland's **Primeval World Diorama**; Progressland presented 32 Audio-Animatronic family members in what Disneyland guests would know as the **Carousel of Progress**; and, most ambitiously, a life-size President Lincoln stood up and delivered a speech to the amazement of nearly everyone in attendance.

With the hydraulics and electronics quickly improving, by the mid-1970s Audio-Animatronic figures populated every corner of the park. There were brainy Mission Control engineers talking to guests in **Flight to the Moon**, personable pirates cavorting through **Pirates of the Caribbean**, banjo-pickin' bears in the **Country Bear Jamboree**, bike-riding birds in **America Sings**, and so many more for so many years now that it's hard to remember a time when Audio-Animatronic figures *weren't* on display.

"People get more out of [Audio-Animatronics] than if there were a real actor there," said Disney Legend **John Hench** in Thomas and Johnston's *Disney Animation*. Advanced A-A characters, he said, "actually do a better job—there's something *super* human about them."

By the time Indiana Jones swung through **Indiana Jones Adventure** in 1995, the art and technology of Audio-Animatronics was so advanced that the truly lifelike Indy didn't simply dazzle guests, he confused some of them into believing he was an actual person. Dazzlement and believability—two words that initially inspired the creation of Disneyland and then came to describe Disney's remarkable achievements with Audio-Animatronics.

Aunt Jemima's Pancake House,
aka Aunt Jemima's Kitchen

MAP: Frontierland, Fr-7

DATES: August 9, 1955–1970

Back in the 1950s and '60s, Quaker Oats sponsored a restaurant that brought a "gracious 'Old South' setting" (according to an original place mat) to the western tip of

Frontierland. Aunt Jemima's Pancake House opened a few weeks after the rest of the park did, its location about 75 feet from the nearest bank of the **Rivers of America** and another 75 from the spot where the **Swiss Family Treehouse** would rise up in 1962. A huge, 22-ton Monterey Bay fig tree, craned into place in front of the restaurant, offered shade for alfresco dining.

Besides its great pancakes and waffles topped with Aunt Jemima syrup, the restaurant was known for having Aunt Jemima herself on hand. Aunt Jemima was only a Quaker Oats character, of course, first played in public early in the century by a former slave who died in 1923. Seven women assumed the character over the decades, including Aylene Lewis, who portrayed her at Disneyland. As Aunt Jemima, Lewis would greet guests, visit tables, and, as declared on the place mats, "send you on your way with a cheerful 'You all come back!'"

Early in 1962, the restaurant temporarily closed. Expanding into the space next door where **Don DeFore's Silver Banjo Barbecue** had been, it reopened in July as Aunt Jemima's Kitchen. The restaurant had two doorways, since it straddled the corner between Frontierland and **Adventureland**. The Frontierland entrance incorporated plantation architecture, while the Adventureland entrance featured a thatched, jungle-themed roof. Quaker Oats ended its participation at Disneyland in 1967, but the park sustained the Aunt Jemima theme until 1970, when the restaurant was remodeled and renamed the **Magnolia Tree Terrace**.

Autopia, aka Tomorrowland Autopia, aka Autopia, Presented by Chevron

MAP: Tomorrowland, T-12

DATES: July 17, 1955–ongoing

Of the four Autopias that have existed in Disneyland, the one in **Tomorrowland** was the only Autopia up and running on **Opening Day**. This original Autopia track curled across approximately three unlandscaped acres of Disneyland's eastern edge, with most of the track design attributed to Disney Legend **Marvin Davis**.

With the nation's interstate highway system developing rapidly in the '50s, most of the Disneyland **souvenir books** from that decade labeled the driving attraction as Autopia Cars and Freeway. The 1959 book renamed it "Super Autopia Freeway," differentiating the D-ticket (see **ticket books**) **Tomorrowland** original from **Fantasyland's** C-ticket **Junior Autopia** (opened in 1956) and B-ticket **Midget Autopia** (1957). The large **Fun Maps** of the '60s and beyond used the site-specific designation Tomorrowland Autopia to avoid confusion with the **Fantasyland Autopia** that debuted in 1959.

During these early years the Richfield Oil Corporation, "the official gasoline of Disneyland" and the company that in 1970 would become the "R" in ARCO, was the sponsor of the Autopia, and the Richfield name was prominently displayed on the signage at the site. In 2000 the Chevron Corporation became the sponsor of the redesigned attraction that has been operating ever since as Autopia, Presented by Chevron.

The 1956 souvenir book called the Autopia "Disneyland's cars of the future," though it's hard to see how these small, slow, noisy, gas-powered autos driven mostly by kids were futuristic. Fun, yes; futuristic, no. For the first decade of operation, the track did not have a guide rail running down its center, meaning drivers could veer their cars into each other, pass each other, and in some cases even manage to go against traffic (a persistent legend has Sammy Davis Jr. being chased off the road into some bushes in 1955). Not until 1965 was a center rail installed down the middle of the Autopia freeway to keep cars aligned.

In contrast, the cars themselves, which were mostly designed by Disney Legend **Bob Gurr**, went through many modifications. The earliest sketches show bulbous, heavy fenders and running boards on the cars, just like on classic American autos of the '40s and '50s, thus making the "cars of the future" really more like "cars of the recent past." The Mark I cars that hit the Tomorrowland road in 1955 were modeled on foreign sports cars—Porsches and Ferraris in particular—to give them a sleek, low-slung look that anticipated styles of the next decade, if not quite the next century. Unfortunately, with bodies made of fiberglass and bumpers of soft aluminum, the cars couldn't withstand anything more than slight impacts, even though they usually traveled at less than eight miles per hour. Consequently, when drivers decided to ram other vehicles or bounce off the side of the track, the toll was both disastrous and

immediate—according to the 2007 *Disneyland Secrets, Stories, & Magic* DVD, 95 percent of the cars running at the start of Opening Day were either disabled or broken down by day's end (that is, 38 out of 40 cars were no longer "usable").

Before the end of 1955, two more versions of the Autopia cars—the Mark II and Mark III—arrived with sturdier engines and chassis. Yet another update, the Mark IV, appeared midway through 1956, and an even heavier, slower (hence safer) version came in '59. This iteration, the Mark V, was the longest-lasting design of its time and wasn't replaced until 1965, the same year that the center rail was finally installed on the track.

Since drivers could no longer sideswipe each other, the side bumpers were taken off these cars. Then, in keeping with the dramatic remodel of "new Tomorrowland," new Mark VII Autopia cars debuted in 1967 that were, at over $5,000 apiece, the most expensive yet (by comparison, guests could have bought two brand-new, full-size Ford Mustangs for that price). Looking like little Corvette Stingrays, these Autopia cars were also the most durable and rode the track until the end of the century.

After temporarily closing in 1999, the 2000 version of the attraction opened with a large video screen displaying animations, a grandstand viewing area, new cars that came in three different styles (Dusty, Suzy, and Sparky, to coincide with the TV ads of Chevron, the new sponsor), and a longer, more exciting, and more humorous driving experience. The new layout incorporated the extinct Fantasyland Autopia track, stretched the ride time to over six minutes, and even included a bouncy "off-road" section.

No matter the era, guests of all ages have enjoyed the Autopia experience, and it remains one of the park's most consistently popular attractions (and the only one in Tomorrowland left from Opening Day). This popularity may seem ironic, since most guests have to fight their way through freeway traffic just to get to Disneyland—it seems unrealistic to ask them to wait in line for a chance to get behind the wheel of another car. However, many adults, prominent celebrities, and even **Walt Disney** himself have happily taken the cars for a spin. Kids, naturally, have always jumped at the chance to take the wheel, especially if they were over 52 inches tall and could drive alone.

Decades of nifty enhancements have helped make the Autopia a utopia for trivia fans. Of the original Mark I cars, four were designed to look like patrol cars, with black-and-white color schemes, sirens, and flashing lights. Also, in the '50s and '60s kids could get free Official Drivers Licenses from Richfield Autopia, certifying them as safe drivers (new Chevron Drivers Licenses were offered as of 2000). These days, humorous signs punctuate the trip: there's one that warns of "Mouse Crossing" near a mouse hole, another that designates the road as Disneyland Route 55 (in honor of the inaugural year), and cartoony roadside billboards that advertise clever products. One of the dinky **Midget Autopia** cars is still displayed about a minute into the drive, followed shortly by an ancient car from **Mr. Toad's Wild Ride**. The Autopia roadway may be only about a mile long, but for millions of drivers that's a mile of smiles.

Autopia Winner's Circle

MAP: Tomorrowland, T-10, T-13

DATES: June 29, 2000–ongoing

Once again tying in a store with a nearby attraction, Disneyland opened the small Autopia Winner's Circle shop next to **Autopia** in 2000. The new shop's debut was timed to the reopening of the 45-year-old Autopia, which had temporarily shut down for a remodel to accommodate its new sponsor, Chevron. With its motoring souvenirs (including models of the cute cars from Chevron's TV commercials) and an actual Autopia car on display, the store made for a nice pit stop for automotive fans. Guests could also get the photos for their Autopia Drivers Licenses taken here.

Back in 2000, the Winner's Circle was located close to the lagoon where guests had once lined up for the **Submarine Voyage**, which closed in 1998. But with the submarines scheduled to resurface in mid-2007, and the Winner's Circle space slated to become the subs' **queue** area once again, in late 2006 the Winner's Circle relocated to its current position next to **Innoventions**, where the **Mad Hatter of Tomorrowland** had once set up shop.

Avenue of the Flags

MAP: Tomorrowland, T-2

DATES: March 1956–September 1966

On **Opening Day**, flags from all the states in the union—there were only 48 in 1955—flew on tall aluminum flagpoles in the star-shaped **Court of Honor** deep inside **Tomorrowland**. A year later, the newly created **Astro-Jets** needed a home, so the flagpoles were uprooted, the Court was adjourned, and the Astro-Jets touched down.

The flagpoles, meanwhile, were re-installed in a prominent new location that needed some kind of dramatic statement: the 150-foot-long walkway that connected the **Hub** and the entrance to Tomorrowland. At one time a science-inspired sculpture rising up from the middle of a wide fountain had been planned for this walkway, but as construction invoices lengthened and deadlines shortened in the frantic spring of 1955, the sculpture concept was abandoned.

While not as imaginative as the sculpture-fountain combination, the flagpoles were a convenient and patriotic addition to the landscaped walkway, soon dubbed the Avenue of the Flags. When they were installed in '56, the flags were placed in the numerical order in which their states had been admitted to the Union; three years later both Alaska and Hawaii were added to complete the 50. Mounted six feet up each flagpole was a black plaque identifying the state and its date of admission, ordinal number among the states, and motto. Crowning the Avenue of the Flags was Old Glory, flying at the Tomorrowland end of the walkway right in front of the **Clock of the World**; 250 feet behind the clock soared the majestic *Moonliner*, with the Astro-Jets twirling nearby. In September 1966 the flags were lowered and removed as construction began on futuristic new Tomorrowland gates that would debut 10 months later.

Babes in Toyland Exhibit

MAP: Town Square, TS-9

DATES: December 17, 1961–September 30, 1963

Babes in Toyland, Disney Studios' first big-budget, live-action musical, hit the 1961 **holiday season** accompanied by lots of holiday hoopla. With Annette Funicello, America's sweetheart, starring alongside teen idol Tommy Sands and Disney mainstay Tommy Kirk, the picture was expected to be a blockbuster, and so a walk-through *Babes in Toyland* Exhibit was installed in the **Opera House** on **Town Square**.

This was the first public exposure to the Opera House's interior. From **Opening Day** in 1955 and onward for the next six and a half years, the Opera House doors were locked because the interior space was being used to store lumber for the park's construction projects. However, three days after *Babes in Toyland* opened in theaters, the Opera House's doors opened to guests. Inside the building were some of the actual sets and props from the movie, including the Mother Goose Village and the Forest of No Return, plus **cast members** dressed like Bo Peep, anthropomorphic trees, and other movie characters.

The exhibit proved to be only slightly more long-lasting than the movie, which failed at the box office. There was no mention of the exhibit in any of the Disneyland **souvenir books** of the early '60s, and within a year of its opening some of the sets were struck. Segments of *The Mickey Mouse Club* TV show were shot on what remained, but by October of '63 the last of the *Babes in Toyland* artifacts were gone, and the Opera House became home to the **Mickey Mouse Club Headquarters**.

Baby Station,
aka Baby Center, aka Baby Care Center

MAP: Hub, H-6

DATES: July 1957–ongoing

On the Fourth of July in 1979, out on a bench in the **Hub**, the first baby was born at Disneyland. Fortunately the park's official Baby Station was nearby. The Baby Station has always been located on East Plaza Street, about 25 feet to the right of what was called the **Red Wagon Inn** back in 1955 and the Plaza Inn as of 1965. Anyone trying to find it could just look for all the baby strollers parked outside.

Though the Baby Station has frontage only about 10 feet wide, the interior is about 50 feet deep. Inside the room, parents can find all manner of helpful supplies and services—everything from pacifiers and baby bottles to diapers and a diaper-changing area (but no babysitters). The Mead Johnson Corporation, maker of Pablum baby cereal, was the establishment's first sponsor, and thus the park's 1958 **souvenir book** listed the site as the Pablum Baby Station. However, by '61 it was called simply the Baby Station, followed later by Baby Center, Gerber Station, Gerber Baby Care Center, and Car-

nation Baby Care Center. In 2007, the name was Disneyland Baby Care Center, hosted by Nestlé. No matter the name, this facility has always had an adorable baby picture on the wall. The baby? None other than 10-month-old **Walt Disney**.

Baker, Buddy
(1918–2002)

The rollicking "Grim Grinning Ghosts" theme music in the **Haunted Mansion**? That's the work of prolific composer Buddy Baker, who wrote the music for hundreds of Disney attractions, movies, and TV shows.

Norman Dale Baker was born in Missouri in 1918. After earning a Ph.D. in music, he played with noted big bands and began composing music for television. Hired at Disney Studios in 1954, he wrote and/or arranged music for *The Mickey Mouse Club* show, the **Disneyland TV series**, and dozens of Disney films.

At Disneyland, in addition to composing the Haunted Mansion music, Baker wrote the background music for **Great Moments with Mr. Lincoln**, the **Carousel of Progress**, the **Monorail**, the **PeopleMover**, **Adventure Thru Inner Space**, and **Innoventions**. He also arranged a simple **Sherman Brothers** ditty into a multi-lingual anthem for **It's a Small World**. And it was his "Swisskapolka," a composition for the film *Swiss Family Robinson*, that played inside the **Swiss Family Treehouse**. Later accomplishments included numerous compositions at Walt Disney World and Tokyo Disneyland. Having received an Oscar nomination and numerous prestigious music awards, Buddy Baker was named a Disney Legend in 1998. He died in Sherman Oaks, California in 2002 at age 84.

Baloo's Dressing Room

MAP: Fantasyland, Fa-19

DATES: March 15, 1991–September 8, 1991

Disney Afternoon, the 1990s TV show, spawned Disney Afternoon Avenue, the temporary area in **Fantasyland** that opened in 1991. Throughout that summer, while walking north from the **Storybook Land Canal Boats** toward **It's a Small World**, guests could interact with popular cartoon characters. One of these characters was Baloo, co-star of 1967's *The Jungle Book* and Disney's *TaleSpin* cartoons. The affable bear had his own hangout located in the back of Fantasyland, at the base of the train overpass.

Baloo's Dressing Room was a popular meet-and-greet site with *TaleSpin*-themed décor. After six months, Baloo and the rest of the Avenue regulars left as bigger plans emerged for the area. Two years later those plans were realized, and Baloo's spot at the train tracks became the tunnel walkway into **Mickey's Toontown**.

Bandstand

MAP: Hub, H-2; Adventureland, A-4

DATES: July 17, 1955–1962

Other than a pretty photo in Disneyland's 1955 **souvenir book**, the bandstand got little mention in the park's early literature. It was, however, a topic of much discussion in mid-1955.

As he re-created small-town midwestern America on **Main Street**, **Walt Disney** was aware that a traditional bandstand was a mandatory accessory. Location was the issue. Before **Opening Day** the bandstand, a cozy open-air gazebo where live music could be performed, sat in **Town Square** as one of the first structures incoming guests would see. Unfortunately, that was the problem—the bandstand obscured the

view of **Sleeping Beauty Castle** from the Main Street train station. So, before any guests ever saw the bandstand in Town Square, a 65-foot flagpole was installed as the cynosure of Town Square, and the bandstand was relocated to a spot alongside the **Hub** halfway between the entrances to **Frontierland** and **Fantasyland**. There it stood on Opening Day and for about a year after, a little white, wooden structure about 15 feet tall with a short staircase, pastel roof, decorative railings and finials, and a flagpole on top.

The **Disneyland Band** played at the bandstand every day, to audiences sitting on nearby park benches. Realizing that the bandstand was becoming increasingly popular, in 1956 Walt Disney had the area transformed into the **Plaza Gardens**, which featured a bigger stage and a dance area. Meanwhile, the bandstand was relocated again, this time to a Southern-styled resting area at the far tip of Adventureland called **Magnolia Park**. The bandstand played on for six more years until a 1962 expansion of the **Jungle Cruise** encroached on its section of Magnolia Park. Happily, the old bandstand was bought before it was dismantled, and today it lives on at a nursery in nearby Newport Beach called Roger's Gardens. In 2010, sharp-eyed Disneyland guests may have spied a small illustration of the bandstand (with two **America Sings** characters inside it) on the rotating exterior of **Innoventions**.

Bank of America,
aka Bank of Main Street, aka Annual Pass Center, aka Annual Passport Processing Center

MAP: Town Square, TS-10

DATES: July 17, 1955–2009

Walt Disney knew guests would need lots of money to enjoy Disneyland to the fullest, so he wisely installed a bank within the park, but not just anywhere—it was located within one of the very first buildings guests encountered as they entered the park. Situated on the first floor of the handsome **Opera House** building, in its early years the 35-foot-long Bank of America had another serious organization, **Town Square Realty**, as its immediate neighbor to the north. Around the south corner was a nostalgic mural reminding bank customers that "a penny saved is a penny earned."

Inside the bank, the main room had the feel of a traditional financial institution, replete with teller windows and conservative décor; however, this particular B of A always functioned a little differently from other branches. For instance, it was one of the few in America open on Sundays and holidays (and not many other banks required their customers to pay a park admission fee to gain access). From **Opening Day** in 1955 until mid-1993, guests could open a genuine B of A account inside and also get checks with Disneyland images on them.

After Bank of America ended its participation at Disneyland in 1992 (the same year the bank stopped sponsoring **It's a Small World**), in July of '93 the B of A became

the B of MS for eight more years. The Bank of Main Street, though, wasn't a true bank with bank accounts; instead, it was more of an information center that also happened to exchange currency, cash small checks, and offer ATM access.

In 2001, though it still looked like a bank with teller windows and still sported the Bank of Main Street name out front, the bank bega focusing more on selling Annual P ports. Four years later, the B ceased all bank functions and existed solely as the Annual Pass Center, the place where guests could buy the various year-long plans that offer frequent admission to the park at discounted prices.

The space closed in 2009 and reopened later that year as the **Disney Gallery**, which had formerly been located in **New Orleans Square** (Annual Pass Center functions, meanwhile, relocated to the **Plaza Pavilion**). Unbeknownst to most pedestrians walking by the old bank building, the curtained windows on the second floor front the sound rooms that generate the park's public-address announcements.

Bathroom of Tomorrow

MAP: Tomorrowland, T-22

DATES: April 5, 1956–August 30, 1960

One of the more unusual exhibits in Disneyland's history was born nine months after **Opening Day**. The Bathroom of Tomorrow was located at the end of the row of buildings on the right as guests entered **Tomorrowland**; this row already housed the science displays in the **Hall of Chemistry** and the **Hall of Aluminum Fame**, so one more exhibit about life in the near-future must have seemed appropriate.

The Crane Plumbing Company installed a 20-foot-wide bathroom that looked like something from an industrial trade show. From behind a railing, guests inspected the bathroom and all its fixtures, with everything done in yellow and some parts plated with 24-karat gold. Flush with enthusiasm, Crane added to the excitement with separate laundry facilities and a kids' play area called Fun with Water (a colorful mobile, plus guest-controlled fountains and spigots).

While it's easy to joke in retrospect about an archaic exhibit called the Bathroom of Tomorrow, it was at least a serious attempt at showing how technology would impact the modern world. Disneyland, remember, wasn't built merely to entertain, but also to educate, even if the lessons did involve a posture-enhancing toilet seat. In mid-1960 the Bathroom of Tomorrow became the Bathroom of Yesterday when it was replaced by uncomplicated **Fun Fotos** displays.

Bear Country

MAP: Park, P-14

DATES: March 24, 1972–
November 23, 1988

Bear Country, the seventh major land in Disneyland, was added in 1972 after the plans for a Disney ski resort in California called Mineral King were abandoned. An elaborate show with singing **Audio-Animatronic**

bears would've been performed in one of the Mineral King buildings, but when the ski dream ended, so did the show, at least for the next five years. In 1971 the **Country Bear Jamboree** opened in Walt Disney World, and that success prompted a new Bear Country back in Anaheim.

Veteran guests recognized Bear Country as a familiar Disneyland name. Since 1960, there had been a small **Frontierland** site called Bear Country along the route traversed by the **Mine Train**. This early Bear Country featured realistic bears fishing in a lake and lasted until 1977, when it was obliterated by the **Big Thunder Mountain Railroad** construction.

In the spring of '72, the "real" Bear Country opened on the land that had been home to the **Indian Village** from 1956 to 1971. Bear Country, however, extended beyond the area of the Indian Village, which was bordered on the west by the **Santa Fe & Disneyland Railroad**. Over half of Bear Country's 3.5 acres spread *under* the train tracks, pushing westward through Disneyland's perimeter **berm** into what had been an employee parking lot. One of the results of this expansion was Bear Country's entrance and exit—they were in the same location, so there was only one way in and out. Every other existing land—Adventureland, Frontierland, Fantasyland, Tomorrowland, Main Street, and New Orleans Square—had at least two pathways to neighboring areas. But Bear Country uniquely rounded into a cul-de-sac that didn't lead anywhere else in the park.

Built for approximately $8,000,000, Bear Country cost almost half of what it cost to build all of Disneyland back in the mid-'50s. Disneyland's 1972 **souvenir book** played up Bear Country's arrival with a colorful back cover that read, "A whole new land . . . a wild new band" and a two-page spread that described the new area as "a lighthearted blend of the authentic with the fanciful." The 19th-century Pacific Northwest inspired Bear Country's rustic design: the buildings were made out of wooden planks and exposed timbers, old-fashioned fonts decorated the store fronts, and transplanted trees grew thick and tall. The entrance into Bear Country was marked by a wooden sign supposedly created by J. Audubon Woodlore, a park ranger from old Disney cartoons who declared this to be "a honey of a place" and then joked about its scratching, hibernating, tree-climbing residents. Also to the left of the entrance was a cave, home to an ever-snoring but never-seen Rufus Bear.

When it opened, Bear Country had only one significant new attraction: the **Country Bear Jamboree**, a musical extravaganza performed by 18 Audio-Animatronic bears that were accompanied by a variety of A-A animals. Bear Country's other new establishments were **Teddi Barra's Swingin' Arcade**, **Ursus H. Bear's Wilderness**

Outpost, the **Golden Bear Lodge**, and the **Mile Long Bar** (the two holdovers from the Indian Village were the **Indian Trading Post** and the **Indian War Canoes**, the latter renamed Davy Crockett's Explorer Canoes).

For some line-weary guests, the absence of high-profile attractions was welcome, because it meant Bear Country would remain a relatively quiet, rural, relaxing corner of the park. But the attenuating crowds concerned park officials, and after a decade they began working on a major new attraction. The arrival of **Splash Mountain** brought a name change to the whole area—since late 1988, Bear County has been known as **Critter Country**, and the name on the mailbox out front has changed from Rufus Bear to Brer Bear.

Bell Telephone Systems Phone Exhibits

MAP: Tomorrowland, T-5

DATES: 1960–1982

In 1960, Bell Telephone Systems started sponsoring the prominent **Circarama** theater in **Tomorrowland**. While redesigning the pre- and post-show areas of the five-year-old theater, Bell installed interactive phone exhibits that fulfilled the Tomorrowland mission statement printed in Disneyland's **souvenir books**. Tomorrowland, it read, was intended to offer a "living blueprint of our future."

For Bell, that blueprint included the wonders of dialing long distance. Thus the park's 1960 souvenir book announced a new "demonstration of coast to coast Direct Distance Dialing. . . . Bell Telephone System representatives will dial cross country to local Weather Bureaus as a stop watch records the time necessary to complete the call." Also part of the theater's exhibits was "a dimensional mural" of movie screens that told the story of communications. In 1964, Bell added a Picture-Phone, which guests could observe but not actually try out with their own personal calls (what friends with Picture-Phones could visitors have called, anyway?). The idea of seeing whom you're talking to may have seemed attractive at the time, and it was a moderately interesting spectacle to watch, but obviously the Picture-Phone on display did not find its way into every American home.

Around 1967, Bell added devices that guests really could use: small "phone rooms" called Chatterboxes. In a Chatterbox, a group sat in a booth in front of a large pay phone, dialed any phone number, paid the charge via coins, and then talked conference-style to the dialee via a microphone mounted on the Chatterbox phone. Having a group conversation in a phone booth with no cumbersome handset to pass around was a fun novelty back then, and the speakerphone idea really did come to pass. One drawback to the Chatterbox was that the calls could only be made one way—a sign clearly announced that the phones did not accept incoming calls, which meant if one group wanted to tie up a Chatterbox for a long time, they'd be pumping lots of quarters into the slot.

Other options in the Bell exhibits included the Dial a Character wall, where guests could pick up phones and hear recordings of Disney characters talking on the other end, and a phone that enabled listeners to hear what their own voices sounded like. Naturally, actual Bell phones that guests could buy were also displayed. Bell hung up its Phone Exhibits around 1982 when it withdrew from the theater and the airline PSA flew in as the new sponsor.

Bengal Barbecue

MAP: Adventureland, A-3

DATES: June 4, 1990–ongoing

The instantly popular Bengal Barbecue replaced **Sunkist, I Presume** in 1992. The location is in the heart of **Adventureland** across from **Indiana Jones Adventure**. While Sunkist offered juices and snacks, the Bengal Barbecue has always provided more substantial fare to hungry guests (the sign, clutched in the jaws of a large tiger's head, helps makes that point). The highlight is the selection of marinated skewers—beef, chicken, and vegetables—that come with various sauces. Following the Adventureland theme, side dishes are called Extra Provisions and have included SSS-inamon Snake Twists and Tiger Tails (cinnamon twists and breadsticks, respectively). Also in keeping with the local color is the décor—the counter and tables sit under a thatched jungle roof.

Berm

MAP: Park, P-Perimeter

DATES: July 17, 1955–ongoing

In order to enhance the illusion that Disneyland is a complete world in itself, a tall earthen barrier, known as the berm, wraps around the perimeter of the park. "The terraced embankment which completely encloses Disneyland," explained the park's 1955 book *The Story of Disneyland*, "was designed to keep the outside world from intruding upon you."

Walt Disney knew how effective a berm could be—he'd already built one around a section of Disney Studios in Burbank. Later, to shield his Holmby Hills neighbors from the elaborate one-eighth-scale miniature railroad he ran on a half-mile of track behind his house, Disney surrounded his backyard with another embankment.

Disney included a tall berm in his plans for Disneyland even when it was in the design stages; the famous concept drawing executed by **Herb Ryman** in 1953 showed an unlandscaped dirt wall as Disneyland's boundary. Subsequent construction over the decades (including the addition of

> ## Attractions and Lands "Beyond the Berm"
>
> - Bear Country/Critter Country
> - The Haunted Mansion (show building*)
> - Holidayland
> - Indiana Jones Adventure (show building)
> - It's a Small World (show building)
> - Mickey's Toontown
> - Monorail (track from the park to Disneyland Hotel)
> - Pirates of the Caribbean (show building)
>
> *"Show building" refers to a structure outside the park where much of an attraction actually takes place, even if its façade and entrance are inside Disneyland.

Bear Country and **Mickey's Toontown**) has pushed the berm outward, changing its shape and original 1.3-mile length. But back when it did outline the rounded triangle that was Disneyland's initial shape, the berm defined the park's actual boundaries. The maximum north-south distance of the 1955 park (from the **Main Street** train station to the northern tip of **Fantasyland**) was about 1,900 feet, or just over one-third of a mile; the maximum east-west distance (from the **Frontierland** berm to the eastern berm behind Tomorrowland's **Autopia**) was some 2,150 feet—approximately two-fifths of a mile. Over 50 football fields could've fit within the original berm.

Planted along the berm are dense stands of trees and shrubs to help block outside distractions. While the foliage and the 12 to 20-foot-high berm do keep pedestrians inside the park from seeing the world beyond, the berm has never been high enough to prevent guests on the **Matterhorn**, the extinct **Skyways**, and other elevated attractions from seeing Anaheim buildings nearby. And it hasn't always managed to keep nonpaying guests out. On **Opening Day**, bermcrashers found sneaky ways to get over it; by now, virtually every section of the berm and its supplemental fence has been tested by climbers, fence-cutters, and even tunnelers. But the dirt berm has always successfully fulfilled one other vital function: it's the support for the main train tracks circling the park.

Bibbidi Bobbidi Boutique

MAP: Fantasyland, Fa-7

DATES: April 17, 2009–ongoing

Kids needing the full royal treatment can get it at this **Fantasyland** salon. Having debuted in Florida three years earlier, the Bibbidi Bobbidi Boutique came to Anaheim in 2009 and moved into a large retail space inside the Sleeping Beauty Castle courtyard.

Formerly the site of the **Tinker Bell Toy Shoppe**, the location has an imposing column outside to mark its entrance, two separate doorways for easy access, enticing window displays, and a detailed cottage décor. The Bibbidi Bobbidi name, of course, is taken from the Fairy Godmother's song in *Cinderella*.

Inside, walls of merchandise fit for a princess—tiaras, dresses, bags,

and jewelry—draw little girls in like magnets. Farther back, the salon offers plush chairs and is staffed by **cast members** who provide fairy-tale makeovers. The package deals, which usually require reservations and are priced from around $50 to $200, include everything from princess hairstyles, makeup, and nail polish to gowns, wands, and shoes. Hidden mirrors magically open up to reveal the enchanting results. For under $15, boys can get transformed into knights with a new hairstyle, a shield, and a sword.

Big Game Safari Shooting Gallery

MAP: Adventureland, A-2

DATES: June 15, 1962–January, 1982

There had already been shooting galleries on **Main Street** and in **Frontierland** when another one opened in **Adventureland** in 1962. The Adventureland version was the largest of the three shooting galleries and occupied a prominent space next to the **Adventureland Bazaar**. The attraction went by several names during its two-decade existence, including Safari Shooting Gallery, Big Game Safari, and Big Game Shooting Gallery. It had a jungle theme, naturally, that included a thatched roof and bamboo decorations. Elephants, rhinos, hippos, snakes, and jungle cats were among its exotic targets. No tickets were required to pick up an "elephant rifle"—this was a "pay to play" attraction that cost a quarter for a tube full of lead pellets.

The guns were limited in their range of motion, of course, to keep the barrels away from guests. But the use of pellets meant that the target area had to be repainted every night to look fresh for the next day's shooters. Another pellet problem was the toxic lead dust they generated, a gradually accumulating threat to **cast members** breathing the gallery air for long spells. The Big Game Gallery shut down in 1982 when a major remodel filled that stretch of Adventureland with new shops.

Big Thunder Barbecue, aka Festival of Foods, aka Celebration Roundup and Barbecue

MAP: Frontierland, Fr-20

DATES: December 14, 1986–January 21, 2001; April, 2009–ongoing

Seven years after the **Big Thunder Mountain Railroad** debuted, a rustic, cafeteria-style restaurant called Big Thunder Barbecue opened directly north of the rowdy railroad. Previously, this section of **Frontierland** was called the **Painted Desert**, a sun-bleached territory explored by mule packs and mine trains. The restaurant was within the **Big Thunder Ranch** area and shared the same Wild West theme. Recreating 19th-century American frontier life, the Big Thunder Barbecue offered alfresco dining on picnic tables near old-fashioned chuck wagons and a fire pit. Barbecued ribs, chicken, turkey legs, a "Trail Boss Sampler" of meats, and corn on the cob satisfied even the hungriest trail hand.

From June 21, 1996 until April 18, 1998, the restaurant's name was changed to Festival of Foods and the theme was augmented with gypsy décor to echo the 1996 animated movie *The Hunchback of Notre Dame*. (Exactly why an outdoor barbecue restaurant in **Frontierland** was suddenly echoing 15th-century France was never entirely clear.) In May 1998, the name and theme reverted back to the Big Thunder Barbecue, Georgia-Pacific's Brawny became the sponsor, and the food was temporarily accompanied by the musical stylings of **Billy Hill and the Hillbillies** on a small outdoor stage.

In early 2001, the restaurant finally closed to the public, though it was still occasionally fired up for corporate functions and private picnics. A farewell sign announced that "we have moved down the trail a bit" to a "new hacienda, **Rancho del Zocalo**." However, in April 2009 the ol' ranch rebounded, this time with a new name—Celebration Roundup and Barbecue—and a new *Toy Story* theme, with movie characters circulating and performing in the restaurant. The updated menu included new vegetarian options in addition to the hearty barbecue fare. In 2011, an all-you-can-eat *prix fixe* menu boasted $19.99 lunches and $24.99 dinners of barbecue meats, beans, and corn bread.

Big Thunder Mountain Railroad

MAP: Frontierland, Fr-21

DATES: September 2, 1979–ongoing

For several years in the 1970s, tantalizing concept art for a new Big Thunder Mountain Railroad attraction was displayed on **Main Street**, inside **Disneyland Presents a**

Preview of Coming Attractions. In the fall of 1979, the preview became a reality (which, unfortunately, can't be said for all the ideas presented in that Coming Attractions room). Big Thunder was the third major mountain constructed in Disneyland after **Opening Day** (**Matterhorn Mountain** debuted in 1959, **Space Mountain** in 1977). Requiring two years of construction, the Big Thunder Mountain Railroad took longer to build than the entire original park did (from 1954–1955), and with a price tag approaching $16 million, it cost almost as much.

The E-ticket (see **ticket books**) attraction was heralded as an instant classic. Its two-acre site is located in the large area in Frontierland formerly known as **Nature's Wonderland**, previously traversed by, among other attractions, plodding pack mules. Some of the old rocks, landscaping, and desert props from that earlier area were retained, but the dominant Big Thunder feature was brand new. Standing 104 feet high, the central mountain is about three-fourths as tall as Matterhorn Mountain and borrows its dramatic, soaring orange buttes from Utah's Bryce Canyon National Park.

As a high-speed roller coaster, the Big Thunder Mountain Railroad was designed to compete with other Southern California theme parks that were wowing '70s teens

with rapidly proliferating variations of highly kinetic roller coasters. Big Thunder's half-mile-long track is steep, tightly curved, and wet, thanks to a splash area similar to the one at the end of the **Matterhorn Bobsleds**. Though they average only about 30 miles per hour during their three-minute trip, the half-dozen runaway trains seem faster and definitely put the "wild" in Wild West. The rollicking trains are noisy, too: according to *The Imagineering Field Guide to Disneyland*, Steven Spielberg recorded their raucous sounds to accompany the mine-cart chase in *Indiana Jones and the Temple of Doom*.

More than just thrills, though, Big Thunder has always offered humorous details and frontier allure. Before guests board the trains, they encounter little details that add to the Western theme, such as a sign that touts Big Thunder as "the biggest little boom town in the West" with a steadily decreasing population, an exposed wall of dinosaur bones, a miniature of the Rainbow Ridge town that once graced the loading area for the old mine train, and the little train engines named U. B. Bold, I. M. Brave, U. R. Courageous, U. R. Daring, I. M. Fearless, and I. B. Hearty. Along the track itself are threatening rockslides, swarms of menacing bats, and assorted mechanical wildlife. Frontier flair is everywhere: an "old coot" narrates the attraction, genuine Old West antiques decorate the **queue** area, and up until 2010 a derelict engine and cars from the old **Mine Train** could be seen crashed in the "woods" nearby.

Several much-publicized accidents over the years have tarnished Big Thunder's legacy. But the "wildest ride in the wilderness" is so consistently popular that variations have been installed in other Disney parks, albeit with the Monument Valley-style landscaping that was originally intended for Disneyland.

Approximate Speeds of 14 Attractions

40 mph
Splash Mountain

25–30 mph
Big Thunder Mountain Railroad
Monorail
Rocket Rods
Space Mountain
Viewliner

20 mph
Gadget's Go Coaster
Matterhorn Bobsleds

8–10 mph
Autopia

4–6 mph
King Arthur Carrousel
Main Street Vehicles
PeopleMover

1–3 mph
Skyway to Fantasyland/Tomorrowland
Submarine Voyage

Big Thunder Ranch,
aka Festivals of Fools, aka Little Patch of Heaven

MAP: Frontierland, Fr-19

DATES: June 27, 1986–ongoing

The unused area of **Frontierland** behind 1979's **Big Thunder Mountain Railroad** was finally developed in 1986. Themed to match the noisy railroad nearby, the serene Big Thunder Ranch looked like a working frontier ranch from the 1880s, complete with log cabin, stables, and "the happiest horses on Earth," according to nearby signs. The most-photographed subject at the attraction was most likely Mickey Moo, a white cow with a natural black patch on its hide that resembled Mickey Mouse's head.

On June 21, 1996, the ranch got a makeover and a new name based on the Disney movie *The Hunchback of Notre Dame*: the Festival of Fools, an acclaimed 28-minute pageant of music and effects that retold the *Hunchback* story. The elaborate multi-stage show ran for almost two years. During this time, the little log cabin was turned into a shop called Esmeralda's Cottage.

The Big Thunder Ranch name and theme reappeared on May 30, 1998. Six years later, Little Patch of Heaven was added to the ranch, referencing the 2004 animated movie *Home on the Range*. The log cabin, renamed Pearl's Cottage after one of the movie's characters, began offering "Crafts & Fun!" to visitors. Within two years, however, Little Patch of Heaven disappeared and Pearl's name was removed from the cabin.

These days, the area is once again referred to as the Big Thunder Ranch. The outdoor performance space is now called the Festival Arena, where special events, such as 2011's **Family Fun Weekends** and the *Pirates of the Caribbean* movie premiere, are occasionally held. The cabin, now called Miss Chris' Cabin (after the "proprietor" of the ranch) is often used for kids' coloring activities. Live farm animals, including goats and lambs, are available for petting most of the year, but these cute critters get a winter break when husky, well-antlered reindeer are brought in for **Santa's Reindeer Round-Up**. Georgia-Pacific is Big Thunder Ranch's longtime sponsor; their "Washin' Station" not only stocks Brawny Paper Towels, it gives official directions on washin' up.

Billy Hill and the Hillbillies

DATES: 1987–ongoing

A Disneyland legacy over two decades long has established Billy Hill and the Hillbillies as one of the park's most lasting and popular forms of entertainment. Mixing bluegrass tunes with slapstick humor, the nascent group began as the Barley Boys (Barley, Charlie, Farley, Gnarley, Harley, and Ed), hosting pig races and entertaining guests at **Big Thunder Ranch** during the 1987 **State Fair** promotion. A year later, freshly renamed Billy Hill and the Hillbillies, the brothers (all of whom are called Billy) moved their guitars, banjos, fiddles, mandolins, harmonicas, and bass to the outdoor stockade area of **Frontierland**. After relocating to **Critter County** in 1989 for the debut of **Splash Mountain**, in the early '90s the Billys moved into the **Golden Horseshoe Saloon** and alternated appearances with the Golden Horseshoe Variety Show. Late in the decade the group temporarily returned to Big Thunder Ranch, but since 2003 they've been fixtures at the Golden Horseshoe.

With their daily schedule of five half-hour performances, the Billys have now played over 20,000 Disneyland shows (leader Kirk Wall has played in nearly all of them, and says that, with all the improvisation, no two shows have been identical). The full roster of Billys, all of them stellar bluegrass players, includes about a dozen members to accommodate all the shows the group performs. The repertoire includes everything from classic bluegrass favorites to modern songs given the bluegrass treatment. Billy Hill and the Hillbillies recorded a live CD a few years back, and occasionally will perform as the Billys in other concert venues around Southern California.

Blair, Mary
(1911–1978)

It's a Small World, one of the most popular attractions in Disneyland's history, was given color and style by the prolific artist Mary Blair. Her imaginative art, which is simultaneously childlike and sophisticated, was a perfect match for a fanciful cruise past the children of the world.

Blair was born Mary Robinson in 1911 in McAlester, Oklahoma. She graduated from a Los Angeles area art school in 1933 and soon got a job at MGM Studios in the animation department. She was married in 1934 and in 1940 began working in the animation department at Disney Studios.

Over the next two decades, Blair enhanced the color palettes of such films as *Cinderella*, *Alice in Wonderland*, and *Peter Pan*. Her art also greatly influenced Eyvind Earle and the other Disney animators who were creating a new look for *Sleeping Beauty* (Blair and some of her bold illustrations are shown in the film's 2008 DVD). She contributed to Disney movie sets and costume designs before leaving the company in 1953 to start a career as a freelance illustrator for ads and children's books.

In the '60s, at the invitation of **Walt Disney**, Blair styled It's a Small World, which was originally built for the 1964–1965 New York World's Fair before it was installed in **Fantasyland** in 1966. Blair also had a great influence on Disneyland itself; the park's exuberant color was inspired by her designs. The main buildings in **Tomorrowland** were decorated in 1967 with huge, beautiful tile murals of Blair's joyous art, and the main Tomorrowland walkway, designated the **Corridor of Murals**, was a tribute to her work. Blair's importance to the park was underscored in 1965 when she became one of the few artists to make an appearance on the TV show *Walt Disney's Wonderful World of Color*, where she was shown working on lighting effects for It's a Small World. She later created an enormous mural for the Contemporary Resort at Walt Disney World.

Blair died in 1978 at age 66 in Soquel, California. Inducted as a Disney Legend in 1991, she was the subject of a biography called *The Art and Flair of Mary Blair* in

2003 and a **Disney Gallery** exhibition in 2011. Today, Disneyland visitors will find a nice little tribute to Blair inside It's a Small World: perched on the Eiffel Tower is a cheery doll dressed to look like her, holding a balloon.

Blast to the Past Celebration

DATES: Spring 1988–spring 1989 (seasonal)

To jump-start the 1988 and 1989 summer seasons, Disneyland introduced an elaborate celebration called Blast to the Past. This springtime spectacular followed on the heels of the **Circus Fantasy** of 1986 and the **State Fair** of 1987 and '88. At a time when the 1950s was a popular decade in the media (*Happy Days* was a TV hit all the way through 1984, and *Grease* and *Back to the Future* were blockbuster movies in 1978 and 1985, respectively), Blast to the Past featured rockin' music, colorful costumes, special give-aways, and themed **parades**, all of which evoked the innocent bygone days of poodle skirts and sock hops. The celebration even extended to the park's décor, which was altered dramatically. Blast to the Past signs were added over the **entrance** tunnels underneath the **Main Street** train station; an enormous jukebox joined the **Hub**; a scene featuring palm trees and a sandy beach appeared in front of **It's a Small World**; and a nostalgic name, Rainbow Diner, was given to **Tomorrowland Terrace**.

From March to June, daily **parades** of hot rods and classic motorcycles wended their way from **Fantasyland** to Main Street, and on weekends a Main Street Hop presented legions of costumed dancers cavorting to a spiffy soundtrack while confetti showered down on them from above. What's more, hit bands from the '60s, including Herman's Hermits and the Turtles, performed on the **Videopolis** stage; the venerable **Dapper Dans** transformed themselves into the doo-wop group Danny and the Dappers; and the park sold a special collection of familiar songs reworked for Disney characters (Donald Duck's "Quackety Quack" instead of "Yakety Yak," for instance). There were plenty of prizes—the Guess-o-Rama offered an opportunity to win a car, and, thanks to a cross-promotion with McDonald's, guests could win discounted admission to the park. And there were lots of special events—the park set world records for mass hula-hooping and mass twisting.

The festival peaked on May 20, 1989, when the TV special "Disneyland Blast to the Past" aired just a month before the celebration itself became a thing of the past.

Blue Bayou

MAP: New Orleans Square, NOS-4

DATES: March 18, 1967–ongoing

Though **New Orleans Square** was officially dedicated and opened to the public on July 24, 1966, its showpiece restaurant—indeed, the park's showpiece restaurant—didn't open for another eight months. When it did, it was instantly hailed as a landmark dining experience. Because it is incorporated within a major attraction, the

Blue Bayou is truly *sui generis*.

The attraction, of course, is **Pirates of the Caribbean**. The revolutionary cruise and the Blue Bayou debuted in Anaheim on the same day in 1967. The entrance to the Blue Bayou is adjacent to the Pirates' exit. Inside the Blue Bayou building—and guests really are inside a building, despite the restaurant's al fresco feel—the illusionary setting is a terrace in front of a small Southern town situated along a quiet, crepuscular riverbank. Here the ambience is always serene, the time is always twilight, and the delta moon is always radiant, no matter what the real weather, season, or time of day is like outside. Nearby, crickets chirp, fireflies meander, and shallow boats of park visitors float past lazily; overhead, thin clouds drift slowly across an indigo sky that's punctuated several times a minute by shooting stars. For visual spectacle, the Blue Bayou can't be beat by any other indoor restaurant in Disneyland.

The Blue Bayou is the only restaurant inside Disneyland that takes (and usually requires) reservations. Its menu is something of a collectible and can usually be taken home upon request. And the candlelit tables are welcome departures from all the quick-stop food counters in the park outside.

Over a million of the Blue Bayou's Le Spécial de Monte Cristo sandwiches have been sold, making it the restaurant's most popular lunchtime entrée. Dinner may include crab cakes, steak Diane, pork loin, prime rib, mahi mahi, Cajun gumbo, or jambalaya; for dessert, pecan pie or chocolate mousse cake. Unlike the food at many other establishments in Disneyland, these gourmet dishes aren't served buffet-style. Instead, they're brought to guests' tables by Disneyland **cast members**.

Great scenery, food, and service. No wonder the Blue Bayou is still Disneyland's premier restaurant destination.

Blue Bird Shoes for Children

MAP: Main Street, MS-13

DATES: July 17, 1955–1957

Main Street was always meant to evoke **Walt Disney's** own small-town childhood. An old-fashioned children's shoe store was a natural for the nostalgic avenue.

Gallen-Kamp ran Blue Bird Shoes on the eastern side of Main Street, where Chester Drawers now resides. But guests were most likely far too distracted by Disneyland's many attractions to want to spend time shoe shopping, and the store made an early exit from park history just two years after its opening.

Blue Ribbon Bakery

MAP: Main Street, MS-6

DATES: April 6, 1990–January 5, 2012

Guests who love the smell of sticky buns in the morning used to flock to the Blue Ribbon Bakery. Blue Ribbon was the second bakery to be installed on **Main Street**; in the '50s, **Puffin Bakery** occupied the same west-side stretch next to the **Penny Arcade**, until the **Sunkist Citrus House** replaced it in 1960. When Sunkist closed in 1989, the Blue Ribbon Bakery took over a year later.

In January 1997 the bakery temporarily closed. When it reopened three months later it had acquired a new sponsor, Nestlé Toll House, and had traded places with the **Carnation Ice Cream Parlor**, jumping from the middle of the block to the corner of West Center Street and Main Street (the ice creamery switched to the space where the Blue Ribbon Bakery had been and reopened with a new name, the **Gibson Girl Ice Cream Parlor**).

No matter where it was located, the bakery was always a popular breakfast destination specializing in delectable baked temptations like fresh muffins, scones, croissants, biscotti, and humongous cookies. The bakery also whipped up gourmet sandwiches, as well as exotic coffees and specialty beverages for the holidays.

After two decades on Main Street, the bakery finally closed so the adjacent Carnation Café could supplement its outdoor tables with some prime indoor seating.

Boag, Wally
(1920–2011)

Originally signed to a two-week contract at Disneyland in 1955, Wally Boag went on to enjoy a record-setting career at the park that lasted almost three decades.

What kind of record did he set? The Guinness-verified world record kind. Boag was one of the stars of the longest-running stage show in history, the *Golden Horseshoe Revue*, which he co-wrote. Boag then performed in the revue approximately 40,000 times—from 1955 until his last performance on January 28, 1982.

Comedian Steve Martin has singled out Boag as a major inspiration for his own career. In his memoir, *Born Standing Up*, Martin writes that Boag "wowed every audience every time" as he "plied a hilarious trade of gags and offbeat skills such as gun twirling and balloon animals" while maintaining an air of "amiable casualness."

Born in 1920 in Portland, Oregon, Boag learned his trade as a teenage dancer and comedian in vaudeville theaters across the country. MGM Studios gave him small roles in several films before he auditioned in front of **Walt Disney** in 1955 to work at the **Golden Horseshoe**. Instantly popular as the show's Traveling Salesman and Pecos Bill characters, the quick-witted, acrobatic Boag charmed audiences three times a day in the *Golden Horseshoe Revue*. He also guest starred on the TV shows *Disneyland* and *The Mickey Mouse Club* and appeared in such Disney films as *The Absent-Minded Professor* and *The Love Bug*. Veteran guests might recognize Boag as the voice of Jose the parrot in the **Enchanted Tiki Room**. He was also one of the main creative forces working on the **Chinatown** area that was planned in the late '50s but never built.

Boag and his two Golden Horseshoe costars, **Fulton Burley** and **Betty Taylor**, were inducted as Disney Legends in 1995. Wally Boag died at age 90 in 2011, one day before **Betty Taylor** died.

Bonanza Outfitters

MAP: Frontierland, Fr-2

DATES: June 29, 1990–ongoing

The **Pendleton Woolen Mills Dry Goods Store**, a **Frontierland** fixture since 1955, finally closed after almost 35 years of meeting guests' flannel needs. Two months later, just in time for the 1990 summer season, Bonanza Outfitters opened in Pendleton's same large location some 50 feet inside the Frontierland gates and to the right of **Pioneer Mercantile**. The store still has the same wooden sidewalk out front and the same kind of rustic interior it had in its Pendleton days, and the clothes are still frontier-friendly. Cowboy boots, countrified kitchen supplies, and Western-themed gifts have supplemented the expected Disney wares at times. However, the current merchandise seems to be the usual T-shirts, pins, and hats (some old-fashioned farm dresses still manifest the frontier theme).

Bone Carving Shop

MAP: Frontierland, Fr-1

DATES: Ca. 1956–ca. 1964

In the 1950s and '60s, the park's **souvenir books** and maps sometimes listed the Bone Carving Shop in **Frontierland** as either Bone Jewelry or Bone Craft. The shop was inside the **Davy Crockett Arcade**, which was the first main building on the left as guests entered Frontierland. Crockett's arcade went through several remodels, and during one of them the Bone Carving Shop got remodeled out of existence as the building evolved into **Davy Crockett's Pioneer Mercantile**.

Bookstand

MAP: New Orleans Square, NOS-3

DATES: Ca. 1966–ca. 1973

Over the years Disneyland has provided many small establishments that sell books and postcards. One of them, simply called the Bookstand, stood in **New Orleans Square** on Royal Street, near the **Pirates of the Caribbean** exit. The Bookstand has never been mentioned in the park's **souvenir books** (which the Bookstand sold), and only briefly did it turn up on some maps between 1966 (when New Orleans Square opened) and 1973 (when the Bookstand disappeared in a building renovation).

Boyajian, Chuck
(1917–2004)

Guests have always admired and appreciated the immaculate cleanliness of Disneyland, which is known as the tidiest, most sanitary park in the world. Early on, **Walt Disney** made cleanliness a part of his Disneyland dream, as noted in *The Quotable Walt Disney*: "When I started on Disneyland, my wife used to say, 'But why do you want to build an amusement park? They're so dirty.' I told her that was the point—

mine wouldn't be." Once the park opened, James B. Stewart's *Disney Wars* pointed out, "no tradition was more hallowed than Walt's habit of personally picking up any scrap of paper or refuse that he detected on his frequent visits to Disneyland. Walt was obsessed by cleanliness." There was a motive behind Disney's fastidiousness—he felt that a glistening park would inspire guests to help keep it pristine.

One man was in charge of establishing and maintaining the park's spotless reputation—Chuck Boyajian. Born in 1917, Boyajian grew up in Ohio and later served in the Navy during World War II. He worked at Disneyland from **Opening Day** until 1981 as the manager of custodial operations, creating procedures, setting standards, and training **cast members**.

To maintain radiant cleanliness even when Disneyland was packed with guests, Boyajian's crews worked efficiently and unobtrusively. In the early years his crews had extra days for cleaning, because during the off-season the park was closed on

Mondays, and sometimes on Tuesdays, too (Disneyland has been open seven days a week since 1986). Some cleaning problems were anticipated—Walt Disney decreed that no peanuts in shells would be sold, because he knew from his visits to other amusement parks that there would be pieces of broken shells everywhere. But other problems quickly presented themselves—chewing gum being one of the toughest, since it is difficult to remove quickly in the hot sun. (Gum joined the list of things not sold in the park.) Diane Disney Miller, Walt Disney's daughter, named other problematical products in *The Story of Walt Disney*: candy with cylindrical sticks ("because people might slip on those discarded sticks") and spun candy ("because children get it all over everything"). And, as always, the sheer volume of trash (about 20 tons on an average day, 40 on busy days) was an issue.

Ultimately, Boyajian's methods were so successful that he was brought on board to help set and meet the same standards in the Disney areas at the 1964–1965 New York World's Fair, Walt Disney World in 1971, and Tokyo Disneyland in 1983. Chuck Boyajian died at age 86 in 2004, one year before he was inducted as a Disney Legend.

Brer Bar

MAP: Bear Country/Critter Country, B/C-5

DATES: July 17, 1989–April, 2003

When **Bear Country** was renamed **Critter Country** in 1988, many of the establishments in the area were also renamed. The **Mile Long Bar** was one of them, adopting the name Brer Bar, which echoed the *Song of the South* stylings of nearby **Splash Mountain**. The bar's location, the northern tip of the wide building at the back of Critter Country, didn't change. Nor did the food—like its predecessor, the Brer Bar was a quick-stop food spot for hot dogs, cookies, Mickey Mouse-shaped pretzels, and drinks. In 2003 the Brer Bar was swallowed up by a remodel that introduced **Pooh Corner** to the area.

Briar Patch

MAP: Bear Country/Critter Country, B/C-10

DATES: December 1988– February 1996; October 1996–ongoing

Located in a back corner of **Frontierland**, the **Indian Trading Post** was a longtime holdover from the days of the old **Indian Village**. The rustic Trading Post cabin lasted from 1962 all the way through 1988. Finally, with **Critter Country** replacing **Bear Country**, the Indian arts, crafts, and jewelry shop moved out and Briar Patch moved in.

Like the nearby **Brer Bar**, the Briar Patch took its name from the "Zip-A-Dee-Doo-Dah" theme of **Splash Mountain**, the area's major attraction. The Briar Patch also adopted some of the ride's décor—Brer Rabbit's carrots grow down through the roof into the store's interior. Souvenirs, toys, clothes, sunglasses, and gifts were originally sold on the shelves of the Briar Patch, but changes were made in early 1996, when the store briefly became **Critter Country Plush** and filled up with new merchandise. Eight months later, the Briar Patch name returned, but the plush toys stayed. In 2004 the store temporarily closed for yet another change, one that retained the Briar Patch name but replaced much of the plush with big hats.

Briar Rose Cottage

MAP: Fantasyland, Fa-30

DATES: May 29, 1987–July 15, 1991

In the late 1980s, guests who walked through **Sleeping Beauty Castle** and into **Fantasyland** found an enchanting store on their immediate right. The name, of course, is a reference to the beautiful Briar Rose, who was cursed by wicked Maleficent in the Disney movie *Sleeping Beauty*. Previously, this choice location next to **Peter Pan Flight** had been the home of **Mickey's Christmas Chalet**, a charming spot selling holiday ornaments. The Briar Rose Cottage was no less charming, and its merchandise (Disney-themed figurines and collectibles) no less ornamental.

In mid-1991, evil conquered good when the **Disney Villains** store took over this spot.

Broggie, Roger
(1908–1991)

Roger Broggie, the man known throughout Disney Studios for his mechanical genius, was born in Massachusetts in 1908. Broggie grew up in Illinois, learned how to work industrial tools and machines, and subsequently headed west to join the burgeoning film industry of the 1930s. In 1939 Broggie landed at Disney Studios, where he developed special cameras and photographic equipment and eventually ran the company's machine shop. Away from the studio, he helped **Walt Disney** create an elaborate miniature train, the famed Carolwood Pacific, in Disney's Holmby Hills backyard.

This train experience presaged Broggie's involvement with Disneyland. Broggie was instrumental in the development and construction of the original **Santa Fe & Disneyland Railroad**. That success propelled him to help develop other major attractions at the park, including the ground-breaking **Great Moments with Mr. Lincoln** and the novel 360-degree films for the **Circarama** theater, as well as the classic *Mark Twain Riverboat*, sleek **Matterhorn Bobsleds**, charming **Casey Jr. Circus Train**, and futuristic **Monorail**.

Broggie also contributed to the special effects for the film *20,000 Leagues Under the Sea* and to Florida's EPCOT Center before he finally retired in 1975. Roger Broggie was named a Disney Legend in 1990, one year before he died in Los Angeles at age 83. In tribute, one of the train engines at Walt Disney World is named after him. *Walt Disney's Railroad Story*, a handsome book about Broggie and Disney trains, was written by his son, Michael Broggie, in 1997.

Bruns, George
(1914–1983)

Several of the 20th century's most popular songs were composed by George Bruns for Disney projects. An Oregonian born in 1914, Bruns took piano lessons as a child, studied brass in high school, and ultimately mastered a dozen different instruments. After playing with big bands and working for Portland radio stations, Bruns traveled to Los Angeles in 1934 to work first for Capitol Records and later for Disney Studios. Bruns was a prolific composer of Disney film scores, including three that earned Oscar nominations: *Sleeping Beauty*, *Babes in Toyland*, and *The Sword in the Stone* (he also shared an Oscar nod for a song in Disney's *Robin Hood*). His most famous screen composition, however, was for the **Disneyland TV series** "The Ballad of Davy Crockett."

At Disneyland, Bruns is celebrated as the composer of one of the park's most famous songs: "Yo Ho (A Pirate's Life for Me)." Bruns wasn't just a writer of music *for* the park; he was also a performer *in* the park, playing tuba with the popular **Firehouse Five Plus Two** jazz band.

After retiring from Disney Studios in '75, Bruns returned to Oregon to teach and make more music. In 1983 he died at age 68, and was inducted as a Disney Legend in 2001.

Burley, Fulton
(1922–2007)

Born in 1922 in Ireland but raised in Canada, Fulton Burley was around lucky horseshoes for most of his long showbiz career. In 1943, having already appeared in several MGM films, he auditioned over the phone and got the lead in Broadway's *Diamond Horseshoe Revue*. Burley and actor **Wally Boag** both played fliers in the 1945 movie *Thrill of a Romance*; 17 years later, Boag invited Burley, who was appearing in Las Vegas, to come to Disneyland's **Golden Horseshoe**, where Boag was already starring in the successful *Golden Horseshoe Revue*.

At the Golden Horseshoe, Burley's rich tenor voice, comedic skills, and Irish accent were a hit for the next 25 years. Burley also appeared at special Disney functions and live shows and provided the vocals for the parrot Michael in the **Enchanted Tiki**

Room. In 1955, eight years after he retired, Burley was inducted as a Disney Legend along with the two other stars of the *Golden Horseshoe Revue*, Wally Boag and **Betty Taylor**. In 2007, 84-year-old Fulton Burley died of heart failure in Carlsbad, California.

Burns, Harriet
(1928–2008)

Harriet Burns was born in Texas in 1928. After graduating with an art degree from Southern Methodist University, she continued her studies at the University of New Mexico before moving to Southern California in the early '50s. There she was employed by a company that helped design TV show sets and Las Vegas hotels.

In 1955 Burns started working for Disney Studios on *The Mickey Mouse Club* TV show (she's credited as the designer of the show's actual clubhouse). Switching to Disneyland projects, she was one of the original model makers for the park's attractions and thus was a key contributor to **Sleeping Beauty Castle**, the **Storybook Land Canal Boats**, the **Enchanted Tiki Room**, **New Orleans Square**, the **Submarine Voyage**, the **Jungle Cruise**, **Great Moments with Mr. Lincoln**, **Pirates of the Caribbean**, and the **Carousel of Progress**. Even while creating Lincoln's head, pirate hair, mermaid costumes, and Tiki Room birds, Burns contributed to such Disney films as *Darby O'Gill and the Little People* and *Babes in Toyland*.

Burns retired in 1986 and lived in Santa Barbara, California until her death in 2008. Today she is remembered not only as a Disney Legend (she was inducted in 2000), but as something of a pioneer—Burns was Disney's first female Imagineer. **Walt Disney** even introduced her to national TV audiences on several episodes of *Walt Disney's Wonderful World of Color*. "His enthusiasm," she wrote in *Disneyland . . . The Beginning*, "left us all inspired." Her own unique contributions were further acknowledged with an "H. Snrub" gravestone outside the **Haunted Mansion**.

Buzz Lightyear Astro Blasters

MAP: Tomorrowland, T-4

DATES: March 17, 2005–ongoing

Needing a hit **Tomorrowland** attraction that would generate some positive buzz after the problematic **Rocket Rods** expired in 2001, Disneyland designers looked to other Disney theme parks for inspiration. Buzz Lightyear's SpaceRanger Spin at Walt Disney World and Buzz Lightyear's Astro Blasters at Tokyo Disneyland were already high-flying successes, so the theme for the next installation seemed obvious.

In Disneyland, the Astro Blasters zoomed into the former pre-show and theater rooms of the old **Circarama** theater. What was a **Mary Blair**-designed tile mosaic on the curving exterior became a painted mural showing speeding rockets, floating space mountains, and fantastic planets. Inside, the attraction features characters and themes from *Toy Story*, all intensified by bright neon colors (Buzz himself makes an appearance as a sophisticated **Audio-Animatronics** character). As described on the sign out front, the attraction is "an interactive adventure in which you travel aboard slow-moving spaceships that you can spin while helping Buzz Lightyear battle the evil Emperor Zurg." The "spaceships," a new iteration of the **Omnimover** system first developed in the '60s, are indeed slow, but guests really can spin them 360 degrees.

What makes this four-and-a-half-minute ride popular enough to necessitate the **FASTPASS** ticket center outside is the interactive shoot-'em-up element. As passengers wend through the 10 different space scenes, they use their own "laser cannons" to blast away at different targets with various point values. Point totals display inside the cockpit, and rankings from Star Cadet to Galactic Hero are posted at the end of the ride.

Calico Kate's Pantry Shop

MAP: Frontierland, Fr-27

DATES: 1965

This sounds like a charming store created by Disney designers, but actually Calico Kate's Pantry Shops had already been established elsewhere before one opened in Disneyland. The first Calico Kate's was a countrified gift shop that opened in Colorado in 1959. An Arizona spin-off opened a few years later. The business was begun and run by a couple whose daughter designed the Calico Kate character. Disneyland's 1965 **souvenir book** listed a Calico Kate's in **Frontierland**, but Kate's gifts and collectibles were gone in about a year.

Canal Boats of the World

MAP: Fantasyland, Fa-15

DATES: July 17, 1955–September 16, 1955

Long before there was a Disneyland, **Walt Disney** collected miniatures. Consequently, among his first Disneyland ideas was one that set a little boat gliding quietly through a setting decorated with adorable miniature buildings. He'd already seen something similar while on vacation in Europe. Unfortunately, the Disneyland version didn't live up to anyone's expectations, at least not at first.

The canal in the title of Disneyland's short-lived 1955 attraction Canal Boats of the World referred to

Names of the Original Canal Boats

1. *Annie Oakley*
2. *Bold Lochinvar*
3. *Gretel*
4. *Lady Guinivere (sic)*
5. *Lady Katrina*
6. *Lady of the Lake*
7. *Lady of Shallot*
8. *Nellie Bly*

a winding river dug into one acre at the back of **Fantasyland**. The "world" was going to be made up of tiny, detailed international buildings that were to line the riverbanks. Early concept drawings also portrayed low-slung canal boats entering a colorful mound of "candy" called **Rock Candy Mountain** as a scenery option. In addition, a Bruce Bushman drawing made in 1954 positioned Monstro the Whale at the end of the ride so boats could slide from his mouth to a splashdown near the unloading dock. But when the attraction debuted on **Opening Day**, no miniature buildings, candy mountain, or Monstro slide were in place.

Disappointingly, the view from the eight boats as they toured the narrow canals was basically of desolate dirt banks (although guests could watch the **Casey Jr. Circus Train**, which circled the same area). What's more, the primitive outdoor motors on the boats were so loud that they preempted the narration of the skippers.

Two months after its opening, the original Canal Boats cruise sank into history but, happily, Walt Disney's idea survived. Nine months later, the wonderfully remodeled **Storybook Land Canal Boats** opened with quieter boats, lavish landscaping, and the kind of delightful miniatures Disney had originally desired.

Candle Shop

MAP: Main Street, MS-3

DATES: 1958–ca. 1977

Disneyland's Candle Shop once stood in the back of the big **Crystal Arcade** building on the western side of **Main Street**. Starting with the 1958 edition, the park's **souvenir books** consistently played up the Candle Shop with prominent photos that made the interior look as colorful as a candy store. According to the captions, "a rainbow of color" filled the Candle Shop: colorful candle displays hung from the ceilings, lined the walls, and filled the shelves and display tables. Among the hundreds of offerings were fun seasonal favorites (October pumpkins, November turkeys, etc.), plus candles shaped like food, spirals, and tiki heads. In the mid-'70s, the Candle Shop's flame flickered out and the store disappeared during a Crystal Arcade remodel.

Candy Cart

MAP: New Orleans Square, NOS-7

DATES: Ca. 1966–ca. 1995

Disney-themed sweets were the main focus at this little outdoor candy stand in **New Orleans Square** near the **Creole Café** (as it was called before it became Café Orleans). In the mid-'90s, the cart got a new name, **Royal Street Sweets**, with an expanded list of merchandise.

Candy Palace, aka Candy Palace and Candy Kitchen

MAP: Main Street, MS-9

DATES: July 22, 1955–ongoing

Five days after **Opening Day**, the Candy Palace opened on the western side of **Main Street**. During that first year, the Candy Palace was also called Candyland (the 1956 Disneyland **souvenir book** listed both names). Just south of the candies was the **Penny Arcade** entrance, and to the north was Coke's **Refreshment Corner**. In 1997, the Palace got renovated and renamed the Candy Palace and Candy Kitchen.

Pedestrians cruising Main Street have always been tempted by the confections on display in the Candy Palace's windows and display kitchen (space around the kitchen was increased in early 2012 to accommodate all the viewers). Today the ever-popular candy counters serve up lots of nostalgic treats like caramel apples, candy canes, and fudge, plus new creations made on-site. Guests and historians have long surmised that vents in front of the store pump out candylicious scents like vanilla and peppermint into the Main Street air.

Captain EO, aka Captain EO Tribute

MAP: Tomorrowland, T-19

DATES: September 18, 1986–April 6, 1997; February 23, 2010–ongoing

Few Disneyland attractions have left the park and then returned later, but *Captain EO* is one of those few.

After successful screenings at Walt Disney World, the *Captain EO* film flew into the **Magic Eye Theater** in **Tomorrowland** in the fall of 1986. The look of the film and its plot drew on themes from such movies as *Alien*, *Star Wars*, and even *The Wizard of Oz*. But it was the film's remarkable cast that garnered most of the attention: Michael Jackson, the world's biggest recording star at the time, portrayed the title astronaut, and Oscar-winner Anjelica Huston played the galaxy's Supreme Ruler. Both performed under the guidance of Oscar-winning director Francis Ford Coppola, and the film was produced by *Star Wars* creator George Lucas.

Jackson's weapons against his wicked space foe were his singing and dancing, aided by a freakish alien crew with cuddly names like Idee, Odee, Hooter, Geex, and Fuzzball. Guests wearing the requisite 3-D glasses watched objects jump out at them and laser beams fire over their heads while Jackson's music filled the theater.

Estimates place the cost of this effect-laden extravaganza at over $17 million, which works out to about $1 million per minute of finished film.

Touting its exciting new attraction, Disney launched the movie with a star-studded premiere in 1986 and aired a making-of TV special called "*Captain EO Backstage*" in 1988. However, the big crowds of the late '80s dwindled down in the mid-'90s as the shine came off Jackson's lustrous superstardom.

In early 1997, *Captain EO* was sent packing and another 3-D Walt Disney World import, **Honey, I Shrunk the Audience**, successfully jumped to the West Coast. Then, about eight months after Jackson's death in mid-2009, *Captain EO* (now called *Captain EO* Tribute) reopened in the same theater it had once occupied, with Kodak as its 2010 sponsor. Officials termed this tribute a "limited engagement," but audience enthusiasm has kept the show going beyond 2011.

Card Corner

MAP: Main Street, MS-14

DATES: June 1985–October 1988

From 1956 until 1985, the prime corner location at the northeast tip of **Main Street** was an information center called **Carefree Corner**. In mid-1985 the spot became a card shop known as Card Corner, its sponsor Gibson Art Co. Gibson had already sponsored one other eponymous greeting card shop on Main Street from **Opening Day** until 1959—**Gibson Greeting Cards**, located on the corner of Main Street and East Center Street.

Advertisements for the new Card Corner displayed four old-time illustrations of sample items inside the shop—greeting cards for Thanksgiving, Easter, Valentine's Day, and the **holiday season**. This second card shop on a Main Street corner lasted over three years. Gibson was later sold to American Greetings, and Card Corner was replaced by Carefree Corner, back for another run that lasted until the mid-'90s.

Carefree Corner

MAP: Main Street, MS-12

DATES: August 1956–spring 1985; November 1988–November 1994

For decades, guests have used the name Carefree Corner to refer to the prominent corner location where the east side of **Main Street** runs into the **Hub**. The signage on that corner building has supported the cheery reference, but technically this spot has served a slightly less carefree function as Disneyland's official information center.

When it opened in mid-1956, the site was hosted by the Insurance Companies of North America and offered, according to the park's 1957 **souvenir book**, "road maps, hotel-motel information, places of interest to see." It wasn't until the 1958 souvenir book came out that the location was referred to as Carefree Corner.

The corner stayed carefree until 1974, when INA's sponsorship ended and the site became known as the Hospitality Center. In 1985, Gibson Greeting Cards moved in and added a new name, **Card Corner**. When Gibson left in '88, the Carefree Corner sign returned until it was replaced again in '94 by the current resident, the **Main Street Photo Supply Co.** The six-year Carefree Corner revival of the '80s and '90s marked one of the few times that an extinct Disneyland shop has reopened in its original location, with its original name.

Back when the building was INA's Carefree Corner, the interior was an open, un-cluttered room that brought to mind a turn-of-the-century hotel lobby. Guests could relax on a round velvet banquette in the middle of the open room, get information about the park or the surrounding area from helpful **cast members** in old-fashioned costumes, and sign the official registration book. For years INA gave away its own small park maps and brochures that today are collectors' items.

Disney Legend **John Hench** is credited as the designer of the building's impressive exterior, three sides of which angle around the corner to form an inviting entrance set back from the street. For a long time the upper floor displayed a large circular insignia that read, "Founded 1792," the year INA issued its first insurance policy.

Carnation Café

MAP: Main Street, MS-5

DATES: March 21, 1997–ongoing

When the venerable **Carnation Ice Cream Parlor** closed in January 1997, it took three months for Carnation to open a new business on **Main Street**. When it did, the new café was just a few steps south of the Ice Cream Parlor's former location. Situated in West Center Street (where the **Flower Mart** had once spread its outdoor floral displays) the Carnation Café's patio tables quickly became one of the best people-watching spots on Main Street.

As the only table-service restaurant on the street, the Carnation Café has the most complete menu in the immediate area. Breakfast features huge sticky buns, tasty croissants, and Mickey Mouse-shaped waffles; lunch and dinner offerings include meatloaf, pasta, soups, gourmet sandwiches, and fancy salads, followed by tempting desserts and gourmet coffee beverages. In 2012 the outdoor café gained some choice indoor tables when it spread into the corner space formerly occupied by the **Blue Ribbon Bakery**.

Carnation Ice Cream Parlor

MAP: Main Street, MS-6

DATES: July 17, 1955–January 4, 1997

Carnation, the dairy company founded in 1899, has been associated with Disneyland for as long as the park has been open. Carnation's first enterprise at Disneyland was the popular Carnation Ice Cream Parlor on **Main Street**. The site was the northwest corner of Main and West Center Street, in the same block as the **Penny Arcade**. In those days, West Center was filled with the **Flower Mart's** fragrant displays.

The original Carnation building was (and still is) a three-story structure wrapped around the street corner, with such elegant touches as a mansard roof, dormer windows, and a widow's walk. So picturesque was the 1890s-style interior, it was often spotlighted in Disneyland's **souvenir books**. For years the books featured the same prominent photo of a wholesome family sitting happily at the counter while a female **cast member** in an old-fashioned costume served them.

In 1977 Carnation expanded into West Center Street, pushing the Flower Mart to the other side of Main and into East Center Street. The parlor's new outdoor patio area on West Center offered a relaxing spot for alfresco dining with tableside service. The menu featured fancy salads, Mickey's Chicken Pot Pie, and various sandwiches, but it's the indulgent dessert list that visitors remember—especially the gigantic sundaes named after Disneyland attractions (the Big Thunder, the Matterhorn, etc.).

Some 20 years later, Carnation closed its Ice Cream Parlor and opened instead the outdoor **Carnation Café**. Simultaneously, the **Blue Ribbon Bakery** moved into the corner building where Carnation had served up its memorable ice cream treats for over 40 years.

Carousel of Progress

MAP: Tomorrowland, T-14

DATES: July 2, 1967–September 9, 1973

Disneyland's Carousel of Progress was an import from the 1964–1965 New York World's Fair. There, **Walt Disney** had his Imagineers devise an ambitious time machine for General Electric called Progressland, which featured an auditorium that rotated around a stationary circular stage. On the stage were depictions of four different decades of American life populated by 32 **Audio-Animatronic** figures, all of them showing how electricity (the sponsor was G.E., remember) had improved domestic life. Progressland was a crowd-pleasing hit in New York, so after the fair closed, Disney brought it to Anaheim.

In Disneyland, Progressland was originally meant to be a walk-through exhibit in **Edison Square**, a new land intended to go behind the eastern blocks of **Main Street**. When Edison Square failed to materialize, Progressland was installed with a new name, Carousel of Progress, in a new building, the Carousel Theater. Built where the large **Space Bar** had stood on the eastern edge of **Tomorrowland**, the 200-foot-wide, two-story structure looked like a stack of immense pancakes wrapped by a swooping ramp and adorned on the side with a thin sculpture that sported—what else?—the G.E. logo.

Inside this free attraction, **cast members** ushered guests into a small 240-seat theater on the ground floor. The Carousel of Progress show began with an infectious theme song, "There's a Great Big Beautiful Tomorrow" by **Richard and Robert Sherman**. The theater, one of six surrounding the stage, then rotated to the first **Audio-Animatronic** (A-A) scene featuring a typical family at home. The year was approximately 1890, and in the room were A-A parents, two A-A children, an A-A cousin, A-A grandparents, an A-A dog (named Rover, Buster, and Sport throughout the show), and such turn-of-the-century devices as a gramophone and gas lamps.

At the conclusion of the brief presentation, the theme song began to play as the theater spun and the audience moved ahead in time by three decades. (Meanwhile, the next audience, seated in another 240-seat theater on the building's perimeter, was wheeled into position to see the 1890s scene). The audience watched as presumably the same family, now updated to the 1920s, used electric lights, an electric fan, and other electric gadgets.

Cue the music, and the theater moved to the 1940s stage and a scene filled with handy appliances (Grandma now wore a hearing aid). The next stage displayed a late '60s scene, with a self-cleaning oven and a color TV with a "built-in video tape recorder."

The final speech and the reprised theme music that followed seemed like the show's finale, but there was actually one last act to go, this one up the Speedramp to the second floor. Upstairs, guests walked past an incredibly detailed model of Progress City, Walt Disney's dream of the ideal city of the future. The model was huge, covering almost one-sixth of an acre and containing over 4,000 buildings, 20,000 miniature trees, thousands of individual vehicles, soaring skyscrapers, a climate-controlled downtown area, an airport, a theme park, and a sports arena, as well as "a welcome neighbor"—a G.E. nuclear power plant. (At one time in the planning stage, ride vehicles were considered that would have toured guests around the enormous model.) Narration and lighting cues directed guests' attention to various parts of Progress City. Visitors left the Carousel of Progress building with the optimistic theme music playing in their ears and hopeful feelings swelling in their hearts.

Disney Legends **Roger Broggie**, **Marc and Alice Davis**, **Blaine Gibson**, **John Hench**, **Sam McKim**, **Wathel Rogers**, and **Herb Ryman** were the main contributors to the Carousel of Progress. Despite the huge commitment of space and energy required to create it, the attraction wasn't spotlighted in the park's **souvenir books**, which instead focused on more easily grasped Tomorrowland highlights like the **Submarine Voyage** and **Autopia**.

After opening in the remodeled Tomorrowland in mid-1967, and after playing to 3,600 guests an hour at its peak, the Carousel stopped in the fall of 1973. For a show so complex, advanced, and confident, it is surprising that it barely lasted six years. Once again it moved across the country, this time to Walt Disney World, where Walt Disney's dream of Progress City was becoming the reality of EPCOT. Disneyland's Carousel Theater didn't stay dark long, however—**America Sings** opened there the following June.

Carriage Place Clothing Co.

MAP: Main Street, MS-1

DATES: Ca. 1993–ongoing

This handsome little clothing store can be accessed from within the big **Emporium**, which presides over the first western corner of **Main Street**. Tucked away near the **Fire Department**, the Carriage Place has its own attractive doorway on the side of the Emporium facing **Town Square**. Self-proclaimed "Clothiers of Distinction," the store sells Disney-themed shirts, hats, and small gifts.

Carrousel Candies

MAP: Fantasyland, Fa-5

DATES: Ca. 1983–ongoing

In addition to its many major edifices, **Fantasyland** also hosts a small candy cart called Carrousel Candies. Operating on a variable schedule, the cart is located in the **Sleeping Beauty Castle** courtyard, near the **King Arthur Carrousel** (hence the cart's name). Disney-themed specialty sweets made at "Goofy's Candy Factory" were originally available here, but now the cart's goodies are mostly comprised of traditional candy, souvenirs, and royal accessories. The cart's look has changed, too, a tall, compact pink coach replacing its original wide blue wagon.

Casa de Fritos, aka Casa Mexicana

MAP: Frontierland, Fr-24

DATES: August 11, 1955–April 1, 2001

Three weeks after **Opening Day**, Casa de Fritos made its **Frontierland** debut on the corner where the big **River Belle Terrace** stands today. In 1955 the River Belle Terrace location was dominated by **Aunt Jemima's Pancake House**, with a small space next door for Casa de Fritos.

Just a year later, however, the thriving little Casa was looking to expand. In mid-'56 it jumped Frontierland's main walkway and replaced the **Marshal's Office** to the north, the site it still occupies. **Don DeFore's Silver Banjo Barbecue** eventually moved into the old Fritos spot by Aunt Jemima's.

Fritos, of course, is the crunchy snack made by Frito-Lay, something guests were reminded of as soon as they entered the restaurant. Inside was a large replica of the former Fritos cartoon mascot, the Frito Kid, which stood next to a clever vending machine that dispensed little bags of the fried tortilla chips. As for the restaurant's original menu, to modern eyes it looks like standard Mexican fare—tacos, burritos, and enchiladas—that one would expect at any decent Mexican restaurant. But back in the '50s, Mexican food wasn't as commonplace as it is now; a hacienda-style restaurant with outdoor tables probably seemed fairly exotic at the time, especially to visitors who didn't live in the western U.S. or come from south of the border.

Over the years the restaurant gradually expanded toward **Mineral Hall**. Finally, after a brief closure in 1982, it reopened that October with a larger outdoor space, more authentic-looking Mexican architecture, a new name (Casa Mexicana), and a new sponsor, Lawry's. The name, décor, sponsor, and menu were revised again when the restaurant became the **Rancho del Zocalo Restaurante** 19 years later.

Casey Jr. Circus Train

MAP: Fantasyland, Fa-13

DATES: July 31, 1955–ongoing

The sturdy little train from *Dumbo* almost got derailed before it got going at Disneyland. Initially planned as a slightly faster, roller coaster-style attraction, early test runs through an acre of hills in the back of **Fantasyland** raised serious safety questions. Although the Casey Jr. Circus Train was shown in TV coverage of the park's **Opening Day** festivities, the train didn't really begin carrying passengers for two more weeks as workers flattened the track layout to make the three-and-a-half-minute trip smoother, slower, and safer.

When it did finally open to the public, Casey Jr. was a whimsical little train

headed by a colorful engine that was followed by a line of circus-themed cars. Disney Imagineers Bruce Bushman and **Roger Broggie** are credited with developing the two adorable trains that shared the track. The trip wasn't much at first, though; that first year, the tracks passed across the barren dirt banks that lined the waterways of the **Canal Boats of the World**. Once the remodeled **Storybook Land Canal Boats** attraction hit the water in the summer of '56 with a full complement of miniature buildings along its shores, the views from the Casey Jr. train were as charming as the train itself.

Though it was never more than a B-ticket attraction (see **ticket books**), Casey Jr. has always had enough delightful detail to make it a Fantasyland favorite. Who isn't cheered up by the passenger car labeled "Monkeys," for instance, or the beautiful sleigh-style cars transplanted from the original merry-go-round that became the **King Arthur Carrousel**? Who wouldn't sing along to the swingin' theme song written by Frank Churchill (who worked on *Snow White and the Seven Dwarfs*) and Ned Washington (*Pinocchio*)? Who isn't inspired by the audible "I think I can" mantra? This isn't just a train trip; it's therapy.

Veteran guests may remember that the whole track got replaced in 1989; careful observers might recognize that the propulsion for the Casey Jr. train is provided by the car *behind* the decorative engine, not the engine itself; and adults may lament that the cramped cages are more suitable for kids. But happy passengers won't mind how the train came to be, what's driving it, or how tight the seating arrangements are, so enchanting is Casey's journey.

Castle Arts

MAP: Fantasyland, Fa-3

DATES: Ca. 1983–ca. 1987

The Arribas brothers, Tomas and Alfonso, were master glass cutters who learned their craft in Spain. After meeting **Walt Disney** at the 1964–1965 New York World's Fair, they opened several shops in Disneyland, followed later by locations in other Disney parks around the world. One of their Disneyland shops was located inside **Sleeping Beauty Castle**, where guests walked from the drawbridge toward the castle's courtyard. Previously this spot had been the **Arts and Crafts Shop**, and in the late '80s

Major Attractions and Exhibits
Added in the 1950s
(after Opening Day)

1955   Casey Jr. Circus Train; Circarama theater; Conestoga Wagons; Dumbo
         the Flying Elephant; Flight Circle; Mickey Mouse Club Theater; Mike Fink
         Keel Boats; Phantom Boats; 20,000 Leagues Under the Sea Exhibit

1956   Astro-Jets; Indian War Canoes; Junior Autopia; Mine Train; Skyway to
         Fantasyland/Tomorrowland; Storybook Land Canal Boats; Tom Sawyer
         Island

1957   Frontierland Shooting Gallery; Holidayland; House of the Future; Motor
         Boat Cruise; Sleeping Beauty Castle Walk-Through

1958   Alice in Wonderland; Grand Canyon Diorama; Midget Autopia; Sailing
         Ship *Columbia*; Viewliner

1959   Fantasyland Autopia; Matterhorn Bobsleds; Monorail; Submarine
         Voyage

it would become the **Castle Christmas Shop** before transforming into the **Princess Boutique** a few years later. Beautiful glassware and cut-glass sculptures of Disney characters have long been an Arribas specialty.

Castle Candy Kitchen, aka Castle Candy Shoppe

MAP: Fantasyland, Fa-4

DATES: 1958–1994

Over the years, many businesses have occupied spots along the well-traveled walkway through **Sleeping Beauty Castle**. From 1958 until the mid-'60s, the Castle Candy Kitchen took up the right-hand side of that walkway, with the **Arts and Crafts Shop** on the opposite side. Kids could stock up on Castle Candy's array of distinctive sweets before hitting the attractions up ahead in Fantasyland. The name was changed to Castle Candy Shoppe around 1967 before being replaced by the **Heraldry Shoppe** in 1995.

Castle Christmas Shop

MAP: Fantasyland, Fa-3

DATES: Ca. 1987–ca. 1996

This choice location on the left-hand side of the walkway through **Sleeping Beauty Castle** belonged to the cozy **Castle Arts** store for much of the 1980s. After the nearby **Mickey's Christmas Chalet** closed in 1987, the Castle Christmas Shop replaced Castle

Arts to satisfy guests looking for holiday ornaments. A decade later, the shop relocated to **New Orleans Square** as **La Boutique de Noël**. Meanwhile, back at the castle, the **Princess Boutique** filled the vacant space along the interior walkway.

Cast Members

Disneyland employees are called cast members. Usually seen wearing garments themed to the area where they work, cast members include ride operators, store cashiers, food servers, security personnel, **parade** performers, parking attendants, and roving street sweepers. They have their own unions, parking lots, cafeterias, and store (Company D, selling discounted Disney merchandise a few miles from Disneyland). Cast members employed in 1955 even have their own club, Club 55. The number of Disneyland cast members has swelled dramatically over the years from about 600 on **Opening Day**, to 6,200 in 1970, to over 13,000 in the 21st century.

Though cast members come from all around the world, most are hired from a large pool of local applicants. Many are college-age kids, though older adults and even retirees are also employed at the park. Because the supply of applicants has usually overwhelmed demand, Disneyland has nearly always been able to be selective, choosing people who are smart, attractive, personable, poised, and available for evening/weekend/holiday hours. Among former cast members who worked in Disneyland in their pre-celebrity days are Steve Martin, Kevin Costner, Michelle Pfeiffer, Teri Garr, and Debra Winger.

Of all the jobs in the park, the one usually considered the "coolest" is the wisecracking **Jungle Cruise** skipper (think of a swaggering Costner, a one-time Jungle Cruiser). The most uncomfortable jobs are most likely those inside hot, cumbersome costumes. These character costumes can weigh as much as 40 pounds, and

many afford the wearers extremely limited vision as they navigate curbs and crowds. Bruises and abrasions are the badges frequently worn at the end of the day by these walk-around cast members (David Koenig's *Mouse Tales* books describe stabbings and costumes set on fire, Richard Stayton's *Unknown California* tells of frequent attacks on the Seven Dwarfs and the Three Little Pigs, and Trevor Allen's one-man show *Working for the Mouse* includes anecdotes about kids punching and kicking Allen when he worked as a costumed character). Many of the costumes, incidentally, are worn by dancers, and often the Mickey and Pinocchio costumes are worn by women. Guests today might struggle to identify some of the retired character costumes from the past, including the albatross Orville from *The Rescuers* and characters from *The Black Hole*. Also, fewer characters seem to be roaming the park anymore, as Disney officials now tend to position characters in specific areas.

In Disneyland's first year, some job functions, especially those taking place in the **parking lot** and in the custodial and security departments, were contracted to outsiders, but performance inconsistencies soon led to extensive Disney-oriented training for everyone. Cast members adhere to the strict code of conduct that's taught in a weeklong "Traditions" orientation held in the Disney University offices behind **Space Mountain**. Politeness, smiles, and practiced answers to questions are the traditional tools used to deliver happiness, safety, and reassurance to guests. A

wholesome, clean-cut image is also required, though how that image is defined has gradually changed. According to a decades-old manual, men weren't allowed to have mustaches (even though **Walt Disney** had one) and had to wear black shoes and socks. Women had to wear stockings and couldn't wear eye shadow, eyeliner, fake eyelashes, or earrings in pierced ears. In 2000, however, men were finally allowed to wear mustaches, a decade later they could leave their casual shirts untucked, and in 2012 they were permitted to wear short beards. As of 2010, women no longer have to wear pantyhose with their skirts, and can now wear capri pants and sleeveless tops.

Despite the park's attempts at conformity, cast members are able to reveal their individual personalities. Many stories have arisen over the years about pranks played upon one another, impulsive swims in the waterways, store merchandise rearranged into **Hidden Mickeys**, and playful nicknames for various attractions and characters (of the latter, cast members routinely refer to the Jungle Cruise elephant spraying water as Bertha and the **Matterhorn** yeti as Harold).

The fact that employees are referred to as cast members is indicative of the park's intention to make the Disneyland experience similar to a theatrical show. In the park's vocabulary, the term "guest" has always been used in place of "customer." "Costume" has also be used instead of "uniform," "backstage" for behind-the-scenes areas, and "onstage" for areas in view of guests. From 1955 to 1962 cast members wore name tags with impersonal numbers on them, but those name tags now include first names for friendly identification (names are helpful when guests want to leave comments about cast members, which they can do at **City Hall**). To honor their contributions to 50 years of Disneyland success, in 2005 the Walt Disney Company presented each cast member with a memory-filled 64-page book called *The Magic Begins with Me*.

The cast members seen during operating hours are not the only employees working at Disneyland, of course. After closing, over 600 horticulturists, painters, welders, electricians, divers, and custodians hit the park to fix/clean/repaint/test everything for the next day's activities. Every inch of the park is walked, all the waters are explored, every vehicle and track is closely inspected, and all surfaces are cleaned, hosed down, or sanitized. Store shelves are restocked, restaurant kitchens are replenished, and many still-working light bulbs are replaced (about a quarter million Disneyland light bulbs are changed every year). Before the park opens, an early morning Resort Enhancement team installs special decorations and checks every window and balcony display. All of this work is done in an empty park so it won't have to be performed during the day in view of guests, thus maintaining Disneyland's carefully cultivated reputation of impeccable service, immaculate cleanliness, and undiminished illusion.

Character Foods, aka Character Food Facilities

MAP: Fantasyland, Fa-10, Fa-27

DATES: 1955–1981

For a quarter century, two **Fantasyland** fast-food huts shared the name Character Foods. One hut was in a small courtyard on the northern side of the old **Mickey Mouse Club Theater**. This location would eventually open up to become the walkway to **Frontierland**. The second hut was on the other side of Fantasyland, near **Alice in Wonderland** and today's **Mad Hatter of Fantasyland**. Both stands were circular and topped with a striped, circus-style cone.

The eatery's name referred to the snacky menu items named after the stars of Disney animation. The Character Foods stand near Frontierland disappeared in 1979; the other location was eaten up by the extensive Fantasyland remodel that ended in 1983.

Character Shop

MAP: Tomorrowland, T-22

DATES: Summer 1967–September 15, 1986

The massive **Tomorrowland** remodel that began in 1966 brought an end to the **20,000 Leagues Under the Sea Exhibit** and the adjacent **Fun Fotos** displays. A year later, one of the largest stores in the park, the Character Shop, opened in their combined spaces. Next door was **Adventure Thru Inner Space** (later **Star Tours**), and outside was the **Tomorrowland Stage** (later the ramp to **Space Mountain)**.

Its size and prime corner location made the Character Shop an instant must-visit for guests searching for clothes and gifts. Described in 1969's *Walt Disney's Disneyland* as a "Disney-themed toy and merchandise mart," the store featured rows and rows of displays and a ceiling hung with futuristic abstract shapes. Adding even more character to the Character Shop was the **PeopleMover**, which skimmed quietly through the back of the store, about 10 feet above the floor.

Just as it had appeared during a major Tomorrowland upheaval, so too did the shop disappear during another Tomorrowland revamp. Late in 1986, only a few months before the adjacent Star Tours opened, the Character Shop was replaced by the space-themed **Star Trader** store.

Charles Dickens Carolers

DATES: 1956–ongoing

Since 1956, a singing group called the Charles Dickens Carolers, or simply the Dickens Carolers, has enhanced Disneyland's winter holiday celebrations. Although its cast of singers continually changes to include new members, the lineup typically consists of four (two men, two women) or eight (four and four) performers at a time, all dressed in elegant 19th-century costumes: felt top hats, topcoats, and scarves for men, and long-sleeved hoop dresses, bonnets, and hand muffs for women.

The Dickens Carolers have performed up and down **Main Street** and in front of the Christmas tree in **Town Square**, as well as in Disney-owned businesses adjacent to Disneyland. The a cappella group generally sticks to traditional carols but also occasionally includes more modern favorites, such as "Rockin' Around the Christmas Tree" and other special requests. In recent years the group has abandoned the Dickens title and is now known as the Holiday Carolers, making more appearances in the Disney hotels than in Disneyland itself.

Chicken Plantation,
aka Plantation House, aka Chicken Shack

MAP: Frontierland, Fr-10

DATES: July 17, 1955–January 8, 1962

On **Opening Day**, Swift, a meat-packing company established in the 1850s, sponsored three Disneyland locations. Two, the **Market House** and the **Red Wagon Inn**, were located on **Main Street**; the third, the Chicken Plantation or Plantation House, was on the far edge of **Frontierland**.

The Chicken Plantation occupied a distinguished-looking two-story building overlooking the **Rivers of America**. Interestingly, the building was schizophrenic. Viewed from the east, it appeared to be a white mansion, with dormer windows projecting from the roof, a decorative wooden balcony circling the perimeter, and about 20 outdoor tables spreading across an expansive patio. Conversely, when viewed from the Disneyland trains to the west, the restaurant appeared to have rough-timber construction more appropriate to the Frontierland wilderness.

The specialty here was a fried chicken dinner for under two dollars, so popular that when the building was demolished in 1962 to make way for the **Haunted Mansion**, take-out meals were offered from a temporary Chicken Shack in front of the construction site.

China Closet

MAP: Main Street, MS-13

DATES: Spring 1964–ongoing

The eastern side of **Main Street** has always featured some form of a china shop. Formerly the **Ruggles China and Glass Shop**, the store has been called the China Closet since 1964. Though the name changed, the location didn't—it's still one door south of what is now the **Main Street Photo Supply Co.**

Inside, the room opens to both the photo store and **Crystal Arts**. The China Closet sells Disney-themed glass statues, frames, and mugs. Snow globes and delicate ornaments supplement the selection around the holidays. Guests not interested in the shop's wares will find welcome solace on the cozy porch out front, which offers wooden chairs and a bench for a brief rest from the busy street.

---

11 Serene Hideaways
Quiet, often shaded places slightly off the beaten path:

Critter Country	Hungry Bear Restaurant's lower deck
Frontierland	Benches near the Frontierland entrance Big Thunder Trail East-facing docks on Tom Sawyer Island Walkway behind Fowler's Harbor
Hub	Garden at First Aid Walkway west of Sleeping Beauty Castle
Main Street	Porch at China Closet
Mickey's Toontown	Toon Park
New Orleans Square	Court des Anges near portrait artists Fountain south of the Haunted Mansion

---

Chinatown

MAP: Main Street, MS-17

DATES: Never built

East Center Street, the little lane that divides **Main Street** into separate blocks, would look vastly different had the plans for Chinatown come to fruition. Unlike the rest of Main Street, which was built to echo turn-of-the-century American architecture,

Chinatown was going to look like a real Chinese neighborhood. According to concept drawings by Disney Legend **Herb Ryman** in the late 1950s, and as seen in the 1960 Disneyland **souvenir book**, Chinese shops and eateries and an arcade would have lined the East Center cul-de-sac next to the **Market House**. An **Audio-Animatronic** stage show presented in an elegant Chinese restaurant would have featured a philosophizing Confucius and singing birds.

By the summer of 1960, the Chinatown plan had faded away as attentions turned to other Disneyland developments. The idea for singing Audio-Animatronic birds survived, however, and flew over to **Adventureland**, landing three years later inside the **Enchanted Tiki Room**.

Chip 'n Dale Tree House

MAP: Mickey's Toontown, MT-4

DATES: January 24, 1993–ongoing

Located in the far corner of **Mickey's Toontown**, the Chip 'n Dale Tree House is a fun mini-playland for young children. The tree house is a small, cute, and architecturally askew structure built in a gnarled tree studded with oversize acorns. Kid-size stairs pass the chipmunks' mailbox, enter a charming wooden passageway, and climb to the house and balcony some 15 feet off the ground.

Originally a Tree Slide provided the route down from the tree house, and an Acorn Ball Crawl gave kids under 48 inches tall a place to go nuts in a pit filled with acorn-shaped plastic balls. In 1998 the slide and pit were removed, leaving the tree house as a walk-through attraction, this time with stairs as its exit. Though the fun may have been reduced slightly, at least there's no time limit on playing.

Chocolate Collection, aka Chocolate Rue Royale

MAP: New Orleans Square, NOS-5

DATES: Ca. 1980–ca. 1995

Throughout the 1980s, the Chocolate Collection sold imported chocolate confections deep in the heart of **New Orleans Square**. Prior to its opening, **Le Forgeron** and **La Boutique d'Or** had occupied this spot at the back of Royal Street.

Nestlé sponsored the Chocolate Collection until the mid-'80s, at which point the unsponsored business took the name Chocolat Rue Royale.

Circarama, aka Circle-Vision, aka Circle-Vision 360, aka World Premiere Circle-Vision

MAP: Tomorrowland, T-5

DATES: July 18, 1955–September 8, 1997

In 1952 *This Is Cinerama* introduced American audiences to multiple-screen movies. The non-Disney documentary showed footage shot from the front of a roller coaster, the cockpit of a swooping plane, and other dramatic locations, all projected on three connected screens that partially wrapped around the audience.

Within a few years, major motion pictures (including the Oscar-nominated *How the West Was Won*) were utilizing the Cinerama three-screen projection system. An impressed **Walt Disney** decided he would go Cinerama one better at Disneyland; soon Disney Legend **John Hench** was drawing up a concept illustration with Grand Canyon images displayed in the round.

Three years after *This Is Cinerama*, on the day after the park's **Opening Day**, Disney's film *A Tour of the West* debuted in the new Circarama building near the **Tomorrowland** entrance. Instead of filming with three forward-facing cameras à la the Cinerama process, Imagineers mounted *11* 16mm cameras in a circle on top of an American Motors car (American Motors was one of Circarama's sponsors). Directed by Disney Legend **Peter Ellenshaw,** the film took viewers from Beverly Hills to Monument Valley, a 12-minute scenic drive played up in the 1956 Disneyland **souvenir book** as "an exciting travel picture."

The film was an instant hit. Despite having to stand the entire time with no rails to lean against, audiences loved being at the center of a 360-degree movie that surrounded them with images. The seemingly unrelated displays lining the inside of the theater—cars made by American Motors and refrigerators made by Kelvinator—didn't exactly enhance the experience, but they did establish a tradition of exhibits in the pre- and post-show areas that would be fully developed later. Plus, since this was a free attraction requiring no A-B-C ticket from the Disneyland **ticket book**, nobody was really complaining about the extraneous decorations, no matter how superfluous they were.

Five years later, a new 360-degree movie, the 16-minute *America the Beautiful*, expanded the tour to include aerial footage and shots from across the whole country. It was even more popular than its predecessor. Bell Telephone Systems was the sole sponsor, adding fun **Bell Telephone Systems Phone Exhibits** into the pre- and post-show areas. Late in 1964 the name Circle-Vision replaced Circarama as a way to avoid any confusion—and any legal entanglements—with Cinerama.

A major remodel of the theater began in early 1967 and lasted into June. The attraction's name changed again, this time to Circle-Vision 360. *America the Beautiful* was also revised to include two minutes of new footage, the number of screens went from eleven to nine larger screens, and the pre-show area was radically reworked. Guests now waited in a colorful room filled with upholstered blocks with flags displaying abstract representations of all 50 states hanging from the ceiling. Three times per hour, a **cast member** conducted a playful identify-the-flags quiz with guests, a suitable activity for a movie showcasing American landscapes. The female cast members wore patriotic outfits of red, white, and blue featuring blue skirts, red jackets, red tights, and white gloves. Inspired by the patriotic vision and fun quiz, guests eagerly stood at the new railings inside the theater and enjoyed a fire truck's crazy careen through San Francisco, a wild ride through the Waikiki surf, and more.

After Bell withdrew its sponsorship in 1982, the theater closed again in early '84. For the July 4th reopening, the theater again got a new name, and this time it got an all-new film. With the airline PSA on board, World Premier Circle-Vision began showing an eight-minute short called *All Because Man Wanted to Fly*, followed by *American Journeys*, a 21-minute documentary offering more slices of American life. Later this longer film alternated with an import from Walt Disney World, *Wonders of China* (*China* played in the mornings, *Journeys* in the afternoons).

In mid-1989 PSA canceled its flight, but another airline, Delta, immediately took over sponsorship for seven years, with both movies still on the bill. Finally, on New Year's Day in 1996, Delta took off and World Premiere disappeared from the theater's name. That July, *America the Beautiful* returned for one last glorious sprint to the theater's finish line.

Circle-Vision closed for good on September 8, 1997, to be replaced first by the short-lived **Rocket Rods** and then by **Buzz Lightyear Astro Blasters**. Disney Legend **Roger Broggie** is considered the main architect of Disney's 360-degree filming process (with assistance from **Ub Iwerks**, Eustace Lycett, and other masters of Disney cinema). Today, Circarama/Circle-Vision is fondly recalled as one of the best theater experiences in the park's history.

Circus Fantasy

DATES: Winter 1986–spring 1988 (seasonal)

Even before Circus Fantasy debuted in January of 1986, circus themes had already been plentiful in Disneyland's history. Dumbo's Circusland and an Interplanetary Circus had been on the drawing boards for a while; **Dumbo the Flying Elephant** and the **Casey Jr. Circus Train** had been operating since mid-1955; the **Mickey Mouse Club Circus** had appeared in late 1955 for about six weeks; and that same year, daily circus **parades** had frolicked down **Main Street**.

Like the **State Fair** and **Blast to the Past** promotions that followed it, Circus Fantasy was an attempt to speed up ticket sales during what were traditionally slow months of the year. For the winter and early spring months of 1986, 1987, and 1988, Circus Fantasy filled Main Street and the **Hub** with real circus acts. There were elephants and professional clowns, a high-wire act across Main Street, stilt-walkers, a motorcycle daredevil, and more—all the requisite attractions expected at an actual circus. Circus on Parade trumpeted daily down Main Street and a circus-themed show filled the **Videopolis** stage. When park attendance rose in the summer, the circus acts were put on hold until ticket sales began to drop again in the fall.

Some of the circus activities were shown on a TV special called "Disneyland's All-Star Comedy Circus" in 1988, the same year Blast to the Past replaced Circus Fantasy as the new spring promotion.

City Hall

MAP: Town Square, TS-4

DATES: July 17, 1955–ongoing

Since **Opening Day**, City Hall has been a handsome presence along the west side of **Town Square**. About 30 feet south of the building is the **Police Station**, with a closed one-story structure connecting it to City Hall; about 40 feet north is the **Fire Department**, connected to City Hall by a row of **restrooms**. These adjacent buildings differ significantly from those shown in a 1953 **Marvin Davis** concept illustration that placed a fire station and hospital to the left and a Hall of Records to the right.

Disney Legend **Harper Goff**, who designed Disneyland's City Hall, based the look on a similar building in his Colorado hometown. Spreading approximately 45 feet wide, City Hall has two main stories crowned by a mansard roof and widow's walk, with a central rectangular tower rising yet one more story. Sturdy red bricks and ornate white trim give the structure a dignified look, while the row of slender columns out front adds a graceful touch to the entryway. In the evening, decorative white lights define the upper stories attractively. Inside City Hall's lobby are displays of art, photos, and official proclamations.

In some ways, City Hall has indeed served as the park's official headquarters. The first Disneyland **souvenir books**, which labeled the building both Town Hall and City Hall, identified it as the place to locate lost children, the park's security officers, and First Aid. Eventually City Hall became home to **Guest Relations**, the information

Disneyland Measured in Football Fields
(100 yards = 1 FF)

1. City Hall to Opera House = .75 FF
2. Enchanted Tiki Room to Tarzan's Treehouse = 1 FF
3. Hub to Golden Horseshoe = 1 FF
4. Tom Sawyer Island Rafts to *Mark Twain* dock = 1 FF
5. Grand Canyon Diorama = 1 FF
6. Pirates of the Caribbean to Splash Mountain = 2 FF
7. Hub to Pirates of the Caribbean = 2 FF
8. Hub to Innoventions = 2 FF
9. Main Street train station to Hub = 2.5 FF
10. Tom Sawyer Island north–south = 2.5 FF

center for guests looking for foreign-currency exchanges, maps, local phone directories, and entertainment schedules. Also available are binders that identify the park's flora and provide recipes for the dishes served in Disneyland's restaurants. Rarely noticed by guests are the tall, century-old eucalyptus trees behind the building. These were saved from the original groves that preceded Disneyland, making them perhaps the oldest living things in the park.

Clarabelle's Frozen Yogurt

MAP: Mickey's Toontown, MT-8

DATES: January 24, 1993–ongoing

Clarabelle, Disney's cartoon cow, got her own yogurt stand in 1993. Located in **Mickey's Toontown** next to **Pluto's Dog House**, the little blue building has a distinctive white awning speckled with irregular black spots. Clarabelle's counter offers a small menu of "udderly refreshing" yogurts, desserts, and soft drinks.

Clock of the World,
aka World Clock

MAP: Tomorrowland, T-3

DATES: July 17, 1955–September 1966

Short on dramatic attractions for **Tomorrowland** in 1955, **Walt Disney** added some inexpensive spectacle with the futuristic Clock of the World. Standing inside a landscaped circle at the entrance to Tomorrowland, the clock was comprised of a 15-foot-tall cylinder pinched in the middle like an hourglass. A world map wrapped around the upper half of the hourglass, and a blue base formed the bottom half. Around the top of the cylinder were the hours 1–24, and attached to the very top was a sphere that showed half the sun facing the crescent moon.

The early Disneyland **souvenir books**, which sometimes referred to the structure as the World Clock, played up the exhibit with photos of captivated guests pointing and staring at it. Their fascination, supposedly, was in the clock's ability to tell the time, right to the minute, for any location on the planet.

Evidently guests attending the park after the late 1960s no longer needed this information; time ran out for the Clock of the World in 1966, and it was dismantled for that year's major remodeling of Tomorrowland. In 2010, the rotating exterior of the **Innovations** building displayed a small rendition of the old Clock of the World.

Clock Shop

MAP: Fantasyland, Fa-3

DATES: 1963–ca. 1969

Disneyland's 1968 **souvenir book** showed off the Clock Shop with a nice color photo of a family surrounded by ornate cuckoo clocks, plus the caption "The Castle Clock Shop leaves no doubt about the time, especially at the start of a new hour." Actually, the Clock Shop *did* seem to leave doubt about the time—of the dozen clocks with readable faces in the photo, only two were set for the same time, which means that a cuckoo clock was probably cuckooing every few minutes.

The shop itself was located inside the entrance to **Sleeping Beauty Castle**, a spot formerly taken by the **Arts and Crafts Shop**. A 1970 map of **Fantasyland** restored the Arts and Crafts Shop to its previous position inside the castle arches.

Club Buzz

MAP: Tomorrowland, T-9

DATES: May 2001–November 2006

What had been the space-themed **Tomorrowland Terrace** since 1967 became the movie-themed Club Buzz in 2001. Borrowing names from the nearby **Buzz Lightyear Astro Blasters** attraction, the eatery was also called Club Buzz: Lightyear's Above the Rest. Club Buzz combined casual dining and entertainment, just as the Terrace had in the previous century. The large curving food counter offered an "out-of-this-world menu" of breakfast plates, sandwiches, fried chicken, salads, and "the best burgers in the galaxy."

As guests ate, a kid-friendly show named *Calling All Space Scouts: A Buzz Lightyear Adventure* was performed on the Club Buzz stage. As with the old Tomorrowland Terrace, this stage rose up from below ground level. However, the top of this stage was decorated not with sleek white planter boxes, but with an elaborate futuristic sculpture in blue, silver, and purple. The heroic astronaut Buzz Lightyear hosted the new show, which featured a confrontation with the evil Emperor Zurg.

In 2007, when the new *Jedi Training Academy* moved in, Club Buzz reverted back to its original design and former name, Tomorrowland Terrace.

Club 33

MAP: New Orleans Square, NOS-4

DATES: June 15, 1967–ongoing

One of Disneyland's worst-kept secrets is the presence of a private restaurant in **New Orleans Square**. The name Club 33 has long been the subject of speculative guesses by fans, who have come up with a wide range of explanations—everything from 33 being the number of original Disneyland sponsors to 33 somehow representing Mickey Mouse's initials (or Mickey Mouse's ears) when the digits are turned sideways. According to official explanations, the name is derived from the actual address, 33 Royal Street, on the ground-level doorway to the right of the **Blue Bayou**.

There used to be another private dining room in the back of the **Red Wagon Inn** on **Main Street**, but it one was much less elaborate than what now exists in New Orleans Square. Club 33 was originally meant to be used by the Disney family in conjunction with their **apartment** above the nearby **Pirates of the Caribbean**, but **Walt Disney** passed away before the club and apartment were completed. When it was finished, Disneyland executives used Club 33 to entertain VIPs and business associates. Within a few years, it became a private club with a paid membership of under 500 people.

Today, membership is both expensive (the initiation fee is now over $10,000 per individual, plus over $3,500 a year in annual dues) and hard to come by (the waiting list was finally cut off at 1,000). In 2007 Disneyland raised the number of members to 500, but applicants can still expect to wait a decade for membership.

Club 33's interior is said to be the most elegant and fascinating dining space in the park. Once members have been identified and admitted through the Club 33 door on Royal Street, an elevator takes them upstairs, where wooden floors, crystal chandeliers, artifacts from Disney movies, and antiques purchased by Walt and Lillian Disney await, as well as a gourmet buffet. The floor plan wraps around the heart of New Orleans Square, from the Blue Bayou area to the space across Royal Street above Café Orléans. Two lavishly decorated dining rooms overlook the **Rivers of America**. At one time some kind of interactive **Audio-Animatronics** arrangement was going to be installed in the Trophy Room, and microphones were even placed in chandeliers for instant communication between staff and guests. That plan, however, never evolved past the experimental stage.

Besides its luxurious décor and magnificent views, Club 33 offers unique amenities that no other Disneyland restaurant does: it's the only one to serve alcohol; it indulges guests with gifts to help them remember their visits; and it offers the impeccable service of Disneyland's most highly trained food servers.

Naturally, there's never been any description of Club 33 in Disneyland's **souvenir books**, and although many people have heard of it and even more have unknowingly walked right by the entrance, only a very few will ever be able to say they've been inside.

Coats, Claude
(1913–1992)

A San Franciscan born in 1913, Claude Coats earned a degree in architecture and fine arts at USC and then studied at an art institute in Los Angeles. Hired at Disney Studios in 1935, he became one of the company's most gifted artists, known especially for his sublime background paintings in classic animated films like *Pinocchio*, *Fantasia*, and *Peter Pan*.

Switching to Disneyland projects in 1955, Coats was a key contributor to popular attractions throughout the park. He helped paint the displays and backgrounds on early **Fantasyland** attractions like **Mr. Toad's Wild Ride** and **Snow White Adventures**. He also designed almost everything in the original **Alice in Wonderland** attraction and created the Rainbow Caverns interiors for the **Mine Train** in **Frontierland**, underwater scenes for the **Submarine Voyage** in **Tomorrowland**, and the backdrop for the **Grand Canyon Diorama**. In the mid-'60s he contributed interior designs to **Adventure Thru Inner Space**, the **Haunted Mansion**, and **Pirates of the Caribbean** (**Walt Disney** called Coats "the Imagineer in charge of the Pirates project" in a 1965 episode of *Walt Disney's Wonderful World of Color*).

Before retiring in 1989, Coats also helped with many attractions at Walt Disney World. He died in 1992, a year after he was honored as a Disney Legend.

Coin Shop, aka Stamp and Coin Shop

MAP: Main Street, MS-15

DATES: Ca. 1957–1960

The narrow Center Street intersects **Main Street** just past the **Market House**. Starting around 1957, a little Coin Shop briefly operated next to the **Pen Shop** in the East Center cul-de-sac. Disneyland's 1957 **souvenir book** introduced the Coin Shop and the 1959 edition renamed it the Stamp and Coin Shop, but subsequent souvenir books never mentioned any kind of coin, stamp, or coin-and-stamp business again. The shop disappeared in the 1960 remodel that delivered a big **Hallmark Card Shop** on the corner of Main and East Center.

Cole of California Swimsuits

MAP: Main Street, MS-11

DATES: 1956–1957

Formerly a silent-movie actor, Fred Cole created his fashionable line of swimwear in

1923. After his suits became popular in the Hollywood community, in 1956 he opened a little shop on **Main Street** in the west-side block dominated by Coke's **Refreshment Corner**. But as enduring as the Cole line has been (Cole swimsuits are still made today), the Disneyland location was short-lived. By 1958 the store was gone, replaced by the first **Mad Hatter of Main Street** shop.

Conestoga Wagons

MAP: Frontierland, Fr-21

DATES: August 1, 1955–September 13, 1959

The Conestoga Wagons were part of the original **Frontierland**, back when the **Painted Desert** was being explored by mules and mine trains. The wooden wagons were replicas of the horse-drawn vehicles driven across America in the middle of the previous century. Each Disneyland wagon was pulled by at least two horses, held about a dozen guests, and, true to the pioneer spirit, had "Westward Ho!" or "Oregon or Bust" painted on its canvas top.

From the summer of 1955 until 1958, a ride in a Conestoga Wagon cost a B ticket from the Disneyland **ticket book** or 25 cents; in 1959, the price rose to a C ticket. Heading north to the **Painted Desert** and back, the trip approximated the route of Disneyland's **Stage Coach**. Ironically, the wagons and the stage expired on the same day and for the same reason—unreliable power plants. The horses, unfortunately, were sometimes startled by unexpected noises; though this Frontierland area was presented as a desert wilderness, train whistles, "blank" gunfire, amplified announcements, and other random sounds emanated from the park all around it. Fearful of spooked horses blocking stalled wagons—or panicked horses galloping off with runaway wagons—officials quietly retired the Conestogas after the summer of '59. The **Mule Pack** and **Mine Train** continued to explore the new and improved **Nature's Wonderland** until everything surrendered to the **Big Thunder** installation in the late '70s.

Corridor of Murals

MAP: Tomorrowland, T-5, T-23

DATES: 1967–1998

For over three decades, beautiful tile mosaics greeted guests as they passed through the metallic entrance into **Tomorrowland**. The mosaics adorned two large, curving buildings that faced each other—the Circle-Vision 360 theater on the left and the **Adventure Thru Inner Space** building on the right. On each building, hundreds of square feet of wall space were covered with one half of a large artwork called *The Spirit of Creative Energies Among Children*, thus giving this stretch of Tomorrowland the name Corridor of Murals.

Mary Blair, the principal designer of **It's a Small World**, created the murals. Her mosaics depicted children in international costumes frolicking in colorful scenes, with a big smiling sun, an ocean, trees, ribbons of color, and various abstract shapes composed in the style of **It's a Small World**. The theme and execution might have seemed better suited to **Fantasyland** than Tomorrowland, but the murals did help humanize what were otherwise rather sterile buildings.

Unfortunately, neither section of the Corridor of Murals survived the century. The half on the Adventure Thru Inner Space building disappeared when **Star Tours** opened in 1987 and added its own artwork to the building's exterior. The Circle-Vision half was lost to the 1998 **Rocket Rods** remodel that included a new transportation-themed painting on the building's wall.

After dismantling Blair's work, Disneyland sold off the tile pieces to fans. Even if Blair's designs no longer fit in with Tomorrowland's future, they are still cherished reminders of Tomorrowland's past.

Cosmic Waves

MAP: Tomorrowland, T-20

DATES: June 22, 1998–January 2002

The interactive fountain called Cosmic Waves must have seemed like a good idea when the Disneyland designers first conceived it. Who wouldn't have fun jumping among thin jets of water shooting up intermittently from the ground, especially on a blazing summer day? And who wouldn't want to try to rotate a big wet marble sitting in the middle of all the action? Unfortunately, the reality proved to be less cosmic than expected.

Cosmic Waves opened with the remodeled **Tomorrowland** in mid-1998, its lo-

cation a 60-foot-wide circular plaza near the *Moonliner*. The plan was for kids to run between the fountain's five-foot-high water jets without getting wet. Additionally, kids could team up to push on a giant six-ton granite ball that stayed in place as it turned slowly. It turned out, however, that *experiencing* the water, was more fun than *avoiding* the water, leaving parents and **cast members** to deal with soaking wet kids who hadn't thought to bring bathing suits.

By the end of 2001, as Cosmic Waves became more like a Cosmic Bath, the park turned off the fountain. Though the water no longer spurts, the stone ball can still be taken for a spin.

Cottrell, Bill
(1906–1995)

Bill Cottrell was the first Disney employee to be recognized for 50 years of service. He was born in South Bend, Indiana, in 1906. After graduating from Occidental College in Los Angeles and working briefly for the creator of *Krazy Kat* comics, he became a cameraman at Disney Studios. Within a few years he was working on Disney's cartoons and animated movies, ultimately making major contributions to *Snow White and the Seven Dwarfs*, *Pinocchio*, and *Peter Pan*, among others.

As a key ally (and brother-in-law) of **Walt Disney**, Cottrell was instrumental in bringing the Disneyland dream to life and was said to be Disney's "right-hand man." In addition to planning and overseeing many projects, Cottrell wrote scripts for some of the attractions and added many important details, including naming the individual **Jungle Cruise** boats and developing the Disneyland lexicon that renamed "rides" as "attractions" and "customers" as "guests."

Cottrell was later promoted to president of the company's design and development department (today's Imagineers) and was named a Disney Legend in 1994, a year before he died at age 89.

Country Bear Jamboree,
aka Country Bear Playhouse

MAP: Bear Country/Critter Country, B/C-4

DATES: March 24, 1972–September 9, 2001

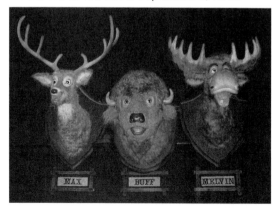

Like **Space Mountain**, the Country Bear Jamboree existed in Walt Disney World before it debuted in Disneyland. Actually, an attraction like the Country Bear Jamboree would have appeared first in California's Sierra Nevada mountains, had Disney's plans for a new resort called Mineral King not been scuttled in 1966.

When the Jamboree did finally open in Anaheim, it was the E-ticket showpiece (see **ticket book**) of the new **Bear Country** area built west of **Frontierland**. While other Disney Legends worked on the attraction, the bears and their distinctive personalities were mainly the creations of artist **Marc Davis**, who drew up the original character designs. Disney artist Al Bertino inspired the taciturn Big Al character.

Dubbed "the wildest show in the wilderness" on its ornate **attraction poster**, the rollicking 15-minute Jamboree featured 18 **Audio-Animatronic** bears singing approximately a dozen short, countrified songs on a gaudy stage. Among the tunes were the familiar "Ballad of Davy Crockett" and the heartbreaking "Tears Will Be the Chaser for My Wine," with such comical numbers as "My Woman Ain't Pretty (But She Don't Swear None)" sprinkled into the mix. Henry, an amiable, top-hatted bear with a starched collar and bow tie, was the putative emcee; "Zeke and Zed and Ted and Fred and a bear named Tennes-

> ### Movies Based on Disneyland Attractions
>
> 1. *The Country Bears* (2002)
> 2. *The Haunted Mansion* (2003)
> 3. *The Haunted Mansion* (2012)
> 4. *Pirates of the Caribbean: Curse of the Black Pearl* (2003)
> 5. *Pirates of the Caribbean: Dead Man's Chest* (2006)
> 6. *Pirates of the Caribbean: At World's End* (2007)
> 7. *Pirates of the Caribbean: On Stranger Tides* (2011)
> 8. *The Hill* (projected for 2013)
> 9. *Magic Kingdom* (projected for 2013)
> 10. *Mr. Toad's Wild Ride* (in development)
> 11. *Jungle Cruise* (in development)

see" formed the Five Bear Rugs; Bunny, Bubbles, and Beulah were the singing Sun Bonnets; and cute Teddi Barra swung down from the ceiling with her feather boa to knock out "Heart, We Did All That We Could." Gomer played an upright piano topped with a honey pot, Sammy the coonskin hat popped up to join in the fun, and Big Al stole the show with his languid rendition of "Blood on the Saddle." Max, Melvin, and Buff, a trio of talking trophy heads mounted on the wall, added to the vaudeville-style festivities.

In 1975, Wonder Bread replaced Pepsi-Cola as the Jamboree's sponsor. In '84 the bears performed their first Country Bear Christmas Show, which subsequently reappeared each **holiday season**. (In the show, a bear named Rufus was identified as the dim-witted stage manager—fans recognized him as the owner of the mailbox at the entrance to Bear Country.) In February 1986, the bears starred in the new Country Bear Vacation Hoedown. Five months later, after Wonder Bread withdrew its sponsorship, the theater was officially renamed the Country Bear Playhouse.

The Hoedown held strong for another 15 years, but ultimately the crowds began to dwindle and in 2001 park officials put the show in permanent hibernation. The replacement for the Country Bear attraction, **The Many Adventures of Winnie the Pooh**, starred another bear, and he too was an import from Walt Disney World.

Fans of the original bears got to have one more look at them in theaters when *The Country Bears*, a movie based on the Jamboree's characters, debuted in 2002. The bears received a satirical treatment in 2009 when they made a guest appearance in an episode of *The Simpsons* in chains, costumes, and bad moods.

Court of Honor

MAP: Tomorrowland, T-8

DATES: July 17, 1955–March 1956

The Court of Honor was a short-lived exhibit in the heart of **Tomorrowland**. Its location was in the plaza 50 feet west of **Innoventions**. The "court" was a large, star-shaped flower box; the "honor" was represented by the 48 flags of all the states in the union (back then, Alaska and Hawaii had not yet been admitted). The flags waved from atop tall flagpoles planted among the greenery, with six poles for each of the star's eight points and an even taller pole in the center displaying Old Glory.

What any of this had to do with Tomorrowland, which the 1956 **souvenir book** described as "the realm of the unexplored," was unclear. While **Walt Disney** certainly loved to celebrate patriotism, perhaps this tribute to America's past and present landed where it did only out of a desperate need to fill empty Tomorrowland space for **Opening Day**. In March of 1956, the eight-month-old flags and poles were relocated to the newly constructed **Avenue of the Flags** at the Tomorrowland entrance. Within a few weeks the **Astro-Jets** touched down for a long stay where the Court of Honor had been.

Creole Café, aka Café Orléans

MAP: New Orleans Square, NOS-7

DATES: July 24, 1966–ongoing

From the summer of 1966 until 1972, the Creole Café was a choice spot for **New Orleans Square** dining. Entered from Royal Street, the café was halfway between the **Pirates of the Caribbean** entrance and the **French Market** restaurant. Since it jutted out in the direction of the **Rivers of America**, it was highly visible to anyone walking the main thoroughfare from **Frontierland** toward the **Haunted Mansion.**

In 1972 the Sara Lee Corporation took over sponsorship of the café and changed the name first to Sara Lee's Café Orleans and then to the simpler Café Orleans. Marie Callender's briefly sponsored the restaurant in 1987. Over the years, the relatively inexpensive meals have included sandwiches, crêpes, chicken dishes, gumbo, and salads. Though the menu has changed often and the days and hours of operation have varied, the riverside setting has never been anything but picturesque. Café Orleans is serviced by the same giant underground kitchen facility that provides the food for the **Blue Bayou**, **Club 33**, and other nearby eateries.

Cristal d'Orleans

MAP: New Orleans Square, NOS-6

DATES: July 24, 1966–ongoing

In the heart of **New Orleans Square** is a beautiful crystal shop that is as old as New Orleans Square itself. The sponsors are the Arribas brothers, the same master craftsmen behind the current **Crystal Arts** on **Main Street** and the extinct **Castle Arts** shop formerly in **Fantasyland**. Their Cristal d'Orleans has two door-ways, one on Orleans Street across from **Mlle. Antoinette's Parfumerie**, and the other on Royal Street across from **Le Bat en Rouge**. Like all Arribas shops, glassware, vases, jewelry, paperweights, and delicate Disney-themed sculptures are among the shimmering creations on display, with an engraving service available to personalize items.

Critter Country

MAP: Park, P-14
DATES: November 23, 1988–ongoing

With a dramatic new **Bear Country** attraction debuting in just eight months, in late 1988 Disney officials decided to change the name of this corner of the park to Critter Country. The new name de-emphasized the bears and threw the spotlight on all the various critters of the soon-to-arrive **Splash Mountain**.

The Critter Country description in the 2000 Disneyland **souvenir book** inventoried the animals: "Here amid shady trees and cool streams is a world where the rabbits, bears, opossums, foxes, alligators, owls, and frogs are just as social and neighborly as they can be." Building on that theme, several of the area's businesses surrendered their old ursine identities to new critter-oriented names—**Ursus H. Bear's Wilderness Outpost** became **Crocodile Mercantile**, for instance.

Despite all the new Southern fauna, Critter Country continued to host musical bears in the **Country Bear Playhouse** until 2001, when another bear replaced them in the new **The Many Adventures of Winnie the Pooh** attraction. No matter what animals rule this land, the lush vegetation has always made Bear Country/Critter Country a quiet, rural contrast to its jazzy, urbane neighbor, **New Orleans Square**.

Critter Country Fruit Cart

MAP: Bear Country/Critter Country, B/C-2

DATES: Ca. 2000–ongoing

Standing along the **Rivers of America** near **Splash Mountain**, this is the most remote of Disneyland's three fruit carts. Like the **Main Street Fruit Cart** and **Indy Fruit Cart**, the Critter Country Fruit Cart peddles simple, healthy snacks. Besides fresh fruit and juices, guests can also stock up on muffins, cookies, and sodas.

Critter Country Plush

MAP: Bear Country/Critter Country, B/C-10

DATES: February 1996–October 1996

Located next to **Splash Mountain**, the rustic **Briar Patch** cabin has been a **Critter Country** fixture from 1988 until the present—with one major interruption. In February 1996 the store changed its stock from handcrafted gifts and clothes to modern plush toys, and changed its name to Critter Country Plush. Despite the ongoing popularity of its merchandise, the store barely lasted eight months—by Halloween, a sign announcing the Briar Patch's return was already in place. The plush toys, however, stayed in the shop until 2004, when many of them were removed in favor of souvenir hats.

Crocodile Mercantile

MAP: Bear Country/Critter Country, B/C-7

DATES: November 23, 1988–April 2003

On the same day that **Bear Country** was renamed **Critter Country**, **Ursus H. Bear's Wilderness Outpost** was renamed Crocodile Mercantile. Its location at the back of Critter Country was the same, as was much of the souvenir, T-shirt, and toy merchandise.

In 2003 Crocodile Mercantile, the **Brer Bar**, and **Teddi Barra's Swingin' Arcade** were all remodeled and merged into a single store called **Pooh Corner**.

Crump, Rolly

(1930–)

Born in 1930 near Pasadena, California, Roland Crump began his career at Disney Studios 22 years later as a young artist working on such animated films as *Peter Pan* and *Sleeping Beauty*. During the '60s, he contributed to numerous structures all around Disneyland, including the **Enchanted Tiki Room** (he sculpted, painted, and installed

most of the tiki gods), the **Tomorrowland Terrace** (his abstract forms crowned the roof), and the **Adventureland Bazaar** (he created the overall look).

At the 1964–1965 New York World's Fair, Crump had a hand in practically all of Disney's exhibitions. For the fair's **It's a Small World** building, he designed some of the dolls inside and the 12-story *Tower of the Four Winds* outside. When It's a Small World moved to Anaheim in '66, Crump helped design the flamboyant façade, especially the oversized exterior clock that still marks every 15-minute period with a march of mechanical puppets. Among his other Disneyland efforts were stages and floats for some of the elaborate **parades**. A mid-'60s episode of *Walt Disney's Wonderful World of Color* featured Crump and some of his creations for the park's Museum of the Weird (which would later become the **Haunted Mansion**). In the early '80s he was one of the leaders of the complex **Fantasyland** renovation.

Outside of Disneyland, Crump was a key designer at Walt Disney World. He also helped develop theme projects for other companies, and eventually formed his own design firm. Returning to Disney in 1992, Crump helped remodel EPCOT before retiring in '96. Eight years later, Rolly Crump was named a Disney Legend.

Crystal Arcade

MAP: Main Street, MS-3

DATES: July 17, 1955–ongoing

Since **Opening Day**, **Main Street** has had two arcades on its western side, but only one—the **Penny Arcade**—has kept generations of kids mesmerized with games. The other, the Crystal Arcade, dominates the middle of Main's first western block. How many kids have walked under the Crystal Arcade's big, bright letters expecting to find the same kind of amusements that are in the Penny Arcade 150 feet to the north? What they've found instead is a collection of shops, which has included the **Candle Shop** and the **Story Book Shop**. An actual **Glass Blower** was also a prominent inhabitant of the Crystal Arcade in its first decade.

A 1995 remodel opened up the interior to make it more like an extension of the **Emporium** next door. Filled with plush toys and souvenirs, the room still has glittering crystal chandeliers, justifying the arcade's name. A 2005 renovation revitalized the grand blue-green exterior, and the 2006 **souvenir book** featured photos of the Crystal Arcade at its best—in the evening, when the semi-circular entrance glows with golden lights.

Crystal Arts

MAP: Main Street, MS-13

DATES: 1972–ongoing

After meeting and impressing **Walt Disney** at the 1964–1965 New York World's Fair, Tomas and Alfonso Arribas, two Spanish brothers who were master glass cutters, opened several shops in Disneyland. Their first was **Cristal d'Orleans** in **New Orleans Square**, and their second was Crystal Arts on **Main Street**. Later the brothers would open a third Disneyland shop—**Castle Arts**—as well as additional stores in other Disney parks.

On Main Street, Crystal Arts sits next door to the **Silhouette Studio** in a space that was once home to Timex's **Watches & Clocks**. Delicate glassware and Disney character figures, bells, vases, and lamps make the interior of Crystal Arts sparkle. At times the shop has displayed an opulent crystal sculpture of **Sleeping Beauty Castle**, priced at around $20,000 (**cast members** here claim that one of these was purchased in recent years by actor Nicolas Cage). Custom creations and free engraving are also offered.

Daisy's Diner

MAP: Mickey's Toontown, MT-8

DATES: January 24, 1993–ongoing

Daisy, Donald Duck's girlfriend, has a boat named after her in Toon Lake. She also has her own diner over by **Goofy's Gas Station**. "Diner" is a misnomer for guests expecting a blue plate special and old-fashioned banquettes. Daisy's Diner is a simple counter serving fast pizzas, garden salads, and basic beverages to go, with outdoor tables conveniently located nearby.

Dalmatian Celebration

MAP: Town Square, TS-7

DATES: November 28, 1996–January 5, 1997

Disney's live-action version of *One Hundred and One Dalmatians* premiered in New York on November 18, 1996; to help promote the new movie, Disneyland opened Dalmatian Celebration 10 days later. The spot for the spots was just to the right of the prominent **Disney Showcase** store, which occupied the corner where **Main Street** stretches northward from **Town Square**. Formerly the Dalmatian Celebration location had been utilized by various eateries, among them the **Town Square Café**.

Guests entering the park through the east tunnel couldn't miss the new area themed to Disney's biggest movie of the year. Inside, they found lots of movie-related activities, including spots-on-the-face-painting and photo opportunities with a menacing Cruella De Vil. The biggest surprise was the presence of actual puppies for guests to meet.

Once the **holiday season** ended, so did the six-week promotion. The internal rooms became off-limits offices, and the external space a character-greeting area. Dalmatian Celebration wasn't the first time Disneyland had gone to the dogs—from the late 1950s to the mid-'60s, a one-day Kids Amateur Dog Show fetched a few more guests every spring.

Dapper Dans

DATES: 1957–ongoing

To many Disneyland fans, **Main Street** wouldn't be Main Street without the Dapper Dans. This lighthearted, all-male barbershop quartet has been performing in the park since 1957, though not always with the same singers. Over a hundred have performed as one of the Dans, many of them rotating between Disneyland and other Disney parks. The group's formula has changed only slightly since the late '50s, consisting of four smiling gentlemen in colorful striped suits who harmonize sentimental songs, usually a capella, to evoke sweet memories of the turn of the 20th century. The Dans' extensive

29 Long-Lasting Park Performers

Adventureland
Alturas
Royal Tahitians
Trinidad & Tobago Showboat Steel
    Orchestra

Main Street
All-American College Band
Charles Dickens Carolers
Coke Corner Pianist
Dapper Dans
Disneyland Band
Keystone Cops
Sax Quintet

Fantasyland
Make Believe Brass
Royal Jesters

Frontierland
Big Thunder Breakdown Boys
Billy Hill and the Hillbillies
Firehouse Five Plus Two
Laughing Stock Co.
Strawhatters

Tomorrowland
Kids of the Kingdom
Krash
Trash Can Trio

New Orleans Square
Bayou Brass Band
Bilge Rats & Bootstrappers
Gloryland Brass Band
Jambalaya Jazz Band
Jolly Roger
Orleans Street Band
River Rascals
Royal Street Bachelors
Side Street Strutters

repertoire emphasizes barbershop standards and Disney classics (the most-requested song dates is reportedly from Disneyland's infancy, but it isn't a Disney song—it's "Lida Rose" from the 1957 musical *The Music Man*).

Popular as they were from the start, the Dans weren't shown in the park's **souvenir books** until 1968, when a photo presented them wearing white jackets, carrying straw boater hats in hand, and riding their crowd-pleasing quadcycle. The Dapper Dans appeared on the *Strike Up the Disneyland Band* vinyl LP in 1969, and their own *Shave and a Haircut* CD came out in 2000. Onscreen, they've appeared in several Disney-produced TV shows and specials, such as a 1962 "Disneyland After Dark" episode that showed the group entertaining a Main Street crowd with a humorous rendition of "Carry Me Back to Old Virginny." Fans of *The Simpsons* may recognize the Dans' vocals in the episode about Homer's a capella group, the Be Sharps, and movie fans might remember the Dapper Dans' performance as the singing busts in *The Haunted Mansion*.

Date Nite

DATES: June 1957–ongoing

In the park's early history, Date Nite was a pleasant summer tradition. This musical event began in June of 1957 as a way to fully utilize Disneyland after dark. That first month, the park stayed open on Fridays and Saturdays until midnight, but in July and August the hours extended until 1:00 AM.

The goal was to draw in young couples for a sophisticated dance concert. The lovely outdoor **Plaza Gardens** in the northwest corner of the **Hub** provided the location, and the Date Niters (officially the Elliot Bros. Orchestra) provided the music. These 10 musicians, all wearing red jackets and white pants, included a half-dozen brass instrumentalists, a stand-up bass player, a pianist, a drummer, and a vocalist. The group's 1958 album *Date Nite at Disneyland* showed off their repertoire of Gershwin, Johnny Mercer, and Rogers and Hart standards, with "Goodnight Sweetheart" as a romantic coda.

Starting with the park's 1958 **souvenir book**, Date Nite was consistently featured with a photo of well-dressed, happy couples dancing in front of the orchestra and an accompanying caption: "A gay twirl with your best girl to the dance rhythms of Disneyland's popular Date Niters orchestra is a Summertime evening favorite."

The Date Niters knocked out a swingin' song for a national TV audience on a 1962 episode of *Walt Disney's Wonderful World of Color*. A few years later, the Date Nite concept was abandoned, but the trend of evening entertainment at Disneyland had been set and would even be extended throughout the week. Concerts at the Plaza Gardens later continued with such shows as the Cavalcade of Bands in the '60s and the Big Bands at Disneyland series in the '80s.

Davis, Alice
(1929–)

Alice Davis and her husband, Marc, were instrumental in making Disneyland the beloved park it is. Born in 1929 in Escalon, California, Davis was an art student when she met her future husband. She worked as a fashion designer for most of the '50s until Marc invited her to work on costumes for Disney movies, which led to a job researching and designing hundreds of Velcro-lined costumes for Disneyland's **It's a Small World**. (Alice told a convention audience in 2010 that It's a Small World was her favorite park project because, as a child of the Great Depression, she'd never had dolls to play with, and with this attraction she finally had hundreds.) In 1965 she began creating costumes for buccaneers in **Pirates of the Caribbean**, using Marc's drawings for ideas. Later she worked on costumes for Flight to the Moon and the **Carousel of Progress**. Still affiliated with Disney, she's appeared at special events in recent years and continues to consult. Davis was named a Disney Legend in 2004.

Davis, Marc
(1913–2000)

One half of the husband-and-wife Davis team, Marc Davis enjoyed a long career with Disney. Marc was one of the legendary "nine old men" (a nickname bestowed by an appreciative **Walt Disney**) whose art propelled Disney's classic animated films. Born in Bakersfield, California in 1913, Davis studied at several art institutes before settling in at the Disney Studios in 1935. For the next 26 years he worked on films from *Snow White and the Seven Dwarfs* to *One Hundred and One Dalmatians*, creating along the way such memorable movie characters as Tinker Bell and Cruella De Vil.

Davis joined the Disneyland team in 1961, and his creative talents are still seen and heard all over park. He wrote jokes for the **Enchanted Tiki Room**, invented comic scenes for the **Jungle Cruise** and **It's a Small World**, added animals and settings to **Nature's Wonderland** in **Frontierland**, drew up the musical bruins for the **Country Bear Jamboree**, developed characters and scenes for **America Sings**, and painted the humorous portraits in the **Haunted Mansion's** "stretching room."

His finest work may have been **Pirates of the Caribbean**. Davis' original concepts became actual scenes in the attraction: the trio of jailed pirates trying to lure the dog holding the key; the pirate skeleton pinned to the wall by a sword, a seagull nested in his hat; the pirate struggling under a mountain of hats and booty as he steps onto a shaky launch. In the 10th anniversary episode of *Walt Disney's Wonderful World of Color* in 1965, Davis was introduced to a national TV audience, along with highlights of the coming Pirates and Haunted Mansion attractions.

Davis officially retired in 1978 but stayed on to help with EPCOT and Tokyo Disneyland. Elected as a Disney Legend in 1989, he died in Southern California in 2000.

Davis, Marvin
(1910–1998)

When it came to creating Disneyland's layout and overall design, Marvin Davis probably worked as closely with **Walt Disney** as any other Disney employee. Davis was right there in the inner circle as plans for the nascent park began to take shape; he's often credited with drawing up the first aerial view of Disneyland as we now recognize it. His 1953 illustration assigned the park practical building arrangements, stretched **Main Street** from the **entrance** up to the **Hub**, and branched lands out from the Hub's spokes.

Like several other Disney Legends who contributed to Disneyland, Davis got his start working on movies. He was born in 1910 in New Mexico, won awards in college as an architecture student, and got a job in 1935 as an art director at 20th Century Fox. Twenty years later, he joined the Disneyland design team.

In addition to helping determine the park's overall structure, Davis planned many specific areas and attractions over the next decade. He came up with over 100 variations of the main **entrance**, executed early designs of Main Street buildings and **Sleeping Beauty Castle**, translated Walt Disney's own rough sketch of **Tom Sawyer Island** into detailed plans, and contributed to the look of both **New Orleans Square** and the **Haunted Mansion**.

Davis also directed Disney movies and TV shows, including *Babes in Toyland* and *The Mickey Mouse Club*, picking up an Emmy in 1962 for art direction and scenic design. In the late '60s and early '70s, Davis steered the planning and design of Walt Disney World before he retired in 1975. Davis was named a Disney Legend in 1994, four years before he died in Santa Monica at age 97.

Davy Crockett Arcade,
aka Davy Crockett Frontier Arcade

MAP: Frontierland, Fr-1

DATES: October, 1955–1985

Sustaining the momentum of the Davy Crockett craze that was sweeping the nation in 1955, the Davy Crockett Arcade replaced the **Davy Crockett Frontier Museum** in the fall of that year. The location—just inside the **Frontierland** gates, in the building to the immediate left—didn't change, and for a while not much else inside the arcade did either, since the museum's wax figures remained on display until the following June.

The Davy Crockett Arcade wasn't for game-playing the way a modern arcade is (although Davy's did have a coin-operated pistol shootout game). Instead, Crockett's building was a collection of subdivided spaces occupied by a changing roster of retailers: the Mexican Village, Squaw Shop, Leather Shop, Frontier Rock Shop, Frontierland Hats, Frontier Print Shop, Western Emporium, and a souvenir stand (according to a small 1970 Frontierland map, these last five shared the arcade that year). Much of the interior space looked like the inside of a 19th-century frontier building, utilizing lots of pitted stucco and rough wood.

The whole enterprise was renamed the Davy Crockett Frontier Arcade in 1985. Two years later it was dubbed **Davy Crockett's Pioneer Mercantile**. This repeated reference to Davy Crockett illustrates his enduring appeal—other than Walt Disney himself, no other real person has been invoked more often in the names of Disneyland's attractions and stores.

Davy Crockett Frontier Museum

MAP: Frontierland, Fr-1

DATES: July 17, 1955–October 1955

To capitalize on the success of the three Davy Crockett episodes that began running on the ***Disneyland* TV series** in late 1954, Imagineers started spreading the Crockett theme throughout **Frontierland**. First up in the summer of '55 was the Davy Crockett Frontier Museum, a large building to guests' immediate left as they entered Frontierland's stockade gates. The museum displayed a collection of Crockett-themed exhibits, the highlight being a detailed re-creation of a meeting between Crockett (who resembled Fess Parker, the actor who portrayed Crockett on the *Davy Crockett* TV show), his sidekick George Russel (a Buddy Ebsen lookalike), and Andrew Jackson (a dead ringer for Andrew Jackson) inside Jackson's headquarters. The full-size wax figures were dressed in detailed frontier costumes, a row of rifles stood along the wall, historic art lined the rough-timber interior, and a period flag and wax sentry added authenticity.

Elsewhere in the museum, a coin-guzzling pistol-shooting game and shops selling Crockett-themed items (coonskin caps, buckskins, and other souvenirs) competed for attention. Three months after opening, the museum was re-billed as the **Davy Crockett Arcade**, and eight months after that the wax figures were relocated to Fort Wilderness on **Tom Sawyer Island**.

Davy Crockett's Pioneer Mercantile,
aka Pioneer Mercantile

MAP: Frontierland, Fr-1

DATES: 1987–ongoing

What was known for three decades as the **Davy Crockett Frontier Museum** and then the **Davy Crockett Arcade** became Davy Crockett's Pioneer Mercantile in 1987. For all three enterprises, the location was the big rough-timbered building guests encountered as they entered **Frontierland**. The store offered a wide range of toys, polished rocks, videos, souvenirs, books, and hats. Woody from *Toy Story*  and Pocahontas from *Pocahontas* have been strong presences among the merchandise over the years; when other Disney character dolls are sold in the store, they're usually wearing Western duds.

Eventually Davy Crockett was dropped from the name of the store, so it exists today as simply Pioneer Mercantile, connecting through its interior to **Bonanza Outfitters** next door. The Mercantile still evokes the pioneer spirit with a wood ceiling, rustic lighting fixtures, and a faux tree blended into the décor. Guests can still buy '50s-style coonskin caps "made of all new materials."

15 Disneyland Attractions, Shops, and Exhibits Named After Real People
(not including Walt Disney)

Marie Antoinette, French queen: Mlle. Antoinette's Parfumerie

Davy Crockett, frontier hero: Davy Crockett Arcade, aka Davy Crockett Frontier Arcade; Davy Crockett Frontier Museum; Davy Crockett's Explorer Canoes; Davy Crockett's Pioneer Mercantile

Don DeFore, TV and film actor: Don DeFore's Silver Banjo Barbecue

Mike Fink, pre-Civil War keelboat brawler: Mike Fink's Keel Boats

Joe Fowler, admiral and Disney Legend: Fowler's Harbor, aka Fowler's Landing

Gibson brothers, four Victorian Scottish printers: Gibson Greeting Cards

George Keller, circus entertainer: Keller's Jungle Killers

Jean Laffite, 19th-century pirate: Laffite's Silver Shop

Abraham Lincoln, U.S. president: Great Moments with Mr. Lincoln

Jimmy Starr, movie publicist: Jimmy Starr's Show Business Souvenirs

Mark Twain, American author: *Mark Twain* Riverboat

Linus Yale and Henry Towne, inventors and lock manufacturers: Yale & Towne Lock Shop

A Day at Disneyland
(1982)

In the tradition of previous Disney-produced documentaries like *Disneyland, U.S.A.* and *Gala Day at Disneyland*, *A Day at Disneyland* offered a state-of-the-park tour that celebrated favorite attractions and locations. But unlike the earlier two featurettes, both of which were released into theaters in pairings with Disney films, *A Day at Disneyland* was released on video in June of 1982 and was intended to be more of a souvenir keepsake.

Populating the 40-minute documentary were many Disney characters who frolicked through the park. Viewers watched Goofy float through the **Jungle Cruise**, Hook and Smee sail with the **Pirates of the Caribbean**, and more. Footage of now-extinct attractions like the **20,000 Leagues Under the Sea Exhibit** and **Skyway to Tomorrowland** adds a touch of nostalgia for modern viewers. A 1994 re-release included scenes of two 1990s enhancements, **Mickey's Toontown** and **Fantasmic!**

Discovery Bay

MAP: Frontierland, Fr-22

DATES: Never built

In the 1970s, it seemed like a whole new area was heading to Disneyland. Inside **Disneyland Presents a Preview of Coming Attractions**, a **Main Street** exhibit space that displayed models and art for possible future attractions, guests were discovering Discovery Bay.

Discovery Bay was to be a new body of water located somewhere between **Fantasyland** and **Frontierland**, possibly in the space later filled by the **Big Thunder Mountain Railroad**. Small waterfront buildings would have evoked the spirit of the 19th-century Barbary Coast, while the half-submerged *Nautilus* would have echoed a classic Disney movie (*20,000 Leagues Under the Sea*). Dominating the Discovery Bay imagery was a giant hangar with the sleek 200-foot airship *Hyperion* from the 1974 Disney movie *Island at the Top of the World* emerging for some unexplained purpose.

Was it a walk-through exhibit? Some kind of balloon-ride attraction? And the "looping upside-down on a magnetic roller-coaster" experience mentioned in the book *Walt Disney Imagineering*—where and what was that? Unfortunately, the public never got answers to any of these questions. The *Island* movie sank at the box office, and Discovery Bay went unrealized, though elements did turn up later at Disneyland Paris.

Disney Afternoon Avenue

MAP: Fantasyland, Fa-22

DATES: March 15, 1991–November 10, 1991

The success of the *Disney Afternoon* TV series led to a new **Fantasyland** area called, appropriately, Disney Afternoon Avenue. This temporary exhibit was built in early 1991 along 400 feet of walkway between **Matterhorn Mountain** and **It's a Small World**. Afternoon Avenue's cartoony structures represented Duckburg, USA, a brightly-colored small town that was a sort of early version of **Mickey's Toontown** (which would open two years later).

As with Toontown, guests could explore the cute buildings and meet and take pictures with Disney characters, including Scrooge McDuck, King Louie, and Baloo (**Baloo's Dressing Room** was at the far northern end, near It's a Small World). Several other nearby attractions—**Fantasyland Autopia**, **Videopolis**, and the **Motor Boat Cruise**—joined in on the *Disney Afternoon* theme by adding some temporary décor.

The whole enterprise peaked with the airing of a TV special, "Disney Afternoon Live! at Disneyland," on September 14, 1991. Never intended to be a long-term presence in the park, Disney Afternoon Avenue closed two months later.

Disneyana

MAP: Main Street, MS-4, MS-19

DATES: January 9, 1976–ongoing

Recognizing that rare Disney collectibles were hot commodities, Disneyland opened its own memorabilia shop in 1976. Originally, Disneyana was where the **Hurricane Lamp Shop** had once stood, a small location next to the **Crystal Arcade** on **Main Street**. At first the Disneyana shop specialized in rare vintage pieces, but eventually the line of merchandise expanded to become mostly limited-edition contemporary pieces.

Needing more room, on May 30, 1986, Disneyana switched places with the **Jewelry Shop**—the jeweler took Disneyana's west-side spot on Main Street, and Disneyana moved into the east-side space between the **Main Street Cinema** and the **Market House**. Disneyana is still there and remains a fascinating destination for Disneyphiles interested in animation cels, statues, and other collectibles.

Disney Clothiers, Ltd.

MAP: Main Street, MS-14

DATES: March 23, 1985–ongoing

For a quarter century, the **Hallmark Card Shop** has occupied the large corner where East Center Street divides **Main Street** into two blocks. In 1985 Disney Clothiers, Ltd.—"where good style is always in fashion"—moved into this prime retail spot across from the **Market House**. The clothing selection has varied from infantwear,

T-shirts, and jeans to fashionable sweaters, jackets, and dresses, all adorned with Disney themes. Bath products and linens have both appeared on the shelves, even though the sign out front announces "clothing with character—a Main Street tradition since 1905." Two signs outside identify different rooms within Disney Clothiers, including Castle Brothers ("collegiate fashions") and Chester Drawers ("togs for toddlers"). Antique sports equipment, including golf clubs and skis, hangs in Castle Brothers, while Chester Drawers looks like a baby's nursery. All the rooms inside the store are connected, and Castle Brothers and Chester Drawers both open into **Crystal Arts** to the north.

Disney Dollars

DATES: May 5, 1987–ongoing

Scrooge McDuck was on hand when Disney Dollars debuted at Disneyland on May 5, 1987. Created by marketing whiz **Jack Lindquist**, the new currency arrived by armored truck and yielded immediate results—so popular were the bills, they were soon found at Walt Disney World and in Disney Stores across America.

Since that 1987 debut, guests have bought and used the bills just like they're real money—and, in a sense, they are. Available at Disneyland's **City Hall**, Disney Dollars can be used throughout the park, and can be exchanged at any time for cash at full monetary value.

The bills themselves have undergone many revisions. The first series of Disney Dollars came in two denominations: a $1 Mickey bill with **Sleeping Beauty Castle** printed on the back, and a $5 Goofy bill featuring the *Mark Twain* Riverboat on the

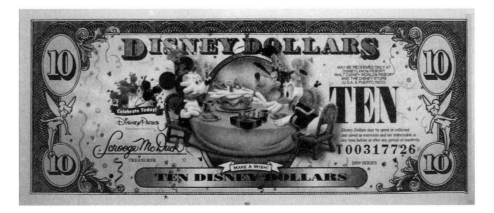

back. Two years later, a $10 Minnie Mouse bill was added that featured several Disneyland attractions on its back.

Further revisions came in 1993, when **Mickey's Toontown** imagery was added, and in 1997, when Mickey sported his *Fantasia* costume on the $1 bills, Goofy wore a tuxedo on the $5 bills, and Simba (of *The Lion King* fame) replaced Minnie on the $10 bills. All were backed with Walt Disney World imagery (the Florida park was celebrating its silver anniversary at the time).

Redesigns continued into the 21st century, too. In 2000 Mickey was dressed up for a millennium New Year's party; in 2002 he transformed into the whistling Mickey from *Steamboat Willie*; and in 2005 he was temporarily replaced by Chicken Little. In 2007 the park began offering singles with *Pirates of the Caribbean* movie themes (a skull on the front, a pirate ship on the back), plus singles, fives and tens featuring Ariel, Aurora, and Cinderella, respectively. Disney Dollars in 2011 showed variations on a party theme with different Disney characters. A small drawing of Tinker Bell has always adorned the front of the every bill.

Fun as they may be, the creation of the bills is extremely sophisticated. They're made using complicated engraving and printing processes that rival those used for actual U.S. currency. The bills have anti-counterfeiting security symbols worked into their art, and the serial numbers on them are real (numbers beginning with an A are from Disneyland; those with a D are from Walt Disney World).

And the signature on all the Disney Dollars? Treasurer Scrooge McDuck.

Disney Gallery

MAP: New Orleans Square, NOS-1; Town Square, TS-10

DATES: July 11, 1987–August 7, 2007; October 2, 2009–ongoing

What was intended to be a private **apartment** in **New Orleans Square** for **Walt Disney** and his family was finally opened to the public in 1987 as the Disney Gallery. The area was originally called the Royal Suite due to the discreet entrance on Royal Street intended for the Disney family alone.

Public entry was via outdoor stairways leading up to the second-floor gallery, a dramatic entrance built when the walkway to the ground-floor **Pirates of the Carib-**

bean was remodeled in 1987. Upstairs, the Disney Gallery interior spread out over various rooms and short hallways that surrounded a small patio. The luxurious furnishings, elegant moldings, and parquet floors all approximated the 3,000-square-foot apartment as it would have looked, had it been finished for the Disney family in the 1960s. The ornate iron railing outside the art rooms still has the initials WD and RD curled into the filigree as tributes to the Disney brothers.

But it was the art, not the architecture, that compelled frequent repeat visits. Changing displays of Disneyland-related paintings and drawings lined the walls, and glass cases held detailed models of Disneyland buildings and attractions. Typically the artwork represented a specific theme, such as the inaugural "The Art of Disneyland 1953–1986" exhibit, 1997's "A Look at the Future—Tomorrowland: 1955–1998" installation, 2002's display of Mickey Mouse imagery, and 2007's "Inspired by Disneyland" show.

The room to the immediate right of the gallery entrance was called the Disney Gallery Collector's Room and sold Disneyland-inspired books, prints, and note cards. Art on Demand consoles enabled guests to select art that could be mailed home or picked up later. Special events, such as book signings or new releases of limited-edition art, were also occasionally held in the Disney Gallery. Furthermore, the **cast members** here took evening reservations for the balcony outside, where guests could sample desserts and enjoy an uncrowded view of that night's **Fantasmic!** presentation.

With little notice, the 20-year-old Disney Gallery permanently closed in the summer of 2007. That fall, a thorough remodel converted the historic space into a lavish 2,600-square-foot overnight suite for 2008's **Year of a Million Dreams** promotion. The Disney Gallery, meanwhile, relocated to a prominent space in **Town Square** formerly occupied by the **Bank of America**. Today, the gallery operates in this location, in three beautifully appointed rooms. An elaborate vault, left over from the building's banking days, stands open in the front room, and the cashier operates out of an old teller cage. Display cases and original art fill the back rooms. Special exhibits have included a tribute to **Mary Blair** and a "Day One Disneyland" show devoted to the park's early plans.

Disneyland After Dark

DATES: 1957–ongoing

To entice guests to stay—and dine—at the park after sundown, Disneyland started lighting up the nighttime skies with fireworks in 1957. A few years later, the park further courted guests by inaugurating special Disneyland After Dark programs  that ran until midnight. Early 1960s brochures listed "the greatest show in town," to be put on every summer evening. The festivities included bands, dancing, "special entertainment," and more, transforming the park into a "date night destination" for teens and a "mecca for adults, too" (according to **Martin Sklar's** 1964 book *Walt Disney's Disneyland*). A 1962 "Disneyland After Dark" episode of *Walt Disney's Wonderful World of Color* showcased all the activity, paying special attention to the musical acts.

Despite all the attention it was receiving, the annual **souvenir books** didn't have a Disneyland After Dark section until 1965, when a single page showed how "Disneyland becomes a different world after dark." Subsequent books expanded the coverage to multiple pages and sometimes included a long quote from Walt Disney about "the new kind of magic and excitement" at night. Decades later, in *Disneyland: The First 50 Magical Years*, narrator **Steve Martin** seconded Disney's sentiment with his own reverie about the park's lights coming up at dusk.

New nighttime enticements have been added to Disneyland over the years, including the rockin' **Tomorrowland Terrace** in 1967, the **Main Street Electrical Parade** in 1972, **Videopolis** in 1985, and more. Interestingly, the Disneyland After Dark name has also been used outside of Anaheim. An '80s Danish rock band called itself Disneyland After Dark until Disney lawyers called for a name change; under the moniker D-A-D, the group has continued releasing new records into the 2000s.

Disneyland Band

DATES: 1955–ongoing

Since **Opening Day**, the Disneyland Band has helped evoke the feeling of small-town America on **Main Street**. Uniformed marching bands have a long tradition in popular culture, of course, and in 1957 they got a boost when *The Music Man*, the nostalgic tale of a small Iowa town starting up its own marching band, became a Broadway hit. At Disneyland, the band is 16 instruments strong, including lots of brass and a big bass drum. The uniforms vary but usually feature bright red or white jackets with ornate trim, pants with gold stripes down the sides, and sturdy, brimmed hats adorned with feathers on the front.

According to the "Disneyland Data" section in the 1956 **souvenir book**, the band gives 1,460 concerts annually (that's about four a day, every day of the year). Naturally, players have rotated in and out over the years; usually about 20 are available at a time, and some of the band's members have occasionally dressed up in costumes to play in combos like the Keystone Cops and the **Strawhatters**. However, the bandleaders have rarely changed. The very first leader, **Vesey Walker**, lasted 15 years. Subsequent bandmasters have included Jim Barngrover, James Christensen, and Stanford Freese.

Since its inception, the Disneyland Band has been a picturesque target for the park's official photographers. The annual souvenir books routinely spotlight the band with big photos and enthusiastic text, and the 1956 featurette *Disneyland, U.S.A.* showed band members playing their instruments while spinning in teacups in the **Mad Hatter's Mad Tea Party**.

In addition to marching in **parades**, the band used to perform concerts in the long-gone **bandstand**. They have also appeared at special park events and at the late-afternoon flag-lowering ceremonies in **Town Square**. The band has also been featured in several albums over the years, among them *Walt Takes You To Disneyland* (1958), *Strike Up the Disneyland Band* (1969), and *I Love a Parade* (1974). Not surprisingly, the "Mickey Mouse March" is the band's most-performed song, even though the band's 400-song repertoire includes everything from polkas to waltzes.

Enduringly popular, the Disneyland Band delivered performance number 50,000 in 1982, and by now it's closing in on 4,000 total miles marched through the park.

Disneyland Fun: It's a Small World
(1990)

Like 1982's **A Day at Disneyland**, 1990's *Disneyland Fun: It's a Small World* was released on video, not in theaters, by the Walt Disney Company. Presented by an animated Professor Owl (star of the Oscar-winning cartoon *Toot, Whistle, Plunk and Boom;* see page 350), the 29-minute video featured dozens of Disney characters playing in Disneyland. However, because *Disneyland Fun* was part of the Disney SingAlong Songs series, those characters also sang and danced as lyrics showed on the screen.

Although the songs target children, the scenery still satisfies adults, simply because it includes so many extinct attractions. The **Rocket Jets**, **Swiss Family Treehouse**, **Tahitian Terrace**, **Skyway to Fantasyland**, **PeopleMover**, **Mike Fink Keel Boats**, **Fine Tobacco**, and Fort Wilderness on **Tom Sawyer Island** are all on view in the video, as well as the original **Star Tours** and **It's a Small World** attractions. Additionally, the cameras take prolonged tours of the **Jungle Cruise**, **Big Thunder Mountain Railroad**, **Splash Mountain**, **Matterhorn Bobsleds**, and **Haunted Mansion**. Sharp-eyed viewers will note that **Sleeping Beauty Castle** at one time had front walls covered in ivy.

Disney timed the *Disneyland Fun* summer video release to coincide with the park's 35th anniversary. Fifteen years later, the DVD came out in time for the park's 50th.

Disneyland Presents a Preview of Coming Attractions, aka Disneyland Showcase

MAP: Main Street, MS-20

DATES: April 1973–July 22, 1989

Originally the **Wurlitzer Music Hall**, and later **The Legacy of Walt Disney** occupied this highly visible corner on the eastern side of **Main Street**. But from 1973 until 1989, it was filled with the closely studied exhibits of Disneyland Presents a Preview of Coming Attractions. Here, fascinated guests could linger over detailed models, concept illustrations, and even videos depicting proposed developments for the park. Among the tantalizing plans were some that were fully realized (**Space Mountain** and **Big Thunder Mountain Railroad**), and some that never materialized at all (**Discovery

Bay and Dumbo's Circusland). In 1980 the room spotlighted the park's silver anniversary, and in 1981 it was renamed the Disneyland Showcase.

The exhibit closed for three months of 1989 while it was converted into a retail store called **Disney Showcase**. Some of the Coming Attractions displays appeared later in the **Disney Gallery**.

Disneyland: The First 50 Magical Years

MAP: Town Square, TS-9

DATES: May 5, 2005–ongoing

Disney Legend Steve Martin starred with Donald Duck in this celebratory film, released in 2005 to coincide with Disneyland's 50th anniversary. Martin, who once worked in the park's **Main Street Magic Shop**, delivered humorous, affectionate narration for the 17-minute film, which included footage of **Walt Disney** and Disneyland's construction. According to **cast members**, Martin's scenes were filmed at sound stages made to look like Disneyland locations.

Disneyland: The First 50 Magical Years originally played in the **Opera House** on **Main Street**, in the large theater previously occupied by **Great Moments with Mr. Lincoln**. When Lincoln returned in 2009, the film moved from the Opera House to a TV screen in the lobby, where today it is surrounded by historical displays and rare artworks from Disneyland's past.

Disneyland TV Series
(1954–1983)

Television was a great ally to **Walt Disney** as he ramped up work on Disneyland in 1954. Debuting nine months before Disneyland opened, the weekly *Disneyland* show on the ABC network worked like an extended infomercial for the park, making its layout and themes famous even while the park was still being built. What's more, the TV show helped finance Disneyland—ABC also presented a loan that went toward the park's construction. For ABC, the benefits were reciprocal—its *Disneyland* show was an instant hit and immediately bolstered the fledgling network, which at the time floundered far behind its rivals, NBC and CBS.

That Walt Disney, a successful movie producer, even deigned to venture into television was unique at the time. Rival studio heads ignored the new medium disdainfully, but Disney embraced it. His rapid and long-lasting success on the smaller screen presaged the later TV successes of movie moguls like Irwin Allen, Steven Spielberg, and George Lucas.

Disney launched his first regular prime-time show, *Disneyland*, in 1954's fall season on Wednesday nights. After only 20 episodes, *Newsweek* labeled it "an American institution." The triumphant show lasted for a record 29 years, won seven Emmy Awards, and eventually played on all three major networks, switching from Wednesday to Sunday nights. It also changed its name a total of five times. Those names were: *Walt Disney Presents* (1958–1961), *Walt Disney's Wonderful World of Color* (1961–1969), *The Wonderful World of Disney* (1969–1979), *Disney's Wonderful World* (1979–1981), and *Walt Disney* (1981–1983).

Throughout its long history, the show frequently presented episodes devoted to Disneyland. On the premiere episode, called "The Disneyland Story," Walt Disney explained the park-to-be by showing maps, models, and illustrations. He also described his goals for Disneyland: "We hope it'll be unlike anything else on this earth. A fair, an amusement park, an exhibition, a city from Arabian Nights, a metropolis from the future. In fact, a place of hopes and dreams, facts and fancy, all in one . . . A place of knowledge and happiness."

The list of Disneyland-themed episodes includes:
• October 27, 1954—"The Disneyland Story," the premiere episode that introduced the coming park
• February 9, 1955—"A Progress Report/Nature's Half Acre," an aerial tour seven months into park construction
• July 13, 1955—"A Pre-Opening Report from Disneyland," aka "A Further Report on Disneyland," shown four days before **Opening Day**
• February 29, 1956—"A Trip Through Adventureland/Water Birds," spotlighting the **Jungle Cruise**
• April 3, 1957—"Disneyland the Park/Pecos Bill," an aerial tour of Disneyland
• April 9, 1958—"An Adventure in the Magic Kingdom," a guided tour led by an animated **Tinker Bell**
• May 28, 1961—"Disneyland '61/Olympic Elk," showing recent park additions
• April 15, 1962—"Disneyland After Dark," showcasing nighttime music (Louis Armstrong, the four Osmond Brothers, and more), plus **fireworks**
• September 23, 1962—"*Golden Horseshoe Revue*," the popular **Frontierland** show celebrating its 10,000th performance
• December 23, 1962—"Holiday Time at Disneyland," a tour of the holiday-themed park by Walt Disney
• May 17, 1964—"Disneyland Goes to the World's Fair," a preview of Disney attractions at the 1964–1965 New York World's Fair
• January 3, 1965—"Disneyland's Tenth Anniversary," with **Miss Disneyland** (Julie Reihm) helping show off the upcoming **Pirates of the Caribbean** and **Haunted Mansion** attractions
• December 18, 1966—"Disneyland Around the Seasons," presenting the newly opened **New Orleans Square** and **It's a Small World**

- January 21, 1968—"Disneyland—From the Pirates of the Caribbean to the World of Tomorrow," previewing **Tomorrowland** changes
- March 22, 1970—"Disneyland Showtime," a celebration of the new **Haunted Mansion** with the Osmond Brothers and Kurt Russell

Outside of the weekly show, many Disney-produced TV specials showcased the park, among them:

- July 17, 1955—"Dateline: Disneyland," a live presentation of Opening Day festivities hosted by Bob Cummings, Art Linkletter, and Ronald Reagan for an estimated 90,000,000 viewers
- June 15, 1959—**"Disneyland '59,"** aka "Kodak Presents Disneyland '59," a live salute to the new **Matterhorn Bobsleds**, **Monorail**, **Motor Boat Cruise**, **Fantasyland Autopia**, and **Submarine Voyage**
- April 10, 1974—"Sandy in Disneyland," starring Sandy Duncan
- July 11, 1974—"Herbie Day at Disneyland," Bob Crane, Helen Hayes, and Volkswagens promoting the film *Herbie Rides Again*
- April 3, 1976—"Monsanto Presents Walt Disney's America on Parade," with Red Skelton
- December 6, 1976—"Christmas in Disneyland with Art Carney," featuring Sandy Duncan and Glenn Campbell
- March 6, 1980—"Kraft Salutes Disneyland's 25th Anniversary," with Danny Kaye
- June 28, 1984—"Big Bands at Disneyland," the first of 12 music shows airing on the Disney Channel
- February 18, 1985—"Disneyland's 30th Anniversary Celebration," starring Drew Barrymore and John Forsythe
- May 23, 1986—"Disneyland's Summer Vacation Party," featuring comedians Jay Leno and Jerry Seinfeld
- September 20, 1986—"Disney's *Captain EO* Grand Opening," with Patrick Duffy, Justine Bateman, and the Moody Blues
- February 12, 1988—"Disney's Magic in the Magic Kingdom," with George Burns
- November 13, 1988—"Mickey's 60th Birthday," with John Ritter and Carl Reiner
- December 11, 1988—"Disneyland's All-Star Comedy Circus," featuring circus stars
- February 4, 1990—"Disneyland's 35th Anniversary Celebration," starring Tony Danza and the Muppets
- September 14, 1991, "Disney Afternoon Live! at Disneyland," spotlighting **Splash Mountain**
- July 10, 1993—"Disneyland Presents: Tales of Toontown," showing off the new **Mickey's Toontown**
- March 4, 1995—"40 Years of Adventure," hosted by Wil Shriner, showing the new **Indiana Jones Adventure** attraction
- May 23, 1997—"Light Magic: A Spectacular Journey," showing the short-lived spectacular
- December 12, 1998—"Holiday Greetings from Disneyland: The Merriest Place On Earth," hosted by Wil Shriner
- February 1, 2000—"Disneyland 2000: 45 Years of Magic," hosted by Ryan Seacrest

- October 14, 2003—"Disneyland Resort: Behind the Scenes," airing on the Travel Channel

While many park traditions were shown on the *Disneyland* TV series, at least one tradition was initiated by the show itself. From the premiere episode onward, each show opened with an animated Tinker Bell splashing sparks with her wand. The public's expectations for that sight at Disneyland led to the appearance of a **Tinker Bell** character who soared over **Fantasyland** on summer nights beginning in 1961.

Disneyland, U.S.A.
(1956)

Released into movie theaters for the 1956 winter holidays alongside *Westward Ho the Wagons*, this Cinemascope featurette was essentially a 42-minute Disneyland commercial. It examined the park from the air via spectacular helicopter footage, showed off the new Disneyland Hotel, and presented a walking tour of all the lands.

Extensive scenes of extinct attractions (such as the **Skyway to Fantasyland**), plus long looks at areas that have been much-modified over the decades (the **Jungle Cruise** back when the skipper's spiel was serious, **Fantasyland** with its original medieval decor), make his essential viewing for Disneyland fans. Winston Hibler, who also wrote the words on the dedication plaque in **Town Square**, co-wrote and narrated the film's text. In 2007 *Disneyland, U.S.A.* was included on a compilation DVD called *Walt Disney Treasures: Disneyland Secrets, Stories & Magic*.

Disney, Roy O.
(1893–1971)

Without the advice and efforts of his older brother, Roy, **Walt Disney** never would have been able to make his Disneyland dream a reality.

Roy Oliver Disney was born in Chicago in 1893, about eight years ahead of Walt. Several years before Walt would hold the same job, teenage Roy worked as a "news butcher," selling inexpensive items on trains. After Roy moved to Hollywood, he invited Walt to join him, and in 1923 the brothers co-founded an animation company. In this partnership, their roles would generally stay the same for the rest of their lives—Roy's financial wizardry supporting Walt's creative genius. Though occasionally distressed by his brother's risky and expensive plans, Roy stayed fiercely loyal to Walt and for over 40 years served as CEO of their company (which eventually became the Walt Disney Company).

During his career, Roy supervised the company's lucrative merchandise licensing, negotiated the groundbreaking contract for the ***Disneyland* TV series** in the 1950s, and in 1953 found and won over the investors who would back Disneyland's construction. Significantly, Roy Disney was the first person to buy a Disneyland admission ticket—ticket #000001—which he purchased for $1.

After Walt Disney's death in 1966, Roy assumed leadership of the impending Walt Disney World and guided the immensely complex project through the construction stage to its 1971 opening. He died of a cerebral hemorrhage just two months later. Several Disney tributes honor his memory: his initials are curled into the metal balcony above Disneyland's **Pirates of the Caribbean**, a Disney Studios building and a Walt Disney World train engine are named after him, and a statue in the Florida park depicts him sitting on a bench next to Minnie Mouse. His son, Roy E. Disney (1930–2009), was a top Disney executive who was named a Disney Legend in 1998.

Disney Showcase

MAP: Main Street, MS-20

DATES: October 27, 1989–ongoing

Guests walking north from **Town Square** are welcomed to the eastern side of **Main Street** by the eminent Disney Showcase. There's a lot of history on this busy corner. In 1955, the **Wurlitzer Music Hall** sold piano rolls here; later, the space displayed **The Legacy of Walt Disney**, followed by the fascinating exhibits of **Disneyland Presents a Preview of Coming Attractions**. Just before the holidays in 1989, the distinguished building became the Disney Showcase. Announced by an ornate sign, that retail store endures today as a popular destination for movie- and Disneyland-themed clothes, sportswear, pins, and other gifts.

Disney Vacation Club Information Desks

MAP: Frontierland, Fr-18; Hub, H-1; Mickey's Toontown, MT-12; New Orleans Square, NOS-10; Tomorrowland, T-8

DATES: Ca. 2006–ongoing

Scattered around Disneyland are "Information Desks" to coax guests into joining the Disney Vacation Club. The desks (at five locations in 2011) are themed to their respective surroundings—the Tomorrowland location, for instance, is shaped like a spindly flying saucer. After getting basic information on over 500 timeshare properties around the world, guests are then invited to attend an "open house" presentation at the nearby Disneyland Hotel for further details.

Disney Villains

MAP: Fantasyland, Fa-30

DATES: July 16, 1991–June 21, 1996

When the sweet **Fantasyland** store known as **Briar Rose Cottage** closed, the sinister Disney Villains store opened soon after. The location was the same—just through the **Sleeping Beauty Castle** entrance and to the right in the castle's courtyard—but the theme was completely inverted to showcase the wicked characters from the Disney film collection. The beauty-obsessed queen who tormented Snow White, malevolent Maleficent from *Sleeping Beauty*, Pan-chasing Captain Hook, and puppy-chasing Cruella De Vil were all presented for sale in clothing and gift form.

Five years after it opened, the Disney Villains shop was replaced by **Quasimodo's Attic**, following the theme of that year's *Hunchback of Notre Dame* film. Some of the villain merchandise returned when the **Villains Lair** shop opened here in 1998.

Disney, Walt
(1901–1966)

Walt Disney was a man of many contrasts. Born on December 5, 1901, he experienced a peripatetic childhood dominated by a stern father and hard work. Yet when he memorialized his youth it manifested as Disneyland's sweet, happy **Main Street**. A high school dropout, Disney later aggressively promoted education and drove the development of the California Institute of the Arts. He had a nostalgic love of American folklore and history, but he eagerly embraced a utopian future humming with high-tech gadgets and sleek new transportation.

Stridently patriotic, Disney also championed global "small world" unity. He was an extravagant traveler who toured South America, took frequent European vacations, and flew by private jet later in life. But if given his choice, his preferred meal might have been chili out of a can, his preferred activity riding his miniature train around his backyard. The movies he produced were often about making and keeping friends, but he himself remained distant from longtime associates and rarely socialized. The affable, charismatic exterior Disney displayed in public belied a churlish, impatient, sometimes irascible personality known around his studio. The same man who demanded intense loyalty also made ruthless business decisions that cut loose some longtime employees.

The kindly, wholesome image Disney cultivated as the world's fairy tale-loving uncle was offset by a private man with a volatile temper who enjoyed nightly cocktails and chain-smoked. He banned employee mustaches, but wore one himself. Disney is remembered by many as being conventional and old-fashioned, but actually, many of his business and creative decisions were daring and bold. "I'm corny," he freely admitted; yet he was a prescient innovator who pushed for cartoons synchronized to sound, the first full-color, three-strip Technicolor cartoon, the revolutionary multi-plane camera, the groundbreaking **Audio-Animatronics** technology, and a "surround sound" forerunner called Fantasound that made him Hewlett-Packard's first-ever customer (according to *Variations on a Theme Park*).

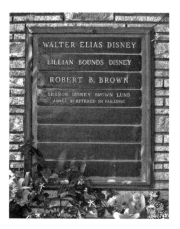

Contrasts even marked Disney's death. Urban myth dictates that he was cryogenically frozen before he died so he could be revived when there was a cure for the cancer that was killing him, but it was cremation, not freezing, consumed him after he died on December 15, 1966. And while Disney promoted himself as one of the common people with ordinary tastes, during his lifetime this versatile colossus was bestowed with hundreds of major international honors, his name was on one of the world's biggest entertainment companies and the world's most famous theme park, and upon his death he was extolled as few people in history have ever been.

Many of these contrasts came into play as Walt Disney invented and built Disneyland. The spark for a "magical realm," historian Dale Samuelson speculated in *The American Amusement Park* in 2001, may have been struck by Walt's father, Elias, a carpenter who helped build the fabulous World's Columbian Exposition (Walt wasn't born yet, but undoubtedly profound stories of Chicago's monumental 1893 World's Fair and the "White City" circulated ever after through the Disney household). The Walt Disney Family Museum has stated that the park was conceived as early as Walt's "Kansas City years," which came in the 1920s. Certainly Walt Disney's visits to San Francisco's Golden Gate Exposition in 1939, to Michigan's charming Greenfield Village in 1940 and '48, and to Chicago's Railroad Fair in '48, fanned the creative flames.

By the late 1940s, Walt Disney, already famous as a pioneering moviemaker, had begun making notes for a small amusement park on the seven-acre plot next to his movie studio in Burbank. Those early ideas included a village based on his Midwestern hometown of Marceline, Missouri, plus a railroad station, opera house, movie theater, farm, Indian village, and merry-go-round, as well as carnival rides and ponies. The ideas were still modest, as were his descriptions of "a three-dimensional thing that people could come and visit." As he wrote, at that stage it was still just an "amusement enterprise," and "a little dream" of a "magical little park."

Finances were a pressing concern for an undertaking so experimental and expensive. Millions of dollars would be required—and that was just the seed money to get a firm start. At the time, Walt Disney wasn't exactly flush; his track record at theater box offices had been dreadful in the early '40s, when *Fantasia* and *Pinocchio* were costly, labor-intensive flops and World War II sealed off the lucrative European markets. (Although the Walt Disney Company was making millions in the 1930s and '40s and had earned 30 Oscar nominations, it never got out of serious debt until the '50s.) So, rather than risk his studio, Disney risked himself. His daughter, Diane Disney Miller, wrote in *The Story of Walt Disney*: "In the end he put his own money into it, not the studio's money. He hocked his life insurance and raised $100,000 and . . . paid a draftsman out of his own pocket to lay out what he'd planned."

To keep the project advancing, Disney sold his newly built Palm Springs vacation home and borrowed from friends, ultimately pouring about a quarter-million of

his own dollars into what was still just an idea. Major corporate sponsors were eventually recruited. Most importantly, **Roy Disney**, Walt's older brother, negotiated the complex television deal that brought ABC in as both an investor and a means to promote the un-built park with a Disney-produced TV show. The show debuted in 1954 with the simple title *Disneyland* and quickly became ABC's top-rated program.

In the early '50s, the park moved steadily from vague dream to realistic plan. After Disney himself visited Copenhagen's immaculate Tivoli Gardens in 1950, he dispatched **Harper Goff** to amusement parks throughout Europe. Upon his return, Goff started drawing up detailed illustrations of what was to be called either Disneylandia or Mickey Mouse Park. This was to be a much larger Burbank enterprise with double-digit acreage that would include an island in a lake, trains, a stagecoach, **Skull Rock**, canal boats, and a circus. Looking ahead, Disney installed horse trainers Owen and Dolly Pope in a trailer at the Disney Studios to start building Western-style carriages and to gather animals for the coming park.

In 1952 Disney began calling his park Disneyland and his ideas continued to grow; a rocket and a submarine were added to the plans. That same year he formed WED (Walt E. Disney) Enterprises to assemble and sequester his core design team, recruiting as members some of the animators and art directors from his movie studio, including designer **Bill Cottrell**, art directors **Richard Irvine** and **Marvin Davis**, layout artists Goff and **John Hench**, and more. These were the pioneers who would revolutionize amusement parks and amusement park rides.

On March 27, 1952, Burbank's *Daily Review* newspaper broke the story about the Burbank park-in-the-making with this headline: "Walt Disney Make-Believe Land Project Planned Here—$1.5 million dreamland to rise on site in Burbank." But that plan soon changed. Within a year, Disney realized that the Burbank plot was too limited for his ambitious dreams, especially after the city council coolly rebuffed his unusual plans. Consequently, in 1953 he paid the Stanford Research Institute $25,000 to pinpoint Southern California's best site for the park. SRI's **Harrison Price** found the spot, 38 miles south of Burbank—Anaheim, where weather, freeway access, and cheap land were favorable variables in his formula for success.

Disney first saw the Disneyland site that fall and soon began to buy up the land for around $4,500 an acre—$700,000 total—reportedly acquiring 160 acres of Anaheim orchards from 17 different farmers.* Moving with alacrity on his unified assemblage, in the spring of '54 Disney removed 12,000 orange trees, had the telephone poles cleared from the area and their lines buried, designated 100 acres for the **parking lot**, and prepared to build his park. Anaheim's *Bulletin* newspaper officially announced the switch to Orange County on May 1, 1954.

Realizing that his own designers could execute his ideas better than any outsiders, Disney released the architectural firm he'd hired to draw up plans, and expanded his core design group. Long brainstorming sessions with those designers, who later became known as the Imagineers, ensued throughout 1954. To observers, the resilient and resourceful Disney was in his element, happily working off his own nervous energy with an all-consuming new project that demanded tenacious focus.

Before construction began, Disney sent Harper Goff and a team of designers back out to amusement parks, fairs, zoos, museums, and other tourist areas around the country for more ideas and inspiration. Disney himself made additional scouting trips to other parks (among them the nearby Knott's Berry Farm) to watch the crowds and step off measurements of park geography. He also consulted with numerous experts in the amusement industry, several of whom derisively predicted failure and delivered their standard advice: sell alcohol, add a Ferris wheel and simple carnival games, don't waste money on landscaping and non-revenue-producing structures like **Sleeping Beauty Castle**, don't stay open more than four months a year, etc. To those unimaginative disbelievers who ran gimcrack carnivals, "real" and "ideal" were trains traveling on perpendicular tracks.

Disregarding the unsettling suggestions of the "experts," ignoring the recession of 1953 and '54, and relying on his own intuition and rectitude (as he had often done in his movie-making career), Disney finally broke ground on his Anaheim park in mid-July of 1954. Unlike nearly every subsequent event in Disneyland's history, there was no fanfare, no initial spade-turning ceremony. For this reason, the official ground-breaking date is disputed—some say it was July 12, 1954, while others claim it was July 16th. Walt's daughter, Diane Disney Miller, stated in *Disneyland . . . The Beginning* that it was the 17th, architectural historian Karel Ann Marling pinpointed the 21st, and Michael Broggie (son of **Roger Broggie**) wrote that it happened in August 1954. The deadline, however, is indisputable; TV commitments placed the finish line at July 17, 1955.

With the hourglass officially upended, work progressed for the next year, steadily

---

* Various books over the years, including some published by Disney itself, have given different numbers for the size of the Disneyland plot in 1955. Estimates have ranged from a low of 73 acres (according to Art Seidenbaum's book, *Los Angeles 200*), to a high of 244 acres (*National Geographic* in 1963). Rebecca Cline, the director of the Disney Archives, definitively stated in a letter to the author that "Disneyland and its parking lot covered 160 acres by July 17, 1955." See www.encycoolpedia.com for more discussion of the park's 1955 acreage.

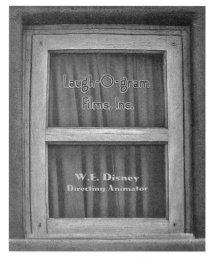

at first, then hurriedly, and finally frantically, especially in the last weeks, when construction stretched around the clock. Over 2,500 construction workers put in long hours, and even Walt Disney's wife, Lillian, picked up a broom to sweep off the decks of the **Mark Twain** **Riverboat** in the final days.

Incredibly, despite spiraling costs that drove the price above $17 million (over $140 million in today's dollars), despite labor strikes and bad weather and daily construction problems, and despite being told by his own staff that he needed to postpone the opening until autumn, Walt Disney finished his park on time. That is, it was at least finished enough to *look* finished. Some of the attractions, including the **Casey Jr. Circus Train** and **Rocket to the Moon**, were ready only for viewing, not for riding. **Tomorrowland** had to be swathed in balloons and bunting to camouflage its empty buildings. Still, the remarkable park was open for business right when Walt Disney said it would be, and an instantly-seduced America quickly set the turnstiles spinning at a record-setting pace.

Meanwhile, Disney himself was a creative whirlwind stirring multiple pots. During the mid-'50s—when he was so deeply immersed in detailed Disneyland planning and construction that he was actually living in an **apartment** at the park much of the time—he also oversaw ongoing production of his studio's most ambitious animated film yet, *Sleeping Beauty*. At the same time, he completed the 1953–1956 films *Peter Pan*, *20,000 Leagues Under the Sea*, and *Lady and the Tramp*, produced numerous documentaries and dozens of cartoons, and created his new TV show with its landmark Davy Crockett character. Busy as Disney and his company were, there was no drop-off in quality—the Disney productions made during this time earned 13 Oscars nominations.

Although Walt Disney didn't do all of this single-handedly, he was extremely (some said obsessively) involved in everything his company did, and routinely worked all day and late into the evening. His mantra: "Get a good idea and stay with it. Dog it and work at it until it's done, and done right." When Disney did neglect something and allowed others to run with it—the 1951 film *Alice in Wonderland*, for instance—it was usually derided by critics as one of the studio's lesser efforts.

With Disneyland, the arc of Disney's career was finally complete. He had begun with unrefined sketches and transitioned first to silent black-and-white cartoons, then to

singing color cartoons. He'd leapt to full-length animated features, live-action movies, and documentaries. Then he had topped it all off with the real-life world of Disneyland.

When Disneyland opened in mid-1955, it wasn't the first American theme park. Walter Knott had launched his Ghost Town in 1940, Indiana's Santa Claus Land had debuted in 1946, and the ocean-themed Marineland of the Pacific had opened in 1954. But Disneyland was the cleanest, safest, most efficient, most scrupulously planned, and most totally immersive park anyone had ever seen—as well as the most imaginative. It wasn't merely a fair, a village, an "island" like Coney, or even a park in any traditional sense—it was a *land*, an entire kingdom of possibilities.

The 60-acre triangle was bursting with archetypal imagery from Disney movies and kids' dreams—pirates and princesses, cowboys and stage coaches, rockets and rivers, majestic castles and quaint towns, cool little cars and cozy little boats, twirling teacups and flying elephants—with enough exhibits, **parades**, and live music added in to enable everyone to find something to enchant/engage/entertain them no matter what their age or disposition was. The conspicuous presence of dozens of respected sponsors like Coca-Cola and TWA eased concerns about quality and helped make the untried park a little more familiar.

Though there were certainly fast, exciting experiences to be had here that held the potential for chaos and terror, everything somehow seemed orderly and family-friendly. Many attractions were related to a noble American heritage or to timeless fairy tales, and most espoused traditional values even while celebrating wonderful new technology. Everything was either fun, patriotic, or educational, or even all three. Even the revolutionary switch-back **queues**, cleverly doubling back upon themselves and offering eye candy to sweeten the line-waiting experience, seemed entertaining, even comforting, and were thus another expression of Walt Disney's people-pleasing philosophy. "All I want you to think about," he told his designers, "is that when people walk through or ride through or have access to anything that you design, I want them, when they leave, to have smiles on their faces. Just remember that; it's all I ask of you as a designer."

A smile. Disneyland guests would be confronted with cemeteries, pits, dungeons, demons, oncoming trains, abominable snowmen, headhunters, pirate skeletons, witches, ghosts, and many other villains, but they'd still leave merry. Ultimately what Disney sought wasn't the most thrilling, or the most terrifying, or the most educational, or even the most fun park in history—his kingdom, he famously declared, would be "the happiest place on Earth."

What his daughter Diane Disney Miller called his "insatiable, omnivorous curiosity" drove Disney to nurture Disneyland for all the rest of his days (to "plus" the park was his own invented verb). Miller quoted him: "The way I see it, my park will never be finished. It's something I can keep developing and adding to. A movie is different. Once I've wrapped it up and have turned it over to Technicolor to be processed, I'm through with it. As far as I'm concerned the picture I've finished a few weeks ago is done. There may be things in it I don't like, but if there are I can't do anything about them. I've always wanted to work on something alive, something that keeps growing. I've got that in Disneyland. Even the trees will grow and be more beautiful every

year." Thus, Disney the perfectionist tinkered persistently with every detail in every corner of his endlessly regenerable park, even to the very end of his life. In mid-'66, just months before his death, he approved the designs for two of his most ambitious attractions yet, **Pirates of the Caribbean** and **Adventure Thru Inner Space**, while simultaneously pushing forward the long-gestating **Haunted Mansion** and Walt Disney World projects, devising a new California ski resort (Mineral King, never built), and overseeing production on his last major films, *The Jungle Book* and *The Happiest Millionaire*. All this, even as he lived with constant pain and failing health.

Not everyone has accepted the park with equal glee, of course. Rarely does anyone disparage the park's incontrovertible craftsmanship, but some carping critics loudly deride what they see as meretricious artifice and saccharine sweetness; others vilify the rampant merchandising and sky-high prices. Condescending detractors use the adjective "Disneyfied" pejoratively, and accusations that Walt Disney was a calculating phony with his ear eagerly cocked to the silvered sirens of the marketplace are often supported with Disneyland as Exhibit A.

Though he was occasionally assailed by anhedonic intellectuals, Disney didn't seem to care. After all, he hadn't created his extraordinary park for them. Fortunately most of the public, for whom Disneyland was built, loved it from **Opening Day** and made it an instant and lasting financial success. Boosted by the 1950s' propitious surge in both disposable personal income and the number of American children, and helped by low gas prices and a new freeway system that put Anaheim within easy driving distance of millions of people, Walt Disney's teetering pre-Disneyland company was in the black soon after the park opened. In 1956, its first full year, the park generated $10 million, according to Richard A. Schwartz in *The Fifties*; within a decade, the total was more than 20 times that, which was more than Disney movies were making. By 1965 Disneyland, according to Kirse Granat May's *Golden State, Golden Youth*, was "the number-one tourist destination in the entire country" with an "overall park attendance equal [to] one-fourth of the total population of the United States." Historian Andrew Rolle called the young park "the largest tourist attraction in the world." Even today, more than 55 years after it opened, Disneyland still draws around 15-million guests annually (averaging some 40,000 people every single day of the year, most of them repeat visitors).

"I'm not interested in pleasing the critics," Walt Disney once said. "I'll take my chances pleasing the audiences." Yet another contrast, one that worked for him in movie theaters and again in Anaheim, and one that has kept Walt Disney in the rarified pantheon of beloved geniuses. Ultimately, the words on the dedication plaque in **Town Square**—"a source of joy and inspiration to all the world"—apply as much to the revered man who spoke them as they do to the wondrous park he was describing.

Dixieland at Disneyland

MAP: Frontierland, Fr-16

DATES: October 1, 1960–1970

One of the most exuberant musical events at Disneyland was the Dixieland at Disneyland concert series held each fall from 1960 to 1970. Requiring a special ticket that included admission to the park and attractions, Dixieland at Disneyland featured live performances by world-renowned jazz musicians. Among the stars were Louis Armstrong, Kid Ory, and Al Hirt, plus Disneyland's own **Firehouse Five Plus Two** and the **Strawhatters**.

For the first five years, the shows were held evenings at the **Rivers of America** in **Frontierland**. With crowds lining the riverbanks, musicians played either on the southern tip of **Tom Sawyer Island** or out on the water on rafts and **Mike Fink Keel Boats**. The grand finale involved **fireworks** and the *Mark Twain* paddlewheeling past the cheering audience while the musicians and a 200-person choir performed "When the Saints Go Marchin' In." An ensuing **parade** carried musicians through the park for more celebrating.

The show was updated in 1963 to include Mardi Gras-style floats, singers, and dancers. For the last half of the '60s, the show moved to **Main Street**, where the bands performed on wagons and then embarked on a park-touring parade. The undeniable star of any show was Louis Armstrong, who first performed at Disneyland in 1961 and racked up a half-dozen park engagements during the '60s. The king of jazz's raft was specially designed with a huge crown on top, and Satchmo himself would wear a crown while leading the festivities.

Donald's Boat, aka *Miss Daisy*

MAP: Mickey's Toontown, MT-2

DATES: January 24, 1993–ongoing

Maximum play, minimum complexity. That seems to be the philosophy behind many **Mickey's Toontown** attractions, including Donald's Boat. Named for Donald Duck's girlfriend, *Miss Daisy* sits in little Toon Lake like a big colorful duck. Entry via a walkway takes guests past Donald's mailbox and into the hull. Inside, the boat reveals itself as a simple walk-through—or, more accurately, a simple play-through—attraction. The charming interior reminds guests who this craft's owner is, and the exterior decks offer room for kids to run around.

Nifty details abound to quack up the young clientele: Donald's sailor suit hanging on the laundry line between the masts, a speaker shaped like a duck's bill, etc. No minimum height requirement makes this a good spot for children to burn up excessive energy while parents rest in the nearby shade.

Don DeFore's Silver Banjo Barbecue

MAP: Frontierland, Fr-6

DATES: June 15, 1957–September 1961

Almost two years after Disneyland's **Opening Day**, the self-proclaimed "finest barbecue this side of the Mississippi" opened in **Frontierland** next door to **Aunt Jemima's Pancake House**. This ground-floor space was previously the site of **Casa de Fritos**, which had vacated in 1956 in favor of a more prominent Frontierland location.

The restaurant was named after the popular Emmy-nominated actor best known in the 1950s as Thorny, the Nelsons' neighbor on *The Adventures of Ozzie and Harriet*. On the national TV broadcast of Disneyland's Opening Day ceremonies, DeFore was briefly seen in an **Autopia** car and on the **Casey Jr. Circus Train**. In his Silver Banjo restaurant, DeFore himself was the chef, and his brother Verne was the manager. The Silver Banjo referred to one of DeFore's prized personal possessions (a

fortunate choice, since another name he considered for his eatery was Don DeFore's Bean Palace).

Barbecued ribs, chicken, pork, and fish were the restaurant's specialties, all prepared on the premises in a kitchen so small it was chided by fire marshals for code violations. After the Silver Banjo closed in 1961, the interior space was engulfed in an expansion that transformed Aunt Jemima's Pancake House into Aunt Jemima's Kitchen, while the front areas became the **Malt Shop and Cone Shop**.

Dream Machine

DATES: 1990

Always ready to celebrate any anniversary divisible by five, Disneyland debuted the Dream Machine 35 years after **Opening Day.** As they entered, guests received special tickets decorated with smiling Disney characters. Each ticket granted a pull on the Dream Machine's lever. Stationed at the **Hub**, the Dream Machine looked like a giant, wildly decorated cake but worked like a slot machine. Usually the winners got free food and beverages, but occasionally they won videos, toys, or watches. Sometimes the prize was extravagant—flights to any location in America, for instance—and once a day it was a new Chevy. Guests who won the car watched it rise up from inside the cake while Mickey danced around it and confetti rained down. The car inside the cake, though, was only a duplicate of the actual prize—guests had to go pick theirs up from a dealer later on.

Duck Bumps

MAP: Fa-6

DATES: Never built

As shown in **Bill Martin's** color illustration in 1954, Duck Bumps was to be a watery attraction located in **Fantasyland** near the **King Arthur Carrousel**. Duck Bumps placed 11 ring-shaped boats in a pool for "bumper-car" maneuvering. A Donald Duck head was mounted on a tall pole attached to each boat. Adjacent to this attraction was a 20-foot windmill called *The Old Mill*, named after the landmark 1937 cartoon, but neither the Bumps nor the Mill ever made it past the drawing table.

Dumbo the Flying Elephant

MAP: Fantasyland, Fa-11, Fa-14

DATES: August 16, 1955–ongoing

An attraction based on *Dumbo*, Disney's 1941 film, was present in early Disneyland plans. Although the ride was always intended to have spinning elephants, there was a considerable difference between what appeared in the first drawings and what appeared at **Fantasyland** in 1955.

Originally the elephants were pink, representing the pink elephants (not Dumbo himself) parading through the movie's hallucination sequence, and their ears were going to flap. Timothy Mouse was slated to stand atop a circus-themed column in the middle, and ultimately the whole attraction was supposed to be in operation on **Opening Day**.

Problems with time, budget, and flawed prototypes created an attraction that was both different and delayed. Almost a full month after the rest of Disneyland opened, Dumbo the Flying Elephant finally debuted 10 gray elephants, all wearing collars and colored hats. There were no flapping ears, and Timothy was nowhere to be found.

For the next 27 years, Dumbo spun as a minute-and-a-half attraction in the far western corner of Fantasyland. Back then there was no connecting walkway to **Frontierland**, making the Dumbo corner more of a Dumbo cul-de-sac.

Kids loved the aerodynamic elephants because they could control their own altitude with the same kind of cockpit-lever system used to elevate the **Astro-Jets** in **Tomorrowland**. The colorful **attraction poster** included this rhyme: "Whirling and twirling way up in the blue . . . elephants fly, and so can you!" One guest who wouldn't whirl and twirl was former President Truman, a Democrat who refused to board the ride during a visit in 1957 and be photographed on an attraction that evoked Republican Party symbolism.

Changes started to come two years later, when the price in the old Disneyland **ticket books** rose from B to C. Later, Timothy was added to wield his whip from atop a shiny silver ball. In the '70s, plans for an expansion called Dumbo's Circusland were announced with a display inside **Disneyland Presents a Preview of Coming Attractions** on **Main Street**. Although Circusland never became a reality, Dumbo did undergo a significant modification that relocated the elephants about 75 feet to the northeast. This was the extensive 1982–83 Fantasyland remodel that replaced the **Pirate Ship Restaurant** and **Skull Rock** with Dumbo and opened up the attraction's cul-de-sac as a shortcut to Frontierland. Dumbo now had his own vintage band organ, too—a refurbished antique that pumped out Disney classics.

Another revision came in 1990, when the whole attraction was beautifully refurbished. Instead of 10 elephants, there are now 16 (originally built for Disneyland Paris, they were brought to Anaheim first and Paris got its own elephants later). Additionally, Timothy lost his silver-ball platform but gained a colorful hot-air balloon to stand on. The whole attraction now sits in a lovely fountain setting where the charming elephants whirl and twirl more attractively than ever.

Edelweiss Snacks

MAP: Fantasyland, Fa-22

DATES: September 25, 2009–ongoing

Just when there didn't seem to be any more space for new structures inside **Fantasyland**, in 2009 a new A-frame cottage arose along the walkway next to **Fairytale Arts**. Swiss-themed like the nearby **Matterhorn Bobsleds**, Edelweiss Snacks serves up turkey legs, chimichangas, corn on the cob, and other take-away snacks.

Edgren, Don
(1923–2006)

Don Edgren installed streaking rockets inside **Space Mountain**, took **Pirates of the Caribbean** underground, and figured out how **Matterhorn Mountain** could carry bobsleds. Whatever the Imagineers dreamed up, Edgren, leader of the park's engineering team, got it built.

Edgren was born in Los Angeles in 1923. Upon graduating high school, he joined the Air Force and flew 45 combat missions in World War II. Returning to Southern California afterwards, he began working at an engineering firm that was readying Disneyland for **Opening Day**. Edgren worked as a field engineer at the busy construction site. A few years later, Edgren helped construct the Matterhorn and incorporate bobsleds tracks into the unique structure.

In 1961 Edgren started working full-time for Disney. His team's biggest challenge may have been Pirates of the Caribbean—what was originally designed as a walk-through exhibit became a subterranean boat ride requiring elaborate waterways and a new "show building" beyond the park's perimeter **berm**.

Away from Disneyland, Edgren supervised Disney exhibits at the 1964–1965 New York World's Fair. Later, he became chief engineer at Walt Disney World and leader of that park's Space Mountain project. Afterwards, he moved to Japan to help build Tokyo Disneyland before finally retiring in 1987.

Don Edgren was named a Disney Legend in 2006, just a few months before he died of a stroke at age 83.

Edison Square

MAP: Hub, H-4

DATES: Never built

The same 1958 **Fun Map** that laid out a detailed plan for **Liberty Street**, an area that was never built, also portrayed another **Main Street** spin-off that was intended to open in 1959 but never made it beyond the drafting table. Whereas Liberty Street would have run roughly parallel to Main Street, designers imagined another new side street, this one situated at the north end of Main Street, running perpendicular to its right for two blocks.

As shown on the '58 map, **Edison Square** began at the **Hub**, continued eastward for a block as a narrow street, and then ended in a cul-de-sac behind **Tomorrowland**. The theme of this new area was to be American progress as propelled by Thomas Edison—a statue of the scientist would have graced Edison Square's center, his life story told with a series of dioramas surrounding the figure.

Unlike Main Street, which was a commercial area of colorful shops and eateries, Edison Square was intended to look more like a mature residential neighborhood of attractive two-story homes from the early 20th century. Inside each building was a theater, leading guests through decades of electronic progress. According to the map, the four theaters would have been named American Home: Pre-Electricity, American Home: Advent of Electricity, Contemporary Living, and The Electronic Age. **Audio-Animatronic** figures would have occupied the four stages.

Unfortunately, the technology needed to pull all of this off wouldn't be perfected until the mid-'60s. By then Edison Square had been stricken from the park's plans. However, visitors may recognize the attraction's planned theme of electronic progress, its sponsor (General Electric), and Audio-Animatronic figures as the cornerstones of the **Carousel of Progress** that eventually spun in Tomorrowland in 1967.

Ellen's Gift Shop

MAP: Main Street, MS-13

DATES: 1955–1957

In the mid-'50s, a little shop called Ellen's sold small gifts next to **Gibson Greeting Cards** on **Main Street**. Today the big **Disney Clothiers, Ltd.** store engulfs much of this block.

Ellenshaw, Peter
(1913–2007)

Peter Ellenshaw painted beautiful backgrounds for Disney movies and extraordinary Disneyland artworks. Born in London in 1913, Ellenshaw pursued his love of art even while working in a car garage as a teen, landing a job painting sets for various English films.

A 1947 meeting with **Walt Disney**, who was in England to start work on *Treasure Island*, brought Ellenshaw an invitation to create detailed background paintings for the movie as well as for *20,000 Leagues Under the Sea* a few years later. For the former, Ellenshaw painted English coastlines and dock areas that were shown behind the main action; for the latter, he depicted Vulcania, the secret island shown behind the submarine. In both movies, Ellenshaw's work looks more like realistic photographs than paintings.

Following these early successes, Ellenshaw enjoyed a long Disney career as a matte artist and production

designer and won an Oscar for his memorable cityscapes in *Mary Poppins*.

Before Disneyland was built, Ellenshaw painted one of the park's original maps, a majestic four-foot-by-eight-foot overhead view that depicted its overall triangular shape with lands spreading out from the **Hub** (it also included some details that were never realized, such as a hot-air balloon). The map was featured on the ***Disneyland TV series***, and was used on the first-ever Disneyland postcard and the cover of the 1955 **souvenir book**. For **Tomorrowland**, Ellenshaw created the detailed backdrop for **Space Station X-1**, an attraction that offered a view of Earth from space. A couple years later he directed *A Tour of the West*, the **Circarama** theater's first film.

Peter Ellenshaw was elected a Disney Legend in 1993. Three years later, a book of his art, *The Garden Within*, was published, and in 2002 he appeared in the special features on the *Swiss Family Robinson* DVD.

Ellenshaw died in 2007 in Santa Barbara, California at age 93. His son, Harrison Ellenshaw, is an Oscar-nominated visual effects artist who has worked on several *Star Wars* films.

El Zocalo, aka El Zocalo Park

MAP: Frontierland, Fr-23

DATES: 1958–1963

When Disneyland was in its infancy, Zorro was one of Disney's most popular characters, thanks to the 1957–1959 TV series. El Zocalo incorporated some of Zorro's south-of-the-border style.

Zocalo is the traditional Spanish word for town square. In **Frontierland**, El Zocalo covered about a fifth of an acre near the landing for the ***Mark Twain* Riverboat**. There were no real attractions in El Zocalo, but there were certainly some in close proximity, including the **Mule Pack** and **Stage Coach**. Some Mexican gifts were sold in the little plaza, and **Casa de Fritos**, located nearby, offered Mexican food to guests.

Though the original El Zocalo was gone by 1964, in the 21st century the name has enjoyed something of a resurgence. Casa de Fritos, later Casa Mexicana, reopened in 2001 as the Rancho del Zocalo Restaurante. A small stage and some landscaping now fill the old Zocalo site, and the park was the center of the Three Kings Day celebration held January 6–8, 2012. The flag-decorated sign sometimes displayed above the stage reads, "El Zocalo Park, dedicated 55," an affectionate tribute to Disneyland's own history.

Emporium, aka Disneyland Emporium

MAP: Main Street, MS-2

DATES: July 17, 1955–ongoing

Just as a small American town's main street probably contains a sizeable department store, so too does Disneyland's **Main Street** have its expansive Emporium. Inside this attractive building is over 4,000 square feet of souvenirs, gifts, hats, clothing, jewelry, and more. Everything is on view in an open room given even more character by the deep-brown woodwork along the walls and the beautiful light fixtures added in a 2011 refurbishment. For added interest, up by the ceiling the balconies use old-fashioned artifacts and figures to display nostalgic scenes, such as a barber with a child and a woman in a milliner's shop.

The Emporium is located 800 feet south of **Sleeping Beauty Castle**, on the corner of Main and **Town Square**. Since this is one of the last stores before the Disneyland exit, it offers guests a final chance to splurge on whatever they don't already have with whatever money they haven't already spent. To maximize shopping opportunities, the Emporium is accessible from many areas on the block; guests can reach it from within the **Carriage Place Clothing Co.** next door and from other shop interiors to the north.

The Emporium's exterior is as impressive as anything inside. A white balcony wraps around its corner, and the handsome mansard-style upper stories are dotted with ornamented circular windows. At night, thousands of lights outline the building with electric splendor. Most memorably, the big rectangular windows on the ground floor are filled, not with merchandise and mannequins, but with imaginative dioramas depicting characters and settings from recent Disney films. This tradition began in 1969 to promote a re-release of *Peter Pan*; since then, dozens of movies have been emulated with detailed artwork and puppets. These "Windows of Enchantment" are changed after-hours by a team of artists and designers who make the Emporium the best window-shopping in Disneyland.

Enchanted Chamber

MAP: Fantasyland, Fa-3

DATES: 2008–ongoing

In 2008 **Tinker Bell & Friends** moved out of **Sleeping Beauty Castle**, and the Enchanted Chamber moved in. The small L-shaped shop still has three entrances—one along the drawbridge walkway and two in the castle's courtyard—though usually only two doors are open at a time. Instead of Tink's fairy themes and merchandise, the Enchanted interior now displays medieval-style decorations and an array of accessories, autograph books, dolls, and playsets to entice young princesses.

Enchanted Cottage Sweets & Treats

MAP: Fantasyland, Fa-17

DATES: 2004–November 2009

It was not all that enchanted, nor was it really a cottage, but the Enchanted Cottage snack stand did bring in a lot of business, most likely due to its location next to the big outdoor stage in the back of **Fantasyland**. The eatery had cycled through many different names, including **Yumz**, Meeko's, Louie's, Fantasyland Theater Snacks, and Troubadour Treats, the theme changing to match whatever theatrical presentation was running next door. No matter what the name has been, the stand has always been a quick stop for fast food.

When *Snow White—An Enchanting Musical* opened in 2004, the woodsy Enchanted Cottage Sweets & Treats, sponsored by Nestlé, was born. A new Bavarian menu was created to match the Snow White story, including sausages, pretzels, German chocolate cake, and more. All of the items were given fanciful names, like Diamond Mine Delight and Magic Wishing Apple. Outdoor patio seating, specialty coffee drinks, and souvenir containers all added to the enchantment.

Even though the **Princess Fantasy Faire** replaced the *Snow White* show in 2006, the cottage retained its name until it was transformed into the **Troubadour Tavern** in late 2009.

Enchanted Tiki Room

MAP: Adventureland, A-11

DATES: June 23, 1963–ongoing

A tidal wave of tiki culture surged onto American shores in the late 1950s as

restaurants, cocktails, movies, TV shows, music, and fashion all drew inspiration from the South Seas. In 1963 that tiki wave splashed into the first building on the left in **Adventureland** with the debut of the Enchanted Tiki Room.

As fun and timely as the tiki theme was at its opening, the Tiki Room's real significance was its advancement of **Audio-Animatronic** technology. Previously Disneyland had displayed moving animals on the **Jungle Cruise** and in **Nature's Wonderland**, but those had employed simple, repetitive motions viewed at a distance. Inside the Tiki Room, the A-A characters sing and move with sophisticated subtlety just a few feet from over 200 pairs of watchful eyes. The 17-minute show (later tightened to about 15) showcases 225 moving birds, drumming tiki figures, chanting tiki masks, and singing blossoms, all within an air-conditioned tropical hut where fountains bubble inside, a rainstorm rages outside, and an elaborate "birdmobile" descends from the ceiling. The songs include "Hawaiian War Chant," "Barcarole," and the sing-along "Let's All Sing Like the Birdies Sing." Hosting the festivities are Fritz, Jose, Michael, and Pierre, four wise-cracking A-A macaws of international heritage.

The birds themselves still appear incredibly lifelike, thanks to their varied movements and real feathers. The lively presentation has brought glowing reviews, especially in its first decades. A 1963 issue of *National Geographic* called the Tiki Room "a tremendous show" and gave it over two pages and three big photos. Disneyland's own 1963 **souvenir book** proclaimed it "a new dimension in entertainment."

The Tiki Room is actually a scaled-down version of what had been originally planned. Designers first envisioned a restaurant with an after-dinner bird show, but when the plan proved to be unworkable, the entertainment was expanded into an entire attraction. The Tiki Room **attraction poster** makes a reference to what might have been: "Tiki talk say, 'Better go! Wondrous food! Wondrous show!'" Another nov-

elty was the initial ticket pricing: guests didn't need the usual A–E tickets from the **ticket books**, but rather separate 75-cent tiki tickets (by the mid-'60s, admission to the hut had changed to an E ticket).

The Tiki Room's success inspired **Walt Disney** to sprint ahead with his next Audio-Animatronic attraction—the 1964–1965 New York World's Fair exhibits, which included a realistic Abraham Lincoln. Back at Disneyland, United Airlines took over sponsorship for the Tiki Room from 1964 to 1973, followed by Dole Pineapple from 1976 onward. (Dole added a pre-show video about pineapples and also began sponsoring the **Tiki Juice Bar** next door.) After years of neglect, a major renovation in 2005 upgraded the Tiki Room's interior and exterior.

Many Disney Legends contributed to the Tiki Room's legacy. **Rolly Crump** and **Marc Davis** worked on the whole project from its inception; **John Hench** drew up colorful design sketches and invented the rising-fountain concept; **Wally Boag** from the **Golden Horseshoe** wrote the script and voiced both Jose the macaw and the talking bird that used to sit in front of the building; **Fulton Burley**, also a Golden Horseshoe regular, did the vocals for the Irish macaw, Michael; **Thurl Ravenscroft**, later a prominent **Haunted Mansion** presence, vocalized Fritz, the German macaw; the **Sherman Brothers** wrote the infectious "Tiki Tiki Tiki Room" theme song; and **Harriet Burns** created the birds' intricate plumage.

Though the Enchanted Tiki Room may seem tame to 21st-century audiences, it is well-loved by veteran guests who recognize its significance and enjoy the classic entertainment it offers.

Entrance, aka Main Gate

MAP: Park, P-5

DATES: July 17, 1955–ongoing

"Walt understood the function of an entranceway, or threshold," said **John Hench** in the book *Remembering Walt.* "The threshold is supposed to embrace you. It's where you feel like you're entering some very special place." This architectural philosophy wasn't new in 1955, but Disneyland's distinctive entrance sure was.

Against the advice of seasoned operators of fairs and parks around the country, **Walt Disney** opened Disneyland with only one entrance. Whereas many "experts" thought there needed to be a variety of convenient ways to get into the park, Disney thought that multiple entrances might confuse guests, and reasoned that he'd be better able to control the visitors' initial Disneyland experience if he welcomed them through a single portal.

The result was the wide entrance at the southern tip of the park. For decades, guests were guided to this point from a huge **parking lot** to the south and via footpaths to the west and east. Freestanding ticket booths are still scattered across the clean, open plaza in front of the park turnstiles, the Monorail still glides some 25 feet above, and the **Main Street** train station still beckons ahead to the north. Stretching 200 feet to the left of the turnstiles are one-story buildings that house, among other things, lockers and **restrooms**; to the right is a shorter row that culminates with pet kennels.

Once their admission tickets have been bought, guests stream into Disneyland through 32 covered turnstiles arranged in a slight semicircle. Guests then find themselves 75 feet from a giant Mickey Mouse face, carefully formed out of planted flowers

Major Attractions and Exhibits Added in the 1960s

1960 Pack Mules Through Nature's Wonderland; Skull Rock and Pirate's Cove; Western Mine Train Through Nature's Wonderland

1961 Babes in Toyland Exhibit; Flying Saucers

1962 Big Game Safari Shooting Gallery; Swiss Family Treehouse

1963 Enchanted Tiki Room

1965 Great Moments with Mr. Lincoln

1966 It's a Small World; Primeval World Diorama

1967 Adventure Thru Inner Space; Carousel of Progress; PeopleMover; Pirates of the Caribbean

1969 The Haunted Mansion

in a colorful 25-foot-wide parterre. Park photographers and characters are often milling about this picturesque area. For decades the smooth concrete here was red; many observers have speculated that this was Disney's way of extending an inviting "red carpet" to his guests. Today, feet are still greeted by reddish pavers.

Even at this stage, when guests have paid their way into the park and have passed through turnstiles, the park is still not clearly visible. Revelation comes once guests walk through one of the two tunnels on either side of the manicured Mickey garden. Each of these arched tunnels is decorated on the inside with eight beautiful **attraction posters**, and each is topped with a plaque that quotes Walt Disney's declaration about the wonders just ahead: "Here you leave today and enter the worlds of yesterday,

tomorrow and fantasy." The tunnels lead guests under the train tracks and into **Town Square**, where **Main Street** and all its enticements await.

Thankfully, Disneyland has nearly always been able to keep its posted hours, so guests can rely on the entrance gates being open as scheduled. There have been about a dozen unscheduled closures in Disneyland history, however. Most of these have been the result of extreme winter weather conditions. One death led to the sudden closure of the park—not Walt Disney's passing in 1966, as one might expect, but John F. Kennedy's assassination in 1963. Park officials also closed the park on September 11, 2001, in response to that morning's terrorist attacks. More recently, on the morning of March 3, 2012, Disneyland officials called the Orange County bomb squad in response to a "suspicious" (but ultimately benign) package found near the entrance; during the subsequent lockdown, no guests could enter or leave the park for three hours.

Evans Brothers (Jack and Morgan)
(Unknown–1958) (1910–2002)

Many Disneyland guests love the park's landscaping and ornamental flower gardens almost as much as they love its attractions. Those guests can thank Morgan "Bill" Evans and his brother, Jack, the men who first planted Disneyland's flora.

Gardening was always a big part of the Evans' lives. Jack and Bill grew up in a Santa Monica home that had a huge garden filled with exotic plants. Upon returning from the Merchant Marine Academy in the late '20s, Bill studied geology in college. In 1934 he helped turn the family garden into a thriving business that supplied rare plants to the growing Hollywood community, including such luminaries as Clark Gable and Greta Garbo.

In 1952 **Walt Disney** invited the Evans brothers to do the landscaping around his large home near Beverly Hills (which housed Disney's famous Carolwood Pacific miniature railroad in its backyard). Two years later, an impressed Disney recruited the brothers to be Disneyland's chief landscape architects.

With a budget of about a half-million dollars and input from notable landscapers like Ruth Shellhorn, the Evans brothers transformed the bulldozed orange groves into a verdant, beautifully manicured park. Among the thousands of plants and flowers brought in were some mature trees Bill Evans rescued after they were uprooted by local freeway construction. The goal, according to Bill's 1965 book *Walt Disney Disneyland World of Flowers*, was to create "a perennial welcome mat of flowers" that bloomed all year long. The brothers also had to meet all the special landscaping requirements for the park's unique attractions (imagining the landscaping of the future for **Tomorrowland** was especially difficult, Evans wrote).

According to one story, the Evans brothers intentionally planted trees upside-down along the riverbanks of the **Jungle Cruise** so their twisted, exotic-looking roots would spread above ground. Another tale, related in the Bob Thomas biography *Walt Disney: An American Original*, recounted the last frantic days before the opening, when the brothers were running out of time, money, and plants; with some of the berm behind **Fantasyland** still bare, Walt Disney requested little signs with long Latin names to disguise the weeds as desirable specimens. Ultimately, the brothers filled Disneyland with over 750 varieties and species of plants, of which, Evans wrote, only five percent were native to California.

Jack Evans died in 1958. In Bill's *World of Flowers* book, Walt Disney remembered how Jack "worked mightily to create authentic and delightful landscapes" throughout Disneyland. Bill Evans continued to supervise Disney landscaping and to train the company's landscape architects. So valuable was his knowledge that he was asked to consult on Disney parks around the world even after he retired in 1975. Bill Evans was named a Disney Legend in 1992, 10 years before he died at age 92.

Fairytale Arts

MAP: Fantasyland, Fa-23

DATES: December 2006–ongoing

Fairytale Arts is a collection of open booths stretching alongside the **Fantasyland** waters, formerly toured by the **Motor Boat Cruise**. Run by Kaman's Art Shoppes (a company that has been providing artists for amusement park projects since the 1970s), the booths cover about 60 feet of waterfront walkway. The arts—including personalized calligraphy and exotic face-painting— would fit right into the Renaissance Faire. Nearby is Fantasia Freeze, a cart that cools off guests with tart ice drinks.

Family Fun Weekends

DATES: January 14, 2011–March 6, 2011

When **Main Street** was blocked off for renovation in early 2011, guests were temporarily denied the daily **parades**. To compensate, Disneyland launched a short-lived program called Family Fun Weekends. Held for eight consecutive three-day weekends from January 14th to March 6th, the event was initially staged in **Frontierland** at **Big Thunder Ranch**. There, an outdoor performance space called the Festival Arena was transformed every weekend with a different theme.

First up was Fiesta Disneyland, featuring mariachi music and local artisans presenting their wares. Next came the Kickin' Country Weekend, a celebration of country and western costumes, music, food, and crafts. The third weekend, Character Fan Days, filled the area with roaming Disney characters, including some that are rarely seen anymore, such as the bears from the Country Bear Jamboree. Lunar New Year was the theme of the last two February weekends. Finally, the revelry shifted to **New Orleans Square** for three weekends of Mardi Gras celebrations.

The success of the Family Fun Weekends in 2011 led to new Disneyland events a year later. Centered in front of **It's a Small World** from January 20 to 29, 2012, the Happy Lunar New Year Celebration promoted Chinese, Korean, and Vietnamese cultures via musical performances, themed foods, and meet-and-greets with Mulan and other Disney characters. Then, the New Orleans Bayou Bash brought live jazz, specialty foods, "Tiana's Mardi Gras Procession," and more to New Orleans Square for five Mardi Gras weekends in February and March of 2012.

Family Reunion

DATES: 1980

In 1980 a new Family Reunion theme unified Disneyland's celebration of its silver anniversary. For the event, former **cast members** were invited for a special night of entertainment and festivities on April 11th. On TV, Danny Kaye hosted a March special called "Kraft Salutes Disneyland's 25th Anniversary" (Michael Jackson was one of the guests). A new Family Reunion Parade and a 25-hour party that lasted from 12:01 AM on July 17th until 1:00 AM on July 18th were additional highlights.

Fantasia Gardens

MAP: Fantasyland, Fa-23

DATES: January 1993–2006

Nearly every major animated movie produced by Disney Studios from the 1930s to the '50s has been echoed by a Disneyland attraction—except *Fantasia*. In 1993, the 1940 classic finally found a home in the park, on the east side of Small World Way in **Fantasyland**. Formerly the **Motor Boat Cruise** had putted around this area north of the **Matterhorn**. Soon after the last motor boat sailed, the landscaping and fountains of Fantasia Gardens filled in what had been the boats' loading area.

Like the **Topiary Garden** outside **It's a Small World**, some of the bushes in the Fantasia Gardens formed recognizable shapes, notably the hippo and crocodile characters from *Fantasia*. A snack stand nearby made this a convenient rest stop until everything was closed off in 2006 so that **Fairytale Arts**, and later a temporary designated smoking area, could set up here.

Fantasmic!

MAP: Frontierland, Fr-16

DATES: May 13, 1992–ongoing

"Some imagination, huh?" So concludes Mickey Mouse at the end of Fantasmic!, and it's doubtful anyone could disagree. Originally intended to be called either *Imagination* or *Phantasmagoria*, Fantasmic! is an elaborate, state-of-the-art outdoor music and pyrotechnic show that almost defies definition.

To install the stage and create the special effects, in 1992 the **Rivers of America**

waterway in **Frontierland** was drained, the southern tip of **Tom Sawyer Island** was re-built, and the island's Mill was relocated. After the first year proved to be overwhelmingly successful (but also overwhelmingly crowded), terraced walkways were added near Frontierland and **New Orleans Square** to accommodate the thousands of guests who gather nightly along the riverbanks to witness the mesmerizing 22-minute show.

The complicated multimedia presentation incorporates many different elements, usually including over 50 **cast members** (most taking on multiple roles) and featuring thrilling music and sound effects, 30-foot-tall spotlight towers, 125 special effects that can generate six-foot flames, 11 floating watercraft, and an assortment of smoke machines, lasers, black lights, and water cannons. The show also features a 100-foot-long snake, a crocodile 25 feet wide by 17 feet tall, a 20-foot-tall Ursula (from *The Little Mermaid*), an appearance by the ***Mark Twain*** Riverboat and/or the **Sailing Ship *Columbia***, and, as of 2009, a 40-foot-tall fire-breathing mechanical dragon. Some of the most innovative elements of the production are huge water screens on which full-color animated images are projected. The screens, which are 30 feet tall by 50 feet wide by four inches thick, require thousands of gallons of water to create.

The Fantasmic! plot follows the hero, Mickey, in his sorcerer's costume as he battles various Disney villains, resulting in a tour of classic Disney movies from *Snow White and the Seven Dwarfs* to *Beauty and the Beast*.

One possible drawback of Fantasmic! is that it is canceled in any inclement weather (wind would soak viewers with water from the water screens). Up until a 2007 remodel, the public's best view was from a balcony outside the nearby **Disney Gallery**, which once offered a special vantage point for those with reservations.

The park's **souvenir books** have justifiably touted the pioneering Fantasmic! experience as "one of the most complex and technically advanced shows ever presented." Just as the **Main Street Electrical Parade** reinvented nighttime entertainment in the '70s, so too did Fantasmic! reinvent it in the '90s.

Fantasy Faire

MAP: Hub, H-2

DATES: 2013–ongoing

The **Plaza Gardens** was a stylish (if underused) entertainment venue for 55 years. This prime location next to **Sleeping Beauty Castle** finally closed in 2011; that same year, plans were announced for Fantasy Faire, a medieval village square projected to open in 2013. Fairy tale cottages, a tower inspired by *Tangled*, a meet-and-greet area for Disney princesses, live entertainment, interactive experiences, and evening dances all combine to make Fantasy Faire one of Disneyland's biggest additions in years.

The buildings and activities may be new, but the alliterative Fantasy Faire name isn't, having been used for a gift shop and for the **Princess Fantasy Faire** area in **Fantasyland**.

Fantasy Faire Gifts,
aka Fantasy Shop,
aka Fantasy Emporium,
aka Fantasy Gift Faire

MAP: Fantasyland, Fa-9, Fa-16

DATES: Ca. 1955–ca. 1981; ca. 1996–ongoing

In Disneyland's early decades, a little shop shared a building with the **Mickey Mouse Club Theater** in **Fantasyland**. At various times, park maps called the shop Fantasy Faire Gifts, the Fantasy Shop, Fantasyland Emporium, and Fantasy Gift Faire. Small and castle-themed, it lasted until the early '80s, when a major renovation introduced Pinocchio designs and the **Village Inn** restaurant.

After disappearing for over a decade, the shop returned in the mid-'90s. Today it is located near **It's a Small World** as a free-standing shop called Fantasy Faire Gifts. Like an open-air convenience store, Fantasy Faire stocks film, postcards, candy, hats, plush toys, pins, and other souvenirs.

Fantasyland

MAP: Park, P-16

DATES: July 17, 1955–ongoing

Fantasyland fans may be surprised to know how fortress-like this most charming of lands appeared at its inception. In 1953, 10 months before construction began, **Herb Ryman** drew up a detailed sketch of the park as envisioned by **Walt Disney**, who coached Ryman through the two-day creative process.

That landmark drawing depicted

Fantasyland atop a high plateau. Imposing walls, turrets, and battlements ringed an enormous vertical castle in the center, making Fantasyland look more like a Fantasyempire. A crooked moat wound its way completely around the plateau's perimeter, isolating it from the rest of Disneyland. Other details were far less formidable, such as the carousel located in front of the castle.

A few months before the park was built, Disney artists created a smaller study of a circular "Fantasy Land" that looked a bit more like the land today's guests see. The area stretched from a structure very much like **Sleeping Beauty Castle** up to a big lagoon with an island in the middle. Some attractions on this revised map (a "Mother Goose Fun Thru," Nemo's sub from *20,000 Leagues Under the Sea*, and an undefined attraction called Pinocchio Square) were never built. Another Fantasyland proposal that never materialized was Bruce Bushman's concept drawing of a Ferris wheel, derived from the 1937 cartoon *The Old Mill*.

Clearly Fantasyland went through many design changes, but one theme endured through all the revised plans: movies. More than any other area in the park, Fantasyland celebrates classic films. Within a few years of its opening, Fantasyland already included two *Dumbo* attractions (the airborne elephants and the Casey Jr. train), two *Alice in Wonderland* attractions (the indoor ride and the spinning teacups), Mr. Toad's Wild Ride from the 1949 film *The Adventures of Ichabod and Mr. Toad*, and attractions echoing *Snow White*, *Peter Pan*, and *Sleeping Beauty*, plus a theater that played Disney cartoons.

Walt Disney probably had several strategies in mind as he was infusing Fantasyland with his movies. Certainly the buildings and attractions would be marvelous ways to promote his films, including old favorites like *Snow White* and *Dumbo*, and new additions like *Peter Pan* and *Sleeping Beauty*.

More importantly, with so many attractions and lands—**Adventureland** and **Tomorrowland**, in particular—that would be unfamiliar and overwhelming to 1955 guests who had never been to a theme park before, Walt Disney perhaps sensed that the familiar cartoon faces featured in Fantasyland would be a welcome comfort. The same general strategy—acclimating, orienting, and comforting guests before introducing them to the unfamiliar—most likely influenced the placement of **Main Street**, which eases guests into the park with a stroll down a

gentle, recognizable avenue.

In addition to this connection with Disney films, Fantasyland stirs up idyllic, dreamy memories of childhood fantasies shared by anyone who is, or was, a kid. Disneyland literature emphasizes this collective memory—the park's **souvenir books** have called Fantasyland "the happiest kingdom of them all," "a magic land that takes you back to childhood," and a "carefree kingdom" "where dreams could actually come true." When introducing Fantasyland on the ***Disneyland TV series***, Walt Disney declared that here you could do "anything your heart desires, because in this land hopes and dreams are all that matter." That's a whole lot of happiness, magic, childhood memories, dreams, hope, and heart for the little six-acre section of the park.

Unfortunately, 28 years would pass before the Fantasyland Walt Disney had envisioned would actually be built. With **Opening Day** approaching, time pressures and budget restrictions forced Disney to abandon his idea of uniting the Fantasyland attractions with traditional village architecture. Instead, he had his artists create medieval-style façades, so at least the front of the attractions would appear village-like. These façades, plus banners and pennants installed along the roofs, gave Fantasyland the atmosphere of an Old World fair.

The medieval look would last for decades, but within a year of opening some major changes were already arriving. The delightful **Storybook Land Canal Boats** replaced the dreary old Canal Boats, the scenic **Skyway to Fantasyland** drifted above, and **Junior Autopia** cranked up to the east. In 1957 the passageway to the **Sleeping Beauty Castle Walk-Through** opened and a smaller **Midget Autopia** began motoring. In 1959, Disneyland's tallest structure, **Matterhorn Mountain**, was installed, flanking Fantasyland near the new **Fantasyland Autopia**. Seven years later, Fantasyland expanded dramatically northward when **It's a Small World** pushed past the train tracks and the park's perimeter **berm**.

In 1983, a massive $50 million remodel transformed the heart of Fantasyland into what Walt Disney had originally visualized. Some old attractions were retired (the **Pirate Ship Restaurant**, **Skull Rock**, and the Fantasyland Theater); others were relocated (Dumbo, the Mad Tea Party, and the King Arthur Carrousel); tired attractions got a facelift (Snow White, Peter Pan, and Alice); and a new one was added (**Pinocchio's Daring**

Journey). In addition, everything within the castle courtyard got a makeover to approximate the movies the attractions were based upon. Consequently, the exterior of **Mr. Toad's Wild Ride** really looked like Mr. Toad's wild home, the Pinocchio building evoked Geppetto's alpine village, etc.

Walt Disney's intended Fantasyland had finally come to life. He must have believed it eventually would—after all, according to part of one Fantasyland dedication plaque he created (but never placed in view), "Fantasyland is dedicated . . . to those who believe that when you wish upon a star, your dreams come true."

Fantasyland Autopia, aka Rescue Rangers Raceway

MAP: Fantasyland, Fa-22

DATES: January 1, 1959–1999

Tomorrowland's **Autopia** became so popular that three more Autopias followed it. After the smaller **Junior Autopia** and **Midget Autopia** were built for children, the Fantasyland Autopia for older drivers opened in 1959. With roadways spread across the park's northeast corner, the new Fantasyland Autopia entrance was located on the main walkway behind the **Matterhorn**, near the **Motor Boat Cruise**.

The park's **souvenir books** sometimes described this attraction as the Super Autopia Freeway with "the latest Mark V cars." Mark V was a reference to the fifth iteration of Autopia car design and matched what was running concurrently nearby in Tomorrowland's Autopia. In fact, from 1959 until 1991 the Fantasyland and Tomorrowland Autopias were almost identical in many ways, sharing sponsorship (Richfield Oil Corporation), similar layouts (cars were side-by-side in some places), and price (usually a C ticket from the Disneyland **ticket book**).

The biggest difference between the two Autopias came in March of 1991, when the Fantasyland version was briefly renamed the Rescue Rangers Raceway in accordance with a temporary re-theming that installed **Disney Afternoon Avenue** in **Fantasyland**. The Fantasyland Autopia name was restored eight months later and lasted until 1999, at which point the attraction was closed so it could be merged into Tomorrowland's heavily remodeled Autopia, Presented by Chevron.

Fashions and Fabrics Through the Ages

MAP: Tomorrowland, T-23

DATES: March 1965–December 1965

To keep up with the styles of the future, guests need to understand the styles of the past. Or so it seemed in 1965, when **Tomorrowland** welcomed a fashion exhibit, of all things, into its pantheon of unusual displays. Like its neighbors the **Bathroom of Tomorrow** and the **Hall of Aluminum Fame**, Fashions and Fabrics Through the Ages was an industrial show added to promote a needed sponsor, in this case the formidable multibillion-dollar Monsanto chemical company founded in 1901.

Lasting only nine months in 1965, Fashions and Fabrics was the shortest-lived of the four Disneyland attractions and exhibits sponsored by Monsanto (the others were the **Hall of Chemistry**, which opened in 1955, the **House of the Future** in 1957, and **Adventure Thru Inner Space** in 1967). Monsanto set up the exhibit adjacent to its Hall of Chemistry in the first right-hand building inside the Tomorrowland entrance. The fashions on view were all women's garments, most of them historical, shown in wall displays or on mannequins. The exhibit began with ragged animal skins worn by cavewomen, and continued on from the exotic attire of ancient Egypt and Renaissance Europe to the fine dresses of the 18th, 19th, and 20th centuries. The exhibit culminated with synthetic spacewear (the synthetic angle dovetailed nicely with the chemical advances being showcased in the Monsanto hall next door).

At the end of 1965, the Monsanto fashion exhibit was removed so the entire building could be gutted in preparation for 1967's **Adventure Thru Inner Space**.

FASTPASS

DATES: 1999–ongoing

Already a triumph in Walt Disney World and Disneyland Paris, the FASTPASS ticketing system came to Disneyland just before Thanksgiving in 1999. The first attraction to get a FASTPASS ticket distribution machine was **It's a Small World**. Soon many of Disneyland's other top attractions—**Space Mountain**, **Splash Mountain**, etc.—had their own FASTPASS machines, and guests happily took advantage of them to avoid standing in lines.

Anyone who has ever waited 90 minutes for a busy attraction can appreciate how advantageous FASTPASS reservations are. All a guest has to do is show up at the popular attraction of his choice and insert his park admission ticket or annual pass into the accompanying FASTPASS machine. He'll then receive a free FASTPASS ticket that will allow him to bypass the regular line and board more quickly when he returns at the time designated on the ticket.

The system doesn't always work effortlessly, especially when overwhelming crowds form a FASTPASS **queue** in addition to the regular line. Also, each guest is allowed to obtain only one ticket at a time and must wait for the designated time to arrive before getting another one.

Typically, FASTPASS really does enable guests to jump past a long line to the front of a big attraction. Disney executives have discovered another advantage— many FASTPASS ticket holders, who normally would have spent hours waiting in lines, now have free time on their hands for shopping and dining until their reservation times arrive.

The FASTPASS system has been so successful that the amusement park industry lauded it with a Breakthrough Innovation award in 2001.

FASTPASS Attractions

Nine attractions offering FASTPASSES in 2011:

Adventureland:	Indiana Jones Adventure
Critter Country:	Splash Mountain
Frontierland:	Big Thunder Mountain Railroad
Mickey's Toontown:	Roger Rabbit's Car Toon Spin
New Orleans Square:	The Haunted Mansion
Tomorrowland:	Autopia, Presented by Chevron; Buzz Lightyear Astro Blasters; Space Mountain; Star Tours

50th Anniversary Shop

MAP: Fantasyland, Fa-3

DATES: May 2005–November 2006

Concurrent with the celebrations planned for Disneyland's 50th birthday, in 2005 the **Princess Boutique** in **Fantasyland** was transformed into the 50th Anniversary Shop. The location was the same—inside the **Sleeping Beauty Castle** entrance—but the merchandise switched from princess accoutrements to 50th anniversary souvenirs and collectibles, including some sold exclusively in the shop. Once the partying subsided, the shop was reopened as **Tinker Bell & Friends** in late 2006.

Fine Tobacco

MAP: Main Street, MS-19

DATES: July 17, 1955-June 3, 1990

For its first 35 years Disneyland maintained a genuine tobacco shop, squeezed between the **Main Street Magic Shop** and the **Main Street Cinema**. A tobacco shop, complete with a wooden Indian out front, would have been a natural component of a small-town street at the turn of the century, making a shop that sold cigarettes, cigars, and pipes an authentic addition to Main Street. In a nod to tradition, Fine Tobacco handed out complimentary matchbooks; some of these included a depiction of the shop's exterior, while others had an old-fashioned lamppost printed on the front and a cigar-store Indian on the back.

In the politically correct '90s, however, Fine Tobacco's days were numbered. The shop closed at the beginning of the decade, replaced by the **Patented**

Pastimes collectibles shop and later the **20th Century Music Company** store. Sale of tobacco elsewhere in the park concluded at the end of the decade, and within a few years there were only a handful of spaces designated as smoking areas. As a tribute to the past, Fine Tobacco's wooden Indian still stands watch in his usual place along Main Street, just as he has since 1955.

Fire Department, aka Fire Station

MAP: Town Square, TS-5

DATES: July 17, 1955–ongoing

An attractive two-story brick building trimmed in white stone, the Fire Department (or Fire Station) has stood proudly to the right (north) of **City Hall** since **Opening Day**. Displayed on the ground floor is the Fire Department's horse-drawn "fire engine" (Disneyland's **souvenir books** have also dubbed it "an old-time hose and chemical wagon"). This beautifully appointed red wagon was one of the original **Main Street Vehicles** that cost only an A ticket from the Disneyland **ticket book** for a ride to the **Hub**.

In the summer of 1960, the horse-drawn wagon was withdrawn from service and permanently parked inside the Fire Department, where it has been on view along with displays of actual firefighting equipment, a potbelly stove, and antique fire extinguishers ever since. Although kids aren't allowed to play with any of the displays, they are encouraged to climb on the fire wagon. The horses that once pulled the wagon were moved to the park's **Pony Farm**, but their Fire Department stalls remain intact and are still adorned with the names Bess and Jess—the building's first equine employees.

Upstairs and off-limits to the public is a private **apartment** for **Walt Disney** and his family. Also off-limits is the park's real fire department, located in an unseen building behind the **Opera House** on the opposite side of **Town Square**; though it may look authentic, the Fire Department on Main Street has never been used to fight fires.

Firehouse Five Plus Two

DATES: 1955–1971

The rollicking septet known as the Firehouse Five Plus Two was a summertime staple at Disneyland for 15 years. The group traveled all over the park, playing in **Town Square**, inside the **Golden Horseshoe**, on the streets of **New Orleans Square**, and while riding in **parades**. Their signature look was a fireman's outfit—a bright red shirt, white suspenders, and an authentic fire helmet—and their signature sound was guest-friendly Dixieland jazz punctuated by bells, whistles, and sirens.

As with the **Dapper Dans**, membership varied during the group's career. Among the longtime players were Danny Alguire (cornet), **George Bruns** (tuba), **Harper Goff** (banjo), Ward Kimball (trombone, and the band's leader), Johnny Lucas (trumpet), Clarke Mallery (clarinet), Monte Mountjoy (drums), Erdman Penner (tuba), George Probert (saxophone), Dick Roberts (banjo), and Frank Thomas (piano). Kimball and Thomas were two of the famed "nine old men," the influential animation team nick-named by **Walt Disney**.

The Firehouse Five Plus Two formed in the late 1940s as a lunchtime, after-work, and weekend hobby for a few Disney animators and technicians. For their early per-formances at parties, they went by the names Huggajeedy Eight and then the San Gabriel Valley Blue Blowers. In 1949 the group developed its good-time firehouse theme, complete with an old fire engine for photos. During the '50s, it performed live on TV variety shows, on radio shows, and in nightclubs. The group also got airtime when it was featured in the 1955 *Dateline Disneyland* TV special, which introduced the nation to the newly completed park.

Additionally, throughout the 1950s and '60s the group recorded a dozen albums. One of them, 1962's *At Disneyland*, was recorded live at the Golden Horseshoe. The songs included numerous popular stomps and rags, and the cover showed the boys hamming it up while sitting in the **Fantasyland** teacups.

The Firehouse Five Plus Two recorded its last album in 1970 and disbanded a year later.

Fireworks

DATES: Summer 1957–ongoing

Episodes of the *Disneyland* **TV series** began with an animation of fireworks exploding over the park in 1954. However, Disneyland itself didn't actually have this pyrotech-nic ability until the summer of 1957. According to the book *Disneyland: The Nickel Tour*, the fireworks were the brainstorm of entertainment director **Tommy Walker**, who was trying to persuade guests to linger in the park for dinner.

Disneyland's first fireworks show was called Fantasy in the Sky, launched by pyrotechnicians from the northern area of the park where **Mickey's Toontown** would eventually be built. At the time, the beautiful bursts of kaleidoscopic color, syn-chronized to music and visible in some Anaheim neighborhoods, were state of the art. Disneyland's **souvenir books** were quick to show off the fireworks with dazzling photos and text about the "cascade" of effects and "shower of color." The captions also noted how the appearance of **Tinker Bell** drew "the curtain on daytime fun" by "shining the footlights on nighttime magic." Tink, actually a 71-year-old female circus aerialist named Tiny Kline, joined the fireworks show in 1961.

In the 21st century the fireworks show was re-themed and renamed several times, each including an ever-present ellipsis: Believe . . . There's Magic in the Stars (2000); Believe . . . In Holiday Magic (2001); Imagine . . . A Fantasy in the Sky (2004); and Remember . . . Dreams Come True (2005). These later shows added narration, new

moves for Tinker Bell, and the most complex, expensive pyrotechnics yet. In a nostalgic nod to its past glory, the original Fantasy in the Sky show returned briefly in 2005 and 2006 for several special events. Themed fireworks are also presented on Halloween and during the winter holidays, and as of 2009 the Magical show has sent Dumbo and other flying characters aloft.

Fireworks fans can find several samples of fireworks music on Disney recordings. The Fantasy in the Sky music made it onto *Walt Disney Records: The Official Album* (1997), while the music of the 21st-century fireworks shows appeared on later CD collections of park-related songs.

The show's schedule has stayed fairly uniform. The presentation lasts about a half hour, and fireworks are usually launched every night in the summer and on weekend nights year-round for a total of about 250 shows per year. A painted sign on a **Frontierland** wall reminds viewers all day long what to expect at night: Laod Bhang.

First Aid and Lost Children

MAP: Town Square, TS-4; Hub, H-4

DATES: 1955–ongoing

Back in 1955, the facilities for First Aid and Lost Children were both headquartered in **City Hall**. The park map pinpointed the specific location and offered descriptions of the two services: "A doctor and registered nurses are always in attendance" at the former, and "experienced attendants" "maintain a special playground" at the latter.

Starting in 1958, the park's **souvenir books** placed the First Aid and Lost Children rooms north of **Main Street**, on the eastern side of the **Hub**. To alleviate guests' anxieties, an early First Aid sign depicted a cartoon Alice (wearing a nurse's hat) and the White Rabbit attending to guests, with Pluto looking on; the sign for Lost Children showed various Disney characters leading kids to safety by the hand.

These days, the First Aid sign offers no cartoon graphics—just sedate text and a red cross. First Aid is in its own building off of the Hub, near the **Plaza Inn**. Inside are registered nurses who treat injuries, dispense free aspirin, and offer anti-nausea remedies. There are also rooms with beds for a short rest, and refrigerators for guests to store their medications. Most medical matters are pretty routine; blisters are still the primary malady.

The Lost Children area used to be located next door to First Aid, but that space is now the Wish Lounge for kids served by the Make-A-Wish Foundation. Today's Lost Children room is actually a subsection of the **Baby Station** (aka Baby Care Center) next to the **Main Street Photo Supply Co**. Here children have an attractive waiting area where they are tended to by entertaining **cast members** and shown Disney books and movies to help pass the time.

Flagpole

MAP: Town Square, TS-6

DATES: July 17, 1955–ongoing

Since **Opening Day**, a flagpole has been located in the center of **Town Square**. But that wasn't the original plan. **Walt Disney** intended to place an old-fashioned **bandstand** in that spot—in fact, one was briefly installed there. However, just days before the park officially opened, Disney realized that the gazebo-like structure blocked guests' view of **Sleeping Beauty Castle** as they entered the park. Disney relocated the bandstand to the other end of **Main Street** and had a stately 65-foot-tall flagpole erected in its place, surrounded by a 25-foot-wide flower bed.

Today, the flags of the United States and California fly from the top of the flagpole and are occasionally lowered to half-mast—for September 11th observances, for example. Interesting details add some colorful history to the flagpole area. The ornate base is said to have been rescued by **Emile Kuri** from under an electric light

pole that was knocked down in a car accident. Two authentic 19th-century French army cannons are positioned nearby, 40 feet away from the flagpole and 90 feet from each other. Seating around the flagpole is provided by old restored park benches from San Francisco. A respectful, patriotic flag-lowering ceremony usually attended by the **Disneyland Band** or the **Dapper Dans** is held daily around dusk (**City Hall** provides the specific times). Disney characters also frequent this area for meet-and-greet visits.

On the flagpole's base is a plaque that quotes Walt Disney's Opening Day dedication speech:

DISNEYLAND

TO ALL WHO COME TO THIS HAPPY PLACE:

—WELCOME—

DISNEYLAND IS YOUR LAND.

HERE AGE RELIVES FOND MEMORIES

OF THE PAST . . . AND HERE YOUTH MAY SAVOR

THE CHALLENGE AND PROMISE OF THE FUTURE.

DISNEYLAND IS DEDICATED

TO THE IDEALS, THE DREAMS, AND THE HARD

FACTS WHICH HAVE CREATED AMERICA . . . WITH THE

HOPE THAT IT WILL BE A SOURCE OF JOY

AND INSPIRATION TO ALL THE WORLD.

JULY 17, 1955

Incidentally, this isn't the only flagpole erected at Disneyland. In the 1950s, flags for every state decorated the **Court of Honor** and the **Avenue of the Flags**. Today's guests will find another tall flagpole inside the entrance to **Frontierland**.

Flight Circle, aka Thimble Drome Flight Circle

MAP: Tomorrowland, T-21

DATES: September 1955–January 1966

The Flight Circle was a free exhibit that opened about two months after the rest of Disneyland. Located in the plaza area in front of the **Moonliner** rocket, the exhibit's paved circle was about 75 feet in diameter, had the four compass points marked in the center, and was surrounded by a chain-link fence. Guests stood behind this fence to watch demonstrations of motorized model planes, cars, and boats. (Most of the planes were the type that whirled around in a circle by an operator holding a long cable.) Model-plane manufacturer Wen-Mac (the original partners were name Wenland and McRoskey) was the first sponsor; Cox Manufacturing, a 10-year-old company that constructed a line of Thimble Drome model vehicles that burned Thimble Drome "glow fuel," assumed sponsorship in 1957 and renamed the exhibit the Thimble Drome Flight Circle (the boats were nearby, motoring around a small pond).

Anyone who heard the loud, droning planes in the park can attest to their annoying noise, but somehow the exhibit proved popular enough to stay in operation for over a decade. An illustrious moment came when the **Rocket Man** took off from the exhibit location in late 1965. A few months later, most of Tomorrowland was closed for major remodeling. Eventually some of the Flight Circle real estate became a walkway, and part of it was transformed into the **PeopleMover's** loading area.

Flight to the Moon

MAP: Tomorrowland, T-16

DATES: August 12, 1967–January 5, 1975

The original **Rocket to the Moon** in **Tomorrowland** took guests on simulated lunar flights from July of 1955 to September of 1966. After closing for a major refurbishment, the attraction opened the following summer with a new sponsor (McDonnell-Douglas, replacing Douglas Aircraft), a new ticket price (D instead of C from the Disneyland **ticket book**), a new neighbor (the Carousel Theater and its **Carousel of Progress** show), and a dramatic new presentation.

The updated Flight to the Moon simulator basically worked the same way as its predecessor by showing a receding Earth on one screen and an approaching moon on another. But the new journey was much more authentic and technically advanced. In addition to accommodating more guests, the attraction boasted more and better effects inside the ship (including a brief moment of weightlessness), and offered views of astronauts on the moon.

Even more impressive was an elaborate new Mission Control area on display before the launch. Previously, the pre-flight area had been confined to a plain room where a short film was shown; now it was a complex, computer-lined area populated with **Audio-Animatronic** scientists. This busy team was headed by a sophisticated A-A character named Tom Morrow, the Director of Mission Control. Morrow described the about-to-launch Lunar Transport Flight 92 and directed guests to look at wall monitors and catch humorous footage of a supposed UFO that turned out to be a clumsy incoming bird. As ambitious as the Flight to the Moon update was, it still fell short of the bold concept illustration sketched out by artist Bill Bosche, who had originally depicted the flight heading to Saturn and beyond.

Two years after it debuted, the Flight to the Moon was superseded by the real drama of Apollo 11. As the sight of actual astronauts walking, riding, and even swinging a golf club on the moon became more commonplace in the '70s, attendance for Disneyland's lunar flight began to dwindle, leading to 1975's new and improved **Mission to Mars**. Flight to the Moon's flight director, Tom Morrow, became a featured character in **Innoventions**, and **Redd Rockett's Pizza Port** now serves meals in the spot where Flight to the Moon once launched its guests.

Flower Mart, aka Flower Market

MAP: Main Street, MS-5, MS-17

DATES: 1957–ca. 1995

Fresh-cut flowers wouldn't have lasted long in the California sunshine or survived a whirl on the teacups. Fortunately, artificial flowers could do both. In 1957, Disneyland added the beautiful little Flower Mart, or Flower Market, to **Main Street**.

Sold out of open-air carts on wheels, "the world's finest natural flowers not grown by nature" were mobile and so had two different locations. Originally, the

Flower Mart was located halfway down the western side of Main Street, filling the middle of the small, intersecting West Center Street. The plastic posies remained there until the **Carnation Ice Cream Parlor** on the corner expanded into West Center in 1977, sending the flower carts across the way to East Center Street, where **portrait artists** had formerly set up their easels.

The Flower Mart vanished quietly in the mid-'90s. In its heyday, over a dozen different blooms were available, even through the mail.

Flying Saucers

MAP: Tomorrowland, T-18

DATES: August 6, 1961–September 5, 1966

Showing more ambition than practicality, Disneyland debuted its unique space-age bumper car ride in mid-1961. UFOs had been a hot topic throughout the '50s, when sightings headlined newspapers and bug-eyed Martians invaded America's drive-in movie screens. Thus the time seemed right for Flying Saucers to invade Disneyland.

The park's promotional literature played up the attraction: "Fly Your Own Flying Saucer" at the "Space Terminal," touted the **attraction poster**; "Each guest pilots his own ship in free flight," announced the 1961 **souvenir book**; "Space travel" at a "space station," captioned the '62 book for its Flying Saucers photo; "Choose a 'flight pattern' . . . and away you go," exhorted the '65 book. All intriguing descriptions, to be sure.

In reality, Disneyland's Flying Saucers probably should have been called the Hovering Saucers. Operating in a circular, open-air platform that covered a third of an acre next to the **Rocket to the Moon** attraction, the **Bob Gurr**-designed saucers were small, one-seat hovercraft six feet in diameter.

The Saucers got airborne when they were lifted up by high-powered jets of air generated by large motors under the platform. When they hovered successfully, the 64 saucers (in two fleets of 32) could lift a few inches off the ground. Though they had no controls—only handles—inside their cockpits, the saucers could be steered independently by guests, who only had to lean to dip their saucers in any direction—even into other saucers for some bumper-bashing.

Unfortunately, persistent problems with the air jets led to lots of ground time for the E-ticket attraction (see **ticket books**). Body weight was an issue; small guests couldn't get their saucers to dip anywhere, while some larger guests couldn't even get off the ground. Other guests occasionally turned their saucers completely over, risking a crash. Too often, guests couldn't go anywhere because the whole system would shut itself down.

Some five-million pilots gave the saucers a test flight, but after five years of headaches and extremely loud noise, Disney designers finally grounded the troublesome ride in 1966 and remodeled the whole area as the **Tomorrowland Stage** in 1967.

Fortuosity Shop

MAP: Main Street, MS-4

DATES: October 3, 2008–ongoing

The prime corner location on Main Street that was once the **Upjohn Pharmacy** and then **New Century Watches & Clocks** became the Fortuosity Shop in 2008. Named after a sanguine song from the 1967 Disney movie *The Happiest Millionaire*, the shop specializes in customized Disney watches, just as it did in its New Century days. Handbags, shirts, hats, and gifts supplement the timepieces in the front of the shop, while rings, bracelets, and cameo fill the displays in a smaller side room.

40 Pounds of Trouble
(1962)

The first major movie to be filmed in Disneyland was made, not by Disney, but by Universal Pictures. Released in 1962, *40 Pounds of Trouble* is a light family comedy starring Tony Curtis and Suzanne Pleshette. The 19 minutes of sunny Disneyland scenes include aerial footage, a ride on the **Matterhorn Bobsleds**, and extinct park attractions such as the **Skyway**, but they are more notable for their fabrications—for

6 Theatrical Movies Featuring Disneyland

The Boys, a celebration of the Sherman Brothers' lives and music from Walt Disney Productions, 2009 (three minutes of footage)

Disneyland, U.S.A., featurette from Disney, 1956 (42 minutes)

Exit Through the Gift Shop, Banksy's Oscar-nominated documentary from Paranoid Pictures, 2010 (six minutes)

40 Pounds of Trouble, feature film from Universal Pictures, 1962 (19 minutes)

Gala Day at Disneyland, featurette from Walt Disney Productions, 1960 (27 minutes)

That Thing You Do!, Tom Hanks' Oscar-nominated feature film from 20th Century Fox, 1996 (15 seconds)

instance, in the film, the **Monorail** disembarks passengers at **Town Square**, and guests who board **Peter Pan Flight** also get to go through the **Mr. Toad** and **Snow White** attractions.

40 Years of Adventure

DATES: 1995

Disneyland had lots to celebrate in 1995, and celebrate it did with its wide-ranging 40 Years of Adventure promotion. Back in '95, **Mickey's Toontown** still felt new, the 1994 blockbuster *The Lion King* was winning Oscars, the Lion King Celebration was packing **Main Street** by day, and the **Main Street Electrical Parade** was still running at night.

Best of all, 1995 welcomed the debut of the biggest single attraction since 1989's **Splash Mountain**—the landmark **Indiana Jones Adventure**. Indy's exciting arrival was heralded with a TV special in March, bold emblems on the 1995 **Fun Map** and **souvenir book**, and a new gift shop (**Indiana Jones Adventure Outpost**) showcasing 40 Years of Adventure merchandise. Additionally, a unique "time castle" was buried in front of **Sleeping Beauty Castle** on July 17th, the 40th anniversary of **Opening Day**.

Fowler, Joe

(1894–1993)

Joe Fowler, the man in charge of building Disneyland, was born in Maine in 1894. After graduating from both the Naval Academy and MIT, Fowler worked as a naval architect, designing the World War II aircraft carriers *Lexington* and *Saratoga*, and heading two dozen naval shipyards in the '40s.

Fowler retired from the U.S. Navy in 1948 as a rear admiral, but an introduction to **Walt Disney** brought him an invitation to oversee construction of Disney's new Anaheim project. He joined the Disneyland team in April 1954, began construction three months later, and a year later had the vast park ready for guests.

Once Disneyland opened, Fowler supervised operations into the next decade and had a hand in every building project in the park. Within a few years, he was leading the way on several exceedingly complex Disneyland developments—the **Matterhorn**, the **Submarine Voyage**, and the **Monorail**. In the '60s, Fowler took on **New Orleans Square**, the **Haunted Mansion**, **Pirates of the Caribbean**, and the heavily remodeled **Tomorrowland**, all built while the park was still open for business.

By the late '60s, Fowler was in charge of construction at Walt Disney World. As a senior VP, he also ran the entire Imagineering department, designing new attractions before he finally managed to retire for good in 1978.

Fowler, nicknamed "Can-Do" for his optimism, was inducted as a Disney Legend in 1990, three years before his death at age 99. At Disneyland, **Fowler's Harbor** in **Frontierland** is named after him.

Fowler's Harbor, aka Fowler's Landing

MAP: Frontierland, Fr-13
DATES: June 14, 1958–ongoing

Fowler's Harbor is the name of the dock along the **Rivers of America** where the **Sailing Ship** *Columbia* is often moored. Years ago, the **Mike Fink Keel Boats** launched just south of this dock, and the **Indian War Canoes** launched just north.

The dock's name is a tribute to **Joe Fowler**, the Navy admiral who supervised the construction of Disneyland and stayed on as a top Disney executive until 1978. Back in 1955, the little dock area was an informal, unnamed location for servicing the *Mark Twain*. However, when the *Columbia* began berthing there in 1958, it was christened Fowler's Harbor (or occasionally, Fowler's Landing).

Small structures at the harbor are decorated with **Frontierland**-themed façades, including one that reads, "Fowler's Inn." For a while, one sign at Fowler's Harbor promoted a nonexistent restaurant called Maurie's Lobster House, named after Joe Fowler's wife. The serene 100-foot-long path that winds behind Fowler's Harbor offers picturesque views of **Tom Sawyer Island.**

France, Van Arsdale
(1912–1999)

One of Disneyland's hallmarks is extraordinary customer service. Van Arsdale France was the man who first instructed the park's employees in conduct, and along the way he created many of the training techniques still used throughout corporate America.

France was born in Seattle in 1912 and earned a college degree in liberal arts 22 years later before holding a number of jobs and establishing himself as a labor relations expert in the 1940s. Beginning his Disneyland career four months before the park opened, France and his assistant, **Dick Nunis**, who would later become the president of Walt Disney Attractions, converted an abandoned house near the Disneyland construction site into a training center called the Personnel Annex (the Disneyland Hotel was later built on the property). France's task was to make Disneyland **cast members** the most efficient and congenial employees anywhere. Just as a clean park would inspire guests to avoid littering, polite employees, **Walt Disney** believed, would inspire guests to be on their best behavior. "You can design, create, and build the most wonderful place in the world," he once said, "but it takes people to make the dream a reality."

To accomplish Disney's ambitious goals for Disneyland employees, Van France established Disney University, which first convened in small trailers before moving to an office building outside the park's southeast corner. There, France wrote the manuals that set procedures and attitudes for decades to come. These manuals, with names like "You're on Stage at Disneyland" and "The Spirit of Disneyland," taught Disneyland philosophy first and specific job skills second. Cast members learned how to create happiness before they learned how to serve food or park cars. France reinvented workers as actors and actresses in an elaborate show where all customers, not just the famous ones, were treated as special guests.

Among his other duties in the park's first decade, France briefly supervised **Tomorrowland**, helped resolve traffic issues on the nearby streets, smoothed relations with the community, put together *Backstage Disneyland* (the first magazine for cast members), and set up the Disneyland Alumni Club. Though he officially retired in 1978, France stayed on as a consultant and spokesman. His autobiography, *Window on Main Street,* was published in 1991. Named a Disney Legend three years later, Van France died in Newport Beach in 1999.

Frees, Paul
(1920–1986)

Guests may not know the name, but they certainly know the voice. Born Solomon Frees in Chicago in 1920, Paul Frees was a D-Day veteran who performed thousands of radio, TV, and movie voices in a career stretching from the '40s to the mid-'80s. Movie buffs recognize him as the narrator of *War of the Worlds* (1953), the voice of the talking rings in *The Time Machine* (1960), and even as Tony Curtis's "Josephine" voice in *Some Like It Hot* (1959). Fans of Disney movies will also recall his vocals from *The Absent-Minded Professor* and *The Monkey's Uncle,* among others. On TV, he gave voices to many memorable cartoon characters, including Boris Badonov, Ludwig von Drake, and John and George on the Beatles' cartoon show. He also voiced several famous characters in commercials, among them the Pillsbury Doughboy and Froot Loops' Toucan Sam.

Many more movies and cartoons followed, but it was at Disneyland that Frees found his biggest audience. Since the late '60s, he has been heard by hundreds of millions of visitors on a variety of landmark attractions—he has voiced the Ghost Host in the **Haunted Mansion**, the "auctioneer" and other rogues in **Pirates of the Caribbean**, and the shrinking scientist in **Adventure thru Inner Space**. He was also the original narrator for **Great Moments with Mr. Lincoln**.

Paul Frees died of heart failure in 1986; two decades later he was named a Disney Legend.

French Market
MAP: New Orleans Square, NOS-10
DATES: July 24, 1966–ongoing

The French Market has been an attractive dining destination since **New Orleans**

Square opened in 1966. The location, *c'est magnifique*. From its corner near the **Haunted Mansion**, the restaurant's patio with 50-plus tables offers alfresco dining and expansive views of the **Rivers of America**, and is located next to a small stage for live jazz.

The restaurant's menu has changed considerably, from the open-face turkey-on-white sandwiches served in the late '60s to the more sophisticated Creole cuisine served today. Roast beef, salmon, jambalaya, and "signature clam chowder" served in sourdough bread bowls are some of the buffet favorites. Stouffer's, the frozen-food company that also sponsored the **Plaza Pavilion** and the **Tahitian Terrace**, was the longtime host here.

Frontierland

MAP: Park, P-15

DATES: July 17, 1955–ongoing

Covering some 20 acres and about 33 percent of Disneyland in the 1950s, the original **Frontierland** was the largest of the park's first five lands. Even after **New Orleans Square** and **Bear Country** carved into Frontierland in the '60s and '70s, it was still bigger than either **Tomorrowland** or **Adventureland**. Much of this vast Frontierland acreage was and is accessible only by boat, mule, or train, since the **Rivers of America**, **Tom Sawyer Island**, the **Painted Desert**, and **Nature's Wonderland** have sprawled over large portions of the territory.

Early in the planning stages, **Walt Disney** decreed that one of the park's lands would be inspired by "America's frontiers." Disneyland's **souvenir books** added temporal boundaries, declaring these to be the frontiers "from Revolutionary days to the great southwest [*sic*] settlement" (the late 1700s to the late 1800s), where guests would "experience the high adventure of our forefathers who shaped our glorious history." True to that frontier spirit, the land was positioned in the western half of the park, and vast regions appeared to be undeveloped—yet this "wilderness" was carefully constructed, and plenty of attractions added over the decades have transformed Frontierland into Funtierland.

Like Adventureland, the neighbor with a main entrance 30 feet to the south, Frontierland has an entrance from the **Hub**. The portal, which spans a shallow pond, was built with real logs to look like the gates of a frontier stockade. Pre-opening concept drawings by both Bruce Bushman and **Herb Ryman** depicted guests passing teepees before they entered the gates of the fort, but ultimately teepees were placed on the far-west edge of Frontierland in the **Indian Village**.

Once under the stockade gates, guests find themselves 40 feet from a flagpole with a plaque presented to Walt Disney by the American Humane Association in 1955. Guests then walk toward a small, Western-style "downtown" that looks straight out of the 19th century, featuring wooden sidewalks, small shops, an exuberant saloon, and a shooting gallery. Images of cowboy boots and horseshoes are stamped into the pavement, and country music drifts through the air. Even the brown metal **trash cans**, painted to look as if they were made out of planks, contribute to the theme.

Some 300 feet from the Frontierland gates roll the Rivers of America. More stores and restaurants line the walkway toward New Orleans Square on the left, Tom Sawyer Island appears straight ahead, and an expansive wilderness area stretches to the right. Plying the river's waters is an array of watercraft—everything from a grand paddlewheeler to simple canoes. In the '50s, a **Marshal's Office** stood along the main walkway, a **Miniature Horse Corral** bordered the **Frontierland Shooting Gallery**, and the wilderness to the north was explored by a horse-drawn **Stage Coach**, a lumbering **Mule Pack**, rustic **Conestoga Wagons**, and an old-fashioned **Mine Train**. More Old West realism materialized every day in the form of a staged "shootout" between Sheriff Lucky and Black Bart in front of the **Golden Horseshoe**.

While the basic building architecture has remained the same over the decades, massive changes have uprooted the low-capacity transportation systems that used to explore the desert wilderness. The biggest modifications began in 1979 when a sweeping renovation added the high-speed, high-capacity, high-tech **Big Thunder Mountain Railroad** to the Nature's Wonderland area, followed a few years later by the **Big Thunder Barbecue** and **Big Thunder Ranch** (as well as a new pedestrian path into the back of **Fantasyland**). The stockade at the front gate has been remodeled twice, first in 1980 and again in 1992, and the nightly shows have graduated from **Dixieland at Disneyland** jazz concerts to the elaborate **Fantasmic!** presentation.

Even with the all the modernization, Frontierland has stayed faithful to Walt Disney's original vision. His inspirational articulation of that vision would have been shown on the land's 1955 dedication plaque, had it ever been installed: "Frontierland is a tribute to the faith, courage, and ingenuity of the pioneers who blazed the trails across America." Five decades later, the old frontiers of the past are still thrilling guests.

Frontierland Miniature Museum

MAP: Frontierland, Fr-1

DATES: Never built

Walt Disney's love of miniatures, most obviously manifested in the **Storybook Land Canal Boats** over in **Fantasyland**, almost found expression inside the **Frontierland** gates.

According to some early concept drawings, the museum and stockade entrance would have shared the same style of hewn-log architecture. Inside the museum, guests would have found displays of miniature towns, houses, and people, plus a small mechanical dancing man that foreshadowed the later **Audio-Animatronic** figures of the '60s. Many of these displays (and the mechanical man) were actually created, and in fact, back before a Disneyland plan was even under discussion, Walt Disney intended to send them on tour around the country.

Ultimately, a museum did open in the park, but its theme was something that mid-'50s TV audiences could more easily relate to—the King of the Wild Frontier. In 1955 the **Davy Crockett Frontier Museum** opened in the spot now occupied by Pioneer Mercantile.

Frontierland Shooting Gallery,
aka Frontierland Shootin' Arcade,
aka Frontierland Shooting Exposition

MAP: Frontierland, Fr-26

DATES: July 12, 1957–ongoing

Two years after the park opened, the success of the **Main Street Shooting Gallery** prompted Disneyland executives to add a rootin' tootin' rifle range to **Frontierland**.

The Frontierland Shooting Gallery opened along the right-hand side of Frontierland's main walkway, in a 45-foot-wide spot where the **Miniature Horse Corral** had been. The rifles fired lead pellets at frontier-themed metal targets that had to be laboriously repainted every night. To keep the guns from being aimed too far from the targets, they were positioned in a cradle—although the sheer weight of the rifles was enough to keep kids aiming them forward. As with the later **Big Game Safari Shooting Gallery**

in **Adventureland**, visits to the Frontierland Shooting Gallery required quarters, not admission tickets.

Concerned with the hazardous lead dust generated by the pellets and the high maintenance of the gallery, in the spring of 1985 Imagineers installed 18 new electronic rifles that fired infrared beams and new targets that also produced humorous sound effects. The gallery got a new name, too—Frontierland Shootin' Arcade.

The name and effects were updated once more with the 1996 debut of the Frontierland Shootin' (later Shooting) Exposition. The mining town of Boot Hill was the new target, and the effects included a skeleton that popped up when guests hit a graveyard shovel. Today, some of the Boot Hill tombstones have playful epitaphs reminiscent of those at the **Haunted Mansion**: "An arrow shot straight n' true/made its mark on Little Lou," says one.

Frontier Trading Post

MAP: Frontierland, Fr-27

DATES: July 17, 1955–1987

From 1955 until the late '80s, guests who walked from the **Hub** through the **Frontierland** stockade gates found the Frontier Trading Post on their immediate right (this store is not to be confused with the similarly named **Indian Trading Post**, which existed over in the **Indian Village** from '62 until '88). The Frontier Trading Post had a rustic wood-plank design that fit right in with this stretch of walkway by the rowdy **Frontierland Shooting Gallery**. From its small space the Trading Post sold frontier souvenirs, many of them related to the Davy Crockett craze that overwhelmed America in the mid-'50s. The store's wooden Indian still stands outside, but in 1987 the Trading Post name was traded for the **Westward Ho Trading Company**.

Fun Fotos

MAP: Tomorrowland, T-22

DATES: 1960–1965

In Disneyland's first decade, whenever vacancies opened up inside the exhibit buildings along the right-hand side of **Tomorrowland**, Fun Fotos were installed as temporary, inexpensive space fillers. The **American Dairy Association Exhibit**, **Bathroom of Tomorrow,** and **Hall of Aluminum Fame** all got replaced at one time or another by Fun Fotos.

The fun of the fotos was twofold: guests got their pictures taken in front of painted Disneyland-themed backgrounds, and those Polaroids were then developed "while you wait" (quick-developing photos were still a novelty back then).

All the Fun Fotos disappeared around 1966, when the buildings were completely remodeled for **Adventure Thru Inner Space** and the **Character Shop**.

Fun Maps

DATES: 1958–ongoing

Old poster-size park maps are among the most evocative Disneyland collectibles. Called Fun Maps and sold at the park, these visually rich souvenirs recreate fond memories and build eager expectations; many a fan has studied the maps for hours to recall previous visits and dream of the next one.

The first Fun Map sold in the park was drawn by Disney Legend **Sam McKim**, who seemed to specialize in park cartography (he also drew the **Tom Sawyer Island** maps). This 1958 map positioned the Disneyland Hotel in one corner ("designed and priced for family fun") and **Walt Disney's** face and his **Opening Day** speech in another. It also had a compass featuring **Tinker Bell** and a legend to point out **restrooms,** telephones, "future developments," and more. Best of all, detailed drawings and captions saturated the park layout with information. Nearly everything in Disneyland was labeled, even some things not usually identified ("Swan Lake" is the name of the Sleeping Beauty Castle moat, according to the 1958 map). The map also depicted **Holidayland** west of **Frontierland**, the "heliport" outside of **Tomorrowland**, and attractions that were never actually built in Disneyland, such as **Adventures in Science**, **Edison Square**, and **Liberty Street**.

By the '90s, though the maps were basically the same as they'd always been, they showed a range of design differences. For one thing, the size shifted from year to year (maps have usually been around 30 inches wide by approximately 40 inches tall). Some of the maps included drawings of Disney characters around their perimeters. Some years, the maps had far fewer captions, making them much less useful. The scale was inconsistent—**Jungle Cruise** animals might be as big as buildings, and **Sleeping Beauty Castle** would sometimes be shown approximately the same height as the **Matterhorn**, even though the castle is actually about half as tall as the mountain.

The maps weren't being updated very frequently, either—a Fun Map purchased new in 1994 had actually been drawn in 1989; thus, it didn't include **Mickey's Toontown**, which had opened in 1993, and it still included the **Mile Long Bar**, which had been renamed in 1989. Cartoon heads were still sprinkled around the edges, though many guests would have been hard-pressed to identify little-known characters like Horace Horsecollar. A year later a new 1995 map spotlighted Disneyland's 40th anniversary and the new **Indiana Jones Adventure**, but that map also had problems—until a quick revision and reprint, the '95 map gave the wrong date for Disneyland's **Opening Day**.

A Fun Map available for purchase in 2011 changed size again, this time to 27 inches by 34 inches. Walt Disney's face was back, and so were many more captions, exemplified by the nine named sections of the **Grand Canyon Diorama**. Nomenclature continued to be slippery; what most guests call the **Hub** had been called the Plaza on the '58 Fun Map, the Plaza Hub on the '89 map, and the Central Plaza on the 2011 version.

Gadget's Go Coaster

MAP: Mickey's Toontown, MT-3

DATES: January 24, 1993–ongoing

Gadget's Go Coaster is a kid-size version of a rowdy outdoor roller coaster. This fun attraction is located at the west end of **Mickey's Toontown** near the **Chip 'n Dale Tree House**, with part of its track venturing over a small pond.

Gadget, of course, refers to Gadget Hackwrench, the mouse inventor from the *Chip 'n' Dale Rescue Rangers* TV show. The roller coaster is supposed to be one of her clever inventions, and it's also supposed to represent the world from a mouse-eye view. Guests are placed inside big acorns for a trip on what looks like a Tinker Toy track that quickly turns past oversized displays like gigantic pencils, combs, matchbooks, and more.

Lasting just under a minute, the brief 700-foot-long trip is perhaps the shortest ride in the park, but it's a popular one. Unfortunately, with only two trains on the track (one rollercoastering at around 20 mph while new passengers load in the other), and with each train holding a maximum of only 16 guests at a time, lines can get long here. Appropriately enough for an attraction targeted to young children, the sponsor, Georgia-Pacific's Sparkle Paper Towels, helps parents clean up messes.

Gag Factory

MAP: Mickey's Toontown, MT-9

DATES: January 24, 1993–ongoing

Comedians might suggest that a place named the Gag Factory probably sells really bad food, but actually this is a clever retail store in the downtown section of **Mickey's Toontown**. The factory décor includes a brick interior and gears on the walls.

The gags here include a talking mailbox and bendable jail bars out front, a painted interior wall that reads, "Do not paint on this wall," and the motto *Carpe Gag 'Em* above the door. The shelves used to be full of crazy toys, practical jokes, and magic tricks, but these days the merchandise has

Approximate Ride-Times of Disneyland Attractions

1 Minute or Less
Gadget's Go Coaster, Rafts to Tom Sawyer Island

90 Seconds–Under 3 Minutes
Casey Jr. Circus Train, Jolly Trolley, King Arthur Carrousel,
Mad Hatter's Mad Tea Party, Matterhorn Bobsleds, Mr. Toad's Wild Ride,
Peter Pan Flight, Snow White Adventures

3–5 Minutes
Alice in Wonderland, Big Thunder Mountain Railroad,
Buzz Lightyear Astro Blasters, Casey Jr. Circus Train, Indiana Jones Adventure,
The Many Adventures of Winnie the Pooh, Pinocchio's Daring Journey,
Rocket Rods, Roger Rabbit's Car Toon Spin, Space Mountain, Star Tours

6–9 Minutes
Adventure Thru Inner Space, the Haunted Mansion, Jungle Cruise,
Skyway to Fantasyland/Tomorrowland (round trip), Splash Mountain,
Storybook Land Canal Boats, Submarine Voyage, Autopia,
Western Mine Train Through Nature's Wonderland

10–15 Minutes
Country Bear Jamboree, Great Moments with Mr. Lincoln,
Indian War/Davy Crockett's Explorer Canoes, Finding Nemo Submarine Voyage,
It's a Small World, Light Magic, *Mark Twain* Riverboat, Mike Fink Keel Boats,
Mission to Mars, Mule Pack, Rocket/Flight to the Moon, Sailing Ship *Columbia*,
A Tour of the West film.

16–20 Minutes
America the Beautiful film, *Captain EO* film, Enchanted Tiki Room,
Honey, I Shrunk the Audience film, *Magic Journeys* film, PeopleMover,
Pirates of the Caribbean

21+ Minutes
American Journeys film, America Sings, Fantasmic!, Festival of Fools,
Santa Fe & Disneyland Railroad

shifted to less joke-y jewelry, mugs, clothes, and hats. The Gag Factory added the first-ever Disney dime-press machine in 2005, some two decades after the first Disney penny-press machine was installed on **Main Street**. This store connects to the adjacent **Toontown Five & Dime**, making this block a funtastic shopping destination.

Gala Day at Disneyland
(1960)
This 27-minute documentary was released in movie theaters on January 21, 1960.

Like an earlier Disney featurette, 1956's *Disneyland, U.S.A.*, *Gala Day at Disneyland* was essentially an extended commercial for the park's newest attractions. Key among these were the **Monorail**, **Matterhorn Bobsleds**, and **Submarine Voyage**, all of which had debuted the previous summer as Disneyland's first E-ticket attractions (see **ticket books**). **Parades**, **fireworks**, **mermaids**, and Richard Nixon also got some screen time.

Garden of the Gods

MAP: Fantasyland, Fa-22

DATES: Never built

Looking for ways to enhance the slow-moving **Motor Boat Cruise** in **Fantasyland**, in the '60s Disney designers considered adding pastoral design elements from the movie *Fantasia*. For Garden of the Gods, artist **Marc Davis** designed Olympian sculptures that incorporated peaceful fountains. Boats shaped like swans and rail cars shaped like steeds were considered for transportation. Classical music from the movie was slotted for the soundtrack.

Unfortunately, before such serene scenes made it into Disneyland, reality hit home: the tracks of **Fantasyland Autopia** circled all around these waterways and would have intruded loudly upon the bucolic gardens. However, the *Fantasia* theme did ultimately arrive in this area in 1993; when the Motor Boat Cruise finally sank into the past, the lush landscaping of **Fantasia Gardens** took root.

Geppetto's Arts & Crafts,
aka Geppetto's Toys & Gifts,
aka Geppetto's Holiday Workshop

MAP: Fantasyland, Fa-9

DATES: May 25, 1983–2004; 2006–2007; 2010

The village-themed architecture that surrounds **Pinocchio's Daring Journey** once embraced a Pinocchio-themed gift shop as well. Next to the attraction's exit to **Fantasyland** was a store named after Pinocchio's toy-making father.

Dense with charming Old World details, Geppetto's Arts & Crafts was designed to look just like the cozy toy shop in the classic movie. In its first incarnation, lots of marionettes, figurines, and old-fashioned cuckoo clocks dominated Geppetto's place. In the mid-'90s the shop's name switched to Toys & Gifts and focused more on plush toys and dolls, with same-day, custom-made dolls as its specialty. Geppetto's was also the site of special toy-related events and frequent appearances by Disney princesses.

Ten years later the toy maker and his creations moved out and **Names Unraveled**, formerly a cart that operated elsewhere in Fantasyland, moved in. In 2006, the sign above the door announced a new name: Geppetto's Holiday Workshop. However, early in 2007 the store closed again. When it reopened in 2010, it did so as **Geppetto's Candy Shoppe**, selling sweets instead of toys.

Geppetto's Candy Shoppe

MAP: Fantasyland, Fa-9

DATES: May 26, 2010–October 2010; fall 2011–ongoing

Poor Geppetto—his Disneyland stores never seem to pan out. After starting out in 1983 with **Geppetto's Arts & Crafts**, then moving on to toys, gifts, and holiday items until 2007, the old toymaker tried selling candy in 2010. Pre-packaged sugary sweets filled the adorable little store for a summer, but in October of 2010 the space was transformed into **Tangled**, a meet-and-greet area for the stars of the Disney movie of the same name.

Gibson, Blaine
(1918–)
Blaine Gibson's childhood hobby was sculpting; eventually his hobby became his career. Born in Colorado in 1918, Gibson began working in the animation department at Disney Studios in 1939. He's listed in the credits of many of the company's classic films and cartoons from the '40s to the early '60s, including *Peter Pan*, *Sleeping Beauty*, and *One Hundred and One Dalmatians*. Even while working at the studio by day, he continued to take sculpting classes at night, and in 1954 **Walt Disney** invited him to start making models for Disneyland attractions.

Over the next three decades, Gibson supervised the sculpture department and created hundreds of works that were transformed into the **Audio-Animatronic** characters in such diverse attractions as the **Enchanted Tiki Room**, **Great Moments with Mr. Lincoln**, and the **Haunted Mansion**. Gibson's Timothy Mouse creation rode the top of **Dumbo the Flying Elephant**, his fair maiden graced the bow of the **Sailing Ship** *Columbia*, and his little demons lined the fiery finale of **Mr. Toad's Wild Ride**.

In 1965 Gibson appeared on *Walt Disney's Wonderful World of Color* alongside some of his pirate sculptures for **Pirates of the Caribbean**. Later he sculpted representations of all the chief executives for the Hall of Presidents at Walt Disney World, and later still, after he'd retired in 1983, he created *Partners*, the famous bronze statue of Walt Disney and Mickey Mouse installed in Disneyland's **Hub** in 1993. That same year, Blaine Gibson was named a Disney Legend in celebration of his four decades as one of the company's master artists.

Gibson Girl Ice Cream Parlor

MAP: Main Street, MS-7

DATES: March 21, 1997–ongoing

The 1997 shuffle of ice cream parlors and bakeries along **Main Street** landed a new dessert spot, the Gibson Girl Ice Cream Parlor, next to the **Penny Arcade**. The **Blue Ribbon Bakery** had been located there until early '97; when Blue Ribbon moved to the corner space where the **Carnation Ice Cream Parlor** had been, the Gibson Girl took the vacant space in the middle of the block.

Gibson Girls, of course, were the curvy pin-ups created by American illustrator Charles Dana Gibson in the early 20th century. The curvy-pin-up element didn't get recreated inside the ice cream parlor (except for a few discreet drawings), but the early-20th-century part sure did. From the ornate display fonts and striped awning outside to the old-fashioned lighting fixtures and soda fountain inside, this is a place where the time travel is as enticing as the desserts.

An expansion in early 2012 added more space to the Gibson Girls interior. A four-foot-tall glass elephant imported from Disneyland Paris makes for an interesting conversation piece in the back dining room, but most guests who pack the place throughout the day are probably more focused on the shop's sweets. "Old-fashioned hand scooped ice cream" and "a perfect treat for someone sweet" are touted on the signage outside, referring to the sundaes, ice cream cones, floats, sodas, and lemonade available. The shop doesn't offer many ice cream flavors, but what they've got is served up generously (publicists claim that in one year Gibson Girl sells enough ice cream to build a full-size **Matterhorn Mountain**).

Special creations for the holidays are big hits, as are the homemade waffle cones sold year-round. Not surprisingly, two ice cream companies, Nestlé and Dreyer's, have been the sponsors.

Gibson Greeting Cards

MAP: Main Street, MS-14

DATES: July 17, 1955–1959

Gibson stores sold charming cards and postcards printed by an Ohio-based company that was originally launched in 1850. The Gibsons, four Scottish brothers, began their business printing up labels and business cards. In the 1880s they added a new product, **holiday season** greeting cards, to their line and established themselves as one of the country's biggest card companies well into the next century.

At Disneyland, the Gibson Art Co. has had two different stores in two **Main Street** locations (neither store was in any way related to the **Gibson Girl Ice Cream Parlor**). The first store, Gibson Greeting Cards, debuted on **Opening Day** and lasted until 1959. This initial location was at the corner of Main Street and East Center Street where **Disney Clothiers, Ltd**. now sits.

The **Hallmark Card Shop** took over for Gibson in 1960, and Gibson disappeared from Main Street until mid-1985, when its **Card Corner** filled the spot that had formerly been known as **Carefree Corner. John Hench**, the influential designer and Disney Legend, designed the first Gibson location.

Gift-Giver Extraordinaire Machine

DATES: 1985–September 1986

To celebrate its 30th anniversary, in 1985 Disneyland displayed a running tally of ticket sales in anticipation of the arrival of guest number 250 million. Out in front of the park stood the "Incredible Countdown Clock," designed with gears shaped like Mickey's ears and a counter with nine digits.

Throughout the year, every 30th guest who walked through the gates won an instant prize. For some lucky winners, the prize was a chance to take home a new car, determined by a spin of the Gift-Giver Extraordinaire Machine in the **Hub**. This showy device was the precursor of the **Dream Machine**, the slot machine cake created for the park's 35th birthday five years later. As it worked out, every 30 thousandth guest got a new car (about a car a day), and the 3 millionth guest got a new Cadillac (there were over 12,000,000 guests that year, which meant over 400 cars and four Caddies were given out). Winners collected their prizes (except for the actual cars) at the Prize Redemption Center next to the **Opera House** doorway.

The idea for the birthday prize giveaways is credited to the park's longtime marketing chief, Disney Legend **Jack Lindquist**. Lindquist's goal was to spark 1985 attendance after a disappointing 1984 (that year's L.A. Olympics had kept many guests away from the park). After a February TV special and months of generous giveaways, Disneyland attendance jumped 22 percent over the previous year's tally, and that 250 millionth guest finally walked through the gates on August 24, 1985.

The Gift Giver Machine didn't stop giving, however, until September of '86. Prizes that year included airline tickets, videocassettes, watches, color TVs, and "the official car of Disneyland '86," a Pontiac Firebird.

Give a Day, Get a Disney Day

DATES: 2010

A short but sweet off-season promotion for 2010, Give a Day, Get a Disney Day enabled guests to earn free entrance into Disneyland by volunteering. After registering and performing any of a number of community volunteer options, guests could then exchange a voucher for either park admission or a special **FASTPASS** ticket. Numerous promotions and TV commercials helped spread the word. The word did indeed spread fast and far: less than 10 weeks after it debuted on January 1st, the Give a Day program closed abruptly on March 9th. Disney officials, touting the program's success, claimed that a million volunteers had taken advantage of this unique opportunity.

Glass Blower

MAP: Main Street, MS-3

DATES: 1955–1966

For over a decade, **Main Street** housed a glass blower who had his own shop. His name was Bill Rasmussen, and he leased a space in the rear of the **Crystal Arcade**. There Rasmussen created delicate, whimsical glass figurines in full view of guests. He even worked in full view of the whole nation when he appeared on an episode of *The Mickey Mouse Club*.

Rasmussen left Disneyland in 1966 and opened a series of shops in San Francisco, Boston, Honolulu, and other American cities (he called his Hawaiian shop the Little Glass Shack). Meanwhile, back in Disneyland, other glass blowers filled Rasmussen's Crystal Arcade spot into the '70s.

Goff, Harper
(1911–1993)

Movie fans know Harper Goff's *Nautilus* from a memorable Disney film; Disneyland fans know his widespread designs all over the park. And jazz fans might know his contributions as the banjo player in the **Firehouse Five Plus Two**.

The multi-talented Harper Goff was born in 1911. His Fort Collins, Colorado upbringing found its way into Disneyland—several of the buildings he designed for the park, including **City Hall**, were based on actual buildings in his hometown. After attending art school in Los Angeles, Goff moved to New York and in the '30s drew illustrations for *Esquire* and other popular magazines. Back in Hollywood in the '40s, he became a set designer at Warner Bros. and worked on *Casablanca* and *Captain Blood*, among other film favorites. Moving to Disney Studios in the '50s, Goff was instrumental in establishing the story and creating the designs that made *20,000 Leagues Under the Sea* an Oscar-winning classic.

Goff was involved with the nascent Disneyland project even before Anaheim was set as the park's location. At **Walt Disney's** behest, he took several trips around the country to gather information about other amusement parks, fairs, and museums; it was his research that informed the earliest Disneyland plans.

As one of the first designers on the project, in 1951 Goff drew up concept art for a 16-acre Burbank park that would have featured boats on a lake, an island, a circus tent, a frontier town, and a train ride. As the Anaheim plans came to fruition, Goff oversaw construction on the **Jungle Cruise** and created the interior for the **Golden Horseshoe**, in addition to countless other contributions. Later he helped create EP-COT in Florida, and was still consulting on Disney theme parks into the early 1990s.

Named a Disney Legend in 1993, 81-year-old Harper Goff died that same year in Los Angeles. He's memorialized in Disneyland with a window above the **Adventureland Bazaar**.

Golden Bear Lodge, aka Hungry Bear Restaurant

MAP: Bear Country/Critter Country, B/C-3

DATES: September 24, 1972–ongoing

One of the most serene dining experiences in the park debuted in 1972 as the Golden Bear Lodge, located just inside the entrance to **Bear Country**, a large plot adjacent to the **Country Bear Jamboree**. Since the big two-story restaurant was positioned along the **Rivers of America**, its upper and lower terraces offered scenic views of the passing river traffic.

By 1977 the lodge had a new name—the Hungry Bear Restaurant—as well as a large sculpture of a bear greeting guests. The restaurant has always been a counter-service establishment serving burgers, hearty sandwiches, salads, and desserts; a 2011 menu update added some popular new items, especially an acclaimed Fried Green Tomato Sandwich for vegetarians.

Golden Horseshoe

MAP: Frontierland, Fr-4

DATES: July 17, 1955–ongoing

The beautiful Golden Horseshoe has been delighting guests since **Opening Day**. Situated on a prominent **Frontierland** corner that juts toward the **Rivers of America**, the Golden Horseshoe is an eye-catching two-story structure, particularly radiant when it was painted white with gold trim (in 2010 the colors were softened to yellows and creams). The decorative finials on the roof and the long balcony with a turned balustrade add timeless elegance, while the wooden sidewalk out front grounds the building in frontier history.

Disney Legend **Harper Goff** created the glamorous interior, basing his designs on a saloon set he had already drawn up for the 1953 Doris Day film *Calamity Jane*.

The approximately 2,500-square-foot room features a curtained stage flanked by private boxes, a main floor with dining tables, and a curling balcony that forms a horseshoe shape (there's also a prominent golden horseshoe mounted above the stage).

The bar along the right-hand side serves up burgers, chili, snacks, and elaborate desserts that guests can take to their tables.

Several shows and sponsors have been involved with the Golden Horseshoe over the decades. The lighthearted *Golden Horseshoe Revue* began running on July 17, 1955 and continued for over 50,000 performances until October 12, 1986, with Pepsi-Cola the sponsor for all but the last four years. After Eastman Kodak took over sponsorship from 1982 to '84, the unsponsored revue continued deep into 1986. On November 1, 1986 the *Golden Horseshoe Jamboree* began an eight-year run, the last four sponsored by Wonder Bread. As of December 18, 1994, various acts and special presentations have appeared on the Golden Horseshoe stage, including *Woody's Roundup* (a 1999 *Toy Story*-themed show), the *Golden Horseshoe Variety Show* (2000), and **Billy Hill and the Hillbillies**.

But it's the original *Golden Horseshoe Revue* that established the building's golden reputation. It was called "the Grandest Show in the West" and "Dazzlin' Rootin' Tootin' Fun" on the **attraction poster**, "the most scintillating shows in Disneyland" in the 1955 **souvenir book**, and "the world's longest-running live stage show" in the *Guinness Book of World Records*.

The show's original stars were singers Judy Marsh and Donald Novis and comedian **Wally Boag**. Marsh played Slue-Foot Sue (who was noted on the sign out front as the building's owner) but was soon replaced by the spunky **Betty Taylor**. Irish tenor **Fulton Burley** took over for Novis from 1964 to '86. The enduring Boag stayed with the show as Sue's boyfriend, Pecos Bill, from its inception until 1982 (Taylor, Burley, and Boag would all be named Disney Legends in 1995). Supporting the actors was a small live band and a changing line-up of high-kicking cancan girls wearing gaudy dresses, colorful headwear, and black garters.

So popular was the *Golden Horseshoe Revue* that it was spotlighted in a 1962 episode of *Walt Disney's Wonderful World of Color* in honor of its 10 thousandth performance. **Walt Disney** was a fan, frequently catching the show from his private box adjacent to the stage (today's guests can use that same box). Later Golden Horseshoe shows—the *Jamboree*, the *Variety Show*, and Billy Hill—have been popular, but it's unlikely that anything will last as long the original *Golden Horseshoe Revue*.

14 Official and Unofficial Streets Inside Disneyland

1. Big Thunder Trail (walkway connecting Fantasyland and Frontierland)

2. East Center Street/West Center Street (intersects Main Street at the Market House)

3. East Plaza Street/West Plaza Street (separates the Hub from Main Street)

4. Esplanade (diagonal walkway between New Orleans Square and the Rivers of America)

5. Front Street (north-south alley on the west side of New Orleans Square)

6. Main Street (north-south street connecting Town Square and the Hub)

7. Matterhorn Way (north-south walkway between Alice in Wonderland and Matterhorn Mountain)

8. Mill View Lane (walkway around Fowler's Harbor)

9. Neighborhood Lane (residential street in Mickey's Toontown)

10. New Orleans Street (east-west walkway connecting the Golden Horseshoe and the River Belle Terrace)

11. Orleans Street (diagonal street in the center of New Orleans Square)

12. Royal Street (southernmost street in New Orleans Square)

13. Small World Way (wide walkway from Storybook Land Canal Boats to It's a Small World)

14. Tomorrowland Way (the Innoventions Dream Home is at 360 Tomorrowland Way)

Goofy's Bounce House,
aka Goofy's Playhouse

MAP: Mickey's Toontown, MT-1

DATES: January 24, 1993–ongoing

No frowns are allowed in this interactive structure. Located near the entrance to **Mickey's Toontown**, Goofy's Bounce House launched with the rest of Toontown in January 1993. Designed to look, uh, goofy, the lopsided Bounce House appears, from the outside, as a wildly discombobulated residence where all the angles are askew and a car has bashed into Goofy's mailbox. Inside, the building was originally constructed as a playpen for toddlers. To ensure it was used by only the youngest kids, there was a height maximum of four feet four inches tall, making this one of the few attractions that put an *upper* limit on a guest's height.

Within the structure, a **cast member** supervised the kids, who literally bounced off the walls. And the floor. And the furniture, since everything was inflated and made for play. The charming décor (a kite flying inside the house, and a nutty piano, to name two) and the wacky noises inside added to the silly fun.

After temporarily closing on January 7, 2005, on March 5, 2006 the Bounce House reopened as Goofy's Playhouse with an additional play area outside. Today, everything out in the yard is still screwy, suggesting the builder is a klutz, but the garden now grows pre-carved pumpkins, bell peppers that are actual bells, and ears of popcorn, suggesting the gardener is a genius. The house's interior has lost its bounce and is now more of a quiet sitting area. After all the climbing, crawling, and sliding outside, kids can cool off with icy beverages from Goofy's Free-Z Time, a trailer with flat tires that is always parked next door but only occasionally open.

Goofy's Gas Station

MAP: Mickey's Toontown, MT-7

DATES: January 24, 1993–ongoing

This toontastic rest stop in the heart of **Mickey's Toontown** offers bathrooms, water fountains, a playful car to sit in out front, and opportunities to meet the Goof himself. As with everything else in Toontown, the real fun is discovering all the humorous details worked into the décor—for example, the fish swimming inside the gas pumps, the talking water fountains, and the sign that reads, "Did we goof up your car today?" A list posted outside the station identifies the Goofy Water on tap here, including everything from Liquid Water to High Water.

Gracey, Yale
(1910–1983)

It's no coincidence that one of the characters in the 2003 film *The Haunted Mansion* is named Master Gracey; in fact, the whole eerie building carries the Gracey name. Yale Gracey created many of the memorable special effects in Disneyland's **Haunted Mansion.**

Born in China in 1910, Gracey grew up in Shanghai and studied art in California. His Disney career began in 1939 at the Disney Studios, where he worked as an art director and layout artist on films and cartoons spanning *Pinocchio* in 1940 to *Babes in Toyland* 20 years later.

Throughout the '40s and '50s, Gracey supplemented his studio commitments with hours spent devising homemade gadgets and models. An impressed **Walt Disney** invited him to bring his gadget-making talents to new attractions at Disneyland. During the '60s, Gracey added special effects to the **Carousel of Progress** and the **Pirates of the Caribbean** attractions, among others (one specific example of his ingenuity is the fiery Pirates finale that seemingly burns down the town). Though he retired in 1975, Yale Gracey continued to consult on special effects at Walt Disney World. In 1983, he died in Los Angeles at age 73; 16 years later he was inducted as a Disney Legend.

Grad Nite

DATES: June 15, 1961–ongoing (seasonal)

The long-running party known as Grad Nite is a marketing concept created in the early '60s by Disney Legend **Milt Albright**. His idea was to invite graduating high school seniors from the L.A. area to Disneyland in the late spring, charge them a special fee, keep the park open to them all night long, and sell them special souvenirs.

Obviously, filling a late-night park full of jubilant teenagers was a recipe for disruption, so to ensure proper conduct Disneyland had several strictly enforced rules, in addition to the usual no-drinking and no-bad-behavior rules. Teenage guests had to arrive on school buses with chaperones; shorts and T-shirts weren't allowed; nobody could leave the park before dawn; and nobody could nap in the park. However, as Disneyland officials soon discovered, rules are made to be broken.

The inaugural Grad Nite was held on June 15, 1961 for over 8,000 local students, who paid $3.95 each to get in. Within a few years, tens of thousands of students were coming from all over the country to party at Grad Nite. Within two decades, over 150,000 were joining in on several different spring nights. Unfortunately, the kids were enjoying the party much more than the park's security personnel. Alcohol consumption, minor vandalism, and overly affectionate couples were persistent problems that kept adults on continual alert.

Walt Disney acknowledged the challenge in a *Walt Disney Conversations* talk with Bill Ballantine about Grad Nite: "Over 50,000 young kids—the boys in coat-and-tie, the girls all in party dresses—the park is theirs. *Beautiful!* And of them all, there are only fifty or a hundred characters that we have to take care of." "Take care of" alluded to keeping intractable "characters" in a holding area or removing them from the park altogether.

Despite the occasional troublemakers, Grad Nite continues on today. Additional precautions over the years have included a "friendly frisk" at the entrance, closure of some dark attractions, and periodic sweeps through theaters to clear out drowsy teens. New events have included a Blast Off pre-party before the main party begins, special **fireworks** shows, new dance areas, big-name musicians, a new sponsor (Honda), and, starting in 2013, a new Grad Nite location (Disney California Adventure).

Even though the list of rules and dress codes is longer than ever, the event continues to be a popular tradition (the 5 millionth Grad Niter arrived in 2009). For many teens, high school isn't over until they've graduated Grad Nite.

Grand Canyon Diorama

MAP: Tomorrowland, T-17

DATES: March 31, 1958–ongoing

While Disneyland's **souvenir books** have always located this attraction in their **Main Street** section, and while the images and animals in the diorama seem more suited to **Frontierland**, the beautiful Grand Canyon Diorama is actually situated in **Tomorrowland** behind **Space Mountain**. The diorama lines one interior wall of a long tunnel that sits along the perimeter railroad track just east of the Main Street station.

Like many other attractions in the park, the Grand Canyon Diorama was inspired by a Disney movie—in this case, the Oscar-winning 1958 documentary *Grand Canyon*. As in that documentary, the diorama pairs visually stunning images with the clip-clopping of horses to portray the "On the Trail" passage from Ferde Grofé's *Grand Canyon Suite*. The Grand Canyon Diorama presents a 90-second pass along one rim of the immense canyon. The view includes a sunrise, ancient cliff-dweller ruins, a storm, a 180-degree rainbow, and a sunset, all separated from the train by a wall of glass.

Combining a detailed 300-foot-wide, 34-foot-tall background painting with dozens of foreground animals and hundreds of rocks, bushes, and other props, the diorama was touted for years as the longest in the world. With a 1958 price tag estimated at $375,000, it was also most likely one of the world's most expensive; certainly it is still one of the world's most realistic.

Disney Legend **Claude Coats** was its primary creator and painter, while the cougar, eagles, skunks, mule deer, snakes, and other desert animals were the products of a taxidermist (none of them are **Audio-Animatronic** machines). A 1968 issue of *Vacationland* magazine proclaimed that creating the Grand Canyon canvas took 4,800 man hours and 300 gallons of paint.

At the official opening, a band, park officials, and Native Americans in native dress dedicated the new D-ticket attraction (see **ticket books**) with a blessing-of-the-trains ceremony. The diorama has changed very little since then. However, it got a mighty supplement in 1966 when the new **Primeval World Diorama** and its impressive Audio-Animatronic dinosaurs were added onto the next section of train track, thus doubling the diorama drama.

Grandma's Baby Shop

MAP: Main Street, MS-13

DATES: July 17, 1955–September 1955

A charming shop for infant clothes and accessories was born on **Opening Day**. Unfortunately, Grandma's Baby Shop, still an infant at barely two months old, was the first store on **Main Street** to fold. By autumn, the **Silhouette Studio** had taken over Grandma's spot near today's **Disney Clothiers, Ltd.**

Great Moments with Mr. Lincoln

MAP: Town Square, TS-9

DATES: July 18, 1965–spring 2005; December 2009–ongoing

A decade of advances in **Audio-Animatronic** technology culminated in 1964 with the creation of a mechanical Abraham Lincoln. Lincoln was originally planned for the Hall of Presidents in the **Liberty Street** area, an attraction that never came to be at Disneyland (Liberty Square and the Hall of Presidents would exist later at Walt Disney World). When the A-A Lincoln did appear for the first time in public, it was being used by the State of Illinois in its pavilion for the 1964–1965 New York World's Fair.

The life-size electronic effigy incorporated everything Disney designers had learned from the mechanical animals they'd made for Disneyland's **Jungle Cruise**, **Nature's Wonderland**, and **Enchanted Tiki Room**. Lincoln, however, was by far the most ambitious Audio-Animatronic project yet. Not only did he look and sound exactly like the very famous, very dignified public figure (Lincoln's life mask was the model for the face), he also had a wide range of complex motions. Mid-1960s viewers, expecting a sitting Lincoln figure that would merely swivel its head and perhaps blink, must have been utterly astonished to see the Great Emancipator stand up, move his arms, and deliver an impassioned speech that utilized hand gestures and remarkably subtle facial movements.

The August 1963 issue of *National Geographic* called Lincoln's realism "alarming," detailing the engineering wonders of the 14 hydraulic lines running through the body and 16 air lines working inside the mechanical head to produce 15 different facial expressions. Some members of the press were so amazed by the verisimilitude that they invented their own details about what Lincoln could do, crediting the seemingly sentient figure with walking around and shaking hands with front-row guests.

While the robotic Lincoln couldn't do all that, designing the A-A figure to per-

form as he did was an extreme challenge to Disney's Imagineers. Over two years of development went into the project; yet even in final testing Lincoln was still capable of flattening a chair when he sat on it. After the public's overwhelmingly positive reception at the fair, Walt Disney had an even more sophisticated Lincoln rushed to Disneyland's **Opera House** for the park's 1965 **Tencennial**. Great Moments with Mr. Lincoln opened as an E-ticket attraction, though anyone under 17 years old could get in free thanks to a special coupon in kids' **ticket books**. The 13-minute show, presented by Lincoln Savings & Loan, began with a short biographical film, featured a dramatic monologue by the electronic Lincoln that blended excerpts from four of the former president's speeches, and ended with a 50-foot post-show mural that celebrated American freedom.

Although most audiences loved the presentation, some elite academics were scathing in their sardonic criticism of Disney's Lincoln, insisting that the robotic figure diminished the venerated president (Richard Schickel's provocative and much-discussed 1968 book *The Disney Version* unleashed a particularly venomous attack).

Mr. Lincoln "retired" on New Year's Day in 1973, when **The Walt Disney Story** moved into the Opera House. However, fans were so insistent about bringing the president back that Lincoln returned in 1975, generating the longest title of any attraction so far: The Walt Disney Story, Featuring Great Moments with Mr. Lincoln. Updates in 1984 and 2001 enhanced the presentation with new special effects and better sound. Starting in 2005, the celebratory movie *Disneyland: The First 50 Magical Years* temporarily replaced Lincoln, but a further-enhanced Lincoln returned in 2009.

Lincoln's voice was performed by Royal Dano, a character actor with a long career in movies and TV shows. Dano, who was 42 when he first recorded the Lincoln vocals, died in 1994 at age 71. **Paul Frees** spoke the original narration introducing the attraction, and **Buddy Baker** provided the heart-swelling music. As for the mechanical president, Disney Legends **Roger Broggie**, **Harriet Burns**, **Marc Davis**, **Blaine Gibson**, **Bob Gurr**, and **Wathel Rogers** helped make Great Moments great.

Guest Relations

MAP: Town Square, TS-4, P-7

DATES: 1955–ongoing

Disneyland's 1956 **souvenir book** was the first to note the existence of Guest Relations inside **City Hall**. It's still there, serving as an information center for guests who have questions, are looking to file a complaint or a compliment about a **cast member**, or require maps of the park or the surrounding area. Disney Legend **Robert Jani** originally headed up Guest Relations, with another Disney Legend, **Cicely Rigdon**, taking over in the '60s.

Outside the park, a second Guest Relations office has existed since the mid-'80s for visitors who have not yet walked through the gates. This office was originally located in a small building to the right of the main **entrance** to Disneyland, but Guest Relations then moved to the left of the main entrance to Disney California Adventure. There the media, **Club 33** members, and anybody else who needed answers before entering the park could get help. While construction was underway at Disney California Adventure in 2011 and 2012, this Guest Relations office relocated to a nearby ticket booth.

Gurr, Bob
(1932–)

Any guest who's ever ridden in any of Disneyland's trains, bobsleds, or **Autopia** cars knows Bob Gurr's work. Gurr is the man who created and engineered the park's transportation.

Born in Los Angeles in 1932, Gurr grew up fascinated with machines and automobiles. After graduating from college in 1952 with a degree in industrial design, he promptly started his own company and found himself consulting on the new Autopia in **Tomorrowland**. Soon Gurr was designing the attraction's cars. From then on, he worked full-time to make a reality of the elaborate vehicles dreamed up by **Walt Disney**, including such diverse devices as the hovering **Flying Saucers** and the old-time **Main Street Vehicles**.

In the '50s, Gurr transformed an automobile into the **Viewliner** train, redesigned a boxy German monorail train into Disneyland's sleek **Monorail** (and even piloted the first test drive), drew up the original passenger coaches for the park's railroad, made **Mr. Toad's** wild cars, and built the bobsleds for **Matterhorn Mountain**. In the '60s Gurr designed several old-time electric runabouts for Walt Disney's personal use and was one of the wizards behind **Great Moments with Mr. Lincoln**. He also worked on the **Omnimover** pods for **Adventure Thru Inner Space** and the **Haunted Mansion.**

Retiring from Disney in 1981, Gurr worked on creations for other theme parks and special events, among them the King Kong attraction at Universal Studios and the UFO at the '84 Summer Olympics. Still a consultant on Disney attractions, Bob Gurr was named a Disney Legend in 2004.

Hallmark Card Shop

MAP: Main Street, MS-14

DATES: June 15, 1960–January 6, 1985

Three business have operated out of the attractive building designed by John Hench on the northeast corner of Main Street and East Center Street. Two of those businesses were card shops, starting with **Gibson Greeting Cards** from 1955 to 1959. When Gibson bid farewell, the Hallmark Card Shop took over in mid-1960.

It was probably only a matter of time before Hallmark showed up at the park. Founded in 1910, the company had been making Disney-themed greeting cards since 1931. Also, its headquarters were in Kansas City, where **Walt Disney** had spent some of his childhood and later started his Laugh-O-Gram animation company. Disneyland's Hallmark Card Shop continued for almost a quarter of a century, closing in early 1985 to make way for a big new retailer, **Disney Clothiers, Ltd.**

Hall of Aluminum Fame

MAP: Tomorrowland, T-24

DATES: December 1955–July 1960

In Disneyland's first year, **Walt Disney** needed some **Tomorrowland** sponsors who could provide their own exhibits, thus freeing him to concentrate his time and money on other aspects of the park. Five months after **Opening Day**, the Kaiser Aluminum & Chemical Company debuted its shiny Hall of Aluminum Fame in the same educational-exhibit building that already housed Monsanto's **Hall of Chemistry**. This building, prime real estate just inside the Tomorrowland entrance, would eventually house **Star Tours**.

Early **souvenir books** described Kaiser's walk-through Hall as an "entertaining exhibit" of "today's and tomorrow's uses of the vital metal." Guests first encountered a sign announcing "the brightest star in the world of metals" next to a 40-foot slanting aluminum cylinder that looked like a giant telescope, complete with oversize dials and two narrow finder scopes mounted along the top.

The telescope was actually the entrance to the Hall—guests walked through the base and entered a room lined with displays showing the history and uses of aluminum. A six-foot-wide "time sphere" in the center of the room presented images of men using and even wearing aluminum. Above the room, a cascade of aluminum stars streaked past exposed rafters and beams. Enjoying the proceedings from a pedestal near a wall was a three-foot-tall grinning aluminum pig named Kap. Wearing work clothes and holding a wrench, Kap made a cute mascot (though he was not a Disney character). "Kap" was an acronym for Kaiser Aluminum Pig, "pig" being the term for the impure base alumina that is refined into pure aluminum. Like the Hall itself, Kap was a strained attempt at making science and industry entertaining to kids and laypeople.

Five years after its opening, the lights dimmed on the brightest metal's exhibit in favor of less cerebral **Fun Fotos** displays.

Hall of Chemistry

MAP: Tomorrowland, T-24

DATES: July 17, 1955–September 19, 1966

Of the four Monsanto attractions that existed in **Tomorrowland** in the 1950s and '60s, the Hall of Chemistry was the only one to debut on **Opening Day** (the **House of the Future** opened two years later, followed by **Fashions and Fabrics Through the Ages** in '65 and **Adventure Thru Inner Space** in '67).

The Hall of Chemistry's big rectangular building inside Tomorrowland's entrance was adorned on the outside with the red Monsanto logo and space age atoms. Inside, the Hall was a free walk-through exhibit that featured informational displays demonstrating how the modern world benefited from chemical engineering. Oversized test tubes, electrified wall displays, and a metaphorical arm reaching across the ceiling all contributed to the educational experience. "Carpet makes it home" was Monsanto's pitch for synthetic floor coverings.

As pedestrian as the Hall of Chemistry sounds today, it did last for over a decade and must have educated millions of visitors. The attraction finally gave way in 1966 and was replaced by the dramatic Adventure Thru Inner Space attraction the following year. Today's guests will find **Star Tours** where corporate chemistry was once celebrated.

Halloween Time

DATES: September 29, 2006–ongoing

Other Southern California parks began celebrating Halloween with month-long activities as far back as 1973, the year Knott's Berry Farm debuted its seasonal "Knott's Scary Farm" transformation. Surprisingly, Disneyland didn't do any park-wide Halloweening during the 20th century. However, in the 21st century Disneyland executives decided to scare up some off-season crowds of their own. On September 29, 2006 it was finally time for Halloween Time.

The Disney difference was the target audience; while other parks aimed their Halloween attractions at teens and offered intense thrills and chills, Disneyland captured the family audience with gentler activities that were as fun as they were scary. Those activities have included special shows at the temporary Woody's Halloween Roundup in **Frontierland**, a seasonal re-theming of **Space Mountain** with Ghost Galaxy décor, special Halloween-themed foods, and a playful Haunted Mansion Holiday overlay (continuing a **Haunted Mansion** tradition begun in 2001). In recent years a Halloween Screams fireworks display and a costume party for special ticket-holders have added to the nighttime festivities. Pumpkins, naturally, appear everywhere in the park, beginning with a 16-foot-tall Mickey-shaped jack-o'-lantern on Main Street and continuing with hundreds of smaller pumpkins in every corner of the park. In addition, windows and lampposts are adorned with Halloween décor, and stores are stocked with spooky items.

Once Halloween is over and Halloween Time runs out, there is barely a month left to transform the park for the winter holidays with elaborate new decorations. So popular is Halloween Time that it's been starting earlier every year (on September 16th in 2011). And that hoped-for surge in October attendance? It jumps about 40 percent compared to pre-Halloween Time years, with comparable spikes in merchandise and food sales.

Happiest Homecoming on Earth

DATES: May 5, 2005–September 30, 2006

In honor of its 50th birthday, Disneyland staged the Happiest Homecoming on Earth, a comprehensive celebration that lasted from May 5, 2005 through September 30, 2006. Julie Andrews served as the official ambassador for the 18-month party. Among the special events and new shows were celebratory decorations appearing on **Sleeping Beauty Castle** and other significant buildings; Walt Disney's Parade of Dreams, held daily; a nightly fireworks spectacular called Remember . . . Dreams Come True; and *Disneyland: The First 50 Magical Years*, a new documentary featuring Steve Martin and shown all day long in the **Opera House**. Disneyland welcomed one new attraction in 2005 (**Buzz Lightyear Astro Blasters**), the reopening of updated favorites, and a plethora of 50th-anniversary merchandise.

On July 16th, 2005 fans started lining up for entry the next morning—the 50th anniversary of **Opening Day**. Elsewhere, Disney parks around the globe honored the Disneyland tradition with Happiest Celebration on Earth festivities of their own. One day after Disneyland's 50th-birthday party ended, the **Year of a Million Dreams** promotion began.

Harbour Galley

MAP: Bear Country/Critter Country, B/C-1
DATES: July 1989–ongoing

In 1989 a small counter-service eatery called the Harbour Galley opened near the **Haunted Mansion**. The riverfront location was on a walkway named Mill View Lane, a reference to both Disney Legend **Joe Fowler** (this was reportedly the name of the

street he lived on in Florida) and the Old Mill over on **Tom Sawyer Island**.

As the maritime sign out front announced, the Harbour Galley offered "delectable seafood specialties," including Cajun popcorn shrimp, fish and chips, and chowder. Unfortunately, business was often so slow that the Harbour Galley was frequently closed. In mid-2001, while still retaining its name, the restaurant transformed into a McDonald's outlet serving only fries and beverages (an abbreviated McMenu similar to the one in **Westward Ho Conestoga Wagon Fries** from 1998 to 2008). After closing in September 2008, the Harbour Galley reopened nine months later, with a small soup and salad menu replacing everything from McDonald's.

The Haunted Mansion

MAP: New Orleans Square, NOS-12

DATES: August 9, 1969–ongoing

One of the most eagerly awaited days in park history was the debut of the Haunted Mansion. The public had been hearing about the attraction since 1961 and had been staring at its gleaming, unfinished exterior in **New Orleans Square** since 1963. When it finally opened at the height of the summer tourist season in 1969, the exciting new attraction drew some of Disneyland's largest crowds ever.

Tentative plans for some kind of haunted house had actually preceded those for Disneyland itself—**Harper Goff's** 1951 concept drawing depicted a haunted mansion on a hill, and **Marvin Davis's** 1953 illustration placed a rickety haunted house at the end of **Main Street**.

Two years after Disneyland opened, **Ken Anderson** came up with a basic design and a story to go with it. Expecting a New Orleans section to be built in Disneyland at some point, Anderson drew a Southern mansion and invented a plot that included the Headless Horseman and a murderous sea captain who ended up hanging himself (most of this plot was abandoned in the end, but some individual elements endured, such as the hanging corpse seen early in the attraction).

As building designs evolved, **Walt Disney** quickly rejected any that portrayed dilapidated mansions reminiscent of the creepy haunted houses in films. Disneyland structures, he decreed, would not look run-down and neglected. In 1961, Disney announced that the Haunted Mansion would open within two years, and in fact, an elegant, three-story mansion with four stately columns was built in 1963 near **Adventureland**. Guests were tantalized, and all decade long the park's **souvenir books** touted the attraction with an eerie painting by **Sam McKim**.

In reality, work on the Haunted Mansion had stopped. Dedicating himself and his design team to creating four new attractions for the 1964–1965 New York World's Fair, Walt Disney put the Haunted Mansion on indefinite hold. He stirred up excitement once again when he re-announced it in 1965 on an episode of his *Wonderful World of Color* TV show, and even mentioned specific details, such as a Museum of the Weird (which was never built). But not until 1967 was real Mansion construction underway and accelerating.

Using ideas approved by Disney before he passed away in 1966, an all-star team of future Disney Legends ran with the project: **John Hench** was the overall supervisor; **Bill Justice** developed **Audio-Animatronic** ghouls; **Fred Joerger** made plaster models; **Rolly Crump**, **Bill Martin**, and **Yale Gracey** designed scary special effects; **Marc Davis** added whimsical touches; **Claude Coats** designed the spooky interiors; and **Buddy Baker** and **X Atencio** wrote the "Grim Grinning Ghost" theme song sung by

Thurl Ravenscroft and the Mello Men (Atencio also penned the Ghost Host's script).

From its genesis to its actual debut, the Haunted Mansion underwent two major revisions. The first came when it gradually transformed from being completely frightening to being a half-scary/half-funny "happy haunt" attraction. The second came when it changed from a walk-through exhibit into an **Omnimover** attraction. The Omnimover system—basically semi-enclosed pods on a conveyor belt—had already proven itself as a safe, efficient way to move crowds through the popular **Adventure Thru Inner Space** attraction in **Tomorrowland.** Realizing that pedestrians would move too slowly through the mansion's interiors (especially if those pedestrians were frightened or fascinated), designers decided to convey thousands of "foolish mortals" per hour via Omnimover "Doom Buggy" pods that would swivel on pre-programmed command.

Once inside the building and past the foyer, guests step into a "stretching room" that lowers them 15 feet down in an elevator to a 90-foot subterranean walkway. This is the "portrait gallery." Besides showing off clever intaglio busts and double-image paintings, what the gallery really does is lead guests under the park's railroad tracks, effectively taking them beyond the perimeter of the park's original layout to a one-acre "show building" next door. There, 131 Doom

---

The Haunted Mansion's Main Outdoor Cemetery

Interred in the Wall:

Theo Later
U. R. Gone
Ray N. Carnation
Dustin T. Dust
Levi Tation
I. M. Mortal
G. I. Missyou
I. Trudy Departed
I. L. Beback
Rustin Peece
M. T. Tomb

Pets with Tombstones:

Bat: "Freddie the Bat, 1847, We'll Miss You"
Dog: "Buddy, Our friend until the end"
Fish: "October 10, 1867"
Frog: "Old Flybait, He Croaked, August 9, 1869"
Pig: "Rosie: She was a poor little Pig but she bought the Farm, 1849"
Rat: "In Memory of My Rat Whom I Loved, Now He Resides in the Realms Up Above"
Skunk: "Beloved Lilac, Long on Curiosity . . . Short on Common Scents, 1847"
Snake: "Here lies my snake whose fatal mistake was frightening the gardener who carried a rake"
Spider: "Here lies Long Legged Jeb, Got tangled up in his very own Web"

Buggies carry guests through haunted hallways, past the haunted attic and haunted ballroom, into a haunted cemetery, and back to an exit ramp.

Next to Pirates of the Caribbean, the Haunted Mansion was the most ambitious and complex attraction of its time. Just before it opened to the public in mid-1969, the anticipation was so intense that stories circulated about viewers who had died of fright on preview tours. When the attraction finally opened, guests were welcomed by elegantly dressed **cast members** who intensified the suspense with their uniformly somber demeanor (they are encouraged *not* to smile).

The Haunted Mansion quickly became the park's most popular attraction—on August 16, 1969, one week after officially opening, a record 82,516 guests roamed Disneyland—all of them, it seemed, ready to line up for hours to get scared for eight minutes by Haunted Mansion horrors (that attendance record lasted for almost two decades; though Disneyland stopped giving attendance figures in 1984, it's believed that the record was finally eclipsed in 1987, when **Star Tours** debuted).

Over the years, a large group of loyal fans has unearthed and disclosed some of the Haunted Mansion's secrets: Walt Disney himself considered doing the narration later performed by **Paul Frees**; the Madame Leota floating-head illusion is the face of Leota Toombs, a Disney Imagineer (the voice is provided by veteran actress Eleanor Audley, who added vocals to the films *Cinderella* and *Sleeping Beauty*); the organ in the ballroom is the one used in the film *20,000 Leagues Under the Sea*; the humorous tombstones formerly in the cemetery out front referred to actual Imagineers; in addition to the main pet cemetery in the **queue** area to the left of the building, there's a small hidden cemetery to the right; the singing busts have names—Cousin Algernon, Ned Nub, Phineas P. Pock, Uncle Theodore, Rollo Rumkin (Walt Disney's visage is not on a broken bust, as rumored, that's actually singer Thurl Ravenscroft); the cake on the banquet table has 13 candles; the maritime weathervane atop the Haunted Mansion refers to the original murderous-mariner storyline; and at one time live cast members in costume (including a suit of armor) would jump out at guests to enliven the experience for repeat visitors (one "secret" that's been long-rumored but is untrue concerns the horse-drawn hearse out front—it's not from Brigham Young's funeral).

The venerable mansion gets revised occasionally. In 2001, the building was dressed up with *The Nightmare Before Christmas* décor for the Haunted Mansion Holiday; in 2006, high-tech updates in the attic caused portraits to vanish before guests' eyes. The soundtrack has also been revised. But no matter how it changes, the Haunted Mansion continues to exert an irresistible pull on guests, and they still "hurry ba-ack, hurry ba-ack," just as the Little Leota figure near the exit has encouraged them to do for over four decades.

Hench, John
(1908–2004)

Many historians have concluded that no person other than Walt Disney, had more influence on Disney theme parks, or understood them better, than John Hench. And no one appreciated Disneyland more than this erudite designer. "Disneyland is our greatest achievement," Hench wrote in *Designing Disney*. "Disneyland was first and set the pattern for others to follow."

An Iowan born in 1908, Hench attended art institutes in New York, San Francisco, and Los Angeles before joining Disney Studios in 1939. There he worked as an artist and story editor for almost 20 years on animation classics like *Fantasia*, *Dumbo*, and *Peter Pan*. Hench also helped with the Oscar-winning special effects on *20,000 Leagues Under the Sea*.

In 1954 Hench started designing Disneyland projects and shaping the park's aesthetics, which meant that everything from attraction layout to garden landscaping to color schemes was within his purview. He was the designer or chief planner for the **Moonliner**, the **Snow White Wishing Well and Grotto**, **New Orleans Square**, the **Carousel of Progress**, **Tomorrowland**, the **Haunted Mansion**, and many buildings on **Main Street**. **Cast member** costumes, **queue** areas, **attraction posters**, and even **restrooms** were sketched by John Hench. The nation got a glimpse of him working on **Plaza Inn** interiors on a 1965 episode of *Walt Disney's Wonderful World of Color*.

Hench, however, was quick to point out that **Walt Disney** was the real designer of everything in Disneyland. "By the time you got your ideas back from Walt," Hench said in *Remembering Walt*, "you wouldn't recognize them as your own. . . . In the end, the production was all his."

Outside Disneyland, Hench was Walt Disney's right-hand man in developing the opening and closing ceremonies of the 1960 Olympic Games. He also helped with the new exhibits for the 1964–1965 New York World's Fair and was a key contributor as other Disney parks opened around the world. As Mickey Mouse's official portrait artist, he created new commemorative paintings for the star's 25th, 50th, 60th, and 70th birthdays.

Named a Disney Legend in 1990, John Hench was long respected as the wise mentor to younger Imagineers. In 1999 one of Disneyland's greatest contributors celebrated a 60-year Disney career, and in 2003 he eloquently summarized what he'd learned in a retrospective book called *Designing Disney*. The following year John Hench died in Burbank at age 95.

Heraldry Shoppe, aka Castle Heraldry
MAP: Fantasyland, Fa-4, Fa-30
DATES: Ca. 1995–ongoing
Over the years, **Fantasyland** has offered several resources for genealogical research.

While the now-absent **Names Unraveled** service looked up names, the current Heraldry Shoppe enables guests to investigate family history. The Heraldry Shoppe has also been called Castle Heraldry due to its original location within the entrance to **Sleeping Beauty Castle**. After a decade there, it moved into the castle courtyard next to **Peter Pan Flight**, a prominent spot that once upon a time housed **Merlin's Magic Shop**. **Three Fairies Magic Crystals** replaced the Heraldry Shoppe inside the castle in 2006.

Heraldry got its start in the Middle Ages as a way for English families to trace their heritage, establish their ruling status, and define their coats of arms. At Disneyland, guests can learn the geographic and historical origins of their family name, check out the family crest, and purchase an attractive hard copy of all the pertinent information. Also available are souvenir coats of arms, $150 swords, personalized plaques, and more.

Kids may get bored in this regal shop, but adults will be fascinated. Operated by a lessee, the Historical Research Center, the shop occasionally closes even when other Fantasyland shops are open.

Hidden Mickeys

The term Hidden Mickey is something of a misnomer, since the Mickeys that are supposedly hidden are actually in plain sight. A Hidden Mickey is a three-circled shape patterned after Mickey Mouse's silhouetted head and round ears. However, simple mouse ears placed on a different character, or the appearance of Mickey's oversized gloves or shoes, can also qualify as Hidden Mickeys.

The Hidden Mickey concept probably started on a small scale at Disneyland in the 1970s when Disney Imagineers planted a few for their own amusement. But as interest in Disneyland trivia intensified over the decades, the Imagineers began incorporating Hidden Mickeys into Disneyland's architecture and attractions with increasing

frequency, to be discovered by enthusiastic guests. By now, dozens of Hidden
Mickeys of varying sizes, shapes, and
subtlety are scattered throughout the park. Several unofficial fan websites catalogue
new Hidden Mickeys as they appear in the park.

Hidden Mickeys are distinguished from "actual" Mickeys that have been obviously
worked into the décor or design (the large parterre at the **entrance**, for example)
or that constitute the shape of a product (a Mickey Mouse-shaped lollipop wouldn't
count). Finding a true Hidden Mickey usually requires careful observation and repeat
visits for confirmation.

For Disneyland's 50th Golden Anniversary in 2005, 50 additional blue and gold
Hidden Mickeys were incorporated into the park in various locations. These temporary
Mickeys were much more conspicuous than their hidden brethren, and in fact **City
Hall** even provided a list of locations to help guests find them all.

Hills Bros. Coffee House and Coffee Garden

MAP: Town Square, TS-7

DATES: June 13, 1958–December 1976

Eight months after Maxwell House closed its coffee shop on **Town Square**, Hills Bros., a San Francisco coffee company founded in the early 1900s, reopened it. Because it had an expanded outdoor area, the park's **souvenir books** dubbed this the Hills Bros. Coffee House and Coffee Garden. The location was ideal for a morning coffee business, since it faced guests as they entered the park through the east tunnel and headed to **Main Street**. In 1976 Hills Bros. headed for the **Market House**, and the **Town Square Café** took over this spot as a full-service sit-down restaurant.

Hobbyland

MAP: Tomorrowland, T-20

DATES: September 4, 1955–January 1966

For over 10 years, the open area south of the **Flight Circle** in **Tomorrowland** was the site of a freestanding retail area known as Hobbyland. If Hobbyland were in place today, it would begin outside the **Star Trader** store and extend to **Cosmic Waves**.

Lackluster in design, Hobbyland was nothing more than about a dozen countertops separated by aluminum struts that supported temporary fiberglass roofs. What interested its devotees, however, was the Hobbyland treasure they could mine. Hobbyland's jewels were its model kits. Guests sifted through a comprehensive collection that included everything from cars and ships to rockets and dinosaurs, plus some of the motorized vehicles from the nearby Flight Circle.

In 1966 this whole area was closed off for the extensive Tomorrowland remodeling that would put the **PeopleMover** and new walkways where Hobbyland's simple booths had once dazzled model-makers.

Holidayland

MAP: Park, P-13

DATES: June 16, 1957–September 1961

One of Disneyland's most unusual areas wasn't actually in the park. Holidayland was located outside Disneyland's perimeter **berm**, in a field west of **Frontierland**.

Holidayland's nine acres were devoted to simple, inexpensive outdoor family fun. Minimally landscaped, the area offered refreshment stands, picnic tables, a baseball field, volleyball nets, a children's playground, and horseshoe pits, as well as square dancing (plans for ice skating and some other seasonal activities never came to fruition). Swift, the same company that sponsored the **Market House**, **Red Wagon Inn**, and **Chicken Plantation**, sold picnic baskets (which, surprisingly, included beer). Dominating Holidayland was a traditional red-striped circus tent where special events, ranging from bingo to performances by the Mouseketeers, could be held. This tent was the same one used for the short-lived **Mickey Mouse Club Circus** in **Fantasyland**.

Holidayland was intended to attract big family reunions or, ideally, corporations that could buy up to 7,000 tickets for their employees and hold day-long company picnics. Admission to Holidayland, unfortunately, did not include admission to Disneyland. It did, however, include access to a special Disneyland entrance where a park admission ticket could be purchased and then a path into Frontierland could be taken under the train tracks. This was the only time in Disneyland's history that guests could enter the park in a location other than the front gates or via the **Monorail** station in **Tomorrowland**.

Disney Legend **Milt Albright**, who would later devise more successful group-sales strategies, supervised Holidayland in its early years. Ticket sales for this isolated area were always a challenge, and so in the fall of 1961, its circus tent already destroyed in a storm, Holidayland closed. Guests still visit the old Holidayland site, though they aren't aware of it; this is where the "show buildings" for the **Haunted Mansion** and **Pirates of the Caribbean** are hidden.

Holiday Season

DATES: November 24, 1955–ongoing (seasonal)

The winter holiday season is one of the park's best-attended times of the year. Since 1955, the centerpiece of the celebration has been a perfectly symmetrical, 60-foot-tall artificial tree erected in **Town Square**. At one time the tree was entirely white, but guests today will find a green tree densely decorated with thousands of lights and lavish ornaments.

For its first holiday season, the park held a festival called Christmas at Disneyland from November 24, 1955 until January 8, 1956. The festival featured a special holiday **parade** and a concert held daily in an open space west of **Sleeping Beauty Castle** called the Christmas Bowl. As described on a 1955 promotional flier, this holiday concert featured "leading church and school choral groups from all over the West." When the Christmas Bowl site became home to the **Plaza Gardens** in 1956, the strolling **Charles Dickens Carolers** took holiday music to **Main Street**.

Disneyland's winter celebration has continually expanded over the decades. From 1961 until the mid-'70s, a sparkling 44,000-pound star, helicoptered into position and visible from the Santa Ana Freeway, topped the **Matterhorn** until energy concerns ended its long run. Moreover, several TV specials, such as 1976's "Christmas in Disneyland with Art Carney," have spread the cheer far outside the park. "Disneyland Around the Seasons," a 1966 episode of *Walt Disney's Wonderful World of Color*, showcased that year's holiday parade and Candlelight Procession.

The latter event has become the season's inspirational highlight. First performed in

1958, the Candlelight Procession sends legions of carolers and candles down a garlanded **Main Street**. Culminating the procession is a dramatic retelling of the traditional story of Christmas. Dozens of celebrities have served as the event's narrator, starting with actor Dennis Morgan for the first decade and then diversifying to include such stars as John Wayne, Henry Fonda, Mickey Rooney, Cary Grant, Charlton Heston, Dick Van Dyke, and Gregory Peck. Equally emotional is the Massed Choir Ceremony that combines local choirs, the Charles Dickens Carolers, an orchestra, and the Living Christmas Tree stacked with volunteer **cast members** who audition and then practice together as a choir.

The park's holiday season parades are among the most popular of all the holiday events. Parades from previous decades include the Christmas in Many Lands Parade (1957–1964), Fantasy on Parade (1965–1976 and 1980–1985), and the Very Merry Christmas Parade (1977–1979 and 1987–2000). These have included such familiar favorites as marching toy soldiers, dancing gingerbread cookies, and Disney princesses with their princes.

During the holidays, Disneyland twinkles with beautiful decorations and lights, and there are celebrations around every corner. The sheer variety of joyous events ensures the park's popularity—there's literally something for everybody, no matter what the age or interest. Here's a partial list of 2010's holiday proceedings: Believe . . . In Holiday Magic Fireworks Spectacular, including "snow" for the finale; the **Haunted Mansion** Holiday, with Jack Skellington dressed as Sandy Claws; festive foods, such as "snowman shortbread," in the **Blue Ribbon Bakery**; new holiday gifts and collectibles sold in the park's stores; a twice-daily Christmas Fantasy Parade; Mr. and Mrs. Claus with live reindeer in **Frontierland**; dozens of decorated Christmas trees of various sizes scattered throughout the park; **Sleeping Beauty Castle** adorned with "icicles" and special illumination; and 50,000 holiday lights decorating the **It's a Small World** façade. All of this is on display in addition to Disneyland's regular shows, attractions, and live entertainments—even Scrooge would be impressed.

Honey, I Shrunk the Audience

MAP: Tomorrowland, T-19

DATES: May 22, 1998–February 2010

Replacing the decommissioned *Captain EO* in the **Magic Eye Theater** was *Honey, I Shrunk the Audience*, a Kodak-hosted 3-D movie that debuted with the rest of the remodeled **Tomorrowland** in 1998.

Like *EO*, *Honey* had been shown in Florida before it was brought west to Anaheim. During the film's 18 minutes, guests wore the obligatory 3-D glasses and met emcee

Dr. Nigel Channing (Eric Idle of *Monty Python's Flying Circus*). Channing then brought in the Imagination Institute's Inventor of the Year, Professor Wayne Szalinski (Rick Moranis, reprising his role from the *Honey, I Shrunk the Kids* and *Honey, I Blew Up the Kid* movies). Soon the nutty but well-intentioned Szalinski accidentally miniaturized the theater to lunchbox size, and merriment ensued as the audience viewed everything in the

film—the cast, the props, a dog, a lunging snake—as if it were gigantic.

Technologically more advanced than *Captain EO*, *Honey I Shrunk the Audience* was synchronized with several special effects built into the theater itself, such as jets under the seats that blasted air around audience members' feet to simulate scurrying mice. But *EO*, it turned out, wasn't gone for good. Michael Jackson's death on June 25, 2009, revived interest in the pop star and catalyzed the return of *Captain EO* in early 2010.

House of the Future

MAP: Tomorrowland, T-1

DATES: June 12, 1957–December 1, 1967

In *The Graduate*, Benjamin Braddock (played by Dustin Hoffman) received one key word of advice as he considered his coming career: plastics. Anyone who saw Disneyland's House of the Future might have summarized modern living the same way.

The second Monsanto-sponsored attraction at Disneyland (after the **Hall of Chemistry**), the House of the Future was a free walk-through exhibit located outside the entrance to **Tomorrowland**. The attraction stood on a 256-square-foot raised platform surrounded by contemporary gardens and a winding pool that collectively covered about a quarter of an acre. The pool wasn't just there for aesthetics—its water was part of the building's cooling system.

From above, the 1,280-square-foot, three-bedroom, two-bath home was shaped like a graceful plus sign. Its four compartmentalized modules were each eight feet tall and sixteen feet long and extended from a central core outwards over open air. These smooth, streamlined modules ("half jet fuselage, half legume," according to writer P. J. O'Rourke) could be supplemented with additional modules to accommodate the expanding family. An optional rotating platform enabled inhabitants to spin their house to face any direction.

During its decade-long existence, the House of the Future welcomed some 20 million guests (more than the entire population of California at the time). Instead of a fun, Disney-designed attraction, guests found a serious mass-produced tract home designed by MIT and Monsanto engineers to show off technological advances from

Monsanto's Plastics Division. One of the strengths of the house was, in fact, its strength: when it came time to dismantle the entire structure in 1967, engineers discovered that the four extending wings of the house had drooped less than a quarter-inch, despite all the heavy traffic. The two-week demolition had to be done by hand with crowbars and saws, because the wrecking ball swung at the house merely bounced off its sides.

Pre-recorded narration playing inside the home bragged that nearly everything on view was artificial and adjustable. Fixtures in the bathroom and shelves in the cabinets could be raised or lowered at the push of a button, and the climate-controlled air could be instantly warmed, cooled, purified, or scented. The futuristic communications included an intercom, push-button speaker phones, picture phones, a sound system in the shower, and a large, wall-mounted TV screen. Interior illumination was provided by "panalescent fixtures," "trans-ceiling polarized panels," and mobile lights that could "bathe each room with the glow of natural sunlight." The sleek furniture was made from vinyl and urethane, the drapes from nylon. Highlights in the "step saver" kitchen included an "ultrasonic dishwasher" and a microwave oven.

Although the House of the Future may seem silly or dated now, at the time it was an ambitious attempt to make the spirit of the space age real and practical, which is what **Walt Disney** would later try to do with the **Monorail** and **PeopleMover**. While the **Astro-Jets**, **Autopia**, and other Tomorrowland attractions entertained guests as fanciful rides, the House of the Future educated visitors as a working vision of what the future could be. After the House of the Future closed in 1967, the **Alpine Gardens** were established over the landscaped grounds, and a souvenir stand incorporated part of what had once been the futuristic patio. The seeds planted by the House of the Future later blossomed into the Progress City model inside the **Carousel of Progress**.

Hub, aka Plaza Hub, aka Central Plaza

MAP: Park, P-10J

DATES: July 17, 1955–ongoing

All the earliest concept drawings of the full-size Disneyland park depicted a broad center axis as the organizing principle for the overall layout. **Walt Disney** wanted his guests to walk through a cozy, familiar setting—**Main Street**—before they ventured into his unknown lands. Once past Main Street, guests would arrive at the park's chief terminal, from which all other areas could be accessed. Situated 800 feet north of the

Main Street train station, this terminal, the park's nucleus, is called the Hub.

Labeled as the Plaza Hub on 1989's **Fun Map**, and formally called the Central Plaza today, Walt Disney himself called this location "the Plaza, or the Hub," when he introduced a model of the park on his *Disneyland* TV series. The single word Plaza might confuse 21st-century guests who have seen signs for the Main Entry Plaza (located outside Disneyland's turnstiles) and the Sunshine Plaza and Gateway Plaza (located inside Disney California Adventure). Not only does the term Plaza Hub both describe and pinpoint the location of this central open space, it also reaffirms its connection to the various Plaza-named establishments that have surrounded it, such as the Plaza Inn and the Plaza Gardens (there have been no Hub-named restaurants).

Known to most guests as simply the Hub, the area is both a departure point and a meeting point. Radiating out from the Hub like the spokes of a wheel are six main walkways: one taking guests south to Main Street, two heading west to **Adventureland** and **Frontierland**, two going north toward **Fantasyland**, and one heading east to **Tomorrowland**. Smaller walkways also lead to a number of main restaurants, including the **Plaza Pavilion** to the southwest, the **Plaza Gardens** to the northwest, and what was once the **Red Wagon Inn** (now the Plaza Inn) to the southeast.

It's very unlikely that a guest could avoid crossing the Hub circle at least once during a park visit. Few guests, however, *want* to avoid the Hub. Its circular expanse covers about 35,000 square feet (four-fifths of an acre), and it's beautifully landscaped with trees, shrubs, flowers, and benches. The central position of the Hub make it one of the park's best spots to people-watch, view **fireworks**, and admire vehicles (**Main Street Vehicles** round the Hub on their trips back to **Town Square**). In addition, **popcorn carts**, cappuccino stands, and character greetings are usually available along the sidewalks. A helpful Information Board near the Plaza Pavilion offers up-to-the-hour information about **parades**, shows, and wait-times (plus a large Braille map, installed in the summer of 2011). Along the southern border of the Hub are West and East Plaza Street, home to the **Refreshment Corner** piano player, the **Baby Station**, and other sites.

As of 1993, the **Partners** statue of Walt Disney and Mickey Mouse has stood on a pedestal in the Hub's center. The placement is significant. This dignified tribute to the park's origins wasn't installed in Town Square, or outside the highly visible **entrance**, or in Fantasyland (reputed to be Walt Disney's favorite area), or in any of the other key locations around the park. *Partners* is at the heart of the Hub, and thus at the very heart of Disneyland itself.

Hurricane Lamp Shop

MAP: Main Street, MS-4

DATES: 1972–1975

In 1972 a **Main Street** room formerly part of the corner **Upjohn Pharmacy** became home to the Hurricane Lamp Shop. Victorian hurricane lamps with glass chimneys and oil-burning wicks might have seemed like appealing items for turn-of-the-century Main Street, but guests would soon "glow" out of them. In 1976 the **Disneyana** shop replaced the non-Disney lamps with Disney collectibles.

Indiana Jones Adventure

MAP: Adventureland, A-6

DATES: March 3, 1995–ongoing

Debuting in 1995, Indiana Jones Adventure was the first major new attraction in **Adventureland** since 1963's **Enchanted Tiki Room**. As with *Captain EO* and **Star Tours**, Indiana Jones Adventure was the result of a fruitful pairing of Disney and George Lucas.

Plans for the attraction actually began in the mid-'80s, back when the second Lucas-produced Indiana Jones movie, *Indiana Jones and the Temple of Doom*, was busy establishing itself as a huge hit in theaters. Various Disney designers took a crack at incorporating elements from the Indiana Jones films into some kind of Disneyland adventure. Some of the early concept drawings showed battered vehicles careening along a cliff above a lava-filled ravine; others included a roller coaster-style mine-car chase. Nearly all the early plans incorporated the rolling boulder sequence from *Raiders of the Lost Ark*.

When Indiana Jones Adventure finally opened, it had accumulated the highest price tag for any Disneyland attraction ever (most estimates are over $100 million, about six times the total cost to build the entire park in the mid-'50s). Before construction began in 1993, designers first reshaped the adjacent Jungle Cruise river to make room for the three-story temple structure (some of it underground) and its elaborate **queue** area. Stretching a half-mile, this was the longest line in Disneyland history.

The real achievement, however, wasn't the construction of the building as much as the engineering of the cars, which are the park's most complex vehicles. Created to look like well-used jungle jeeps from 1935, the 16 vehicles dip, swerve, shake, tilt, accelerate and brake all along the 2,500-foot track, making for a crazy and unpredict- able ride (and somewhat dangerous—in its first year, the vehicles generated so many minor injuries that designers quickly added several safety modifications). What's more, each vehicle carries its own computer that instigates random bumps, fire flash- es, and other effects to create 160,000 possible variations of the Indy experience.

Once they leave the "archaeological dig" at the boarding area, the trucks speed up to 13 miles per hour and whip guests through a perilous three-and-a-half-minute journey inside the Temple of the Forbidden Eye. Snakes, rats, bugs, fire, blow guns, a collapsing bridge, that famous rolling stone, and sophisticated **Audio-Animatronic** Indiana Jones figures await (an Indy at the end, updated in September 2010, is one of the most lifelike A-A machines ever made). Pumping through the on-board audio systems are realistic sound effects, Indy's voice, screaming mummies, and the familiar movie music, all propelling the excitement to unprecedented heights.

Just as the film versions were in movie theaters, the Indy ride at Disneyland was an instant hit. Publicized on a 1995 TV special called "40 Years of Adventure," the exciting new attraction drew the biggest crowds since 1987's Star Tours debut. Fans have always loved the delightful little details that add to the authenticity and fun. Among them: Sallah, one of Indy's movie sidekicks, delivers the pre-boarding instruc- tions; the **queue** area displays coded symbols ("maraglyphics") deciphered via special decoder cards; one of the queue-area crates is addressed to Obi Wan, a character from another Lucas movie; the jungle trucks don't really go in reverse, even though an illusion suggests they do; and, in the finest **Hidden Mickey** tradition, one of the skeletons often sports mouse ears. These and many, many other surprises make this ride one of the most thrilling and inventive additions to the park in a generation. To paraphrase one of the movie ads upon which it is based—if adventure has a name, it must be Indiana Jones Adventure.

Indiana Jones Adventure Outpost

MAP: Adventureland, A-2

DATES: Spring 1995–ongoing

Capitalizing on the massive attention brought to **Adventureland** by **Indiana Jones Adventure**, Indiana Jones Adventure Outpost debuted across from the ride's entrance in 1995. The Outpost's interior is about 45 feet wide and 20 feet deep, and it opens to South Seas Traders next door. Indy's Outpost replaced the **Safari Outpost**, which had been selling khaki safari gear for almost 10 years. Once the Indy name was on it, the Outpost began selling classic fedoras, whips, maps, and archaeological artifacts.

Indian Trading Post

MAP: Frontierland, Fr-15

DATES: July 4, 1962–December 1, 1988

The rustic little store known as the Indian Trading Post joined the seven-year-old **Indian Village** in **Frontierland** on 1962's Independence Day. The picturesque location near the **Rivers of America** offered guests swell views of boats on the water and kids on **Tom Sawyer Island**. Inside the Trading Post were authentic Indian crafts, such as turquoise jewelry, clothing, and pottery. Despite the 1972 remodeling in this area that replaced the Indian Village with **Bear Country**, the Indian Trading Post was left untouched, its Indian theme still appropriate for the new land set in the Pacific Northwest woods of the 1800s. However, the Indian Trading Post didn't survive the 1988 remodel that replaced Bear Country with **Critter Country**—a week after the critters arrived, the Trading Post became the equally rustic but more Disney-esque **Briar Patch**.

Indian Village

MAP: Frontierland, Fr-15

DATES: July 1955–October 1971

In 1955 a realistic Indian Village opened just a tomahawk's throw from the **Chicken Plantation** restaurant at the western edge of **Frontierland**. From there guests could see the southern tip of what would soon be called **Tom Sawyer Island**.

For the first few months, the Indian Village consisted of a small collection of teepees and simple wooden structures that recreated the dwellings of various 19th-century Plains Indians. Unlike most of Disneyland, the village had dusty dirt paths winding through it instead of paved sidewalks.

Inside the Indian Village, actual Native Americans demonstrated their customs and performed such ceremonial dances as the Eagle and the Mountain Spirit. The result was a touch of frontier authenticity in an area of the park that was otherwise only an imitation of the frontier experience (Disneyland's 1985 hardcover **souvenir book** proudly noted that the "authentic dances from such tribes as the Apache, Navajo, Comanche, and Pawnee" were "performed with the permission of the respective tribal councils and the U.S. Bureau of Indian Affairs").

Within a year, the Indian Village was

relocated farther north along the river's west bank, a spot opposite the center of Tom Sawyer Island. This was a larger space with more development, including a ornate dance circle, additional teepees, lodges, a burial ground, and the **Indian War Canoes**. Demonstrations of archery and displays of arts and crafts added to the fun. A 1962 remodel of the village expanded the location and brought in the **Indian Trading Post**.

The park's **souvenir books** often showed photos of "full-blooded Indians" performing "tribal dances," Chief Shooting Star in his elaborate native garb, and canoes paddling past painted teepees. In one happy photo, **Walt Disney** poses in front of a tribal drum, wearing a ceremonial headdress with his gray suit and smiling broadly. The Indian Village was showcased on a 1970 episode of *The Wonderful World of Disney*, but dwindling interest and mounting labor problems meant the village's days were numbered. In the fall of 1971, the Indian Village was dismantled so this corner of Frontierland could be transformed into **Bear Country**.

Indian War Canoes,
aka Davy Crockett's Explorer Canoes

MAP: Frontierland, Fr-14

DATES: July 4, 1956–ongoing

Of all the many cars, boats, trains, and carts guests can ride in at Disneyland, only one has required its passengers to help with the actual propulsion. That's what Indian War Canoes in **Frontierland** asked of its guests, starting on Independence Day in 1956.

Like the *Mark Twain*, the D-ticket (see **ticket books**) canoes made an approximately 12-minute trip around **Tom Sawyer Island**, but the canoes deferred right-of-way to bigger, less mobile watercraft. The canoes launched from the northernmost dock along the western bank of the **Rivers of America**, a spot near the **Indian Village** and opposite the central section of Tom Sawyer Island.

The canoes weren't made by Disney, coming instead from a canoe-building company in Maine. Originally, the 35-foot-long, one-ton vehicles had small motors to supplement the paddlers. These, however, were soon eliminated, so all power had to come from the dozen guests and two strong-armed **cast members** in each boat.

On May 19, 1971 the Indian War Canoes got a more politically correct name, though Davy Crockett's Explorer Canoes was basically the same attraction. They've operated irregularly because of weather concerns, and there was some talk that they'd be permanently retired in the late '90s. However, today the canoes still exist as rustic throwbacks to Disneyland's earlier, simpler years.

Indy Fruit Cart

MAP: Adventureland, A-7

DATES: Ca. 1995–2006

Of the various fruit carts that have been stationed throughout Disneyland, one of the most memorable was the Indy Fruit Cart parked at the west end of **Adventureland**. Themed to the nearby **Indiana Jones Adventure**, the cart was shaped like a battered World War II jeep, complete with dings and faded paint. The menus lodged into the steering wheel and chained to the body announced various fresh fruit selections that were supplemented with nuts, chips, and juices. This healthy haven was towed away around 2006.

Innoventions

MAP: Tomorrowland, T-14

DATES: July 3, 1998–ongoing

A quarter of a century after the **Carousel of Progress** show stopped spinning, and a decade after **America Sings** sang its last song, Innoventions opened in the big, round Carousel Theater at the back of **Tomorrowland**.

Innoventions wasn't a daring risk for the park—it had already been a success at Walt Disney World before it came to Anaheim. At Disneyland, the attraction continues to be an ever-changing, multi-faceted presentation of innovative edutainment. Innoventions focuses on the future—not the distant future, but the future nonetheless, even if that future sometimes seems like it's only about 10 minutes away.

In its first decade, Innoventions spread displays of gadgets and games, many of which were already on the market, out across its 30,000 square feet and two big floors. Subdivided zones pertaining to modern living—entertainment, home, transportation, information, and sports/recreation—grouped exhibits together thematically, with each zone sponsored by major companies like Yamaha and Pioneer. The content of the zones was frequently updated, making each Innoventions visit a new experience. Typically there was a ring of exhibits circling the slowly rotating perimeter that were demonstrated by **cast members** (one complete revolution still takes about 18 minutes). In the central hub were hands-on games, quizzes, gadgets, and computers for guests to linger over. The upstairs floor offered more exhibits, corporate displays, and the exits.

Throughout the building, guests may have seen voice-activated appliances, the latest PlayStation games, an imaging program that ages a just-taken photograph, a tree made out of circuit boards, a futuristic car, and virtual-reality exercycles. As of 2008, the interior space has been dominated by the 5,000-square-foot Innoventions Dream Home, a variation of the **House of the Future** that lasted 10 years near Tomorrowland's entrance. Sponsored by Microsoft and other companies, the home displays high-tech, well-furnished rooms used by the fictional Elias family (Elias was both Walt Disney's middle name and

> ## A Dozen Disneyland Imports from Walt Disney World
>
> 1. Astro-Orbitor
> 2. Buzz Lightyear Astro Blasters
> 3. *Captain EO*
> 4. Country Bear Jamboree
> 5. FASTPASS
> 6. *Honey, I Shrunk the Audience*
> 7. Innoventions
> 8. *Magic Journeys*
> 9. The Many Adventures of Winnie the Pooh
> 10. Mile Long Bar
> 11. Space Mountain
> 12. *Wonders of China*

his father's first name). Innoventions guests will also hear long spiels about next-generation cars coming from a major sponsor, Honda. What guests won't find inside Innoventions are **restrooms**—evidently those haven't been innovented yet.

The Carousel Theater is usually filled with **Audio-Animatronic** figures—there were over 100 for America Sings—but now only one prominent A-A character is on view. He's a doozy, though. Hosting the proceedings is a wise-cracking robot with Nathan Lane's voice, transparent skin, and a see-through lab coat. Called Tom Morrow, he recalls the similarly named flight director in the old **Flight to the Moon** attraction. Another nostalgic nod to the past is the **Sherman Brothers'** familiar "There's a Great, Big, Beautiful Tomorrow" tune, bolstered with new lyrics. Outside, the theater's exterior salutes the past with banners showing old Tomorrowland attractions, a nice reminder that innovation is nothing new at Disneyland.

International Street

MAP: Town Square, TS-7

DATES: Never built

From 1956 to 1958, a sign on a tall wooden fence near the **Opera House** announced that a new area called International Street was under construction. Behind the fence, visible to curious guests through small viewing holes, were photographs of what the street would look like when finished. According to the photos, International Street would run parallel to the eastern row of buildings along **Main Street**, lined with architecture and shops inspired by a half-dozen countries.

Actually, what guests were seeing through the viewing holes was a scaled-down version of something called International Land, which was intended for Disneyland's northeast corner beyond **Tomorrowland**. Roughly triangular in shape, International Land, as depicted in the book *Disneyland: Then, Now, and Forever*, would be surrounded by water and connected to the rest of the park by three bridges. Some kind of transportation system curled through the five-acre triangle, and several large buildings graced the interior.

Although neither International Street nor International Land was built, similar concepts did find expression two decades later in Walt Disney World. At Disneyland, announcements for the upcoming International Street were replaced in 1958 by plans for **Liberty Street**, but those too would soon pass.

Intimate Apparel, aka Corset Shop

MAP: Main Street, MS-13

DATES: 1955–December 1956

Ever since Disneyland opened, one of the most restful places along **Main Street** has been an elevated porch along the eastern side of the street near the **Hub**. Today,

guests who take a rest on the bench and chairs here probably don't realize that this little porch, only about 18 feet wide and five feet deep, originally belonged to the Intimate Apparel shop (also called the Corset Shop in the park's 1956 **souvenir book**).

In case the euphemistic Intimate Apparel name didn't register with 1950s guests, the sign above the porch at the time clearly spelled out what was available inside—"Brassieres" and "Torsolettes." The sponsor was the H-M Company, better known at the time as Hollywood-Maxwell or "the Wizard of Bras." H-M had created, and was selling at Disneyland, the "strapless Whirlpool bra" that "makes the most of you." Not only that, Intimate Apparel even told the history of women's undergarments via an in-store exhibit.

Some experts speculate that the porch was built as a buffer to keep the window displays a few feet back from young pedestrians; others suggest that the porch was intended as a seating area for gentlemen while their ladies shopped for unmentionables inside. It's also possible that the porch was simply provided as an inviting rest stop on a busy commercial street. In any case, H-M abandoned the porch and closed up shop in Disneyland in late 1956, at which point the **Ruggles China and Glass** shop next door spread into the vacant room.

Irvine, Richard

(1910–1976)

Imagineers have led the way to new Disneyland attractions, and Richard Irvine led the Imagineers. Born in 1910 in Salt Lake City, his family moved to California 12 years later. Irvine attended Stanford University, USC, and an art institute before getting a job in the budding film industry. Working as an art director for the next two decades, he contributed to such notable films as *Miracle on 34th Street*, Disney's *The Three Caballeros*, and *Sundown*, the latter earning him an Oscar nomination.

Joining the Disneyland designers in 1952, Irvine worked with outside architects to create the park. However, Irvine soon realized that the best people to design a park that would translate themes from stage and screen were the people already working on Disney films. Accordingly, **Walt Disney** gathered many of his top animators, artists, set designers, and craftspeople into his own newly formed design department, which would eventually be called Imagineering.

For the next 20 years, Irvine headed this team in the creation of every Disneyland attraction, including sophisticated classics like **Pirates of the Caribbean**. After Walt Disney died in 1966, Irvine became the master planner for Walt Disney World, where one of the old-fashioned steamboats is now named after him.

Irvine retired in 1973 and died three years later in Los Angeles. He was named a Disney Legend in 1990. His daughter-in-law, Kim Irvine, is an acclaimed Disneyland art director who has worked on everything from **Rivers of America** to the **Disney Gallery**.

It's a Small World

MAP: Fantasyland, Fa-21

DATES: May 28, 1966–ongoing

It's a Small World was launched on a very large stage—the 1964–1965 New York World's Fair, where over 10 million visitors joined "the happiest cruise that ever sailed 'round the world."

However, what those visitors saw wasn't what was originally planned; the happy cruise went through a major change before it ever launched. The main concept was always a charismatic boat ride past hundreds of singing **Audio-Animatronic** dolls from six continents. However, initially the international dolls were going to sing all the various national anthems on all those continents. This would have resulted in a disharmonious jumble as guests listened to one anthem as they approached the next.

Instead of a multitude of overlapping melodies, a single anthem was written by **Richard and Robert Sherman** to fill the entire trip with a 15-minute reminder that it was indeed a small world after all. The Shermans originally intended their song to be played as a slow ballad, but the playful spirit of the cruise demanded a bouncier tempo.

The building in New York was vastly different from what was constructed in

Anaheim. For the fair, It's a Small World was in the Pepsi-Cola pavilion, where the relatively bland exterior was dressed up with signage and an elaborate 120-foot-tall, 100-ton artwork in front. This structure, called the *Tower of the Four Winds*, had mobile elements that expressed "the boundless energy of youth," according to its designer, Disney Legend **Rolly Crump**. At Disneyland, that structure is now echoed with an artistic sign out front made of twisting, bending metal tubes.

Anaheim's acre-and-a-half Small World building supplanted the old train depot at the back of **Fantasyland** and extends well beyond the park's perimeter **berm**. The multifarious façade is an intricate, smile-inducing collage of moving shapes that evokes grand monuments—the Taj Mahal, the Eiffel Tower, etc.—from around the world.

Wonderful and whimsical, this isn't architecture, it's *lark*-itecture. Designed by several Disney Legends, among them **Mary Blair**, the exterior has undergone several paint revisions that have taken it from white-and-gold and white-and-blue color schemes to a sweet rainbow of candy pastels. The gold trim is made of actual 22-karat gold leaf, and some of the fancy decorations are enlarged duplicates of personal jewelry owned by the designers. A lavish **Topiary Garden**, a complex cuckoo clock that chimes with marching toy soldiers every 15 minutes, and the Disneyland trains, which pass across the building's layered frontage, all add to the fanciful fun. As charming as the cruise is, the trip itself is almost unnecessary because there's so much to see on the building's exterior.

Inside the building, the winding, 1,400-foot river, laid out by Disney Legend **Claude Coats**, meanders past over 300 singing dolls and about 250 kinetic toys and effects. Everything is scattered across dozens of **Marc Davis**-created scenarios to illustrate how happiness is a global emotion, whether it's experienced by island kids on surfboards, Dutch girls clacking their wooden shoes, giggling hyenas in Africa, skating Scandinavians, or a Chilean flautist. **Alice Davis's** adorable doll costumes put the fun in functional—they're fastened with Velcro for easy access whenever mechanisms need repair.

Veteran guests may remember the sponsor's cheery reminder at the exit that no matter where in the world they went, Bank of America would be there. B of A, which helped fund Disney film projects dating back to *Snow White* in 1937, sponsored It's a Small World until 1992, when Mattel took over (in recent years, Sylvania displays a slogan about "making our Small World brighter").

Since 1997, beautiful seasonal decorations have been added for It's a Small World Holiday, still a winter favorite; additionally, in 2008 a major refurbishment brought updated boats and new dolls to the festivities.

After debuting in New York in 1964, It's a Small World got two big pages in Disneyland's 1965 **souvenir book** a year *before* the attraction even opened in Anaheim. At its Disneyland premiere in '66, international children ceremoniously poured water from each of the world's oceans into the Small World river while press photographers merrily clicked away. The E-ticket attraction (see **ticket books**) even had its own soundtrack album, complete with a colorful 10-page booklet. In 1999, It's a Small World became the first Disneyland attraction to get the new **FASTPASS** ticket-distribution system, a significant sign that "the happiest cruise" is still as adored and adorable as ever.

It's a Small World Toy Shop

MAP: Fantasyland, Fa-20

DATES: December 18, 1992–ongoing

To cash in on the high volume of pedestrian traffic emerging from **It's a Small World**, two stores sit near the exit of the famous attraction. The smaller store slightly farther away is **Fantasy Faire Gifts**, and the larger one right in the path of departing guests is the It's a Small World Toy Shop. For most of its history, the Toy Shop was sponsored by Mattel, which also sponsored It's a Small World. This meant the store has sold lots of Mattel toys, not all of them Disney-related. Hot Wheels cars, games, and Barbie dolls have occasionally populated the shelves.

Today, plenty of Disney dolls, statues, and toys for tots fill the store. The building's fanciful design echoes the playful scenes displayed along the banks of the Small World cruise.

Iwerks, Ub
(1901–1971)

One of the great Disney animators was also a key creative force behind several major Disneyland attractions. Ubbe "Ub" Iwerks was born in Missouri in 1901, the same year as **Walt Disney**. Working at the same Kansas City art studio, the two teens met and soon started up a commercial art business. The short-lived company soon led to a bigger one called Laugh-O-Gram Films in 1922, with Iwerks working as the chief animator. A few years later, the two friends reunited in Hollywood at the new Disney Brothers Cartoon Studio, where Iwerks worked on the "Alice Comedies," became the first person to draw Mickey Mouse, and single-handedly animated Mickey's first cartoon, *Plane Crazy*.

After pioneering the *Silly Symphonies* series of the late '20s, Iwerks left the company during the '30s to create his own cartoons. However, his Flip the Frog and other characters weren't as successful as those he'd created with Disney, and so he returned in the early '40s. Heading the studio's research and development team, Iwerks devised new cinematic advances that propelled imaginative live-action/animation combinations. These special effects would memorably flourish in *Mary Poppins* and win him two Oscars for his technical achievements. Iwerks is listed in the credits of dozens of Disney classics, among them *Cinderella* and *Sleeping Beauty*, plus Alfred Hitchcock's *The Birds*.

At Disneyland, Iwerks brought his technological wizardry to three of the biggest attractions of the 1960s: the **Circle-Vision 360** theater in **Tomorrowland**, **Great Moments with Mr. Lincoln** on **Main Street**, and **It's a Small World** in **Fantasyland**. In the **Haunted Mansion**, the illuminated floating head in the séance room and the singing busts in the graveyard are based on projection systems Iwerks devised.

After working on the Hall of Presidents for Walt Disney World, Ub Iwerks died in 1971 at age 70. He was inducted as a Disney Legend, along with the first fleet of great Disney animators, 18 years later.

Jani, Robert
(1934–1989)

Robert Jani, Disneyland's longtime entertainment specialist, invented imaginative productions that redefined the **parade** concept. Jani was born in Los Angeles in 1934 and graduated from USC two decades later. In 1955 he started working at Disneyland as the first person to lead **Guest Relations**, an information and problem-solving department based in **City Hall**. Jani then served two years in the army. Upon his return, he eventually rejoined Disneyland in '67 as its director of entertainment.

At Disneyland, Jani's two most famous creations are **America on Parade**, the patriotic spectacular of the mid-'70s, and the legendary **Main Street Electrical Parade**, which ran for over two decades. The Electrical Parade was probably the most popular parade in the park's history. However, the unique nighttime concept was initially a tough sell to Disney execs, as Jani explained on the 2007 DVD *Disneyland Secrets, Stories & Magic*.

In addition to these park productions, Jani produced several prominent non-Disney events, including Super Bowl halftime shows, New York's 1976 Bicentennial Celebration, massive **holiday season** shows at Radio City Music Hall, and numerous TV specials. Though he retired in 1978, Jani stayed on to consult on Disneyland Paris and Disney-MGM Studios.

After fighting Lou Gehrig's disease, Bob Jani died in Los Angeles in 1989 at age 55. He was named a Disney Legend in 2005.

Jemrock Shop, aka Jemrocks and Gem Shop

MAP: Main Street, MS-3

DATES: 1956–1957

Listed among the earliest stores on **Main Street** is the small Jemrock Shop (also called the Jemrocks and Gem Shop) open for only two years in the mid-'50s. Its location inside the **Crystal Arcade** was appropriate for a lapidary business. But by the time the 1958 Disneyland souvenir book came out, all mention of the Jemrock Shop was gone.

Jewel of Orléans

MAP: New Orleans Square, NOS-9

DATES: 1997–May 2011

A list of the prettiest shops in Disneyland's history would have to include Jewel of Orléans in **New Orleans Square**. The shop featured a decorative ceiling, ornate wall details, exquisitely embellished mirrors, lace curtains, and a glittering chandelier found in the Crescent City by Walt and Lillian Disney. All of this combined to evoke a Parisian setting—an appropriate reference, given that the former longtime occupant of this space was the French-themed **Mlle. Antoinette's Parfumerie**, and next door is the **French Market** restaurant.

For the first dozen years of its operation, the shop was run by the Jacobs family, owners of an antique jewelry business called Dianne's Estate Jewelry. Their Disneyland shop sold glittering Victorian bangles and cameos, vintage pocket watches, Edwardian pendants and necklaces, Art Deco trinkets, Tahitian pearls, and even some Disneyland-related pieces. The Jewel of Orléans felt more like a museum than a shop, especially since some of the items cost tens of thousands of dollars.

A sluggish economy took its toll, however, and in early 2010 Jewel of Orléans lost its sparkle, closing for six weeks. Upon reopening, the French name and beautiful décor were the same, but the Jacobs family had departed. Disney was now running things, and the merchandise was completely different. Instead of antiques, the shop started selling new jewelry and handbags from high-profile designers, as well as chic Ray-Ban sunglasses. When the shop finally closed in 2011, Mlle. Antoinette's returned with her perfumes.

Jewelry Shop, aka Rings & Things

MAP: Main Street, MS-19

DATES: 1955–1986

Starting in 1955, a small space near the Market House on Main Street was occupied by the Jewelry Shop. In 1970 the Jewelry Shop absorbed the adjacent space that had been the **Yale & Towne Lock Shop**. New signs were posted announcing the slightly more specific Rings & Things. In 1986, Rings & Things switched locations with the **Disneyana** shop across the street. The new location was the corner building that had once been the **Upjohn Pharmacy**; the new name was **New Century**, an umbrella title applied to both New Century Jewelry and New Century Timepieces next door.

Jimmy Starr's Show Business Souvenirs

MAP: Town Square, TS-8

DATES: March 23, 1956–September 20, 1959

Nicknamed Stage Door Jimmy, Jimmy Starr was a longtime Hollywood insider who started working in the movies in the 1920s. Starr eventually held jobs in several different fields, working as a newspaper gossip columnist, publicist, novelist, screenwriter, and actor.

From the spring of 1956 to the fall of '59, a collection of Starr's Hollywood memorabilia filled a leased space just north of the **Opera House**. Disneyland's **souvenir books**, evidently figuring that guests might not know who Jimmy Starr was, listed his shop as Show Business, Show Business Souvenirs, and Motion Picture Souvenirs. Inside the store, guests could view some movie props and buy photos, autographs, and other collectibles.

By no means a retail super Starr, the shop closed in 1959 and later reopened as **Wonderland Music**. Starr died in 1990 at age 84.

Joerger, Fred
(1913–2005)

Designers and architects make two-dimensional drawings of new Disneyland attractions and buildings. During his time working for Disney, Fred Joerger turned those drawings into intricate three-dimensional models.

Born in 1913, Joerger graduated in 1937 with a fine arts degree from the University of Illinois. After moving to Los Angeles, Joerger started building models at Warner Bros. Studios. In 1953 he joined Disneyland's model-making team, which included Disney Legends **Wathel Rogers** and **Harriet Burns**. Among Joerger's first creations was a model of the **Mark Twain Riverboat**, followed quickly by elaborate miniatures of the **Jungle Cruise**, **Sleeping Beauty Castle**, **Main Street** buildings, villages for the **Storybook Land Canal Boats**, and many more early attractions, all before any of them were constructed. His 3-D **Matterhorn** rendering led to the construction of the park's tallest structure, and his **Haunted Mansion** model was the precursor to one of Disneyland's most famous attractions. Joerger also contributed models of movie sets to Disney Studios, among them detailed miniatures of the *20,000 Leagues Under the Sea* submarine.

In addition to building models, Joerger was an expert at sculpting the faux rocks that added realistic atmosphere to such Disneyland attractions as **Tom Sawyer Island** and **Pirates of the Caribbean**. His rock work was acknowledged on a Haunted Mansion tombstone that read, "Here lies Good Old Fred, a great big rock fell on his head."

After working on Walt Disney World, Joerger retired in 1979, though he later consulted on EPCOT and Tokyo Disneyland. He was named a Disney Legend in 2001, four years before he died in L.A. at age 91.

Jolly Holiday Bakery Café
MAP: Hub, H-1

DATES: January 5, 2012–ongoing

The venerable **Plaza Pavilion** was once a prominent restaurant, but in recent years it served as the more mundane Annual Passport Processing Center. With passport functions transferred out to the ticket booths as of August 2011, in early 2012 the building was reborn as a new *Mary Poppins*-themed dining experience called the Jolly Holiday Bakery Café. "Practically perfect pastries" and other delights with spoonfuls of sugar in them were the menu's star attractions. The presence of this big new bakery signaled the end of the **Blue Ribbon Bakery** on **Main Street**; that prime corner location became indoor seating for the adjacent **Carnation Café**.

Jolly Trolley

MAP: Mickey's Toontown, MT-12

DATES: January 24, 1993–2006

In **Mickey's Toontown**, public transportation was once provided by the wacky Jolly Trolley. "It's clean! It's fun! It bounces a lot!" read the sign for this attraction, and few guests would have disagreed. Looking like little toy versions of the beautiful horse-drawn streetcars that still roam **Main Street**, these happy vehicles were built with soft curves and painted bright red with gold trim. They also sported cartoon-ish wind-up keys on top. About 10 guests at a time could fit inside for the scenic fountain-to-fountain ramble across Toontown. What put the jolly in the trolley was the series of gentle jiggles, dips, and bumps as it drove along its 800-foot track.

Appropriately enough for this cheery ride, **cast members** wore bright blue conductor uniforms with big yellow buttons, red bow ties, and snappy multi-colored hats. Disneyland's **souvenir books** of the '90s nearly always showcased the photogenic Jolly Trolley, which seemed incapable of taking a bad picture.

The trolleys fell out of favor in the mid-2000s as concerns for guest safety increased. The trolleys went from having two cars, to single cars, to no cars as the ride was quietly chained up as a photo op and a **Disney Vacation Club** site.

Jones, Mary

(Dates unknown)

The head of Disneyland's Community Relations started working at the park in 1962 as a secretary. Within a few months of being hired for her clerical skills, Mary Jones was heading Community Relations, a department that worked with local leaders to assure Disneyland's happy coexistence with its neighbors. Jones began by administering awards for community service; later, she established the Community Action Team to support nonprofit organizations and also formed Operation Christmas to bring holiday celebrations into children's hospitals. Jones also served as the liaison with consulates and the State Department when foreign dignitaries and royals wanted to visit the park, leading to many impressive photo opportunities that broadened Disneyland's international appeal.

Jones retired from Disneyland in 1986 but continued with the local government to set up and run the Orange County Office of Protocol, continuing the community work she'd pioneered at the county's most-visited destination. Mary Jones was inducted as a Disney Legend in 2005.

Jungle Cruise

MAP: Adventureland, A-8

DATES: July 17, 1955–ongoing

The Jungle Cruise was arguably Disneyland's most important early attraction. Until the 1962 arrival of the nearby **Swiss Family Treehouse**, the cruise was the only major attraction in all of **Adventureland**. What's more, since it covers approximately three acres, the Jungle Cruise has always been one of Disneyland's largest attractions—and one of the most heavily promoted. Before any park construction began, **Walt Disney** was boldly describing an explorer's boat ride down a lush "river of romance." Months before the park opened, the *Disneyland* **TV series** previewed the coming cruise with footage of Disney taking a car through the dry riverbed while he touted the wonders to come.

Once the park opened, the official **souvenir books** devoted more space and photos to the nine-minute Jungle Cruise than to any other attraction. Calling it the Explorer Boat Ride, River Boat Ride, Jungle River Boat Ride, Jungle River Boat Safari, and finally (in 1959) the Jungle Cruise, the early souvenir books liberally mixed colorful photos with enthusiastic text that described how "adventure lurks at every bend" of this "jungle wonder world." In 1969's *Walt Disney's Disneyland*, writer **Martin Sklar** named it "Disneyland's finest achievement." If **Sleeping Beauty Castle** was the park's most iconic structure, the Jungle Cruise was its signature attraction.

As with the **Painted Desert** area of **Frontierland**, the Jungle Cruise incorporated themes and images from Disney's True-Life Adventure films of the '50s—in this case, the 75-minute documentary *The African Lion*. The original **attraction poster** for the Jungle Cruise emphasized the connection with this line: "For true life *adventure*, ride the Jungle River." However, what the poster's imaginative artwork depicted—a colossal elephant towering over guests who were standing in a boat—wasn't exactly "true life."

Disney Legend **Harper Goff** laid out the four-foot-deep river and drew some of the first concept sketches of the scenery that would appear along its teeming banks, taking some of his ideas from another '50s movie, the Oscar-winning *The African Queen*. Africa, however, isn't the only setting of the Jungle Cruise. In addition to the

Congo and Nile, scenes along the waterway suggest other international rivers like the Amazon and the Mekong. Landscapers **Morgan "Bill" Evans and Jack Evans** made creative use of exotic greenery as they planted the dense foliage that soon filled the area to resemble real jungles of the world. Today there are more than 700 trees and over 40 different kinds of plants (representing six continents) in the Evans' jungle.

Early plans called for real animals to populate this wilderness, but that idea was quickly scotched when designers realized that jungle wildlife usually sleeps all day, and even those beasts not sleeping would probably be hiding from noisy, intrusive boats. Dozens of realistic mechanical animals and jungle natives eventually went on display, among them majestic elephants, writhing snakes, charging hippos, statuesque giraffes, half-submerged crocodiles, and dancing headhunters. Though their motions were relatively simple and repetitive, these machines were considered advanced special effects in the '50s, and they gave the Jungle Cruise its unique thrills.

The Jungle Cruise has been updated at least 10 times since 1955. Veteran jungle cruisers may recall that at one time the jungle river and Frontierland's **Rivers of America** were briefly linked by a small canal, and the old one-story boathouse had a square lookout tower on the roof for **cast members** to survey the river. In 1962 the playful elephants and their bathing pool were added to the waterway. The African Veldt, **Marc Davis's** "lost safari" climbing away from a rhino, and the Cambodian ruins all joined the fun by '64, and then a dozen years later the gorillas started playing in the abandoned camp. In 1994, with **Indiana Jones Adventure** under construction next door, Imagineers re-routed part of the river and built a new two-story **queue** area at the dock. This wooden structure, made to look old and abandoned, intentionally sags to suggest that nature is reclaiming what man has encroached upon. Guests waiting inside will hear old-time music and see period artifacts from the 1930s.

The gas-powered boats have also undergone several revisions. Early on, spotlights were added to allow night cruises. The boats' gleaming white exteriors and red-and-white striped roofs were replaced with more drab-looking paint and canvas coverings

Jungle Cruise Boat Names

1. *Amazon Belle**
2. *Congo Queen**
3. *Ganges Gal**
4. *Hondo Hattie*
5. *Irrawaddi Woman**
6. *Kissimmee Kate*
7. *Magdalena Maiden*
8. *Mekong Maiden**
9. *Nile Princess**
10. *Orinoco Adventuress*
11. *Swanee Lady**
12. *Ucayali Una*
13. *Yangtze Lotus*
14. *Zambesi Miss*

*Original 1955 boat.

to give them a weathered look and evoke the Indiana Jones aesthetic. The 27-foot boats have always held about 32 passengers and have always been guided by rails hidden under the river water, which is made to look cloudy and green.

One key aspect of the Jungle Cruise that separates it from other Disneyland attractions is the comical patter spoken by the wisecracking skippers. Initially these cast members, wearing safari garb and brandishing blank-loaded pistols, delivered serious narration about the cruise and its dangerous inhabitants, but after a few years that narration, with the blessing of park officials, was played for laughs. The purpose, perhaps, was to deflate the menace of the realistic spiders, jungle beasts, and savages with bursts of humor. The cruise eventually became a nonstop joke-fest that begins before guests are even in their seats. By now, most guests can recite one or two of the corny gags that have been repeated thousands of times: the crocs looking for a handout; the rare view of the back side of water; Trader Sam, the attraction's mascot who will trade two shrunken heads for yours; and the most dangerous part of the trip, the return to civilization. Much of this is scripted, but skippers have a long tradition of ad-libbing new material, especially on the last run of the night. Kevin Costner, Robin Williams, and Nixon's press secretary, Ron Ziegler, are all said to have been Jungle Cruise skippers in their youth. These might be fanciful legends to go along with entertaining stories of boats that have sunk and skippers who have swung from ropes in the trees, but they are part of the reason guests have always been fascinated with this beloved Disneyland classic.

Junior Autopia

MAP: Fantasyland, Fa-23

DATES: July 23, 1956–September 15, 1958

Of the four Autopias that have chugged through Disneyland's history (Tomorrowland's **Autopia**, **Fantasyland Autopia**, and **Midget Autopia** are the others), Junior Autopia came and went the quickest. Capitalizing on the popularity of the 1955 Tomorrowland original, Disneyland opened a second version, Junior Autopia, in 1956 to accommodate younger, shorter drivers who couldn't handle the bigger Tomorrowland cars.

Located in the **Fantasyland** area where the **Mickey Mouse Club Circus** had briefly operated, the Junior Autopia site was a little farther north of the Autopia in Tomorrowland. The track layout for the Junior Autopia was not as elaborate as the layout for Tomorrowland's Autopia, and it was safer, too— to help guide novice drivers, the Junior track had a center rail, a feature not included in the Tomorrowland Autopia back then. The cars of the Junior and Tomorrowland Autopias were basically identical (sleek, **Bob Gurr**-designed sports cars with fiberglass bodies), except for extended gas pedals and higher seats to make the Junior cars more child-friendly.

About 26 months after opening, Junior Autopia closed for a major remodel. The site reopened in 1959 as the larger Fantasyland Autopia, with some of the land taken over by the waters of the **Motor Boat Cruise**.

Justice, Bill
(1914–2011)

Animator, programmer, Imagineer—Bill Justice wore many hats as a key Disney employee for over four decades. Born in Ohio in 1914, Justice was raised in Indiana and graduated from an Indiana art institute in 1935. Two years later he was living in Southern California and starting a long career with Disney Studios.

Working on animated films, Justice contributed memorable scenes and characters to such classics as *Fantasia*, *Bambi* (Thumper was his creation), and *Peter Pan*. Along the way he directed the opening animation for *The Mickey Mouse Club* TV show, co-created the special opening titles for such popular Disney films as *The Shaggy Dog* and *The Parent Trap*, and designed the nursery sequence in *Mary Poppins*.

In 1965 Justice began working on Disneyland attractions, especially those involving sophisticated **Audio-Animatronic** figures like **Great Moments with Mr. Lincoln**, **Pirates of the Caribbean**, the **Haunted Mansion**, **Mission to Mars**, **America Sings**, and the **Country Bear Jamboree**. Justice also designed costumes for the park's walk-around characters and devised floats for the elaborate **parades**.

After working on Walt Disney World and Tokyo Disneyland, Justice finally retired in 1979. His 1992 autobiography, *Justice for Disney*, recounted his 42-year Disney career. Bill Justice was inducted as a Disney Legend in 1996; he died in 2011, one day after celebrating his 97th birthday.

Keller's Jungle Killers

MAP: Fantasyland, Fa-22

DATES: February 19, 1956–September 7, 1956

Killers in **Fantasyland**? Well, sure. If real guns could be fired in the **Main Street Shooting Gallery**, why not show some dangerous animals east of the **Storybook Land Canal Boats**? What's really surprising is that Keller's Jungle Killers weren't located in the jungle-themed **Adventureland**.

When the short-lived **Mickey Mouse Club Circus** bailed from Fantasyland in early 1956, one of the circus attractions, Keller's Jungle Killers, stayed on through the summer. George Keller's B-ticket attraction (see **ticket books**) featured, not mechanical replicas, but actual jungle cats in a cage. The beasts may have been killers at one time, but they weren't after being declawed and sedated. As Jack Lindquist noted in his book *In Service to the Mouse*, the real danger was a sleepy cat slumping onto Keller and crushing him.

Wearing sparkly outfits, Keller himself interacted with the leopards, lions, and tigers. His most famous stunt, which he often performed in fairs around the country, was placing his head inside a lion's mouth. After departing Disneyland, Keller briefly joined the Ringling Bros. Barnum & Bailey show in 1959 before suffering a heart attack a year later.

Back in Fantasyland, meanwhile, Keller's former site was extensively remodeled from 1956 to 1959. **Junior Autopia** took over as the area's first new attraction.

Ken-L Land Pet Motel,
aka Kennel Club, aka Pet Care Kennel

MAP: Park, P-7

DATES: January 18, 1958–ongoing

To accommodate pet owners who might otherwise leave their animals sitting in sun-baked cars, Disneyland added a pet care facility in 1958. Conveniently accessible directly from the **parking lot**, the kennel was located in a small building to the right of the **entrance**. Pets couldn't be left overnight, but they could be stay for an entire day in "airy, individual enclosures" for modest fees (for years that daily fee was under $1, including food, but by 2011 the service cost $20). Over the years everything from lizards to goldfish to pigs have stayed in one of the 100-plus enclosures.

When the kennel first opened, it was called the Ken-L Land Pet Motel. Five different pet food companies have hosted and remodeled the kennel over the decades. Ken-L Ration sponsored its Pet Motel from 1958 to 1967, and Kal Kan created the Kennel Club from 1968 to 1977. After an unsponsored period, Gaines renamed it the Pet Care Kennel from 1986 to 1991 before Friskies restored the Kennel Club name in 1993. Finally, Purina took over in 2002 and kept the Kennel Club signage. In 2010 no sponsor was named at a discreet entrance called simply the Disneyland Kennel Club.

Khrushchev in Disneyland
(Never made)

Many presidents and royals have toured Disneyland over the decades, but possibly the most famous visit by a dignitary was one that never happened. Before embarking on an 11-day tour of America in 1959, Soviet Premier Nikita Khrushchev requested that he be taken to "the fairy-tale park," as he called it. Mid-tour, government officials (not park officials) denied the request, saying they couldn't assure security on the busy Saturday set for his visit.

The incident drew international attention when an irate Khrushchev complained loudly about the rejection. On September 19th, the afternoon when he would have been at Disneyland, he threw a temper tantrum in front of journalists and celebrities. What, he wondered aloud, did the park have to hide? His wild guesses included "cholera," "rocket-launching pads," and "gangsters." Denied Disneyland, was he now supposed to "commit suicide"?

Walt Disney later said he'd been looking forward to showing off his new submarine fleet to the Communist leader. In the '60s Disney briefly considered developing a movie about the whole affair, a comedy to be called *Khrushchev in Disneyland*. Peter Ustinov was to play the petulant premier, who would have been shown inventing his own plan to dodge security and sneak into the park.

Kids of the Kingdom

DATES: Ca. 1968–1986

Kids of the Kingdom was an energetic musical ensemble put together by Disney in the late '60s to perform in Disneyland. The Kids weren't exactly kids the way the pre-teen Mouseketeers were; these Kids were college-age singers and dancers. They usually performed on the large **Tomorrowland Stage** and appeared at special events in other park locations.

Wearing colorful matching outfits, the co-ed Kids belted out upbeat, choreographed versions of Disney classics, show tunes, and other popular songs. Their eponymous album in 1968 on Vista Records was titled *Young Singing Stars of Disneyland*. The cover showed 14 well-groomed, white-sweatered performers, half of them holding Mickey balloons, all of them smiling in front of **Sleeping Beauty Castle**.

Two years later, the Kids were introduced to a national audience on a 1970 episode of *The Wonderful World of Disney* TV show. On that "Disneyland Showtime" episode, the Kids, actor Kurt Russell, the **Dapper Dans**, and the Osmond Brothers celebrated the new **Haunted Mansion**. Although the Kids' Disneyland run ended by the time their stage became the **Magic Eye Theater** in 1986, a Florida version of the group continued to perform at Walt Disney World.

King Arthur Carrousel

MAP: Fantasyland, Fa-5, Fa-6

DATES: July 17, 1955–ongoing

A carousel near the center of Disneyland is also central to the park's history. **Walt Disney** always maintained that some of his ideas for a new kind of amusement park came while he was waiting near a Griffith Park merry-go-round that his daughters were riding (in 2010 the **Opera House** debuted a display of the actual bench he had been sitting on at the time).

When it finally came time to build his own park, Disney placed his carousel in a most telling place. Not only is it in the middle of the castle courtyard, where it pumps out gaiety, music, and color as if it were **Fantasyland's** beating heart, but it is in a

conspicuous location where it can be seen from hundreds of feet away. Guests on **Main Street** can look across the **Hub** to see the glittering lights of the King Arthur Carrousel through the castle's archway, an alluring sight that draws them into Disneyland's fairy-tale fantasy.

Regarding the carousel's name, several points need clarification. While King Arthur refers to the same legend that was the basis of Disney's *The Sword in the Stone*, the main imagery decorating the carousel isn't from that 1963 movie—it's from 1959's *Sleeping Beauty*, represented by nine hand-painted scenes circling the carousel's core. Also, while the attraction uses an old spelling variation of the more familiar "carousel," the meaning—a whirling ride with moving horses—is identical. Carousels differ from merry-go-rounds, which are similar but usually include a variety of animals and benches, some of which don't move up and down.

Ironically, Disneyland's carousel was originally a merry-go-round. It was built in 1875 and was in Toronto, Canada when Walt Disney bought it. After he transported it to his new park, Disneyland designers took off the non-equine animals and seats and added over two dozen horses purchased from other carousels, including one on Coney Island (during the renovation, some of the removed seats were added onto the cars of the **Casey Jr. Circus Train**). Ultimately, Disneyland's carousel opened with 68 hand-carved, hand-painted, antique wooden horses arrayed in 17 rows of four. All the horses seem to be leaping, an effect Disney designers created when they attached new legs to some of the horses that previously had four on the floor. And all the prancing steeds are now a gleaming white, thanks to new paint applied in the 1960s over the previous shades of black, tan, cream, and brown. Brightly colored saddles, jewels, and other details help distinguish each horse. For its first three decades, the carousel's rollicking music came from a calliope, and it only cost an A ticket from Disneyland's **ticket book** for a two-minute, four-miles-per-hour spin.

In the early '80s, the King Arthur Carrousel was remodeled along with the rest of Fantasyland. First, Imagineers relocated the carousel north by about 20 yards to open up the congested area near the castle. This move put the carousel closer to **Mr. Toad's Wild Ride** and pushed the twirling teacups next to **Alice in Wonderland**. Next, the music transformed when the Disney classics playing next door at **Dumbo the Flying Elephant** became the same soundtrack for the carousel.

What hasn't changed in over 50 years is the affection guests have for the King Arthur Carrousel (especially one famous guest, Julie Andrews, whose initials and Mary Poppins silhouette adorn the saddle on "Jingles"). The carousel is still shown off in modern **souvenir books** as prominently as it was in the books of the '50s. It still gleams from six hours of polishing on the brass poles every single night and frequent touch-ups of the horses. And it still warms hearts with its traditional pleasures, regal style, and timeless beauty, making it the perfect centerpiece for Fantasyland's rich buffet.

10 Relocations Within Disneyland

All of these attractions moved from one spot in the park to another:

1. Astro-Jets (two Tomorrowland sites)
2. Bandstand (from the Hub to Adventureland)
3. Disney Gallery (from New Orleans Square to Town Square)
4. Disneyana (two Main Street sites)
5. Dumbo the Flying Elephant (two Fantasyland sites)
6. Indian Village (two Frontierland sites)
7. King Arthur Carrousel (two Fantasyland sites)
8. Le Bat en Rouge (two New Orleans Square sites)
9. Mad Hatter's Mad Tea Party (two Fantasyland sites)
10. Names Unraveled (three Fantasyland sites)

King Triton Gardens, aka Triton Gardens

MAP: Tomorrowland, T-1

DATES: February 1996–August 17, 2008

The former grounds for the **House of the Future** and the **Alpine Gardens** were re-landscaped into the splashy King Triton Gardens in 1996. Also called simply the Triton Gardens, this beautiful area was named after the ocean monarch from the 1989 Disney movie *The Little Mermaid*. The Triton Gardens sported several statues of the character to establish whose gardens these were; one water-spouting representation of the king stood in the middle of the pond, and his smiling daughter Ariel perched on a rock.

Kids loved the fountain jets that shot playful streams of water over the walkway. At night, iridescent lights made the gardens and waters look especially lovely. Parents appreciated the quiet 300-foot walkway that led around the pond. In a small clam-shaped area called Ariel's Grotto, the lovely red-haired mermaid herself was often on hand to sign autographs.

In the fall of 2008, the King was deposed and his gentle gardens were revamped into the new **Pixie Hollow** meet-and-greet area. Triton lives on, however, over at Disney California Adventure, where his six-foot-tall statue crowns the entrance to the Little Mermaid attraction.

Knight Shop

MAP: Fantasyland, Fa-30

DATES: August 16, 1997–October 3, 1998

This Middle Ages-themed shop replaced **Quasimodo's Attic** after the excitement over 1996's *Hunchback of Notre Dame* movie died down. The Knight's location was the same as Quasimodo's, greeting guests in the castle courtyard just before they flew with Peter Pan. The shop's merchandise included daggers, swords, and armor accoutrements. Disneyland planners must have thought that knight supplies matched nicely with the **Princess Boutique** nearby. A year later, however, the Knight went over to the dark side when it was transformed into the **Villains Lair**, a return of the bad guys formerly in the **Disney Villains** store.

Kodak Camera Center,
aka GAF Photo Salon, aka Polaroid Camera Center

MAP: Main Street, MS-13

DATES: July 17, 1955–November 1994

Disneyland's allure for camera and film company sponsorship is obvious—most guests carry cameras with them during their visits. They may also wish they had brought a camera and so need to buy one, or lose the one they had brought with them and need to replace it. In pre-digital days, those insatiable cameras gulped film and needed to be replenished often. The Kodak Camera Center met all of these camera and film needs from the **Main Street** space where Castle Brothers now resides. Not only did the store sell both still and movie cameras, it rented them, too. To inspire even more picture-taking and film-buying, Kodak posted helpful signs around the park to prompt especially scenic photographs.

In 1970, the General Analine Film Corporation replaced Kodak as the sponsoring company and operated the shop as the GAF Photo Salon until 1977. Polaroid got into the picture at the end of the decade and renamed it the Polaroid Camera Center. Finally, in a new development that yanked the camera saga back to its origins, Kodak reappeared as the sponsor from 1984 until 1994, at which point the whole operation got a new name—**Main Street Photo Supply Co.**—and was relocated to the building known as **Carefree Corner**.

Kuri, Emile
(1907–2000)

Anyone who watched movies made any time from the 1930s to the 1970s probably saw the work of Emile Kuri, one of Hollywood's most prolific set directors. Among the 100-plus films he contributed to were the classics *It's a Wonderful Life* and *Shane*, plus three Hitchcock movies. As the main decorator for Disney Studios, Kuri also helped design the sets and décor for dozens of live-action Disney films and TV shows. His long Hollywood career brought him an Emmy and eight Academy Award nominations for Art Direction/Set Direction (two of the nominations were for *Mary Poppins* and *The Absent-Minded Professor*); one of his two Oscar wins was for his imaginative *Nautilus* sets in *20,000 Leagues Under the Sea*.

Emile Kuri was born in Mexico in 1907. When his family moved to Los Angeles, Kuri found work as a duster in a Hollywood furniture store, which led to chance meetings with filmmakers and eventually his film career. In the 1950s Kuri began working on Disneyland. He's responsible for the **Plaza Inn's** elegant interior, the old-fashioned lampposts on **Main Street**, the flagpole in **Town Square**, and the furnishings on the **Sailing Ship Columbia**, to name just a few prominent park features. Several of his projects are rarely seen by guests, including the interior of **Club 33** and **Walt Disney's** private **apartment** overlooking Town Square. Kuri also assisted on the Disney attractions at the 1964–1965 New York World's Fair, consulted on Walt Disney World, and even decorated Disney's own homes. Emile Kuri died in 2000 at age 93.

La Boutique de Noël

MAP: New Orleans Square, NOS-5

DATES: Ca. 1998–March 2006

The larger of the two Christmas shops that existed simultaneously in **New Orleans Square** (**L'Ornement Magique** was the other), La Boutique de Noël was located in the spot where **Le Gourmet** had once been. Filled with colored lights, stocking holders, and ornaments, La Boutique offered Noël all year long. For guests who couldn't visit during the winter season, it was a nice sampling of Disneyland holiday cheer. Discounts were available in the off-season, but unfortunately the shop entered its own permanent off-season in 2006. **Le Bat en Rouge** moved from the other end of Royal Street into this space.

La Boutique d'Or

MAP: New Orleans Square, NOS-5

DATES: Ca. 1974–ca. 1980

After **Le Forgeron** withdrew its metal merchandise from the back of **New Orleans Square** in the mid-'70s, La Boutique d'Or brought in its bold gold. Jewelry, home décor, and other golden goods made this a glittering stop across from **Le Gourmet** on

Royal Street. A different kind of indulgence followed when the **Chocolate Collection** moved in around 1980.

Laffite's Silver Shop

MAP: New Orleans Square, NOS-6

DATES: Ca. 1966–1988

Jean Laffite has a presence inside the **Pirates of the Caribbean** attraction, where Laffite's Landing is the launching dock for its boats. He is also remembered out on **Tom Sawyer Island**, though there his name is spelled "Lafitte." Additionally, for about two decades the early 19th-century privateer had his own namesake shop in **New Orleans Square**. Tucked in behind what was then the **Creole Café**, Laffite's Silver Shop offered a wide array of silver items, all of them ready for engraving right on the premises. Laffite la-left when the Creole Café, renamed Café Orleans, expanded into its space in 1988.

La Mascarade d'Orléans

MAP: New Orleans Square, NOS-9

DATES: Ca. 1985–ongoing

From its corner at the back of **New Orleans Square**, La Mascarade d'Orléans beckons like a fanciful Parisian confection. After it replaced **Marché aux Fleurs, Sacs et Mode** in the mid-'80s, La Mascarade introduced elaborate Mardi Gras masks as the shop's specialty. A 1999 makeover transformed La Mascarade into a vintage shop that sold artistic items, including beautiful candles and regal princess hats. In recent years the room has become a center for pin traders, and in 2011 there was also a display of Vinylmation, "the new Disney collectible." But as a reminder of the long history here, "Sacs et Mode" is still painted on the outside of the building.

La Petite Patisserie

MAP: New Orleans Square, NOS-8

DATES: 1988–ca. 2004

One of the hidden jewels in **New Orleans Square** was La Petite Patisserie, a hard-to-find spot that wasn't always open but was always satisfying when it was. More of a walk-up window than a true dining location, "the little pastry shop" was behind **Café Orleans** and faced **Jewel of Orléans**.

The patisserie was famous for its four different kinds of waffles, which it served on a stick. Waffle variations ranged from the simple Royal (sprinkled with powdered sugar) to the decadent Mascarade (coated in dark and white chocolate). Non-alcoholic daiquiri slushies and delectable cappuccinos made this an indulgent stop for guests lucky enough to find it, and to find it open. With the Patisserie gone, this section of Orleans Street now offers an attractive outdoor seating area.

Leather Shop

MAP: Frontierland, Fr-1

DATES: Ca. 2000–ongoing

The two separate rooms of the Leather Shop flank the doorway of the big Pioneer Mercantile building just inside the **Frontierland** gates. Often only one of the Leather Shop's rooms is open at a time. Both offer small leather items, especially keychains and bracelets, plus some pewter and silver objects (the room on the left also sells cowboy hats and hat bands). **Cast members** here can also personalize guests' purchases.

Le Bat en Rouge

MAP: New Orleans Square, NOS-3, NOS-5

DATES: October 2002–ongoing

Le Bat en Rouge is a retail spin-off of the popular Haunted Mansion Holiday, which brings *The Nightmare Before Christmas* theme to the **Haunted Mansion**. In 2001, the first year of that holiday celebration, a cart outside the Haunted Mansion sold *Nightmare* souvenirs. A year later, the cart disappeared and the souvenirs relocated to a scary-looking shop near the **Royal Street Veranda**. Formerly the **One-of-a-Kind Shop** and **Le Gourmet** had occupied this space. In 2006, Le Bat flew again, this time to the spot near the **Blue Bayou** where **La Boutique de Noël** had been.

Le Bat en Rouge, of course, is a playful take on Baton Rouge, the Louisiana capital within 100 miles of New Orleans and thus a suitable identity for a space in New Orleans Square. Jack Skellington is the store's star, but there are lots of other creepy Halloween-appropriate books, posters, clothes, figurines, skeletons, and skulls on display.

Le Chapeau

MAP: New Orleans Square, NOS-9

DATES: 1966–ca. 1974

Disneyland has never lacked hat shops. Most have been dominated by the usual Disney souvenir hats and mouse ears, but not the elegant Le Chapeau in **New Orleans Square**. The women's hats formerly on display here on the corner behind the **French Market** were mostly fine, feathered, frilly creations suitable for Mardi Gras. For men, there were derbies, top hats, and other handsome styles available. Some of the expected Disney hats were also sold, but they weren't as prominent as the more expensive merchandise.

In the mid-'70s Le Chapeau became another French-themed store with a different name: **Marché aux Fleurs, Sacs et Mode**.

Le Forgeron

MAP: New Orleans Square, NOS-5

DATES: 1966–ca. 1974

Early in the history of **New Orleans Square**, Le Forgeron occupied a spot at the end of Royal Street. Named after the French word for "blacksmith," the shop offered old-fashioned metal and leaded-glass objects for the home. Paired with **Le Gourmet** across the street, Le Forgeron made it possible for guests' homes to be decorated with authentic-looking styles evoking the French countryside. A shop evoking a glittery French jewelry store, **La Boutique d'Or**, replaced Le Forgeron in the mid-'70s.

The Legacy of Walt Disney

MAP: Main Street, MS-20

DATES: January 15, 1970–February 11, 1973

In 1970 the prominent **Main Street** corner formerly occupied by the **Wurlitzer Music Hall** was transformed into a celebration of the life and achievements of **Walt Disney**. The Legacy of Walt Disney offered biographical information and displays of some of the awards, tributes, and honors Disney received in his lifetime. After three years, the displays were moved to the **Opera House** for a new presentation called **The Walt Disney Story**. Back on Main Street, the Legacy corner became **Disneyland Presents a Preview of Coming Attractions** and later, the high-profile **Disney Showcase** store.

Le Gourmet, aka Le Gourmet Shop

MAP: New Orleans Square, NOS-5, NOS-3

DATES: 1966–ca. 2002

Le Gourmet, or Le Gourmet Shop, filled a large space at the end of Royal Street

Major Attractions and Exhibits Added in the 1970s

1970 The Legacy of Walt Disney

1972 Country Bear Jamboree

1973 Disneyland Presents a Preview of Coming Attractions; The Walt Disney Story

1974 America Sings

1975 Mission to Mars; The Walt Disney Story, Featuring Great Moments with Mr. Lincoln

1977 Space Mountain

1979 Big Thunder Mountain Railroad

near the **Blue Bayou**. A photo in Disneyland's 1968 **souvenir book** showed studious shoppers examining "rare culinary items," which included fine kitchen accessories for connoisseurs. Everything from copper pots, potholders, and chef hats to wooden utensils, dish towels, and Aunt Sally's Creole Pralines was sold here, much of it adorned with Disneyland or New Orleans Square logos.

After about three decades, part of this space ceased to be a mecca for gourmands and instead became a mecca for holiday decorators when **La Boutique de Noël** moved in; **Port d'Orleans** also filled some of the space with gourmet sauces and coffees. Le Gourmet, meanwhile, moved to the other end of Royal Street next to the **Royal Street Veranda**. There it stayed until **Le Bat en Rouge** started haunting this spot in 2002.

Le Petit Chalet

MAP: Fantasyland, Fa-22

DATES: 1997–ongoing

Matching the theme of the adjacent **Matterhorn**, the Swiss-styled Le Petit Chalet gift shop is definitely petite, made up of not much more than several open counters under an alpine roof. Gifts have included small items like Disneyland-themed dolls (including a yeti from the mountain next door), hats, autograph books, disposable cameras, and the princess-style merchandise found elsewhere in **Fantasyland**.

Let the Memories Begin

DATES: January 1, 2011–ongoing

Let the Memories Begin was a 2011 park-wide marketing promotion that replaced

2010's **What Will You Celebrate?** Cynics could point out that the public's Disneyland memories really began in 1955, not 2011. Still, the Memories campaign did present some new interactive opportunities: guests could share their photos and stories on Disney websites, and a new nighttime show called **The Magic, the Memories, and You!** splashed photos of guests across the **It's a Small World** façade. For most of 2011 and up to mid-January 2012, a colorful signboard with more smiling photos dominated the broad walkway between Disneyland and Disney California Adventure. A new promotion called One More Disney Day, focused on 24 hours of Leap Day activities lasting from February 29 to March 1, supplemented the Memories campaign in 2012 and drew overnight capacity crowds.

Liberty Street

MAP: Town Square, TS-7

DATES: Never built

First announced in 1958 with a sign in **Town Square**, Liberty Street was a coming attraction that would have expressed Walt Disney's unabashed patriotism. Originally, **International Street** had been announced on the sign, but when enthusiasm for that idea cooled, the Liberty Street concept heated up. According to a 1958 **Fun Map**, Liberty Street would have run roughly parallel to **Main Street**, starting on Town Square's northeast corner from a spot next to the **Wurlitzer Music Hall**. From there, Liberty Street would have headed north toward **Edison Square**, an area that was also never built.

The 1958 map showed Liberty Street laid out as a quaint small-town avenue that dog-legged to the right. There were no spinning rides on this street, no little cars or cute boats—just a dignified, historically accurate presentation of an American colony in the late 1700s. Listed on the map were these Liberty Street structures: U.S. Capitol in Miniature, Colonial Shoppes, Hall of Presidents, Declaration of Independence Diorama, Boston Observer Print Shoppe, Paul Revere's Silver Shop, Griffin's Wharf, Glass Shoppe, and Blacksmith. Griffin's Wharf appeared to be a small dock where several sailing ships were tied up. What looked like a prominent church steeple stood at the entrance to Liberty Street, and an even more imposing building called Liberty Hall towered over the cobblestone cul-de-sac at the back end (supposedly a Liberty Bell would have tolled from the top of Liberty Hall). A color illustration in the 1958, '59, and '60 **souvenir books** labeled that cul-de-sac as Liberty Square, with a Liberty Tree and Liberty Hall as the two dominant features.

Although the full Liberty Street area never blossomed as intended, some of its seeds did disperse elsewhere into the park. The U.S. Capitol model actually exists and has been featured inside the Opera House since the mid-'70s. The Audio-Animatronic technology needed to create the Hall of Presidents didn't exist in the late '50s, but by 1965 a solitary Abraham Lincoln figure was up and talking in **Great Moments with Mr. Lincoln**. The full Hall would later be built in Walt Disney World.

Light Magic

DATES: 1997–1998

The 1997 replacement for the long-running **Main Street Electrical Parade** was the short-lived Light Magic show. Unlike its venerated predecessor, Light Magic is remembered today as a summer debacle, though in some ways it was a precursor to modern street spectaculars like 2010's Celebrate! A Street Party. Promoted as "a spectacular journey," Light Magic moved four big portable stages—each covering 900 square feet and standing 25 feet tall—through **Main Street** and presented almost a hundred performers who danced and interacted with the crowd. The "light magic" was supplied by innovative fiber optics and strobe lights. Screens for movie clips and confetti cannons added to the 14-minute spectacle, but many guests left disappointed (and many kids left frightened by the bizarre costumes). With the plug pulled on Light Magic after only four months, a new *Mulan*-themed **parade** arrived in 1998.

Lilliputian Land

MAP: Fantasyland, Fa-22

DATES: Never built

Long before the **Storybook Land Canal Boats** cruised past tiny buildings, **Walt Disney** wanted to build an entire land devoted to miniatures. Coney Island's Dreamland area had already presented something similar in the early 1900s—Lilliputia (or "Midget City," as it was nicknamed), a small-scale community built on a third of an acre and populated by 300 very short people who lived and worked in front of fascinated spectators.

Disneyland's version, though larger in size, was a little simpler. Named after Lilliput, the tiny kingdom in *Gulliver's Travels*, Disney's Lilliputian Land appeared on a park map drawn by **Marvin Davis** in September of 1953, some 22 months before Disneyland opened. Davis's rendering showed Lilliputian Land as a two-and-a-half-acre rounded triangle sandwiched between **Fantasyland** and **Tomorrowland**. The area had its own entrance from the **Hub** as well as a curving track for a small railroad, a winding river for canal boats, and plenty of small hills and trees.

Later that month, **Herb Ryman** drew his famous Disneyland map under Walt Disney's watchful eye. His map also featured a Lilliputian Land east of Fantasyland. However, once Disney decided to include small mechanical figures, he realized the

Audio-Animatronic technology he needed was still years away, so the Lilliputian Land idea was scrapped. Instead, a less ambitious attraction, the **Canal Boats of the World**, debuted inside Fantasyland on **Opening Day**. Within five years, some of the acreage originally reserved for Lilliputian Land would be partially occupied by the **Matterhorn,** the **Submarine Voyage**, and the **Fantasyland Autopia.**

Lindquist, Jack
(1927–)

According to the tribute posted in his **Main Street window**, Jack Lindquist is Disneyland's "Honorary Mayor" and "Master of Fun." Before earning those titles, Lindquist, born in Chicago in 1927, was a child actor with roles in the *Our Gang* comedies of the early '30s. Two decades later he was serving in the Air Force and then attending USC.

After starting at Disneyland in 1955 as the park's advertising manager, Lindquist later headed the marketing department and eventually became the park's first president. He championed some of Disneyland's signature promotions, concepts, and expansions, among them **Disney Dollars**, **Sky-fest**, the **Gift-Giver Extraordinaire Machine**, **Blast to the Past**, the **Tencennial**, and **Mickey's Toontown**. During Lindquist's time at Disneyland, virtually every corner of the park was improved or promoted by one of Lindquist's ideas or decisions. As testament to Lindquist's significance, Charles Ridgway's book *Spinning Disney's World* identifies him as a passenger in the inaugural boat that first cruised through **It's a Small World** in 1966.

In the 1970s and '80s, Lindquist was a key contributor to the marketing and promotional plans for Disney parks around the world. A year after his 1993 retirement, Lindquist was named a Disney Legend. His memoir, *In Service to the Mouse*, was published in 2010. A tribute to Lindquist in the form of a grinning pumpkin still sits outside **Goofy's Bounce House** in Mickey's Toontown.

Little Green Men Store Command

MAP: Tomorrowland, T-6

DATES: March 2005–ongoing

Aliens have arrived, and they've got their own store. The Little Green Men Store Command is located next to the exit from the **Buzz Lightyear Astro Blasters** attraction—an appropriate home for a store with a *Toy Story* theme. The store's name, of course, is a takeoff on Buzz's Star Command. A large photo collage of Buzz hung outside the shop during Disneyland's golden anniversary.

Formerly the **Premiere Shop** had filled this space, and like its predecessor Little Green Men Store Command still exhibits spaceships from the extinct **Rocket Jets** (formerly black and white, the two on display are colorfully repainted and used as display cases). Light fixtures are shaped like Saturn, and wall murals depict legions of smiling three-eyed aliens. Pin traders will find a large selection of pins and accessories, while Buzz Lightyear

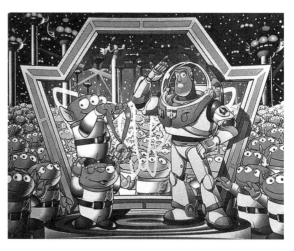

fans will find plenty of toys and clothes that celebrate their galactic hero.

Little Red Wagon

MAP: Hub, H-5

DATES: Ca. 1995–ongoing

This snack stand isn't the kind of wagon that is towed around by a horse or a child—it's a food wagon, more like an old-fashioned catering truck. Usually it's parked in the southeast corner of the **Hub** (a location that has some historical wagon-related significance). Originally the adjacent Plaza Inn was called the **Red Wagon Inn**, sponsored by Swift, the meat-packing company with a logo that incorporated a red wagon. Today, the Little Red Wagon specializes in popular hand-dipped corn dogs and snacks.

Locker Area, aka Main Street Lockers & Storage

MAP: Main Street, MS-1; Park, P-3; Main Street, MS-16

DATES: July 17, 1955–ongoing

A locker area has been available in the park since **Opening Day**, but it's changed locations and names several times. The first location was a small building in **Town Square** to the right of (but not attached to) the **Fire Department**. Disneyland's early

souvenir books labeled this original locker area the Bekins Van & Storage Locker Area and the Bekins Locker Service. In 1963 another moving company moved in and the site became known as both the Global Van Lines Locker Area and the Global Locker Service (though the signs on the building read Lost & Found and Parcels). This lasted until 1979, to be followed on June 1, 1980 by the National Car Rental Locker Area until January 2, 1990. During these years, a second locker area appeared about 150 feet west of Disneyland's **entrance;** guests still use this handy storage before they enter the park.

In the early '90s, when the Emporium was remodeled and expanded to include the **Carriage Place Clothing Co.**, the Town Square locker area moved to the little side street by the **Market House**. The current Main Street Lockers & Storage has a big gold key planted in a lock above the door and displays of antique luggage mounted on the shelves inside. Lockers are available on a first-come, first-serve basis, with daily fees for different size lockers ($7 to $15 in 2011). The room's walls are lined with lockers, in addition to four long islands of extra compartments for a total of over 2,700 lockers. Phones, phone card machines, postcard machines, and "charging lockers" for electronic devices are also available.

Outside the locker area is a subtle but entertaining feature—according to signs, some of the upstairs rooms belong to a dentist, and the realistic sounds of a dental office can be heard from the street.

L'Ornement Magique

MAP: New Orleans Square, NOS-5

DATES: October 10, 1998–February 2012

For over a decade, L'Ornement Magique filled a charming little location at the back of **New Orleans Square** with holiday cheer. No matter the season, guests could always buy elaborate handcrafted ornaments created by New York-based artist Christopher Radko.

Radko is famous for his delicate glasswork—the *New York Times* dubbed him the "Czar of Christmas Present." At Disneyland, much of his work featured Disney characters, and many of his ornaments were created exclusively for the park. In its final years the shop offered beautiful ornaments by an array of designers before it closed in early 2012.

Lost and Found

MAP: Town Square, TS-9; Main Street, MS-16, MS-1; Park, P-2

DATES: July 17, 1955–ongoing

Lost and Found might just be the most peripatetic office in Disneyland. The park's 1956 **souvenir book** listed Lost and Found as "above **Opera House**," an upstairs location guests couldn't actually access. The '57 book instructed guests looking for Lost and Found to "Inquire Security Office" but didn't identify where that office was (the **Police Station** in **Town Square** may have been a guest's best guess, but large **Fun Maps** showed the **Security Office** and Lost and Found just off of **Main Street**, near the **Market House**). For the next decade there was not a single mention of the Lost and Found in the park's souvenir books.

In actuality, in the early 1960s Lost and Found, as announced by a sign on the building, had been relocated to the Global Van Lines locker area in the northwest corner of Town Square (the 1968 souvenir book finally acknowledged this location). In the '90s Lost and Found relocated once again, this time back to East Center Street and the nearby Market House; guests could find it by using the small, free maps that are still handed out at the turnstiles. For the 21st century, Lost & Found (with an ampersand) then moved outside the park into the Esplanade area near Disney California Adventure; in 2011 it moved once more, this time to a spot west of Disneyland's turnstiles between the **Locker Area** and the **Newsstand**.

No matter where it's been located, the Lost and Found office has stayed busy. Something like 400 items a day are turned in at Lost and Found—everything from umbrellas, sunglasses, and wallets to medication, expensive jewelry, and cameras (on average, a cell phone is turned in every 20 minutes). In addition to returning lost items to their owners, the office matches them up with their finders, too—a guest who finds an item can bring it to Lost and Found, fill out a form, and claim the item if it isn't picked up within two months.

Love Bug Day

DATES: March 23, 1969; June 30, 1974

DVDs of Disney's *The Love Bug* include brief snippets of film showing an unusual day in Disneyland history. Love Bug Day was first held on March 23, 1969 to celebrate the box office triumph of *The Love Bug*, which had debuted late in '68 but had gone into wide release in March of '69.

The event had two main parts. The first, held out in the **parking lot**, involved a contest whereby guests decorated their own VW Beetles in order to win a new one. Some of these vehicles were so heavily laden with giant ears, noses, legs, eyes, signs, and paint that they looked more like weird alien creatures or psychedelic hallucinations than popular cars.

The second part of Love Bug Day was a **parade** featuring all the wildly disguised Beetles, with music provided by the **Disneyland Band**. Since the cars were coming from the parking lot, this parade began in **Town Square**, cruised northward up **Main Street**, and ended in front of **It's a Small World**. There, the star of *The Love Bug*, Dean Jones, presented the winning Beetle-decorator with the keys to a new car. This wasn't the first time cars had overrun Main Street, by the way—in 1956 the Antique Automobile Parade had sent old Model Ts chugging from the **Hub** to Town Square.

Five years later, with *Herbie Rides Again* in theaters, Disneyland held a second Love Bug Day on June 30, 1974, again with a contest and a parade. Two weeks later, it turned up on a TV special called "Herbie Day at Disneyland," featuring lots of Volkswagens and one of the film's stars, Helen Hayes.

While there were no more Love Bug Days, there were more *Love Bug* movies, plus a 1982 TV series.

Lunching Pad

MAP: Tomorrowland, T-8

DATES: 1977–1998

In the year **Space Mountain** opened, a small snack bar with a space age theme settled in right beneath the **PeopleMover's** second-story loading area. Though it wasn't always open, the Lunching Pad was a handy hot dog/popcorn/soda spot for guests on the go. A small snack stand called the **Space Bar** had stood here previously.

The Lunching Pad lasted two decades, but in the extensive 1998 remodel of **Tomorrowland** it blasted off for good and was replaced by the **Radio Disney** broadcast station.

Mad Hatter of Fantasyland

MAP: Fantasyland, Fa-27

DATES: 1956–ongoing

Three separate Disneyland areas—**Fantasyland**, **Main Street**, and **Tomorrowland**—have featured Mad Hatter hat shops. Though they opened on different dates, the shops all operated simultaneously for over 40 years. The first Mad Hatter opened in 1956 in Fantasyland's castle courtyard. The shop was tucked into a corner of the building that held **Mr. Toad's Wild Ride**, putting the hats about 75 feet from their namesake attraction, the **Mad Hatter's Mad Tea Party**.

Two years later another related attraction, **Alice in Wonderland**, opened about 75 feet to the east of the Mad Hatter's spot, putting three Alice-related establishments within easy walking distance of each other. In 1983 the three were placed even closer together to form a cozy Alice corner. The twirling teacups were moved nearer to

Alice in Wonderland, and the Mad Hatter hat shop was swung around from the castle courtyard to an adjacent cottage where it still operates. Underscoring the connection is one of the teacups in the hat store's front garden.

Hats, of course, are the Mad Hatter's specialty, including everything from adorable princess hats and baseball caps to the famous Mickey and Minnie ears that can be personalized with embroidered names. And yes, the shop carries the signature Mad Hatter hat with the "10/6" shillings/pence price on the outside. The interior's second story displays lots of antique hats, and the sales counter features a pretty nifty trick—a grinning Cheshire Cat that periodically appears in the wall mirror.

Mad Hatter of Main Street

MAP: Main Street, MS-11; Town Square, TS-8

DATES: June 1958–ongoing

A Mad Hatter hat shop has existed on **Main Street** since 1958, but not always in the same location. The first one, which opened two years after the **Mad Hatter of Fantasyland**, was near the **Hub** at the north end of Main Street. Also called Mad Hatter Hats, the shop was around the bend from Coke's **Refreshment Corner** on little West Plaza Street.

This shop offered classic Disney-themed hats—pirate hats, Donald Duck caps, mouse ears, etc. In 1963 a remodel of this Main Street building meant the hat shop had to go—and go it did, to a more prominent location next to the **Opera House**. It's still there today, presenting guests with their first chance inside the park to try on such zany headwear as a Goofy-eared hat or a jester's cap with bells.

Mad Hatter of Tomorrowland,
aka Mod Hatter, aka Hatmosphere

MAP: Tomorrowland, T-22, T-13

DATES: 1958–December 2006

A 1958 **Fun Map** placed a Mad Hatter hat shop at the **Tomorrowland** building that held the **Bathroom of Tomorrow** and other exhibits. This was Disneyland's third Mad Hatter, and it sold the same kind of merchandise as the versions in **Fantasyland** and on **Main Street**. When Tomorrowland underwent extensive remodeling in 1966 and 1967, the Mad Hatter re-emerged in a showy location and with a hip name. The new freestanding building was next to the massive **Carousel of Progress** structure, and the new name, appropriately enough for the psychedelic '60s, was the Mod Hatter. As cool as the name sounded, the merchandise was basically unchanged.

In the '80s the name went less mod and more space-y when it changed to Hatmosphere. Mickey's sorcerer hats, whimsical sun hats, and the ubiquitous mouse ears were among the many hats 'n' caps available until 2006, when the **Autopia Winner's Circle** relocated to this space. While a few hats are still available among the car-related items, the move brought to a close almost 50 years of Tomorrowland hat history.

Mad Hatter's Mad Tea Party

MAP: Fantasyland, Fa-6, Fa-25

DATES: July 17, 1955–ongoing

One of the original **Fantasyland** attractions that debuted in 1955, the Mad Hatter's Mad Tea Party has gone through several changes. Preliminary concept drawings showed basically what guests see now: a whirl of teacups with an *Alice in Wonderland* theme that echoes the 1951 Disney film. The most conspicuous stylistic differences between what was drawn and what was built concerned the track layout and the attraction's centerpiece. One early illustration showed 20 teacups circling a central hub, as if they were on a racetrack with banked curves.

When it opened, the Mad Tea Party and its colorful teacups were positioned in the **Sleeping Beauty Castle** courtyard to the west of **Mr. Toad's Wild Ride**, a location now occupied by the **King Arthur Carrousel**. Originally the main platform upon which the cups spun was gray; later it was painted with a giant, red-and-orange psychedelic

spiral. Guests instantly took to the crazy cups, enthusiastic about the price (initially only a B ticket from Disneyland's **ticket book**) and the control wheel in the center of each cup that enabled riders to spin them faster or slower, clockwise or counterclockwise. So frantic is the action that many guests don't realize the 90-second Mad Tea Party is one of the shortest rides in the park.

Promoting the Mad Tea Party has always been pretty easy for Disneyland publicists—the attraction is easily understood and basically sells itself. An early **attraction poster** placed Mickey, Minnie, and Alice characters in cups, with a tagline about spinning "into the fun-filled world of Wonderland." The park's **souvenir books** showed off the teacups with large, colorful photos of twirling, laughing people, telling readers that they would "whirl and spin at a dizzy pace." Interestingly, though, the souvenir books couldn't settle on the attraction's name, listing it in different places as the Mad Tea Party, Mad Hatter's Tea Party, Mad Hatter Tea Party Ride, and Mad Hatter Tea Cup Ride.

A legend that's grown over the years is that the "dizzy pace" of the ride is dizzier in some cups than it is in others; guests are constantly testing out spin rates to determine which cups are the fastest (of today's 18 cups, the purple and orange ones seem to get the most votes). Something that isn't a legend is the frequency with which guests stumble out and get sick after a vertiginous reel—Disneyland's website warns riders that it's "best to eat after you spin" and "guests who are prone to motion sickness should not ride." As a precaution, the Mad Tea Party shuts down in the rain so guests won't slip as they stagger away from their cups.

In early 1982, Disney designers shut down the teacups for over a year so they could be relocated near the **Alice in Wonderland** attraction about 150 feet to the east. The carousel, which was already in the castle courtyard, moved north to fill the Mad Tea Party's former location, and the teacups filled what had once been an empty walkway. New party lights were strung above the cups, and the "Very Merry Un-Birthday" song from the *Alice* film was piped in to enhance the connection. One thing the attraction doesn't have that is found at other Disney parks is a teapot at the center of the whirling platform. Most guests, though, either don't notice or don't care.

While it may seem nauseating and perplexing to some older guests, millions still enjoy the thrills that have kept this particular party going for over five decades.

Magic Eye Theater

MAP: Tomorrowland, T-19

DATES: May 1986–ongoing

The big outdoor site that had hosted the **Flying Saucers** and the **Tomorrowland Stage** finally went indoors in 1986 when the 575-seat Magic Eye Theater opened. This new building, located to the right of **Space Mountain**, was one of the first major Disneyland projects completed under the Michael Eisner regime that began in 1984.

Most guests know the biggest attractions that have played inside the Magic Eye, but few can name its initial offering. *Magic Journeys* was a Kodak-sponsored 3-D movie that was imported from Walt Disney World in 1984 for a two-year run, first on the **Space Stage** and then for four months at the Magic Eye. Billed as "a 3-D Film Fantasy" on

Major Attractions and Exhibits Added in the 1980s

1983
Pinocchio's Daring Journey

1985
Magic Eye Theater; Videopolis

1986
Big Thunder Ranch; *Captain EO*

1987
Disney Gallery; Star Tours

1989
Splash Mountain

the **attraction poster**, the 16-minute film enabled guests, especially children, to "soar on the wings of imagination."

Magic Journeys, though, was just a placeholder until the star attraction was ready for his 3-D close-up at the Magic Eye. *Captain EO*, another Florida import, debuted in September of '86 with a whirlwind of publicity, thanks to the superstar talent involved—singer Michael Jackson, producer George Lucas, and director Francis Ford Coppola.

A decade later, with audiences dwindling, *EO* was replaced with another popular film, **Honey, I Shrunk the Audience**, jetted in from Orlando. *EO* turned the tables, however, when it replaced *Honey I Shrunk the Audience* in 2010.

Magic Kingdom Club

DATES: 1957–2000

In the 1950s, many businesses implemented marketing programs that offered corporate discounts to their biggest customers. None of these programs, however, was as successful as Disney's Magic Kingdom Club. Founded in 1957 by **Milt Albright** of the Group Sales department, the MKC offered discounts similar to what theaters and other theme parks were offering—around 15 percent—but Disneyland's club seemed more stylish and significant. When companies signed up for the MKC, their employees submitted formal applications to join, a process that enhanced the value of the free membership card they eventually received.

Besides cheaper admission tickets, members also got hotel discounts and received a free quarterly magazine. So successful was the MKC that within five years it had over a million card holders from dozens of major companies. Before the program ended in 2000, it had spread to other Disney parks, expanded its discounts to a long list of vacation services, and counted over five million members.

The Magic of Disneyland

(1969)

Released in October of 1969, this 16mm color documentary gave a general overview of Disneyland. All the expected attractions were shown, notably some that are long-gone, including the **PeopleMover**, **Skyway**, **Flight to the Moon**, and more. Climbers on the **Matterhorn**, park entertainers, and a live **Tinker Bell** in flight are additional highlights. Some of the aerial shots and other scenes are included among the special features on *The Love Bug* DVD.

The Magic, the Memories, and You!

DATES: January 28, 2011–ongoing

Disneyland began a new marketing campaign called **Let the Memories Begin** on

January 28, 2011. The showpiece of the new promotion was a nightly multimedia event entitled The Magic, the Memories, and You! During this eye-popping 10-minute presentation, images of happy guests were projected onto the façade of **It's a Small World** for all to see, with background music and perfectly synchronized special effects evoking magic and memories. Several updates to the show added new imagery, such as a romantic segment for the weeks surrounding Valentine's Day in 2012.

Magnolia Park

MAP: Adventureland, A-4

DATES: July 17, 1955–1962

In Disneyland's early years, a small, serene rest area known as Magnolia Park was located on the far western edge of **Adventureland**. Guests strolling through Magnolia Park were flanked by the **Rivers of America** to the north and the **Jungle Cruise** to the south.

The closest thing to a permanent attraction that Magnolia Park ever had was the decorative **bandstand** that was placed there in 1956 after it had been removed from the **Hub**. In 1958, a series of special outdoor promotions for Disney's *Zorro* TV series was also performed in Magnolia Park.

Four years later Magnolia Park disappeared as redevelopments supplanted its valuable real estate. First, a Jungle Cruise expansion pushed a new elephant bathing pool into what had been the southern part of Magnolia Park. By the end of '62, the new **Swiss Family Treehouse** was dominating the park area. Next came **New Orleans Square**, which in '63 overwhelmed the park with major excavations and construction. In what might be seen as a tribute to the long-lost little park, **Aunt Jemima's** Adventureland restaurant became the **Magnolia Tree Terrace** in 1970. Today, the scenic fountain area between the **Haunted Mansion** and the **French Market** is informally called Magnolia Park (though no official signage announces it).

Magnolia Tree Terrace

MAP: Frontierland, Fr-7

DATES: 1970–1971

As the '60s turned into the '70s, one prominent Frontierland restaurant underwent a quick succession of name changes. Quaker Oats had sponsored **Aunt Jemima's Pancake House** in the '50s and '60s, and Oscar Meyer began sponsoring the same site with the new name **River Belle Terrace** in 1971. But between these two eras, the building spent a year as the unsponsored, upscale Magnolia Tree Terrace. This pretty name referred to **Magnolia Park**, which is what the area off the tip of **Adventureland** had been called before **New Orleans Square** arrived. The restaurant's corner location has always been conspicuous and attractive, offering views of the river only 75 feet away.

Main Street Cinema

MAP: Main Street, MS-19

DATES: July 17, 1955–ongoing

Since 1955 the Main Street Cinema has presented short films in a stylish brick building along the southeastern block of **Main Street**. Just to the north is a locked doorway that's supposedly the home of the Disneyland Casting Agency, where, according to a sign on the door, "It takes People to Make the Dream a Reality." A prominent marquee projecting out from the building announces the program, and the beguiling Tilly from Marceline (the boyhood home of **Walt Disney**) is always present in her ticket booth.

Inside the theater, movies and cartoons play on six small screens in one wood-paneled room, with an oval riser in the center to help kids get a clear view. Like the Circle-Vision 360 theater that once existed in **Tomorrowland**, the Main Street Cinema doesn't have seats, only railings that standing guests can lean on. Back when Disneyland used **ticket books**, admission to the Main Street Cinema initially cost only an A ticket (rising to a B in 1960).

For the first three decades, the program offered black-and-white silent movies, each lasting only 10 or 15 minutes, and each dating to the earliest years of film history. Vintage newsreels added interest and authenticity. In the '80s the selection changed to early Disney animation, including *Steamboat Willie*, the 1928 cartoon that made Mickey Mouse a star. In July 2010, five of the theater's six screens were devoted to a rare eight-minute color film that depicted Disneyland in its earliest years; the sixth screen looped **Opening Day** footage from the national TV broadcast.

Long-Running Programs at the Main Street Cinema

Silent Films:
1. *A Dash Through the Clouds* (1912), Mack Sennett's drama about biplanes
2. *Dealing for Daisy* (1915), a William S. Hart Western
3. *Fatima's Dance* (year uncertain), Fatima's risqué belly dance
4. *Gertie the Dinosaur* (1915), Winsor McCay's cartoon, one of the first ever made
5. *The Noise of Bombs* (1914), a Keystone Kops comedy
6. *Shifting Sands* (1918), a Gloria Swanson melodrama

Disney Cartoons:
1. *The Dognappers* (1934)
2. *Mickey's Polo Team* (1936)
3. *The Moose Hunt* (1931)
4. *Plane Crazy* (1928)
5. *Steamboat Willie* (1928)
6. *Traffic Troubles* (1931)

Main Street Cone Shop

MAP: Main Street, MS-16

DATES: Ca. 2000–ongoing

Halfway down **Main Street**, on the little side street called East Center, hides this little hot weather delight. Sponsored by Dreyer's, the Main Street Cone Shop isn't always open, but when it is (usually on hot afternoons) it serves up cold, tempting summertime treats. The ice cream bars are shaped like Mickey, sundaes come with assorted toppings, and root beer floats are served in souvenir cups. Umbrellas offer shade for the outdoor seating amidst humorous sound effects emanating from the upstairs offices of E. S. Bitz, D.D.S., the "painless dentist."

Main Street Electrical Parade

DATES: 1972–1996

It's hard to describe the Main Street Electrical Parade to anyone who never saw it, because it was unlike traditional **parades**. Yes, it included floats, but no marching bands. The recorded narration enthusiastically described it as a "spectacular festival pageant of nighttime magic and imagination in thousands of sparkling lights and electro-syntho-magnetic musical sounds." Close, but still not enough.

The Electrical Parade was the brainchild of **Robert Jani**, Disneyland's longtime director of entertainment. Though Jani produced many of the events that are now treasured memories for millions of guests, the Electrical Parade was his signature creation. His inspiration was a display of electrified scenes that had helped inaugurate Walt Disney World in 1971. For Disneyland, Jani put elaborate two-dimensional scenes on unseen motorized carts, outlined everything with a total of a half-million lights, and had hidden **cast members** drive the glittering vehicles down a darkened **Main Street** toward **Town Square**.

Another Disney Legend, **Bill Justice**, designed many of the mechanical floats. These included a train and scenes from Disney classics like *Cinderella*, *Dumbo*, and *Pinocchio*. The memorable electronic music that emanated from loudspeakers was a 1967 non-Disney composition called "Baroque Hoedown," supplemented with snippets of other songs, all played on the futuristic Moog synthesizer.

The Main Street Electrical Parade debuted on the park's 27th birthday in 1972 and ended two dozen years later. Its career was twice interrupted—in 1975 and '76 a special **America on Parade** celebration commemorated the bicentennial; when the Electrical Parade returned, it was 10 minutes longer, with new, more spectacular three-dimensional displays, notably the one celebrating the title character from *Pete's Dragon* (the late '70s also welcomed a 50th birthday float for Mickey and a rousing patriotic climax). The second interruption came in '83, when the Flights of

Fantasy Parade landed for two years. During the Electrical Parade's 24-year run, several floats were retired, among them those for **It's a Small World**, the movie *Return to Oz*, and the birthday cake for Mickey's 60th birthday in 1988.

When Disneyland officials announced that the Main Street Electrical Parade's last performance would come in mid-October of 1996, the fan response was so strong and the surge in attendance so great that the parade's final run was extended to November 25th. Afterwards, some of the bulbs from the floats were sold off for charity. Replacing the Electrical Parade the following spring was **Light Magic**, a hugely promoted but hugely disappointing street spectacle. In 2001 a modified version of the Electrical Parade reappeared in Anaheim, but not at Disneyland (hence the name change). Disney's Electrical Parade cruised through Disney California Adventure to help spark attendance at the new park.

Main Street Fruit Cart

MAP: Main Street, MS-17

DATES: Ca. 2000–ongoing

Parked at the busy intersection of **Main Street** and East Center Street is the highly visible, highly tempting Main Street Fruit Cart. Here strolling guests can get healthy snacks on the go, including pieces of fresh fruit and fruit juice, all arrayed on 20-foot-long shaded displays. Behind the Fruit Cart are the slightly more sinful temptations of the **Main Street Cone Shop**.

Main Street Magic Shop

MAP: Main Street, MS-19

DATES: 1957–ongoing

The Magic Kingdom's most enduring magic store is tucked into a cozy spot along the southeastern block of **Main Street**. In 1957 the young Main Street Magic Shop had **Fine Tobacco** as its neighbor to the north. When Main Street Magic opened, it was the second magic supply store in the park—**Merlin's Magic Shop** in **Fantasyland** was two years older, but it pulled the disappearing-store trick in 1983. At night, the Magic Shop's sign stands out on Main Street—while nearly every other sign is outlined in pretty white lights, this one is outlined in garish blue and yellow.

And though the sign announces MAGIC, there's more here than meets the eye—scar makeup, disguises, toys, and gag gifts offer additional amusements.

Still, it's the display of magic tricks that offers a genuinely magical experience. Right before guests' very eyes, skillful **cast members** will demonstrate card tricks, coin tricks, and other sleight-of-hand illusions. Although they won't explain the tricks, the magicians will point out the how-to books that do. As shown in the movie *Disneyland: The First 50 Magical Years*, Disney Legend Steve Martin worked the Main Street Magic Shop's counter in the '60s, developing a rudimentary magic act that would lead to his professional career (Martin's memoir *Born Standing Up* has him working in both of Disneyland's magic shops).

In recent years the Main Street Magic Shop lost some of its luster and started selling generic Disney merchandise. However, a retailer called Houdini's Magic Shop, already established in Las Vegas, New York, San Francisco, and Downtown Disney, took over shop operations in 2009 to restore the magic that guests had enjoyed for over 50 years.

Main Street Photo Supply Co.

MAP: Main Street, MS-12

DATES: November 19, 1994–ongoing

At the northeast end of **Main Street**, the prominent building formerly known as Carefree Corner has been the Main Street Photo Supply Co. since 1994. As the sign above the door announces, "a picture is worth a thousand words" in this Kodak-sponsored shop. Whether guests are shooting still photos or making movies, this is the best-developed photography center in Disneyland.

"Photo Supply" doesn't begin to suggest the wide range of photo-related products here—everything from disposable cameras, film, and various batteries to View-Master reels, Disney frames, and photo books. In addition, the shop offers cameras to rent, film-processing services, camera repair, and battery chargers. Finally, this is where the photos taken of guests by park photographers—such as the portraits taken with the famous mouse himself inside **Mickey's House**—can be picked up.

Main Street Shooting Gallery

MAP: Main Street, MS-8

DATES: July 24, 1955–January 1962

Walt Disney wanted to keep traditional (and traditionally tacky) midway amusements out of his magnificent park, but at least one midway perennial—the shooting gallery—found its way in. The first and shortest-lived of Disneyland's three major shooting galleries, the Main Street Shooting Gallery debuted just after **Opening Day** (the **Frontierland Shooting Gallery** opened in 1957, and the **Big Game Safari** version five years after that).

On **Main Street**, the shooting gallery was located inside the **Penny Arcade**. Today that seems like an odd place to put a rifle range—after all, most of Disneyland's **souvenir books** have included Walt Disney's quote about Main Street representing "carefree times." Evidently those carefree times involved actual .22-caliber weapons, since that's what guests fired. Even kids got to handle the guns—souvenir books from 1959 to '62 included back-cover illustrations of a smiling adult handing a rifle to a gleeful child.

By early 1962, with another shooting gallery already established in **Frontierland** and another one coming soon to **Adventureland**, the live ammo was discharged from Main Street and replaced by the more urbane pleasures of the remodeled Penny Arcade and its associated shops.

Main Street, U.S.A., aka Main Street

MAP: Park, P-9

DATES: July 17, 1955–ongoing

Main Street, U.S.A. is often used as an all-inclusive heading for three identifiable areas in Disneyland's southern half. In fact, many people automatically assume that Main Street, U.S.A. (shortened throughout this book to Main Street) includes everything from the park's **entrance** up to **Sleeping Beauty Castle** 1,000 feet to the north. Certainly the park's **souvenir books** have supported the notion that the **Town Square** and the **Hub** are on Main Street, as their photos and descriptions have usually been gathered together under a single Main Street heading. However, to throw a fuller spotlight on each separate area, we've defined Main Street as the two-block business district between the rectangular Town Square and the circular Hub. This smaller, more manageable Main Street begins at the **Emporium** and ends at the **Refreshment Corner** 350 feet away.

Within this concentrated Main Street area are two distinct intersecting streets. The iconic Main Street, about 32 feet from curb to curb and lined with candy-colored buildings, is divided in half by the narrower Center Street. Center itself is divided into West Center (at today's **Fortuosity Shop**) and East Center (at the **Market House**). In addition to Main and Center, a third street, Plaza, runs from west to east across the north end of Main. Plaza Street divides the Main Street district from the Hub and is within the latter's domain.

The two blocks of Main Street constitute the most densely developed acreage in the park. With no large attractions filling up space, there are far more doorways and businesses here than anywhere else. And, visually at least, this is also Disneyland's least-changed area. Dozens of businesses here have opened and closed or opened and relocated, yet the exterior architecture remains basically as it's been since 1955. The same can't be said of the park's other lands, all of which have undergone massive remodelings and expansions.

Even in the first stages of planning his park, **Walt Disney** knew that he wanted a long entranceway that funneled guests through a charming recreation of a turn-of-the-century small American town. This strategy, he felt, would help orient guests to the park and ease them into the stranger lands that lay ahead. If the guests themselves didn't live in a small town, thought Disney, surely their relatives did, or their ancestors had, or they'd seen one in popular movies or TV shows. Thus they'd feel comfortable walking into one at Disneyland. Theoretically, the same small-town sweetness that had made Andy Hardy one of the most enduring film characters of the '40s would work in Anaheim in the '50s and beyond.

And so, the early concept drawings for Dis-neyland always included something called Main Street. But renderings of the picturesque street varied considerably. For one thing, two additional major streets, **International Street** and **Liberty Street**, were almost built in the area, branching off from Main Street. Designers, however, had abandoned both ideas by the early '60s. Some proposals also called for residential homes and a little red schoolhouse. The famous **Herb Ry-man** drawing of the 45-acre park, as Walt Disney envisioned it in 1953, placed an enormous, high-steepled church on Main Street. A **Marvin Davis** sketch that same year showed open-air court-yards inside some of Main Street's buildings, and one 1956 concept drawing put a "Disneyland Dog Pound" on Main Street, which would have provid-ed a comical photo opportunity echoing a scene from *Lady and the Tramp*.

Unlike other lands in the park that derive from screen entertainment (the Davy Crockett TV character shaped **Frontierland**; Disney's ani-mated movies spread across all of **Fantasyland**) Main Street derived from Walt Dis-ney's own life. Ultimately, what he built was a delightful evocation of the Midwest town he grew up in: Marceline, Missouri. The Disneyland version, however, is much more idealized and generic. It's not Main Street, Marceline; it's Main Street, U.S.A., a place that everybody, not just Missourians, can identify with. "Here is the America of 1890–1910," read the introductory text in the park's early souvenir books, not "Here is Marceline."

Disneyland's Main Street has included most of the features that would have been found in any small town's commercial center in the years bracketing the *fin de siè-cle*—an apothecary, a tobacconist, a movie theater, candy stores, bakeries, jewelers, horseless carriages, etc. But Disney didn't merely recreate what he remembered—he improved upon it. At its best, everything in Main Street sparkles, runs perfectly, and stays fresh. In fact, the street is so polite and pretty that it's more like a gentle Disney movie of what a turn-of-the-century town would have been like, had all the defects and blemishes of the real world been expunged. Indeed, like a detailed movie set, the impeccable façades and varied color schemes suggest individual buildings and store fronts, but in reality the interiors of the buildings are all connected and open to each other, making it possible to walk north–south for hundreds of feet, from one shop to the next and the next without venturing outside.

On Main Street, the buildings feel safer and cozier than real buildings because the architects designed them that way. The original Imagineers, remember, were art directors from Disney Studios, so they employed visual tricks from the movies as they planned out Main Street. Just as the park's railroad is 5/8 the size of a real train, and just as Sleeping Beauty Castle has larger blocks at the bottom than at the top to give the illusion of towering height, so too do the multi-story buildings on Main Street play with perspective. All along the street, the ground floors are approximately 90 percent of the regular size, to make doorways slightly less intimidating and shops a little more inviting to anxious guests (especially kids). The second floors, then, are all about 90 percent the size of the ground floors, making them about 80 percent of the normal size. Although none of these second stories can be entered by guests, the illusion is visible from the street. Finally, third floors are about 80 percent the size of the second floors, making them about 60 percent of the regular size and giving the whole Main Street area a snug, comfortable atmosphere. A small town? Yes, in more ways than one.

Adding to the warm feeling along Main Street is the bright paint on the buildings, which are all multicolored and frequently touched up to keep everything looking fresh. Every building boasts splendid architectural elements—beautifully adorned upper-story windows, decorative mansard roofs, striped awnings, turned finials, and ornate iron railings, all of it put there after designers studied old books and historic sites to get the details of the idyllic past just right.

Main Street is full of intriguing sights, smells, and sensations. Rounded trees add greenery, but they aren't so big that they block views. Century-old gas lamps purchased from St. Louis and Baltimore light the sidewalks, and new vehicles evoking vintage buggies and trolleys drive by frequently. There are old-time musicians, fragrant scents, and the joyous feeling of slow, unhurried exploration (no whirling rides here). Studious guests can try to decipher the proprietors identified on upper-story **Main Street windows**, or they can linger over the Emporium's wonderful window displays. At night, the white trim lights that have been outlining all the buildings since 1956 create an ambiance that is pure delight. Walt Disney declared that his favorite time of day at Disneyland was dusk, when the skies were darkening and the lights were coming up. Anyone who has seen Main Street by twilight would find it hard to disagree with him.

As if all that weren't enough, Main Street is filled several times a day with buoyant **parades**. In addition, special events occasionally fill the street with unique fun. From 1957 until 1964, for example, Main Street hosted the California State Pancake Races. This friendly competition was an inexpensive entertainment that supported

Quaker Oats, sponsor of **Aunt Jemima's Pancake House** in **Frontierland**. For the pancake race, two dozen housewives sprinted from the Hub to Town Square while flipping pancakes over ribbons draped across the street. The winner won $100, a plaque, and a gift basket. So popu-

lar were these races that celebrity judges, marching bands, and Disney characters eventually joined the festivities. Other special events have included "ice skating" on a synthetic Main Street pond for a 1974 TV audience and a 2002 swimming demonstration by Olympic athletes in a full-length Main Street pool.

Although some of these activities may sound corny, it's typical of the old-fashioned fun that has distinguished this old-fashioned area. Main Street may be just a nostalgic fantasy, but for many guests it's the best one in Disneyland.

Main Street Vehicles

MAP: Park, P-8, P-9, P-10

DATES: July 17, 1955–ongoing

Adding immeasurably to the atmosphere on **Main Street** are its various old-time vehicles. Since 1955, six varieties of public transportation have traveled up and down Main Street from **Town Square** to the **Hub**, all of them moving at three to four miles per hour, and all of them costing only an A ticket from the Disneyland **ticket book** to ride back in the day. No matter the vehicle, pick-ups and drop-offs are made at either end of the route, and all the rides are one-way.

Only three types of conveyances were in service on **Opening Day**, all of them towed by horses: the horse-drawn fire wagon, surrey, and streetcar. The gleaming red fire wagon, or fire engine as it was also called, was "an old-time hose and chemical wagon" pulled by two horses. There was only one fire wagon, and of all the Main Street Vehicles, it had the shortest career. After only five years of service, it was retired in mid-1960 to Town Square's **Fire Department**, where it has been on display ever since. The second Opening Day vehicle was the horse-drawn surrey, which lasted until 1971. This horse-drawn cart with tall wooden wheels carried eight to ten passengers spread out over three bench seats. The third vehicle dating to 1955 is the beautiful streetcar, which continues to run to this day. Two streetcars can operate at a time, their wheels spinning in the metal tracks that are grooved into Main Street (the street has two sets of these tracks to enable the streetcars to pass each other). As big as these vehicles are—and they are big, each holding up to 30 passengers and weighing up to two tons—each one is pulled by just a single horse, usually a Percheron or a Belgian.

Observant guests will find the names of the horses on their bridles.

Horsepower of a different kind was introduced to Main Street on May 12, 1956, when a shiny, red horseless carriage, the first of two, hit the street. Seven months later, a second horseless carriage with bright yellow paint also chugged along the Town Square-Hub route. Although both motorcars were put together meticulously to look like antiques from about 1903, underneath the exterior

are modern cars built by Disney Legend **Bob Gurr**. Each has a fringed top, toots a bulbous "ah-oo-gah" horn, and carries a half-dozen passengers on two bench seats.

In the summer of '56 a huge green double-decker bus called the omnibus was added to the roster of Main Street Vehicles. It was supplemented by a second omnibus on Christmas Day in 1957. Built by Bob Gurr, the Disneyland omnibuses look old but contain modern machinery—in fact the only true antique on it is the old-fashioned horn. Modeled after the big buses that toured Manhattan in the '30s, the omnibus is fully capable of today's freeway speeds. This gentle giant isn't always in service, but when it is it offers a matchless view of the Main Street area for up to 45 passengers at a time.

The last vintage vehicle to appear was another Gurr creation—the motorized fire truck that began carrying small groups of guests on August 16, 1958. To deliver his creation to the park, Gurr actually drove the truck down the freeway for almost an hour, from Disney Studios where it was built to Anaheim. Inspired by turn-of-the-century fire engines, the fire truck carries lengths of hose along its sides and has a bell mounted at the rear (the siren has been replaced by a horn).

Now over 50 years old, all the motorized Main Street vehicles are still cruising on Main Street. While these aren't the most thrilling vehicles guests will ride in at Disneyland, they are among the most charming and historically significant.

Main Street Windows

MAP: Park, P-9

DATES: July 17, 1955–ongoing

Many guests know that the names on the upper-story windows along **Main Street** pay tribute to real people, most of them Disney employees who contributed to Disneyland in some significant way. Typically, the windows identify a "proprietor" and then give a brief description of a fictional business supposedly operating behind the window. That descriptive text is usually a clue as to what the real-life Disney employee did at the park. For instance, the window for **Wally Boag**, the long-time comedian at

Names on the Main Street Tribute Windows
As of 2011, with their actual Disneyland-related occupations:

Milt Albright, accountant/manager
Charles Alexander, construction supervisor
W. F. Allen, executive at Upjohn Pharmacy, an early sponsor
Hideo Amemiya, Disneyland Hotel executive
American Broadcasting Company, TV network
Ken Anderson, artist
X Atencio, artist/writer
Renie Bardeau, official park photographer
H. Draegart Barnard, Walt Disney's doctor
Wally Boag, comedian
Chuck Boyajian, custodial superintendent
Charles Boyer, artist
C. Randy Bright, writer/executive
Roger Broggie, engineer
Harriet Burns, model maker
Bruce Bushman, artist
Cast members, honoring the long history of park employees
John Louis Catone, communications services
Royal Clark, treasurer
Claude Coats, artist
Renie Conley, costume designer
Ray Conway, construction
Jim Cora, executive
W. Dennis Cottrell, planner/designer
Roland F. Crump, artist
Don DaGradi, writer
Alice Davis, costume designer
Marc Davis, artist
Marvin Davis, architect/designer
Elias Disney, father of Walt Disney
Walt Disney (in Mickey's Toontown)
Ron Dominguez, executive
Don Edgren, engineer
Peter Ellenshaw, artist
Greg A. Emmer, executive
Morgan "Bill" Evans, landscape architect
Orlando Ferrante, executive
Van Arsdale France, guest services
Blaine Gibson, sculptor
Donald S. Gilmore, chairman of Upjohn Pharmacy, an early sponsor
Harper Goff, architect/designer (in Adventureland)
Bob Gurr, engineer

Jacob Samuel Hamel, engineer
John Hench, artist
Glenn Hicks, attractions operator (in Frontierland)
Alexander Irvine, doctor
Richard Irvine, art director/designer
Robert F. Jani, entertainment planner
Fred Joerger, model maker
Bill Justice, artist/engineer
Emile Kuri, decorator
Fred Leopold, lawyer
Gunther R. Lessing, lawyer
Jack Lindquist, marketing/executive
Mary Anne Mang, community relations
Ivan Martin, prop builder
Bill Martin, art director/designer
Sam McKim, artist
Edward T. Meck, publicist
Christopher D. Miller, Walt Disney's grandson
George Mills, carpenter
Seb Morey, taxidermist
Dick Nunis, executive
Fess Parker, actor (in Frontierland)
George Patrick, art director
C. V. Patterson, executive at Upjohn Pharmacy, an early sponsor
Bob Penfield, cast member from Opening Day to mid-1997
Cicely Rigdon, supervisor of Guest Relations
Wathel Rogers, model maker/engineer
Jack Rorex, construction
L. H. Roth, construction
Wade B. Rubottom, art director
Herb Ryman, artist
Gabriel Scognamillo, art director
Richard Sherman and Robert Sherman, composers
Cash Shockey, painter
Martin Sklar, writer/executive
E. G. Upjohn, president of Upjohn Pharmacy, an early sponsor
Ray Van De Warker, attractions/management
Robert Washo, designer
Frank Wells, executive
William T. Wheeler, engineer
George Whitney, designer/manager
Ed Winger, supervisor of paint department
John Wise, engineer
Gordon Youngman, lawyer

the **Golden Horseshoe**, states that his business is "Golden Vaudeville Routines"; for **X Atencio**, "The Musical Quill—Lyrics and Librettos" references his musical contributions to the **Haunted Mansion** and other attractions. Some tribute windows are not on Main Street at all: actor Fess Parker and designer **Harper Goff** are honored in **Frontierland** and **Adventureland**, respectively.

Not all of the tribute windows have names on them—some on Main Street have no text at all, and some identify a fictional business (Piano Lessons, Massage Parlor) without naming a specific proprietor. Two of the windows represent **Walt Disney's** relatives: his father, Elias, who died 14 years before Disneyland opened, and his grandson, Christopher Miller, who was born in 1954 while Disneyland was being built. Walt Disney himself does not have a Main Street window, but he does have a window at the **Mickey's Toontown** library: "Laugh-O-Gram Films, Inc. W. E. Disney, Directing Animator."

Malt Shop and Cone Shop

MAP: Frontierland, Fr-6

DATES: Ca. 1958–ca. 1970

A Malt Shop and Cone Shop tandem seems like a natural for **Main Street**, but actually this pair existed for about a decade in **Frontierland**. The location was next door to **Aunt Jemima's Pancake House** in the space previously occupied by **Don DeFore's Silver Banjo Barbecue**. Both the Malt Shop and Cone Shop were fast-food counters. The first served up hot dogs and burgers along with the malts, and the second served up ice cream to go. A 1970 remodel replaced these two eateries with another pair, the equally small and fast **Wheelhouse and Delta Banjo**.

The Many Adventures of Winnie the Pooh

MAP: Bear Country/Critter Country, B/C-4

DATES: April 11, 2003–ongoing

After almost 30 years, the ursine entertainers of the **Country Bear Jamboree** finally retired in 2001. Replacing them was another bear, this one the rotund star of A. A. Milne's whimsical stories and Disney's animated films. Like the Country Bear Jamboree, the Many Adventures of Winnie the Pooh originated in Florida, where it had replaced Mr. Toad's Wild Ride. When fans protested the threatened removal of **Mr. Toad's Wild Ride** from Disneyland, Pooh found a home in **Critter Country**. There the

attraction was set up as an indoor ride with an outdoor line.

To experience the Many Adventures, guests sit in adorable beehive-shaped "beehicles"—each with its own name—and venture for three and a half minutes into the verdant Hundred-Acre Wood. Along the way are visits with Pooh's animal friends, including Tigger, Rabbit, and Eeyore, plus an inevitable search for "hunny," a Heffalump-and-Woozle dream, and a party (Christopher Robin was not invited, it seems, as he's nowhere in sight).

A visual treat for children, the attraction is filled with bright colors, gentle bounces, friendly faces, heartwarming sentiments, and delightful **Sherman Brothers** music. Fans of the old Jamboree will enjoy a glimpse of the three heads of Max the deer, Melvin the moose, and Buff the buffalo still mounted on a darkened wall just past the Woozles. What's more, Pooh's balloon ride is accomplished via the same mechanism that once carried Teddi Barra, one of the singing Country Bears, aloft on her swing.

Marché aux Fleurs, Sacs et Mode

MAP: New Orleans Square, NOS-9

DATES: 1975–ca. 1985

"Flower Market, Stylish Bags" was a shop located for over a decade in the back of **New Orleans Square**. Previously **Le Chapeau** had been on this corner behind the **French Market**. The merchandise was just as French and frilly as the hats that had previously lined the shelves. Fancy handbags, accessories, and some hats were offered, plus film and a few other supplies. **La Mascarade d'Orléans** brought Mardi Gras masks here in the mid-'80s.

Market House

MAP: Main Street, MS-18

DATES: July 17, 1955–ongoing

The nostalgic Market House has been a **Main Street** staple since **Opening Day**. Wrapping around the southeast corner of Main and East Center Street, the Market House exterior has three street-facing sides, two of brick, and one of wood. The building's four stories are topped with a mansard roof and a widow's walk, making it one of the most imposing structures on Main Street. A 1954 concept drawing labeled it a combination "grocery store" and "meat market"—ultimately, it was designed as a handsome 1890s general store.

The ground-floor interior has always been a fascinating room to explore and is in some ways more like a museum than a retail space. An ornate potbellied stove invites guests to relax over a game of checkers. Swirling candy sticks stand in decorative jars, pickle barrels are scattered around the hardwood floors, and kitchen supplies, gourmet foods, and a huge selection of mugs line the shelves. Cocoa and coffee drinks are served to guests by costumed women in long, old-fashioned dresses. One delightful touch added in 1974: the antique phones here convey gossipy party-line conversations.

Swift & Company, the meat packager, was the original sponsor (Swift also sponsored two early Disneyland restaurants, the **Red Wagon Inn** and **Chicken Plantation**). The park's 1956 and '57 **souvenir books** called the building Swift's Market House, with the added description "meats and groceries" (just how many groceries were purchased and lugged around the park is debatable). Later the Hills Bros. name was established out front, but in recent years the Market House has remained unsponsored. Dignified signs declare the store's wares: Canned Fruits and Vegetables, Coffee, Candy, Preserves, Canned Goods and Spices. As always, thanks to the absence of Disney-themed T-shirts, hats, and modern souvenirs, this remains one of the most genuine old-time locations in Disneyland.

Mark Twain Riverboat

MAP: Frontierland, Fr-17

DATES: July 17, 1955–ongoing

Nearly every description of the *Mark Twain* includes the words "stately" and "majestic." The graceful white ship certainly is both. As the first large paddlewheeler built in America since the early 20th century, it's also historic. And at 105 feet long and 150 tons, it rivals the magnificent **Sailing Ship *Columbia*** as Disneyland's single most imposing watercraft.

Walt Disney wanted a resplendent riverboat in his park long before Disneyland was built—early concept drawings always included something that looked like the *Mark Twain* circling what appeared to be the **Rivers of America**. Tellingly, when the ship's landing was built, it was placed in a highly visible location at the end of the main **Frontierland** walkway so that guests would be able to see the docked, dazzling

Mark Twain from the **Hub**. This tempting vision drew many a diffident newcomer deep into the wild frontier.

The ship's illustrious history began with the steel hull, built at shipyards in nearby Long Beach. Meanwhile, the wooden decks and ornate superstructure were constructed at Disney Studios in Burbank, trucked down to Anaheim, and then added to the hull inside the park. While the twin-smoke-stacked *Mark Twain* is an authentic-looking replica of the larger stern-wheelers that plied the Mississippi in the 19th century, it isn't architecturally perfect—some parts were built proportionally to a smaller scale than other parts, in accordance with the specific safety and maritime needs at Disneyland. The ship can hold over 350 passengers, though when it debuted there was no official loading capacity. Thus there are old tales of **cast members** accidentally overloading the boat until it almost capsized when all the guests shifted to one side to view the riverbank.

Disneyland's Watercraft

Attached to Rails:
1. Canal Boats of the World/Storybook Land Canal Boats (1955/1956–ongoing)
2. Jungle Cruise (1955–ongoing)
3. *Mark Twain* Riverboat (1955–ongoing)
4. Motor Boat Cruise (1957–1993)
5. Sailing Ship *Columbia* (1958–ongoing)
6. Submarine Voyage/Finding Nemo Submarine Voyage
    (1959–1998/2007–ongoing)

Free-Floating:
7. Indian War Canoes/Davy Crockett's Explorer Canoes (1956–ongoing)
8. It's a Small World (1966–ongoing)
9. Mike Fink Keel Boats (1955–1997)
10. Phantom Boats (1955–1956)
11. Pirates of the Caribbean (1967–ongoing)
12. Rafts to Tom Sawyer Island (1956–ongoing)
13. Splash Mountain (1989–ongoing)

Stationary:
14. Donald's Boat, aka *Miss Daisy* (1993–ongoing)
15. Pirate Ship Restaurant (1955–1982)

On July 13, 1955 the *Mark Twain* made a prominent trial voyage at a party thrown by Walt Disney and his wife to celebrate their 30th wedding anniversary. Four days later, actress Irene Dunne christened the ship during televised **Opening Day** ceremonies. From then on it has endured as one of Disneyland's iconic attractions. Strangely, in its first three decades the *Mark Twain* swung back and forth from being a C, D, and even briefly an E attraction. The views have also changed dramatically over the decades, but the lovely, serene trip hasn't varied significantly. Powered by steam and propelled by its stern paddlewheel, the ship travels on a submerged track around, appropriately enough, the island named after one of Mark Twain's greatest characters, Tom Sawyer. On its 12- to 14-minute journey the ship travels about a half-mile and takes in panoramic views of island wilderness and attractions in Frontierland, **New Orleans Square**, and **Critter Country. Audio-Animatronic** animals and **Mike Fink Keel Boats** are among the additional sights along the water's edge.

Naturally, the *Mark Twain* has often been a star attraction for special events. In its 50-plus years and 260,000-plus miles, the ship has been specially decorated for holidays, paraded jazz combos in front of shoreline guests, and been incorporated into **Fantasmic!**. From November 2009 to January 2010, the *Mark Twain* hosted Tiana's Showboat Jubilee!, a spirited Mardi Gras-style musical celebration coinciding with the release of *The Princess and the Frog*. At one time the ship sold mint juleps on board, and occasionally a lucky guest still gets invited to visit the wheelhouse. But most guests don't need anything special to enliven the experience—on a hot day, a quiet voyage on cool waters aboard the stately, majestic *Mark Twain* is plenty special enough.

Marquee

MAP: Park, P-1

DATES: 1958–ongoing

For over 40 years a magnificent marquee graced the automobile entrance to the Disneyland **parking lot**. Surprisingly, there was no big sign there on **Opening Day**, and in fact the first true marquee wasn't installed along Harbor Boulevard until 1958. When it did go up, the marquee offered a friendly and memorable welcome to drivers.

The sign was in three parts. The top section spelled out the Disneyland name, with the letters mounted separately in different-size rectangles and spelled out in a fantasy-style font. Underneath that line was a wide horizontal section that read "The happiest place on Earth," and underneath that was a board with manually placed letters listing that day's hours and special events. Stretching skyward from the sign was a row of flagpoles festooned with stiff banners. It wasn't the biggest park marquee ever built (that honor probably goes to New Jersey's Palisades Amusement Park, which had a 400-foot-wide electrified sign big enough to be read 50 miles away), but the Disneyland marquee might have been the most beloved.

After some 30 years, a new marquee went up in the same spot on October 6, 1989. This one was essentially the same as the original, save for the new electronic billboard in the bottom third. This sign was replaced in 1996 with a dazzling new one, with all-new components. The Disneyland name was now spelled out in white letters on a blue background. While the letters were still written in the same fantasy font, and while they were still mounted in separate rectangles, those rectangles were now all approximately 14 feet high for a more uniform look. Underneath the first line, a white-on-pink sign reprised the "happiest place on Earth" tag line, and below that the new computerized billboard featured flashier announcements. Crowning the marquee were six small pink, yellow, and blue banners and, in the center, an 18-foot-tall gold castle within a blue circle. From the street to the top of the gold castle, the marquee stood about six stories tall. For a few years in the '90s, customers could temporarily rent the electronic billboard through the Disney catalog and have a private message photographed as a keepsake.

On June 14, 1999 this large marquee flashed its last announcement; the whole thing was removed the next day in anticipation of construction for Disney California Adventure. After the sign was dismantled into separate pieces, the Disneyland letters, the "happiest place" section, and the gold castle were auctioned off on eBay, with actor John Stamos placing one of the winning bids.

A less imposing marquee now greets pedestrians along Harbor Boulevard. The eastern walkway into Disneyland is marked by a 20-foot-wide, 15-foot-tall blue aluminum banner, with a "thank you for visiting" sign on the back. Of note to fans is **Walt Disney's** star in the sidewalk here. Placed in 2006, this was the inaugural star on a new Anaheim/Orange County Walk of Stars.

Marshal's Office

MAP: Frontierland, Fr-25

DATES: July 1955–July 1956

Adding authenticity to **Frontierland** was a small one-story Marshal's Office that once stood at the far end of the row that holds today's shooting gallery. Decorated with small flags, the office was primarily used as a backdrop for photos. The sign on top of its slanted roof read, "Willard P. Bounds, Blacksmith and U.S. Marshal." In the book *Disneyland: The Nickel Tour*, Bounds is identified as a real-life frontier marshal **Walt Disney** actually knew—his father-in-law.

After a year the nearby Mexican restaurant **Casa de Fritos** relocated into this spot with a newer, bigger building.

Martin, Bill
(1917–)

Many of the original Disneyland designers were moviemakers recruited from Disney Studios, but Bill Martin was a moviemaker recruited from 20th Century Fox, where he'd worked as a set designer. Martin was an Iowan born in 1917. When his family moved to Southern California, he studied architecture and design at local colleges and art institutes until he was hired to work as a Hollywood art director. After serving in the Air Force, Martin continued his career at Fox until he joined the Disneyland planning team in 1953.

It's said that Martin had a hand in everything at the park. One of his tasks was to create the original **Fantasyland**—its layout, its look, and its attractions. Working with other Disney Legends like **Ken Anderson**, Martin designed most of the indoor "dark rides" that are still favorites today, including **Peter Pan Flight** and **Mr. Toad's Wild Ride**. A few years later he was in on the creation of the **Nature's Wonderland** area, the **Fantasyland Autopia**, and the **Submarine Voyage** while also laying out the long, looping path of the **Monorail**.

In the '60s Martin was a key architect of **New Orleans Square** and its two landmark attractions, the **Haunted Mansion** and **Pirates of the Caribbean**. He also helped design **Walt Disney's** New Orleans Square **apartment**, a decorous space that later became the **Disney Gallery**. Martin rose to the position of vice president of design in '71, supervising plans and contributing designs for Walt Disney World. Formally retired as of 1977, he stayed on as a consultant and was eventually named a Disney Legend in 1994.

Matterhorn Bobsleds
MAP: Fantasyland, Fa-24

DATES: June 14, 1959–ongoing

Nowadays guests appreciate the fun and aesthetics of the thrilling Matterhorn ride, but few people realize how innovative this attraction was when it debuted in 1959. Before then, all roller coaster-type rides placed long trains on wooden tracks with wide curves. In contrast, the bobsleds of Disneyland's first true thrill ride used small, sleek vehicles, not on wooden tracks, but on hollow metal tubes that made the ride both quieter and smoother.

It was wilder, too—since the metal tubes could be bent easily, the ride had

tighter curves. Furthermore, the Imagineers placed more than one bobsled at a time on the track, an important strategy for cutting down on wait times (when the single bobsleds were later doubled up into pairs, the Swiss-costumed **cast members** could fill them with over 1,500 guests per hour). Disney Legend **Bob Gurr** is credited as the main designer of the little two-toned bobsleds, while another Disney Legend, **Fred Joerger**, made numerous models of **Matterhorn Mountain** with various track layouts. The result of their efforts was a revolution in ride design and the very definition of an E-ticket attraction (see **ticket books**).

The bobsleds run on two tracks that climb through the inside of the Matterhorn to a point about two-thirds of the way up. They then glide down quickly around and through the mountain for a total distance of about 2,100 feet. For decades guests have tested their theories that one track is faster than the other, but ultimately the speed has more to do with the load inside the sleds than it does with the tracks (the track on the Fantasyland side is slightly longer and has tighter curves). During the two-and-a-quarter-minute trip, the sleds on both tracks travel at an average speed of barely 20 miles per hour. The speed certainly *seems* faster, though, and riders can grab only quick glimpses of the spectacular scenery.

When the Matterhorn opened, its bobsleds quickly got famous as the park's hottest vehicles, and held on to that reputation until **Space Mountain** opened in 1977. So special were they that on the day they debuted, **Walt Disney**, his family, and Vice President Richard Nixon took the first ride. One of the special touches that has made the trip distinctive is its climax—a sudden, splashy swoop through a "glacier lake" (as described in the Disneyland **souvenir books**). No other Disneyland ride had an effect like this in the late '50s. The splashdown not only creates a great visual effect for riders and pedestrians but also decelerates the speeding sleds (before the lake was in place, test rides culminated in sandbags and bales of hay).

At the end of the trip, the pre-recorded voice of **Jack Wagner** cautions riders to "remain seated please"—fans of the band No Doubt will recognize his request as the 11-second introduction to the song "Tragic Kingdom."

Matterhorn Mountain

MAP: Fantasyland, Fa-24

DATES: June 14, 1959–ongoing

For many guests arriving via the Santa Ana Freeway, their first view of Disneyland has often been a quick glimpse of the Matterhorn. The memorable mountain has been a Disneyland icon since 1959, when it opened after less than a year of construction. Along with the **Mono-rail** and **Submarine Voyage**, it was one of the year's three major additions to the park.

Like dozens of other Disneyland attractions, the mountain was inspired by Disney movies—a 1955 documentary called *Switzerland* and a 1958 feature called *Third Man on the Mountain*. In addition, **Walt Disney** had already made several trips to the actual Matterhorn and had been enchanted by it, so when the idea for a snow-capped hill with a toboggan ride occurred to him in late 1956, by 1957 that idea had evolved into a taller snow-capped mountain with a roller coaster ride, and by late 1958 it had grown into the majestic Matterhorn with its revolutionary **Matterhorn Bobsleds**.

The name evolved right along with the plan—as noted in *Disneyland: The Nickel Tour*, what began as Snow Hill became Snow Mountain, then Mount Disneyland, Disneyland Mountain, Sorcerer's Mountain, Magic Mountain, Fantasy Mountain, Echo Mountain, the Valterhorn (adapting Walt's name), and finally Matterhorn Mountain.

The Matterhorn was created on a barely used, barely landscaped picnic mound called Holiday Hill. This 20-foot-tall bump, straddling the Fantasyland/Tomorrowland border, was built up with dirt excavated from the **Sleeping Beauty Castle** moat. The location makes the European mountain clearly visible from the all-American **Main Street**, a potentially jarring sight that bothered some designers, but not Walt Disney. The location also places the mountain in the middle of lots of park traffic. Not including the bobsleds, five other kinds of vehicles have passed close by over the years—the **Motor Boat Cruise**, the **Fantasyland Autopia**, the **Submarine Voyage**, the **Alice in Wonderland** caterpillar cars, and the looping Monorail. Additionally, the old **Skyway** trams actually passed through, not around, the mountain.

During the planning phase, Disney Legend **Fred Joerger** made many models to get the mountain's shape correct from all perspectives. As it grew, the construction project gobbled up over 2,000 steel girders for the frame, with no two girders identical in size and shape. Four acres of cement, smoothed by hand, covered the construction like gray skin, with 2,500 gallons of white resin adding permanent "snow" to the upper half. The finished mountain, its landscaped grounds, and its alpine-themed **queue** area created a circular park footprint of about one and a half acres. The mountain stands precisely 147 feet tall, which is 1/100th the height of the actual Matterhorn. Not only is it still the tallest structure in Disneyland, for a while Disneyland's Matterhorn was the tallest structure in the county until a building boom in the '60s built up the surrounding skyline. Forced perspective, the same movie-making technique that makes Sleeping Beauty Castle look taller than it really is, also makes the Matterhorn seem to stretch higher than it really does. Here, the trick is in the trees, which get gradually smaller the farther up the mountain they "grow."

The mountain has many unique features. For one thing, its placement between two lands has meant that Disneyland's **souvenir books** have listed it first in Tomorrowland (for its first nine years) and then in Fantasyland. Also, the mountain has been regularly ascended by trained alpine climbers. According to a 1963 issue of *National Geographic*, climbers scaled the Matterhorn eight times a day. Occasionally, they've even made their ascents dressed as Disney characters or Santa Claus. There are 30 routes to the summit, with views revealing Catalina Island and, on the clearest days, the Hollywood sign some 40 miles away.

One no-longer-hidden secret about the climbers is that they have had their own small basketball court about 100 feet up inside the Matterhorn. It's not a full-size court, just a flat surface with a mounted hoop so that climbers and workers can take a break without having to go down to the park. At least one local radio station has broadcast its show from the court inside the mountain.

Another distinctive feature of the Matterhorn is its interior elevator. Besides carrying maintenance workers, this elevator lifts **Tinker Bell** to a platform for her glide above Fantasyland. Tink's flight isn't the only nighttime event to feature the Matterhorn. From 1961 until the mid-'70s, a 22-ton sparkling star, visible from the nearby freeway and neighborhoods, adorned the mountain's apex over the winter holidays.

The 15 Tallest Structures in Disneyland History

1. Matterhorn Mountain (147 feet)
2. Space Mountain (118)
3. Big Thunder Mountain (104)
4. Splash Mountain (87)
5. Rocket Jets tower (85)
6. Skyway to Tomorrowland tower (85)
7. Sailing Ship *Columbia* (84)
8. Pirate Ship Restaurant (80, estimated)
9. Sleeping Beauty Castle (77)
10. Original *Moonliner* rocket (76)
11. Swiss Family Treehouse (70)
12. Flagpole in Town Square (65)
13. Astro-Orbitor (64)
14. Christmas tree (60)
15. 1998 *Moonliner* rocket (53)

Today's bobsled riders may not realize that in the '60s and '70s, riders could clearly see the support beams inside the Matterhorn. A 1977–1978 remodel added new "ice cave" features that blocked off the exposed beams, and also introduced the Abominable Snowman creature as a scary presence throughout the ride. Another aesthetic improvement came when the Skyway trams were shut down and their mountain openings were sealed off in 1994. Also, at some point two slender spires were added to the summit to serve as a lightning rod and a beacon to aircraft. A 2012 update enhanced the effects inside the attraction, added a fresh coat of paint to the mountain's exterior, remodeled the loading areas, and put new three-seat bobsleds on the tracks.

The Matterhorn is unique in the history of Disney parks. Unlike other Disneyland mountains—**Splash**, **Space**, and **Big Thunder**, which all exist in other Disney parks around the world—the mighty Matterhorn has never been duplicated, an appropriate tribute to the first, and some say still the most beautiful, Disney pinnacle.

Maxwell House Coffee Shop

MAP: Town Square, TS-7

DATES: December 1, 1955–October 8, 1957

Almost five months after Disneyland opened, the Maxwell House Coffee Shop debuted on **Town Square** between the **Wurlitzer Music Hall** on the corner and the **Opera House** building. A charming coffee house facing guests as they entered the park in the morning must have seemed like the perfect blend of location and timing. So perfect that after Maxwell House left in 1957, **Hills Bros.** stepped in eight months later.

McGinnis, George
(Dates unknown)

Futuristic vehicles may have been George McGinnis's specialty, but he also contributed to some of the old-style attractions at the park. After studying engineering and design in college in the early '60s, this Pennsylvanian was invited to work on the **Tomorrowland** remodel of 1966–1967. Among other projects, McGinnis designed the whirling vehicles that updated the old **Astro-Jets** into the new **Rocket Jets**, and created the Mighty Microscope that greeted guests inside **Adventure Thru Inner Space**.

Moving to Walt Disney World projects, McGinnis designed that park's PeopleMover in the late '60s. Back at Disneyland, he was one of the key designers of **Space Mountain**, and a decade later he redesigned the **Monorail** with a sleek and luxurious Mark V train. During this time, McGinnis also joined Disney moviemakers to work on *The Black Hole*; his four robot characters are included in the sci-fi production.

Throughout the '80s and '90s, McGinnis continued to help with a wide variety of significant vehicles and attractions at Disney parks throughout the world, including Disneyland's new **Snow White Adventures** cars and the **Indiana Jones Adventure** jungle trucks. McGinnis was elected to the National Inventors Hall of Fame in 2001.

McKim, Sam
(1924–2004)

One of the best souvenirs a guest can take home from Disneyland is a large, beautifully illustrated **Fun Map**. Artist Sam McKim drew the first of these in the 1950s; veteran guests may also recall his smaller **Tom Sawyer Island** map, which was a free **Frontierland** handout until 1976. Over the decades McKim also drew many, many detailed concept drawings for other attractions and buildings that eventually found their way into the park.

A Canadian born in 1924, McKim and his family moved to Southern California in 1935. Related to an MGM casting agent, he was soon getting jobs as a child actor in numerous Westerns. After serving in World War II, studying at Los Angeles art colleges, and winning medals during the Korean War, Sam McKim became an artist in Hollywood. In the mid-'50s he drew set sketches for 20th Century Fox until a layoff sent him over to Disney Studios, where he was hired temporarily to sketch upcoming Disneyland attractions. McKim ended up staying with the company for the next three decades, often working closely with **Walt Disney** himself. Today McKim's drawings of Frontierland, the **Golden Horseshoe**, **Main Street**, the **Monorail**, **New Orleans Square**, and more still inspire Disney designers and artists.

Outside of Disneyland, McKim worked on live-action Disney films of the '50s and '60s as a storyboard artist. He also drew concept illustrations for the 1964–1965 New York World's Fair and several Walt Disney World attractions. Though he retired in 1987, five years later he drew a lavish park map for the debut of Disneyland Paris. McKim was elected a Disney Legend in 1996, eight years before he died of heart failure at age 79.

Meck, Edward
(1899–1973)

Eddie Meck was working in promotions long before he became Disneyland's publicist. Born in Wisconsin in 1899, Meck began his career with Pathé Frères, an early film company that specialized in dramas and made the *Perils of Pauline* serials and the Harold Lloyd comedies. After publicizing those movies in the 1920s, Meck jumped to Columbia Pictures in the '30s and pushed Frank Capra's films to Oscar-winning success.

Meck joined the Disneyland team in the spring of 1955 and helped build the **Opening Day** excitement to a fever pitch. He did it, not with the fantastic stunts and invented publicity gimmicks that heralded other big premieres and events of that era, but with simplicity, letting the beauty and diversity of the park speak for itself. Throughout his Disney career, Meck's idea was to invite the global press (flying them in when necessary) and let them each find their own topics. After all, there were plenty of unique ways to enjoy Disneyland—why not let the writers discover those pleasures for themselves?

The result was a flood of gushing travel articles in national newspapers and magazines, and quickly Disneyland surged to its longstanding position as a top tourist attraction. Working out of Disneyland's **City Hall**, Meck also invited lots of celebrities to come share in the fun, leading to plenty of well-publicized photos. In 1971 his soft-sell approach introduced the media to Walt Disney World, where Meck himself set up the new publicity department.

Meck died in 1973 at age 74. He was inducted as a Disney Legend 22 years later.

Meet Me at Disneyland
(1962)

During the summer of 1962, KTTV, an independent TV station in Los Angeles, aired a one-hour show on Saturday nights called *Meet Me at Disneyland*. Thirteen episodes ran from June 9 to September 8, all of them shot live in the park with TV announcer/actor Johnny Jacobs as the host. Filled with attractions and entertainment, the show featured performances by such Disneyland groups as the **Dapper Dans** and the **Firehouse Five Plus Two**. Non-Disney acts like the Osmond Brothers and special guests like astronaut John Glenn also made appearances.

Merlin's Magic Shop

MAP: Fantasyland, Fa-30

DATES: July 17, 1955–January 16, 1983

The first of Disneyland's two magic shops, Merlin's Magic Shop in **Fantasyland** was ready for its debut on **Opening Day**, about two years before the **Main Street Magic Shop** opened. However, while the shop on **Main Street** has never closed down, the one in Fantasyland was replaced after 27 years of business.

Merlin's occupied a great location in the **Sleeping Beauty Castle** courtyard, right next to **Peter Pan Flight**. The building is still there, featuring a half-timbered, peak-roofed, European-village exterior as if from an old fairy tale—a suitable look for a magic shop named after the wizard character in *The Sword in the Stone*. Inside the shop were magic tricks, how-to books, and practical jokes, with enthusiastic **cast members** ready to demonstrate sleight-of-hand illusions right at the counter.

As fun as Merlin's was, it didn't survive the huge Fantasyland renovation of the early '80s and was replaced by **Mickey's Christmas Chalet**.

Mermaids

MAP: Tomorrowland, T-11

DATES: June 14, 1959; summer 1965–summer 1967 (seasonal)

For decades, the beautiful **attraction poster** for the **Submarine Voyage** depicted a looming, lavender-colored sub with lithe, long-haired mermaids swimming underneath it. For three summers in the mid-'60s, mermaids really did splash around in the submarines' lagoon.

Originally eight of these sirens, attractive local swimmers wearing ocean-themed halter tops and svelte neoprene mermaid tails, were part of the celebratory festivities promoting the new submarine attraction when it launched in June 1959. Six years later, after conducting auditions in the Disneyland Hotel pool, Disneyland officials brought mermaids back to frolic in the **Tomorrowland** waters and stretch out on the surrounding rocks.

Entertainment specialist **Tommy Walker** is usually credited with developing the mermaid idea, though its provenance probably goes back to 1947, when Florida's Weeki Wachee Springs began presenting underwater shows with live mermaids. In the late 1940s and '50s, Mermaids were also a recurring topic in movies such as *Mr. Peabody and the Mermaid*, *Miranda*, and *Mad About Men* (not to mention that one of the era's top film stars, Esther Williams, was nicknamed the Million Dollar Mermaid).

At Disneyland, the Tomorrowland mermaids were a popular feature, but extensive exposure to the lagoon's chlorine eventually became a concern. When some of the male guests felt compelled to jump into the water after the alluring mermaids, park officials had finally had enough and whistled everyone out of the pool in 1967.

Mickey Mouse Club Circus

MAP: Fantasyland, Fa-22

DATES: November 24, 1955–January 8, 1956

Many Disneyland attractions that debuted in 1955 thrived for decades, but a few early ideas were utter flops. One of these was the Mickey Mouse Club Circus, which on paper must have seemed like an appealing attraction to **Walt Disney**, a longtime circus-lover. In November of '55, two circus tents went up in the northeast corner of **Fantasyland**, an area that would later be filled by the **Junior Autopia**. The official circus opened on Thanksgiving Day with a **parade** down **Main Street** and an hour-and-a-quarter show in heated tents.

Theoretically, fans of *The Mickey Mouse Club* TV show should have been fans of the circus acts—Jimmie Dodd, the TV host, was the ringmaster, and the Mouseketeers (who, according to a promotional flyer, were "clowning, riding elephants, and in an Aerial Ballet") were among the stars. Additionally, a dozen professional acts presented a total of 150 animals and performers, including camels, ponies, trained seals, dogs, trapeze artists, equestrians, and "Bob-O the Disneyland Clown."

11 Attractions and Exhibits Permanently Closed Within One Year of Debuting

1. Canal Boats of the World (July 1955–September 1955)
2. Davy Crockett Frontier Museum (July 1955–October 1955)
3. Court of Honor (July 1955–March 1956)
4. Marshal's Office (July 1955–July 1956)
5. Phantom Boats (August 1955–January 1956)
6. Mickey Mouse Club Circus (November 1955–January 1956)
7. Keller's Jungle Killers (February 1956–September 1956)
8. Fashions and Fabrics Through the Ages (March 1965–December 1965)
9. Disney Afternoon Avenue (March 1991–September 1991)
10. Toy Story Funhouse (January 1996–May 1996)
11. Dalmatian Celebration (November 1996–January 1997)

Unfortunately, the circus stands, which had the capacity to hold 2,500 guests, were rarely half-full and often were barely occupied at all. Guests, it turned out, wanted to explore the unique park, not sit and watch a typical circus that cost an extra fifty cents for acts they'd already seen in their hometown. What's more, several of the animal acts were problematic (some animals actually escaped at one point), and a few of the professional circus performers weren't exactly consistent with the wholesome Disney image.

After only six weeks, the Mickey Mouse Club Circus was dismantled, though some of its elements did linger at the park. The big cats stayed on as **Keller's Jungle Killers**, and the main tent moved to the picnic grounds of **Holidayland**, just outside of **Frontierland**.

Mickey Mouse Club Headquarters,
aka Mickey Mouse Club Shop

MAP: Town Square, TS-9

DATES: Fall 1963–1964

After the **Babes in Toyland Exhibit** left the **Opera House** in September of 1963, the Mickey Mouse Club Headquarters set up shop, selling Mouseketeer photos and souvenirs while serving as club headquarters where new members could enroll and get membership cards. The timing for a Mickey Mouse Club Headquarters might have seemed off to many guests—after all, *The Mickey Mouse Club* TV show had been canceled in 1959, so the only episodes on TV in '63 were reruns. The headquarters itself was canceled in 1964, and the next year this space was finally filled by something that would last—**Great Moments with Mr. Lincoln**.

Mickey Mouse Club Theater,
aka Fantasyland Theater

MAP: Fantasyland, Fa-9

DATES: August 27, 1955–December 20, 1981

The Mickey Mouse Club TV show was still 10 weeks away from airing when the Mickey Mouse Club Theater opened in **Fantasyland**. The theater covered about 5,000 square feet in the **Sleeping Beauty Castle** wing where **Pinocchio's Daring Journey** is today. On **Opening Day** the theater made it into the national TV coverage—not for anything having to do with the theater itself, but for the debut of the Mouseketeers outside.

The theater's exterior carried the same medieval festival theme common to the castle courtyard at the time. By late August the air-conditioned, 400-seat, B-ticket theater was showing half-hour blocks of cartoons from 11 AM to closing, but no live Mouseketeers. Starting on June 16, 1956, a half-hour show called *3D Jamboree* offered a 3-D Mouseketeer movie, 3-D cartoons, and 3-D glasses. The promo poster declared that the show was "all in color~all in music~all in fun." Behind the scenes, the theater was also used for official meetings and training sessions.

With no new episodes of the original *Mickey Mouse Club* being made after 1959, the Mickey Mouse Club Theater finally got a new name in 1964. Rechristened the Fantasyland Theater, it continued to show cartoons on a varying schedule until December 20, 1981, when it was closed permanently for construction that would produce Pinocchio's Daring Journey. The Fantasyland Theater name would live on, however—in mid-1995 it became the new name of **Videopolis**.

Mickey's Christmas Chalet

MAP: Fantasyland, Fa-30

DATES: May 25, 1983–May 17, 1987

When **Fantasyland** was remodeled extensively in the early '80s, several venerable attractions and shops disappeared. Among them was Merlin's Magic Shop, which had been purveying magic tricks since 1955. Replacing the magic of Merlin was the magic of Christmas. Located in the same old world-style building next to **Peter Pan Flight**, but freshened up with new paint and flower boxes, Mickey's Christmas Chalet opened as a year-round, holiday-themed store filled with decorations and ornaments (not all of them adorned with Disney characters).

Four years later, the holiday merchandise was relocated to the **Castle Christmas Shop**, a nearby room within the castle's entryway. Moving into Merlin's and Mickey's old spot was the charming **Briar Rose Cottage**.

Mickey's House

MAP: Mickey's Toontown, MT-5

DATES: January 24, 1993–ongoing

For decades many guests wondered where Mickey Mouse lived in Disneyland and where they could meet him. They found out in early 1993, when the mouse who started it all got his own fascinating home at 1 Neighborhood Lane in the new **Mickey's Toontown** area.

It turns out that Mickey lives in a bright yellow bungalow with bulbous columns, white and green trim, peaked dormer windows, curved walls, and sloping roof lines. Outside, his garden is exquisitely maintained and outlined by a white picket fence. Inside, Mickey splurged on beautiful hardwood floors. The mouse's house contains famous books revamped with mouse-related titles (*Random Mouse Dictionary*, *Mice Station Zebra*, etc.), a Mouseway player piano with **Hidden Mickeys** on it, a smiling old-time radio, a TV that plays cartoons, Mickey's passport with Disney-related stamps, and Pluto's bed and water bowl. Throughout the house are clever architectural flourishes and design details that leave no doubt as to whose home this is (Imagineers must have been laughing constantly as they came up with all the delightful gags and puns). A garage outside holds the star's sports equipment, tools, and garbage cans.

The walk-through mouse house is actually a lead-in to the attraction's signature event. Out back is the Movie Barn, a rustic prop-filled building where cartoons are supposedly still being made. A small stand-up theater plays Mickey's highlights, and old posters line the walls. To the delight of kids, the main mouse, dressed in a natty tuxedo, is available in his dressing room all day long to greet guests and take photos. For adults and Disney fans, Mickey's House is a wonderfully imaginative, amazingly detailed museum worthy of careful study.

Mickey's Toontown

MAP: Park, P-17

DATES: January 24, 1993–ongoing

Since the early '90s, Disneyland's **souvenir books** have spent many colorful pages enticing guests to explore the land to the far north.

How far? Mickey's Toontown exists completely outside the **berm** that defines the park's original perimeter. Formerly this area beyond **Fantasyland** was the site of a narrow road that led to the park's **Pony Farm** and storage facilities. A tunnel through the berm now provides the gateway into Toontown. A population counter above the tunnel pretends to keep track of incoming guests, but the wacky digits also include blanks, question marks, and random spinning.

Toontown was the first entirely new themed land added to Disneyland since 1972's **Bear Country**. It's also the smallest of the park's lands: Toontown measures only 200 feet from the back of Toon Park up to the door of the Third Little Piggy Bank, and 500 feet from Chip 'n Dale Tree House in the west to Roger's Fountain in the east, an area totaling under three acres. Originally called Mickeyland in the early plans, Toontown derives

from a small character-greeting area that was successful at Walt Disney World. The concept was then greatly expanded upon at Disneyland to include themes, designs, and gags from the blockbuster Disney movie of 1988, *Who Framed Roger Rabbit*. Toontown stands today as the least-changed land in the park—whereas dozens of stores have moved in and out of **Main Street** and dozens of attractions have come and gone in the other lands, Toontown exists today almost exactly as it did when it opened.

Toontown debuted in 1993 with a special ceremony attended by Disney CEO Michael Eisner and comedian Harry Anderson. At the opening, guests were informed that the hilarious little Toontown village had supposedly existed for over 50 years but was only now being revealed to visitors. As an animation destination, everything in Mickey's Toontown is designed primarily for kids (like most cartoons) but can also be appreciated by adults (like the best cartoons). And, as in cartoons, the brightly-colored buildings here don't have right angles or straight lines and instead appear swollen or inflatable.

Many of the locations in Toontown are scaled-down versions of places that exist elsewhere in Disneyland. For instance, Toontown has its own City Hall and Fire Department, a walk-through tree house, a roller coaster-style attraction, a car-driving attraction, and a large boat, plus inexpensive snack stands and souvenir stores. Like other small towns, Toontown is divided into a downtown district (to the east) and a residential neighborhood (to the west), with mass transit (the now-defunct **Jolly Trolley**) connecting the two. Downtown includes stores, fast-food eateries, and kid-friendly attractions like **Roger Rabbit's Car Toon Spin**, while the star-studded neighborhood boasts the wacky homes of Mickey, Minnie, Goofy, and Chip and Dale, all of them appearing appropriate for their owners but none of them copied from specific Disney cartoons. Two fountains provide centerpieces for the plazas, and rolling hills (adorned with a Hollywood-style sign) provide the backdrop.

Throughout Toontown, random objects produce silly sounds and effects. Stand on a manhole cover near the Five & Dime and weasel voices will call out at you. Drink from a water fountain and it will utter wisecracks. A plunger at the Fireworks Factory, doorbells at the Electric Company, a Dalmatian pup occasionally peering out of the firehouse, interactive mailboxes, a street sign announcing Wrong Turn O.K., a blank sign announcing that it is merely a Blank Sign—like the rest of Disneyland, Toontown rewards deliberate exploration with delightful surprises.

Midget Autopia

MAP: Fantasyland, Fa-16

DATES: April 23, 1957–April 3, 1966

Following in the slipstreams of Tomorrowland's popular **Autopia** (opened in 1955) and **Junior Autopia** (1956), the Midget Autopia debuted in 1957 as a destination for the youngest drivers of all—preschoolers. The Midget track was laid out near the **Storybook Land Canal Boats** in **Fantasyland**; formerly a relatively undeveloped eating area, this location would be eliminated in favor of wide walkways leading to **It's a Small World**.

Whereas the other two Autopias banned the smallest guests from driving the cars, the Midget Autopia actually invited them to take the wheel (adults weren't even allowed in the cars). In contrast to the sleek Tomorrowland and Junior Autopia sports cars, the Midget Autopia bodies were rounder and friendlier-looking, like cartoon cars with two steering wheels side-by-side. The Midget cars didn't run on internal combustion like their bigger, noisier siblings did; the tiny cars were electric and ran under the control of ride operators (like the cars on **Mr. Toad's Wild Ride**). And unlike the other Autopias, which touted their tracks as freeways, the Midget Autopia track was a gentle, winding road that at one point crept through a little building.

After the attraction was dismantled in 1966, the cars and displays were donated to Marceline, Missouri, **Walt Disney's** hometown. In Marceline's Walt Disney Park, the cars ran as a kiddie ride until they were eventually removed. One of the Midget Autopia cars is on display in a local Marceline museum; another is mounted on a pedestal alongside the track in Disneyland's current Autopia, giving 21st-century guests a glimpse at 1950s fun.

Mike Fink Keel Boats

MAP: Frontierland, Fr-12

DATES: December 25, 1955–May 17, 1997

For over 40 years, keel boats operated in **Frontierland** waters. Many guests today

wouldn't even know what a keel boat was unless they'd seen the "Davy Crockett's Keel Boat Race" episode of the old ***Disneyland* TV series**.

In the late '50s, however, everyone would have recognized a keel boat as a small, old-fashioned wooden houseboat, since that popular TV episode helped propel the nation's Crockett craze. On the show, tough guy Mike Fink raced his ramshackle *Gully-whumper* against Davy's *Bertha Mae*. To the vanquished went the spoils—Mike, an actual historical figure, lost the fictional race but won a long-running Disneyland attraction.

The *Gullywhumper* began operating in Disneyland on Christmas Day, 1955, to be followed three months later by the *Bertha Mae*. Both boats were the actual vessels used on the TV show, both were powered by modern diesel engines, and both cruised freely without any submerged guide rails. About 30 guests sitting inside and on the roof could take the 11-minute, C-ticket tour (see **ticket books**) of the **Rivers of America**. By 1958 the wooden originals had been replaced by fiberglass replicas that could better stand the constant wear and tear (and also added two open windows).

The boats' route around **Tom Sawyer Island** was basically the same one taken by the ***Mark Twain***, but the keel boats launched from the opposite side of Frontierland. Home for the keel boats was a rugged dock on the southwestern riverbank by **Fowler's Harbor**. The keel boats kept an irregular schedule, operating mostly during the summer and on the busiest days. Things got really irregular when the two boats were temporarily pulled from service in the fall of '94. Then, after returning the following spring, a near-disaster led to their abrupt demise. In May 1997, a possibly overloaded *Gullywhumper* capsized suddenly, dumping frightened guests into the water and sending several to the hospital with minor injuries. Both boats were immediately shut down, and eventually the attraction was permanently closed.

Disney auctioned off the *Bertha Mae* for $15,000 in 2001, and two years later the *Gullywhumper* was installed along the river as stationary scenery. In 2010 the boat was moved to the back of Tom Sawyer Island, showing that Mike Fink had retired to what was formerly the island's ever-burning cabin.

Mile Long Bar

MAP: Bear Country/Critter Country, B/C-5

DATES: March 24, 1972–July 17, 1989

Debuting in 1972 with the rest of **Bear Country** was the Mile Long Bar, an eatery that served up cider, ice cream, and lightweight snacks. Like some other Bear Country attractions, the Mile Long Bar had already thrived at Walt Disney World before it opened at Disneyland right next to **Teddi Barra's Swingin' Arcade**. Its brown, two-story exterior looked appropriately countrified, and the interior, thanks to an arrangement of mirrors at either end of the bar, created the "mile long" illusion the name referred to. In 1989 that name was changed to **Brer Bar** to match the theme of its new neighbor, **Splash Mountain**.

Mineral Hall

MAP: Frontierland, Fr-24

DATES: July 30, 1956–December 1962

In the late 1950s, guests exploring the little **Frontierland** area called **El Zocalo** would have discovered a dignified, two-story white building at the back of the square. Mineral Hall showed and sold exotic rocks and minerals, highlighting the

Disneyland's Arcades, Bars, Boutiques, and More

In this encyclopedia's 544 main entries, there are two Cottages (Briar Rose, Enchanted), two Galleys (Captain Hook's, Harbour), five Corners (Art, Card, Carefree, Pooh, Refreshment), three Outposts (Indiana Jones Adventure, Safari, Ursus H. Bear's Wilderness), and four Terraces (Magnolia Tree, River Belle, Tahitian, Tomorrowland). Here are 10 more classifications of 52 Disneyland establishments (each one listed has its own encyclopedia entry) and their years of operation.

Arcade
Crystal _____ (1955–ongoing)
Davy Crockett _____ (1955–1987)
Frontier Shootin' _____
  (1957–ongoing)
Penny _____ (1955–ongoing)
Pirate's _____ (1967–1980)
Starcade (1977–ongoing)
Teddi Barra's Swingin' _____
  (1972–2003)

Bar
Brer _____ (1989–2003)
Dairy _____ (1956–1958)
Mile Long _____ (1972–1989)
Mint Julep _____ (1966–ongoing)
Space _____ (1955–1966)

Tiki Juice _____ (1976–ongoing)
Yacht _____ (1957–1966)

Boutique
Bibbidi Bobbidi _____
  (2009–ongoing)
La _____ de Noël (1998–2006)
La _____ d'Or (1974–1980)
Princess _____ (1997–2005)

Club
_____ Buzz (2001–2006)
_____ 33 (1967–ongoing)
Kennel _____ (1968–1977;
  1993–ongoing)
Yacht _____ (1955–1957)

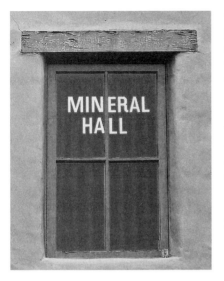

merchandise with black lights to draw out spectacular colors. So impressive was this display that dazzled guests could even buy the lights along with their mineralogical wonders so they could recreate the show at home.

After Mineral Hall closed in late 1962, the restaurant next door, **Casa de Fritos**, gradually expanded into the space. Eventually some of the old hall was converted to offices that were closed to the public. Today, however, guests can still find a nostalgic Mineral Hall window at today's **Rancho del Zocalo Restaurante**.

Gardens
Alpine _____ (1967–1995)
Fantasia _____ (1993–2006)
Hills Bros. Coffee House and Coffee
    _____ (1958–1976)
King Triton _____ (1996–2008)
Plaza _____ (1956–ongoing)
Topiary _____ (1966–ongoing)

Hall
City _____ (1955–ongoing)
_____ of Aluminum Fame
    (1955–1960)
_____ of Chemistry (1955–1966)
Mineral _____ (1956–1962)
Wurlitzer Music _____ (1955–1968)

House (not including tree houses, playhouses, funhouses)
American Egg _____ (1978–1983)
Aunt Jemima's Pancake _____
    (1955–1970)
Plantation _____ (1955–1962)
Goofy's Bounce _____
    (1993–ongoing)

Hills Bros. Coffee _____ (1958–1976)
_____ of the Future (1957–1967)
Market _____ (1955–ongoing)
Mickey's _____ (1993–ongoing)
Minnie's _____ (1993–ongoing)
Opera _____ (1955–ongoing)
Pluto's Dog _____ (1993–ongoing)
Sunkist Citrus _____ (1960–1989)

Inn
Red Wagon/Plaza _____
    (1955–ongoing)
Village _____ (1983–ongoing)

Tavern
Oaks _____ (1956–1978)
Troubadour _____ (2009–ongoing)

Trader(s)
South Seas _____ (1984–ongoing)
Star _____ (1986–ongoing)
Tiki Tropical _____ (1955–ongoing)

Mine Train, aka Rainbow Caverns Mine Train, aka Western Mine Train Through Nature's Wonderland

MAP: Frontierland, Fr-21

DATES: July 2, 1956–January 2, 1977

Almost one year after 1955's **Opening Day**, the first of several railroad attractions began chugging through **Frontierland's** wilderness. Ultimately, this land would one day be traversed by the high-speed **Big Thunder Mountain Railroad**, but back in the '50s it was explored at the more sedate speeds of the Mine Train—a common nickname for the Rainbow Caverns Mine Train.

Built for under a half-million dollars, the little Mine Train was closer in size and spirit to **Fantasyland's** cozy **Casey Jr. Circus Train** than it was to a full-size railroad. At 30 inches wide, the track was six inches narrower than the 36-gauge track of the train that circled Disneyland. Guests sat in open cargo cars behind a small, old-fashioned engine run by an electric motor. Along the quarter-mile journey the sights included the **Conestoga Wagons**, **Stage Coach**, and **Mule Pack**, which also served this same dusty territory.

The highlight of the whole trip—the feature that gave the Rainbow Caverns Mine Train its name—was exclusive to train passengers. Rainbow Caverns was a resplendent cave with black lights installed to illuminate neon-colored waterfalls and glowing pools of luminescent water. **Claude Coats** and **John Hench** are acknowledged as the Imagineers behind the caverns. According to the Disneyland Data page in the 1957 **souvenir book,** approximately 270,000 gallons of water were circulated every hour to create the seven multi-colored waterfalls.

The complex visual effects inside the caverns, accompanied by choral mood music, were impressive enough to survive the makeover that hit the rest of the attraction at the turn of the decade. After closing down in October 1959, the railroad reopened on May 28, 1960 as the Western Mine Train Through Nature's Wonderland, a nine-minute, D-ticket ride (see **ticket books**). **Nature's Wonderland** was the result of an extensive re-landscaping of the arid terrain to accommodate over 200 new **Audio-Animatronic** animals in river and mountain settings. As with other Disneyland railroads, **Walt Disney** was actively involved in the design of this one, in both of its iterations. **Roger Broggie** was in charge of building the train sets.

In 1977, the Mine Train was finally pulled from service to make way for the **Big Thunder Mountain Railroad**. For years a relic of the old days was still on view from the southeastern side of **Tom Sawyer Island**—a buckled Mine Train locomotive and a couple of askew cars appeared to have crashed among Frontierland brush.

Miniature Horse Corral

MAP: Frontierland, Fr-25

DATES: July 1955–July 1957

The Miniature Horse Corral was an early, inexpensive **Frontierland** exhibit. The ponies, donkeys, and miniature horses behind the rough-hewn wooden fences were meant for viewing and petting, not for riding, making this area a precursor of the petting zoo that later appeared in **Big Thunder Ranch**. The quiet corral closed in July 1957 and was quickly replaced by the noisy **Frontierland Shooting Gallery**.

Minnie's House

MAP: Mickey's Toontown, MT-6

DATES: January 24, 1993–ongoing

Appropriately enough, Mickey Mouse's girlfriend has her own adorable walk-through exhibit right next to his residence in **Mickey's Toontown**. Like the other homes in the neighborhood, Minnie's House is a bungalow-style structure with a curved roof, stone chimney, rounded columns, and white picket fence. But whereas **Mickey's House** is a sunny yellow, Minnie's is painted a romantic lavender, with hearts and frills decorating the walls and furnishings.

As with all the other attractions in Toontown, Minnie's place invites interactivity by offering an array of gizmos to touch and gags to discover. Knock out a tune on the pans on the stove, explore a variety of cheeses in the Cheesemore fridge, check Minnie's e-mails on her heart-shaped computer (with an eight-key keyboard), play at her makeup table, and flip through her magazines (including *Mademouselle*). Out back is a special wishing well that generates a familiar giggly voice, and Minnie herself is usually on the premises for photos and autographs.

Mint Julep Bar

MAP: New Orleans Square, NOS-11

DATES: July 24, 1966–ongoing

Guests may come to the Mint Julep Bar for the mint juleps, but they'll probably stay for the fritters. This little snack counter, tucked away in the back of the **French Market** restaurant in **New Orleans Square**, has been offering some of the park's tastiest baked goods for over 40 years. As the bar's name suggests, mint juleps are its famous specialty, and they are indeed cool, tasty concoctions with "a hint of lime flavor," though purists will decry the absence of bourbon (only one restaurant inside Disneyland serves alcohol, and it's not open to the public—the nearby **Club 33**). It's possible, though, that the Mint Julep Bar's virgin version of the drink is more historically accurate, anyway. After all, the name derives from *julab*, the Persian word for "rose water," not "hard liquor." Additional to-go items include dessert treats and fancy coffee drinks.

Miss Disneyland,
aka Disneyland Ambassador to the World

DATES: 1965–ongoing

During Disneyland's first decade, **Walt Disney** tried to handle all park-related media events and public appearances by himself. But by the mid-'60s, the increasing demands on his time (especially with Walt Disney World in the serious planning stages) necessitated additional official Disneyland representatives to meet with the media and the public.

Starting in 1965, Disneyland established a position that was called, for the first few years, Miss Disneyland; later the title was changed to Disneyland Ambassador to the World. From 1965 until 1994, the position was given only to female **cast members**, who were selected on the basis of their appearance, personality, and poise. Each year a new Miss Disneyland/Ambassador to the World would represent the park in **parades**, on TV shows, and at special events.

The first Miss Disneyland, selected in 1964 but serving in 1965 to help promote the park's **Tencennial**, was a 21-year-old Texan named Julie Reihm. Reihm was a local college student who had been a Disneyland **Tour Guide** for two years. On January 3, 1965 she co-starred in the *Walt Disney's Wonderful World of Color* TV series. For the "Disneyland 10th Anniversary" episode, Reihm, wearing her Tour Guide uniform, helped preview the coming **Pirates of the Caribbean** and **Haunted Mansion** attractions by commenting on the attractions alongside **Walt Disney**. Disney Legend **Jack Lindquist** wrote in his memoirs that Reihm was "perhaps the best Disneyland ambassador ever," the one who "set the standard that still stands." She's also, according to Lindquist, the only one to have been given a new car along with her title.

Connie Swanson, another Tour Guide, was the second Miss Disneyland. While Swanson didn't appear on the *Wonderful World of Color*, she did travel extensively on behalf of the park. Melissa Taylor, the Disneyland Ambassador of 1985, circled the globe on a 30-day flight with Mickey Mouse to celebrate the park's 30th anniversary. In 1995 the Ambassador title went plural, and since then an Ambassador to the World team has been selected, with men also included in the mix. Actress Julie Andrews was named an honorary "Disney Ambassador to the World" in 2005 as part of Disneyland's 50th anniversary celebration.

Mission to Mars

MAP: Tomorrowland, T-16

DATES: March 21, 1975–November 2, 1992

Once man landed on the moon in 1969, Disneyland's **Flight to the Moon** attraction might as well have been called Flight to the Mundane. So Disneyland's designers did what NASA would eventually do—target a new heavenly body. Thus, in 1975 an upgraded, enlarged flight-simulation attraction called Mission to Mars debuted in Flight to the Moon's space next to **Tomorrowland's** big Carousel Theater.

Considering how different Mars is from the moon, the two flights were surprisingly similar. The sponsor, the McDonnell-Douglas aerospace company, hadn't changed, and neither had the price—both rides required a D-ticket from the park's **ticket book**. The pre-show Mission Control area for the Mars mission looked and operated the same way it had for the moon flight—in fact, Disneyland's **souvenir books** of the late '70s used the same photo for the Mars mission that they'd used for the earlier lunar expedition—a picture showing banks of computers attended by **Audio-Animatronic** figures. Overseeing these mission controllers was Mr. Johnson (no longer Tom Morrow from the lunar mission), a dignified mechanical scientist with a headset, glasses, lab coat, and clipboard. Johnson discussed space travel and the Mars vehicle, played the incoming-bird gag that Tom Morrow had used before the moon flight, and then excused everyone for boarding.

As with the Flight to the Moon, over 100 guests sat in a circular theater and watched two screens, one on the floor and one on the ceiling, that showed them where they'd been and where they were going. Small screens positioned around the edge of the theater provided additional views of the 15-minute journey. After lift off (felt through the seats with a lowering-raising effect), and after the moon came into view on the overhead screen, a speedy jump through hyperspace brought the Red Planet quickly into range. Camera probes beamed back surface details of the Martian canyons and mountains until a sudden meteor shower impelled the main ship to dash back to Earth.

Although the visuals were still exciting and the synchronized seats nicely simulated G-forces, by the mid-'70s guests were underwhelmed by the whole space-travel experience. They'd been watching real Gemini and Apollo missions on TV since the early '60s, and those TV audiences had become so small and disinterested that some of the later flights weren't even televised.

Tomorrowland's last Mars mission returned home for good in 1992. A dramatic attraction called Alien Encounter was considered for the space, but it was deemed too big for this location and ended up in Walt Disney World instead. In early '96, the **Toy Story Funhouse** was temporarily installed at the Mission site, but that spring fling came down by summer. Finally, along with the big remodel of Tomorrowland in '98, the old Mission to Mars building reopened, this time serving up lunch instead of interstellar space flight. **Redd Rockett's Pizza Port** still operates here in the shadow of the *Moonliner*.

Mlle. Antoinette's Parfumerie

MAP: New Orleans Square, NOS-9

DATES: 1967–1997; May 28, 2011–ongoing

As shown in Disneyland's 1968 **souvenir book**, this elegant little shop has always had a beautiful, heavily French interior, boasting such features as a sparkling chandelier, ornate mirrors, and display cases lined with delicate bottles. Located in **New Orleans Square**, the shop fit right in with its neighbors—especially the stylish **Le Chapeau** next door. In Mlle. Antoinette's, "ladies," as specified in the souvenir book, "blend their own exclusive perfumes," aided by trained perfumers who mixed customized fragrances and kept the formulas on file for return visits. Brand-name perfumes were also sold in the shop.

Some 30 years after it opened, the Parfumerie was replaced by the equally sumptuous **Jewel of Orléans**. When Jewel abruptly closed in 2011, Mlle. Antoinette's quickly stepped back in. Sponsoring the shop is the LVMH Group, the conglomerate behind many luxury items (the initials stand for Louis Vuitton Moët Hennessy). Although the Parfumerie doesn't offer custom blends like it did in the old days, there are many exalted perfumes for sale here.

Gone/Not Gone

Eight attractions, shops, and eateries that closed "permanently"
(not just for a remodeling) and reopened later in the same location:

1. Arts and Crafts Shop (ca. 1958–ca. 1963; ca. 1970–1982)
2. Briar Patch (1988–1996; 1996–ongoing)
3. *Captain EO*; *Captain EO* Tribute (1986–1997; 2010–ongoing)
4. Great Moments with Mr. Lincoln (1965–1973; 1975–2005; 2009–ongoing)
5. Mlle. Antoinette's Parfumerie (1967–1997; 2011–ongoing)
6. Sleeping Beauty Castle Walk-Through (1957–2001; 2008–ongoing)
7. Submarine Voyage; Finding Nemo Submarine Voyage (1959–1998; 2007–ongoing)
8. Town Square Café (1976–1978; 1983–1992)

Monorail,
aka Disneyland-Alweg Monorail, aka Disneyland Monorail

MAP: Tomorrowland, T-10

DATES: June 14, 1959–ongoing

The debut of the magnificent Monorail in June of 1959 was an auspicious moment in Disneyland history. Of the three new E-ticket (see **ticket books**) vehicles that began running that month (the **Matterhorn Bobsleds** and **Submarine Voyage** were the others), the Monorail was the only one intended to be a serious advance in American transportation. The other two attractions were no doubt wonderful, but the Monorail was especially

significant. So significant, in fact, that Vice President Nixon was on hand for the ribbon-cutting honors. So significant, it was awarded a special plaque by the American Society of Mechanical Engineers in 1986. So significant that, unlike every other vehicle in the park that either stayed on its original course or was eventually closed (à la the **PeopleMover**), the Monorail's service was actually *expanded* to cover more than three times its original length. While other vehicles made memories, the Monorail made history.

Walt Disney and his staff didn't invent the monorail-on-an-elevated-track concept. Various monorails had been successfully built and demonstrated in America since 1876, the year a steam-powered monorail debuted at Philadelphia's Centennial Exposition. Some eighty years later Alweg, a design company named for the initials of its Swedish founder, Dr. Axel Lennart Wenner-Gren, began testing advanced monorail train and track designs in Germany. When a vacationing Walt Disney saw a boxy monorail train run on a rural test track near Cologne in '57, he quickly partnered with Alweg to construct a new, streamlined Disneyland version. "I think monorail is going to be the rapid transit of the future," Disney said in *Walt Disney Conversations*, "and we'll be giving a prevue of it."

Disney Legend **Bob Gurr**, who designed most of the park's vehicles, created a tapered, futuristic train that would be as exhilarating to watch as it would be to ride. **John Hench** enhanced Gurr's pencil drawings with color and effects to make the Monorail look like a horizontal rocket ship. **Roger Broggie** and his engineering team built the first Monorail at the Disney Studios, and **Bill Martin** laid out the track approximately where the **Viewliner** had been. For all of these Imagineers, the goal wasn't merely to create an attraction for fun, stylish sight-seeing; it was to create a meaningful alternative to public transportation, an all-electric train that would glide smoothly and silently along an elevated "highway in the sky" and convey guests in and out of Disneyland's interior.

But that's not how the Monorail first operated. When it opened, there was only one three-car train, called *Monorail Red* (the trains have usually been identified by their colors), and there was only one stop, next to the submarines in **Tomorrowland**. This meant that only 82 passengers, not hundreds at a time, were starting and stopping at the same point. From the Tomorrowland station guests looped for eight-tenths of a mile around the lagoon, **Autopia**, and **Matterhorn Mountain** (the view even included some of Anaheim). It was a scenic journey, but not a vital one.

The Monorail's operation was splendid. Speeds were usually in the 20–35 miles per hour range, though the Monorail could have easily doubled those numbers had its drivers been allowed to cut loose. Just as impressive as the quiet, smooth ride was the clean, elevated track, rising from about 12 feet above the Autopia road to about 20 feet above Fantasyland walkways. And everybody loved the train's low, booming horn. With crowds quickly filling *Monorail Red* to capacity, a second train, *Monorail Blue*, joined

the route three weeks after the debut of its predecessor. But still, the world's first daily public monorail was a Tomorrowland-only ride.

Expansion plans, however, were in the works. On April 10, 1961 the Monorail was temporarily shut down so the track could be dramatically extended outside the park to the Disneyland Hotel. Reopening on June 1st, the Monorail now traveled on a 2.3-mile-long track that left Tomorrowland, ventured along Harbor Boulevard and over the **parking lot**, crossed a public street (West Avenue), and reached a new Monorail station at the hotel, where the train dropped off and picked up guests for a return journey back to the park. Each one-way trip (park to hotel, hotel to park) took about two and a half minutes. The new route added elevation to the ride as it rose to about 25 feet above Disneyland's **entrance**. The new route also increased the Monorail's significance—by delivering guests from one station to another, it had become the mass-transit system Walt Disney had always intended it to be.

Not only was the route different, so was the vehicle. Another passenger car joined the train, upping capacity to 108 guests, and a new train, *Monorail Gold*, joined the line. These Mark II trains also included a nifty new design feature: little bubble canopies over the first cars. More revisions were to come—the Mark III Monorail debuted in 1969 with a fifth passenger car (127 riders total), larger windows, and bucket seats instead of benches. Plus there was a fourth train, *Monorail Green* (not all the trains operated simultaneously, instead subbing for each other during the frequent maintenance periods).

Everything about the Monorail was cool. **Cast members** on the attraction dressed like pilots and flight attendants. The breathtaking **attraction poster** showed *Monorail Red*, the lagoon, the *Moonliner*, and the Matterhorn all at once, adding up to one of Disneyland's best promotional images ever. And for years the **souvenir books** featured colorful photos of the Monorail and bold text about "the future in city mass transportation."

The advances kept coming. The Mark IV Monorail never made it to Disneyland, debuting in Orlando instead, but the Mark V came to Anaheim in 1987 with a new shape created by **George McGinnis**. *Monorail Purple* featured automatic sliding doors, air conditioning, and a new Alweg-less name—it was now simply the Disneyland Monorail (Alweg had encountered financial problems in the '60s and had been taken over by another company).

In 2001, concurrent with the arrival of Disney California Adventure, an updated Monorail station in Downtown Disney replaced the one that had been built at the Disneyland Hotel. Then, on August 21, 2006, the entire Monorail line ceased operations for four months to accommodate the construction of the new Finding Nemo Submarine Voyage. Once the subs resurfaced in 2007, one of the Monorail trains was painted bright yellow and decorated with portholes and text to help publicize the attraction. All-new Mark VII Monorails that hearken back to earlier, sleeker designs went into service in February 2008. These Rhode Island-built/Vancouver-assembled trains sport new colors, tinted windows, and window-facing bench seats that offer panoramic park views.

Unfortunately, the urban revolution that Walt Disney hoped his 1959 monorail would begin never arrived. While several other Alweg monorails went into service (most notably one in Seattle), other major cities (most disappointingly Los Angeles) never adopted them, making the one in Disneyland all the more special. The first of its kind built in America, the longest-lasting of its kind, and always a majestic sight anytime it streams into view, Disneyland's Monorail is still the grand symbol of an optimistic future.

Moonliner

MAP: Tomorrowland, T-15

DATES: July 17, 1955–ongoing

Just as the *Mark Twain* draws guests westward into **Frontierland**, so too did the original *Moonliner* rocket, visible from the **Hub**, compel pedestrians to venture eastward into **Tomorrowland**. The *Moonliner* wasn't a ticketed attraction, and guests couldn't go inside it, but by its very design and placement it was a dramatic invitation to come explore the world of the future. Most of the early concept drawings that rendered aerial views of the proposed park showed a rocket standing tall in the eastern section of Disneyland. In 1954 **Herb Ryman** sketched a spindly rocket that looked a lot like the elegant design that **John Hench** eventually drew up. When its pieces were assembled just a few weeks before **Opening Day**, the *Moonliner* towered an imposing 76 feet high, right in front of the low-slung **Rocket to the Moon** attraction.

Unlike the actual moon rockets that fired from the Florida coast in the 1960s and '70s, the *Moonliner* had no separate stages, capsule, cluster of engines at the bottom, or adjacent support gantry. What it did have were three legs, a slender, tapered shape, a cockpit near the top, two rings of portholes, horizontal red stripes on its white hull, and a corporate sponsor, TWA ("the Official Airline to Disneyland"). While the *Moonliner* technically wasn't what moon rockets typically turned out to be, it sure looked like what everyone in the '50s imagined a cool rocket *should* look like.

What's more, theoretically the *Moonliner* was going to do more than what actual rockets of the '60s did. It wasn't supposed to be just a one-time disposable vehicle that visited the moon for a quick scientific visit and returned as a single tiny capsule on parachutes. This was a *liner*, a futuristic ship that conveyed travelers back and forth between the earth and the moon, with lunar bases waiting at one end, reusable launch pads at the other, and the ultimate frequent flyer miles in between. Something so sleek and optimistic perfectly symbolized Tomorrowland; it was often featured in **souvenir books** and **attraction posters**, and on the Rocket to the Moon poster, the *Moonliner* rose proud and tall in the foreground, its needle nose already in the stars.

Somehow, such an important symbol barely lasted a decade. In mid-1962 Douglas Aircraft took over sponsorship, painted its name down the side of the rocket, and replaced its horizontal red stripes with vertical blue ones. Incredibly, four years later the beautiful *Moonliner* was deemed expendable and was dismantled during the major remodel of Tomorrowland. The rocket's site was assumed by the sprawling Carousel Theater. (Douglas, meanwhile, was acquired by McDonnell to become McDonnell-Douglas, which sponsored 1967's **Flight to the Moon.**)

Thirty-two years later, the park welcomed back a *Moonliner* replica. At 53 feet tall, this 1998 version was only about two-thirds the size of its classic predecessor. The small size of the new rocket isn't readily apparent because of its new location about 20 yards from its previous spot. The rocket now sits on top of the roof of the **Spirit of Refreshment**. Since this snack stand is sponsored by Coca-Cola, the red stripes have returned to the *Moonliner* to echo the red-and-white livery of Coke cans. On hot days the rocket's base sprays a cooling mist down on guests.

While it's not the awe-inspiring spectacle it once was, most fans will agree that a stunted *Moonliner* that advertises cola is better than no *Moonliner* at all.

Motor Boat Cruise,
aka Motor Boat Cruise to Gummi Glen

MAP: Fantasyland, Fa-22

DATES: June 1957–January 11, 1993

After unending maintenance problems finally sank the infamous **Phantom Boats** in 1956, a new boat ride opened at the start of summer in 1957. Whereas the Phantom Boats had toured the big lagoon in **Tomorrowland**, the Motor Boat Cruise crept along a new **Fantasyland** waterway that was carved into land where the **Mickey Mouse**

Club Circus had formerly operated. When the new **Fantasyland Autopia** and **Monorail** opened in 1959, their pylons and overpasses carried them right over the motorboats. Walls of oleander along the banks shielded external views, keeping this a cozy cruise.

Even though the boats looked like sleek

Oldest Attractions to Be Retired

21 years old: Mine Train (1956–1977)
28: PeopleMover (1967–1995)
29: Country Bear Jamboree/Playhouse (1972–2001)
30: Rocket Jets (1967–1997)
36: Motor Boat Cruise (1957–1993)
37: Swiss Family Treehouse (1962–1999)
38: Skyway to Fantasyland/Tomorrowland (1956–1994)
39: Submarine Voyage (1959–1998)
40: Fantasyland Autopia (1959–1999)
42: Circarama/Circle-Vision theater (1955–1997)

little speedsters—all of them with aerodynamic shapes, open cockpits, brightly colored hulls, and white decks—the Motor Boat Cruise was to boating what Autopia was to driving. The boats operated on a submerged guide rail and so offered limited returns no matter how much effort was put into cranking the wheel. In addition, the gas pedal had little effect on the whole experience (some have suggested that all it did was increase engine volume). Kids probably enjoyed the illusion of control, while adults could relax, peruse the rocky river, enjoy the disparate vehicles that slipped through the vicinity, and take comfort in knowing that they'd only spent a B ticket from the park's **ticket book** for this attraction. For years, photos in the park's **souvenir books** showed boats easing past big boulders in mild waters. In the accompanying caption—"Steering through rapids is fun on the Motor Boat Cruise"—"rapids" was undoubtedly a technical term meaning "gentle waves."

Somehow, with Disneyland moving to new high-tech, high-speed, high-profile roller coaster attractions in the 1970s and '80s, the mild motorboats lasted into the '90s. Just before they ended, the boats underwent a major change in 1991. From March to November, the Motor Boat Cruise got a new name—Motor Boat Cruise to Gummi Glen—and new scenery, painted plywood images of Gummi Bears in support of the Gummi's TV show. By Thanksgiving, the attraction was again called simply the Motor Boat Cruise, and by February of '93 the boats and the waterway had been replaced by the lush landscape of **Fantasia Gardens**.

Mr. Toad's Wild Ride

MAP: Fantasyland, Fa-28

DATES: July 17, 1955–ongoing

Whereas the other two original **Fantasyland** dark rides are either enchanted with wondrous airborne views (**Peter Pan Flight**) or have effectively reduced a classic story to its most emotional elements (**Snow White Adventures**), Mr. Toad's Wild Ride had one simple goal: to make guests laugh. The park's early **souvenir books** emphasized this intention with its Wild Ride photos, in which everyone was laughing. The Wild Ride cost only a C ticket out of the **ticket books**, but it may have been Disneyland's jolliest attraction.

The Wild Ride is housed in a rectangular building that's shared with **Alice in Wonderland**; in fact, Alice's caterpillar vehicles crawl up onto the second floor above Toad's tracks. A whirling ride has always been out in the courtyard near Mr. Toad—before 1983 that ride was the **Mad Hatter's Mad Tea Party**, and since '83 it's been the **King Arthur Carrousel**. Mr. Toad's theme came from Disney's half-hour animated movie *The Wind in the Willows* (1949), which is based on the classic Kenneth Grahame book. Though the attraction doesn't exactly retell the movie's plot, elements of the film are reprised throughout: the cars are named after key characters (MacBadger, Winky, Cyril, etc.); most of the movie's characters actually appear during the two-minute trip; J. Thaddeus Toad's own home is the ride's preliminary race track; and Toad's madcap movie energy propels the whole Disneyland adventure.

A colorful mural in the loading area foretells some of the hijinks to come. After boarding a stylish but uncontrollable little antique car, riders immediately careen and crash through the hallways, then tear off across the English countryside. Their destination: Nowhere in Particular; their goal: unbridled merriment. The most astonishing portion of the ride is its fiery ending. After a rollicking romp through London's streets, a police chase, a courtroom trial, and a prison getaway, the whole frantic escapade is brought to a sudden crashing halt by the scary approach of a noisy train, and guests wind up . . . in hell (literally—a blazing, demon-populated Hell).

No other Disneyland attraction veers so far from the movie that inspired it (the film ends with Toad happily soaring off in a flying machine) or ends so calamitously (the **Haunted Mansion** sends guests home with a hitchhiking ghost, but that's nothing compared to the eternal burning and poking that culminates the Wild Ride). Perhaps the finale is a warning—drive recklessly like Toad, and you'll suffer dire consequences—but it's so unexpected that it probably evokes more laughter than fear. Whether it's caution or comedy, the ending epitomizes the unpredictable nuttiness that makes Toad's attraction such a fan favorite.

When it was first being planned, the trip was possibly going to be more roller-coaster-ish, but that idea was reined in to make the Wild Ride essentially the same simple, glorious gambol it's been since 1955. Disney Legends were at the core of its creation—**Bill Martin** laid out the basic ride, **Claude Coats** drew the interiors, **Ken Anderson** designed the sets, and **Bob Gurr** built the vehicles. A 1961 update improved some of the interior that had been hastily painted for **Opening Day**. More significantly, a major renovation in 1983 brought new effects to both the interior and exterior. Inside, new areas and gags filled out the escapade. Outside, a stunning new mansion design replaced the medieval-tournament façade that existed throughout Fantasyland but seemed out of step with Toad's Edwardian-era automobile adventures. Toad Hall is now one of the area's architectural highlights, a wonderful multi-chimneyed structure that is as fun as it is fascinating (it also echoes the miniature Toad Hall viewed from the **Storybook Land Canal Boats**).

As beloved as the attraction is, park designers almost eliminated Mr. Toad's Wild Ride in the 1990s when they considered bringing the **Many Adventures of Winnie the Pooh** to Fantasyland. Fortunately Mr. Toad was saved, and Pooh moved into **Critter Country**. Mr. Toad's survival brought a sigh of relief to fans and gave generations of newcomers a chance to decipher the fractured Latin of Toad's family motto, giggle at all the cleverly titled books (*Toadman of Alcatraz*, *Twice Toad Tales*, etc.) on the bookshelves, watch for the Sherlock Holmes silhouette in the upstairs window, take the Toadster's roadster on a rowdy road trip, and experience the surprise of Infernoland for themselves.

Walt Disney himself acknowledged the importance of the Mr. Toad attraction. According to the book *Remembering Walt*, when a park waitress addressed him as Mr. Disney, he reminded her that he was Walt. "There's only one 'mister' in Disneyland," he told her, "and that's *Mr.* Toad."

Mule Pack, aka Rainbow Ridge Mule Pack, aka Pack Mules Through Nature's Wonderland

MAP: Frontierland, Fr-21

DATES: July 17, 1955–February 1, 1973

The Mule Pack debuted on **Opening Day** and enjoyed a surprisingly long run—er, walk. While it's easy to dismiss the mules as unsophisticated leftovers from the 1950s, in actuality some form of this attraction survived into the '70s. Maybe it was the interactivity that guests enjoyed: live animals have been seen through the Disneyland decades in everything from the **Miniature Horse Corral** to the **Dalmatian Celebration**, but the Mule Pack presented the only opportunity to actually *ride* them.

The ride operated from a **Frontierland** loading area that sent guests and their little mules clomping along dusty wilderness trails, with the rowdier **Stage Coach** and **Conestoga Wagons** often in sight. Usually nine mules at a time were strung together in a long line, headed by a cowboy-costumed **cast member** on a lead horse. Kids were the target audience; younger, lighter children were belted to their saddles. Bought for $50 apiece, the mules were kept at night in the park's **Pony Farm**.

In early 1956 the attraction temporarily closed so the wilderness area could be updated and re-invigorated with more landscaping, simple mechanical creatures, and the new train tracks of the **Mine Train**. When the mules returned on June 26th of that year, they had graduated from a C-ticket to a D-ticket attraction (see **ticket books**) and had acquired a new name—the Rainbow Ridge Mule Pack. This lasted until October of 1959, when again the attraction temporarily shut down for a desert remodel. The new Pack Mules Through Nature's Wonderland attraction opened on June 10, 1960, cost an E ticket to board, and included a cool display of dinosaur fossils along the journey.

After that, the attraction didn't change much until the Pack Mules finally packed up in early 1973. By then there were many stories of problems along the trail. Mules had been startled by the sudden train noises, boat whistles, and other surrounding Frontierland sounds. The recalcitrant animals had sometimes nipped guests, and occasionally they'd stopped in their tracks altogether, turning a 10-minute ride into a frustrating ordeal. Indeed, when they were shown in Disneyland's **souvenir books**, the mules never looked happy. Six years after closing, the trails where the little mules had once ambled reopened as the thrilling **Big Thunder Mountain Railroad**.

Names Unraveled

MAP: Fantasyland, Fa-23, Fa-4, Fa-9

DATES: Ca. 1995–ca. 2005

Names Unraveled could also be called Names Well-Traveled, since this little specialty service had three locations in its decade-long existence. It started as a **Fantasyland** cart parked in the walkway north of **Matterhorn Mountain**. In the late '90s it moved to a room inside the **Sleeping Beauty Castle** entrance. After a few years, Names Unraveled relocated to the shop that had been **Geppetto's Toys & Gifts**, over by **Pinocchio's Daring Journey**.

No matter where it was located, Names Unraveled always provided the same service—investigating the derivations of guests' names, and then offering ways to take that information—or just copies of the printed names themselves—home as keepsakes. Hard copy, stationery, plaques, glasses, and more were available until Names Unraveled became Names Unavailable around 2005.

Nature's Wonderland

MAP: Frontierland, Fr-22

DATES: May 28, 1960–January 2, 1977

The biggest change to hit **Frontierland** during the 1960s arrived in the decade's very first year. Nature's Wonderland was the huge, $2.5 million remodel in a barren area that was mostly unnamed, except for a one-and-a-half-acre northern section called the **Painted Desert**. Beginning in 1955, three old-fashioned modes of transportation had left tracks there—the **Mule Pack**, **Stage Coach**, and **Conestoga Wagons**. As of 1956 the **Mine Train** had chugged through on its way to the luminous Rainbow Caverns. All four of these attractions were shut down in 1959 so the desert could be transformed into Nature's Wonderland.

When the Mine Train resumed service on May 28, 1960, Nature's Wonderland

presented guests with a seven-acre area that mixed unspoiled American backcountry with **Audio-Animatronic** technology. To the west, overlooking the **Rivers of America** and **Tom Sawyer Island**, was a new snow-capped, five-story mountain called Cascade Peak. Across the center of Nature's Wonderland was a T-shaped body of water: the upper horizontal part was Bear Country (not to be confused with 1972's **Bear Country**), and the stem was Beaver Valley. To the northeast was the Living (formerly the Painted) Desert. Gone were the Stage Coach and Conestoga Wagons, but back were the mules and the train, both of which would survive into the '70s.

Like the **Jungle Cruise** and the original Painted Desert, Nature's Wonderland took its imagery from Disney Studios' *True-Life Adventures* series. Here, the four inspirations were the half-hour documentaries *Bear Country*, *Beaver Valley*, *The Living Desert*, and *The Olympic Elk* (the first three won Oscars for Best Short Subject). Populating Nature's Wonderland were over 200 new Audio-Animatronic animals, including everything from snakes and birds to beavers and bobcats. Viewed from the train, the landscape offered stunning new views of the Three Sisters and Big Thunder waterfalls splashing down Cascade Peak, wildlife splashing in the rivers, and Old Unfaithful Geyser splashing 70 feet above the desert.

So proud was **Walt Disney** of the new area that he himself had sketched out for his designers that he gave it a special wrap-around cover on the outside of Disneyland's 1960 **souvenir book**. Called "The Story of Nature's Wonderland," this unique outsert detailed the attractions that awaited inside: "Here, in a primitive setting that duplicates the remote wilderness country, you may watch beavers, busy as always, on home-building and tree-cutting chores; coyotes and mountain lions; clown-like bears, romping without a care in the world; Olympic Elk engaged in a battle for survival, just as it is enacted daily in the natural wilderness." A colorful full-page map laid out the entire Nature's Wonderland acreage and spotlighted "exciting wilderness scenes" such as two elk butting heads, a bear using a tree as a back-scratcher, and a moose drinking from a river. In addition, Nature's Wonderland even had its own rustic **attraction poster**. Divided into four sections circumnavigated by train tracks, the poster reinforced the movie connection by labeling its quadrants as Bear Country, Beaver Valley, Living Desert, and Olympic Elk.

Despite all the hullabaloo, by the early 1970s work was already underway to undo Nature's Wonderland. The mules were led away in '73, the train was gone in '77, and **Big Thunder Mountain Railroad** was roaring across the dramatically redesigned landscape in '79. However, some of the old Nature's Wonderland elements endured. Hollow Cascade Peak, gradually deteriorating from within, didn't give way to demolition until 1998, and even today a few of the A-A animals can be glimpsed from Big Thunder's trains.

New Century Watches & Clocks,
aka New Century Timepieces and New Century Jewelry

MAP: Main Street, MS-4

DATES: 1972–July 2008

The **Main Street** corner that had been the **Upjohn Pharmacy** since 1955 became a clock shop called New Century in 1972. Sponsored by the watch-making company Elgin, it was first called New Century Watches & Clocks. When Lorus took over sponsorship in 1986, the store was renamed New Century Timepieces. That same year, the Rings & Things store across the street moved in next door to New Century Timepieces, where there was a small space vacated by the **Disneyana** shop. The Rings name disappeared and new vertical signage declared this entire space to be New Century Jewelry, even though New Century Jewelry and New Century Timepieces both operated inside.

From the outside, the businesses looked separate and had different paint jobs. Inside the building, however, were two rooms wide open to each other, like two halves of one big store. The main corner room offered "Disney traditions in time," meaning vintage-style Disney character watches and Disney-themed clocks from prominent manufacturers. The jewelry cases in the room to the south showed off sparkling rings, bracelets, and gold charms. One unique specialty was on the timepiece side, where an artisan often sat painting $300–$500 customized watch faces in view of guests.

Time ran out on New Century in mid-2008, when the store closed permanently; it reopened as the **Fortuosity Shop** just in time for Halloween.

New Orleans Square

MAP: Park, P-12

DATES: July 24, 1966–ongoing

Walt Disney had long been a fan of New Orleans, and in the late 1950s he believed that a small, graceful replica of its famous French Quarter would fit in nicely at Disneyland. It would be historic and pretty, like **Main Street**, and would present lots of French-themed shops and restaurants to guests. Disney's New Orleans vision wouldn't become a reality until 1966, and it would be the last large-scale Disneyland project dedicated during his lifetime.

Years before New Orleans Square ever opened, Disneyland designers had already infused some of Frontierland and its surroundings with Southern themes. The *Mark Twain* had steamed along the **Rivers of America** since **Opening Day**; **Magnolia Park** and the **Chicken Plantation** restaurant were both on view in the 1950s; until the early '60s, live Dixieland music

was played in a waterfront gazebo; and the mesmerizing exterior of the antebellum-style **Haunted Mansion** was erected in 1963. New Orleans Square would consolidate Disney's Delta dreams into one marvelous neighborhood. Those dreams wouldn't be cheap—the price for New Orleans Square, according to the 2007 *Disneyland Secrets, Stories & Magic* DVD, was about $15 million, almost 90 percent of what it had cost to build all of Disneyland a decade before.

Imagineers began sketching ideas for a New Orleans area in 1957, just two years after Disneyland opened. The park's **souvenir books** began showing preview illustrations of "Old New Orleans" in 1961. Early construction began that same year, but in 1963 work stopped because of the sudden urgency to create new high-profile attractions for the 1964–1965 New York World's Fair. In 1965, a full year before New Orleans Square debuted, public excitement about the new land began to surge. That year's souvenir book devoted a full page of drawings and descriptions to the coming area, showing off the ambitious streets and buildings. When it finally opened in

mid-1966 with a special ceremony attended by Walt Disney and the mayor of New Orleans, New Orleans Square was the first permanent new land added to the park's original roster of Main Street, **Adventureland**, Frontierland, **Fantasyland**, and **Tomorrowland**. It was also the only land at the time not directly connected to the **Hub**. Three days after Walt Disney's death, and a week before Christmas, a 1966 episode of *Walt Disney's Wonderful World of Color* put Disneyland's version of New Orleans before a national TV audience.

That audience saw a compressed idealization of what everyone still imagines a few perfect blocks of New Orleans should look like. But there's far more going on here than meets the eye, because the geography of New Orleans Square isn't as readily apparent as, say, the straight-up-and-down Main Street or the wide-open **Town Square**. Unlike the actual New Orleans, which has streets crisscrossing in a grid pattern, New Orleans Square isn't really square. Three separate blocks angle through the main neighborhood: to the south, a large east-west block houses **Pirates of the Caribbean** and the **Blue Bayou**; north of that, a smaller diagonal block extends southwest to northeast and juts Café Orleans toward the **Rivers of America**; and on the west side, a third block containing the **French Market** aims at the Haunted

> # New Orleans Square Establishments with French Names
>
> 1. Cristal d'Orleans
> 2. La Boutique de Noël
> 3. La Boutique d'Or
> 4. La Mascarade d'Orléans
> 5. La Petite Patisserie
> 6. Le Bat en Rouge
> 7. Le Chapeau
> 8. Le Forgeron
> 9. Le Gourmet
> 10. L'Ornement Magique
> 11. Marché aux Fleurs, Sacs et Mode
> 12. Port d'Orléans

Mansion about 150 feet away. Between the three blocks are two narrow, asymmetrical streets, each only about 15 feet wide. Royal Street separates the Pirates of the Caribbean block from the diagonal Café Orleans block, and Orleans Street separates the Café Orleans block from the French Market block. Bordering New Orleans Square to the west and south is the 75-foot-long Front Street and the railroad track; to the east is Adventureland; to the northeast, the Esplanade and the Rivers of America; to the north, **Critter Country**.

New Orleans Square's diminutive scale keeps everything intimate. The main neighborhood, not including the separate Haunted Mansion, covers only about three acres. Not only are the blocks compact, they're short, too, reaching only two and three stories high. To make the buildings seem bigger than they are, architects have incorporated the same "forced perspective" design they first used on Main Street (the upper stories are built on a smaller scale than the lower stories). Compressed as they may be, the buildings *feel* right. Appreciated more by adults than their fast-moving kids, the French-themed shops and cafés are adorned with authentic design details such as hanging plants, French doors, cozy verandas, and lacy wrought-iron railings. Appropriately, New Orleans Square has no noisy, whirling rides, no huge **Emporium**-style stores, and no towering mountains to rival **Big Thunder** or the **Matterhorn**. Instead, the focus here is on architecture and ambience, shopping and dining, drifts of flowers by the river, and swirls of jazz music in the air. Relaxing, not riding, has always been the area's raison d'être.

Guests still marvel at the wonderful variety of sights and sounds here that evoke the New Orleans spirit. Because the Crescent City itself was named after French royalty (Philippe II, Duke of Orléans) and was once a French colony, many of the businesses in New Orleans Square have either had French names (**La Petite Patisserie**, **Le Chapeau**, etc.) or been named after famous French figures (**Mlle. Antoinette's**

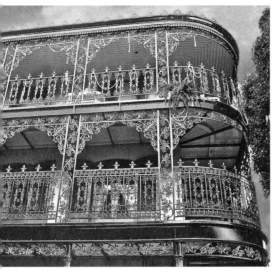

Parfumerie, **Laffite's Silver Shop**). And since New Orleans, the birthplace of Dixieland, is a world-renowned jazz capital, the air in New Orleans Square is often sweetened with the sounds of jazz combos, either playing on the streets or at the French Market. Just as New Orleans plays host to Mardi Gras, so too does New Orleans Square feel like the best place to party. It does, after all, contain Disneyland's best restaurant, the **Blue Bayou**, as well as an eatery named after a cocktail (the **Mint Julep Bar**) and the only in-park restaurant that serves alcohol (**Club 33**). Realistic pre-recorded sounds drift down from the upper windows, just as they do on Main Street— although here, those sounds include a voodoo priestess preparing spells.

More pleasing than the authentic New Orleans touches are the nice surprises that are pure Disney. Guests will turn a corner and find a quiet courtyard with **portrait artists** practicing their craft and potted plants climbing the curving Court des Anges staircase. Tucked behind a building, a hidden counter sells delicious baked goods; wander a street, and you'll find a mysterious doorway marked with the number 33. Above the buildings, some of the roofs are topped with maritime sails, put there both to hide searchlights and to imply where a romantic waterfront awaits. Below the buildings is a subterranean-level honeycomb of tunnels, store rooms, restaurant kitchens, offices, and an employees-only cafeteria. As famous, familiar, and photographed as it is, New Orleans Square is still a place for discovery.

New Orleans Square Lemonade Stand

MAP: New Orleans Square, NOS-12

DATES: 2009–ongoing

Some **cast members** refer to this outdoor vendor as the NOS Lemonade Stand. It's been sitting in the walkway outside the **Haunted Mansion** entrance for a couple of years now, serving up Slurpee-style frozen lemonade and other beverages from a colorful, New Orleans-themed counter. The hours of operation vary and are usually limited to weekends and holidays in the off-season.

Newsstand

MAP: Park, P-4

DATES: July 17, 1955–ongoing

Guests get their first look at Disneyland souvenirs on the western side
of the main **entrance**. In addition to
small gift items, the Newsstand sells
disposable cameras and other necessities for a day at Disneyland. The sign
above the little freestanding building reads both Newsstand and Information because, in addition to selling their wares, **cast members** here can answer questions
and hold Package Express items purchased inside the park for convenient pick-up on
the way out. Additional newsstand structures selling the same type of merchandise
can be found nearby at the two entrance tunnels leading to **Town Square**.

New Year's Eve Party

DATES: 1958–ongoing

Disneyland's winter holidays have nearly always included an all-park New Year's Eve
Party. The New Year's tradition was inaugurated on December 31, 1958 with relatively
modest late-night festivities. Since then, the annual event has been expanded to
include special **parades** (often a preview of bands from the next day's Rose Parade in
Pasadena), creative light shows projected onto **Sleeping Beauty Castle**, a dramatic
countdown, and unique **fireworks**. Crowds have increased over the years; what began
with about 7,500 partygoers in 1958 has sometimes swelled to 10 times that size.
The biggest New Year's Eve gathering ever at the park was probably the one at the
end of 1999, when well over 80,000 guests came to the huge, once-in-a-lifetime millennium celebration.

New York World's Fair Exhibit

MAP: Tomorrowland, T-23

DATES: 1963–1964

In 1963 **Walt Disney** suddenly pulled his Imagineers off their in-the-works Disneyland projects, including **Pirates of the Caribbean** and the **Haunted Mansion**, to
create four big new attractions for the 1964–1965 New York World's Fair. For Disney,
the fair provided an inexpensive way to explore expensive new ideas, since each attraction was being sponsored by a major corporation and was being installed in a
building that Disney himself didn't have to construct. Additionally, once they had
proved themselves to New York audiences, the attractions, or at least some of their
elements, would travel to Disneyland. In a sense, then, the two-year New York World's

Fair was like a free Disneyland research laboratory.

With all four New York attractions on the drawing board, in 1963 a free preview called the New York World's Fair Exhibit opened in Disneyland. It was installed in **Tomorrowland**, in the spot where the Dairy Bar had once stood. The first new development the exhibit displayed was the Wonder Rotunda's Magic Skyway, sponsored by the Ford Motor Co. This attraction's dinosaurs would later appear in Disneyland's **Primeval World Diorama**, and the vehicles would be modified into the **PeopleMover**. The next attraction was General Electric's Progressland, which would become Tomorrowland's **Carousel of Progress**. Third was **It's a Small World** for Pepsi-Cola, the cruise that came to **Fantasyland** in 1966. The final attraction was **Great Moments with Mr. Lincoln** in the Illinois pavilion, which would develop into the attraction of the same name at the Disneyland **Opera House** in 1965.

Disneyland's New York World's Fair Exhibit served two purposes: it helped gauge the public's interest in the upcoming attractions, and it stirred up excitement for Disneyland's immediate future. As they almost always were, Walt Disney's instincts were on target—his four attractions were among the most-visited in New York, and when they moved west they were quickly among the most-visited in Disneyland. In '65, with the New York attractions either already installed at the Anaheim park or coming soon, the Tomorrowland exhibit came down and was replaced by the **Character Shop** after a lengthy remodel. Back in New York, the fair organizers invited Disney to build an East Coast version of Disneyland. But Disney declined; his sights were already set on Florida for his next park location.

Nunis, Dick
(1932–)

A Georgian born in 1932, Dick Nunis was an Academic All-American football player at USC in the early 1950s. Upon graduating in '55, he applied to work at Disneyland two months before **Opening Day**. Hired by **Van Arsdale France**, who was in charge of training new employees, Nunis started as an orientation trainer for the park's first class of **cast members**. Later he was made head of the mailroom, supervisor of **Adventureland** and **Frontierland**, and, ironically, Van France's boss in 1962. Working with France, Nunis developed the park's employee manuals. According to the book *Remembering Walt*, after **Walt Disney** died in 1966, France and Nunis decided to shift the theme of those manuals to a "traditions" concept, "so that Walt's words, traditions and philosophies would go on forever."

Later promotions elevated Nunis to positions as Disneyland's director of operations (it was Nunis who pushed for a new water ride, which finally opened as **Splash Mountain** in 1989) and executive vice president for both Disneyland and Walt Disney World (he oversaw final construction to get the mammoth Florida park open on time). In the 1980s, he oversaw EPCOT, and in the '90s, Disney-MGM Studios. After exactly 44 years of helping to shape the philosophy, growth, and legacy of Disney theme parks, Dick Nunis retired in 1999 as one of the company's top executives. He was named a Disney Legend that same year.

Oaks Tavern

MAP: Frontierland, Fr-5

DATES: 1956–summer 1978

A saloon on the corner (the **Golden Horseshoe**) and a tavern a little farther down the row—in the 1950s, these were the businesses that put the wild in Wild West—right? In **Frontierland**, not so much. The Oaks Tavern was merely a fast-food operation that cooked up chili, burgers, sandwiches, and snacks. Its patio tables overlooked the **Rivers of America** for a scenic dining experience. Last call came to the Oaks Tavern in 1978 when the space was recast as the **Stage Door Café**.

Observatron

MAP: Tomorrowland, T-8

DATES: May 22, 1998–ongoing

The Observatron was added during 1998's major **Tomorrowland** remodel. While it was new to Disneyland, the Obervatron wasn't new to the Disney canon—a similar device had already been operating at Disneyland Paris.

A futuristic kinetic sculpture that looks like a screwdriver mounted to the top of dish antennas, the Observatron sits above the old **PeopleMover** loading area. Disneyland's 2000 **souvenir book** showed off the Observatron with a full-page photo and text declaring that it "signals the quarter hour with an impressive array of movements, lights, and vibrant music." As an elaborate timepiece, the Observatron is like the **It's a Small World** mechanical clock that is unveiled every 15 minutes. Exactly how observers can divine the current time from the whirling Observatron and its elevating antennas isn't quite clear (especially since it rarely operates at all anymore), but the device does make for a curious sight.

Olsen, Jack
(1923–1980)

Many Disneyland items bought in the '60s that are now valuable Disney collectibles were first brought into the park's stores by Jack Olsen. Olsen enjoyed a two-decade career as a key Disneyland executive.

Olsen was born in Salt Lake City in 1923 but raised in California. In the early '40s he went to Penn State before becoming a medal-winning G.I. in World War

II. Returning stateside, he pursued his artistic hobbies while working in L.A. art galleries.

Olsen began working for the Disney Company in 1955, first as an artist at Disney Studios and then as a Disneyland store manager. In his book *Window on Main Street*, **Van Arsdale France**, whom Olsen mentored, called Olsen "a brilliant artist" with a "brilliant mind." From 1960 until 1970 Olsen supervised the company's merchandising division, bringing cool new T-shirts, hats, toys, gifts, novelties, and more to store shelves. It was also his idea to bring **portrait artists** to **Main Street** to draw caricatures of guests. During the '70s, Olsen helped with the merchandising at Walt Disney World, where a Main Street window still identifies him as "the Merchant Prince."

Olsen retired in 1977, and after several years of ill health died in 1980 at age 56. Jack Olsen was named a Disney Legend in 2005.

Omnimover

MAP: Tomorrowland, T-24 and T-4; New Orleans Square, NOS-12

DATES: August 5, 1967–ongoing

Well-known and much-celebrated are the 1960s' most sophisticated attractions, especially **Pirates of the Caribbean** and the **Haunted Mansion**. What's less conspicuous now is the significance of the new Omnimover vehicle system that debuted in 1967.

Before the Omnimover system was invented and implemented, ride vehicles were variations on little miniature cars, trains, boats, and whirling enclosures. As fun as these were, they were limiting. Sitting in open vehicles, guests could look ahead to see other parts of the attraction before they were meant to see them, or even look

behind them to view structural elements they weren't meant to see at all. Music and narration blared through loudspeakers positioned at different stages in the attraction, causing either confusion (when guests had already passed what the narration was about) or a cacophony (when guests heard sounds from other parts of the attraction). What's more, some of these attractions were notoriously slow-loading, since the entire ride had to stop in order to get guests into vehicles (think of the **Mad Hatter's Mad Tea Party**). In the '60s, Imagineers realized that these exciting and very long attractions would soon be handling thousands of guests per hour, and they had to come up with some new way to both improve the experience and move

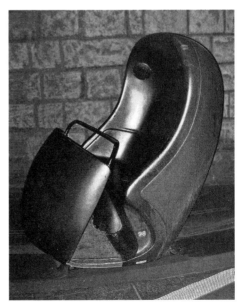

large numbers of guests through the ride efficiently.

Their solution was the Omnimover. The Omnimover actually derived from the vehicles that were first tried at the 1964–1965 New York World's Fair. There the General Motors pavilion and the Disney-designed Ford Magic Skyway both incorporated long trains of vehicles that formed continuous loops, like a closed necklace of little cars. Guests boarded the vehicles from a moving platform, which meant the rides didn't have to stop to load and unload their passengers. The Disney vehicles were otherwise fairly primitive—they didn't move independently, and they didn't have their own individual sound systems. But they soon would.

After a year of development, the park's first iteration of the Omnimover ride system was the Atomobile in **Adventure Thru Inner Space**, a major new **Tomorrowland** attraction that debuted in 1967. As with the New York vehicles, the continuous chain of blue, pod-like Atomobiles had a moving conveyor belt next to it in the loading and unloading areas, and each pod had a self-closing metal bar that helped secure its pair of passengers. To the delight of waiting guests, over 3,000 passengers per hour could now be transported through the world of the molecule.

What's more, Disney Imagineers, particularly **Bob Gurr**, **Roger Broggie**, and **John Hench**, added important new possibilities to the Omnimover's movement (omni, the Latin word for "all," suggested the new range of motion). First, the Atomobiles could spin in any direction on computer command, thus directing the rider's attention to particular sights. In addition, the pods could tilt backward or forward, keeping riders level as the pods went up and down hills. The tilting effect also meant that riders could relax back into their seats when the pods leaned backwards to reveal something up near the ceiling. Plus, with an onboard speaker delivering the narration and music, sound did not have to be blasted through an entire room from large speakers and could instead travel with each individual Omnimover vehicle, to be played at appropriate moments.

A memorable example of how these options all came together occurred at the end of the Inner Space journey when the pods sprung a nifty joke. While moving forward, the pods suddenly swiveled and bent back to direct attention up at a microscope, where a giant eye was peering at riders. Simultaneously, the narrator's voice inside the Atomobile announced, "We have you on visual."

The next Disneyland attraction to use the Omnimover system was the Haunted Mansion two years later. There, black Doom Buggies still convey guests up inclines and down slopes, aim them sideways, and create an effect that has often been described as cinematic. In *The Art of Walt Disney*, author Christopher Finch explains how the Doom Buggy "is used exactly like a movie camera. The rider is traveling through a programmed show which unfolds in time. The choice of where to look is not his to make—it has already been made by the designer, who determines what will be seen, just as a director determines what the movie patron will see." Just as all viewers see the same movie, so do all riders see the same attraction and get the same experience (unless they lean out of the Omnimover pods to sneak looks when they're not supposed to).

Just as Inner Space had a cool closing joke provided by the Omnimover, so too did the Haunted Mansion. At the finale, the Doom Buggies swivel toward a mirror just as the onboard speaker cautions guests to "beware hitchhiking ghosts!"

Another Omnimover attraction opened at Disneyland in 2005. **Buzz Lightyear Astro Blasters** added yet one more dimension—rider control. Guests could now point their vehicles in different directions as they tried to shoot at dozens of different targets during their trip. It was the latest improvement to what was a great techno-logical advancement, one so important that it was awarded its own patent in 1971.

One-of-a-Kind Shop

MAP: New Orleans Square, NOS-3

DATES: July 24, 1966–May 1996

The fascinating One-of-a-Kind Shop opened with the rest of **New Orleans Square** in 1966. Located at the front of Royal Street near the **Royal Street Veranda**, the shop was the first retail space guests encountered in this new Disneyland area. Unlike other park stores that sold replicas of antiques, the One-of-a-Kind Shop sold the real deal—actual antiques that could cost thousands of dollars. The 1968 **souvenir book** confirmed the serious intent of the shop: one photo depicted, not smiling kids, but a mature, well-dressed couple standing underneath the shop's ornate chandeliers.

It's said that the store was suggested, or at least inspired by **Walt Disney's** wife, Lillian, whose love of antiques had already led to the old-fashioned décor inside their **apartment** in **Town Square**. Inside the One-of-a-Kind Shop were items that were, if not truly unique to Southern California, certainly unique to Disneyland, including large spinning wheels, Victorian music boxes, vintage dolls, objects d'art, and old clocks, all of them authentic antiques.

The number of people walking into Disneyland hoping to walk out with a valuable spinning wheel is debatable, but the store did thrive for three decades. In 1995 the merchandise expanded to include reproductions and more generic gift items. A year later, the One-of-a-Kind Shop was the gone-of-a-kind shop, to be replaced in '98 by **Le Gourmet.**

Opening Day

DATES: July 17, 1955

Disneyland's Opening Day has nearly always been declared a failure. That's certain-ly how it was reported by some of the press the next day. **Walt Disney**, ever the demanding perfectionist, nicknamed it Black Sunday. For decades the many minor crises that occurred on July 17, 1955 have been well-chronicled, the park's early flaws and deficiencies well-documented, and the failure of Opening Day generally accepted. Reading historic accounts of Opening Day, one encounters such hyperbolic pronouncements as "everything that could go wrong did" and "nothing was work-ing"—neither of which is actually true.

Looking back, Opening Day seems more like a day filled with minor inconveniences than major traumas. Glitches are not catastrophes: there was no riot, no natural disaster, no park-emptying pandemonium, and not a single major injury. Crowds shown in the TV coverage are generally smiling, excited, and unaware of any problems. Nearly all of the day's difficulties resulted from an overwhelming number of guests who came to the infant park suddenly, even when they were told not to. This may

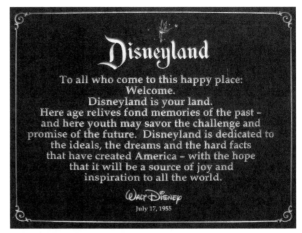

be viewed as success—the success Walt Disney had in building something so alluring that the public had to see it sooner rather than later. Too few visitors, not too many, would have been the real failure, as proven by the ignored advertisements for thousands of embarrassing Broadway openings, forgotten film premieres, and other dead-on-arrival events that litter the fast-moving highway of entertainment history.

Disneyland in mid-1955 was not the Disneyland guests see now, of course. The entire park had been built from scratch in less than a year, still an astonishing feat to contemplate. The run-up to Opening Day had been a frantic sprint to get most of the park functioning, or if not functioning, at least well-disguised as functioning. Having run out of plants, landscapers resorted to decorating existing weeds with little signs adorned with important-sounding Latin names. Lacking time, designers put the **Rocket to the Moon** and **Casey Jr. Circus Train** on view but not in operation. And lacking money, **Tomorrowland** was left undone, its incompletion hidden behind a distraction of balloons and bunting. Today guests might see Disneyland as an efficient entertainment machine, but at the dawn of Opening Day, it was still an unfinished, untried, unrehearsed idea. Workers, in fact, were still applying paint to some of the buildings just hours before the first guests were due.

When they did arrive, those guests arrived *en masse*. Attendance that first sunny Sunday was supposed to be 10,000, and all of the guests were supposed to be dignitaries, celebrities, reporters, Disney employees, and Disneyland sponsors holding special invitations with different entrance times, so admission to the park would be staggered. Alerts had even been posted in the newspapers that the general public would not be admitted to Disneyland on Opening Day, July 17th, but evidently some 20,000 additional fans didn't get the word. With excitement trumping patience, between 28,154 (the official count) and 33,000 (the unofficial tally) people showed up, and most of them arrived early. Though traffic was jammed for miles around, a huge vanguard of unsolicited guests got to the park, either by presenting counterfeit invitations or by sneaking over the **berm**. By mid-afternoon the huge crowd working its way up **Main Street** and streaming off to the different lands was walking shoulder-to-shoulder.

POPULATION
500,000,000

DISNEYLAND ELEVATION 138 FEET

With attendance suddenly triple what it was supposed to be, the inexperienced **cast members** were immediately confronted with food and beverage shortages and an inadequate number of **restrooms** and **trash cans**. Attraction lines quickly bunched up, and some rides were overloaded with guests. Although few people probably knew it at the time, at least one of the watercraft came close to calamity—the *Mark Twain* was so weighted down with extra guests that water splashed onto its decks.

What predicaments the high attendance didn't cause, bad luck did. The intense summer heat caused some of the newly poured asphalt to soften and trap the high heels of women who had dressed up for the opening. With eager crowds waiting, a few of the indoor ride vehicles stopped working altogether. **Van France** wrote in *Window on Main Street* that the doors to **Sleeping Beauty Castle** were inadvertently left unlocked, allowing inquisitive guests to roam through the incomplete interior.

These dilemmas were all new for the Disneyland staff. Awestruck guests were as curious as they were dazzled, and dewy employees were on the front lines trying to solve problems they'd never been trained for. Also remember that back then, not a single person in the world had any familiarity with the practical workings of a huge theme park; Walt Disney was opening his unique, untried vision without benefit of the "spring training" or "out-of-town tryout" that sports stadiums and Broadway theaters employ when they want to experiment with something new before the public sees it.

Compounding the inexperience of the cast members was the inexperience of the TV crews on hand to film the opening. Two dozen TV cameras were scattered around the park for a live coast-to-coast show, the most ambitious broadcast ever attempted. Nobody had ever televised anything so big, so spread out, and so complex before, and it showed. Cues were missed, stars were in the wrong places, and cameras caught activity they weren't supposed to (like actor Bob Cummings spontaneously smooching a dancer, though this conspicuous indiscretion may have been staged to promote Cummings' TV show, for which he played a bachelor photographer). At a time when the total U.S. population was only about 165 million, 90 million Americans tuned in to see what was a humorous, confusing, spontaneous, but ultimately triumphant TV spectacle of unprecedented proportions.

Celebrities were everywhere that day, either being interviewed, walking in **parades**, or enjoying the attractions. Art Linkletter, Ronald Reagan, and Bob Cummings served as jovial TV hosts, and many others celebrities were on hand to celebrate, including Alan Young, Jerry Colonna, Danny Thomas, Frank Sinatra, Sammy Davis Jr., Kirk Douglas, Charlton Heston, Maureen O'Hara, Jerry Lewis, Debbie Reynolds, Eddie Fisher, Fess Parker, Buddy Ebsen, Irene Dunne, Roy Rogers, Dale Evans, Hedda Hopper, California governor Goodwin Knight, Santa Fe Railroad president Fred Gurley, and Annette Funicello with the rest of the Mouseketeers. A laughing Sammy chased Frank in **Autopia**; Fess and Buddy wore frontier costumes and sang; Irene christened the *Mark Twain*; Colonna was the highballin' engineer on Casey Jr.; and Walt Disney roamed the park to make televised speeches.

Just like every Disneyland day since, free entertainment was abundant. During a solemn dedication ceremony, religious speakers spoke and offered a silent prayer, military representatives conducted a flag-raising ceremony, a squadron of planes flew overhead, and doves were sent flying into the sky. Later, the park's first parade wound northward from **Town Square** toward the **Hub**. The procession included soldiers wearing Revolutionary War uniforms, horse-drawn buckboards, a stagecoach, Cinderella's pumpkin coach, Autopia cars, Disney characters, the **Disneyland Band**, the Mouseketeers wearing cowboy gear and hobby-horse costumes, and, bringing up the rear, a Carnation milk truck. During the day, the **Firehouse Five Plus Two** jazz band played atop the **Santa Fe & Disneyland Railroad**. That night's **fireworks** rocketed above **Sleeping Beauty Castle** while a jubilant Walt Disney watched from his Town Square **apartment**. Neal Gabler's *Walt Disney: The Triumph of the American Imagination* summarized the day as "the longest and quite possibly the best of Walt Disney's life."

The next day, Monday the 18th, Disneyland officially opened to the public. How Black could Sunday have been if Monday was as successful as it was? Thousands of guests began lining up before dawn, an enormous traffic jam soon plugged up the nearby freeway, and by the time the turnstiles began twirling at 10 AM the **parking lot** was already full. The first guest to buy a ticket was a 22-year-old college student who had been waiting out front since 2 AM. Walt Disney personally greeted the very first children in line. However, for all the high spirits and éclat that day, some bad luck continued to plague the park when a gas leak forced **Fantasyland** to close early (some sources claim the leak occurred on the 17th, not on the 18th).

On that first Monday morning, several major newspapers published rave reviews of Sunday's special Opening Day events. "Dream Realized—Disneyland Opens," read the July 18th headline in the *L.A. Times*, supplemented with lots of big photos and

Then and Now at 1313 Harbor Boulevard

1955

Hours: 10 AM to 10 PM; open daily all summer; closed some Mondays the rest of the year

Adult admission: $1 (plus additional charges for attractions)

Number of lands: Five (Adventureland, Fantasyland, Frontierland, Main Street, and Tomorrowland)

Number of main attractions: 17 on Opening Day

2012

Hours: Varied, often from 8 or 9 AM to 10 PM or midnight; open daily

Adult admission: $80 (no additional charges for attractions)

Number of lands: Eight (the original five plus Critter Country, Mickey's Toontown, New Orleans Square)

Number of main attractions: 60+

enthusiastic text that called the park "once-upon-a-time land," a "land of magical fantasy," and a "dream come true." However, when several columnists published severe critiques, Walt Disney immediately assembled his top lieutenants to address the writers' issues. Here he was, only one day into Disneyland's history, and already Disney was changing his park. This was the first of thousands of attempts to improve Disneyland after it opened.

"Disneyland is like a piece of clay," Disney declared. "If there is something I don't like, I'm not stuck with it. I can reshape and revamp."

Revamp his team did, working feverishly to solve the traffic problems in the streets, in the restaurants, and on the attractions. Workers quickly attended to the construction that had been left unfinished and landscaping that had been left unplanted. And over the next few weeks, Disney himself courted the press with special invitations and personal apologies.

Hardly anyone could miss the Opening Day sign above the Main Street train station that optimistically announced Disneyland's population as five million people. Skeptics would have wagered that "Disney's Folly" would never draw even a tenth of that number and would close by Christmas.

Disneyland didn't merely survive; it thrived. Attendance, as it had been on Opening Day, was higher for the following months than anyone had expected. According to the Disneyland Data page in the 1957 souvenir book, guest number five million walked through the gates on October 4, 1956, less than 15 months after Black Sunday.

Opera House

MAP: Town Square, TS-9

DATES: July 17, 1955–ongoing

Like **Adventureland**, the Opera House jumped from one side of the park to the other while it was in the planning stages. When it appeared on **Herb Ryman's** large detailed map drawn in 1953 before construction began, the Opera House was clearly shown and labeled on the western side of **Town Square**. The imposing two-story building, of course, ended up on the eastern side, making it one of the first structures guests

meet as they walk into Disneyland through the east tunnel. Today, guests still encounter a long square block that spreads ahead of them about 180 feet from south to north. The Opera House dominates this block and extends about 125 feet back, giving the Opera House a total area of about a third of an acre. The main entrance to the Opera House is in the center of the block and stretches about 35 feet along Town Square; several ground-floor businesses and window displays surround the entrance.

With all the buildings going up in the months leading to **Opening Day**, something had to be finished first, and the Opera House turned out to be that something. Perhaps the main reason it needed to be completed so quickly was because of the way it was going to be utilized, at least in its early years. Although **Walt Disney** originally intended it to be a large, opulent theater, from 1955 until mid-1961 the Opera House was really a working lumber mill, its spacious interior filled with wood and carpentry projects destined for other Disneyland locations.

Starting in '61 and continuing throughout the '60s, the Opera House was put to a variety of uses, none of them having to do with opera. First it was the location for the **Babes in Toyland Exhibit**; next, a temporary TV studio for *The Mickey Mouse Club* scenes; then the site of the **Mickey Mouse Club Headquarters**; and, finally, home to **Great Moments with Mr. Lincoln**. Lincoln arrived in mid-'65, at which point the Opera House really was functioning like the theater it was meant to be.

Lincoln remained until early 1973, when **The Walt Disney Story** temporarily replaced him. Two years later the Great Emancipator returned for the joint Disney/ Lincoln exhibit that continued for the next 30 years. In 2005 the Opera House hosted special exhibits honoring the park's golden anniversary, plus the tribute film *Disneyland: The First 50 Magical Years*. Today, visitors will find elaborate park models and artwork, a flat-screen version of the 50th-anniversary movie, and a special bench that, according to the accompanying plaque, is "the actual park bench from the Griffith Park Merry-Go-Round in Los Angeles, where Walt Disney first dreamed of Disneyland."

No matter what has filled the interior, the Opera House exterior has always stayed dignified, its roof crowned by curling classical ornamentation that makes the structure appear one full story taller than it is. That regal façade was taken in often by one significant fan; the Opera House is the building directly across from the front windows of Walt Disney's private **apartment**.

Our Future in Colors, aka Color Gallery

MAP: Tomorrowland, T-6

DATES: March 1956–January 1963

For its first two years, this exhibit was listed in Disneyland's **souvenir books** as the Dutch Boy exhibit Our Future in Colors. Then, from 1958 to 1963, the books called it simply the Color Gallery. Either way, it had just one location—in the back of the rectangular **Tomorrowland** building that housed the **Art Corner**.

Dutch Boy was a brand name and logo owned by the National Lead Company, a paint manufacturer that was an early Disneyland sponsor. Throughout the summer and fall of 1955, the exhibit's future site was marked by a Dutch Boy statue until construction began that winter for a spring opening. What finally appeared was pretty docile, even by the standards of the child-friendly exhibits found throughout

Tomorrowland. Surrounded by color swatches, guests spun color wheels into new shades. Musical tones accompanied the activity to encourage or discourage possible color combinations.

In 1963 this spot was absorbed into the **Circarama** remodel that would produce a newer, bigger Circle-Vision 360 theater.

Painted Desert, aka Rainbow Desert

MAP: Frontierland, Fr-22

DATES: July 17, 1955–October 11, 1959

In the 1950s, just as **Adventureland** had a **Jungle Cruise** inspired by Disney's *True-Life Adventures* films, so too did **Frontierland** have its own *True-Life* area. The Painted Desert, loosely themed after the Oscar-winning 1953 documentary *The Living Desert*, was an acre-and-a-half spread in the northeast corner of Frontierland. Disneyland's **souvenir books** also referred to this acreage as Rainbow Desert, for its panoply of colors.

The desert being emulated here wasn't the Arabian bleached-sand kind with dunes swelling like ocean waves; Disneyland's desert was styled after the rocky, cactus-studded Arizona landscape. Previewing what the **Big Thunder Mountain Railroad** would speed through in 1979, the Painted Desert had pale orange rock formations crowned with balancing boulders and rough fields of sagebrush. Colorful, bubbling "desert pools" added bright hues, and anthropomorphic saguaro cacti added humor. **Audio-Animatronic** animals weren't displayed yet—any moving creatures were actual birds and lizards that had stopped in for a visit.

From 1956 until 1959 the **Mine Train** slowly traversed the Painted Desert on its way to the spectacular Rainbow Caverns. The Painted Desert and the train both closed in '59, but both reopened the following summer. The desert was reborn as the more animated Living Desert section of the bigger, more sophisticated **Nature's Wonderland**, and the train returned as the Western Mine Train Through Nature's Wonderland.

Parades

DATES: July 17, 1955–ongoing

As discussed in Bob Thomas's *Walt Disney: An American Original,* **Walt Disney** had to convince his own staff that extravagant, expensive parades were a vital part of the Disneyland experience.

"We can't be satisfied," said Disney. "We've always got to give 'em a little more. It'll be worth the

45 Disneyland Parades

1955: Opening Day Parade; Mickey Mouse Club Circus Parade; Christmas Show Parade

1956: Antique Automobile Parade (aka Old Fashioned Automobile Parade)

1957–1964: Christmas in Many Lands Parade

1958–ongoing: Candlelight Procession

1958–1959: Zorro Days Parade

1960–1964: Mickey at the Movies Parade; Parade of Toys

1965–1976; 1980–1985: Fantasy on Parade

1965: Tencennial Parade

1967: Easter Parade

1968: Valentine's Day Party; St. Patrick's Day Parade; Cinco de Mayo Fiesta

1969; 1974: Love Bug Day

1972–1975; 1977–1983; 1985–1996: Main Street Electrical Parade

1975–1976: America on Parade

1977–1979; 1987–2000: Very Merry Christmas Parade

1980–1981: Family Reunion Parade

1983–1984: Flights of Fantasy Parade

1984: Donald Duck's 50th Birthday Parade

1985: Disneyland 30th Anniversary Parade

1986: Totally Minnie Parade

1986–1988: Circus on Parade

1987–1988: Come to the Fair Parade

1990: Party Gras Parade

1991: Celebration USA Parade

1992: World According to Goofy Parade

1993–1994: Aladdin's Royal Caravan Parade

1994–1997: Lion King Celebration

1997: Hercules Victory Parade

1997: Light Magic

1998–1999: Mulan Parade

2000–2005: 45 Years of Magic Parade; Parade of the Stars

2001: Christmas Fantasy Parade

2005: Mickey's Shining Star Cavalcade; Sleeping Beauty's Royal Celebration; Mickey's Magic Kingdom Celebration

2005–2008: Walt Disney's Parade of Dreams

2008–2011: Disney's Celebrate America! A Fourth of July Concert in the Sky

2009–2010: Celebrate! A Street Party

2011–ongoing: Mickey's Soundsational Parade

investment. If they ever stop coming, it'll cost 10 times that much to get 'em back."

But there was more than just a financial concern that drove Walt Disney's passion for parades; he'd loved them since boyhood and had closely observed them whenever one passed down the streets in his hometown of Marceline, Missouri. He transferred that love to Disneyland, where parades have been a daily ritual ever since **Opening Day.** The parades are so popular that the rest of the park often empties out as guests crowd the parade route, making parade-time also a no-line-time at some attractions.

Disneyland parades typically (but not always) begin deep in **Fantasyland**, come past **Matterhorn Mountain** to the **Hub**, and then bend south toward **Town Square**, leaving the public's view through an exit near the **Opera House.** Parades usually last about a half hour and have often culminated with an appearance by Mickey Mouse.

In addition to the daily hometown parades that have been performed most frequently, special parades have celebrated everything from park anniversaries and character birthdays to national holidays and new Disney movies. Any given parade might include vehicles, horses, circus acts, elaborate floats, raised stages with performers, Disney characters, live music, street performers who interact with the crowd, celebrities, and anything else the Imagineers can dream up. The **Main Street Electrical Parade**, the only parade identified on a **Main Street Window**, is probably the most famous of the park's parades; the Candlelight Procession, which debuted in 1958 and still runs every **holiday season**, is the longest-lasting. **Robert Jani**, **Bill Justice**, and **Tommy Walker** are usually named as the park's parade pioneers.

Parasol Cart

MAP: New Orleans Square, NOS-10

DATES: 1990–ongoing

Parked near the **French Market** restaurant in **New Orleans Square** is this pretty, two-wheeled cart selling parasols. While not the sturdiest thing to have while riding fast-paced attractions, a parasol provides lightweight, sophisticated shelter from the blazing summer sun (and makes a frilly gift for a Disney princess). The cart is operated by Rubio Arts, a company that places artists in different art-related concessions around Disneyland (the nearby **portrait artists** are also from Rubio). For under $20, the artists at the parasol cart hand-paint flowers, animals, and other happy patterns (names as well) onto the colorful fabric panels of the parasols. Guests who order customized parasols can pick them up a couple of hours later, after the paint has dried.

Parking Lot

MAP: Park, P-2

DATES: July 17, 1955–January 22, 1998

If the park's parking lot seemed big, it was—in fact, with an area of 100 acres, it was 40 acres bigger than Disneyland itself was in 1955. When it was first built, the lot's capacity was 12,175 cars, all of which entered from Harbor Blvd. on Disneyland's east side and exited 2,000 feet away onto West Street. Most of the original lot wasn't paved, which is perhaps why it cost only 25 cents to park there back in 1955. Other than a couple of areas closest to the **entrance**, the spaces in the dirt lot were marked with chalk.

After a "remodel" and complete paving, the lot was divided into over 15,000 marked spaces. To help guests remember where they left their cars, the parking lot was divided into smaller themed sections that were labeled with character names and pictures. The names were arranged alphabetically, with Alice designated as the first parking area in the northeast corner (near Harbor Boulevard) and Winnie the Pooh as the last in the southwest corner (near the West Street/Katella Avenue intersection). The Bambi section was closest to the ticket booths at the **entrance**; motor homes parked in Eeyore; and a 10-minute handicapped zone was in Donald. **Walt Disney** himself didn't park his car in any of these sections—he had a private spot west of **Town Square**, close to his **apartment** above the **Fire Department**. For his helicopter flights to and from his Burbank studio, he also had a small "heliport," shown outside of **Tomorrowland** on the park's first **Fun Maps**.

For four decades, the tantalizing views of Disneyland from the parking lot—especially of the elevated railroad and **Monorail** trains, both of which pass near the ticket booths—incited quick dashes from the cars to the turnstiles. Guests had the choice of walking across the parking lot to the park or taking the convenient trams that continually circulated to scoop up pedestrians. Requiring no ticket for boarding, these trams were the only free Disneyland vehicles on the entire property. The trams saved footwear, but they didn't always save time, since they took a circuitous route to get to the ticket booths and their top speed was only 11 miles per hour.

One big drawback to the uncovered, unlandscaped parking lot was its lack of shade. Some experts have speculated that the parking lot was intentionally designed to be drab and treeless to throw the color and excitement of Disneyland into high contrast. That thought was a small consolation to anyone who returned to a car during the day and discovered that what they'd parked under the searing Southern California sun wasn't a car but was actually a metal furnace on wheels.

The importance of the immense parking lot to car-driving guests, and to

Disneyland's image, is not to be underestimated. According to James B. Stewart's *Disney Wars*, in the mid-'80s, retired chairman of the board Card Walker vetoed higher parking fees. "The parking lot is the first thing the guest sees. . . . Walt wanted them to think that this is the greatest place on earth." By implication, no park could be considered "the greatest place on earth" without a huge, convenient, inexpensive parking lot nearby.

Even so, after 43 years of service the parking lot was demolished in 1998 to accommodate Disney California Adventure, the Grand California Hotel, and Downtown Disney. During the new construction, the ominous towers that carried high-tension power cables across the parking lot were relocated and made less conspicuous. These days, most drivers avail themselves of the 22-acre Mickey and Friends parking structure to the northwest of Disneyland. This massive edifice, five minutes away by tram, features six levels and spaces for over 10,000 cars, making it one of the largest of its kind in the world. It also offers something that other parking structures don't—a rooftop view of Disneyland's **fireworks** (some visitors favor this viewing location because it puts them near their cars for a quick getaway ahead of the exiting crowds). Three smaller lots with Disney-related names—Simba, Pumbaa, and Toy Story—supplement Mickey and Friends with additional spaces near the park (a fourth lot, Timon, was lost to construction projects at Disney California Adventure). In total, the Disneyland Resort can now accommodate over 29,000 cars.

Partners

MAP: Hub, H-7

DATES: November 18, 1993–ongoing

Disney artist **Blaine Gibson** came out of retirement to sculpt the heralded *Partners* statue that now serves as the centerpiece of the **Hub**. The inspiring bronze statue was installed in a special ceremony overseen by **Roy Disney** and **Jack Lindquist**, both top Disney executives and future Disney Legends. The date of the installation—November 18, 1993—wasn't chosen capriciously. Exactly 65 years earlier, Mickey Mouse had made his debut in *Steamboat Willie*, making this the company's official birthdate for their superstar. Eight years later a re-dedication ceremony was held on December 5th, which would have been the 100th birthday of the company's founder.

From the moment it was unveiled, *Partners* instantly became one of Disneyland's most-photographed features, due in part to its location in front of **Sleeping Beauty Castle**, but also because of the figures it depicts. The statue's two subjects are a smiling **Walt Disney**, who stands about six feet tall, and Mickey Mouse, who is presented as half Disney's size. Disney's left hand holds Mickey's right, and Disney's raised right arm points southward toward **Main Street**. While Disney wears his readily identifiable business suit, playful Mickey sports his trademark short pants with big front buttons, shoes, and gloves. On Disney's tie are the letters STR, the initials of his Smoke Tree Ranch in Palm Springs (Disney had sold the vacation home to help pay for Disneyland's construction, but he re-purchased it later).

The pair stands on a three-foot-tall cylindrical plinth that's surrounded by a 30-foot-wide circular planter bursting with flowers (pre-statue, this circle was filled entirely with blooms). On the southern side of the pedestal is a plaque with the inscription, quoting Walt Disney: "I think most of all what I want Disneyland to be is a happy place . . . where parents and children can have fun, together." After *Partners* went up at Disneyland, similar statues were installed at other Disney theme parks.

Passports

DATES: 1955–1982

From Opening Day until early 1982, the full Disneyland experience required guests to make at least two purchases. One was for park admission, and the other was for supplemental tickets for attractions. For most of this period, attraction tickets were sold in convenient **ticket books**. But because these ticket books were optional, for 27 years it was possible for guests to walk around Disneyland just for the modest admission price, which started out at $1 and for decades was only a few dollars.

In the '70s another theme park about 60 miles away, Magic Mountain, revived a POP (Pay One Price) plan that had been tried elsewhere on a limited basis. One of the earliest big amusement parks, New York's Steeplechase Park, had implemented a POP admission of 25 cents; later, a Los Angeles amusement park called Pacific Ocean Park had tried out a POP plan from 1960 until it closed in 1967. Starting that year, Six Flags Over Georgia offered POP admission for $4.50, followed by Magic Mountain's one-price $5 admission ticket that included entry and unlimited rides.

The advantages of a POP plan were instantly apparent to both the park and its visitors: all guests paid a higher price to get in, but there were no expensive single-ride tickets that had to be carefully monitored during the day. The only guests left out of this equation were those who wanted to pay for admission only, not ride tickets. Those guests must have been few and far between, because by the end of the '70s Disneyland was experimenting with its own all-inclusive, unlimited-attraction admission policy patterned after the one at Magic Mountain.

Originally, the only Disneyland guests to be offered all-inclusive admission tickets were the members of the **Magic Kingdom Club**. By the summer of '82, all adult guests found themselves paying a single price for one-day, unlimited-attraction admission (young children were free, as they are now). The adult price stayed in the teens through most of the '80s, rose to $20 in '87, and has surged past significant price points every few years—$30 in '94, $40 in 2000, $55 in 2005, $60 in 2007—to hit $80 in 2011.

Thankfully, there are ways to reduce the cost of admission, among them Annual Passports, multi-day discounts, various "park hopper" options that combine Disneyland and Disney California Adventure admission, and lower prices for seniors and local residents. Not only have prices changed, but so has terminology—"passport" now applies only to the different annual admission plans.

Patented Pastimes, aka Great American Pastimes

MAP: Main Street, MS-19

DATES: June 15, 1990–1999

Since **Opening Day**, the **Fine Tobacco** shop had been wedged between the **Main Street Cinema** and the **Main Street Magic Shop**. That changed in 1990 when Patented Pastimes, a shop specializing in vintage toys and other collectibles, opened in this small space. Nine months later, the store's name changed to Great American Pastimes, and its merchandise expanded to include nostalgic sports items ("the great American pastime" is one of baseball's nicknames). The approach of a new millennium saw the arrival of a new replacement, the **20th Century Music Company**, in 1999.

Pendleton Woolen Mills Dry Goods Store

MAP: Frontierland, Fr-2

DATES: July 18, 1955–April 29, 1990

Missing **Opening Day** by just 24 hours, the Pendleton store stood for the next 35 years as one of the longest-lasting sponsored stores in the park. The location was about 50 feet within the **Frontierland** gates—guests heading to the **Golden Horseshoe** would have walked past Pendleton's door. The store featured a wooden sidewalk out front and the exterior was appropriately rustic, as if guests were going to hitch up their horses before shopping inside. The interior continued the Old West theme with frontier décor.

When it debuted in Frontierland, Pendleton was already over 40 years old. A respected manufacturer of woolen fabrics and blankets in Oregon, Pendleton had supplemented its line with men's and women's clothes mid-century. In the Disneyland store, flannel shirts, which would prove popular with '60s surfers (the Beach Boys wore them in their early days as the Pendletones), were especially prominent.

In 1990 Pendleton finally left and the store became **Bonanza Outfitters**, another retailer of Frontierland fashions.

Penny Arcade

MAP: Main Street, MS-8

DATES: July 17, 1955–ongoing

Staying true to his desire to recreate what would have existed in small American towns in the early 1900s, **Walt Disney** built a Penny Arcade on Disneyland's **Main Street**. An oversized Indian-head penny, dated 1901, is mounted over the doorway. The arcade's big entrance gapes with tantalizing sights and sounds that invite curious pedestrians to step inside.

The 1957 Disneyland **souvenir book** listed the Penny Arcade in the "rides" category, but the closest thing the building ever had to a major attraction was the **Main Street Shooting Gallery** from 1955 to 1962. Most of the Penny Arcade has always been given over to old-fashioned family fun—simple games, hand-cranked silent movies viewed for only a penny, and bizarre gizmos that were neither games nor movies. Of these latter devices, guests can still try the Electricity Is Life device that hooks them up to a battery, the souvenir coin-pressers, and the beautiful Esmeralda's fortune-telling machine (Esmeralda is popular enough to have her own cloisonné tribute pin).

A 1998 remodel replaced some of the old machines with new video games and space for a candy counter. Unchanged is the classic Orchestron, a century-old mechanical music-maker from Germany that Walt Disney bought before the park opened. Also unchanged is the Penny Arcade's glittering appeal at night, when it seems to burst forth onto the street with bright lights and exuberant activity.

Pen Shop

MAP: Main Street, MS-15

DATES: July 17, 1955–1960

For the second half of the 1950s, a small store selling pens operated on East Center Street, a small lane that intersects **Main Street** at the **Market House**. The Pen Shop was behind the corner **Gibson Greeting Cards** store and opened to the East Center cul-de-sac. Writing instruments were the main items for sale, but there was more to the shop than retail—it also displayed replicas of historical documents and offered handwriting analyses.

The Pen Shop was written off in the 1960 expansion that transformed the Gibson store into the **Hallmark Card Shop**.

PeopleMover,
aka PeopleMover, Presented by Goodyear

MAP: Tomorrowland, T-8

DATES: July 2, 1967–August 21, 1995

"Tomorrow's transportation . . . today!" the PeopleMover's **attraction poster** once declared. For 40 years that optimistic description seemed prophetic. Fondly remembered as one of the coolest little vehicles in Disneyland history, the popular PeopleMover debuted in 1967 with the newly remodeled **Tomorrowland**.

The PeopleMover was certainly one of the most visible of that year's new attractions. Backed by the smooth music of Disney Legend **Buddy Baker**, the little blue, red, green, and yellow cars slid leisurely along a winding, elevated track that took them across the Tomorrowland entrance, into the **Adventure Thru Inner Space** building (where they could be seen by guests standing in line), past the shoppers in the **Character Shop**, in and out of the Carousel Theater, near the submarine lagoon, through the waiting area of the **Circarama** theater, and, as of the late '70s, inside **Space Mountain**. For the price of a D ticket (see **ticket books**), guests got a scenic 16-minute tour of Tomorrowland.

The PeopleMover was truly different from any other futuristic transportation in the park. The book *Walt Disney's Disneyland* pointed out that while the Monorail was "an old idea in a new showcase, the PeopleMover was a new concept developed by Disney engineers and introduced for the first time, anywhere, in Tomorrowland." Those engineers had first experimented with PeopleMover technology in their Magic Skyway ride at the 1964–1965 New York World's Fair. There, the new propulsion concept was used to push unpowered vehicles along a track like factory cars being moved down an assembly line. According to his book *Designing Disney*, Imagineer **John Hench** actually got the idea from a Ford plant, where he watched steel being moved on tracks from area to area.

Two years later a similar system propelled Disneyland's PeopleMover. Unlike the Monorail and other trains in the park, the PeopleMover trains themselves weren't motorized—the track was. Rubber tires mounted every nine feet along the three-quarter-mile track were powered by electricity to push the PeopleMover gently along, at walking speeds ranging from about two to seven miles per hour. Usually four people at a time could fit comfortably on the bench seats inside one of the cars, which had white canopies to shield them from the sun. With the four-car trains running nonstop, and with guests stepping directly into their seats from a moving walkway, almost 4,900 passengers could be moved through the attraction per

Approximate Train Distances

Monorail: 2.3 miles
Santa Fe & Disneyland Railroad: 1.3 miles
PeopleMover, Viewliner: .75–1 mile
Big Thunder Mountain Railroad: .5 miles
Casey Jr. Circus Train: .3 miles
Western Mine Train Through Nature's Wonderland: .3 miles

---

hour. Surprisingly, Goodyear, which made its name selling car tires, sponsored this mass-transit system from 1967 to the end of '81.

Regrettable events marred the PeopleMover's three decades at Disneyland. Tragically, reckless guests trying to move from car to car caused two fatalities in 1967 and 1980. In addition, the attraction got what many people considered to be unnecessary makeovers in '77 and '82, when a "superspeed tunnel" and *Tron* movie effects were incorporated into the trip. The slow-moving trains were finally derailed in the late '90s, to be replaced by the ill-fated **Rocket Rods**.

A ride similar to the PeopleMover still exists at Walt Disney World. Even better, in recent years there's been talk of the PeopleMover being revived at Disneyland, especially since the unused tracks still arc gracefully across Tomorrowland. **Walt Disney** hoped his PeopleMover would be adopted by cities for urban transit, and the system was indeed studied by city planners. However, nobody wanted it except for a single airport, so the PeopleMover exists today as a memory of an ambitious era in Disneyland history.

Peter Pan Crocodile Aquarium

MAP: Fantasyland, Fa-6, Fa-24

DATES: Never built

Had Bruce Bushman's color concept art of 1953 come to be, a large aquarium with a *Peter Pan* theme would have been built in **Fantasyland**. The location would have possibly been the courtyard where the **King Arthur Carrousel** was eventually installed, or perhaps the open area where the **Matterhorn** eventually went up. A Pan-themed aquarium would have given Fantasyland three Peter Pan attractions (**Peter Pan Flight** and the **Pirate Ship Restaurant** both debuted in 1955).

Bushman's art for the Peter Pan Crocodile Aquarium depicted a giant crocodile stretched out in a pool, the croc's head and tail sticking out of the surface. After walking through its gaping jaws and down below the waterline, guests would have entered an aquarium area where live fish swam behind large windows. The closest Disneyland ever actually got to a big aquarium was the **Submarine Voyage**, set in a lagoon filled with mechanical marine life. Bushman's illustration was included in the *Behind the Magic: 50 Years of Disneyland* exhibit held at the Oakland Museum of California in 2006.

Peter Pan Flight, aka Peter Pan's Flight

MAP: Fantasyland, Fa-29

DATES: July 17, 1955–ongoing

Many guests count Peter Pan Flight among their all-time favorite attractions. The enchanting flight over Victorian London to a fantasy island offers one of Disneyland's prettiest views, and for most of its years it has only cost a C ticket from the park's **ticket book**. However, many guests also count Peter Pan Flight among Disneyland's most frustrating attractions; even when park attendance is low, the attraction always seems to have long, slow-moving lines. Then, having waited 45 minutes to board the ride, guests are quickly whisked away from the scenic Never Land vistas before they can really study them. Displeased Peter Pan Flight fans are like sleepers roused prematurely from a sublime dream.

Peter Pan Flight (as it was called from 1955 to 1982) was one of **Fantasyland's** three original indoor "dark" rides. Like **Mr. Toad's Wild Ride** and **Snow White Adventures**, it sends guests into movie environments on small vehicles attached to a track. The Pan innovation is the track's position—rather than winding along the ground, the track hangs from the ceiling to give guests the sensation of flying. The experience is delightful. In the **queue** area a lovely mural piques interest in the Peter Pan story, and the gilded galleons, flying in for boarding and then soaring out of sight, beckon riders to join the adventure.

Peter's famous cry, "C'mon everybody, here we go!" sends guests swooping out the Darlings' nursery window. They're soon floating seven feet above a cityscape that's so detailed it has lighted traffic moving along its roads. At the "second star on the right," with the soundtrack encouraging guests to "think of a wonderful thought," the ships soar to Never Land for bird's-eye views of **Skull Rock**, Captain Hook's ship

anchored in the lagoon, and teepees on a bluff. After 90 wondrous seconds, the final minute features an action-packed encounter with Hook and the rescue of Tiger Lily.

Much of the attraction was enhanced in 1961, and the second section with Captain Hook was dramatically remodeled in 1983 with the rest of Fantasyland. The '83 Pan improvements included the addition of three-dimensional figures, brighter colors, some pieces off the old **Pirate Ship Restaurant**, and Peter himself, previously represented only by his shadow. Outside, a majestic new clock tower marked the entrance, and a new sign declared this Peter Pan's Flight.

Fun details are sprinkled like pixie dust throughout this attraction, including children's toy blocks that spell famous names, bubbling "lava" inside a volcano, and the clock tower's thematic weathervane. All of it adds up to a divine dream in which you can fly, you can fly, you can fly!

Petrified Tree

MAP: Frontierland, Fr-8

DATES: September 1957–ongoing

Guests love finding surprises, and those visiting in 1957 found an *old* surprise in **Frontierland**—a 70-million-year-old surprise, to be exact. That September, the park began to display an authentic petrified tree along the southern tip of the **Rivers of America**.

Before the tree was placed in the park, **Walt Disney** presented it as a gift to his wife, Lillian, in 1956. They had found the mineralized sequoia stump together while on vacation in the Pike's Peak area of Colorado. Disney bought it on the spot from a private seller and had it sent to California as a gift to his wife for their 31st wedding anniversary. Realizing that Disneyland could exhibit it better than she could, Mrs. Disney donated the petrified tree to the park, where it has been an imposing presence ever since. Surrounded by a low metal fence and supported by a metal brace, the white, stony-looking tree stump stands 10 feet tall and weighs five tons. A plaque at the site explains the ancient history of the stump in detail and names Mrs. Disney as the donor.

Phantom Boats

MAP: Tomorrowland, T-10

DATES: August 16, 1955–October 1956

The Phantom Boats have two interesting distinctions—they represent the first attraction ever to be removed from Disneyland, and they're one of the only attractions (**Great Moments with Mr. Lincoln** is another) ever brought back from total extinction.

In mid-August of 1955, the Phantom Boats replaced the temporary Tomorrowland Boats that had been cruising in the Tomorrowland lagoon for about three weeks. Styled like their immediate predecessors, the odd-looking Phantom Boats were slightly futuristic fiberglass vessels with pointy noses, inboard motors, and huge fins (fins being the decade's fab design feature on rockets and cars). Although the boats looked fast, in reality they drove slow. The 14 boats came in two great '50s colors, pink and aqua. The "phantom" in their name had no basis in any apocryphal backstory told to guests—supposedly the name just sounded alluring.

Amazingly, guests were allowed to pilot the boats around the lagoon themselves, sans an on-board **cast member** and with no guide rails or track. Unfortunately, the boats were so problematic that they often stalled out on the water, which perhaps explains why they only cost a B ticket (see **ticket books**). Park officials became so frustrated with the boats' performance (or lack thereof) and their maintenance requirements (almost nightly) that they added a cast member to each boat to serve as a backseat skipper and ensure guests would return safely.

The following January, only five months after their debut, the Phantom Boats were pulled from the lagoon permanently—or so it seemed. Their boats' successors, shallow-draft "airboats" pushed by large airplane props mounted above the water, never made it past the test stages. So, in July of '56, with the lagoon still empty of watercraft and the submarines still almost three years away, the Phantom Boats were resurrected for one last troublesome summer.

By Halloween, the Phantom Boats had become phantoms once again. In mid-1957 the nearby **Motor Boat Cruise** debuted as Tomorrowland's new boat attraction.

Photo Collages

DATES: May 2005–September 2006

To help personalize Disneyland's mammoth golden anniversary celebration, in 2005 and 2006 the park prominently displayed unique artworks that required guest participation. These pieces were large photo collages comprised of thousands of guest photos. The collage concept was announced on Disneyland's 49th anniversary: from July 17th to December 31st of 2004, anyone could submit Disney vacation photos that would be integrated with thousands of others into oversize images depicting Disney-

related scenes. These collages would then be installed at Disneyland from May 2005 to September 2006. Guests whose photos were accepted even received e-mail notifications with the location of the collage that incorporated their photos. Park kiosks also identified photo and collage locations.

Dubbed "The Happiest Faces on Earth . . . A Disney Family Album," the collages were enormously successful. Hundreds of thousand of photos were sent in, and the completed collages were constantly surrounded by groups looking for recognizable faces. The collages varied from enormous wall-size murals (most ambitiously, **Tomorrowland's** glorious *20,000 Leagues Under the Sea* squid-and-submarine display) to smaller poster-size works. The scene from *Steamboat Willie* even included a second collage within the main collage.

The collages included characters from 18 different Disney movies (*Sleeping Beauty* was represented three times, *Toy Story* twice), two different Mickey Mouse cartoons, and four different Disneyland attractions. Typically the collages were posted in areas with thematic connections: *The Lion King* was mounted outside the **Jungle Cruise**, three ghosts hitchhiked at the **Haunted Mansion**, etc.

In all, 28 photo collages went up at Disneyland and remained for about 18 months, with another six collages posted within and outside of Disney California Adventure. Afterward, guests could still see a semblance of the artworks inside the **Opera House** lobby, where a single 10-foot-wide, eight-foot-tall collage of **Walt Disney** and Mickey Mouse, based on a 1966 image, was created from tiny photos of the park.

Pieces of Eight

MAP: New Orleans Square, NOS-3

DATES: Ca. 1980–ongoing

Exhilarated guests still humming "Yo Ho (A Pirate's Life for Me)" can walk straight out of **Pirates of the Caribbean** and say "ahoy matey" to Pieces of Eight, a well-decorated shop filled with pirate treasure. Well, if not exactly pirate treasure, the shop at least offered pirate skulls, weapons, hats, shirts, and other bone-adorned merchandise ready for plundering. There are no buried pirate chests to dig up, but there are open bins filled with glittering gems to scoop out.

Named after the Spanish coin of the 1700s, Pieces of Eight is in the same space where the **Pirate's Arcade Museum** used to be, and as a tribute to that **New Orleans Square** favorite the newer store still has some of the museum's old machines. Notable among these are the metal-stamper, which cranks out personalized coins, and Fortune Red, a fortune-telling pirate who delivers small cards with advice written in pirate lingo.

Pinocchio's Daring Journey

MAP: Fantasyland, Fa-9

DATES: May 25, 1983–ongoing

The major 1982–1983 remodel of **Fantasyland** brought extensive changes to existing attractions and the addition of a new one—Pinocchio's Daring Journey. Disneyland designers had been dreaming of a Pinocchio attraction since the mid-1970s, and

they finally built one in the spot where the Fantasyland Theater had once been. Pinocchio's Daring Journey was new to Disneyland but not to Disney theme parks—the original version had opened a month earlier at Tokyo Disneyland.

Outside, the Pinocchio structure presents a captivating Tyrolean exterior complete with cobblestone walkways, a steeply sloping alpine roof, and a half-timbered façade with a puppet show above the doorway. Inside, guests ride in old-fashioned vehicles through a richly colored three-minute adventure that retells the familiar tale of the wooden boy, Geppetto, Jiminy Cricket, and the Blue Fairy. The attraction incorporates meticulously crafted three-dimensional figures and state-of-the-art ride elements to deliver the animated movie's key plot points. Some of the special effects were derived from other attractions (the effect for the Blue Fairy is the same one that produces **Haunted Mansion** ghosts), and some of the charming architectural details are borrowed from other buildings (the colorful mural and themed weathervane are reminiscent of others nearby). At least one new technical achievement is featured: the first appearance of a hologram in a Disneyland attraction, used here to transform boys into donkeys.

While not a major breakthrough, Pinocchio's Daring Journey is a pleasant trip worthy of the classic film. The lovely **attraction poster** got it right with this line: "Wish Upon a Star and Relive Fantastic Adventures!"

Pin Trading Stations

MAP: Hub, H-1

DATES: April 2000–ongoing

To support fans who were already buying and trading souvenir pins, in 2000 Disneyland started placing Pin Trading Stations—usually colorful carts in walkways or display cases in existing shops—throughout the park. Up until 2011, the large, conspicuous headquarters for pin traders was found at the **Hub** in front of the **Plaza Pavilion**. Here, knowledgeable **cast members** made trades with pin pals, offered encouragement and suggestions, and sold accessories like pin cases and lanyards. Special promotions, such as Mickey's Pin Festival of Dreams in 2007, brought with them some new limited-edition pins. While the Hub headquarters is no longer there, pins and accessories are still sold in many Disneyland shops.

Pirate's Arcade Museum

MAP: New Orleans Square, NOS-3

DATES: February 14, 1967–ca. 1980

The Pirate's Arcade Museum debuted in **New Orleans Square** a few weeks before its famous neighbor, **Pirates of the Caribbean**. Once both were open, dazzled guests leaving the landmark attraction found themselves next to the tempting pirate-themed

Arcade Museum, a room that was much more the former than it was the latter. Most of the arcade games that filled the Pirate's Arcade Museum had pirate imagery worked into their game play and exterior design. Freebooter Shooter, for instance, required guests to blast away at tipsy pirates—a one-dimensional challenge, to be sure, but all arcade games were simpler back then and only cost a dime to play. Elsewhere in the Pirate's Arcade Museum, fans of Disney art fed coins into a postcard machine that sold **Marc Davis's** concept illustrations for Pirates of the Caribbean. Also available was a metal-stamping machine that personalized antique-looking coins.

Fortune Red, a pirate who dispensed fortune-telling cards, proved to be one of the most enduring of the arcade's amusements. As shown in the *Behind the Magic: 50 Years of Disneyland* exhibit at the Oakland Museum of California in 2006, Fortune Red was originally intended to be a full-size, full-body buccaneer with one leg and a parrot, just like Long John Silver from *Treasure Island*, but he ended up as just the upper half of a parrotless pirate. Along with the metal-stamper, he's survived into the 21st century at **Pieces of Eight**, the pirate-themed store that took over this space around 1980.

Pirate Ship Restaurant,
aka Chicken of the Sea Pirate Ship and Restaurant,
aka Captain Hook's Galley

MAP: Fantasyland, Fa-14

DATES: August 29, 1955–August 29, 1982

This nautical eatery was usually called the Pirate Ship Restaurant in early **souvenir books**, but because of its sponsor it was also known as the Chicken of the Sea Pirate Ship and Restaurant. Movie fans who recall Captain Hook from *Peter Pan* have to smile at a restaurant named Chicken of the Sea, seemingly referring to the spineless captain.

The actual Chicken of the Sea, of course, is Starkist Tuna, the staple of the "light meals and snacks" menu presented here. Virtually everything—burgers, sandwiches, pot pies—had tuna in it. Food was ordered and served at a counter within the ship's hull. Guests ate on benches facing a plain pond until 1960, when wooden-keg tables were added and the creepy **Skull Rock** and Pirate Cove were built.

The real fun, though, was the ship itself, which was built to look like an elegant, fully-rigged frigate with a black hull, red-striped sails, and well-appointed decks that guests could tour. From the waterline to the tip of the main mast, the colorful ship towered approximately 80 feet, a height about equal to the **Sailing Ship *Columbia*** in **Frontierland**. The Pirate Ship Restaurant was a **Fantasyland** landmark from 1955 until 1982, though in 1969 it was rechristened Captain Hook's Galley. In the early '80s there was talk of moving the Galley, Skull Rock, and Pirate's Cove over to the **Storybook Land Canal Boats** area. Unfortunately water damage had eroded the ship's wooden hull, and so during the Fantasyland remodel of 1982–1983 it was finally dismantled.

The place where the ship, rock, and cove had been was filled in and given to the relocated **Dumbo** attraction. But the Pirate's Ship Restaurant has never really left Fantasyland, as pieces of the old ship, and Captain Hook himself, are on display inside the nearby **Peter Pan Flight** attraction.

Pirates of the Caribbean

MAP: New Orleans Square, NOS-1

DATES: March 18, 1967–ongoing

Often regarded as Disneyland's best attraction (or certainly one of the top two or three), Pirates of the Caribbean was one of the last attractions **Walt Disney** worked on. It was also the first major attraction to open after he died at the end of 1966.

Discussions about a pirate museum began in the late '50s, and in fact the park's 1958 **Fun Map** even placed a "Wax Museum" approximately where the boat ride would later be built. According to Charles Ridgway's book *Spinning Disney's World*, in 1960 Walt Disney made his first public announcement of the new attraction at the opening ceremonies for **Nature's Wonderland**. A year later the name Pirates of the Caribbean appeared with a preview in the park's **souvenir book**. These early hints suggested that the attraction would be a walk-through "rogues gallery" displaying "famous pirates of the Spanish Main," depicted as drunken buccaneers in a tavern.

Construction on something pirate-ish began in 1961, but the project's construction was interrupted for at least two years so the company could concentrate on Disney exhibits for the 1964–1965 New York World's Fair. Disneyland's 1963 souvenir book then mentioned an upgraded Pirates of the Caribbean presentation featuring a "Bayou voyage," but the shadowy painting of pirates studying a treasure map conveyed nothing about the actual ride experience. Two years later, the 1965 souvenir book raised expectations by describing how **Audio-Animatronic** pirates would "come to life" and "attack, burn and loot a city" in what "promises to be Disneyland's longest and most action-packed attraction." That same year, Walt Disney further fueled excitement by showing off models of the coming attraction to a national TV audience on *Walt Disney's Wonderful World of Color*. While guests were excited for the opening of **New Orleans Square** in mid-1966, everyone was especially primed for Pirates, due the following spring. And they weren't disappointed.

Heralded by an official opening that featured the nearby **Sailing Ship *Columbia*** decked out with a Jolly Roger, the E-ticket (see **ticket books**) Pirates of the Caribbean attraction was the culmination of creative and technological achievement in ride design at the time. No other park in the world had anything nearly as sophisticated, and for that matter, neither did Disneyland. For the first time, Imagineers had implemented Audio-Animatronic humans on a grand scale—previously their A-A figures had been either relatively primitive mechanical animals (as in the **Jungle Cruise**) or a single person viewed from a distance (**Great Moments with Mr. Lincoln**). The Pirates ride, however, featured 75 A-A humans and another 50 or so A-A pigs, donkeys, chickens, and dogs cavorting through realistic settings that included a trip through the bayou, a plunge down two 21-degree waterfalls, a raging storm, a fort and a life-size pirate ship called the *Wicked Wench* lobbing cannonballs at each other, a town engulfed in flames, and a trip back *up* a waterfall. All of this was viewed from only a few yards away, and, even more incredibly, all of it was presented indoors.

The attraction was a *tour de force* of imagination and engineering. Park rides no longer had to be short and compact—this one was slow (about 16 minutes long) and covered 1,800 feet of canals that held 630,000 gallons of water. The 46 shallow boats traversed three levels in two big new buildings, one of them built across what was formerly **Magnolia Park**, the other built outside the park's perimeter **berm**, both buildings covering a total of over 2.5 acres. The cost to create such an elaborate attraction in the mid-'60s? Some $8 million, almost half of what it had cost to build the entire park a decade before.

The press and public immediately recognized the magnitude of Disney's monumental achievement. Disney souvenir books played up the revolutionary pirates with lavish photos and descriptive text. Pirates was also one of only two attractions (**It's a Small World** was the other) to get its own lengthy souvenir booklet in the '60s. TV audiences watched Pirates highlights in 1968, which enticed future guests and made

visitors who had already seen the motley crew eager to experience the ride again.

Designed with scrupulous attention to detail, the attraction rewards repeat visits. Precise detail was born out of necessity, of course, since about 18 guests per *bateau* are drifting, not racing, along the river, carefully analyzing everything they see: the pirates' bloodshot eyes; the **cast members**' costumes at the Laffite's Landing launch site; the moving clouds in the bayou section; the artwork on the walls of the main scenes; and on and on, until their final walk past the dancing fireflies to the exit.

Despite the fact that the pirate behavior on view has always seemed un-Disney-like—what with all the pillaging, wench-auctioning, and heavy drinking—and that these colorful rascals have little in common with the savage cutthroats who are their historical counterparts, the attraction's rollicking spirit and good humor have negated any serious complaints. That spirit and humor was created by a roster of designers and artists that reads now like a who's who of Disney's fabled Imagineers: artist **Marc Davis** generated hundreds of whimsical ideas and concept drawings; his wife, **Alice Davis**, made the costumes; **Richard Irvine** and **Claude Coats** oversaw the art direction and general design; sculptor **Blaine Gibson** made the models; **Roger Broggie**, **Fred Joerger**, and **Wathel Rogers** were the mechanical wizards behind the moving swashbucklers; **Bill Martin** and **Yale Gracey** invented many of the special effects; **George Bruns** and **X Atencio** created the instantly hummable "Yo Ho (A Pirate's Life for Me)" theme song (Atencio also wrote the attraction's script); and **Thurl Ravenscroft** and **Paul Frees** were among the vocal performers.

So revered is the attraction that longtime fans have greeted even the smallest changes warily. The entrance was modified in 1987, and the attraction was closed for two months in 1997 to replace the pirates-chasing-women scenes with pirates-chasing-food scenes. This '90s remodel also added a re-dedication plaque honoring "the original" in the outside **queue** area. Everything was shut down again in 2006 for a June reopening that revealed a remixed soundtrack and new characters from the blockbuster *Pirates of the Caribbean* movies.

Celebrated over the years in books, films, and exhibits, the cherished Pirates of the Caribbean has been duplicated in other Disney parks and appreciated by hundreds of millions of people, and is still thriving as a supreme example of what intelligent theme park entertainment can be.

38 Movies That Inspired Disneyland Attractions, Buildings, and Exhibits

1. *The African Queen*: Jungle Cruise
2. *Aladdin*: Aladdin's Oasis
3. *Alice in Wonderland*: Alice in Wonderland; Mad Hatter's Mad Tea Party; Mad Hatter hat shops
4. *Babes in Toyland*: Babes in Toyland Exhibit
5. *Calamity Jane*: Golden Horseshoe
6. *Davy Crockett, King of the Wild Frontier*: Davy Crockett Arcade; Davy Crockett Frontier Museum; Davy Crockett's Explorer Canoes; Mike Fink Keel Boats
7. *Dumbo*: Dumbo the Flying Elephant
8. *Fantasia*: Fantasia Gardens; Primeval World Diorama
9. *Finding Nemo*: Finding Nemo Submarine Voyage
10. *Home on the Range*: Big Thunder Ranch/Little Patch of Heaven
11. *Honey, I Shrunk the Kids*: Honey, I Shrunk the Audience
12. *Hunchback of Notre Dame*: Festival of Fools; Festival of Foods; Quasimodo's Attic
13. *Indiana Jones* trilogy: Indiana Jones Adventure; Indiana Jones Adventure Outpost; Indy Fruit Cart
14. *The Jungle Book*: Baloo's Dressing Room
15. *The Little Mermaid*: King Triton Gardens
16. *The Many Adventures of Winnie the Pooh*: The Many Adventures of Winnie the Pooh; Pooh Corner
17. *Mary Poppins*: Jolly Holiday Bakery Café

Pixie Hollow

MAP: Tomorrowland, T-1

DATES: October 2008–ongoing

The same year she got her own movie, Tinker Bell got her own outdoor area in **Fantasyland.** The adorable Pixie Hollow stands approximately where the imposing **House of the Future,** bucolic **Alpine Gardens,** and lovely **King Triton Gardens** used to be, between the entrance to **Tomorrowland** and **Sleeping Beauty Castle.**

Borrowing an idea from Tomorrowland's old **Adventure Thru Inner Space** attraction, Tink's cozy enchanted glen is filled with oversize objects to make guests feel that they

18. *One Hundred and One Dalmatians*: Dalmatian Celebration
19. *Peter Pan*: Peter Pan Flight; Tinker Bell & Friends; Tinker Bell Toy Shoppe
20. *Pinocchio*: Geppetto's Arts & Crafts; Geppetto's Candy Shoppe; Pinocchio's Daring Adventure; Stromboli's Wagon
21. *Pirates of the Caribbean*: Port Royal; Pirate's Lair on Tom Sawyer Island
22. *Sleeping Beauty*: Sleeping Beauty Castle; Sleeping Beauty Castle Walk-Through; Three Fairies Magic Crystals
23. *Snow White and the Seven Dwarfs*: Snow White Adventures
24. *So Dear to My Heart*: Frontierland train station
25. *Song of the South*: Briar Patch; Splash Mountain
26. *Star Wars* trilogy: Star Tours; Star Trader
27. *Swiss Family Robinson*: Swiss Family Treehouse
28. *Switzerland*: Matterhorn Bobsleds; Matterhorn Mountain
29. *Sword in the Stone*: Merlin's Magic Shop; Sword in the Stone Ceremony
30. *Tangled*: Tangled
31. *Tarzan*: Tarzan's Treehouse
32. *Third Man on the Mountain*: Matterhorn Bobsleds; Matterhorn Mountain
33. *Tinker Bell*: Pixie Hollow; Pixie Hollow Gift Cart
34. *Toy Story*: Buzz Lightyear Astro Blasters; Club Buzz; Little Green Men Store Command; Toy Story Funhouse
35. *True-Life Adventure* documentaries: Grand Canyon Diorama; Jungle Cruise; Living Desert; Nature's Wonderland
36. *20,000 Leagues Under the Sea*: 20,000 Leagues Under the Sea Exhibit
37. *Who Framed Roger Rabbit*: Mickey's Toontown; Roger Rabbit's Car Toon Spin
38. *The Wind in the Willows*: Mr. Toad's Wild Ride

themselves have shrunk in size. A giant teapot, for instance, serves as the fairy's home, surrounded by huge one-story flowers and mushrooms as big as chairs. Tink herself is regularly on hand for photos and autographs.

Pixie Hollow Gift Cart

MAP: Tomorrowland, T-1

DATES: October 2008–summer 2011

Young girls leaving **Pixie Hollow** were primed to buy sparkly merchandise, but alas, there was no shop located in the immediate area. To fill the void, Disneyland officials wheeled in what was informally called the Pixie Hollow Gift Cart. Parked for almost three years at the Pixie Hollow exit, the elaborate fairy-themed cart and its adjacent display stands sold dolls, wings, wands, wigs, towels, and small gifts, all inspired by Tink and her fairy friends. A small face-painting stand took over this spot in mid-2011.

Plaza Gardens, aka Carnation Plaza Gardens

MAP: Hub, H-2

DATES: August 18, 1956–April 30, 2012

Dining and dancing were at their swingin'est at the Plaza Gardens. Located in the northwest corner of the **Hub**, this spacious half-acre site was also called the Carnation Plaza Gardens in deference to the sponsor.

Though it had a long history, the Plaza Gardens didn't date back to **Opening Day**. That honor went to the old **bandstand**, which occupied the spot from July of '55 until the following summer. As the bandstand's concerts grew more popular that first year, **Walt Disney** decided to relocate it to **Frontierland** and build a big new dance pavilion to keep guests staying and playing after dark.

The result was an old-fashioned wooden building painted a gleaming white. The structure was open on the sides to make the entertainment more visible and inviting to passersby. Guests entered the Plaza Gardens from the Hub by crossing a footbridge spanning a small pond; they then faced a seating area, a stage, and, when it was open, a wide doorway at the back leading to Frontierland. Back when food was served here, a side counter offered cheeseburgers, fries, and enormous ice cream desserts. Occasionally the menu offered items for special events, such as 1969's I Scream Sundaes that celebrated the new **Haunted Mansion**.

More memorable than the menu, however, was the entertainment. Classic swing bands were the traditional performers here ("tried and true favorites for Mom and Dad," boasted the park's 1965 **souvenir book**). Other shows included **Date Nite** concerts with the Date Niters in the late '50s and early '60s, the Cavalcade of Bands concerts beginning in '63, and the televised Big Bands at Disneyland shows of 1984 with, among others, the Glenn Miller and Count Basie orchestras. The Donny-less Osmond Brothers also appeared here in 1961.

Recent decades have brought updates to the Plaza Gardens. The once-white building was painted with red and gold stripes, and in the '90s the Plaza began hosting small stage shows including *The Enchanted Book Shoppe* (1991–1992) and *The Little Mermaid and Her Secret Grotto* (1997–1998). After the summer of '98, the Plaza closed for remodeling, reopening a year later with a wall of **attraction posters** in the back and a new dance show, the Jump, Jive, Boogie Swing Party, sometimes performed four times a night. Small live concerts, often featuring school bands and choirs, were held here some afternoons, but the underutilized venue seemed like a relic of a stylish past.

In 2011 plans were announced to transform the Plaza Gardens site into the **Fantasy Faire**, a fairy-tale village for live entertainment, dancing, and interactive experiences with Disney princesses.

Plaza Pavilion Restaurant,
aka Stouffer's in Disneyland Plaza Pavillion

MAP: Hub, H-1

DATES: July 17, 1955–July 1998

The lovely Victorian-style Plaza Pavilion was an architectural gem in the southwest corner of the **Hub**. In the '50s the Plaza Pavilion was identified more with **Adventureland** than the Hub; in fact it was listed in the early **souvenir books** as the Pavillion (with a double consonant) in the Adventureland section. Although guests entered the eatery from the side facing the Hub, they carried their pasta, gourmet sandwiches, and salads on cafeteria-style trays through the restaurant and out the other side to a patio situated above the banks of the **Jungle Cruise**. In 1962 the restaurant got an unwieldy new name, Stouffer's in Disneyland Plaza Pavillion, and that back patio became the Stouffer's in Disneyland Tahitian Terrace. By 1965 the Stouffer's reference had been dropped and the Plaza Pavilion reverted back to its original name (Stouffer's became the sponsor of the **French Market** in **New Orleans Square** instead). Interestingly, the two exterior décor styles still meet in the middle of the Pavilion's roof, so depending on the angle guests see either turn-of-the-century cut shingles or tropical thatch.

The restaurant was closed for so long that it barely registered with modern guests; when the name Plaza Pavilion did register, it probably wasn't as a dining destination. After serving for a few years as the site of the Junior Chef Baking Experience (in which kids got to don toques and bake their own cookies), from 2009 until July 31, 2011 the building was the site of the Annual Passport Processing Center where guests received their year-long **Passports**. The porch facing the Hub frequently featured a ragtime piano player borrowed from Coke's **Refreshment Corner** next door, and the outside dining area became a large **Pin Trading Station** from 2000–2010. The walkway out front still hosts the information

board where guests can see which rides are closed, what the lines are like, what time **parades** are due, and more.

None of these functions, unfortunately, tapped into the full potential of what used to be a memorable dining experience. But dining finally returned to the building in 2012, when it was transformed into the new **Jolly Holiday Bakery Café**.

Pluto's Dog House

MAP: Mickey's Toontown, MT-8

DATES: January 24, 1993–ongoing

Several restaurants in Disneyland history have been given humorous names (**Lunching Pad**, for instance). The niftiest word play in a name might be Pluto's Dog House, a little snack counter in the heart of **Mickey's Toontown** that, naturally, serves up hot dogs.

The Dog House offers foot-long dogs for adults and kid-size versions for tykes, supplemented with extras like chili, chips, and sodas. Dog-shaped desserts, and alfresco dining help on-the-go guests develop a case of puppy love.

Police Station

MAP: Town Square, TS-3

DATES: July 17, 1955–ongoing

It's the first and last brick building guests will walk past when they enter and exit through Disneyland's west tunnel. The Police Station is one of three "official city buildings" that line up along the western side of **Town Square**; **City Hall** is the main building next door. The one-story structure is the smallest along the row, but it's just as handsome as the others, constructed of red brick and decorated with a yellow balustrade and cream-colored columns.

Despite its name, the Police Station has never been the headquarters for the park's own security personnel. A free map handed out to guests in 1955 located Security Headquarters in City Hall. Similarly, the 1956 **souvenir book** identified City Hall as home base to "45 Security Officers" who were "employed on a full-time basis at Disneyland with eight others on call to protect the Park and its guests." Within a few years, the security officers were moved to another building behind Town Square, out of public view (guests with security concerns are still directed to City Hall). Many of the park's security personnel are as unseen by guests as the security building is—they work undercover to catch shoplifters and vandals.

The Police Station, meanwhile, was actually home to the publicity department,

which needed to be near the **entrance** to greet the media. At one time the front of the building also served as the designated rendezvous for lost guests and their groups. A 2001 brochure handed out at the park identified a kiosk just south of the Police Station as the American Automobile Association's Touring & Travel Services Center, where guests could pick up AAA maps, get park info, and arrange free towing and flat-tire repair. Today, that pretty little kiosk is where guided tours are booked, and the flower-filled garden next to the Police Station is the Guided Tour Garden where **Tour Guides** gather their guests. Signs on the Police Station itself read Guided Tours.

Pony Farm, aka Circle D Corral

MAP: Park, P-17

DATES: July 17, 1955–ongoing

All of the horses, mules, and ponies that have been worked, ridden, petted and paraded in Disneyland over the years have gotten their education at the park's Pony Farm, (now called the Circle D Corral). The Pony Farm used to be located on 10 acres at the back of **Frontierland**—directly behind the **berm**—on land that was later incorporated into **Mickey's Toontown**.

In addition to stables for the horses, the Pony Farm also included a barn and a carpentry shop on the property. In 1980 the Pony Farm was renamed the Circle D Corral. A decade later, in anticipation of the Mickey's Toontown construction, the Circle D acreage was cut in half and relocated farther west, in a location still close to the park but no longer directly behind Frontierland.

In Disneyland's first decade, there was far more equine activity than there is now. Horses pulled **Conestoga Wagons**, the **Stage Coach**, and several **Main Street Vehicles**. Shetland ponies stood in the **Miniature Horse Corral** and a mule train trekked Frontierland trails. Most of these attractions closed within a few years, but several horses can still be seen every day on **Main Street**, where a horse-drawn streetcar has remained as the same nostalgic mode of transportation since 1955.

Even when there were lots of park attractions that needed horses, no horses ever had more than part-time employment. According to the 1956 **souvenir book**, "Disneyland horses punch time cards. No horse is allowed to work over four hours per day or six days a week." These days, that six-day workweek has most likely been reduced to a four-day workweek (the horses, evidently, have a pretty strong union). Some of the horses are rarely used at all—the Lipizzans, for instance, are presented mainly during the **holiday season** and for special wedding events.

Horses are not the only ones to have lived at the Pony Farm/Circle D—so have their trainers. The horses were originally raised by two people who were Disneyland's only full-time live-in residents (the Disneys used their private **apartment** on **Town Square** only part of the time)—horse trainers Owen and Dolly Pope, who began working for **Walt Disney** in the early 1950s. Back then, they were building Western-style carriages and acquiring the horses Disney would need for the small park he was originally planning to build next to his Burbank movie studios. Later, the Popes settled into a small bungalow on the Anaheim property and moved their 200 animals into the Pony Farm's corrals.

The Popes found that one of their main challenges was to get their charges used to distractions. Sudden loud noises—popping **Jungle Cruise** gunfire, shrieking *Mark Twain* whistles, etc.—are still heard without warning throughout the day. To acclimate the animals to the park, the Popes played tapes of shouting voices, a shooting gallery, and other loud noises. Furthermore, they trained the horses to handle the over-friendly crowds that still rush up close for photographs (veteran guests know that polite photo requests made to the operators are nearly always accommodated).

In addition to training the horses, the Popes also took care of the swans that swam daily in front of **Sleeping Beauty Castle**. They also built several of the old-fashioned frontier vehicles used in the park, including the Conestoga Wagons. After getting the Pony Farm started and running successfully, the Popes later left to perform the same function at Walt Disney World. Their former Disneyland home now serves as an office building, and their job of caring for the park's animals (including those that appear at **Big Thunder Ranch**) is covered by dozens of handlers.

Pooh Corner

MAP: Bear Country/Critter Country, B/C-5

DATES: April 11, 2003–ongoing

Guests eager to buy their bear necessities should head straight to Pooh Corner, the park's Winnie the Pooh headquarters. This 120-foot-long **Critter Country** shop fills the large building where the **Mile Long Bar** and **Teddi Barra's Swingin' Arcade** used to be, back when the neighborhood was called **Bear Country**.

Since 2003 Pooh Corner has sold all the plush toys, mugs, cookie jars, and infant clothes any Pooh fan could want (plus lots of candy in a room on the right-hand side). With its adorable interior, the store is decorated like something out of the Hundred-Acre Wood. Outside is Pooh's Thotful Spot, a character-greeting area where guests can take photos with the bear himself.

Popcorn Carts

DATES: Summer 1955–ongoing

Disneyland's early **souvenir books** usually featured photos of an old-fashioned popcorn machine in **Town Square**. Instantly nostalgic and inviting, these carts have always been irresistible. Around eight carts selling popcorn and sodas are scattered throughout the park (the number varies with attendance). Like the **trash cans** and **restrooms**, the popcorn carts are decorated with different themes to match their respective areas. These themes apply both to the carts' colorful exteriors and to their glass display cases. Depending on what attractions are nearby, the little mechanical figure turning the hand crank behind the glass might be a creepy **Haunted Mansion** butler, an explorer, a clown, or another costumed character. Ceramic versions of Disneyland's classic blue-and-white-striped popcorn boxes went on sale in the **Disney Gallery** in 2010.

Port d'Orleans

MAP: New Orleans Square, NOS-5

DATES: Ca. 1995–2002

Part of what used to be the old **Le Gourmet** shop at the back of **New Orleans Square** became a smaller cooking-related shop in the mid-1990s. Disneyland's 2000 **souvenir book** called Port d'Orleans "a lively mart that features items imported directly from Louisiana, such as a variety of spicy Cajun sauces, beignet mixes, and coffees with chicory." A minor remodel in 1999 supplemented the coffees and sauces with lots of souvenirs from the **Haunted Mansion** and other nearby attractions. **Le Bat en Rouge** flew into this space and set up shop in 2002.

Portrait Artists

MAP: New Orleans Square, NOS-5, NOS-6

DATES: Ca. 1986–ongoing

At different times, portrait artists have graced the **Opera House** in **Town Square**, the **Art Corner** in **Tomorrowland**, and Center Street (just off of **Main Street**). In *Window on Main Street*, **Van France** wrote that **Jack Olsen** had the original idea to bring artists into the park to draw quick, lucrative caricatures of its guests.

Today, the portrait artists add a graceful touch to **New Orleans Square**. The artists usually sit with their easels near the charming Court des Anges courtyard behind the **French Market**. Sometimes artists can also be found across from the **Blue Bayou** on Royal Street. Depending on the artist, guests can sit for a profile or a face-on portrait, be depicted in pastels or watercolors, and choose between representational art or a caricature. Scenes from New Orleans Square are usually in the backgrounds of the portraits. The management for these artists is Rubio Arts, the same company that handles the nearby **Parasol Cart** artists.

Port Royal

MAP: New Orleans Square, NOS-3

DATES: 2006–ongoing

In 2006 the spot next to the **Royal Street Veranda** that had been **Le Bat en Rouge** became Port Royal, a name referring both to the street outside and to a location popularized in the *Pirates of the Caribbean* movies. Historically, Port Royal was the Jamaican home of many 17th-century buccaneers and became known as the world's wickedest town. At Disneyland, Port Royal's merchandise, advertised above the doorway as "curios and curiosities," is piratical and souvenir-ish, just like the wares in many other **New Orleans Square** establishments. In addition to offering lots of pirate clothes, hats, and jewelry, the room sometimes has a working doubloon-pressing machine.

Premiere Shop

MAP: Tomorrowland, T-6

DATES: 1963–2005

The Premiere Shop saw a lot of changes during its four decades in the center of all the **Tomorrowland** action. While not as big as the **Character Shop** (now **Star Trader)** across the way, the Premiere Shop was still an appealing shopping destination. It sold California- and sports-themed merchandise until the 1990s, when its shelves were restocked with Disneyland-related clothes and gifts.

In the 21st century the Premiere Shop focused more on pin and lanyard sales. The shop was also supplemented by several cool kiosks. The Disneyland Forever kiosks offered stations where guests could burn their own 10-track CDs with a broad selection of Disney songs, sounds from Disneyland attractions, and other auditory gems. At the Art on Demand kiosks, guests could print out their own customized Disney art.

Little Green Men Store Command replaced the Premiere Shop in 2005, the same year that **Buzz Lightyear Astro Blasters** landed next door.

Price, Harrison
(1921–2010)

Back when Disneyland was still just a drawing on paper, **Walt Disney** was scrutinizing locations for a suitable construction site. He knew it should be in the Greater Los Angeles area—the region boasted warm weather, its five-county population was immense, and his movie studio was already located there—but exactly where in those 4,000 square miles he should build his park was still unclear. Harrison Price, a top business consultant whom Disney treated with "paternal affection," according to the book *Remembering Walt*, is the man who found Anaheim for him.

Price spent three months studying potential locations for Disneyland, among them the west San Fernando Valley (deemed too hot), downtown L.A. (too expensive), and Palos Verdes and the beach communities (too inaccessible). Price narrowed his search to 150 square miles between L.A. and Orange County, and then identified the 10 best available parcels of land in that area. In his report, finalized on August 28, 1953, a 160-acre spread in Anaheim got the top ranking.

It was not an obvious choice. At the time, Anaheim was a sleepy agricultural area—nothing like the crowded city it is now—and it seemed unreasonably far from glamorous Hollywood and other familiar L.A. areas. There were fewer than a hundred hotel and motel rooms in all of Anaheim (in 2011, just the Disney hotels at the Disneyland Resort contained over 2,200 rooms). What's more, at the time most West Coast amusement parks, including eight scattered between San Diego and Santa Monica, were built along scenic Pacific Ocean beaches, so Price was bucking tradition with his inland selection.

After careful consideration, Price declared that within a few decades a map of Southern California's spreading population would show Anaheim at the center (an amazing prediction—the actual center ended up being in Fullerton, just one town over and only four miles away). Growth in Orange County, Price felt, would continue as it had in the 1940s and early '50s, when its population had almost doubled. He was right again—Anaheim's population of 14,000 multiplied by 10 during the '50s (in 2011 it had reached 300,000). Price also recognized that an unfinished north-south freeway project, Interstate 5, would soon pass right through Anaheim, putting the city within easy reach of millions of drivers. He learned that with an annual rainfall averaging only an inch a month, Anaheim's climate was drier than L.A. County's; plus, plenty of flat, undeveloped, and relatively cheap (under $5,000 per acre) land was available. For all these reasons, Harrison Price recommended that Walt Disney build Disneyland in freeway-close, financially friendly Anaheim. History, of course, soon proved Price correct.

Harrison "Buzz" Price was born in 1921 in Oregon, raised in San Diego, and educated at the California Institute of Technology in Pasadena. After serving in the Air Force and working in Peru for three years in the late '40s, Price returned to California to get his graduate degree from Stanford. In 1952 he became a member of the Stanford Research Institute, and soon was consulting on key Disneyland decisions, especially its location. Three years later, with Disneyland a stunning success, Price formed his own consulting company, ERA (Economics Research Associates), and continued doing research for various Disney projects. In the '60s he studied various locations for a "second Disneyland" that would be more convenient to the eastern half of the country. Among the locations he and Walt Disney visited and seriously considered were New Jersey, St. Louis, and the Florida site that ultimately became Walt Disney World. Price also evaluated the Mineral King ski resort in California that was eventually abandoned (the "number-one disappointment" of his career, he claimed), made recommendations for one of Walt Disney's pet projects, the CalArts campus in Southern California, and even advised Disney to buy a company plane to expedite his many travels.

After selling ERA, Price formed another company in 1978, HPC (Harrison Price Company). For the next two decades he continued to research new business developments. Among the many clients he served over his long career are the Six Flags parks, Knott's Berry Farm, Universal Studios, IMAX theaters, the World's Fairs in Seattle and New York, NASA, famous restaurant chains, major aquariums, and Las Vegas megahotels. Price's autobiography, *Walt's Revolution! By the Numbers*, came out in 2003, the same year he was inducted as a Disney Legend. He died in 2010 at age 89.

Primeval World Diorama

MAP: Tomorrowland, T-17

DATES: July 1, 1966–ongoing

About eight years after the **Grand Canyon Diorama** was added along the **Santa Fe & Disneyland Railroad** track, the Primeval World Diorama joined the line. The Primeval exhibit follows the Grand Canyon along the train's route past **Tomorrowland** and ends about 300 feet from the **Main Street** station. Both dioramas are enclosed in long tunnels—the second tunnel for the Primeval World extends about 500 feet, a little longer than the Grand Canyon's tunnel. The combined tunnel experience lasts about 3.5 minutes.

While the first diorama transports train guests to another location, the second transports them to another time—the age of dinosaurs, as it's depicted in the dramatic "Rite of Spring" sequence in *Fantasia*. At slow speed the train crawls past almost four dozen extinct creatures, some 15-feet tall, and all depicted in a prehistoric world. Gigantic brontosaurus necks rise out of a swamp, mouths munching on vegetation. A pterodactyl gazes down from atop a rock. Raptor-esque reptiles sip from a pond. Triceratops babies wriggle out of their eggs. Interestingly, the stirring music in the background isn't Stravinsky's—it's Bernard Herrmann's and comes from his score for *Mysterious Island*, a 1961 adventure film made by Columbia Pictures. The most memorable

encounter, and the one shown on the **attraction poster** and in big photos in Disneyland's **souvenir books**, comes when the towering Tyrannosaurus rex attacks a formidable stegosaurus, a powerful scene straight out of *Fantasia*.

Cavemen, who didn't appear in *Fantasia*, are not included in the diorama. However, cavemen were originally part of the attraction when Disney designers first created it for the Ford pavilion at the 1964–1965 New York World's Fair. **Walt Disney** deemed the fair's **Audio-Animatronic** humanoids too rudimentary in their design and execution for inclusion at Disneyland, especially when compared to his much more sophisticated **Great Moments with Mr. Lincoln** figure (cavemen wouldn't have been historically accurate in this diorama, either, since they followed the extinction of the dinosaurs by tens of millions of years).

Savvy guests long on interest but short on time know a simple trick for catching this attraction at the end of their Disneyland visit. Rather than hopping on board a train at the Main Street station for the long run around the park, they'll catch a quick ride in nearby Tomorrowland, immediately venture back to the primeval past, and then exit the park. Invigorated by the time travel and dazzled by the dinosaurs, they emerge ready to brave the modern world beyond the turnstiles.

Princess Boutique

MAP: Fantasyland, Fa-3

DATES: Ca. 1997–2005

Guests have had several chances to shop in **Fantasyland** for the princesses in their lives. For about eight years, one prime spot was located on the western side of the entrance to **Sleeping Beauty Castle**. Like most of the young clientele shopping there giddily, the Princess Boutique was small, pretty, and princessy—lots of pink, lots of irresistible dresses, and lots of costume jewelry were on display. In 2005 the shop was turned into the **50th Anniversary Shop** for Disneyland's golden anniversary celebration.

Princess Fantasy Faire

MAP: Fantasyland, Fa-18

DATES: November 2006–ongoing

After *Snow White: An Enchanting Musical* closed at the **Videopolis**/Fantasyland Theater in 2006, the large performance space at the back of **Fantasyland** was transformed into a Nestlé-sponsored character greeting area "where happily ever after happens every day." Under a tent roof displaying a starry scene, and on a stage decorated as a castle, throne, and forest, Disney royalty began making frequent appearances.

Many different activities have been held on the

grounds. In the Royal Crafts area, guests could have their hair braided and faces painted, as well as shop for Princess merchandise. Storytelling with Disney Princesses and a Royal Coronation Ceremony were also offered. The most popular activity of all is the Disney Princess Royal Walk, where guests linger with the young beauties and "other royal visitors along an enchanted pathway." The photo opportunities generate long lines of pint-sized princesses and their camera-clicking parents throughout the day. In 2009 some Faire activities were curtailed to make room for even more meet-and-greets.

Professor Barnaby Owl's Photographic Art Studio

MAP: Bear Country/Critter Country, B/C-8

DATES: January 31, 1992–ongoing

Many guests stop to look at the photos on view here at the back of **Critter Country**, but few guests know Professor Barnaby Owl's legacy. The knowledgeable character appeared in two classic *Adventures in Music* cartoons of the '50s: *Melody* and the Oscar-winning *Toot, Whistle, Plunk and Boom* (he also appeared in Disney Sing-Along-Songs videos in the '80s and '90s).

The photos displayed in the good professor's Art Studio are action shots that were snapped as guests began their plunge down the **Splash Mountain** log flume. The sudden realization of what's about to happen—a 52-foot drop, presumably into a briar patch—usually brings interesting expressions to guests' faces. The Art Studio displays all the photos snapped in the last few minutes and offers printed versions for immediate sale in a cardboard frame. In recent years the Art Studio got some notoriety when photos started appearing of women with their shirts open or lifted up, temporarily giving Splash Mountain the nickname Flash Mountain.

Puffin Bakery, aka Puffin Bake Shop

MAP: Main Street, MS-6

DATES: July 18, 1955–June 3, 1960

Had it opened one day earlier, the Puffin Bakery would have been one of the charter businesses to debut when Disneyland did. Even if it did miss **Opening Day**, the Puffin Bakery (also called the Puffin Bake Shop in **souvenir books** at the time) enjoyed an almost five-year run along the western side of **Main Street**, in the same block as the **Penny Arcade**. When the baked goods shop finally went flat in 1960, the **Sunkist Citrus House** moved in. The spot reverted back to its original purpose in the '50s when the **Blue Ribbon Bakery** took over for most of the '90s. Today, the **Gibson Girl Ice Cream Parlor** serves up tasty cold treats in this spot.

Quasimodo's Attic, aka Sanctuary of Quasimodo

MAP: Fantasyland, Fa-30

DATES: June 21, 1996–February 1997

In the summer of 1996, Quasimodo's Attic replaced the five-year-old **Disney Villains** shop in **Fantasyland**. This prominent location in the **Sleeping Beauty Castle** courtyard next to the **Peter Pan Flight** attraction was dedicated to Quasimodo merchandise to help promote that year's *Hunchback of Notre Dame* film. (Simultaneously, two other *Hunchback*-themed locations opened over in **Frontierland—Big Thunder Barbecue** became the Festival of Foods, and **Big Thunder Ranch** became the Festival of Fools.)

By the end of the summer, Quasimodo's Attic had changed its name to Sanctuary of Quasimodo. And by the end of the winter, with the *Hunchback* juggernaut subsiding, the Quasimodo shop closed permanently, its location to be filled six months later by another medieval store, the **Knight Shop**.

Queues

Imagine first-time visitors seeing the young park in the 1950s and '60s. Back then, queues at fairs, amusement parks, sporting events, and movie theaters always seemed to stretch inefficiently and unimaginatively in one long, boring straight line that blocked walkways and entrances to other rides and restaurants. One of the features these novice visitors would have instantly appreciated at Disneyland was its clever management of long lines. Today's guests take for granted the park's distinctive queues because they are now so widely used in myriad industries. But in Disneyland's early years, switchback queues were more than just a novelty—they were a great innovation.

In his book *Designing Disney*, **John Hench** called poorly designed queues "a major design problem" resulting in "irritable, disappointed guests." To fight pedestrian traffic jams and wait-line fatigue, Disneyland created its unique switchback queues. Waiting in a line that doubles back upon itself, guests are usually kept in steady motion, so they don't get completely bored or sore from standing still for long durations. When the queue winds around corners (as in **Indiana Jones Adventure**), guests don't always know how far they are from the head of the line, and thus are not immediately discouraged by the sight of a distant boarding area. Also, as the lines snake back and forth, guests are presented with an ever-changing parade of approaching faces. Some

---

A Dozen Cool Queues

1. Adventure Thru Inner Space (Mighty Microscope and many TV-size display pods)
2. Circle-Vision 360 theater (phone exhibits and flag displays)
3. Big Thunder Mountain Railroad (antiques and the Rainbow Ridge miniature town)
4. The Haunted Mansion (a cemetery with humorous tombstones)
5. Jungle Cruise (a two-story area with safari displays)
6. It's a Small World (a fascinating façade and an elaborate clock)
7. Indiana Jones Adventure (an archaeological dig site and hieroglyphs)
8. Mickey's House (a theater and displays before the main photo op)
9. Roger Rabbit's Car Toon Spin (a comical garage interior)
10. Space Mountain (a spaceship display)
11. Splash Mountain (mountain interiors)
12. Star Tours (*Star Wars* imagery)

---

queues also ameliorate a waiting guest's discomfort by providing shade, drinking fountains, and helpful signs that display wait-times.

Additionally, most of Disneyland's queues actually amplify anticipation for an attraction. Because guests are kept in the vicinity of the attraction they're waiting for, the close proximity offers abundant opportunities for Imagineers to create décor echoing the theme of the attraction. The elaborate queue for the **Jungle Cruise**, for instance, includes historical material that helps put guests in the mood for an old-fashioned jungle adventure. At **Snow White's Scary Adventures**, the creepy queue readies guests for the scares to come. These are just two examples of what the best queues do: work creatively as integral parts of the attractions themselves.

Radio Disney Broadcast Booth

MAP: Tomorrowland, T-8

DATES: March 1, 1999–December 2002

For a few years at the turn of the millennium, Radio Disney operated out of a small glass-walled booth in the middle of **Tomorrowland**. Deejays and broadcast electronics occupied the space underneath the old **PeopleMover** loading platform that had formerly been used for the **Lunching Pad**.

Disneyland's 2000 **souvenir book** explained that, "Through soundproof glass, guests can view Radio Disney's state-of-the-art radio studio and watch daily live broadcasts carried across the nation on 'the radio network just for kids'." Although Radio Disney is still on the air, the Radio Disney Broadcast Booth went silent in the winter of 2002. In 2006 **Tomorrowlanding** landed where the booth had been.

Rafts to Tom Sawyer Island

MAP: Frontierland, Fr-11

DATES: June 16, 1956–ongoing

Guests could see **Tom Sawyer Island** on **Opening Day** in 1955, but they couldn't access it until the summer of '56. That's when the D-ticket (see **ticket books**) Rafts to Tom Sawyer Island began operating their regular service between a dock on **Frontierland's** riverbank and another one on the island's southern tip about 100 feet away. The following summer, a second Frontierland dock close to the **Indian Village** opened up to accommodate more guests, delivering guests to the island's midsection until 1971. No matter which location guests used, the service was about the same, with some

40 or so passengers at a time making the one-minute trip at about four miles per hour. Since the island closes at sundown, the raft crossing is still only made during daylight hours.

The rafts and their promotional materials are designed to appear roughly made. The hand-painted sign at the dock, for instance, that announces rules about strollers and smoking has some of its letters printed backwards. The Tom Sawyer Island **attraction poster** depicts an old log raft reminiscent of the one used for the Mississippi River escape in *Adventures of Huckleberry Finn* (though at Disneyland the rafts are powered by diesel engines). These rafts do not run on underwater tracks and are instead steered by **cast members**. The raft names once alluded to Mark Twain's literary heroes and heroines—*Huck Finn, Injun Joe, Becky Thatcher,* and *Tom Sawyer*. In 2006, the *Huck, Joe,* and *Becky* rafts were renamed *Blackbeard, Anne Bonny,* and *Captain Kidd* to echo the new pirate theme on Tom Sawyer Island.

Rancho del Zocalo Restaurante

MAP: Frontierland, Fr-24

DATES: February 5, 2001–ongoing

Casa Mexicana, the Mexican restaurant born in **Frontierland** in 1982, underwent *cambios grandes* in 2001. Ortega, the chile and salsa company, was the new sponsor, and Rancho del Zocalo was the new name, though an old sign reading "*mi casa es su casa*" still honored the previous establishment. Zocalo refers to the name applied in the 1950s to this section of Frontierland, **El Zocalo** ("the town square"). Though the restaurant has mainly served cafeteria-style Mexican cuisine, the 2001 menu also included some tasty new items, such as smoked ribs and barbecued chicken.

In recent years, with La Victoria as the restaurant's sponsor, the menu has changed again, this time reverting to mostly Mexican dishes supplemented by a few fire-grilled specialties. Today's Rancho is bigger and fancier than the old Casa, with exotic tiles, fountains, a big Zorro mural outside, and elaborate ironwork enhancing the Spanish architecture.

Ravenscroft, Thurl
(1914–2005)

Like **Paul Frees**, Thurl Ravenscroft had one of those resonant voices everyone has heard in movies, TV commercials, and Disneyland attractions for decades. A Nebraskan born in 1914, Ravenscroft served in World War II and then established a Hollywood career as a singer. He was part of several different vocal groups, including the Mello Men and the Johnny Mann Singers (one of his most-loved performances was "You're a Mean One, Mister Grinch" for the holiday classic *How the Grinch Stole Christmas*). As a successful voice actor, Ravenscroft's single most famous line was Tony the Tiger's enthusiastic "they're grrrrreat!"

Ravenscroft sang and voiced characters for numerous Disney movies, among them *Cinderella*, *Mary Poppins*, and *The Jungle Book*. At Disneyland, he provided voices for the **Country Bear Jamboree** (he was the mounted buffalo head), the **Enchanted Tiki Room** (Fritz), and the *Mark Twain* (the narrator). Most famously, he sang lead on the **Haunted Mansion** theme song, "Grim Grinning Ghosts," (his face is still in the quartet of singing busts). Southern California residents also knew Ravenscroft as the narrator of both *The Pageant of the Masters* (a living tableau of artworks held every summer in Laguna Beach) and *The Glory of Christmas* (a holiday spectacular held every winter at Garden Grove's Crystal Cathedral).

Ravenscroft was inducted as a Disney Legend in 1995. He died 10 years later of cancer at age 91.

Redd Rockett's Pizza Port

MAP: Tomorrowland, T-16

DATES: March 21, 1998–ongoing

After **Mission to Mars** stopped flying in 1992, its large **Tomorrowland** building sat empty for four years. The **Toy Story Funhouse** set up here for a brief run in 1996, but two more years would pass before something permanent settled in. Surprisingly, the new arrival wasn't an attraction, but a restaurant serving big portions of fast food. Redd Rockett's Pizza Port and its new neighbor, ***Honey, I Shrunk the Audience***, both

debuted in 1998 in conjunction with a major Tomorrowland remodel. The restaurant's name alludes to both the famous red-and-white rocket on the roof (the ***Moonliner***) and the Space Port that was considered for Tomorrowland in the '60s (**Space Mountain** arose instead in the '70s).

Redd's features cafeteria-style counters and plenty of seating both indoors and out. Buitoni, a Tuscan pasta and sauce company that is now a Nestlé brand, is the sponsor here, so it's no surprise that Italian food dominates Redd's menu. The selections have humorous space-themed names like Mars-inara Pasta and Lunar Cheese Pizza. Proximity to the popular **Starcade** makes this a favorite spot for arcade-happy kids, and the classic **attraction posters** on the walls make it a favorite for nostalgic adults.

Red Wagon Inn, aka Plaza Inn

MAP: Hub, H-3

DATES: July 17, 1955–ongoing

Supposedly **Walt Disney** preferred the posh Red Wagon Inn over any other Disneyland restaurant. In the 1950s, it offered the park's priciest dining experience and was so elegant that it even had its own **attraction poster** featuring its luxurious interior. Photos of its white-trimmed Edwardian exterior made it into all of Disneyland's early **souvenir books**, their captions touting "tempting meals in the beautiful surroundings of Grandfather's day."

The Red Wagon's name derived from the logo of its sponsor, Swift & Company, which also debuted two other Disneyland locations, the **Market House** and the **Chicken Plantation**, in 1955. The full-service Red Wagon offered full-course breakfasts, lunches, and dinners in glitzy, antique-filled rooms lit by crystal chandeliers. It also had a terrace for alfresco dining. Unbeknownst to most guests, there was also a private room with its own entrance for Walt Disney and his VIP guests (this alcohol-serving area was a precursor to the exclusive **Club 33** in **New Orleans Square**). Inside the Red Wagon, some of the opulent furnishings came from a Victorian mansion near downtown Los Angeles.

When Swift ended its sponsorship in July of 1965, the restaurant got a new name, the Plaza Inn, and a new sponsor, the Columbian Coffee Growers. The Plaza Inn is a swank cafeteria serving broasted chicken, pasta, gourmet salads, and fancy desserts among its hearty fare. A 1998 renovation kept the plush Victorian interior but introduced some new menu items, including a prix fixe breakfast with omelets, Mickey-shaped waffles, and the company of Disney characters.

The Plaza Inn, incidentally, is the third Plaza-named restaurant in the immediate area—across the way are the **Plaza Pavilion** and the **Plaza Gardens**. Of this trio, the Plaza Inn is the only one on the **Tomorrowland** side of the **Hub**.

Reel-Ride

MAP: Frontierland, Fr-1

DATES: Never built

If the intriguing legend is accurate, Willis O'Brien, the wizard behind the stop-motion special effects for *King Kong* and other movie classics, once drew up some concept art for an attraction intended for **Frontierland**. Unfortunately, his Reel-Ride was never built. As shown in a 2006 museum exhibition called *Behind the Magic: 50 Years of Disneyland*, a color illustration (purportedly O'Brien's) depicted 10 kids on mechanical horses facing a movie screen. In this attraction-to-be, young buckaroos would have ridden their horses as a rollicking movie of a cowboy star on his horse rolled in front of them. An ungrammatical caption described how the horses were synchronized with "a back-projection on a translucent screen, giving effect of actually traveling through the country. When chase is ended—horses stop."

Had it been constructed and implemented, the three-to-five-minute Reel-Ride might have been the world's first melding of film, motion-simulation, and an amusement park attraction (making it a precursor of **Star Tours**). O'Brien, who was about 68 years old when the 1954 drawing was executed, died in 1962.

Refreshment Corner,
aka Coke Corner, aka Coca-Cola Refreshment Corner

MAP: Main Street, MS-10

DATES: July 17, 1955–ongoing

Since **Opening Day**, Disneyland's most enduring fast-food location has thrived on

the western corner where **Main Street** meets the **Hub**. The Refreshment Corner, also known as Coke Corner and the Coca-Cola Refreshment Corner, bends around the intersection of Main and West Plaza Street toward the **Adventureland** entrance. Inside, the Refreshment Corner opens into the Candy Palace; the outside area with alfresco tables is called the Corner Café. The basic menu initially listed just sodas but was supplemented later by hot dogs and various other snacks.

Three features have secured the lasting popularity of this otherwise simple eatery: its long hours (longer than most food establishments in Disneyland); its charming interior with ornate, turn-of-the-century embellishments; and the presence of affable piano man Rod Miller. Since around 1970, Miller, wearing turn-of-the-century clothes and a consistent smile, played exuberant ragtime piano favorites for over 30 years and chatted with guests on the patio. With Miller now retired, a handful of other pianists currently share the entertainment schedule.

As perky as the Refreshment Corner is in the daylight, it's even brighter after sundown, when the lovely lights and lively music combine to make this one of Disneyland's cheeriest spots. Success here led Coca-Cola to sponsor additional park locations over the decades, including 1967's **Tomorrowland Terrace** and 1998's **Spirit of Refreshment**.

Restrooms

On **Opening Day**, **Walt Disney** almost didn't have working restrooms in Disneyland. A strike by local plumbers forced last-minute negotiations that got the restrooms, but not the water fountains, into operation (Disney made this agonizing choice by acknowledging that guests could forgo the latter, but not the former). A free map handed out to guests that day pinpointed only 10 public restrooms (five men's, five women's) in the entire park that were open; the maps in Disneyland's 1956 **souvenir book** accounted for just a dozen (six and six). Two pairs of restrooms were located on Main Street; the other four main lands had one pair each. Also, the coin-operated stalls in some of the restrooms were converted to free stalls.

Today, Disneyland has over 25 pairs of restrooms. Six pairs are located in the **Main**

Street stretch from the **entrance** up to the **Hub** restaurants. The lands all have at least three pairs each, except for **Critter Country** and **Mickey's Toontown**, which only have one pair each. The size of the restrooms varies from spacious (like those in Critter Country's **Hungry Bear Restaurant**) to cramped (**Tom Sawyer Island**).

What never varies is the cleanliness of the restrooms. **Chuck Boyajian**, the original manager of custodial operations, and his staff raised the bar for cleanliness to a new height that became the industry standard. Even on the busiest days, every bathroom is lightly cleaned every hour in addition to thorough sanitizing cleanings every night. Not only are the facilities spotless, they're also convenient for parents—most restrooms include baby-changing stations, and some even sell baby-changing kits (diapers, wipes, etc.). At the **Hub**, special restroom needs are accommodated inside the Baby Care Center and **First Aid**.

Themed door signs are delightful enhancements to the restrooms. Aliens, for instance, adorn restroom doors in **Tomorrowland**. (Prince, evidently, has his own restroom outside of the **Princess Fantasy Faire** in **Fantasyland**.) What's more, the theme occasionally even extends inside the restrooms; some **Frontierland** restroom interiors feature wooden walls and antique hurricane lamps. The most opulent restrooms are inside **Club 33**, where the ladies' room features gilded seating arrangements that have earn the nickname "thrones."

Rigdon, Cicely
(Dates unknown)

Working her way up from ticket seller in 1957 to Disney Legend inductee in 2005, Cicely Rigdon enjoyed a distinguished Disney career that included over three decades of Disneyland service. In 1959, just two years after being hired at Disneyland, Rigdon headed the new **Tour Guide** program before being promoted to **Guest Relations**, which she supervised in the 1960s and '70s while also training and overseeing the ticket sellers out front. Aside from her many other responsibilities at the time, Rigdon supervised the maintenance of **Walt Disney's apartment** above the **Fire Department**, helped launch the four new Disney attractions at the 1964–1965 New York World's Fair, and worked closely with the park's "Honorary Mayor," **Jack Lindquist**.

In the '70s Rigdon took on training responsibilities at Walt Disney World, and a decade later she was updating the **Miss Disneyland** program to the Disneyland Ambassador to the World program. After 37 years of working at Disneyland, Rigdon retired in 1994.

River Belle Terrace
MAP: Frontierland, Fr-7

DATES: 1971–ongoing

What had been **Aunt Jemima's** restaurant for over a decade and the **Magnolia Tree Terrace** for over a year became the stately, white-trimmed River Belle Terrace in 1971. The location on the corner where **Frontierland** rounds into **Adventureland** has dictated the style of the two restaurant entrances—cream-colored on the Frontierland side, and pale blue on the Adventureland side. Its unique roof has two separate themes to match each land. After a 2007 remodel, the River Belle now stretches all the way back on the Frontierland side toward the **Stage Door Café**, usurping spaces previously occupied by smaller eateries. The interior décor remains as pretty as always, and the umbrella-shaded patio out front still affords guests attractive views of the **Rivers of America**, only 75 feet away.

Oscar Meyer, Hormel, and Sunkist have all been sponsors of the terrace over the years. No matter which company is participating, the cuisine has maintained a down-home flavor, offering lots of basic American food that follows the Mark Twain theme—Aunt Polly's Chicken, Becky Thatcher's Fresh Fruit Plate, etc. In recent years tangy barbecue specialties, signature sandwiches, and "Munch Inc." selections for kids have joined the menu. The highlight of the restaurant, though, has remained the famous Mickey-shaped pancakes, said to have originated here. Disneyland's own literature declares the River Belle Terrace to have been **Walt Disney's** preferred breakfast choice.

Rivers of America

MAP: Frontierland, Fr-9

DATES: July 17, 1955–ongoing

The man-made Rivers of America area is a highly visible, much-traveled section of Disneyland that debuted on **Opening Day**. The waterway, however, might be more accurately called the Rivers of the Midwest, since the Missouri and Mississippi seem to have been the main inspirations for the initial design and landscaping. Though the river area is technically located in **Frontierland**, it is visible from, and bordered by, **New Orleans Square** and **Critter Country** as well. Some of Disneyland's most popular attractions, including the **Big Thunder Mountain Railroad**, the **Haunted Mansion**, and **Splash Mountain** surround the river's perimeter. The river section most often viewed by pedestrians is the southern portion, where **Fantasmic!** is presented. A walk from **Fowler's Harbor** in the southwest corner to the *Mark Twain's* dock spans about 650 feet of pavement.

The overall surface area of the Rivers of America, including the island in the middle, covers about 325,000 square feet. These eight acres represent roughly 13 percent of the total area of the original 60-acre park. Shaped vaguely like a kidney bean around **Tom Sawyer Island**, the waters stretch almost 1,000 feet from the northernmost to the southernmost shore. Measuring across the water from the mainland to the island, the river ranges from about 80 to 100 feet wide. According to Disney legend, the rivers supposedly flow from the hill on Tom Sawyer Island where Tom & Huck's Treehouse is built.

Five watercraft have sailed regularly upon the river (though not all simultaneously): the *Mark Twain*, the *Columbia*, the **Mike Fink Keel Boats**, the **Indian War Canoes**, and the **Rafts to Tom Sawyer Island**. Boats that circumnavigate the island travel about a half-mile through approximately nine million gallons of water only about five feet deep. Despite its shallowness, the river has been the site of an accidental drowning, the tragic result of an inebriated guest entering the waters after dark.

Disneyland: The First Quarter Century describes the main problem with the river's construction. The first time water was pumped into the bulldozed trenches, the water immediately seeped away into the soil. After different types of riverbeds were tried, the river was eventually given a hard clay bottom. These days, the river is drained every few years for cleaning and maintenance. The turbid water that's used to refill the river would be clear if not for a chemical additive that makes it appear murky, thus concealing the submerged tracks that guide the *Mark Twain* and the *Columbia* (and also concealing the hundreds of cameras, pacifiers, sunglasses, and other items accidentally dropped overboard).

One of the misconceptions about the waterway is that it is stocked with fish. It isn't. Occasionally tiny fish are seen in the river, but they haven't been placed there intentionally. The only time park officials introduced fish to the river was in the early years, when a small sealed area at the southern end of Tom Sawyer Island was abundantly stocked and fishing poles were provided for guests who wanted to give fishing a try. The practice was soon abandoned, however, when their odoriferous catches began to stink up the lockers or were abandoned in the park.

Disneyland's 1956 **souvenir book** identified additional fauna along the river: "Flocks of wild geese, mallards, and other birds have found Frontierland's River a safe retreat in their pilgrimages south. The birds pause to rest here, and in some cases stay on for several months." Thus, the desultory ducks often seen drifting along in the waterway aren't **Audio-Animatronic** mechanicals, as some guests might suppose, but are in fact migratory waterfowl visiting Disneyland. The Native Americans and large animals glimpsed around the river—moose, deer, skunks, etc.—are either statues or A-A machines.

A 2010 update to the Rivers of America added details, animals, and landscaping inspired by the Potomac, Rio Grande, and Columbia rivers. As always, the serene waters provide a cooling respite from the busy excitement of the park.

Rock Candy Mountain, aka Candy Mountain

MAP: Fantasyland, Fa-15

DATES: Never built

One of the more sugary ideas considered for the young Disneyland was something called Rock Candy Mountain, also called Candy Mountain. The Burl Ives ballad "Big Rock Candy Mountain" had been a hit in 1949, so the image of an abundantly sweet wonderland was still fresh when Disney designers began drawing concept illustrations in the early 1950s. Although the project gathered momentum late in the decade and was worked on by such Disney Legends as **Claude Coats**, **Harriet Burns**, and **Rolly Crump**, ultimately no mountain of candy ever materialized.

Had it been built, Candy Mountain would have been incorporated into the **Storybook Land Canal Boats** attraction, which had gotten a major remodel and new name in 1956 after its bleak **Opening Day** debut as the **Canal Boats of the World**. As envisioned, sightseers in the boats would have glided into caverns in Rock Candy Mountain and found scenes from a new Disney movie based on one of L. Frank Baum's many *Wizard of Oz* sequels (not to be confused with the 1939 Judy Garland classic). Candy Mountain wouldn't have been the only site in Disneyland's first decade to incorporate props and costumes from a Disney movie—the **20,000 Leagues Under the Sea Exhibit** and **Babes in Toyland** were also walk-through movie exhibits.

Even more colorful than the plans for the interior were those for the mountain's exterior, which at one time was going to be transparent but was later revised to carry a thick coating of artificial candy. Oversized candy canes, gumballs, lollipops, and more would have covered the six-story mountain, and the **Casey Jr. Circus Train** was meant to wrap around the base. Unfortunately, when Disney's *Oz* movie plans collapsed, so did the mountain. As related in *Disneyland: The Nickel Tour*, the miniature model—which had been made with real candy—was taken outside, where birds put a quick end to any Candy Mountain dreams.

Rocket Jets

MAP: Tomorrowland, T-8

DATES: July 2, 1967–January 6, 1997

For four decades some variation of a whirling-rocket attraction stood in the heart of **Tomorrowland**. After debuting as the Astro-Jets in 1956 and then being renamed the Tomorrowland Jets in 1964, the attraction closed in September of '66 while a major remodel redefined all of Tomorrowland. When it reopened just before Independence Day in 1967, the attraction had yet another new name—Rocket Jets—and now required a D ticket from the park's **ticket book** to match the flight's dramatic restyling.

With America's space program in full swing, the decade-old winged cylinders of the Astro-Jets were jettisoned in favor of new Apollo-style rockets. Designed by **George McGinnis**, the sleek new tubes were more bullet-like in appearance, with sharper noses, prominent yellow headlights, and white and black livery reminiscent of NASA's latest spaceships (today, several repainted vehicles are used as display cases in the **Little Green Men Store Command** shop). The redesigned central tower itself looked like one of the imposing Saturn launchers that thrust astronauts into the Florida sky.

Even more impressively, the whole attraction had been lifted three stories off the ground to sit atop the main **PeopleMover** platform. With the center rocket topping out at about 85 feet, guests now rode an elevator (designed to look like the gantry alongside a NASA rocket) to reach the loading area. The fun factor zoomed higher when pilots pushed their vehicles to maximum altitude, soaring some 70 feet above the Tomorrowland pavement.

And soar they would until early 1997, when the rockets were finally grounded and replaced a year later by a spinning sculpture called the **Observatron**. Opening concurrently was a very different expression of the original Astro-Jets idea—the **Astro-Orbitor**, with a new location about 250 feet away at Tomorrowland's entrance.

Rocket Man

MAP: Park, P-18

DATES: December 1965

For a couple of weeks in the winter of 1965, jet-packs were all the rage. At the movies, James Bond soared out of harm's way in the opening sequence of *Thunderball*, the year's winter blockbuster. And at Disneyland, the park's Rocket Man was soaring above the **Flight Circle** in **Tomorrowland** for the holidays. Both Bond and the Rocket Man were using Bell-designed rocket-powered backpacks (also called rocketpacks and rocketbelts) intended for the Air Force. Both pilots wore white helmets, but Disneyland's Rocket Man wore a white flight suit as well (Bond wore his usual natty suit and tie). *Disneyland: The Nickel Tour* identifies the Disneyland rocketeer as William Suitor, the same man who later flew a jetpack at the 1984 Summer Olympics in Los Angeles.

Rocket Rods

MAP: Tomorrowland, T-8

DATES: May 22, 1998–April 27, 2001

"The Rocket Rods zoom above, through, and around Tomorrowland in the fastest and longest attraction in Disneyland Park. This thrilling experience puts guests behind the wheels of high-speed vehicles of the future as they tear along an elevated highway above Tomorrowland."

So read the ambitious description of the Rocket Rods in Disneyland's 2000 **souvenir book**. "Ride the road to tomorrow" was the proud boast at the attraction's entrance. Unfortunately, the Rocket Rods' disappointing reality never matched the printed hyperbole or ambitious concept. What should have been an exciting new 30-mile-per-hour thrill ride for the 21st century barely sputtered through the last year of the 20th. Even more embarrassingly, the Rocket Rods were built to be a high-profile showpiece attraction at **Tomorrowland's** entrance, making their failure all the more glaring.

In the spring of '98, what had once been the **Circarama** theater opened as the Rocket Rods' spiraling **queue** area. Waiting guests learned about the history of transportation from numerous displays, which included vehicles from extinct Disneyland attractions. Guests also heard car-themed music, including a reworked version of "Detroit" from Disney's *The Happiest Millionaire*. The displays and music were fine, but the long wait wasn't, often stretching to well over an hour.

When they finally arrived at the old **PeopleMover** boarding area, guests found sleek, five-passenger hot rods that looked suitably futuristic and were surprisingly loud. Originally called Rocket Rods XPR (Experimental Prototype Rocket), the initials were dropped before guests could start inventing their own acronyms (Extremely Problematic Ride, for instance, or Exceptional Patience Required). Once they headed off along the PeopleMover's elevated tracks, the cars lurched from acceleration on the straightaways to sudden deceleration on the curves for a spastic three-minute trip that was as hard on the vehicles as it was on the passengers.

While some people liked the experience, nobody liked the frequent ride breakdowns. After struggling through three trouble-plagued summers, the attraction "temporarily" closed for repairs in 2000. The following spring, the Rocket Rods moved from Disneyland's future to Disneyland's past and were permanently retired. Four years later, the successful **Buzz Lightyear Astro Blasters** attraction moved into the building; outside, the elevated tracks still stand in mute testament to the fully-realized PeopleMover dream of the '60s and the unfulfilled Rocket Rods dream of the '90s.

Rocket to the Moon

MAP: Tomorrowland, T-16

DATES: July 22, 1955–September 5, 1966

Though it was visible on **Opening Day**, Rocket to the Moon in **Tomorrowland** didn't truly open for five more days. When it did debut, the attraction was sponsored by TWA, but Douglas Aircraft took over sponsorship from 1962 to 1966. The location for the Rocket to the Moon attraction was behind the imposing *Moonliner* rocket; guests boarded inside hemispherical buildings that looked something like observatories.

Early Disneyland **souvenir books** listed the attraction as a "round trip to the moon." Something similar had operated some five decades earlier at Coney Island's Steeplechase Park. There, a ride called A Trip to the Moon used projections of a receding Earth and an approaching Moon to simulate a space voyage that included a landing, views of lunar creatures, and an appearance by a royal Man on the Moon. At Disneyland, the trip was indeed to the moon—but only to lunar orbit, not to the lunar surface itself.

The attraction operated like a low-tech flight simulator. Guests sat in one of two steeply-raked, 104-seat theaters named Diana and Luna. Inside each cylindrical theater, large circular screens were mounted on the center of the floor and in the center of the ceiling. For 15 minutes the screens displayed views of the ship's previous location (the bottom screen began with footage of the launch pad and morphed into a receding Earth) and its approaching target (the top screen showed the oncoming moon), all described by an informative narrator. Simple special effects (such as the raising and lowering of seats), views of a glowing comet and the far side of the moon, and a noisy trip through a meteor shower all made the space trip even more exciting. Disney Legends **Claude Coats**, **Peter Ellenshaw**, and **John Hench** helped create the space experience.

In 1966 the C-ticket (see **ticket books**) Rocket to the Moon flights were scrapped so the more elaborate missions of the D-ticket **Flight to the Moon** could launch a year later. Although the Rocket to the Moon is gone, what remains is one of the most compelling of all the park's **attraction posters**, one that depicts the majestic *Moonliner*, swooping Tomorrowland buildings, a star-spangled sky, and tantalizing text that invites guests to "Blast off aboard a rocket ship on a thrilling trip to the moon and return to Earth."

Roger Rabbit's Car Toon Spin

MAP: Mickey's Toontown, MT-11

DATES: January 26, 1994–ongoing

Roger Rabbit's Car Toon Spin is the signature attraction in **Mickey's Toontown**. After opening in 1994, one year after Toontown's debut, the ride became popular enough to warrant **FASTPASS** ticket distribution.

The Car Toon Spin is similar to the **Fantasyland** dark rides, which feature little vehicles moving through decorated sets with animated movie themes. Roger's ride, however, offers something the **Mr. Toad**, **Snow White**, **Alice**, **Peter Pan**, and **Pinocchio** attractions don't—guest-controlled vehicles. Roger's cars can be spun around a full 360 degrees, like the teacups in the **Mad Hatter's Mad Tea Party.** After entering a garage and climbing into smiling cars designed to resemble the cabs in *Who Framed Roger Rabbit*, guests begin a colorful excursion through that movie's Toontown. The trip gets spinny as soon as the cabs slide through the deadly "Dip" slick the weasels have poured onto the road. From this point on, guests can whirl their cars in a circle, pointing them at anything they pass. Some five minutes and a dozen **Audio-Animatronic** characters

Major Attractions and Exhibits Added in the 1990s

1991 Disney Afternoon Avenue

1992 Fantasmic!

1993 Aladdin's Oasis; Chip 'n Dale Tree House, Donald's Boat; Fantasia Gardens; Gadget's Go Coaster; Goofy's Bounce House; Jolly Trolley; Mickey's House; Minnie's House; *Partners*

1994 Roger Rabbit's Car Toon Spin

1995 Indiana Jones Adventure

1996 Toy Story Funhouse

1998 Astro-Orbitor; *Honey, I Shrunk the Audience*; Innoventions; Observatron; Rocket Rods

1999 Tarzan's Treehouse

later, Roger extricates guests by opening a portable hole that leads back to the garage.

From the entrance to the exit, frenetic energy, zany imagination, and madcap gags burst out of this attraction. The **queue** area rivals **Indiana Jones Adventure** for clever details: a wise-cracking gorilla, a pin-up calendar, a "Dip" recipe, a wall of Disney-themed license plates (2N TOWN, CAP 10 HK, etc.), and many more, making the wait an attraction in itself. The scenery displayed during the cab ride is more detailed than it is in most attractions because of the freedom of movement enjoyed by spinning guests—Imagineers had to create fronts, sides, and backs to everything, since guests would be observing from all directions.

Guests may come for the twirl, but they'll return for the barrage of jokes. Any attraction that culminates with a backwards journey through the Gag Warehouse has just got to be ridden again and again.

Rogers, Wathel
(1919–2000)

"Here rests Wathel R. Bender, He Rode to Glory on a Fender, Peaceful Rest."

This tombstone outside the **Haunted Mansion** was a nifty tribute to Wathel Rogers, a Disney Legend who worked for the company for 48 years. Born in Colorado in 1919, Rogers studied art in the '30s and joined Disney Studios in '39. There he started out as a film animator on such classics as *Pinocchio* and *Bambi*.

After a World War II stint with the Marines, Rogers returned to Disney to help animate *Cinderella*, *Peter Pan*, and *Sleeping Beauty*, among other films. Meanwhile, his expertise as a model-maker qualified him to help **Walt Disney** construct the miniature Carolwood Pacific train on Disney's Holmby Hills property in the early '50s. Rogers then became one of Disneyland's main model-makers, creating small-scale 3-D buildings that would be previewed on the ***Disneyland* TV series** and then be constructed full-size in the park.

During the 1950s, Rogers took on a special task at Walt Disney's request—helping create a mechanical man. Inspired by the lanky build of Buddy Ebsen, Rogers and several others built a nine-inch dancing man who was the prototypical **Audio-Animatronic** figure, setting the stage for the remarkable achievements to come. In the '60s, with technology becoming more sophisticated, Rogers helped make A-A birds for the **Enchanted Tiki Room**, animals for the **Jungle Cruise**, personable buccaneers for **Pirates of the Caribbean**, and Honest Abe himself for **Great Moments with Mr. Lincoln**. While developing new mechanicals for the attraction that would become Disneyland's **Carousel of Progress**, Rogers was shown alongside Walt Disney on national TV to demonstrate how an elaborate programming harness could manipulate the Audio-Animatronic character nearby.

There were still more achievements to come. In the '70s Rogers build an A-A Ben Franklin figure for EPCOT, and in the '80s he organized a team to help solve technical problems in Disney parks. After retiring in '87, Wathel Rogers was inducted as a Disney Legend in 1995, five years before his death in Arizona at age 81.

Royal Street Bachelors

DATES: 1966–ongoing

Disneyland's **souvenir books** have often flaunted photos, some at full-page size, of an authentic jazz combo that "recreates the sounds of old New Orleans" in **New Orleans Square**. This trio is the Royal Street Bachelors, a group that is among the most enduring entertainers in Disneyland history. The Bachelors still play most days of the week,

usually at the intersection of Orleans and Royal Street, or near the **Royal Street Veranda**, or at the **French Market**. The men are typically dressed in classy outfits that can include matching red or green vests, plaid sports jackets, chalk-stripe suits, bow ties, and festive skimmers.

The three Bachelors who currently play at Disneyland aren't the same three who started in 1966. The original trio was comprised of Jack McVea (co-composer of the 1947 hit "Open the Door Richard"), Harold Grant, and Herb Gordy (a relative of Motown Records founder Berry Gordy). McVea was the group's leader, playing the clarinet and the saxophone; Grant strummed a banjo and guitar; and Gordy plucked an upright bass. McVea stayed with the group for 27 years, finally retiring in 1992. A year before he left, a new CD called *The Official Album of Disneyland and Walt Disney World* included 86 seconds of the Bachelors' "Swanee River." This number typified their set, which relied on smooth arrangements of jazz and R & B standards.

In recent years, saxophonist Kenny Treseder has headed the Bachelors, supported by guitarist Terry Evens and bassist Jeffery Littleton (another longtime guitarist, Ernie McLean, died in 2012). Other musical groups that have enjoyed long New Orleans Square careers include the Cajun-style River Rascals, the Bayou Brass Band, and the Side Street Strutters. Except for the Royal Street Bachelors, all these groups seem to have been dropped around 2006.

Royal Street Sweets

MAP: New Orleans Square, NOS-7

DATES: 1995–ongoing

Candy of all stripes, including many with Disney designs, is the specialty at this **New Orleans Square** cart next to **Café Orleans**. In addition to selling sweets, the cart gets into the Mardi Gras spirit to vend sparkly beads, necklaces, and masks. The cart itself changes its look regularly, sometimes appearing as a nostalgic **Main Street** flower cart, and other times like a black coach delivering ghouls to the **Haunted Mansion**.

Royal Street Veranda

MAP: New Orleans Square, NOS-2

DATES: Ca. 1966–ongoing

The Royal Street Veranda is the first dining option offered to guests as they enter **New Orleans Square** from **Adventureland**. Located around the corner from the entrance to **Pirates of the Caribbean**, the little eatery is merely an open counter with outdoor seating offering scenic views of this riverfront area. The Royal Street Veranda is a quick source for food with Cajun flavor—"pot foods" (hearty gumbos, clam chowder, etc.) served in bread bowls, as well as fritters and specialty coffees.

Ruggles China and Glass Shop

MAP: Main Street, MS-13

DATES: July 17, 1955–March 1964

A gift retailer named Phil Papel debuted the Ruggles China and Glass Shop on **Opening**

Day. Filling the small store with imported ceramics and gifts, Papel was successful enough to establish 19 other locations around Southern California. The derivation of the Ruggles name isn't clear—unless, perhaps, it refers to New Hampshire's Ruggles Mine, a major producer of the feldspar used in fine ceramics.

Disneyland's early **souvenir books** listed the Ruggles store as the China Shop, Ceramics & China, the China & Glass Shop, and China & Glass, trying out practically every noun combination that didn't include the actual Ruggles name. The shop's location was one door south of what is today the **Main Street Photo Supply Co**. A year after opening, Ruggles expanded into the adjacent room that became available when **Intimate Apparel** left.

In 1964, the Ruggles China and Glass Shop closed and was quickly replaced by the store that is still operating there today, the **China Closet**.

Ryman, Herb
(1910–1989)

"I look upon Walt as a conductor of one of the world's greatest symphonies," Herb Ryman said in the book *Remembering Walt*, "and I was part of the orchestra."

Humble though he was, the truth is that few artists who contributed to Disneyland were as important as Ryman. On September 26th and 27th of 1953, Ryman drew a detailed aerial view of the unbuilt park while **Walt Disney** described it to him. That landmark sketch—which included a recognizable **Main Street**, a **Hub** with various lands radiating outward from it, a castle, a **berm** with a train, a river with a riverboat, and a **Jungle Cruise**-style attraction—was a key component of the successful presentations **Roy Disney** made to potential investors.

Once Disneyland plans were underway, Ryman was one of the key designers of **Sleeping Beauty Castle**, the Jungle Cruise, Main Street buildings, and later, **New Orleans Square**. On the *Disneyland Secrets, Stories & Magic* DVD, Ryman claimed that

he proposed one of the more notable design changes for the castle—he's the one who spun the top around because he thought it looked better. Afterward, **Walt Disney** agreed that the castle should be built with its original "back" facing the Hub (see **Sleeping Beauty Castle** for more of this story).

Ryman's Disneyland creations were the crowning achievements of his long art career. Born in Illinois in 1910, he studied art before heading west to work in the movies. MGM hired him first, as an illustrator for some of its great '30s films, including *Mutiny on the Bounty*. In 1938 Ryman joined Disney Studios, where he worked as an art director on *Fantasia*, *Dumbo*, and other animated films. He then moved to 20th Century Fox and later traveled extensively with the Ringling Brothers Circus before taking on Disneyland projects, including artwork for New Orleans Square and Disney's exhibits for the 1964–1965 New York World's Fair. Ryman was photographed for a feature story about the park in a 1963 issue of *National Geographic*; the accompanying photo showed him drawing a New Orleans Square concept illustration.

Ryman formally retired from the Disney Company in 1971, but he stayed on as a consultant for projects at other Disney parks. He also created art for the 1977 Disney film *Pete's Dragon*. A year after he died in Los Angeles in 1989, Ryman was inducted posthumously as a Disney Legend. A tree near Sleeping Beauty Castle was planted in his honor, and his art is still frequently displayed in Disneyland.

Safari Outpost

MAP: Adventureland, A-2

DATES: March 1, 1986–January 1995

Starting in 1956, one of the shops at the **Adventureland Bazaar** was a fabric-and-fashions shop called Guatemalan Weavers. Two weeks after that shop closed in 1986, the Safari Outpost opened in its place. The location was at the far west end of the Bazaar, next to the eatery now known as the **Bengal Barbecue**. Wacky for khaki, the Safari Outpost's main merchandise was safari clothing (as expected for a retailer across from the **Jungle Cruise**), but there were also plush animals and toys available for young explorers. In 1995, the same year Indy's major attraction opened nearby, the store became **Indiana Jones Adventure Outpost**.

Sailing Ship *Columbia*

MAP: Frontierland, Fr-17

DATES: June 14, 1958–ongoing

While most guests think that the **Frontierland** theme is focused on America's 19th-century Wild West decades, this area actually gives a prominent nod to America's 18th-century Revolutionary War era. The last major addition to

Frontierland's roster of varied vessels, the majestic *Columbia* is, as described on Disneyland's big **attraction poster**, a "full-rigged, three-masted sailing ship" that takes "a voyage of discoveries on the **Rivers of America**." That voyage began in 1958, the year the ship was dedicated under the supervision of **Walt Disney** and naval officials. For most of the '50s, '60s, and '70s the *Columbia* was a D-ticket attraction (see **ticket books**), occasionally upgraded to an E.

The ship's design was inspired by the original *Columbia*, a privately owned sloop that in 1790 became the first American windjammer to circumnavigate the globe. To some nautical experts, however, the actual design is closer to that of a famous *Columbia* contemporary—the *Bounty*, the infamous ship captained by William Bligh and commandeered by the mutinous Fletcher Christian in 1789. Since the designs for Bligh's *Bounty* were indeed examined during the construction of Disneyland's *Columbia*, it's possible that the park's ship is a blend of both classic vessels. Whatever its backstory, the *Columbia* is a wonderfully appointed replica accurately capturing the spirit of the great age of sail, even if it doesn't accurately replicate the propulsion of that time (despite appearances, engine power, not wind power, drives the ship along the same half-mile submerged track used by the **Mark Twain**). The ship's main mast towers 84 feet, the decks hold 275–300 guests, and the 110-foot-long hull displays 10 cannons, one of which is fired occasionally during the 12–14-minute tour around **Tom Sawyer Island**.

To accommodate the addition of such a large vessel on the Frontierland waterways, the park added a new dock and landing, **Fowler's Harbor**, to the southwest corner of the Rivers of America. To show off the ship's meticulously detailed interior, a walk-through exhibit known as the Below-Decks Museum opened on February 22, 1964. Guests who "mind thy head" (as signs warn) are able to tour the cramped, low-ceilinged quarters endured by ancient mariners.

Today, the *Columbia* sails in daylight hours with narration and sailing music as accompaniment; at night, it has figured prominently as the pirate ship in **Fantasmic!** Occasionally, it has also been transformed into a ghost ship for Halloween-related special events. Despite a dock-side tragedy in 2001 that precipitated new governmental safety regulations, the *Columbia* is still rightfully considered one of the proud flagships of Disneyland's diverse fleet.

Santa Fe & Disneyland Railroad,
aka Disneyland Railroad

MAP: Town Square, TS-1

DATES: July 17, 1955–ongoing

Before the Santa Fe & Disneyland Railroad were built, there was the little Carolwood Pacific. With the help of Disney Legends **Roger Broggie** and **Wathel Rogers**, **Walt Disney** built the one-eighth-scale train in the backyard of his home in Holmby Hills, an upscale neighborhood near Beverly Hills (how upscale? Hugh Hefner's Playboy Mansion is also located in Holmby Hills). That little train, named after the street address,

ran on a half-mile-long track that included a tunnel, trestle, switches, and other realistic features that were sometimes crafted by Disney himself.

Walt Disney's love of railroads, which dated back to his teen years when he worked on trains in the Midwest, was one of the driving passions that inspired him to create a theme park. He wanted to ride, display, and just be around trains; every concept illustration for the unbuilt Disneyland, whether the acreage was a small 16-acre rectangle in Burbank or a 60-acre triangle in Anaheim, included an old-fashioned train running around the perimeter. Naturally, when it came time to design, construct, and operate the railroad line around Disneyland, Walt Disney was closely involved every step of the way. Most of the early **souvenir books** included a photo of him in an engineer's hat and red neckerchief, waving happily from a train.

Like much of the rest of Disneyland, the railroad was built slightly smaller than full-size. Both the train and its track are about five-eighths scale, making Disneyland's railroad—its cars three feet narrower than standard train cars, its doorways closer to six feet tall than seven, its track about 36 inches wide instead of the standard 56.5—friendlier and less intimidating. The trains travel approximately 6,700 feet in a clockwise loop around the park. With stops at three stations along the line, today each round trip begun from the **Main Street** station takes about 25 minutes, making the train tour Disneyland's longest ride.

When it debuted on **Opening Day**, the train had a sponsor, the historic Santa Fe Railroad (more formally known as the Atchison, Topeka, and Santa Fe Railroad). The Santa Fe & Disneyland Railroad also had only two stops—the high-profile Main Street station, and a rustic depot in **Frontierland**. Like the tracks themselves, both stations are perched on the tall **berm** that surrounds the park. Designed by **Bill Martin** and spreading 270 feet from end to end above the Disneyland **entrance**, the Main Street station can hold 300 guests. Its interior displays have included old photographs, as well as the miniature engine and caboose from the Carolwood Pacific.

The diminutive Frontierland station, renamed New Orleans Square/Frontierland station in 1996, is based on a station design used in the Disney film *So Dear to My Heart*. Attentive fans can watch for the real working water tower just outside this station and listen for quiet, telegraph-coded passages from Walt Disney's Opening Day speech. Curiously, the Main Street and Frontierland stations aren't at the same elevation; the sign at the Main Street station marks the park's elevation at 138 feet above sea level, while the Frontierland sign claims it's five feet higher (indicating a gradual downward slope from the back of Disneyland to the front).

The history of Disneyland's railroad is a history of change. A new medieval-looking station joined the line in **Fantasyland** in 1956, but the fanciful little building was removed when **It's a Small World** arose in 1965. Fantasyland then got a new **Videopolis** station in 1985, its location a little further westward from where the earlier Fantasyland station had been; in '93 the Videopolis station became **Mickey's Toontown** depot. In 1958, an uncomplicated, futuristic platform was added to **Tomorrowland**. Further additions to the line arrived in '58 and '66, the years when the tunnels containing the **Grand Canyon Diorama** and the **Primeval Canyon Diorama** opened alongside the track between Tomorrowland and Main Street (the trains slow down noticeably during this portion of the trip for sightseeing purposes). The name of the entire line was simplified to the Disneyland Railroad in the fall of 1974, when the Santa Fe Railroad, which had started carrying only freight instead of passengers, ceased its sponsorship.

Today, the trains are pulled by one of five brightly painted steam engines. Four of the five are named after former presidents of the Santa Fe Railroad—the *C. K. Holliday* (the company's founder), the *E. P. Ripley*, the *Fred Gurley*, and the *Ernest S. Marsh*. The fifth engine, the *Ward Kimball*, is named after a Disney Legend who was a train enthusiast and a close friend of Walt Disney's.

Machinists headed by Roger Broggie built the first two 35-foot-long engines, the *C. K. Holliday* and *E. P. Ripley*, at Burbank's Disney Studios in 1955 for about $100,000; these were the only locomotives operating on Opening Day. The *Fred Gurley* was purchased, not built, by Walt Disney; it dated to 1894 and had been used in Louisiana and sold for scrap before Disney purchased it for $1,200. He spent 30 times that amount for the major overhaul needed before it could go into Disneyland service in March 1958. Built in 1925, the *Ernest S. Marsh* was still chugging along in New Jersey when Walt Disney bought it for $2,000 and had it refurbished. It began circling the park in 1959. The *Ward Kimball* is another refurbished engine that first began running in 1902; renamed and put into Disneyland service in 2005, it was the first engine added to the railroad in 46 years.

Re-dedicated simultaneously with the *Ward Kimball* was the *Lilly Belle*, a lavishly appointed observation car. Named after Walt Disney's wife, the *Lilly Belle* includes potted plants, stained glass, elegant woodwork, and velour-upholstered furniture. Though guests can't ride in it, they can still see the red car when it makes occasional appearances.

In 1955, guests either sat in traditional forward-facing, bench-seat passenger

coaches with windows or stood up in wooden "cattle cars," glimpsing the views from openings or between the horizontal slats (these seatless cars were later retrofitted with benches to make the long trip around the park more comfortable). By the time the Primeval World Diorama opened in '66, some of the cars had been converted to an open-walled design with side-facing seats that afforded better starboard views (side-facing cars are used most frequently today). Upon request, guests are sometimes allowed to sit up near the engineers or in the caboose. All guests can ride on the trains as long as they want without disembarking; many use the train not as a full-circuit journey but as a relaxing way to move around the park. As they ride, guests listen to a pre-recorded, deep-voiced narration about passing attractions voiced by actor Pierre Renoudet (who also went by the moniker Pete Renaday), not **Thurl Ravenscroft**, as is sometimes rumored.

Guests boarding the trains in 1955 bought old-fashioned-looking tickets that had stubs for each leg of the 1.3-mile journey. When A–E **ticket books** went into effect, a ride on the railroad usually cost a D ticket. By now, the number of riders on the well-traveled Disneyland trains tops 300 million, and the 50-plus years of train trips total over five million miles (equaling 10 round-trip flights to the moon). What began as Walt Disney's youthful passion and backyard hobby continues to thrive as one of the most venerated and visited attractions in Disneyland history.

Santa's Reindeer Round-Up

MAP: Frontierland, Fr-20

DATES: November 2005–January 2006; ongoing seasonally

Since 2005, the winter holidays have been celebrated in **Frontierland** with Santa's Reindeer Round-Up. Held from early November to early January, this annual event brings Mr. and Mrs. Claus, live reindeer, and Yuletide festivities to the **Big Thunder Ranch** area. Holiday arts and crafts, sing-alongs, and Disney character meet-and-greets are among the daily events.

Sherman Brothers (Robert and Richard)
(1925–2012) (1928–)

The two men behind such famous Disney songs as "The Bear Necessities" and "It's a Small World" are the Sherman Brothers. Born in 1925 and 1928, respectively, Robert and Richard first lived in Manhattan, where their father worked as a Tin Pan Alley composer. After several cross-country trips, the family settled in Beverly Hills and began learning various musical instruments. Richard attended New York's Bard College, where he majored in music and began composing, while Robert joined the army and earned a Purple Heart in the European campaign. After the war, Robert also studied at Bard College, and when both brothers graduated they teamed up to begin writing songs together.

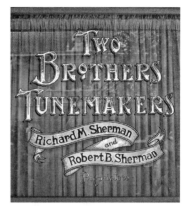

Their partnership would endure as one of the most prolific, successful pairings in music history. "Tall Paul" and "Pineapple Princess," both sung by Annette Funicello, were their first hits. In 1960 the Shermans were hired as Disney Studios' staff songwriters, and soon they were cranking out popular songs and soundtracks for such Disney screen projects as *The Parent Trap*. They also wrote a notable non-Disney hit, Johnny Burnette's "You're Sixteen." In the mid-'60s the Shermans started getting Oscar recognition—their score for *Mary Poppins* and the movie's "Chim Chim Cher-ee," both won Academy Awards. The brothers also wrote the classic songs in *The Jungle Book*, as well as Oscar-nominated music for a non-Disney movie, *Chitty Chitty Bang Bang*. Later Oscar-nominated film projects included *Bedknobs and Broomsticks* and *Tom Sawyer* (for which they also wrote the screenplay).

Disneyland would benefit from several key Sherman compositions. Who doesn't

20 Disneyland-Themed Albums

1. *Echoes of Disneyland* (1955)
2. *Music from Disneyland* (1955)
3. *A Visit to Disneyland* (1955)
4. *Walt Disney Takes You to Disneyland* (1956)
5. *A Day at Disneyland with Walt Disney and Jiminy Cricket* (1957)
6. *Slue-Foot Sue's Golden Horseshoe Revue* (1957)
7. *Meet Me Down on Main Street* (1958)
8. *Dukes of Dixieland at Disneyland* (1962)
9. *Firehouse Five Plus Two at Disneyland* (1962)
10. *The Story and Song from the Haunted Mansion* (1969)
11. *The Haunted Mansion* (1970)
12. *A Christmas Adventure in Disneyland* (1973)
13. *Disneyland's Main Street Electrical Parade* (1973)
14. *America Sings: The Original Soundtrack of the Disneyland Attraction* (1974)
15. *A Musical Souvenir of America on Parade* (1975)
16. *The Official Album of Disneyland/Walt Disney World* (1981)
17. *Big Bands at Disneyland* (1984)
18. *Disney's Happiest Celebration on Earth* (2005)
19. *A Musical History of Disneyland* (2005)
20. *Disneyland Sing-A-Long* (2008)

know their familiar theme songs for the **Enchanted Tiki Room** and **It's a Small World**? Interestingly, the Shermans originally composed the latter as a slow ballad, not as the peppy romp it later became. Other attractions showcasing their music have included **Adventure Thru Inner Space** ("Miracles from Molecules"), the **Carousel of Progress** ("There's a Great Big Beautiful Tomorrow"), and the **Many Adventures of Winnie the Pooh** ("Heffalumps and Woozles" and instrumentals).

By now Richard and Robert Sherman have been awarded several Grammy Awards, have accumulated about two dozen gold albums, had blockbuster shows on Broadway, been named to the Songwriters Hall of Fame, and been inducted as Disney Legends (in 1990). Richard currently lives in Beverly Hills; until his death in March 2012, Robert lived in London, where a popular exhibition of his paintings was held in 2002. The brothers' autobiography, *Walt's Time: From Before to Beyond*, was published in 1998; *The Boys*, a documentary that celebrates their lives while also discussing their long estrangement, was released in 2009.

Ship to Shore Marketplace

MAP: Frontierland, Fr-17

DATES: May 2011–ongoing

The Ship to Shore Marketplace appeared in 2011 next to the dock for the ***Mark Twain* Riverboat** and **Sailing Ship *Columbia***, which explains the stand's maritime theme (decorations include canvas "sails," masts, and shipping crates). Its arrival came almost three years after **Westward Ho Conestoga Wagon Fries** pulled out from a spot a little farther up the walkway in 2008. The menu is similar to the one at **Edelweiss Snacks** in **Fanta-syland**: turkey legs, chimichangas, corn on the cob, "frozen" drinks, and other take-away snacks. A nearby seating area offers views of the river traffic.

Silhouette Studio

MAP: Main Street, MS-13

DATES: January 19, 1956–ongoing

Just a few months after **Opening Day**, **Grandma's Baby Shop** suddenly departed from its tiny 100-square-foot spot on the northeastern side of **Main Street**. Fortunately the business that replaced it has lasted longer than its predecessor—the Silhouette Studio has been operating in Grandma's old location since January of 1956.

The Silhouette Studio primarily does just one thing:

hand-cut black paper silhouettes of guests' profiles. Born in Europe in the mid-1800s, this silhouette art was revived in America in the early 1900s and transplanted to Disneyland in 1955 as an interesting souvenir appropriate to Main Street's turn-of-the-century atmosphere. It's an affordable souvenir, too, because the only added expense is the frame, which can be purchased to enhance and preserve the delicate paper silhouette. What's more, the subject doesn't even have to be in the room, since the artists can work from only a photograph. Amazingly, each customized cut-out is created in only about a minute, with slightly more time needed for group portraits.

Although this enterprise may seem like a minor novelty, it has actually gotten more exposure in the park's **souvenir books** than many other Main Street businesses.

Silver Spur Supplies

MAP: Frontierland, Fr-3

DATES: Ca. 2001–ongoing

When **Bonanza Outfitters** replaced the **Pendleton Woolen Mills Dry Goods Store** in 1990, the single Bonanza Outfitters space actually had two additional businesses operating inside it—the American Buffalo Hat Company and Silver Spur Supplies. After a decade, American Buffalo left and Silver Spur expanded into its empty space, thus establishing itself as its own distinct, two-room store—"the greatest round-up of wares in the West."

The Silver Spur interior still connects to Bonanza Outfitters, and the store's back wall is still dominated by the large wooden buffalo sculpture left over from American Buffalo Hats. A large upside-down canoe hangs from the ceiling, and historic photos of famous frontier figures adorn one wall. Today the Silver Spur is light on the silver and spurs and heavy on the Western clothes, mugs, and pins. To commemorate the store's ongoing success, in 2005 a new Silver Spur pin was issued that depicted cowboy Mickey.

Sklar, Martin
(1934–)

Marty Sklar has been involved in Disneyland since 1955. Born in New Jersey in 1934, he went on to attend UCLA and became the editor of the school's *Daily Bruin*. When he was 21, Disney hired Sklar to create an old-fashioned newspaper called the *Disneyland News* for the park's debut. While this paper was being sold on **Main Street**, Sklar returned to school, graduated, and then joined the Disneyland publicity team in '56.

Working out of offices in **Town Square**, Sklar created a wide range of promotional materials, including *Vacationland* magazine, scripts for Disney TV shows, and text for Disneyland's **souvenir books** (he's listed as the sole author of the authoritative '64 and '69 hardcover editions). In the '60s Sklar worked with **Walt Disney** on new exhibits for the 1964–1965 New York World's Fair, and a decade later he was named vice president, helping to steer the creations of EPCOT and Walt Disney World. Later he was promoted to president and then vice-chairman at Walt Disney Imagineering, roles that placed him in charge of the designers who create new attractions and concepts for Disney theme parks, hotels, and cruise ships. Sklar is credited as being the only Disney employee to have assisted with all 11 Disney parks.

Now formally retired after a 54-year career, Martin Sklar is widely recognized as an authority on everything Disney and is frequently interviewed for documentaries about Disneyland. His decades of leadership brought him recognition as a Disney Legend in 2001, as well as a **Main Street window** on July 17, 2009, the 54th anniversary of the park's **Opening Day**. The tribute window is located outside the **City Hall** office where he once worked.

Skull Rock and Pirate's Cove,
aka Skull Rock Cove

MAP: Fantasyland, Fa-14

DATES: December 1960–1982

Five years after the **Pirate Ship Restaurant** opened in **Fantasyland**, a fully realized lagoon was finally built around the ship. Called both Skull Rock Cove and Pirate's Cove in Disneyland's **souvenir books**, the shallow turquoise pond was shaped like a lopsided rectangle and covered about a quarter-acre. The lagoon and ship were surrounded by prominent attractions—nearby were the **Mad Hatter's Mad Tea Party**, **Dumbo the Flying Elephant**, the **Casey Jr. Circus Train**, and the **Storybook Land Canal Boats**. A **Skyway** tower on the western bank carried gondolas of passengers directly over a corner of the lagoon (but not over the ship). A narrow walkway connected the southern shore to the ship out in the middle of the lagoon, and dining terraces lined the northern shore.

Besides the beautiful pirate ship, the most famous feature of Pirate's Cove was Skull Rock. This artificial formation was a Disney invention for the 1953 *Peter Pan* movie; J. M. Barrie's original play didn't mention a Skull Rock (the only named rock in Barrie's 1904 *Peter Pan* is Marooners' Rock, a lagoon boulder that got swamped at high tide). Disney's Skull Rock probably owes its inspiration to *King Kong*, the 1933 classic that had a Skull Island topped by a prominent skull-shaped mountain. At

Disneyland, Skull Rock was a 30-foot-tall rock-like sculpture rising on the northeastern shore. As shown in aerial photos, Skull Rock shared the same rock formation that currently holds the head of Monstro the Whale.

Skull Rock had what looked like an open mouth, craggy teeth, large open eye sockets that stared toward the ship, and a wide crack down its forehead. Waterfalls poured from the mouth and from either side of the skull. At night, the eyes lit up with an unearthly green color. Abstract volcanic rock sculptures and palm trees surrounded the rock, and trails seemed to wind through the area; all of this landscaping would have made for great climbing if only guests had been allowed to explore it. Unfortunately, this wasn't **Tom Sawyer Island**, so Skull Rock and its rugged terrain were off limits to adventurers.

Skull Rock, Pirate's Cove, and the Pirate Ship Restaurant were all removed in 1982 during the massive Fantasyland remodel. Dumbo's elephants now fly on the site where the glorious pirate ship once sat in its exotic lagoon. A more elaborate Skull Rock can still be found, however, in Adventureland—the Adventureland in Disneyland Paris, that is.

Skyfest

DATES: December 5, 1985

Culminating the celebrations for Disneyland's 30th birthday and timed to **Walt Disney's** birthdate, Skyfest was an ambitious one-day publicity stunt created by Disney Legend **Jack Lindquist**. The goal was to set a new world record by releasing a million balloons simultaneously. The launch was arranged by the GlassHouse Balloon Company, a Costa Mesa outfit owned by Treb Heining. In 1969 a teenage Heining had sold balloons at Disneyland; later it was his idea to put Mickey-shaped balloons inside larger round balloons.

Held on December 5, 1985, Skyfest began in the **parking lot**, where over 3,000 volunteers filled colored helium balloons that were released from locations along nearby Katella Avenue. Later reports had balloons landing as far away as Australia.

Skyway to Fantasyland
and Skyway to Tomorrowland

MAP: Tomorrowland, T-13; Fantasyland, Fa-12

DATES: June 23, 1956–November 9, 1994

Today, most guests wandering near the **Casey Jr. Circus Train** in **Fantasyland** are

oblivious to the alpine chalet on a little hill, half-hidden among lush trees. This chalet is the old Fantasyland station of the extinct Skyway to Fantasyland/Skyway to Tomorrowland attraction. Guests who never got to experience the Skyway may find it hard to appreciate its greatness—but great it was, especially back in the 1950s and '60s, when cable-suspended gondolas were still a decade away from becoming ubiquitous transit systems at ski resorts. Disneyland's **souvenir books** claimed that the Skyway was "the first aerial tramway of its kind in the United States," though a larger and higher-elevated aerial tramway, the Sky Ride, had operated at Chicago's Century of Progress Exposition in 1933.

Like the **PeopleMover** and **Monorail**, the Skyway was an ambitious attempt to introduce efficient public transportation into Disneyland. Unlike any other attraction, the Skyway afforded guests a lingering view of Disneyland from high above the park. The hyperbolic **attraction poster** certainly emphasized the ride's vista views, making it look as if guests were *hundreds* of feet aloft and rising on steeply pitched cables. While the ride was not quite that dramatic, the sight of Disneyland from five stories up in the air was even more breathtaking than it was at ground level, providing a full open-air view of the park's vast expanse.

The Skyway to Fantasyland and the Skyway to Tomorrowland were really the same attraction, operating in opposite directions. Both Skyways ran on the same cable, both shared the same support towers, and both connected the same two stations in Fantasyland and **Tomorrowland**. The Fantasyland station had a Swiss theme, though the inscription on the building came from *Alice in Wonderland*: "'Up above the World You fly, Like a Tea-Tray in the Sky,' said the Dormouse." The futuristic station a quarter-mile away near **Autopia** had a more Spartan design.

Guests could use their D tickets from the park **ticket books** at either station and rode in small red, blue, yellow, and green gondolas with flat roofs and no windows. Over the years, the design changed—while the 1956 originals were cylindrical and included only two individual patio-style chairs, by the mid-'60s the gondolas were rectangular and contained benches for four passengers. In the early years the ride could be taken for either a one-way pass or a seven-minute round trip, but in later decades all trips were one-way only. The altitude varied depending on where the 42 gondolas dangled along their journey, but usually they averaged a height of between 40 and 60 feet (the central suspension tower, standing tall on the hill where the Matterhorn would be built, topped out at 85 feet).

Along the way, guests got incredible views of Tomorrowland and Fantasyland.

Because it would block the Skyway's path when built, the **Matterhorn** was erected in 1959 with a passageway running east–west through its center, enabling visitors to make an exciting trip through the mountain's interior. Inside the Matterhorn, guests witnessed bobsleds hurtling through the mountain on their angled tracks. Also on view below the Skyway were the **Submarine Voyage**, **Alice in Wonderland**, the **Pirate Ship Restaurant**, and the **Casey Jr. Circus Train**.

Fallacious stories of severe accidents and even deaths have long swirled around the Skyway. All of these rumors have been exaggerated, however, and none of them pertain to the reasons the attraction finally closed in the fall of 1994. A more probable reason was the irresistible temptation for some guests to spit, litter, or pour beverages over the side of the gondolas onto visitors below. There was also the more serious possibility of an eventual calamity, plus the presence of the incongruous steel towers and cables in the charmingly remodeled Fantasyland.

After the Skyway's last celebratory run with Mickey and Minnie aboard, the Matterhorn's holes were sealed up, the Skyway towers removed, and the Tomorrowland station disappeared into memory.

Sleeping Beauty Castle

MAP: Fantasyland, Fa-2

DATES: July 17, 1955–ongoing

If Disneyland has a soul, it probably resides within the walls of Sleeping Beauty Castle. Even without seeing the castle in person, people everywhere recognize it as an iconic symbol representing not only Disneyland but the entire Walt Disney Company itself. This was probably true even before the castle was built—back in 1954, a year before Disneyland opened, viewers saw an animated castle in the opening titles of the popular *Disneyland* **TV series** and thus could have easily equated the castle with Disneyland and Disney entertainment. Later, a castle—not Disneyland's castle, but a castle nonetheless—became the centerpiece of the corporate logo that prefaces Disney movies, as well as a prominent feature of countless commercials and print ads.

Pre-construction, the early concept illustrations of Disneyland usually placed some variation of a castle at the park's center. **Herb Ryman's** landmark 1953 illustration depicted a dominating fortress towering hundreds of feet in the air and surrounded by tall, battle-worthy ramparts. What finally arose, of course,

was much smaller. Disneyland's 2000 **souvenir book** explained why the park's "regal sentinel" was scaled downward: "**Walt Disney** recalled that European castles of old were often built to intimidate the peasants. He believed a less imposing castle would appear friendlier and more inviting to Disneyland guests."

Indeed, the castle stands only 77 feet high, making it half as tall as the **Matterhorn**, two-thirds as tall as **Space Mountain**, and one basketball player taller than the **Swiss Family Treehouse**. However, its position at the north end of the **Hub**, where it can be seen from **Town Square**, makes the castle the park's ultimate visual enticement (what Walt Disney called a "wienie"). Guests can also see the twirling, gilded **King Arthur Carrousel** through the castle's entranceway, another alluring wienie drawing them to the castle courtyard.

During the actual design phase in 1954, architects briefly considered using the Snow White story as the castle's theme, but they soon decided on the Disney movie *Sleeping Beauty* instead. Nobody knew at the time exactly what the finalized castle should look like, since *Sleeping Beauty* was still early in production and wouldn't be released until 1959. Thus several European castles served as inspiration, especially Neuschwanstein, a notable Bavarian castle that predated Disneyland by only about 70 years. After reducing that fantastical sky-reaching structure down to a more intimate size, Disneyland designers implemented the same forced perspective techniques they had applied to **Main Street** buildings. For the castle, the optical trick of using bigger blocks at the bottom than at the top makes the cement walls and fiberglass towers appear to be stretching higher than they really are.

The Sleeping Beauty façade is broad, yet intimate. At moat level, the majestic face presented to the Hub spans about 35 feet across the first pair of cylindrical turrets, with the second pair set about 15 feet back toward Fantasyland. A 35-foot-wide circular courtyard in front of the castle offers paths to the **Plaza Gardens** and the **Snow White Wishing Well and Grotto**, plus a famous song lyric embedded in its pavers: "When you wish upon a star, your dreams come true." As depicted in the 1955 souvenir book, the castle has also always had a side entrance/exit that leads to a trail on the west side of the moat.

The drawbridge entrance is the main path into and through the castle. Within this entry are shops visible only upon crossing the moat—no distracting illuminated

signage mars the exterior's integrity. The top portion of the castle, according to a legendary story, was turned around, either by design or by accident, so that what was intended to be the castle's front is actually facing back into **Fantasyland**, not the Hub. Some experts claim Walt Disney asked for this change because more spires would be visible from Main Street; others suggest that he wanted to differentiate his castle from Neuschwanstein; and still others say the reversal was a designer's mistake—or Herb Ryman's idea—that Disney later approved. Whatever the explanation, the castle's architectural details, from the bartizans and crenellations and balistrariae above to the spiraled columns and gothic arches on the courtyard side, all still appear authentic.

The Disney lore is long here: there's 22-karat gold leaf on the spires; for years one spire was colored differently from the rest; what's said to be the heraldic crest of the Disney family adorns the entranceway (some heraldry researchers denounce this claim as apocryphal); a "time castle" was buried in the forecourt on Disneyland's 40th anniversary; a conspicuous bronze marker under the courtyard entrance possibly denotes the park's original geographic center before **Mickey's Toontown** was added (some historians dispute the significance of this marker); the downspouts are animal-shaped; swans occasionally glide across the moat, while swan topiaries grow off to the side; and on and on. The drawbridge, incidentally, has officially been raised and lowered twice—once on **Opening Day**, and again for a rededication in late May 1983 (*The Nickel Tour* noted many raisings and lowerings during that week in May, though only one was for the public ceremony).

Important modifications have been made to the castle since 1955. While guests today expect to see the familiar blue and pink coloring, the castle originally had gray stones at the bottom, and at one time green ivy spread across the front walls. For some celebrations, the castle gets special decorations, such as the gold trim added for the park's 50th anniversary and "icicles" for the winter holidays. Two enduring modifications came in 1957, when the **Sleeping Beauty Castle Walk-Through** debuted and the Fantasy in the Sky **fireworks** began to explode above the turrets on summer nights.

Ultimately, there has been no building more indispensable to Disneyland's history and image than Sleeping Beauty Castle. Upon its completion, artists and writers immediately championed it as the building that best represented the park's truest self, which explains why the castle has been shown on more **souvenir book** covers than all other subjects combined. Guests also

treat the castle differently—they don't usually linger at the entrance to any other land, but they do here. If you ask anyone to think of Disneyland, there's a good chance that person will immediately think of Sleeping Beauty Castle.

Along with the **Opera House**, the castle was one of the first Disneyland buildings to be finished. The Opera House was required for its initial functionality as a lumber mill. The castle, it's said, was required as an inspiration to the park's construction crews—to prove that dreams really could come true, to show them what make-believe looked like, and to remind them, finally, where Disneyland's soul was.

Sleeping Beauty Castle Walk-Through

MAP: Fantasyland, Fa-2

DATES: April 29, 1957–October 7, 2001; November 28, 2008–ongoing

Two years after it opened, **Sleeping Beauty Castle** received a significant enhancement. Not that it was conspicuous from outside the castle—in fact, the entrance to the Sleeping Beauty Castle Walk-Through was so unobtrusive in the castle's inner courtyard that unknowing guests walked right past it.

Inside, the Castle Walk-Through featured narrow stairways that led guests on a walk up into the castle's interior, eastward past 10 beautiful dioramas, across what is now called the "corridor of goons," and down to an eastern exit. The dioramas, designed primarily by **Ken Anderson** and similar to those that were later added in the **Emporium** windows on **Main Street**, retold the story of Disney's *Sleeping Beauty* movie, which didn't open until two years after the Walk-Through debuted. Large illustrated story books with ornate calligraphy, well-executed sets with dreamy colors and cinematic lighting effects, detailed figures with elaborate costumes and precise accessories, and delicate music from the Disney movie all combined to deliver an artistic exposition. An update to the art in 1977 somewhat changed the look, but not the overall spirit, of the dioramas.

One of Hollywood's royals, Shirley Temple, and the **Disneyland Band** graced the Walk-Through's opening ceremonies in 1957. Temple, it's said, donated some of the dolls used in the beautiful tableaux. For the next 44 years, millions of guests investigated the passageway into the castle. Many of those guests, it's safe to say, weren't so much fans of dioramas as they were fans of the famous castle itself and were curious to see what it was like inside

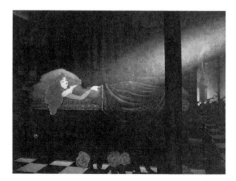

as they crossed through it, west to east. The cooling, calming effect of the dark interior was an additional draw on hot, busy days.

Though only an A-ticket attraction (see **ticket books**) for most of its first two decades, the Castle Walk-Through was always a satisfying charmer. Unfortunately, a temporary closure in 2001 quietly became permanent because of accessibility issues and refurbishment costs. The loss was a disappointing development for anyone looking to recapture some Disneyland history or trying to find some shaded serenity in **Fantasyland**. Fans rejoiced when an upgraded version reopened late in 2008, debuting rejuvenated displays and a new ground-floor viewing room for guests who couldn't negotiate the tight stairways. After such a long absence, the Walk-Through's return was a fairy-tale finish for a classic Disneyland attraction.

Snow White Adventures, aka Snow White's Scary Adventures

MAP: Fantasyland, Fa-8

DATES: July 17, 1955–ongoing

Seemingly innocent but deceptively sinister, Snow White Adventures has been charming adults and terrifying toddlers since **Opening Day**. Throughout its long history, the attraction has survived several name changes: the first **souvenir books** called it the Snow White Adventures Ride, later books amended that to Snow White Adventures, and for a while, the sign above the entrance read Snow White and Her Adventures. The biggest name change, and an acknowledgement of the main issue some parents have always had with the attraction, came in 1983, when it was rechristened Snow White's Scary Adventures. Previously, the only warning about the ride's frightening nature was posted out front, on a small sign that also included a depiction of the witch. As a result, parents generally did not realize that this was not the gentle, song-filled lark they might have expected.

Certainly some happy elements exist inside. Guests are shown what are basically highlights of the classic 1937 Disney movie, including an appearance by the prince and a scene of Dopey, Doc, and the other dwarfs cavorting to the joyous refrain of their "Silly Song." But like the movie, the attraction's imaginative, detailed settings range from the cozy and assuaging (the dwarfs' cottage, the glittering mine) to the dark and menacing (the creepy forest, the castle dungeon). Between the dwarfs' cheery song and the arrival of the passionate prince looms the evil Queen, who yanks the ride to the Dark Side with a witch-transformation scene that has traumatized kids for decades.

Interestingly, like the nearby **Peter Pan** and **Mr. Toad** attractions, the attraction's namesake never appeared among the scenery until 1983's makeover of **Fantasyland**. Early designers hoped guests would realize that *they* were embodying Snow White during the ride, experiencing her adventures the same way they experienced Peter's and Toad's. Few guests saw it that way, however, asking repeatedly where Snow White, Peter, and Toad were, so eventually all three stars were added to the attractions. But even after she was introduced as a physical presence on the cottage staircase, Snow White's appearances were far outnumbered by the witch's repeated manifestations. When the souvenir books featured photos of the ride's revamped interiors, they usually devoted much less space to the young beauty than to Her Royal Ugliness. Scary adventures, indeed.

In addition to changing the name and adding Snow White to the ride, the 1983 remodel resulted in some other notable improvements, including updated woodland vehicles and a longer ride-time. The most obvious change was to the attraction's exterior, where the simple medieval-tournament façade built in the 1950s was supplanted by a complex, well-detailed design that evoked the queen's stone castle, complete with skull decorations and a half-timbered tower over the entrance (the queen herself makes regular window appearances every 24 seconds). Inside the **queue** area, guests are now prepared for the frights to come with eerie voice effects and a dungeon display. Within the attraction, the poisoned apple laced with "sleeping death," which had formerly been a much-stolen prop, has been replaced by a hologram.

Disney Legend **Ken Anderson**, whose career had already arced from the 1937 animated movie to the 1955 attraction, also steered the 1983 enhancement. To adults, Snow White is today more impressive than ever. To kids, it is still one of the most affecting two-minute experiences in Disneyland.

Snow White Wishing Well and Grotto

MAP: Fantasyland, Fa-1

DATES: March 27, 1961–ongoing

Tucked into a quiet corner east of the **Sleeping Beauty Castle** moat, the Snow White Wishing Well and Grotto site has been a bucolic hideaway since 1961. A heart-adorned wooden bridge leads from the northeastern corner of the **Hub** to the old-fashioned, blue-roofed Wishing Well. From the bridge and the well, guests get clear views of the lovely garden Grotto, where a gentle waterfall trickles among white marble statues of Snow White, all seven of the dwarfs, and assorted woodland creatures.

Disney Legend **John Hench** was responsible for this tranquil spot. He also solved the predicament that arose when it came to install the statues, which were created as a gift to **Walt Disney** from an unnamed Italian sculptor. Intended to represent the characters as they appeared in Disney's 1937 movie, all the figures are mistakenly about three feet high—Snow White, of course, should dwarf the dwarfs. To disguise the inaccuracy, she is placed well at the back, the added distance and elevation giving the illusion of proper height disparity.

Romance is in the air here, literally. The Snow White Wishing Well emits a soft, echoing rendition of the movie's "Some Day My Prince Will Come," as sung by the movie's vocalist, Adriana Caselotti (1916–1997). Inspired by the sights and sounds of the garden, "numerous wedding proposals" are offered here, according to a caption in the 2000 **souvenir book**. More fairy tales come true when various Disney princesses make their rounds to sign autographs and have their pictures taken. All the coins tossed into the Wishing Well are given to charity.

South Seas Traders

MAP: Adventureland, A-2

DATES: June 30, 1984–ongoing

Though the **Adventureland** theme suggests exotic jungles and dangerous rivers, guests are, in reality, in the middle of Southern California, one of the world's surfing capitals. Consequently, since 1984 Adventureland has offered South Seas Traders, a beachy-keen shop selling practically everything aspiring surfers could need (except surfboards). The assortment of sun wear, flip-flops, and sunglasses would be appropriate inside a nearby Huntington Beach surf shop. Best bets are the Disney-themed Hawaiian shirts, safari gear, and Shrunken Ned, the "Head Shrink of the Jungle," who dispenses advice. Whether it's summer or not, South Seas Traders is always a fun stop across from the **Jungle Cruise**.

Souvenir Books,
aka Souvenir Guide Books,
aka Pictorial Souvenir Books

The souvenir books referenced throughout this encyclopedia were (and still are) official publications of the Walt Disney Company. As such, they are valuable resources for anyone researching Disneyland history. Sold throughout the park at many stores and souvenir stands, the books have come out nearly every year since 1955, usually with updated photos and text, and frequently with a photo of

Sleeping Beauty Castle on the front.

In early years the books cost only a quarter, a price so low that the profit on each sale was a single penny. Sometimes called souvenir guide books or pictorial souvenir books, most of the souvenir books are laid out horizontally and are approximately 11½ inches wide by 8 inches tall. Typically they have soft covers, 28–38 photo-filled pages, and chapters dedicated to each of the park's lands.

For the Disney Company, souvenir books have served several purposes. First, they have been created as beautiful pictorial keepsakes to help guests recall their visits to the park; perfectly positioned photos, imaginative artwork, and evocative text capture the spirit and atmosphere of the park for those guests who had no cameras or no luck using them (most of the books were published when clunky, unreliable cameras generated as many dark/blurry/misaimed discards as they did treasured photos). The books also welcomed first-time visitors with warm words from an avuncular **Walt Disney**, introduced Disneyland's novel hub-and-spoke layout, and described the kind of thrills to expect from each major attraction. In the early decades, the souvenir books' large maps helped guests envision Disneyland's unique geography. Though the maps usually included a key with lists of attractions, stores, and restaurants, unfortunately the maps did not identify the location of every single item on the list, only a few landmarks. Souvenir books after the '60s didn't include any maps or lists at all, reducing their efficacy as research materials.

While the spirit of the books has been consistent over the decades, the format has changed substantially. The first souvenir book, called *The Story of Disneyland*, was finished before the park was, so it was filled with artist renditions instead of actual photographs. A small 8-inch by 5-inch photo-filled book came out later that year and included a map of freeways that led to the park, revealing how foreign the whole Disneyland concept was in 1955. The '56 and '57 books, both tall verticals, were the first truly educational souvenir books and had on their back covers checklists of everything to see in Disneyland. The books from '58 to '64 all had the same 8-inch by 11-inch horizontal design, covers that blended photos with illustrations, and basically the same interior pages that were sporadically revised to accommodate important new attractions (the **Matterhorn Bobsleds** in 1959, for instance—the '60 book even had a special wraparound cover devoted to the expensive new **Nature's Wonderland** area). These early books also incorporated preview pages that tantalized guests with concept illustrations of future developments such as the **Haunted Mansion**.

At 11 inches by 10½ inches, the '65 book was almost square-shaped, and added heavy design elements and borders to the pages at the expense of large photos. The '68 book returned to the format of the 1958–1964 books; instead of the traditional castle portrait, this souvenir book featured a rather informal photo of Walt Disney signing autographs on **Main Street** (the picture had originally run in *National Geographic* in 1963). In the '70s the books all took on the horizontal format and appeared almost identical with their castle covers, save for the big photo on the back cover featuring the latest high-profile attraction that year—the **Country Bear Jamboree**, **Space Mountain**, etc.

Page counts dramatically increased in the '80s and '90s. While the covers took on creative designs that varied from year to year, the interior layouts during these years didn't change much, and the center maps of the 1950s and '60s were sorely missed. The 2000 book was a small, squarish 8½-inch by 9-inch edition dense with pages and photos. Later books returned to the horizontal format but were no longer just about Disneyland—by covering Disney California Adventure as well, the books devoted less space to the original park and thus were more functional as generic souvenirs than as detailed research tools. These more recent souvenir books still only cost about $10, and older collectible editions (priced from a few dollars for '90s books to over $100 for high-quality '50s books) are still abundantly available from dealers and online sellers as mementos of long-lost attractions.

Interestingly, **Walt Disney** himself became less of a presence in the books over the decades. He's been on many, but far from all, of the covers. Books of the '50s and '60s included his portrait and a welcoming letter, with four or five additional photos showing him laughing as a **Jungle Cruise** skipper, **Autopia** driver, or a participant in other parts of the park. Fewer photos of him appeared from the '70s to the '90s, and the 2000 book didn't include a single photo of the man the park is named after.

Occasionally the softcover books have been supplemented with special hardcover editions that are oriented vertically, are about 9 inches wide by 11½ inches tall, contain over 100 pages, and commemorate special park anniversaries. These hardcover editions broadly re-tell the highlights of Disneyland's long history. While the historical perspective is always interesting, text and photos are often duplicated from book to book, limiting their usefulness. For the researcher, the annual softcover books are more informative because, when compared side-by-side, they provide a more comprehensive picture of the year-to-year changes in Disneyland.

Space Bar

MAP: Tomorrowland, T-14, T-8

DATES: Summer 1955–September 1966

In Disneyland's first summer, a futuristic restaurant called the Space Bar opened on the eastern edge of **Tomorrowland**. The restaurant's name alluded to keyboards and outer space—two components of space age living—but it might also have been a description of the site itself, which did indeed take up a lot of space. So much space, in fact, that in 1961 a Space Bar Dance Area opened out front, and in 1967 the huge Carousel Theater rose above the ruins of the demolished Space Bar.

Early in the planning stages, the Space Bar was going to be called the Stratosnak, its automatic vending service similar to New York's famed Automats. What actually debuted was a small counter-service eatery offering fast food (burgers, chili dogs, sodas, etc.). A wall of vending machines provided some self-serve convenience, and an overall industrial design emphasized convenience over comfort.

A half-dozen years later, the whole enterprise was remade into a bigger, more inviting restaurant without vending machines. Rows of plastic chairs with little side tables provided functional seating on a covered patio with a Tomorrowland view. In 1967 the Space Bar became a displaced bar when the **Carousel of Progress** started spinning inside the Carousel Theater. A smaller Space Bar, reduced to a mere snack stand, reopened that year about 150 feet to the west underneath the loading area of the new **PeopleMover** attraction. A decade later the **Lunching Pad** replaced this Space Bar sequel.

Space Girl and Space Man

MAP: Park, P-18

DATES: Summer 1955–1970s

Space Girl and Space Man roamed Tomorrowland for about two decades. The Space Man role was inaugurated in 1955 soon after Disneyland opened; so popular was the character that crowds would trail along behind him as he walked. Later, Space Girl joined him for Tomorrowland treks. In 2007, **cast members** in the **Opera House** identified this pair as K7 (Space Girl) and K8 (Space Man), setting up a joke about a Space Dog named K9 that was never made.

The fit young space couple rode on attractions, shook hands with guests, and promoted a happy and energetic technological future as the "symbols of Tomorrowland," as they were labeled in Disneyland's '59 **souvenir book**. The pair wore big cartoonish outfits that were definitely futuristic but hardly realistic. The couple's varied wardrobe included clothing made of both white and foil-looking material, silver boots, huge glass helmets with antennae on top, thick padded rings for their forearms and shins, and little oxygen tanks to wear on their backs. Space Girl sometimes wore either a white pantsuit or a short white dress. Silliest of all was her cape—super-fashion taken right out of super-hero comic books.

Randy Bright, one of those cast members who donned the Space Man's silver space suit, later wrote a history of the park called *Disneyland: Inside Story* and eventually oversaw new attractions as vice president of concept development.

Real space men did eventually arrive in Disneyland. In 1969 the **Tomorrowland Stage** broadcast a live TV feed of Apollo astronauts Neil Armstrong and Buzz Aldrin walking on the moon. Eight years later, Scott Carpenter, Gordon Cooper, Wally Schirra, and Alan Shepard were among the astronauts on hand for **Space Mountain's** debut.

Space Mountain, aka Rockin' Space Mountain

MAP: Tomorrowland, T-18

DATES: May 4, 1977–ongoing

Disneyland's second-tallest structure opened in **Tomorrowland** in 1977 at a cost of about $20 million. This dollar figure made Space Mountain the most expensive attraction in the park at the time and the first to cost more than what the entire park had cost to build in 1955. For its money, the Disney Company got a futuristic cone in gleaming white that reached 118 feet high and covered approximately three-quarters of an acre. Space Mountain's crown of slender spires looms high above the southeastern border of the park, and the exterior beams that slope up the mountain's cone intensify the sense of majestic height.

The idea for a roller coaster attraction called the Space Port, which closely resembled Space Mountain but also included tracks spiraling down the *outside* of the structure, was drawn up by Disney Legend **John Hench** around 1964. The Space Port would have been a dramatic new highlight for the mid-decade redesign of Tomorrowland, but the high-priced attraction wasn't doable at the time, not with the nascent Walt Disney World project starting to eat up funds (in addition, computer technology still needed to catch up with the Imagineers' imaginations).

Space Mountain debuted in Orlando in early 1975, where it immediately drew raves from guests and roller coaster aficionados. Construction on Disneyland's Space Mountain began that same year in the area once used by the old **Flying Saucers**. The Anaheim cone was about 60 feet shorter than its Orlando sibling, and its 200-foot diameter about 100 feet smaller. Plus, the Disneyland mountain had only one interior track instead of the two in the Florida version. According to *Disneyland: The First Quarter Century*, over a million man-hours went into Space Mountain's design and construction in Anaheim. The finished product was shown off with a beautiful **attraction poster** of streaking rockets set against a galactic background; the **souvenir books** of the late '70s presented glorious evening photos of the glowing building on their back covers.

Opening in May of 1977 to some of the longest lines in Disneyland's history, Space Mountain propelled the park to an attendance milestone: 1977 was the first year annual attendance eclipsed the 10 million mark. Guests were eager to see the second peak in the park's "mountain range"—the first, the 147-foot-tall **Matterhorn**, had been erected in 1959, 104-foot **Big Thunder Mountain** would follow in 1979, and 87-foot **Splash Mountain** would be built 10 years after that. But Space Mountain wasn't really competing with the Matterhorn or anything else at Disneyland. Instead, it was a contender in the group of

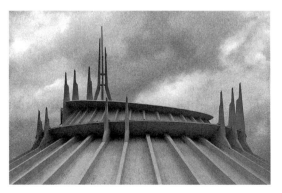

dynamic new roller coasters luring teens to other Southern California theme parks in the 1970s. To zoom ahead of their rivals, Disney designers came up with a unique twist on the coaster concept that has now been validated with 30 years of success.

The Disney innovation of a roller coaster set in the darkness of space is simple in conception but sophisticated in execution. After waiting in a **queue** winding through long, narrow passageways, over 1,800 guests an hour can slip into sleek open-cockpit rockets and hurtle for three minutes through two-thirds of a mile of unlit indoor track. The darkness makes the velocity seem much faster than the 30 miles per hour the rockets reach, and the banked curves and dips seem more thrilling because they're unseen and unanticipated. Air blasts from fans and the rushing

Estimated Costs of 22 Disneyland Projects
(Dollar figures represent approximate costs at the time
and have not been adjusted for inflation.)

- $100–125 million: Indiana Jones Adventure (1995)
- $85 million: Splash Mountain (1989)
- $70 million: Finding Nemo Submarine Voyage (2007)
- $30 million: Star Tours (1987); The Many Adventures of Winnie the Pooh (2003)
- $20 million: Space Mountain (1977); Light Magic Parade (1997)
- $17 million: Disneyland (1955); the Haunted Mansion (1969); *Captain EO* (1986)
- $16 million: Big Thunder Mountain Railroad (1979)
- $15 million: New Orleans Square (1966); Innoventions Dream Home (2008)
- $8 million: Carousel of Progress/Carousel Theater (1967); Pirates of the Caribbean (1967); Bear Country (1972)
- $2.5 million: Submarine Voyage (1959); Nature's Wonderland (1960)
- $1.5 million: Matterhorn Bobsleds (1959)
- $1 million: Monorail (1959)
- $375,000: Grand Canyon Diorama (1958)
- $250,000: Swiss Family Treehouse (1962)

sounds of the rockets themselves intensify the sense of speed. Enhancing the interstellar atmosphere are starry effects (created by floor-mounted disco balls), spinning galaxies, asteroids that have at times looked suspiciously like giant cookies, and a huge loading-area prop that echoes the *Discovery* spaceship from *2001: A Space Odyssey*. Adding heft to the building at its opening were nearby space-themed structures that also debuted in '77, among them the **Space Place** and the **Space Stage**. Adding legitimacy to the whole enterprise were six of the original seven Mercury astronauts who attended the ride's opening day festivities (the seventh, Gus Grissom, had died in an Apollo 1 fire in '67).

Two decades after it opened, Space Mountain started to undergo changes. Fast-paced onboard music was added in 1997. In 1998 the white exterior was painted in the bronzes and greens that adorned other attractions in the remodeled Tomorrowland. In preparation for the park's 50th anniversary, in 2003 the whole attraction closed for two years to replace the track, give the rockets a new look, update the **queue** area with a new silver spaceship, and restore the building's white exterior. The original entrance ramp is gone, replaced with a walkway that goes above the **Magic Eye Theater**. Souvenir photos are now snapped at the end of the trip, much like the pre-splash photos at Splash Mountain, with Spaceport Document Control at the exit handling the transactions.

A nighttime variation of the ride called Rockin' Space Mountain, which debuted as Rock-It Mountain in the summer of 2006, brings new energy, new psychedelic lighting effects, new narration from a rock DJ, and new high-powered music to the space-y interior. And every September and October since 2009, special Ghost Galaxy effects have added Halloween chills to Space Mountain's thrills. If anything, today Space Mountain is farther out of this world than it's ever been.

Space Place

MAP: Tomorrowland, T-16

DATES: Summer 1977–1996

When **Space Mountain** started drawing crowds into **Tomorrowland's** eastern corner, a new fast food restaurant opened up in the base of the Space Mountain complex to feed hungry space travelers. The Space Place was a large counter-service facility with seating for hundreds of guests. Pizza, hot dogs, salads, and ice cream were the main menu items. Special birthday celebrations and group parties were also available. Interestingly, the Space Place served Coke and Pepsi simultaneously—sponsorship arrangements at other Disneyland eateries have usually precluded one of the rival beverages. In fact, for years insiders informally divided the park in two, with Pepsi generally being served in the western half and Coke in the eastern half.

Despite having a busy attraction next door, the Space Place always seemed to have more space than patrons, and as its popularity gradually dwindled its operating hours gradually shrank. Early in 1996 the Space Place was replaced by a temporary new attraction, the **Toy Story Funhouse**. Two years later this area was subsumed within the spacious **Redd Rockett's Pizza Port**.

Space Station X-1, aka Satellite View of America

MAP: Tomorrowland, T-5

DATES: July 17, 1955–February 17, 1960

With more artists than cash available to the park in 1955, **Walt Disney** decided to install an elaborate painting instead of an elaborate attraction in a central building of **Tomorrowland**. In keeping with the land's space age theme, the exhibit room was called Space Station X-1, its position supposedly in orbit above the rotating Earth.

The lovely but overly dramatic **attraction poster** showed guests thousands of miles above the earth with all of North America below, but actually the "space platform" (as the **souvenir books** called it) included a painted representation of the view from only 90 miles above the United States. For three minutes, the round room slowly revolved past a beautiful, detailed landscape painting that surrounded the perimeter. Created by two Disney Legends, **Claude Coats** and **Peter Ellenshaw**, the painting was necessary because photos from space had not yet been taken, since the first true satellite, *Sputnik 1*, wouldn't be launched until October 1957.

Inside Space Station X-1, guests had a broad view that began with the East Coast at sunrise, concluded with the West Coast at sunset, and showcased a daylight panorama of all the mountains and plains in between. Since the entire country was shown in three minutes, this implied that guests were orbiting at about 60,000 miles per hour. Logically impressive, yes, but viscerally thrilling, no, and so admission into the languid, sparsely attended viewing chamber cost only an A ticket from the park's **ticket book**. To keep current with all the exciting satellite developments of '58 (the year of America's own first satellite launch, *Explorer 1*), that year Space Station X-1 was renamed Satellite View of America. Unfortunately, audiences still weren't boarding. Two years later the lights went out on the space exhibit and went up on its **Art of Animation** exhibit replacement just in time to promote Disney Studios' latest animated movies.

Spirit of Refreshment

MAP: Tomorrowland, T-15

DATES: May 22, 1998–ongoing

The reintroduction of the red-and-white *Moonliner*

rocket in 1998 brought with it a new beverage stand with a matching red-and-white logo. That logo, of course, belongs to Coca-Cola, and their **Tomorrowland** counter next to **Redd Rockett's Pizza Port** is called the Spirit of Refreshment. This is Coke's latest Disneyland establishment, the first being the venerable **Refreshment Corner** (aka Coke Corner) on **Main Street**.

If presentation is everything, the Spirit of Refreshment has the most appropriate presentation of any snack stand in the park. Here at the base of a towering rocket, **cast members** will sometimes launch plastic Coke bottles into the air and catch them again before serving.

Splash Mountain

MAP: Bear Country/Critter Country, B/C-9

DATES: July 17, 1989–ongoing

In the 1980s Disneyland designers were eager to put a high-profile thrill ride in **Bear Country**, which had become Bore Country for many guests. Something new and dramatic was needed to reinvigorate, and perhaps even redefine the northwestern corner of the park. That something turned out to be Splash Mountain.

The last and shortest of the four peaks in the Disneyland "mountain range" (also including the **Matterhorn**, **Space Mountain**, and **Big Thunder Mountain**), the 87-foot-high Splash Mountain covers two acres of what was originally the **Indian Village** in **Frontierland**. Though it's in the same "thrill ride" category as the other Disneyland mountains, Splash Mountain is different from the rest in that its thrills aren't apparent until the very end of the ride. While the other mountain attractions are fast-moving roller coasters with rapid twists, turns, and dips, Splash Mountain is, for the first 75 percent of the experience, a gentle musical cruise more akin to **It's a Small World**.

Actually, Splash Mountain's heritage most likely dates back to the early 1900s, when the Old Mill water ride on Coney Island took visitors on a winding, scenic trip. On Splash Mountain, guests drift in hollow log boats for about a half-mile through amiable cavern settings reminiscent of the 1946 Disney film *Song of the South*, with the movie's Oscar-winning hit, "Zip-A-Dee-Doo-Dah," playing in the background near the end of the ride (one of the names originally considered for the attraction was Zip-A-Dee-Doo-Dah River Run). Cute critters ranging from opossum families to croaking frogs sing the happy "How Do You Do" song while a simple plot unfolds about Brer Rabbit eluding the bumbling villains Brer Fox and Brer Bear.

About seven minutes into the 10-minute cruise, however, the mood begins to darken. The singing creatures' faces grow worrisome, ominous vultures appear, and the river leaves its cozy interior and seems to point upward to the distant **Fantasyland** sky. Only in the ride's last moments do guests fully understand what puts the splash in Splash Mountain—a thrilling water plunge reminiscent of another historic Coney Island favorite, the thrilling Shoot-the-Chutes ride. Diving down a 52-foot slope at a 47-degree angle, Splash Mountain's logs hit 40 miles per hour as they zoom beneath an overhang of thorny briars and ram into a pool of water that sends waves splashing across the bow (and usually all over the guests). The logs travel so rapidly that few guests see the sign at the bottom that reads "Drop In Again Sometime."

The **souvenir books** of the late '80s and early '90s proudly touted Splash Mountain as a record-setter, "the world's steepest, highest, scariest, wildest adventure." Signs along the **queue** warn guests that they "may get wet," understating the potential soak factor of a heavily front-loaded log nosediving hard into a splash pool. Atten-

tive guests might notice that some of that splash isn't actually the result of the logs plummeting down, but from water cannons shooting water up into the air. Inside the log, the thrill is perhaps the most intense in Disneyland; from the walkway out front, the screams, five-story nose-dive, explosion of water, and sudden disappearance of the guests and logs create as much concern as fascination. Fortunately, a happy ending built around an enormous set piece, the jubilant *Zip-A-Dee Lady* showboat, brings damp guests, and a laughing Brer Rabbit, home safely.

When it was first dedicated on Disneyland's 34th birthday after five years of planning and construction, Splash Mountain brought with it **Critter Country**, a successful update of the Bear Country theme that had existed since 1972. Lines for the new attraction immediately became some of the longest in Disneyland's history—but just as robust were the glowing reviews from guests. Among the many satisfactual surprises along the way are the **Audio-Animatronic** characters themselves. Over 100 of them populate the caves, most of them recognizable as recycled entertainers from the **America Sings** attraction that once spun inside **Tomorrowland's** Carousel Theater from 1974 to '88. Chickapin Hill is the name of the mountain's peak, and the Brer Bear is voiced by Nick Stewart, the same actor who vocalized the character in the 1946 movie. And just as guests begin their final drop down the mountain, a camera snaps a photo that is viewable at **Professor Barnaby Owl's Photographic Art Studio** just outside the exit. All this and more add up to an immensely popular attraction that at full capacity pumps over 2,000 guests an hour through its caves. Fortunately, **FASTPASS** tickets offer some line relief (for obvious water-related reasons, lines are longer in summer and during the day than in winter and at night).

Some estimate that Splash Mountain cost an extraordinary $85 million to build, but few guests would say it wasn't money well spent. The **attraction poster** gets it right, depicting the three Brers (Fox, Bear, and Rabbit) in a hollow log splashing down the mountain, and only one of the three is laughing.

Terrifying to some, hilarious to others, and entertaining to all, Splash Mountain is a zip-a-dee-doo-dah-dazzler.

Spring Fling

DATES: April 14, 1962–ca. 1972 (seasonal)

Hoping to generate some off-season excitement, Disneyland executives created a special all-park event called the Spring Fling. It was first held on April 14, 1962 and was then repeated one weekend night each spring for about a decade. Though the name conjures images of bright sunshine and gambols among blooming flowers, the Spring Fling was a nighttime event that began at 8:00 or 8:30 PM and continued past midnight to as late as 1:30 AM. Guests needed to buy a special ticket to attend (in 1972 that ticket cost $6 per person), but that admission included "unlimited use of all adventures and attractions." "Unlimited use" was a new concept in the '60s and so made the Spring Flings especially popular. Adding to the fun were special musical acts, dancing, and free prizes. "Get into the Fling of Things," read the welcoming flyer—and guests certainly did, until the fling was finally flung in the early '70s.

> ## 13 Attractions, 13 Theme Songs
>
> 1. Adventure Thru Inner Space: "Miracles from Molecules"
> 2. Carousel of Progress: "There's a Great Big Beautiful Tomorrow"
> 3. Casey Jr. Circus Train: "Casey Junior"
> 4. Enchanted Tiki Room: "The Tiki, Tiki, Tiki Room"
> 5. Grand Canyon Diorama: "Grand Canyon Suite"
> 6. It's a Small World: "It's a Small World"
> 7. The Haunted Mansion: "Grim Grinning Ghosts"
> 8. Mad Hatter's Mad Tea Party: "A Very Merry Un-Birthday (to You)"
> 9. Peter Pan Flight: "You Can Fly! You Can Fly! You Can Fly!"
> 10. Pirates of the Caribbean: "Yo Ho (A Pirate's Life for Me)"
> 11. Mine Train: "The Mine Train Song"
> 12. Rocket Rods: "Magic Highways of Tomorrow"
> 13. Swiss Family Treehouse: "The Swisskapolka"

Stage Coach

MAP: Frontierland, Fr-21

DATES: July 17, 1955–February 10, 1960

Though it must have seemed like a good idea at the time, the Stage Coach proved to be one of Disneyland's more problematic and dangerous attractions. Also occasionally spelled as Stagecoach in the park's **souvenir books**, the three C-ticket coaches

(see **ticket books**) were beautiful wooden vehicles with large yellow wheels, gaudy yellow flourishes along the sides, the name Disneyland Stage Lines painted above the doors, and seating for about a dozen guests (half inside, half on the top, with even a "shotgun" space available next to the coachman). As mentioned in a photo caption in the '57 souvenir book, these were Concord-style stages—that is, they echoed the luxurious design created for the famous overland stagecoaches of the mid-1800s by the Abbot-Downing Company of Concord, New Hampshire. When **Frontierland's** wilderness territory was remodeled and the neighboring **Mule Pack** was rechristened the Rainbow Ridge Mule Pack, the stage was also renamed in June of '56 as the Rainbow Mountain Stage Coaches.

Teams of four horses from the **Pony Farm** pulled the stages through the same area traversed by the mules and the **Conestoga Wagons** (all three attractions loaded their passengers in the vicinity of today's **Big Thunder Mountain Railroad** boarding area). The operation was certainly photogenic—Disneyland's hardcover books included a picture of vice president Nixon smiling from a window, and **Walt Disney** wore a cowboy hat when he posed next to the stage. The hyperbolic **attraction poster** included an illustration of galloping horses, even though they rarely broke out of a trot—at least, they weren't supposed to. Unfortunately, startling noises from trains, ships, and other attractions caused the horses to jump and run occasionally. When several of the top-heavy coaches capsized and spilled guests into the Frontierland dust, the whole enterprise was shut down permanently in 1960.

Stage Door Café

MAP: Frontierland, Fr-5

DATES: September 1, 1978–ongoing

The Stage Door Café is a counter-service option for a quick **Frontierland** meal. For years the fast-food fare didn't stray far from the basic burgers-dogs-fries theme, but lately some more varied items have appeared on the menu, including fish and chips, chicken strips, and gourmet coffee drinks. The café is adjacent to the **Golden Horseshoe** (hence the café's name), and offers views of **Tom Sawyer Island** from its outdoor tables.

Starcade

MAP: Tomorrowland, T-19

DATES: May 4, 1977–ongoing

Guests waiting on line for **Space Mountain** may not realize that the upstairs **queue** takes them past what used to be the upper floor of Disneyland's main video arcade. Called Starcade, in keeping with the rocket themes of **Star Tours** and other space age establishments in the neighborhood, the illuminated complex once spread over two stories and housed hundreds of arcade games; however, the upper story has been closed for years. A 30-foot-long X-Wing fighter from *Star Wars* used to be suspended above the escalator connecting the two floors, but as of 2011 that ship hangs in the **Star Trader** store.

Even with only one floor of games, the Starcade is a popular, noisy place, a perplexing fact to some guests who wonder why anyone would pay for Disneyland admission and then spend time playing indoor arcade games (they've probably wondered the same thing about **Innoventions**, which has offered the same video game consoles as those that guests can play at home). Back in September 1985, *MAD* magazine parodied this same incongruity with a cartoon showing kids being bored inside a Disney park until they finally get to the arcade.

Drawing fans to the current one-story Starcade is a clever mix of addictive faves from decades past and the newest technology available (for $4 a pop), including simulated rides down ski slopes, on race tracks, or into space—"Something for every player," touts the Disneyland website.

Star Tours

MAP: Tomorrowland, T-24

DATES: January 9, 1987–ongoing

In the 1970s Disney's own live-action adventure movies—especially *The Black Hole* and *Island at the Top of the World*—failed to draw the huge audiences of Universal's *Jaws* and 20th Century Fox's *Star Wars*. This meant that in the early '80s, when Disney designers were considering a new attraction to replace the slowly decaying **Adventure Thru Inner Space** in the first right-hand building in **Tomorrowland**, they had to look outside the company's own film oeuvre for successful movie tie-ins.

So fruitful was the resulting pairing with George Lucas that eventually three separate Lucas-assisted attractions would open in Disneyland—the *Captain EO* film of 1986, the following year's Star Tours, and 1995's **Indiana Jones Adventure**. Lucas himself must have enjoyed the irony of landing Star Tours inside Disneyland; not only had he been a frequent park visitor in the 1950s and '60s, but his *Star Wars* script had been rejected by Disney Studios in the mid-'70s.

The curving exterior of the Star Tours building was thematically re-painted with zooming StarSpeeders to distance the new outer space attraction from its old Inner Space days. Inside, Star Tours presents a high-energy amplification of what the old **Rocket to the Moon** attraction had started doing three decades before: sit guests in a flight simulator and show them a movie of a space voyage. Rocket to the Moon, **Flight to the Moon**, and **Mission to Mars** in the '70s all used primitive flexible-seat technology and small circular screens that paled in comparison to the intense gut-wrenching effects possible in the mid-'80s.

In the original Star Tours, 40 guests at a time were strapped into futuristic StarSpeeder 3000s with a first-person view of a wide movie screen in front of them. Ostensibly guests were passengers on a quick, uneventful jaunt to the forest moon of Endor, but unfortunately the novice pilot (voiced by Paul "Pee-Wee Herman" Reubens) quickly lost his way and crashed into the middle of a battle scene straight out of the *Star Wars* trilogies. Intimidating Imperial cruisers loomed, enemy TIE fighters and friendly Rebel X-Wings darted nearby, and explosions echoed as the StarSpeeder burst through a glassy "iceteroid." The ship frantically maneuvered through a lethal dogfight, negotiated the dreaded Death Star's claustrophobic trench, raced up to light speed, and thundered back to its hangar for a final crashing career.

Supplementing the vigorous visuals were the realistic effects delivered by the flight-simulation seats, which shook and shuddered in time with the effects onscreen. So intense was the heart-pounding, six-minute ordeal that **cast members** checked seatbelts as assiduously as if Star Tours were an inverted roller coaster, and the signs out front had some of the longest health warnings in the park.

Throughout the Star Tours experience, obvious and not-so-obvious references

to the *Star Wars* movie universe and Disneyland's own past added fascinating fun to the thrills of the ride. The actual droids from the film, C-3PO and R2-D2, were on hand, with Anthony Daniels reprising his C-3PO vocals. Admiral Ackbar from *Return of the Jedi* supervised the **queue** area, an announcer paged a land speeder with the license plate THX1138 (Lucas's first feature film), and even George Lucas himself made an appearance—his name was pronounced in reverse over the intercom and, in the film played inside the StarSpeeder, he was quickly glimpsed ducking as the ship hurtled toward him and came to a screeching halt (some experts dispute this last Lucas sighting and say it was an anonymous actor). Sharp-eyed and sharp-eared Disneyland fans also picked out the Mighty Microscope from Adventure Thru Inner Space in the film's first hangar sequence, an announcement asking for

Tom Morrow from Flight to the Moon, two armatures from **America Sings** birds in a droid-assembly room, and lots of interesting artifacts floating by on conveyor belts in the queue's Droidnostics Center.

When it debuted in early '87 at a cost estimated to be $30 million, Star Tours generated lines that extended all the way out to **Town Square**. In honor of its newest attraction, Disneyland even presented its inaugural guests with celebratory digital watches; exactly 10 years later, another special commemorative ceremony was held, this one with actress Carrie Fisher on hand. Originally the Mars candy company sponsored the flight, but Energizer later took over, its presence acknowledged with a series of "Keeps On Going" posters near the exit. That exit still leads to an even more conspicuous commercial interest—dizzy with Star Tours visions, departing passengers lurch out of the ride and straight into a "duty free" shop, the **Star Trader** store, and its galaxy of *Star Wars* merchandise.

On July 27, 2010 the first iteration of Star Tours departed for the last time. Officially reopened on June 3, 2011, Star Tours: The Adventures Continue is an acclaimed re-imagining that introduces a revised queue area, new film footage, multiple paths through the plot, and 3-D technology. Now more than ever, Star Tours is a star attraction.

Star Trader

MAP: Tomorrowland, T-22

DATES: November 21, 1986–ongoing

What had been the Character Shop since 1967 became the Star Trader store in 1986. The new store's opening came six weeks before the neighboring **Star Tours** attraction started to take millions of guests into hyperspace. True to **Tomorrowland**, the colorful neon out front shows astronaut Mickey tumbling through space.

Just like the old Character Shop, the Star Trader boasts one of the park's biggest retail interiors. At over 5,000 square feet, it's a space big and tall enough to suspend a 30-foot-long replica of a *Star Wars* X-Wing from the ceiling. The Star Trader has space-themed murals on the walls, glowing 12-foot saucers above the floor, and shelves filled with Star Tours merchandise. The Star Trader, however, offers something no other Disneyland store does—the Force, in force. Hundreds of different *Star Wars*-related items are on display, everything from posters to collectible models. One of the most popular activities here has been the "build your own light saber" kiosk for customized weaponry. When *Toy Story* and *Toy Story 2* became blockbusters in 1995 and '99, merchandise for those films temporarily stocked the shelves throughout this fun store.

State Fair

DATES: Fall 1987–fall 1988 (seasonal)

To boost off-season attendance in the 1980s, Disneyland staged several long-running special events. Between 1986's **Circus Fantasy** and 1988–1989's **Blast to the Past** was a celebration called State Fair. Held in the fall of 1987 and '88, the fair was a spirited simulation of the real thing held annually in most states across the U.S.

Disneyland's State Fair filled **Main Street** and the **Hub** with traditional carnival attractions that ranged from ring-toss games to quilt displays. Guests were divided in their opinions of holding a fair—a rather mundane type of event—at the one-of-a-kind Disneyland. While some visitors were amused by the old-fashioned midway booths and the pig races over at **Big Thunder Ranch**, purists couldn't believe that such ordinary attractions were being prominently showcased in a park famous for its innovation. They also pointed out that **Walt Disney** himself had once declared that Disneyland would be a Ferris wheel-free zone—yet a Ferris wheel for the State Fair stood right at the main **entrance** to the park (in the second year, the 12-seat Ferris wheel was moved to **Frontierland**).

Less popular in its second autumn than it was in the first, Disneyland's State Fair permanently closed with little fanfare, and the park quickly ramped up for its busy **holiday season**.

Storybook Land Canal Boats

MAP: Fantasyland, Fa-15

DATES: June 16, 1956–ongoing

In Disneyland's second summer, **Walt Disney** finally got the charming boat ride he'd wanted all along. Limited on time and money early in 1955, he'd had to settle for the feeble **Canal Boats of the World** attraction that sputtered noisily across one undeveloped acre at the back of **Fantasyland**. However, even as that ignoble attraction was operating, plans were already underway for a huge remodel that began in the fall of '55 and lasted into the following spring. Official dedication ceremonies were held on June 18, 1956, with some of TV's Mouseketeers on hand to help celebrate.

When the seven-minute attraction started up again, it did so with verdant little knolls in place of the muddy slopes that had formerly rimmed the canals. Many of the carefully manicured miniature trees and flowers were planted in their original containers to stunt their growth. A patchwork quilt made of plants lined one hill, and adorable villages and palaces taken from classic Disney animation dotted the once-barren

Names of the Storybook Land Canal Boats

1. *Alice*
2. *Ariel*
3. *Aurora*
4. *Belle*
5. *Cinderella*
6. *Daisy*
7. *Faline*
8. *Fauna*
9. *Flora*
10. *Flower*
11. *Katrina*
12. *Merryweather*
13. *Snow White*
14. *Tinker Bell*
15. *Wendy*

banks. Among the meticulously detailed displays on view were windmills and houses from *The Old Mill* and *Three Little Pigs* cartoons, gardens inspired by *Peter Pan*, Geppetto's village and toy shop from *Pinocchio*, the *Cinderella* castle and coach, and structures from *The Adventures of Ichabod and Mr. Toad* and *Alice in Wonderland*. Built mainly from wood and fiberglass, all the buildings were built on a one-twelfth scale, meaning six-foot doorways became six-inch doorways. So well-crafted were the miniatures that the metal hinges on the tiny doors actually worked (a necessity for changing interior bulbs). To observe such intricate beauty cost only a C ticket from the Disneyland **ticket book** in the 1950s, then a D in the '60s and '70s.

Disney Legends **Morgan "Bill" Evans**, **Ken Anderson**, and **Fred Joerger** designed the new grounds and buildings. A 1994 update added scenes from more recent Disney movies, including *Aladdin* and *The Little Mermaid*, all built with the same careful skill and gentle spirit to keep this a lovely attraction. Among the subtle details guests like to watch for are the blinking eye on Monstro the Whale and the steam he periodically emits from his blowhole. Veteran guests recognize the lighthouse out front as the old ticket booth used in the days when guests had to pay their way for each individual attraction.

As they did in the '50s, guests today observe the scenes while sitting in low-slung *bateaux* similar to those on Northern European canals and rivers (though Storybook

Land's upgraded boats are battery-powered). Costumed **cast members** drive the quiet boats along a track submerged in 465,000 gallons of water. These canal captains deliver live narration just like **Jungle Cruise** skippers do, though the Storybook script isn't fraught with the jungle's dangers and opportunities for punning humor.

Because guests are required to climb in and out of small free-floating boats, over the years this attraction has unfortunately generated a few bumps and bruises. Despite the occasional mishaps, the Storybook Land Canal Boats attraction has endeared itself to millions of visitors, and it's said to have been one of Walt Disney's personal favorites.

Story Book Shop, aka Western Printing Book Shop

MAP: Main Street, MS-3

DATES: July 17, 1955–April 1, 1995

One of the original investors in Disneyland was Western Printing and Lithographing, a Wisconsin company also known simply as Western Publishing. Among Western's imprints were two popular Disney lines that dated back to the 1930s: Little Golden Books and Big Golden Books.

With hundreds of children's titles in its back catalog, Western Publishing was there on Disneyland's **Opening Day** with a children's bookstore on **Main Street**. The Story Book Shop's small site was off the street and at the back of the **Crystal Arcade** building. Mattel bought up Western Publishing in the 1980s, and a decade later the Story Book Shop came to the end of its last chapter. After surviving almost 40 years of changes on Main Street, the shop disappeared during a 1995 remodel of the Crystal Arcade.

Strawhatters

DATES: 1956–ongoing

The Strawhatters were a popular New Orleans-style jazz combo that started playing at Disneyland in 1956. Swingin' Dixieland tunes have always been their core repertoire. In its early years the group generally played on a small gazebo stage in **Frontierland** several times a day; footage of the Strawhatters playing here while the *Mark Twain* glided behind them made it into the 1956 featurette *Disneyland, U.S.A.* (that gazebo was removed in the early '60s). The Strawhatters have also performed at **Grad Nite** and other special events. Today, straw-hatted musicians on **Main Street** often inspire nearby Disney characters to break out some joyous dance moves.

Like the **Dapper Dans**, the Strawhatters have occasionally rotated in new members, but early incarnations of the group usually included a pianist, drummer, trumpeter, trombonist, and clarinetist. The five men were shown in Disneyland's 1965 **souvenir book** wearing gray plaid jackets, black pants, red bow ties, and the straw boaters that lent them their name. Disneyland Records released a Strawhatters record called *Dixieland at Disneyland* in 1957; the group also made it onto the *Slue-Foot Sue's Golden Horseshoe Revue* record that same year.

The group's name isn't unique; a non-Disney TV variety show called *The Strawhatters* aired in the summer in 1953 and '54. Additionally, other groups have used the same name and hats while featuring different instruments (often banjos).

Stroller Shop

MAP: Park, P-6

DATES: July 17, 1955–ongoing

Since **Opening Day**, toddler-laden guests have made the handy Stroller Shop one of their first stops. A prominent location at the **entrance** has always handled the rentals. Originally, guests had to walk through the turnstiles to get a stroller, but as of January 2010, a new location outside and to the east of the turnstiles offers easy access before guests have even entered the park. Renters who lose track of their strollers (but hopefully not the strollees) can get free replacements inside **Tomorrowland** at the **Star Trader** store. Baby Jogger strollers with canopies rented for $15 per day in 2011. Also available at the Stroller Shop are wheelchairs for $32 and ECVs (electric convenience vehicles) for $70.

Stromboli's Wagon

MAP: Fantasyland, Fa-10

DATES: Ca. 1983–ongoing

So the villainous puppet master in *Pinocchio* warrants his own souvenir stand, but the wise Jiminy Cricket doesn't? How does that work? Guests can puzzle over that conundrum while shopping at this elaborately decorated wagon parked at the back of **Fantasyland** near the **Village Haus** restaurant. Candy, sunglasses, postcards, and small souvenirs are the staples here, making the wagon (and the adjacent fruit cart) a convenient stop before heading down the Big Thunder Trail to **Frontierland**.

Submarine Voyage,
aka Finding Nemo Submarine Voyage

MAP: Tomorrowland, T-10

DATES: June 14, 1959–September 8, 1998; June 11, 2007–ongoing

Technically speaking, they weren't submarines. Yes, they looked like real subs, were named after real navy subs, were promoted as "the world's largest peacetime fleet" of subs, and were sponsored by a company, General Dynamics, that actually built subs. But if the true definition of a submarine is a vessel completely *submerged* beneath the water's surface, then what began circling in Disneyland's nine-million-gallon concrete lagoon in June of 1959 weren't true submarines. In point of fact, the eight aluminum vessels were more like 52-foot-long sightseeing buses, carrying 38 passengers and running horizontally via wheels mounted on a rail, the upper half of the ship always, *always* above the waterline. Not that this pedantry mattered, of course, because the

Names of the Submarine Voyage's Subs

1959–1984	1985–1998	2007–ongoing
1. *Ethan Allen*	1. *Argonaut*	1. *Argonaut*
2. *George Washington*	2. *Explorer*	2. *Explorer*
3. *Nautilus*	3. *Nautilus*	3. *Mariner*
4. *Patrick Henry*	4. *Neptune*	4. *Nautilus*
5. *Seawolf*	5. *Sea Star*	5. *Neptune*
6. *Skate*	6. *Seawolf*	6. *Scout*
7. *Skipjack*	7. *Seeker*	7. *Seafarer*
8. *Triton*	8. *Triton*	8. *Voyager*

original Submarine Voyage was a remarkable simulation of the undersea experience.

Built in San Pedro, outfitted at the "Navy Yards" in Disneyland's northeast corner, and introduced simultaneously with the **Matterhorn Bobsleds** and the **Monorail**, the new submarines were part of the first big **Tomorrowland** makeover. Since the ships were based not on futuristic subs but on existing navy vessels, naval officials joined **Walt Disney** for the official June 14th dedication held a week after the subs began cruising. For decades after, eager crowds swarmed the attraction that had cost $2.5 million to build and that even featured live **mermaids** in its lagoon for a couple of years. Whether nosing out from under a waterfall or sliding gracefully through illuminated evening waters, the submarines made vivid postcard subjects; a sub streaking through the depths underwater was transformed into one of Disneyland's most dramatic **attraction posters**.

The subs' **queue** ran underneath the Monorail station, making this a particularly bustling area. After paying with their E tickets from the park's **ticket book**, guests

boarded a sub and descended through a hatch to sit in front of small portholes for a nine-minute voyage. Realistic ship-board sounds and bubbles streaming past the windows recreated a descent into "liquid space," and as each sub putted along at just under two miles an hour, such memorable sights as exotic mechanical fish, the ruins of Atlantis, tethered artificial mermaids, sunken treasure, the polar ice cap, and a googly-eyed sea monster were soon drifting past. Few guests recognized that some of what they saw wasn't in the open lagoon at all but was actually housed in a building underneath the **Autopia** roadway. The subs entered and exited this building by going through cascading waterfalls.

Seemingly nuclear but actually diesel-powered, the subs were a military gray color until 1986, when they were repainted in the yellow color scheme of oceanographic research vessels. Then, deemed out of date in '98, the long-running attraction finally closed, and in 2001 the **Autopia Winner's Circle** shop moved into the subs' queue area. However, the lagoon rail remained in place, suggesting that the missing subs would eventually resurface.

Finally, after a nine-year closure and an upgrade rumored to cost over $70 million, the much-missed subs returned in 2007 as the Finding Nemo Submarine Voyage (Nemo's genial characters were chosen over a theme based on the 2001 Disney movie *Atlantis: The Lost Empire*). The fleet now runs on electricity, not diesel fuel, the speed stays under 1.4 miles per hour for a ride time of about 15 minutes, and the volume of water in the lagoon has dropped by about three million gallons. The new story involves little Nemo, Dory, Crush, a beautiful coral reef made of 30 tons of recycled glass, 126 sea creatures, 10,000 artificial plants, a dazzling erupting volcano, and an Australian narrator who mentions the old attraction's mermaids and sea serpent. The satisfying voyage immediately drew colossal crowds, proving that yesterday can thrive today in Tomorrowland.

Sunkist Citrus House

MAP: Main Street, MS-6

DATES: July 31, 1960–January 3, 1989

For many years a bakery was set in a prime **Main Street** location near the **Penny Arcade**. In the 1950s that bakery was called **Puffin**, and in the '90s it was called **Blue Ribbon**. In between the bakery years, the Sunkist Citrus House used this location to pour glasses filled with orange sunshine. The Citrus House was the first of two Sunkist eateries in the park—the other, **Sunkist, I Presume**, operated almost concurrently in **Adventureland**. When Sunkist came to Main Street in 1960, Puffin's ex-dining room was enlarged to include an adjacent space that had once belonged to the **Sunny-View Farms Jams & Jellies** shop. Despite these interior changes that recast the two rooms as one business, from the outside the Citrus House still looked like two separate establishments with two different paint jobs.

Fresh-squeezed OJ and from-concentrate lemonade were Sunkist's specialties. The refreshing juice bars were frozen favorites, and the short menu was rounded out with coffee and a few baked goods. Everything was served up by **cast members** in colorful striped costumes that included bow ties and green pants for the men and aprons for the women. The Citrus House cooled off hot guests for almost three decades until the Blue Ribbon Bakery took over in 1989.

Sunkist, I Presume

MAP: Adventureland, A-3

DATES: 1962–1992

Two years after the **Sunkist Citrus House** opened on **Main Street**, a nifty outdoor snack shack called Sunkist, I Presume debuted in **Adventureland**. The name, of course, was appropriated from Henry Stanley's famous 1871 meeting with David Livingstone in deepest, darkest Africa. Stanley's first words to the reclusive missionary were "Dr. Livingstone, I presume."

In deepest, darkest Adventureland, Sunkist's location was across from the **Jungle Cruise**; previously the **Tropical Cantina** had occupied the spot. Appropriately enough for the local jungle theme, the little structure featured a thatched roof and its male **cast members** wore Hawaiian shirts and Bermuda shorts while females wore long floral dresses. Sunkist juices, especially the Jungle Julep medley, were the beverages of choice to accompany the hot dogs served here. Behind the scenes, Sunkist, I Presume also made the mint juleps that were served on the *Mark Twain*. Above the scenes, the upstairs balcony was used as an employee break area. The **Bengal Barbecue** replaced replaced Sunkist, I Presume in 1992.

Sunny-View Farms Jams & Jellies

MAP: Main Street, MS-7

DATES: 1955–1957

This small **Main Street** business was listed in the 1956 and '57 **souvenir books**, but it finished out the '50s as an unnamed candy shop. Sunny-View's location was next to the corner **Carnation Ice Cream Parlor**, where it sold jams, jellies, and candied fruit. A small brochure distributed in the shop described Sunny-View's goods as "delicious gifts," while a sign out front announced "preserves of distinction." Jams and candies gave way to juices and juice bars in 1960 when the **Sunkist Citrus House** expanded into this space.

Swiss Family Treehouse

MAP: Adventureland, A-5

DATES: November 18, 1962–March 9, 1999

What had been a landmark Johann Wyss novel in 1812 and a block-bustin' Disney adventure film in 1960 became the world's most elaborate tree house in 1962. At the time, the park needed something to complement the **Jungle Cruise**, which had been operating as **Adventureland's** only high-profile attraction since 1955. The delightful Swiss Family Treehouse was a clever addition to the northern border, where guests round the corner from Adventureland to **Frontierland**.

The tree house took its design and décor from the *Swiss Family Robinson* movie sets and props, which included items salvaged from the Robinsons' sinking ship and home-made creations fashioned from jungle materials. A B-ticket walk-through attraction (see **ticket books**), the tree house included a library, kitchen, private rooms, and viewing platforms, all of it furnished and functional, and all of it toured via 139 steps on the wooden stairways. Most memorable was an ingenious water-delivery system that lifted hundreds of gallons of water per hour to the upper levels using pulleys, bamboo dippers, and bamboo chutes. Throughout the tour, a lively Buddy Baker composition from the movie, "The Swisskapolka," was a buoyant theme song.

Almost as impressive as the tree house was the tree it sprawled across. Play-fully named a *Disneyodendron semperflorens grandis* ("big ever-blooming Disney tree") by its designers, the massive steel-and-concrete structure rose "70 feet over the jungle" and spread "brilliant colored branches 80 feet in width," according to Disneyland's 1964 **souvenir book**. These stats revealed that the tree's width was greater than its above-ground height—but unmentioned was the depth of the foundation "roots," which drove another 42 feet downward and helped give the whole structure a total weight of 150 tons. The 300,000 leaves that adorned the tree were artificial and reddish in color until they faded in the harsh sun and were replaced by green plastic instead. True to the Robinson's heritage, a Swiss flag flew from the top of the tree.

The film's stars were on hand for the dedication, which featured a hand-painted sign in the Jungle Lookout that welcomed guests with this inscription (including the ellipses): " . . . In this compound we often pause to contemplate our small world. . . . Here adventure beckons . . . with every view & every sound, the jungle & its river call out their mystery. . . . invite us to new discovery." That "jungle & river" were indeed visible from the treetops, which afforded spectacular views of Adventureland and the **Rivers of America**.

Cherished as the tree house was for almost four decades, it got a dramatic make-over in 1999 and reopened as **Tarzan's Treehouse**. A few souvenirs have been retained in Tarzan's new domicile in tribute to the departed Robinsons.

Sword in the Stone Ceremony

MAP: Fantasyland, Fa-5

DATES: Summer 1983–ongoing

Along with the much-ballyhooed 1983 architectural re-design of **Fantasyland** came a modest ritual held several times a day 10 feet south of the **King Arthur Carrousel**. The Sword in the Stone Ceremony derives from the 1963 Disney animated movie of the same name. As in the movie and T. H. White's 1938 novel, the fabled sword Excalibur was buried in a stone (at Disneyland, a golden anvil) and could only be extracted by "the true-born king of England."

These days, a **cast member** dressed as Merlin the

Magician auditions crowd members for the regal role of Wart, the story's youthful sword-puller. During the ceremony, another cast member nearby temporarily releases the sword from the anvil, and a boy or girl is heralded as royalty. Afterward, the replaced sword is immovable until the next ceremony. A free "Disneyland Today" brochure from 1986 listed three daily performances, a number that had doubled by the mid-2000s. That brochure also named the Make Believe Brass as the musical accompaniment helping to "manufacture merriment."

Tahitian Terrace,
aka Stouffer's in Disneyland Tahitian Terrace

MAP: Adventureland, A-12

DATES: June 1962–April 17, 1993

In mid-1962 Disneyland opened a new South Seas restaurant. The Tahitian Terrace, also briefly known as Stouffer's in Disneyland Tahitian Terrace, was located just inside the **Adventureland** gates on the left-hand side. The building had existed since 1955 and been filled throughout the decade by the **Plaza Pavilion**. Though the Plaza had faced east toward the **Hub**, it had used the west-facing Adventureland side for the back patio that overlooked the **Jungle Cruise**. This back half became the Tahitian Terrace. The unusual roofing revealed the building's dual function: half the roof was designed in the old-fashioned **Main Street** style, and half was made of tropical thatch.

Until the **Blue Bayou** debuted in '67, the Tahitian Terrace was the fanciest restaurant on this side of Disneyland. Guests sat at outdoor tables, were served by waiters and waitresses, and dined on exotic Polynesian cuisine under the spreading branches of a three-story artificial tree. Cooked in the same kitchen used by the Plaza Pavilion, the Tahitian Terrace menu included island favorites like teriyaki steak, marinated chicken skewers, shrimp tempura, and tropical fruit salad with pineapple ice cream. The famous beverage here was the juicy, non-alcoholic Planter's Punch. At the time, a full dinner, including a drink and dessert, cost under $4.

Live entertainment was included in that price, too. While dining, guests could watch the *Polynesian Revue*, a long-running music-and-dance spectacular featuring hip-swinging hula girls in grass skirts, male dancers dressed like island chiefs, a thrilling walk-on-fire display, and complimentary leis. **Souvenir books** consistently showed colorful photos promoting the restaurant and the show, identifying the entertainers as the "exotic Royal Tahitians dance troupe."

Since it was held outdoors, the *Polynesian Revue* couldn't adhere to a steady year-round schedule, but it managed to stay popular for over three decades. The show and the restaurant finally closed in April 1993, to be replaced three months later by **Aladdin's Oasis**. From 1971 to 2003 Walt Disney World featured its own *Polynesian Revue*, and today guests will also find a Tahitian Terrace at Hong Kong Disneyland.

Tangled

MAP: Fantasyland, Fa-9

DATES: October 15, 2010–ongoing

A month before *Tangled* the movie opened in theaters, Tangled the attraction opened in **Fantasyland**. As a replacement for the toy and candy businesses run by Geppetto, Tangled is a themed meet-and-greet area where guests can get their photos taken with **cast members** dressed as Rapunzel and Flynn Rider. Until early 2012, Rapunzel's famously long hair poured from the top of a tower outside the building and looped across Tangled's roof.

Tarzan's Treehouse

MAP: Adventureland, A-5

DATES: June 19, 1999–ongoing

Just as the **Swiss Family Treehouse** was based on a Disney movie that in turn had originated from a classic book, so too was its replacement, Tarzan's Treehouse, inspired by Disney's cinematic retelling of a popular story. In this case, the movie was *Tarzan* and the book was Edgar Rice Burroughs' 1912 adventure novel *Tarzan of the Apes*.

The Swiss Family Treehouse and Tarzan's Treehouse debuted under very different circumstances. When the original tree house opened in 1962, Disney's *Swiss Family Robinson* movie had already been a huge box-office sensation two years earlier; in contrast, when Tarzan's Treehouse opened on June 19, 1999, Disney's animated *Tarzan* had been in theaters for exactly one day; as the attraction was being planned and built in early '99, nobody really knew if the movie would be a success. Fortunately for Disneyland and the movie studio, the new film and the new tree house were both instant hits.

Since the Tarzan and Robinson story locations are an ocean apart, and since each plot has its own distinct characters, Tarzan's Treehouse is a radical reimagining of the 37-year-old Swiss Family lodgings. Serving as a fun new "foyer," a thin, two-story tree now stands in the **Adventureland** walkway, with a rickety suspension bridge leading guests to the main tree. This immense artificial structure, already 70 feet tall, 80 feet wide, and 150 tons heavy, was modified to stand a little taller and broader. To make the tree appear more African and less Caribbean, it has been adorned with new leaves and hanging moss (it also flies Great Britain's flag now instead of Switzerland's). As always, views from the top can be spectacular for guests who make the 72-step climb.

The tree house itself mirrors the maritime features detailed in the *Tarzan* film, including the ship's bow and the hanging dory. Also new is the presence of the

movie's main characters. None of the Robinsons were shown in their tree house, but Jane, Tarzan, and Sabor the leopard all appear here, as Jane's drawings impart the tale. For younger explorers the coolest enhancement is the hands-on interactivity of the new base camp area, where musical pots and pans are set up as a primitive but enlivening drum kit (*Beauty and the Beast* fans have spotted some recognizable ceramics in this area, too).

As with everything else at Disneyland, the clever details of this attraction delight guests, especially those with emotional attachments to the Swiss Family Treehouse. The Johann Wyss novel sits on a table; some of the old hand-painted signs still hang on the walls; and several of the Robinson's furnishings survived the remodel and remain in the tree house. Especially meaningful is the record playing softly on the ground-level gramophone—it's the familiar "Swisskapolka" song from the 1962 movie.

Taylor, Betty
(1919–2011)

Prior to becoming one of the most beloved entertainers in Disneyland history, Betty Taylor was a singin', dancin' dynamo on nightclub stages. Born in 1919 in Seattle, Taylor had her own professional band while still a teen, landed bit parts in several 1940s movies, and played Vegas with Frank Sinatra in the early '50s. Auditioning at Disneyland in 1956, Taylor quickly landed a lead role in **Frontierland's** *Golden Horseshoe Revue*. She played the saloon's vivacious proprietor, Slue-Foot Sue, alongside such other Disneyland stars as **Wally Boag** and **Fulton Burley**. Taylor's vocal talents and spunky enthusiasm helped make the *Revue* a record-setting favorite, with Taylor herself putting in almost 45,000 performances. She performed for a national TV audience in a 1962 episode of *Walt Disney's Wonderful World of Color*, and in the '70s park guests heard her pre-recorded vocals belting out "Bill Bailey, Won't You Please Come Home" in **America Sings.**

After some 31 years of winning over Disneyland audiences, Taylor formally retired in 1987, though she continued to make special appearances. Taylor, Wally Boag, and Fulton Burley were all inducted as Disney Legends in 1995. One day after Wally Boag died in 2011, Betty Taylor died at age 91 in Washington.

Teddi Barra's Swingin' Arcade

MAP: Bear Country/Critter Country, B/C-6
DATES: March 24, 1972–April 2003

Teddi Barra, her name a play on the legendary silent-screen actress Theda Bara, was one of the **Audio-Animatronic** singing bears in the **Country Bear Jamboree**. Nearby was Teddi Barra's Swingin' Arcade, so named because Teddi swayed on a big swing during her musical number. Inside the small room, the "games of chance" (as the sign out front announced) included both Disney and frontier themes. Charming as they might have been, the selection was so limited

that most gamers sprinted to the expansive **Starcade** instead as soon as it opened in **Tomorrowland** in 1977. Like the **Brer Bar** next door, the arcade was overrun by the 21st-century Winnie the Pooh invasion; **Pooh Corner** now spills into what used to be Teddi's swingin' space.

Tencennial

DATES: 1965

To celebrate its 10th birthday, Disneyland threw itself a year-long party in 1965. The first-ever **Miss Disneyland** helped kick off the Tencennial events with a January appearance on *Walt Disney's Wonderful World of Color*. That episode, called "Disneyland's Tenth Anniversary," featured a televised birthday party with a dancing cake and previews of upcoming park attractions. The year welcomed the debut of one landmark attraction, **Great Moments with Mr. Lincoln**, and a new Tencennial **parade**. Just over the horizon were other major additions: **It's a Small World**, **Pirates of the Caribbean**, and a "new **Tomorrowland**" would all open within two years.

Three Fairies Magic Crystals

MAP: Fantasyland, Fa-4

DATES: November 2006–2008

When the **Heraldry Shoppe** moved out of **Sleeping Beauty Castle** in 2006, the tiny Three Fairies Magic Crystals shop moved in. The first part of the name, of course, alluded to Flora, Fauna, and Merryweather, the fairy trio from *Sleeping Beauty*; "magic" referred to the images lasered into the interiors of small, clear-glass sculptures. Shaped like cubes, spheres, and even mouse ears, the sculptures made pretty gifts. When the **Sleeping Beauty Castle Walk-Through**

reopened in 2008, the Three Fairies shop became a small ground-floor viewing area for guests unable to negotiate the castle's narrow stairways. Inside the 150-square-foot space are display cases and a mini-theater showing the Walk-Through's dioramas.

Ticket Books

DATES: October 11, 1955–1982

During Disneyland's first summer, there were no **ticket books**. Adult admission to the park was $1, children were half of that, and additional admission prices between 10 and 35 cents had to be paid to enter each attraction. Attraction expenses were optional; if guests wanted to simply enter the park and not see any attractions, they could, by paying park admission only. However, this also meant that guests had to wait to buy a separate ticket any time they wanted to ride something, and **cast members** had to perform time-consuming ticket-selling and change-counting duties within the tiny ticket booths stationed outside the attractions.

To make things easier for everyone, on October 11, 1955, Disneyland introduced its first ticket books (sometimes called coupon books). Initially, these books offered a total of eight A, B, and C tickets (or coupons) for $2.50. Nine months later, with **Tom Sawyer Island**, the **Indian War Canoes**, and other new attractions opening in **Frontierland**, the ticket books were expanded to include D tickets; simultaneously, several existing attractions that had previously cost a C ticket, including the **Jungle Cruise** and **Rocket to the Moon**, were reclassified as D-ticket attractions.

The famous high-demand E ticket was added to the ticket books in 1959 to coincide with the debuts of three big park additions—the **Matterhorn Bobsleds**, the **Monorail**, and **Submarine Voyage**. As before, several existing top-tier attractions, including the Jungle Cruise once again, were reclassified for the new higher ticket. For the next 23 years, no further tickets were added to the ticket books. However, new attractions were steadily added to the A–E lineup, and some existing attractions continued to shift around, sometimes going up in cost (**Main Street Cinema**, from A to B), sometimes going down (**Sleeping Beauty Castle Walk-Through**, C to B to A), sometimes doing both (**Snow White Adventures**, C to D to C again). Only a few attractions, notably the A-ticket **King Arthur Carrousel** and **Main Street Vehicles**, never changed their prices.

In 1957, the ticket books briefly included a small Special Bonus Ticket good for one free ride on any attraction. In the 1960s and '70s guests could choose between "Big 10" books with 10 tickets (one A, one B, two C, three D, and three E) or, for a dollar more, "Deluxe 15" books (one A, two B, three C, four D, and five E). If guests left the park with unused tickets, the tickets could be used later but couldn't be refunded for cash. Over the years, several attractions never needed tickets at all because either Disneyland or a sponsor picked up the operating costs; these free attractions included **Adventure Thru Inner Space**, the **Golden Horseshoe** and its *Golden Horseshoe Revue*, the **Carousel of Progress**, and child admission to **Great Moments with Mr. Lincoln**. Conversely, some attractions still charged a separate cash-only fee, even while the lettered-ticket system was in place. Examples include the Mickey

Mouse Club Circus, which cost an additional 50 cents during its brief run in late 1955; **Tom Sawyer Island**, an additional 50 cents in 1956, and a single D ticket thereafter; and the **Enchanted Tiki Room**, priced at an extra 75 cents in 1963 before graduating to an E ticket.

The ticket book system ended in 1982 when all-encompassing **Passports** offered unlimited use of all attractions. Meanwhile, guests holding old tickets from the pre-1982 ticket books have always been able to cash them in toward their cost of admission. Since these individual A–E tickets usually have printed values of less than $1, they're often more valuable as nostalgic collectibles than they are as currency at the ticket booth. Naturally, collectors place the highest premiums on complete, unused ticket books. To get a glimpse of some subtle park history, guests can seek out the large mushroom with the book on top located outside of **Alice in Wonderland**—it's one of several old ticket booths still standing in the park.

Ticketed Attractions, 1955–1982

Ticket prices changed often (Alice in Wonderland, for instance, has been everything from a B to a D). This list gives the prices charged most frequently for attractions.

A Ticket
King Arthur Carrousel, Main Street Vehicles, Satellite View of America, Sleeping Beauty Castle Walk-Through, Space Station X-1, 20,000 Leagues Under the Sea Exhibit

B Ticket
Alice in Wonderland, Art of Animation, Big Game Safari Shooting Gallery, Casey Jr. Circus Train, Conestoga Wagons, Main Street Cinema, Main Street Shooting Gallery, Mickey Mouse Club Theater, Midget Autopia, Motor Boat Cruise, Phantom Boats, Swiss Family Treehouse, Viewliner

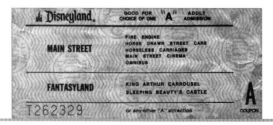

Tiki Juice Bar

MAP: Adventureland, A-11

DATES: Ca. 1976–ongoing

Talk about a match made in **Adventureland**—right outside the entrance to the **Enchanted Tiki Room** is the equally tropical Tiki Juice Bar. The bar has been serving a variety of juices and island-themed refreshments from under its little thatched roof since 1976, the year Dole began sponsoring both the snack stand and the Tiki Room. Unlike many of Disneyland's other quick-stop eateries, this one serves healthy treats like cool pineapple juice and pineapple spears, plus frosty Pineapple Whips that include no ice cream or dairy products. On a scorching summer day, a fortifying stop here is just the thing for overheated explorers heading westward to the **Jungle Cruise** and beyond.

C Ticket
Adventure Thru Inner Space, Astro-Jets, Dumbo the Flying Elephant, Fantasyland Autopia, Frontierland Shooting Gallery, Junior Autopia, Mad Hatter's Mad Tea Party, Mike Fink Keel Boats, Mr. Toad's Wild Ride, Peter Pan Flight, Rocket to the Moon, Snow White Adventures, Stage Coach, Tomorrowland Autopia

D Ticket
Flying Saucers, Indian War/Davy Crockett's Explorer Canoes, *Mark Twain* Riverboat, Mission to Mars, PeopleMover, Flight to the Moon, Rafts to Tom Sawyer Island, Mine Train, Rainbow Ridge Mule Pack, Rocket Jets, Sailing Ship *Columbia*, Santa Fe & Disneyland Railroad, Skyway to Fantasyland/Tomorrowland, Storybook Land Canal Boats

E Ticket
America Sings, Big Thunder Mountain Railroad, Country Bear Jamboree, Enchanted Tiki Room, Great Moments with Mr. Lincoln, The Haunted Mansion, It's a Small World, Jungle Cruise, Matterhorn Bobsleds, Monorail, Pirates of the Caribbean, Pack Mules Through Nature's Wonderland, Space Mountain, Submarine Voyage

Tiki Tropical Traders, aka Tropical Imports

MAP: Adventureland, A-9

DATES: 1955–ongoing

Tiki Tropical Traders, renamed Tropical Imports in the mid-'90s, has been serving up **Adventureland** "curios for the curious" for five decades. Located in an exotic hut near the **Jungle Cruise**, the store used to sell merchandise that was less "Disney plush" and more "jungle unusual," including rubber snakes, bamboo chimes, shrunken heads, exotic shells, and more. In the 2000s, the store added various juices and snacks to its shelves, as well as plush animals, sunglasses, and other sundries.

Tinker Bell

DATES: 1961–ongoing

The fact that a real live Tinker Bell was added to Disneyland in 1961 should come as no surprise—an animated version of the blonde fairy had already graced *Peter Pan* in 1953 (re-released in 1958) and been the delightful (but mute) mascot on the ***Disneyland* TV series** as of 1954. Once **Matterhorn Mountain** went up in 1959, **Walt Disney** knew it was time to bring in Tink.

The plan was to have someone in costume take the elevator and stairway up through the Matterhorn, strap on a harness, and soar 784 feet through the air on a sloping wire from the mountain to a mattress-padded platform in **Fantasyland**, all happening with 25 seconds. Not coincidentally, the person hired for the first flight had already flown in a Tinker Bell costume. At the Hollywood Bowl in 1958, a 4-foot-10-inch circus aerialist named Tiny Kline had made a spectacular 1,000-foot glide from the hills to the stage while dressed as Tinker Bell for a special "Disney Night" concert. Kline, a Hungarian who was born Helen Deutsch, was 68 years old. Her long career in show biz had included stints with the circus and stunts with airborne dirigibles and airplanes for which she had dangled in the air by her teeth.

Kline began performing at Disneyland in mid-'61. Every summer night, she followed a

flood of floating soap bubbles into the Fantasyland sky just before the nightly Fantasy in the Sky **fireworks** show. Kline performed until 1964, the year she died. A series of circus veterans then took up Tink's wand. These later Tinker Bells, who continued the nighttime performances until 1977 and then from 1983 onward, have worn the wings in shows similar to Kline's, but with a few changes. For instance, in 2000's Believe . . . There's Magic in the Stars, Tinker Bell made her descent *during* the fireworks, not before. And Tink doesn't simply glide downwards anymore; instead, she slides back and forth across the sky.

Speculation persists that, at times, the person performing as Tinker Bell has been a man—a rumor that park officials haven't yet confirmed either way.

Tinker Bell & Friends

MAP: Fantasyland, Fa-3

DATES: November 2006–2008

The space within the **Sleeping Beauty Castle** entrance where the **Princess Boutique** and **50th Anniversary Shop** had both been located became a new Tinker Bell gift shop in late 2006. The small, L-shaped store had three doorways—one leading to the castle's main walkway and two toward the castle's courtyard (usually only one of the latter two was open). Although the shop was called Tinker Bell & Friends, Tink dominated the shop without many friends in sight (maybe that was the joke—perhaps she doesn't have many friends). Tink costumes, toys, jewelry, bags, blonde wigs, wands, and more helped girls evoke their inner fairies. The shop took on a new name and new merchandise in 2008 when it became the **Enchanted Chamber.**

Tinker Bell Toy Shoppe,
aka Once Upon a Time . . .
The Disney Princess Shoppe

MAP: Fantasyland, Fa-7

DATES: 1957–April 2009

For over 50 years a charming toy and costume store thrived next to the **Snow White** attraction. The store was first called the Tinker Bell Toy Shoppe—an appropriate name for a cute castle store, considering Tink was sort of a cute castle mascot, thanks to the little blonde fairy's animated appearances at the opening of the *Disneyland* **TV series**. As the largest store in **Fantasyland,** this was the area's main headquarters for enchanting gifts.

The name change in 2002 to Once Upon a Time . . . The Disney Princess Shoppe again reinforced the castle connection. The first half of the new name alluded to the love song "Once Upon a Dream" from the 1959 film *Sleeping Beauty*, while the Princess Shoppe ending appealed directly to the store's target patrons. Little princesses and their parents could find much more merchandise here than in the smaller **Princess Boutique** nearby. Regal dresses, gilded crowns, magic wands, sparkly jewelry and tiaras, detailed dolls and statues, illustrated books, and Disney DVDs filled this store with the stuff dreams are made of. What's more, four classic Disney movie princesses—Snow White, Cinderella, Aurora from *Sleeping Beauty*, and Belle from *Beauty and the Beast*—would stop by to meet, greet, and tell fairy tales. The picture window out front, with its displays of royal wardrobes and accessories, was an irresistible magnet to young girls. In 2009 a remodel and renaming transformed the Disney Princess Shoppe into a salon called the **Bibbidi Bobbidi Boutique**.

Tomorrowland

MAP: Park, P-18

DATES: July 17, 1955–ongoing

Ad astra per aspera—Roman philosopher Seneca's call to reach the stars despite difficulties might've applied to Tomorrowland. No Disneyland area was as problematical in the mid-1950s as Tomorrowland, and no area has undergone as many major revisions since then. The land's main challenge for Disney designers is easy to grasp but difficult and expensive to resolve—to maintain a futuristic, guest-friendly land that continually stays ahead of ever-advancing real-world technological achievements.

Unlike the rest of Disneyland, which is set in the present (**Mickey's Toontown**) or the recent/distant/fabled past (all the other lands), Tomorrowland is set in the future. When the land was first being designed and built, that future was pegged as 1986, the year Halley's Comet would return. The target year was later pushed into the 21st century. Consequently, with Tomorrowland mandated to stay fresh and innovative—"a daring world of hopes and dreams," according to the 1956 **souvenir book**—many more new attractions have been introduced here than anywhere else in Disneyland. **Walt Disney** acknowledged this challenge, commenting that "tomorrow is a heck of a thing to keep up with."

Tomorrowland almost didn't debut on time. Concentrated work on the land didn't begin until there were only six months left before **Opening Day**, making it the last area in the park to be started, and the last to be finished. Lacking adequate funds and time, in July 1955 Tomorrowland only had some empty buildings, the for-display-purposes-only *Moonliner* rocket, the **Circarama** theater, Monsanto's **Hall of Chemistry**, a barely functioning **Autopia**, and not much else ready.

These attractions would be acceptable for a typical amusement park or state fair, but not for the exciting Tomorrowland Walt Disney had imagined, especially when compared to the ambitious descriptions Disney had pitched to potential investors two years before. According to the pitch, this "World of Tomorrow" would preview "some of the wonderful developments the future holds in store," including "a moving sidewalk, industrial exhibits, a diving bell, a monorail, a freeway children could drive, shops for scientific toys, and a Rocket Space Ship to the Moon." Artist **Herb Ryman** had drawn a conceptual Land of Tomorrow entrance that included futuristic architecture and the suspended pods of a new transportation system, as well as some kind of "interplanetary circus." Unfortunately, few of the things originally described and sketched were ready when Tomorrowland opened.

Toward the end of 1954, with the park well under construction, Walt Disney resigned himself to opening Disneyland the following July with "coming soon" signs in front of a closed-off Tomorrowland. Then, early in 1955, he decided to push Tomorrowland to the Opening Day finish line. The desired outcome wasn't completely possible, and the public's first glimpses of Tomorrowland were of festive banners and balloons that camouflaged the embarrassing absence of high-profile, high-tech attractions.

Meanwhile, with guests streaming into the park throughout that first summer, Walt Disney continued to fill the land's approximately 13 acres with more to see and do. Within a month of Opening Day, **Rocket to the Moon** was flying, the **20,000 Leagues Under the Sea Exhibit** was on display, and the **Phantom Boats** were sputtering around the Tomorrowland lagoon. By that fall, **Hobbyland** and the **Flight Circle**, two underwhelming exhibits grounded in the present, were operating. Behind the scenes, Disney had solicited more corporate sponsors, and within six months had brought in Kaiser Aluminum for the **Hall of Aluminum Fame**, the American Dairy Association for their eponymous exhibit space, and the Crane Plumbing Company for the **Bathroom of Tomorrow.** All the exhibits were functional, but hardly inspiring.

Inspirational attractions were on the horizon, however. The spring of 1956 brought the **Astro-Jets** and the **Skyway** to Tomorrowland; 1957 opened the doors

of the **House of the Future**; and 1958 welcomed an attempt at mass transit in the form of the gas-powered **Viewliner** train. A more audacious mass transit system arrived in '59 with the first well-coordinated, large-scale surge in Tomorrowland development. Debuting in June along with the **Matterhorn Bobsleds** (labeled a Tomorrowland attraction at the

> ### Major Attractions and Exhibits Added in the 21st Century
>
> 2003   The Many Adventures of Winnie the Pooh
> 2005   Buzz Lightyear Astro Blasters
> 2007   Finding Nemo Submarine Voyage;
>   Pirate's Lair on Tom Sawyer Island
> 2008   Pixie Hollow
> 2010   Tangled
> 2013   Fantasy Faire

time) and the **Submarine Voyage** was the **Monorail**. The first two were visually stunning, but the electric Monorail was the most significant addition, representing a determined attempt to make Tomorrowland a testing ground for serious experiments in futuristic public transportation.

With this trio of attractions in place simultaneously, in one fell swoop Tomorrowland had electrifying E-ticket (see **ticket books**) options to brag about. And brag the park's marketing department did, filling Disneyland's **souvenir books** with ebullient text and enticing photos. Additionally, this latest and greatest expansion was showcased in much-seen promotional films and TV specials. The Tomorrowland that Walt Disney wanted, one that would be a "living blueprint of our future," was finally here.

Eight years later, a dedication ceremony attended by 1,500 invited guests and celebrities introduced a dramatic "new Tomorrowland." This remarkable update, still one of the favorite moments in Disneyland history for many guests, re-themed the entire land as a shiny "world on the move," as it was called in the park's souvenir books. Inside a dramatic new pair of angular, aluminum entrance gates, the creative **Adventure Thru Inner Space** attraction, new **Rocket Jets**, a new **Tomorrowland Terrace** and **Tomorrowland Stage**, the immense Carousel Theater with its **Carousel of Progress**, and yet one more serious contribution to urban planning, the **PeopleMover**, all replaced familiar landmarks like the *Moonliner*, the Flying Saucers, the Flight Circle, and several long-running exhibits. New Tomorrowland's $20 million price tag (according to the book *Walt Disney's Disneyland*) was about $3 million more than what Disneyland itself had cost to build a decade before, but Imagineers got the impressive results they wanted, and dazzled guests felt like they'd suddenly time-warped from 1967 to the 21st century. Ten years later, **Space Mountain** made them feel like they'd time-warped again into the mind-blowing StarGate sequence of *2001: A Space Odyssey*. Ten years after that, **Star Tours** sent guests light-speeding into *Star Wars* territory. Who knew the future would be so fun?

The '90s brought an even newer "new Tomorrowland," but this one was as controversial as it was exciting. Rather than continually chase an ever-elusive future, Imagineers decided to reinvent a "retro-future"—that is, a future as it might have been imagined a century before. Long gone were the Skyway buckets, the Submarine Voyage, the PeopleMover, and the **Mission to Mars** flight (even the Matterhorn was missing, since the souvenir books had started listing it as a Fantasyland attraction). Jules Verne now seemed to be the main designer of sci-fi attractions like the **Astro-Orbitor**, **Rocket Rods**, and **Observatron**, their warm bronzes and coppers the colors of the Industrial Revolution instead of the stark whites, blacks, and chromes of the space age. And with edible plants filling the flower beds, the future at hand was as healthy and harmonious as it was scientific and gadgety.

Despite all the effort, somehow this future didn't work as well as it could have, and within a few years the disappointing Rocket Rods were Toy Storied out of existence by the fanciful **Buzz Lightyear Astro Blasters**. Space Mountain was being re-painted white, and the submarines were getting new orders to find little Nemo. Rumors suggest that even the PeopleMover may eventually be resurrected. Tomorrowland's future, it seems, is firmly rooted in its past.

Tomorrowlanding

MAP: Tomorrowland, T-8

DATES: 2006–ongoing

What had been the **Radio Disney** booth under the **Observatron** became a new retailer called Tomorrowlanding in 2006. According to the sign outside, this small shop sold "gifts from outer and liquid space," which meant it featured merchandise for the nearby **Star Tours** and **Submarine Voyage** attractions. However, by 2011 Tomorrowlanding seemed to be more of a generic hat store offering items from **Fantasyland** and other areas outside **Tomorrowland**.

Tomorrowland Stage, aka Space Stage

MAP: Tomorrowland, T-19

DATES: 1967–1986

The 1967 "new **Tomorrowland**" introduced an intimate bandstand, the **Tomorrowland Terrace**, for smaller acts, and a showy new venue, the Tomorrowland Stage, for theatrical extravaganzas and nationally known musical groups. The Tomorrowland Stage filled the eastern corner of Tomorrowland, where the **Flying Saucers** had hovered in the early '60s. The stage itself was about 30 feet across and festooned with the same kind of arcs and abstractions that adorned the Tomorrowland Terrace.

The Tomorrowland Stage was a big setting for big shows. Among the large-scale musical spectaculars presented here were *Show Me America* and *Country Music Jubilee*; the book *Disneyland: The First Quarter Century* described the former as a "fast-paced musical comedy" with "more than 120 sparkling costumes" and "favorite American melodies sprinkled with a touch of old-fashioned humor." Stars booked here included Pat Boone, Herman's Hermits, Linda Ronstadt (backed by the newly formed Eagles), and the park's own **Kids of the Kingdom**. One high point was the live big-screen broadcast of the Apollo 11 moonwalk on July 20, 1969. Not only was the event historic, but for most people it was the first time they'd seen a large-scale TV broadcast.

With the completion of **Space Mountain** in 1977, the Tomorrowland Stage was rebuilt as part of the attraction's sleek new architectural complex. That December it also got a new name—the Space Stage, just one of the space-related titles (**Space Place** and **Lunching Pad** were some others) that arrived with the mountain. The kingdom-themed musical *Disneyland is Your Land* began running here in 1985, but a year later the show and the outdoor stage were gone. Starting in 1986, outdoor shows were being held at **Fantasyland's** new **Videopolis** stage, and the Space Stage space was turned into the **Magic Eye Theater**.

Tomorrowland Terrace

MAP: Tomorrowland, T-9

DATES: July 2, 1967–2001; 2006–ongoing

When a "new **Tomorrowland**" opened up in 1967, every addition was conspicuous—except one. Sitting in the open, about 100 feet from the loading area of the **Monorail**, was a futuristic design of some kind. Decorated with artistic pylons and flowing plants, guests could admire the serene 40-foot-long display without really understanding what it was or how it added to the Tomorrowland atmosphere.

Understanding came when, every few hours, the display ascended to reveal itself as the roof of a small oval stage where a spirited music group was already in mid-song as the stage rose up. Sometimes called the Coke Terrace or the Coca-Cola Tomorrowland Terrace in deference to its sponsor, the stage below was decorated with the same sleek arcs and op art abstractions that adorned the sculptural planter on top. The performers included the '60s hit-makers Paul Revere and the Raiders, the pop-oriented Sunshine Balloon, and the beachy boys Papa-Doo-Ron-Ron.

Teens were the target audience, especially at night. During the day, tables in front of the raised stage offered seating for hundreds of guests; at night, the tables were cleared away to open up space for dancing. Back then, Disneyland's **souvenir books** showcased Tomorrowland Terrace's youth appeal with energetic photos.

A counter-service eatery nearby offered fast food staples like burgers, sandwiches, fries, and Cokes (naturally). About a decade after the Tomorrowland Terrace opened, this menu was supplemented with the Tomorrowland-themed Moonburger, and two decades after that (in the late '90s) the lunch and dinner menus were updated with healthier wraps, fruit, and salads.

Coca-Cola shifted its sponsorship from the Tomorrowland Terrace to the nearby **Spirit of Refreshment** when another "new Tomorrowland" remodel arrived in 1998. The Tomorrowland Terrace music and fast food continued to operate, though a new sculpture crowned the roof and the colors were updated to the same warm bronzes of other area attractions like the **Astro-Orbitor**. In 2001 **Club Buzz** reinvigorated the stage and dining area with a new name and a new *Toy Story* show.

The name Tomorrowland Terrace returned in 2006 with a revised menu of sandwiches and burgers called "Flight Command Cuisine" to tie in with the new presentation on the Terrace stage. Sponsored by Hasbro and performed a half-dozen times a day, *Jedi Training Academy* brought *Star Wars* themes and characters to life by training earnest young guests to "master the ways of the Force." Kids still learn the art of lightsaber fencing and square off against Stormtroopers and the two evil Darths, Maul and Vader. The confrontations are more hilarious than terrifying, thanks to the intense kids and fast-paced narration. On recent summer nights, the Tomorrowland Terrace has transformed into the TLT Dance Club, with deejays spinning dance music during the week and live bands often rocking the weekends.

Tom Sawyer Island,
aka Pirate's Lair on Tom Sawyer Island

MAP: Frontierland, Fr-16

DATES: June 16, 1956–ongoing

Walt Disney never produced a movie based on *The Adventures of Tom Sawyer*, but he certainly had an affinity for the novel and shared a midwestern background with its author, Mark Twain. Both men were alive concurrently; Disney was born in Chicago, about 350 miles from Twain's Florida, Missouri birthplace (Disney was eight when Twain died in 1910), and both men grew up in small Missouri towns (Marceline and Hannibal). Both men also created an island in the middle of a river.

Twain's *Tom Sawyer* did not include a place called Tom Sawyer's Island, but it did have a fictional Jackson's Island, "about three miles long and a quarter of a mile wide" out in the middle of the Mississippi River. On the island, Tom, Huck, and their friend Joe Harper cavorted as pirates and escaped "civilization." Reaching the island

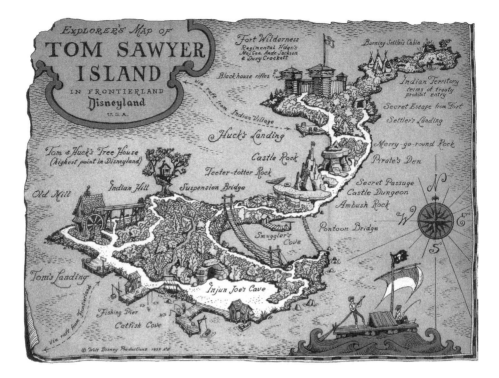

via log raft, the three boys eagerly roamed the woods and found "plenty of things to be delighted with."

Once Disneyland was up and running, in early 1956 Walt Disney turned his attention to the incomplete, visible-but-unvisitable island out in the middle of the **Rivers of America**. Early ideas for the area included a Mickey Mouse Island or a Treasure Island, based on Disney's 1950 movie. Once the Tom Sawyer concept was settled on, Disney did what he typically did for new attractions: he turned over the actual creation to an individual designer, who used his boss's general suggestions to map out the details.

Tom Sawyer Island, however, got some extra attention from Walt Disney. In *Walt Disney: An American Original*, Bob Thomas writes that the island was the only early Disneyland attraction personally designed by Disney himself. Disney did let master planner **Marvin Davis** have first crack at it, but the results weren't satisfactory for him. According to Thomas, Disney took Davis's drawings and worked on them "for hours in his red-barn workshop. The next morning, he laid tracing paper on Davis's desk and said, 'Now that's the way it should be.' The island was built according to his design." Disney's daughter, Diane Disney Miller, wrote in her book, *The Story of Walt Disney*, that her father "kept on adding things until he felt that there weren't any missing parts."

The result is something close to Twain's rough-hewn Jackson's Island. Just as Twain's island was 12 times longer than it was wide, so too is Disney's island long and narrow. Tom Sawyer island stretches 800 feet from top to bottom and varies in width from a trim 50 feet in the middle to about 250 across the northern end, totaling almost three acres. The surrounding shore, most of it belonging to **Frontierland**, is 80–100 feet away, with **Rafts to Tom Sawyer Island** conveying guests back and forth.

Walt Disney added his own flourishes to Twain's undeveloped island, of course. A play structure called Tom & Huck's Treehouse—free of charge, like all other island activities—stands on a hill at the southern tip. In the early decades, the island maps handed out to guests declared this to be the "highest point in Disneyland," meaning it was the highest point guests could access. Some 250 feet north of the tree house was Fort Wilderness, a two-story log structure straight out of a Western movie. In its first years the fort included a passageway down to the trails, a display of Davy Crockett and Andrew Jackson mannequins reused from the **Davy Crockett Frontier Museum**, a refreshment stand, and lookout towers with rifles that delivered bulletless bangs (in the 21st century, age finally caught up with the fort, and it's been closed permanently). Additional island features, all of them shown on the free island maps drawn by **Sam McKim**, included Merry-Go-Round Rock, Pirate's Den, Castle Rock, Smuggler's Cove, Teeter-Totter Rock, shaky pontoon and swaying rope bridges, and a fake cemetery behind the fort. And then there was Injun Joe's Cave.

McDougal's Cave was the scene of the thrilling climax to Twain's *Tom Sawyer*. While writing the book in the 1870's, Twain recalled his childhood days when he'd played in a cave outside of Hannibal. Now a national landmark, this cave was his model for the cave where Tom, Becky Thatcher, and other revelers made a giddy procession into marvelous subterranean rooms with exotic names like the Cathedral and Aladdin's Palace. Twain's vivid descriptions created a "romantic and mysterious" world with "a vast labyrinth of crooked aisles," a "tangle of rifts and chasms," a "multitude of shining stalactites," "glittering crystals," and "fantastic pillars." The Disneyland cave, while not quite as elaborate and only stretching about 100 feet long, captures the natural wonder and adventurous potential of Twain's creation. Guests duck through dimly lit passageways, creep along a dirt floor, negotiate slender side paths, and peer into a "bottomless pit" where somber susurrations echo and the darkness is pierced by stalagmites and stalactites.

When the island finally opened in July of '56, two winners of Hannibal's "Most Typical Tom and Becky of the Year" contest attended the dedication ceremonies. That first year, guests couldn't use any of their A, B, or C tickets from the park's **ticket book** to enter the island—they had to buy special 50-cent tickets for admission. Once on the island, guests could pursue one additional adventure: fishing. Using the park's poles, hooks, and bait, guests fished off the Catfish Cove docks at the island's southern tip. Because they dropped their lines into a penned area of water stocked with live catfish, guests were pretty much guaranteed success. Unfortunately, that was the problem—visitors reeled fish in with ease, but nobody knew what to do with their catch after that. After enough odoriferous carcasses were found abandoned in lockers and bushes, the fishing attraction was closed.

For many guests, Tom Sawyer Island has remained one of the most unique and entertaining locations in Disneyland, and not just because it offers an ideal place to relax on hot days under real trees near cool water. Without any big stores or restaurants on the island, nothing distracts guests from their fun or coaxes cash from their wallets. Also, as a confluence of four different lands (Frontierland, **Adventureland**, **Critter Country**, and **New Orleans Square**), the island offers grand views of such varied landmarks as the **Haunted Mansion**, **Splash Mountain**, the *Mark Twain*, and the *Columbia*. Furthermore, unlike most other attractions, Tom Sawyer Island is not a three-minute experience—guests can stay as long as they want, with dusk the only deadline. And while other attractions bring guests indoors and away from the California sunshine, this one encourages visitors to stay outside in a ludic paradise so low-tech that it's almost *no*-tech. Since there's no set path or pattern to the island adventure, guests get to invent the island experience themselves, with no "safety bar" to stifle imaginative impulses and no limit to where the many hidden areas, secret passageways, and multiple trails will lead.

Not all of those imaginative impulses have ended happily, however. Several guests have tried unsuccessfully to hide on the island overnight (two even drowned in the attempt). More bizarrely, chanting **Yippie Day** protesters invaded Fort Wilderness in 1970 and briefly replaced the Stars and Stripes with their own flag, forcing Disney officials to suspend raft trips to the island.

The inaccessible cabin north of the fort has generated headlines of its own. In 2001 the *L.A. Times* called the cabin "perhaps the most altered attraction" in Disneyland. "For nearly 20 years, the victim of an Indian arrow lay sprawled in front of a burning settler's cabin," explained the paper. "In the 1970s, in the middle of the gas crisis, Disneyland turned off the flames for roughly a decade. . . . In 1984, the park began using a simulated flame and the settler was replaced with a moonshiner passed out on the porch. Then . . . the theme became how an animal habitat was endangered by a fire caused by a careless settler." Today's cabin is still off-limits, but flames no longer flicker. The blaze was finally extinguished in 2007, and in 2010 the cabin was restored to look like Mike Fink actually lives there (one of his famed keel boats is tied up on the shore).

At the island's other end, changes came in 1992 when the southern tip was remodeled to accommodate **Fantasmic!** More dramatically, the entire island closed in 2007 for an extensive renovation that brought out the Bobcats (the earth-moving machines, that is). Reopened on May 25, 2007, Pirate's Lair on Tom Sawyer Island now sports wider paths, a sunken pirate ship, hidden treasure, ghostly apparitions, and other changes with themes from the *Pirates of the Caribbean* movies. A faux Fort Wilderness has been built on the site of the original, but it is for employees only.

Purists may deride any tamperings with Walt Disney's original vision of his Twain-inspired island, but as long as the island still exists at all, it will always be one of the park's best old-school attractions. Missouri's legislature agrees—it has officially annexed Disneyland's island as part of the Show Me State.

Toontown Five & Dime

MAP: Mickey's Toontown, MT-10

DATES: January 24, 1993–ongoing

Sharing a bright yellow **Mickey's Toontown** building with the **Gag Factory** is the Toontown Five & Dime, a cheery retail operation within laughing distance of **Roger Rabbit's Car Toon Spin**. Outside the Five & Dime are some of Toontown's signature jokes and surprises, including talking mailboxes, wacky phones, and a broken clock on the sign outside the clock repair shop. Unfortunately, no items in the Five & Dime cost only five or ten cents, but there are lots of inexpensive pens, key chains, and other small souvenirs, as well as mugs, picture frames, and charm bracelets. More expensive Toon-themed clothes, bags, and plush toys are also available.

Toon Up Treats

MAP: Mickey's Toontown, MT-7

DATES: December 13, 1997–ongoing

About four years after Goofy's Gas Station debuted in **Mickey's Toontown**, a small "snack stop" opened next door. Toon Up Treats is always there, but not always open (only the busy seasons seem to require regular hours). Basic sandwiches, pre-made salads, chips, some desserts, candy, and sodas provide fast fuel for guests on the go, with outdoor seating available nearby.

Topiary Garden

MAP: Fantasyland, Fa-21

DATES: May 28, 1966–ongoing

A topiary is a bush or tree trimmed into some recognizable shape, usually a geometric figure or an animal. An arrangement of many small plants into a single pattern is not considered a topiary, thus the floral quilt planted on the shore of the **Storybook Land Canal Boats** and the large flower-formed face of Mickey Mouse at Disneyland's **entrance** don't qualify as topiaries. Disneyland does boast several true topiaries,

including the joyful pachyderms near **Dumbo the Flying Elephant** and the giant swans outside of **Sleeping Beauty Castle**. But by far the most famous topiaries are the 15 or so gathered in front of **It's a Small World** in **Fantasyland**.

So unusual was this array when it opened in 1966 that the area came to be known as the Topiary Garden. The best views are from the Small World boats, which still loop around the garden to show the garden off from different angles. Three key factors make the Disneyland Topiary Garden so memorable. First and foremost, the whimsical subjects perfectly suit the imaginatively designed building and "the happiest cruise that ever sailed 'round the world." The animals have included a towering giraffe, an elephant balancing on its front legs, a laughing hippo, a fuzzy-headed lion, a prancing reindeer, a rhino with a bird on its back, a dancing bear, a seal balancing a ball, and a three-part sea serpent. There are also densely verdant trees cut into cones, domes, and corkscrews, plus decorative hedges trimmed into cubes and spheres. The fanciful greenery makes the garden look like a child's play area filled with wonderful toys and blocks.

The second factor is the scale of the sculptures. So much work goes into the creation of topiaries that other parks often keep their topiaries small and simple. At Disneyland, the finely detailed sculptures in the Topiary Garden are almost all life-size, each one taking up to two years to grow into its shape.

Finally, painstaking effort is carefully applied to keep the plants in immaculate condition every day of the year no matter what the weather conditions are. Most of the plants are tight-growing, small-leaved shrubs that are meticulously pruned by hand every few weeks. Disneyland's own landscapers and gardeners maintain the topiaries, but a San Diego company called Coburn Topiary & Garden Art claims responsibility for first growing and shaping some of the plants.

Tour Guides

DATES: 1958–ongoing

To help novice guests (or guests short on time) navigate the overwhelming park, a small team of tour guides was added as a Disneyland guest service in 1958. Early on, the tours began at **City Hall** as informal presentations by **cast members** wearing their own casual clothes. But the increasing popularity of the tours resulted in a large team of trained guides, official uniforms, and formalized spiels. By 1960 the Tour Guide program, led by **Cicely Rigdon**, was operating from what was called the Guided Tour Garden, a small landscaped area south of the **Police Station** on **Town**

Square. Conveniently, guests automatically walked right past this location upon entering Disneyland via the west tunnel. A 1964 park flyer described how the "enchanting" guided tours enabled guests to "enjoy several exciting Disneyland rides" while getting "interesting information about Disneyland from your attractive Disneyland Tour Guide." The "Happiness Trip" lasted two hours and cost $3.25 in 1958 and $5.00 in '64; these prices included park admission and a free ticket to use at any other attraction in the park.

Tour guides were first presented in Disneyland **souvenir books** in 1962. That year's book included a photo of one of the female tour guides in the official tour guide uniform: a red-and-black plaid skirt, a red double-breasted vest, a white short-sleeve blouse, red knee-high socks, and black flats; not shown was a cape, a cold weather option. In the photo, the guide's black riding hat and the riding crop in her upraised hand added an equestrian influence to the amalgamation of styles (Walt Disney implied an equestrian connection when he called Tour Guides "guest jockeys" on a '65 episode of his *Wonderful World of Color* TV show). Eventually the Tour Guides became popular and recognizable enough for Disneyland to sell a Tour Guide doll, "a true reproduction of the popular Tour Guide Girls" in the traditional plaid skirt/red vest outfit.

Just as Disneyland has become more complex over the decades, so too have the tours, which now have themes. While they don't automatically move their groups to the front of attraction lines, tours usually include some priority seating for a **parade** or a show, plus extras like pins and free lunches. Tour options in the 21st century have included a "VIP Tour" (a customized tour booked at an hourly rate), a "Welcome to Disneyland Tour" (2½ hours, featuring a general walk through the park), a "Holiday Time Tour" (2½ hours, highlighting winter holiday traditions), a "Discover the Magic Tour" (2½ hours, including an interactive treasure hunt), a "Disney's Myths, Mysteries and Legends Tour" (2½ hours, held at night), and "A Walk in Walt's Footsteps" tour (3½ hours, a fact-filled walk-and-talk with a private lunch and a peek inside **Club 33**). Prices, of course, have escalated; for instance, "A Walk in Walt's Footsteps" cost $64 per person in 2011, a price that did not include park admission.

Town Square

MAP: Park, P-8

DATES: July 17, 1955–ongoing

The early concept sketches of Disneyland were very consistent in their representations of Town Square, and usually what those drawings showed closely resembled the Town Square that was finally built. The famous **Herb Ryman** illustration drawn in 1953, showing a square-shaped one-acre plaza, a triangular third-of-an-acre green

in the center with a soaring flagpole, and a few landmark buildings around the perimeter, was practically a blueprint for Town Square.

As historians have noted, **Walt Disney** carefully crafted Disneyland as if he were a film director laying out movie shots. For example, guests can't see Town Square until it's revealed to them; they enter the park through one of two dark tunnels and then emerge upon a wide, dramatic vista. The move from tight close-up to breathtaking panorama is a cinematic strategy that intensifies the surprise and fixes the sight in guests' memories.

It's no accident that the first view of Disneyland is of an open, relatively calm area. Back in the 1950s, the general public didn't know what Disneyland was or how it was organized, so Walt Disney gave guests a chance to acclimate gradually to his dramatically different park. Town Square, the first land guests came across, was something they would have already been used to—a small-town civic center (at one time planners even considered calling Town Square the Civic Center). Mind-stretching areas like **Tomorrowland** could wait; here at the beginning of the Disneyland experience, it was enough to get one's bearings while being surrounded by such stable institutions as the **Police Station**, **City Hall**, and the **Fire Station** on the west side of the square, Old Glory and inviting benches in the middle, and the **Opera House** and **Bank of America** to the east. Ahead of Town Square stretched an old-fashioned avenue that could have been a street in any American small town. On the horizon, about three full football fields north of the tunnels, was the first fabulous, yet safely distant attraction: **Sleeping Beauty Castle**. Karal Ann Marling called this kind of environment "the architecture of reassurance" in her book *Designing Disney's Theme Parks*. Novice

guests entered Town Square quizzical and left it comforted.

There's one other Town Square strategy worth mentioning. In addition to orienting his guests to their new surroundings, Walt Disney had to manage the crowds. By spreading guests out across a broad square, he nimbly averted the instant bottleneck that would have occurred every day if guests had walked straight from the tunnels into narrow **Main Street**.

In addition to the "civic" buildings, Town Square is also home to formal entertainment and ceremonies. The Opening Day dedication, daily flag-lowering ceremonies, and the lighting of the annual Christmas tree have all been held in Town Square. Because of the wide range of events and its prominent placement at the head of the park, Town Square buildings and ceremonies have been shown in every one of the park's **souvenir books** and virtually every photo book about Disneyland. Old photos reveal little change in the exterior architecture (though some of the interior functions have changed over the decades). Town Square, thankfully, is timeless.

Town Square Café

MAP: Town Square, TS-7

DATES: December 1976–spring, 1978; October 1, 1983–August 23, 1992

The Town Square Café first set up in 1976 as a replacement for the **Hills Bros. Coffee House and Coffee Garden**. This choice site had **Disneyland Presents a Preview of Coming Attractions** on the corner to the west and the **Opera House** block to the east. As a full-service, sit-down restaurant for breakfast and lunch, the unsponsored Town Square Café was the only dining establishment in Town Square.

After two years the American Egg House took over the location. Five years later, the eggs were out and the previous café was back in, this time for almost a full decade. The Town Square Café redux closed in 1992, and four years later the **Dalmatian Celebration** store opened in its place for the **holiday season**. The site has been used as a character-greeting area in the 21st century. Gone but not forgotten, the Town Square Café has been honored with its own beautiful Disney pin.

Town Square Realty

MAP: Town Square, TS-10

DATES: 1955–1960

Listed in all of Disneyland's **souvenir books** through 1959 was, of all things, a business called Town Square Realty (aka simply Real Estate in some of the books). Located to the right of the entrance to the **Opera House**, this was the actual office of an actual realtor who was selling land in Apple Valley, a largely undeveloped area some 80 miles northeast of Anaheim. According to *The Nickel Tour*, the office dispensed information, handed out free Disneyland maps, and gave away little pouches of authentic California dirt. With its novelty wearing off, the realtor departed in 1960; a year later, the space was absorbed into the **Babes in Toyland Exhibit**.

Toy Story Funhouse

MAP: Tomorrowland, T-16

DATES: January 27, 1996–May 27, 1996

With *Toy Story* a hit in theaters as of late 1995, a play area based on the movie went up in **Tomorrowland** in early 1996. The site was next to **Space Mountain** in the old **Mission to Mars** building, which had been closed since 1992. The Toy Story Funhouse was never meant to have a long run at Disneyland—and it didn't, ending about five months later.

Disneyland's version of the Funhouse was based on an interactive exhibit that had been set up for the holidays at the Disney-owned El Capitan Theater in Hollywood, the glitzy movie palace where *Toy Story* was being shown. After seeing the movie, patrons there could explore an exhibit for more *Toy Story* fun. At Disneyland, the Funhouse was spread over several rooms where guests could play video games, negotiate clever obstacle courses, interact with different displays, and buy photos featuring the movie's characters. A gift shop with a *Toy Story* theme also added to the fun. Outside the Funhouse stood a temporary stage where a musical show called *Hamm's All-Doll Revue* was presented regularly to standing-room-only audiences (it wasn't standing-room-only because the show was popular, but because there simply weren't any seats).

With spring about to become summer and Toy Story gone from theaters, the whole Toy Story Funhouse complex was removed in favor of . . . nothing. Two years later, Redd Rockett's Pizza Port would start serving pizzas from the old Funhouse location.

Trash Cans

Writing in his book *Designing Disney*, John Hench noted how the park's original designers "wanted everything that guests experience . . . to be an entertaining part of the story"; thus Hench and his cohorts "took the most basic needs of guests and turned them into attractions." One of those "basic needs" is the urge to unload garbage, especially when guests already have their hands full with bags, strollers, distracted children, A–E tickets from the park's **ticket book** (in the first decades), FASTPASS tickets (in later decades), and more.

Just as another basic need, the use of a **restroom**, is enlivened with a theme appropriate to the area where each particular restroom is located, so too are trash cans given creative decorations that identify them with various Disneyland lands. There have been dozens of different styles of trash cans in the park, including *faux*-bamboo for Adventureland, *faux*-wood for Frontierland, gothic for New Orleans Square, and futuristic for Tomorrowland.

The traditional metal cans themselves are generally of a uniform shape (vertical box) and size (42 inches tall, 20 inches wide), with hinged doors in the upper third. Most have a polite invitation for "Waste Please." A few identify individual locations by name, such as one at **Redd Rockett's Pizza Port**; a few others are shape-specific for the immediate area, such as the tree-stump trash cans on **Tom Sawyer Island**. Nearly every trash can is placed 20-25 steps from another one (supposedly Walt Disney himself paced this distance off). And these days, the trash cans are often accompanied by matching recycling bins. The trash cans are so memorable that a special series of 10 collectible pins was produced in 2001; each pin replicated a different trash can and even had a small swinging door.

Tropical Cantina,
aka Adventureland Cantina, aka Cantina

MAP: Adventureland, A-3

DATES: 1955–1992

Listed in Disneyland's **souvenir books** in the 1950s was a spot in Adventureland called at times either the Tropical Cantina, Adventureland Cantina, or simply the Cantina (the latter name was painted on the building). Whatever the name was, it was always situated across from the **Jungle Cruise.** The signage out front said this establishment served "ice cold tropical drinks." The thatched roof and outdoor tables stayed when the new **Sunkist, I Presume** set up here in 1962.

Troubadour Tavern

MAP: Fantasyland, Fa-17

DATES: November 2009–ongoing

This often-renamed eatery next to the **Videopolis** stage got re-troubadoured in 2009. This counter-service quick-stop started out in 1985 as **Yumz** and ran through three more names before settling on Troubadour Treats for the millennium. In 2004 the arrival of *Snow White: An Enchanting Musical* brought another name, Enchanted Cottage Sweets & Treats, with a fantasy forest theme. Three years after the **Princess Fantasy Faire** replaced *Snow White*, Troubadour Tavern replaced the Enchanted Cottage.

With the new name came new medieval tent décor and new menu items, including baked potatoes and bratwurst. An adjacent patio area still offers seats in the shade to diners. The Troubadour is the second tavern in Disneyland history; from the 1950s to the '70s, the **Oaks Tavern** served up fast food in Frontierland.

20th Century Music Company

MAP: Main Street, MS-19

DATES: June 20, 1999–ongoing

The cigar store Indian standing on the right-hand side of **Main Street** may seem out of place today, but it serves as a reminder of the **Fine Tobacco** shop that was once next to the **Main Street Cinema** during Disneyland's first 35 years. After spending the '90s as various collectibles shops, at the end of the decade the space became a fun and fascinating music store.

Offering "new sounds for a new century," the 20th Century Music Company is all about tunes (not to be confused with toons). Antique instruments are displayed on upper shelves, a century-old, 55-inch-tall symphonion music box stands by the door, and drawings of classical composers hang on the walls.

For Disney aficionados, the store is nirvana (though the band of the same name isn't represented here). The jam-packed room has showcased Disney-related books, sheet music, soundtracks from Disney films and CDs by Disneyland entertainers like the **Dapper Dans** and **Billy Hill and the Hillbillies**. At one time special kiosks enabled guests to burn their own customized discs of Disneyland sounds, speeches, and announcements. In 2011 a wall of iPad accessories and video games was featured in the store.

20,000 Leagues Under the Sea Exhibit

MAP: Tomorrowland, T-23

DATES: August 3, 1955–August 28, 1966

Possibly the very last attraction **Walt Disney** worked on before **Opening Day** was the 20,000 Leagues Under the Sea Exhibit. According to Neal Gabler's *Walt Disney: The Triumph of the American Imagination*, Disney conceived of the exhibit the evening before the park's televised opening and worked on it late into the night with Disney Legend **Ken Anderson**, both of them donning masks for a flurry of 11th-hour spray-painting. They were desperately trying to get something into the **Tomorrowland** building that would one day house **Star Tours**. Unfortunately, this building was, in mid-July of '55, mostly empty, and would remain so for the next two weeks.

When it finally opened in early August, the Leagues exhibit didn't have much to do with the future, which supposedly was Tomor-rowland's domain. Instead, the exhibit offered a walk-through tour of the 19th-century-style sets and props used in Disney's *20,000 Leagues Under the Sea* movie. While a movie set exhibit might seem like a routine concept today, it was unique for its time, and guests were elated to be closer to movie-making magic than ever before. Adding to the excitement was the propitious timing. The immensely popular Disney movie had come out in December of '54, and on March 30, 1955 it had won an Oscar for Best Art Direction—Set Decoration. Thus Jules Verne's tale was still very hot property in the summer of '55.

The sets on display included some of the actual interiors from the *Nautilus*, and among the props was Captain Nemo's famous pipe organ in his lavishly appointed parlor. A large, detailed model of the submarine and Vulcania paintings by **Peter Ellenshaw** contributed cinematic special effects, and a view of the giant squid through the sub's large circular viewing window contributed some genuine thrills. **Harper Goff** designed the sub and some of the sets, while golden-throated **Thurl Ravenscroft** provided the narration.

What was intended to be a temporary Tomorrowland placeholder, and never more than an A-ticket attraction (see **ticket book**), was ultimately so popular that it lasted until 1966 and generated a dynamic **attraction poster** featuring the squid. Finally, after 11 years, the sets were struck to make way for the huge remodel that was on Tomorrowland's near horizon. In Disneyland, a reminder of the exhibit now resides in the **Haunted Mansion**, where a ghostly musician in the ballroom still plays Nemo's pipe organ.

Upjohn Pharmacy

MAP: Main Street, MS-4

DATES: July 17, 1955–September 1970

On **Opening Day**, **Main Street** had a bank, department store, candy shop, general store, and other businesses that would have appeared in an early-1900s downtown area. To add even more authenticity, it also included an apothecary. The Upjohn Pharmacy wasn't a joke—the Upjohn Company was a huge pharmaceutical manufacturer founded in 1886 (they're now part of Pfizer), and the Disneyland pharmacy they sponsored was a detailed recreation of what a pharmacy would have been like at the turn of the last century. A side room displayed the latest in 1955 pharmaceutical technology.

The pharmacy's location was on the corner of West Center and Main, just north of the **Crystal Arcade**. Old-fashioned medicines lined the shelves and antique pharmaceutical equipment decorated the counters and walls, but it was the jar teeming with leeches that riveted guests' attention. While nothing was for sale, jars of all-purpose vitamin pills were freely dispensed.

The Upjohn Pharmacy got a mention and an illustration in the "Special Shows and Exhibits" section of Disneyland's 1958 **souvenir book**. When Upjohn ceased its park participation in 1970, the whole corner site was soon split up and transformed—the side room became the **Hurricane Lamp Shop** and the main pharmacy became **New Century Watches & Clocks**.

Ursus H. Bear's Wilderness Outpost

MAP: Bear Country/Critter Country, B/C-6

DATES: March 24, 1972–November 23, 1988

Disneyland has had three Outposts in its history. Preceding the **Safari Outpost** and **Indiana Jones Adventure Outpost** was Ursus H. Bear's Wilderness Outpost, a new store for the new **Bear Country** that opened in 1972. Its name honors the character who supposedly founded the nearby **Country Bear Jamboree**. *Ursus* is also the Latin word for "bear," and Outpost is the Disney name for "retail store."

The Wilderness Outpost shared the long wooden building in the back of Bear Country with the **Brer Bar** and **Teddi Barra's Swingin' Arcade** (Ursus's spot was in the southwestern corner). The wilderness merchandise available here included country-style gift items, plus the usual T-shirts and souvenirs. In 1988, when Bear Country went Critter, the mammalian Outpost transformed into the reptilian **Crocodile Mercantile** on its way to becoming the Winnified **Pooh Corner** in 2003.

Videopolis, aka Fantasyland Theater

MAP: Fantasyland, Fa-18

DATES: June 22, 1985–October 2006

When the indoor **Magic Eye Theater** replaced the outdoor Space Stage in 1986, Disneyland was left without a venue for large open-air concerts. Voilà Videopolis, a new state-of-the-art concert area that opened in **Fantasyland** even before the Magic Eye was completed. Videopolis, the au courant name capitalizing on '80s videocassette technology, opened west of the nearby **It's a Small World**. A new depot, the Videopolis Station, made the site accessible to train-traveling guests.

Catering to teenagers for its first 10 years, Videopolis offered boisterous nighttime concerts. Bands performed up on a brilliantly lit stage in front of large dance areas totaling 5,000 square feet, a space about the size of a basketball court. Perimeter bleacher seats, light shows, special effects, big video screens, and dozens of monitors circling the dance area all combined to make concerts here just as dazzling

10 Live Stage Shows at the Fantasyland Theater, 1989–2006

1. 1989–1990: *One Man's Dream* (based on the life of Walt Disney)
2. 1990: *Dick Tracy Starring in Diamond Double-Cross* (based on the 1990 movie)
3. 1991: *Plane Crazy* (starring Baloo)
4. Winters of 1991 and 1992: *Mickey's Nutcracker* (for the holidays only)
5. 1992–1995: *Beauty and the Beast* (based on the 1991 movie)
6. 1995–1997: *The Spirit of Pocahontas* (based on the 1995 movie,)
7. 1998–2001: *Animazement: The Musical* (a tribute to Disney animation)
8. 2001–2002: *Mickey's Detective School* (Disney characters search for Pluto)
9. Winters of 2001 and 2002: *Minnie's Christmas Party* (for the holidays only)
10. 2004–2006: *Snow White: An Enchanting Musical* (based on the 1937 movie)

as those in any rock arena. They were just as loud, too, but fortunately the location at Disneyland's northern boundary kept the noise far from guests in the rest of the park.

By the 1990s, however, with teens losing interest, the theater got 1,200 new first-come, first-served floor seats and a new purpose. Instead of live concerts for dancin' teens, Disneyland started trying out live stage shows for seated families. The results were so successful that in 1995 Videopolis received a more traditional theater name. Actually, its new Fantasyland Theater name wasn't all that new—it had been given to the **Mickey Mouse Club Theater** from 1964 to 1981 (the 1983 arrival of **Pinocchio's Daring Journey** in that building made the theatrical appellation available). Later changes to the theater included the addition of a tent high over the seating area in 1998.

The Spirit of Pocahontas was the debut stage show for the revived Fantasyland Theater. Shows usually lasted one or two years and became increasingly spectacular. *Snow White: An Enchanting Musical* boasted Patrick Stewart as the voice of the Magic Mirror, elaborate sets, and a production team straight from Broadway. Late in 2006 the theater finally closed and was reinvented as a new themed area called the **Princess Fantasy Faire**.

Viewliner

MAP: Tomorrowland, T-10

DATES: June 26, 1957–September 15, 1958

Not satisfied with the old-fashioned railroad circling Disneyland, the miniature **Mine Train** chugging through **Frontierland**, and the charming **Casey Jr. Circus Train** winding through **Fantasyland**, **Walt Disney** decided to add a more modern train to the park in 1957. What was modern then, though, hardly looks modern now, and so the inelegant Viewliner is usually remembered as one of the oddest contraptions ever to run on Disneyland tracks.

The new **Bob Gurr**-designed train had lots of similarities to other vehicles. The not-quite-figure-eight track, for instance, was only 30 inches wide, the same as Casey's and the Mine Train's tracks. The Viewliner's sponsor was the Atchison, Topeka and Santa Fe Railroad, as it was for Disneyland's main train. The cab on the front car was a cut-down version of a '54 Oldsmobile 88, which meant a height of under six feet, two swinging car doors, a car-like windshield, and the semblance of a car's blunt nose and headlight assembly. Inside the Viewliner's cab, the engineer shifted gears with an automobile clutch and drove with a steering wheel. The strong, gas-powered V-8 engine from a Chevy Corvette could accelerate the train to about 30 miles per hour and pull five cars behind the locomotive.

When the Viewliner debuted as a B-ticket attraction (see **ticket books**) in Disneyland's third summer, it had two complete trains, one blue and one red, running on the same track. There were stations in Fantasyland and **Tomorrowland**, with each train operating from just one (blue in Fantasyland, red in Tomorrowland). Not only were the trains painted differently, but their 32-passenger cars also had Disney-themed names—*Alice*, *Bambi*, *Cinderella*, *Pinocchio*, and *Tinker Bell* for the Fantasyland cars, and *Mars*, *Mercury*, *Jupiter*, *Saturn*, and *Venus* for the Tomorrowland cars (no *Pluto*, since that name applied both to a Disney character and a heavenly body). The trains looped through the two lands and around the sites of what would become important new attractions in 1959—the **Matterhorn Bobsleds** and **Submarine Voyage**.

Almost 1.5 million guests rode the trains, but just a year after its first run the Viewliner's days were already numbered, once Walt Disney began investigating an experimental new monorail line in Germany. Only 15 months after opening, the Viewliners were closing in mid-1958, and nine months after that Disneyland's **Monorail** was up and running (the Monorail's loading area is still right where the Viewliner's Tomorrowland station had been). Attempts to recycle the Viewliner trains into other civic projects around Los Angeles fell through, and two decades later they were demolished.

Village Inn,
aka Village Haus

MAP: Fantasyland, Fa-11

DATES: May 25, 1983–ongoing

Back when the Fantasyland Theater was drawing guests to the northwest end of the **Sleeping Beauty Castle** courtyard, the closest eateries in the immediate area were the little **Welch's Grape Juice Stand** and the quick-serve **Character Foods** hut. Everything changed in 1983 with the landmark remodel of **Fantasyland**. The theater became **Pinocchio's Daring Journey**, the Welch's and Character Foods eateries disappeared, and the area's main restaurant became the Village Inn. Attached to the back of the Pinocchio building, the Inn got alpine styling, a gabled roof, and eventually a name change to Village Haus.

Two food companies, Sun Giant for the first decade and Minute Maid thereafter, have been the sponsors. Inside, wood carvings and toys punctuate the décor, while elaborate wall murals depict scenes from Disney's 1941 *Pinocchio* movie. The menu has grown increasingly well-rounded over the years, shifting from basic burgers and fries to pizzas, pastas, sandwiches, and salads (a 2011 menu update added some gourmet cheeseburger options along with other new items). Seating is available inside and out, the outdoor tables offering views of the nearby **Casey Jr. Circus Train**. Guests dine unaware that below them is a subterranean maze of storerooms, offices, and food-prep areas.

Villains Lair

MAP: Fantasyland, Fa-30

DATES: October 3, 1998–July 1, 2004

For such a choice location—the first store on the right as guests walk north through **Sleeping Beauty Castle** and into the **Fantasyland** courtyard—this charming building sure has gone through lots of tenants. **Merlin's Magic Shop**, the **Briar Rose Cottage**, **Quasimodo's Attic**, and the **Knight Shop** all operated here with varying degrees of success and varying longevity. One of these past occupants was **Disney Villains**, purveyor of villain-themed merchandise from 1991 to '96. After a two-year absence, the bad guys rebounded in 1998 with a new shop in the old location. This one, Villains Lair, reprised the dark themes from earlier in the decade. After four years of selling lots of scary costume accessories, apparel with images of wicked queens, and creepy glow-in-the-dark gifts, Villains Lair began operating on an infrequent schedule and finally closed completely in 2004. When the **Heraldry Shoppe** moved in, some of the villainous merchandise found its way to other Disneyland stores, among them **Le Bat en Rouge** in **New Orleans Square**.

Wagner, Jack

(1925–1995)

"The Voice of Disneyland" was born in California in 1925. Surrounded by a musical family, Jack Wagner started in show business at a young age and worked for MGM in his teens. As an adult, Wagner got many supporting parts on popular TV shows of the 1950s, among them *Dragnet* and *Sea Hunt*. Fluent in several languages and possessing a warm, resonant voice, Wagner was also a popular radio personality in Southern California, which brought him invitations to do some announcing work for Disneyland's **parades** and special events in the 1950s and '60s.

In 1970 Wagner replaced actor Rex Allen as Disneyland's official announcer. For the next two decades, Wagner's friendly, welcoming voice narrated the train trip around the park, politely requested that riders on the **Matterhorn Bobsleds** "remain seated please," gave cheerful safety spiels at numerous other attractions, delivered official announcements over the park's loudspeakers, and introduced the **Main Street Electrical Parade**. Most of these performances were recorded at Wagner's home studio a few miles from the park.

In addition to his Disneyland work, Wagner produced Disney-themed records and did voiceovers on TV commercials. He also performed the announcements for other Disney theme parks and public entities (such as Orlando International Airport). Jack Wagner retired in 1991 after undergoing vocal cord surgery and died from a heart attack four years later. He was named a Disney Legend in 2005. Since 1991, Wagner's successor as "the Voice of Disneyland" has been Bill Rogers, a voice-over actor who also makes announcements for other Disney parks and projects.

Walker, Tommy
(1923–1986)

The younger half of the father-and-son Walker team was Tommy, born in 1923. Hired as Disneyland's director of entertainment, one of his earliest assignments was to orchestrate the 1955 **Opening Day** festivities, for which he quickly helped invent the famous **fireworks**, **parades**, the winter Candlelight Procession, and other crowd-pleasing special events.

Prior to his Disneyland career, Tommy had been a decorated World War II vet, a USC drum major, and the kicker on the school's football team. He's credited as the composer of the familiar six-note "da-da-da-DUT-da-DUH . . . CHARGE!" fanfare that's still heard in stadiums across America. In 1965 Tommy Walker was identified at the end of a *Walt Disney's Wonderful World of Color* episode as the "Disneyland Coordinator." Two years later, after a dozen years at the park, he left to form his own entertainment company. Walker eventually orchestrated such events as the opening and closing ceremonies of three Olympic Games, Super Bowl half-time shows, the fireworks at the 1986 Statue of Liberty celebration, the Rose Bowl's Independence Day fireworks shows, and special performances at Radio City Music Hall. Tommy Walker died at age 63 in 1986 while undergoing heart surgery.

Walker, Vesey
(1893–1977)

In July of '55, when he was looking for someone to organize and lead a marching band for Opening Day, Tommy Walker didn't have to look outside his own family. Vesey Walker, an Englishman born in 1893, had already led dozens of marching bands in the U.S., including the one for Marquette University. Vesey Walker's original Disneyland gig was supposed to end after two weeks, but it wound up lasting until 1970.

According to Bob Thomas's biography *Walt Disney: An American Original*, **Walt Disney** instructed Walker about the band's repertoire, saying, "I just want you to remember one thing: if the people can't go away whistling it, don't play it." But whistle they did, and Vesey Walker's **Disneyland Band** playing in their crisp uniforms is a fond memory for millions of Disneyland guests. He was also a familiar presence in Disneyland's **souvenir books**—from '55 to '68 he was in every single one, sometimes with two photos, and usually the captions identified him by name. Working in pain in the late '60s, Walker overcame a rare paralyzing disease to make some final park appearances before retiring in 1970. Vesey Walker died seven years later and was inducted as a Disney Legend in 2005.

The Walt Disney Story, aka The Walt Disney Story, Featuring Great Moments with Mr. Lincoln

MAP: Town Square, TS-9

DATES: April 8, 1973–spring 2005

The Legacy of Walt Disney, a tribute to **Walt Disney** and his many accomplishments, ran on Main Street from 1970 to '73. When that corner space became **Disneyland Presents a Preview of Coming Attractions**, the awards and biographical material that had been there moved into the ground floor of the **Opera House**. The new exhibit replaced the Opera House's previous show devoted to another legendary American, **Great Moments with Mr. Lincoln**, though the Great Emancipator wouldn't be gone for long.

Dedicated by Walt's wife Lillian, the Walt Disney Story instantly became one of the park's most absorbing exhibits. As the sign out front announced, the Walt Disney Story included everything "from Mickey Mouse to the Magic Kingdoms" and was "presented free by Gulf Oil." Expanding on the earlier Legacy of Walt Disney displays, the Opera House's lobby area was filled with artifacts and awards that celebrated Disney's diverse roles as an artist, international ambassador of good will, TV pioneer, and filmmaker. Original art from Disney's animated films, props from his TV shows, family photos, early Mickey Mouse merchandise, and even the horseless carriage Walt Disney used in **parades** were all on view.

Disneyland itself was part of the show, as a fascinating high-speed film showed the park under construction. The most unusual display was also the most elaborate—a detailed recreation of Walt Disney's actual office at Disney Studios, with authentic furniture and decorations all accurately in place. (Some biographers state that, even

though this office did exist at the studio, Disney usually preferred to work in a spare side room with a simple desk).

The second part of the exhibit was presented in the 500-seat Opera House theater. There, a 28-minute film retold Walt Disney's life story. Rare film clips and Disney's own narration took guests from his midwestern upbringing all the way up to the beginnings of Walt Disney World in Florida. As entertaining as the film was, guests expressed nostalgia for Mr. Lincoln. So, after closing in February 1975 for a four-month remodel, on June 12, 1975 the exhibit reopened with Lincoln supplementing the film, making this a long presentation with a long compound title: The Walt Disney Story, Featuring Great Moments with Mr. Lincoln. In the 1970s Disneyland's **souvenir books** proudly showed off the entire exhibit with several photos and detailed descriptive text.

Modifications were made to the exhibit over the following decades—a huge, meticulous model of the U.S. Capitol was added to the lobby area, Mr. Lincoln was updated with new technology and a new Gettysburg presentation, and eventually the Disney film stopped showing altogether. For 2005's **Happiest Homecoming on Earth** celebration of Disneyland's 50th anniversary, Lincoln was temporarily retired once again; the theater and signage out front were given to a well-received film called *Disneyland: The First 50 Magical Years*.

Watches & Clocks, aka Timex Shop

MAP: Main Street, MS-13

DATES: July 17, 1955–1972

In 1954, exactly 100 years after its founding, Connecticut's Waterbury Clock Company renamed itself U.S. Time. That was the company's name when its new Watches & Clocks store debuted on Disneyland's **Main Street** on **Opening Day**. The shop's location was a small room one doorway south of the **Silhouette Studio**. Timex watches, which U.S. Time had put on the market at the beginning of the decade, were the store's timeliest attractions; already ads were touting their hardiness as the affordable timepiece that "takes a licking and keeps on ticking." The shop was even informally referred to as the Timex Shop, though Disneyland's **souvenir books** of the 1950s and '60s labeled it Watches & Clocks.

Whatever its name, many of the timepieces on display there had Mickey Mouse faces and are now considered valuable collectibles. Time finally ran out on Watches & Clocks when **Crystal Arts** moved into this space in 1972. Elgin's **New Century Watches & Clocks** across the way would soon become Main Street's primary watch store.

Welch's Grape Juice Stand

MAP: Fantasyland, Fa-9

DATES: 1956–1981

In Disneyland's first three decades, **Fantasyland** had few eateries, and even fewer with a name sponsor. One of the latter was the Welch's Grape Juice Stand (as **souvenir books** usually labeled it). Welch's Foods, the juice company founded in the 1800s, also sponsored the Mickey Mouse Club, and thus the stand's location was especially appropriate—it shared the same building that housed the **Mickey Mouse Club Theater**. Exclusively promoting the company's main product, the Welch's concession was painted with grape-themed murals. The counter sold cold cups of purple, red, and white grape juice, with frozen grape juice bars as an even icier option.

In 1982 the massive remodel that overhauled Fantasyland finally ended the Juice Stand's 26-year run. A year later the beautifully-styled **Pinocchio's Daring Journey** and **Geppetto's Arts & Crafts** opened where the theater and Welch's had been.

Westward Ho Conestoga Wagon Fries

MAP: Frontierland, Fr-18

DATES: November 16, 1998–September 2, 2008

Even though it was a relatively modest little eatery in what seemed like an out-of-the-way spot alongside the **Rivers of America**, Westward Ho Conestoga Wagon Fries had several connections to Disneyland's past. In the 1950s, the Conestoga Wagons attraction operated near this part of Frontierland; some of the wagons had the words Westward Ho! painted on them.

Another connection was to something that still exists today—the similarly named **Westward Ho Trading Company**, which has been operating near the Frontierland entrance since 1987. Both Westward Ho spots echoed *Westward Ho the Wagons*, a 1956 Disney movie about pioneers on the move. The Conestoga Wagon Fries stand actually resembled one of those wooden plains-crossing vehicles from the 1800s.

There was yet one more connection between Conestoga Wagon Fries and something else in Disneyland. The stand's sponsor, McDonald's, occupied another space, the **Harbour Galley**, on the other side of the river in front of **Splash Mountain** until 2008. Both places sold virtually the same thing—McDonald's fries and sodas—until the McSponsorship ended, resulting in the disappearance of Conestoga Wagon Fries (the Harbour Galley continues on but with a different menu).

Westward Ho Trading Co.

MAP: Frontierland, Fr-27

DATES: September 2, 1987–ongoing

After three decades near the **Frontierland** entrance, the old **Frontier Trading Post** was renamed in 1987. The rustic sign out front announced the new shop as the rhyming Westward Ho Trading Co. The first two words allude to *Westward Ho the Wagons*, a 1956 Disney movie starring Fess Parker. Outside stands a five-foot-tall cigar-store Indian, a twin of the statue in front of the **20th Century Music Company** on **Main Street**. Inside, the merchandise used to feature frontier souvenirs but then switched to gourmet chocolates, jelly beans, and cookies. In recent years the store has sold pins, pin-trading accessories, and seasonal ornaments and decorations.

What Will You Celebrate?

DATES: January 1, 2009–December 31, 2010

When the **Year of a Million Dreams** promotion ended after 27 months, Disneyland kicked off 2009 with What Will You Celebrate?, a new campaign that gave guests free admission on their birthdays. Since few guests celebrate Disneyland birthdays by themselves, the additional paid admissions for friends and family (and all that extra celebratory dining and shopping) undoubtedly compensated for the free giveaway, which continued through 2010. A new promotional campaign called **Let the Memories Begin** followed in 2011.

Wheelhouse and Delta Banjo

MAP: Frontierland, Fr-6

DATES: 1974–ca. 1990

In the mid-1970s, these two fast-food eateries replaced **Frontierland's** tiny **Malt Shop and Cone Shop** next door to the **River Belle Terrace**. The Wheelhouse, its name an allusion to the nearby *Mark Twain*, was mainly a weekend spot for burgers, sodas, and ice cream; the Delta Banjo, its name an allusion to a restaurant that had been in this location in the late '50s, **Don DeFore's Silver Banjo**, was a sandwich-and-snacks seller of limited menu and hours. By 1990 both had been lost to remodels.

Wonderland Music, aka Main Street Music

MAP: Main Street, MS-13; Town Square, TS-8

DATES: 1960–1972

After spending a couple of years in the northeastern block of **Main Street** where Chester Drawers is now located, in 1960 the Wonderland Music store settled into a space in **Town Square**. This new location was just north of the entrance to the **Opera House**, a room formerly occupied by **Jimmy Starr's Show Business Souvenirs**. Wonderland sold Disney movie soundtracks and music by Disney entertainers on vinyl records, plus sheet music of Disney songs. Disneyland's **souvenir books** labeled this shop with the generic name Main Street Music, perhaps to help guests better locate it.

Wonderland wandered off in '72, leaving the space vacant for three years until it was used as a hospitality center into the '80s and as an infrequent guest-relations office in the '90s. Today, Disney music can be found nearby in the **20th Century Music Company**.

Wood, C. V.
(1922–1992)

One of the almost-forgotten members of the core Disneyland planning team was Cornelius Vanderbilt Wood, a Texan born in 1922 (some profiles call him an Oklahoman). Wood's background was in industrial engineering. Prior to his Disneyland years, he'd been a manager at the Stanford Research Institute, the same firm where **Harrison Price** worked (Price scouted locations for Disneyland, and Wood then helped persuade Anaheim landowners to sell their plots to Disney). While still in his early 30s, Wood was hired as Disneyland's first general manager to help get the park built. Wood then brought **Joe Fowler** and **Van Arsdale France** onto the nascent Disneyland project; Fowler would rise from a consulting position to become the construction supervisor, and France would eventually be in charge of training all Disneyland employees.

Harrison Price called Wood one of the "boldest, smartest, most shameless and colorful characters ever to career through this business" in his book *Walt's Revolution!* In his memoir *Window on Main Street*, Van France described Wood as a "masterful salesman" who "could easily compete with the legendary P. T. Barnum." France also credited Wood with bringing in corporate lessees like Swift and TWA to help loosen the park's tight financial situation.

It was Wood who oversaw the daily logistics: pre-opening, these included such details as having the official **Opening Day** invitations printed up, and post-opening it meant that Wood and his team were going to run Disneyland, setting everything from park policies to park hours. However, soon after Opening Day, Walt Disney relieved Wood of his duties so that Disney himself, and a hand-picked committee, could supervise daily operations. Some stories suggest they had a serious falling out, possibly because the egocentric Wood was taking credit for designing Disneyland (Wood may have considered himself a star, but his boss was a galaxy). Harrison Price claimed that a separation was inevitable because of Wood's and Disney's immiscible personalities (the scabrous Wood could easily offend with off-color jokes). According to the *New York Times*, the circumstances may even have involved embezzlement.

Wood responded by starting his own amusement parks in Colorado, Massachusetts, and New York. Of these, the Bronx site was the most famous. Called Freedomland U.S.A., and promoted as "the World's Largest Entertainment Center" because it opened on 205 acres (as compared to Disneyland's 160), the park operated from 1960 to 1964. Wood, dubbing himself "the Master Builder of Disneyland," was aided by former Disneyland employees. His park even echoed Disneyland's layout, though Freedomland's themes all derived from American history. Unfortunately, a fire that destroyed some of the buildings before the park opened, a serious ride accident in the first month, and a robbery in the first summer all led to immediate financial problems. When the 1964–1965 New York World's Fair opened in Queens, Freedomland U.S.A. was declared bankrupt, and some its rides were scattered to other amusement parks.

Wood later co-founded the International Chili Society, helped bring London Bridge to Lake Havasu in Arizona, co-designed Lake Havasu City, and even landed a small part in a B movie. Wood died of cancer in 1992. Despite his early contributions to Disneyland, all official references to Wood seem to have been purged from Disney's public literature.

World Beneath Us Exhibit

MAP: Tomorrowland, T-6

DATES: Summer 1955–December 1959

In 1955 the Richfield Oil Corporation sponsored two different locations in Disneyland. One—the **Autopia**—used gas, while the other—the World Beneath Us Exhibit—promoted it.

The World Beneath Us was located on the left-hand side of **Tomorrowland** where **Little Green Men Store Command** is today. Disneyland's 1956 **souvenir book** described the exhibit as a "Cinemascope Technicolor Cartoon & Diorama" telling "the story of oil." That cartoon, titled *The World Beneath Us*, had prehistoric cavemen teaching modern audiences how oil is formed, with dinosaurs alongside to help illustrate the process (the '58 souvenir book emphasized the connection between decaying dinos and plentiful petroleum by placing a drawing of a dinosaur in front of an oil rig). The exhibit ended with a diorama and a map of the L.A. basin that highlighted the oil fields along the coast.

The Richfield exhibit ran out of gas at the end of '59. In May of 1960, the **Art of Animation** exhibit filled the building with a display promoting Disney's animated movies.

Wurlitzer Music Hall

MAP: Main Street, MS-20

DATES: July 17, 1955–September 1968

In the park's first decade, guests streaming northward from **Town Square** onto **Main Street** encountered the Wurlitzer Music Hall on the first right-hand corner. The Wurlitzer space was big, for a big product—this shop housed pianos and organs. It was listed in Disneyland's 1958 **souvenir book** in the "Special Shows and Exhibits" category in back, with text describing "daily organ concerts and display of pianos and organs." Pianos were indeed played in the shop by pianists, mechanical player pianos rolled out traditional tunes, and guests were invited to sing along, though how many bought pianos while at Disneyland is debatable.

The Rudolf Wurlitzer Company pulled out its sponsorship and its instruments in 1968. About a year later the prominent corner was refashioned as an awards-filled celebration called **The Legacy of Walt Disney**.

Yacht Club, aka Yacht Bar

MAP: Tomorrowland, T-10, T-7

DATES: Summer 1955–September 6, 1966

For over a decade Disneyland had its own Yacht Club, though it wasn't as exclusive as it sounds. Basically a place for fast food, the Yacht Club was a freestanding counter-service eatery alongside the **Tomorrowland** lagoon (hence the "yacht" reference). The aquatic theme included an exterior display of nautical pennants; the rest of the building, with its angled roof extending out over its customers, looked more like an old McDonald's franchise.

In 1957 the Yacht Club was transferred to a new site. With the **Viewliner** and its station about to be built, the Yacht Club was lifted and moved about 75 feet away from the lagoon (the **Monorail** station would later stand where the Yacht Club had been). The Yacht Club was renamed the Yacht Bar, though the burgers-and-fries menu stayed about the same. The 1959 **souvenir book** listed a Yacht Bar Dance Area adjacent to the Yacht Bar, a foreshadowing of future developments. In 1966 a major remodel of Tomorrowland sank the Yacht Bar for good; a year later, the **Tomorrowland Terrace** arose nearby with a zesty dance area of its own.

Yale & Towne Lock Shop

MAP: Main Street, MS-19

DATES: July 17, 1955–1964

Looking for sponsors to help launch his park, **Walt Disney** enticed the Yale & Town Lock Company to set up business on the eastern side of **Main Street**. Inventor Linus Yale had patented pin-tumbler locks in the mid-1800s and then partnered with Henry Towne to become America's premier lock manufacturer, successful enough to diversify into forklifts and industrial vehicles.

At Disneyland, the Yale & Towne Lock Shop was located just south of the prominent **Market House**. Y & T was listed in the "Special Shows and Exhibits" section in Disneyland's 1958 **souvenir book**; an illustration showed a lock and a key, and the text described "a complete display of the locksmith's art, from the oldest to the newest." Inside the store, one wall told "The Story of Locks," and another displayed hundreds of keys. As unexciting as all this might sound, the Lock Shop lasted for almost 10 years. Eventually the long-lasting **Jewelry Shop** took over this space.

Year of a Million Dreams

DATES: October 1, 2006–December 31, 2008

In 1971 Disneyland became the site of a special event called the Year of a Hundred Million Smiles. Some special giveaways helped count down the wait for guest number 100 million to walk through the park's turnstiles, a moment that finally occurred on June 17th of that year. Thirty-five years later, as soon as the 18-month celebration of Disneyland's 50th anniversary concluded, the park introduced its Year of a Million Dreams, all of them undoubtedly leading to a million smiles.

Among the million gifts and opportunities offered to guests were special pins and Mickey Mouse ears, free meals in the park, invitations to march along in Disneyland **parades**, and instant **FASTPASS** badges for quick access to attractions. The biggest giveaways were overnight stays in the Mickey Mouse Penthouse at the adjacent Disneyland Hotel and trips to other Disney parks. No purchase was required, and no special qualifications or competitions helped guests anticipate the sudden, surprising appearance of wish-granting Dream Squad members who toted bags with special Year of a Million Dreams logos.

Originally the Year of a Million Dreams was scheduled to last 15, not 12, months, beginning October 1, 2006 and ending December 31, 2007. But halfway through 2007, the promotion's ongoing popularity prompted an extension to the end of 2008. Accompanied by a new name, the Disney Dreams Giveaway dangled a new dream in front of guests—the chance to stay overnight in the **New Orleans Square** rooms formerly occupied by the **Disney Gallery**. On September 18, 2008, the Walt Disney Company, hoping to encourage "celebration vacations," introduced the promotion that would follow the Year of a Million Dreams: 2009's **What Will You Celebrate?**, which gave guests free admission on their birthdays.

Yippie Day

DATES: August 6, 1970

One of the most infamous events in Disneyland's history occurred on August 6, 1970. The International Yippie Pow-Wow, more commonly referred to as Yippie Day, was intended to be a "convention" for members of the Youth International Party (yippies). These anti-establishment protesters hoped to attract publicity with a lineup of bizarre activities that were to be held in the park on the 25th anniversary of the atomic bombing of Hiroshima. While the farcical "planned" activities didn't happen (Porky Pig, a Warner Bros. cartoon character, was not barbecued for an afternoon feast), the 300 protesters did vandalize landscaping, buildings, and cars. They climbed into the rigging of the **Pirate Ship Restaurant** and took temporary control of **Tom Sawyer Island**; they marched while chanting and shouting obscenities; they engaged in shoving matches with guests and security personnel; and they ruined the Disneyland experience for thousands of paying guests.

Disneyland officials, forewarned and expecting the worst, prepared with extra security precautions, which included the presence of hundreds of local police officers in riot gear. **Jack Lindquist's** *In Service to the Mouse* details the park's strong response and the "protecting our own" attitude displayed by the united "family" of **cast members**. Disneyland closed about six hours early and free admission was offered to guests. Eighteen arrests were made (according to the next day's newspapers, though that number was later raised to 23), and the event drew national media attention.

Yumz, aka Louie's, aka Meeko's, aka Fantasyland Theater Snacks, aka Troubadour Treats

MAP: Fantasyland, Fa-17

DATES: June 19, 1985–ongoing

The tradition of serving fast food next to the big outdoor theater at the north end of **Fantasyland** began in mid-1985. That's when Yumz, a small snack stand, opened at about the same time as **Videopolis**, a new dance and concert area. The food at Yumz, just like the music next door, was teen-friendly, including quick-serve nachos, pizza, popcorn, and sodas.

Another tradition here was to match this eatery's name to whatever was happening on the adjacent stage. When Videopolis began presenting a live show called *Plane Crazy*, Yumz briefly changed its name to Louie's (connecting Baloo, *Plane Crazy*, and *The Jungle Book* movie). Yumz was soon restored, and then in '95 everything in this area was revised. Videopolis became the Fantasyland Theater; *The Spirit of Pocahontas* moved onto the stage; and the snack stand was renamed Meeko's after the *Pocahontas* raccoon. Meeko's offered the same basic snack food as its predecessor. After a couple of years, the theater began showing *Animazement: The Musical*, and Meeko's got remodeled first into Fantasyland Theater Snacks and then into Troubadour Treats. In 2004, when *Snow White: An Enchanting Musical* moved into the theater, Troubadour Treats got a new name, some new décor, and a new transformation into the **Enchanted Cottage Sweets & Treats**.

Zorro Days

DATES: April 26–27, May 30–June 1, and November 27–30, 1958; November 26–29, 1959; November 11–13, 1960

To advertise his *Zorro* TV series, which had premiered in October of 1957, **Walt Disney** brought the cast to **Frontierland** for a series of personal appearances. Zorro Day activities were held on three different 1958 weekends (April 26–27, May 30–June 1, and November 27–30), plus weekends in 1959 (November 26–29) and 1960 (November 11–13). The event featured a **parade** down **Main Street** that spotlighted Guy Williams, TV's Don Diego de la Vega (Zorro), on horseback. There was also some swordplay between the Zorro character and his nemesis, Captain Monastario, as they battled on both the **Mark Twain Riverboat** and across Frontierland roofs. Williams, named a Disney Legend in 2011, usually followed these battles with afternoon appearances at **Magnolia Park**. Zorro continued as a Disney presence into the 21st century; the studio brought him back to TV with 1983's short-lived *Zorro and Son* series, and Disneyland still incorporates Zorro imagery in its **Rancho del Zocalo Restaurante**.

In its first decade, promotions for contemporary live-action Disney movies and TV shows weren't unusual at Disneyland—the Mouseketeers from *The Mickey Mouse Club*, Davy Crockett, and the sets from *20,000 Leagues Under the Sea* had all been showcased before Zorro. After Zorro Days, two more movie-related locations, the **Swiss Family Treehouse** and **Babes in Toyland Exhibit**, joined the park in the early '60s. And rooftop battles, it seems, never go out of style—in 2008 another rugged screen star, Indiana Jones, was embroiled in his own rooftop escapades in **Adventureland** to support the latest Indy movie.

Appendix
Land by Land in Disneyland
(entries listed by category)

Adventureland

Attractions
Aladdin's Oasis
Big Game Safari Shooting Gallery
Enchanted Tiki Room
Indiana Jones Adventure
Jungle Cruise
Magnolia Park
Swiss Family Treehouse
Tarzan's Treehouse

Restaurants
Bengal Barbecue
Indy Fruit Cart
Sunkist, I Presume
Tahitian Terrace, aka Stouffer's in Disneyland Tahitian Terrace
Tiki Juice Bar
Tropical Cantina, aka Adventureland Cantina, aka Cantina

Stores
Adventureland Bazaar
Indiana Jones Adventure Outpost
Safari Outpost
South Seas Traders
Tiki Tropical Traders, aka Tropical Imports

Bear Country/Critter Country

Attractions
Country Bear Jamboree, aka Country Bear Playhouse
The Many Adventures of Winnie the Pooh
Splash Mountain
Teddi Barra's Swingin' Arcade

Restaurants
Critter Country Fruit Cart

Golden Bear Lodge, aka Hungry Bear Restaurant
Harbour Galley
Mile Long Bar

Stores
Brer Bar
Briar Patch
Critter Country Plush
Crocodile Mercantile
Pooh Corner
Professor Barnaby Owl's Photographic Art Studio
Ursus H. Bear's Wilderness Outpost

Fantasyland

Attractions
Alice in Wonderland
Baloo's Dressing Room
Canal Boats of the World
Casey Jr. Circus Train
Disney Afternoon Avenue
Dumbo the Flying Elephant
Fantasia Gardens
Fantasyland Autopia
It's a Small World
Junior Autopia
Keller's Jungle Killers
King Arthur Carrousel
King Triton Gardens, aka Triton Gardens
Mad Hatter's Mad Tea Party
Matterhorn Bobsleds
Matterhorn Mountain
Mickey Mouse Club Circus
Mickey Mouse Club Theater, aka Fantasyland Theater
Midget Autopia
Motor Boat Cruise, aka Motor Boat Cruise to Gummi Glen
Mr. Toad's Wild Ride
Peter Pan Flight, aka Peter Pan's Flight
Pinocchio's Daring Journey
Pixie Hollow
Princess Fantasy Faire
Skull Rock and Pirate's Cove, aka Skull Rock Cove
Skyway to Fantasyland and Skyway to Tomorrowland
Sleeping Beauty Castle
Sleeping Beauty Castle Walk-Through

Snow White Adventures,
    aka Snow White's Scary Adventures
Snow White Wishing Well and Grotto
Storybook Land Canal Boats
Sword in the Stone Ceremony
Tangled
Topiary Garden
Videopolis, aka Fantasyland Theater

Restaurants

Carrousel Candies
Castle Candy Kitchen, aka Castle Candy Shoppe
Character Foods, aka Character Food Facilities
Edelweiss Snacks
Enchanted Cottage Sweets & Treats
Geppetto's Candy Shoppe
Pirate Ship Restaurant, aka Chicken of the Sea Pirate Ship and Restaurant,
    aka Captain Hook's Galley
Troubadour Tavern
Village Inn, aka Village Haus
Welch's Grape Juice Stand
Yumz, aka Louie's, aka Meeko's, aka Fantasyland Theater Snacks,
    aka Troubadour Treats

Stores

Arts and Crafts Shop
Bibbidi Bobbidi Boutique
Briar Rose Cottage
Castle Arts
Castle Christmas Shop
Clock Shop
Disney Villains
Enchanted Chamber

Fairytale Arts
Fantasy Faire Gifts, aka Fantasy Shop, aka Fantasy Emporium,
    aka Fantasy Gift Faire
50th Anniversary Shop
Geppetto's Arts & Crafts, aka Geppetto's Toys & Gifts,
    aka Geppetto's Holiday Workshop
Heraldry Shoppe, aka Castle Heraldry
It's a Small World Toy Shop
Knight Shop
Le Petit Chalet
Mad Hatter of Fantasyland
Merlin's Magic Shop
Mickey's Christmas Chalet

Names Unraveled
Pixie Hollow Gift Cart
Princess Boutique
Quasimodo's Attic, aka Sanctuary of Quasimodo
Stromboli's Wagon
Three Fairies Magic Crystals
Tinker Bell & Friends
Tinker Bell Toy Shoppe, aka Once Upon a Time . . . The Disney Princess Shoppe
Villains Lair

Frontierland

Attractions
American Rifle Exhibit and Frontier Gun Shop
Big Thunder Mountain Railroad
Big Thunder Ranch, aka Festivals of Fools, aka Little Patch of Heaven
Conestoga Wagons
Davy Crockett Arcade, aka Davy Crockett Frontier Arcade
Davy Crockett Frontier Museum
Fantasmic!
Fowler's Harbor, aka Fowler's Landing
Frontierland Miniature Museum
Frontierland Shooting Gallery, aka Frontierland Shootin' Arcade, aka Frontierland
Shooting Exposition
Golden Horseshoe
Indian Village
Indian War Canoes, aka Davy Crockett's Explorer Canoes
Mark Twain Riverboat
Marshal's Office
Mike Fink Keel Boats
Mine Train, aka Rainbow Caverns Mine Train, aka Western Mine Train Through
Nature's Wonderland
Mineral Hall
Miniature Horse Corral
Mule Pack, aka Rainbow Ridge Mule Pack, aka Pack Mules Through Nature's
Wonderland
Nature's Wonderland
Painted Desert, aka Rainbow Desert
Petrified Tree
Rafts to Tom Sawyer Island
Rivers of America
Sailing Ship *Columbia*
Santa's Reindeer Round-Up
Stage Coach
Tom Sawyer Island, aka Pirate's Lair on Tom Sawyer Island

Restaurants

Aunt Jemima's Pancake House, aka Aunt Jemima's Kitchen
Big Thunder Barbecue, aka Festival of Foods, aka Celebration Roundup
and Barbecue
Casa de Fritos, aka Casa Mexicana
Chicken Plantation, aka Plantation House, aka Chicken Shack
Don DeFore's Silver Banjo Barbecue
Magnolia Tree Terrace
Malt Shop and Cone Shop
Oaks Tavern
Rancho del Zocalo Restaurante
River Belle Terrace
Ship to Shore Marketplace
Stage Door Café
Westward Ho Conestoga Wagon Fries
Wheelhouse and Delta Banjo

Stores

Bonanza Outfitters
Bone Carving Shop
Calico Kate's Pantry Shop
Davy Crockett's Pioneer Mercantile, aka Pioneer Mercantile
El Zocalo, aka El Zocalo Park
Frontier Trading Post
Indian Trading Post
Leather Shop
Pendleton Woolen Mills Dry Goods Store
Silver Spur Supplies
Westward Ho Trading Co.

Hub, aka Plaza Hub, aka Central Plaza

Attractions

Baby Station, aka Baby Center, aka Baby Care Center
Bandstand
Fantasy Faire
First Aid and Lost Children
Partners

Restaurants

Jolly Holiday Bakery Café
Little Red Wagon
Plaza Pavilion, aka Stouffer's in Disneyland Plaza Pavillion
Red Wagon Inn, aka Plaza Inn
Plaza Gardens, aka Carnation Plaza Gardens

Main Street, U.S.A., aka Main Street

Attractions

Carefree Corner
Disneyland Presents a Preview of Coming Attractions, aka Disneyland Showcase
The Legacy of Walt Disney
Main Street Cinema
Main Street Shooting Gallery
Main Street Vehicles
Main Street Windows
Penny Arcade

Restaurants

Blue Ribbon Bakery
Candy Palace, aka Candy Palace and Candy Kitchen
Carnation Café
Carnation Ice Cream Parlor
Gibson Girl Ice Cream Parlor
Main Street Cone Shop
Main Street Fruit Cart
Puffin Bakery, aka Puffin Bake Shop
Refreshment Corner, aka Coke Corner, aka Coca-Cola Refreshment Corner
Sunkist Citrus House

Stores

Blue Bird Shoes for Children
Candle Shop
Card Corner
Carriage Place Clothing Co.
China Closet
Chinatown
Coin Shop, aka Stamp and Coin Shop
Cole of California Swimsuits
Crystal Arcade
Crystal Arts
Disneyana
Disney Clothiers, Ltd.
Disney Showcase
Ellen's Gift Shop
Emporium, aka Disneyland Emporium
Fine Tobacco
Flower Mart, aka Flower Market
Fortuosity Shop
Gibson Greeting Cards
Glass Blower
Grandma's Baby Shop

Hallmark Card Shop
Hurricane Lamp Shop
Intimate Apparel, aka Corset Shop
Jemrock Shop, aka Jemrocks and Gem Shop
Jewelry Shop, aka Rings & Things
Kodak Camera Center, aka GAF Photo Salon, aka Polaroid Camera Center
Locker Area, aka Main Street Lockers & Storage
Main Street Magic Shop
Main Street Photo Supply Co.
Market House
New Century Watches & Clocks, aka New Century Timepieces and
    New Century Jewelry
Patented Pastimes, aka Great American Pastimes
Pen Shop
Ruggles China and Glass Shop
Silhouette Studio
Story Book Shop, aka Western Printing Book Shop
Sunny-View Farms Jams & Jellies
20th Century Music Company
Upjohn Pharmacy
Watches & Clocks, aka Timex Shop
Wurlitzer Music Hall
Yale & Towne Lock Shop

Mickey's Toontown

Attractions
Chip 'n Dale Tree House
Donald's Boat, aka *Miss Daisy*
Goofy's Bounce House, aka Goofy's Playhouse
Goofy's Gas Station
Gadget's Go Coaster
Jolly Trolley
Mickey's House
Minnie's House
Roger Rabbit's Car Toon Spin

Restaurants
Clarabelle's Frozen Yogurt
Daisy's Diner
Pluto's Dog House
Toon Up Treats

Stores
Gag Factory
Toontown Five & Dime

New Orleans Square

Attractions
Disney Gallery
The Haunted Mansion
Pirate's Arcade Museum
Pirates of the Caribbean
Portrait Artists

Restaurants
Blue Bayou
Candy Cart
Chocolate Collection, aka Chocolat Rue Royale
Club 33
Creole Café, aka Café Orleans
French Market
La Petite Patisserie
Mint Julep Bar
New Orleans Square Lemonade Stand
Royal Street Sweets
Royal Street Veranda

Stores
Bookstand
Cristal d'Orleans
Jewel of Orléans
La Boutique de Noël
La Boutique d'Or
Laffite's Silver Shop
La Mascarade d'Orléans
Le Bat en Rouge
Le Chapeau
Le Forgeron
Le Gourmet, aka Le Gourmet Shop
L'Ornement Magique
Marché aux Fleurs, Sacs et Mode
Mlle. Antoinette's Parfumerie
One-of-a-Kind Shop
Parasol Cart
Pieces of Eight
Port d'Orleans
Port Royal

Tomorrowland

Attractions

Adventures in Science
Adventure Thru Inner Space
Alpine Gardens
American Dairy Association Exhibit, aka Dairy Bar
American Space Experience
America Sings
Art of Animation
Astro-Jets, aka Tomorrowland Jets
Astro-Orbitor
Autopia, aka Tomorrowland Autopia, aka Autopia, Presented by Chevron
Avenue of the Flags
Bathroom of Tomorrow
Bell Telephone Systems Phone Exhibits
Buzz Lightyear Astro Blasters
Captain EO, aka *Captain EO* Tribute
Carousel of Progress
Circarama, aka Circle-Vision, aka Circle-Vision 360, aka World Premiere
    Circle-Vision
Clock of the World, aka World Clock
Club Buzz
Corridor of Murals
Cosmic Waves
Court of Honor
Fashions and Fabrics Through the Ages
Flight Circle, aka Thimble Drome Flight Circle
Flight to the Moon
Flying Saucers
Grand Canyon Diorama
Hall of Aluminum Fame
Hall of Chemistry
Honey, I Shrunk the Audience
House of the Future

Innoventions
Mad Hatter of Tomorrowland, aka Mod Hatter, Hatmosphere
Magic Eye Theater
Mermaids
Mission to Mars
Monorail, aka Disneyland- Alweg Monorail , aka Disneyland Monorail
    Moonliner
New York World's Fair Exhibit
Observatron
Our Future in Colors, aka Color Gallery

PeopleMover
Phantom Boats
Primeval World Diorama
Radio Disney Broadcast Booth
Rocket Jets
Rocket Man
Rocket Rods
Rocket to the Moon
Skyway to Fantasyland and Skyway to Tomorrowland
Space Girl and Space Man
Space Mountain, aka Rockin' Space Mountain
Space Station X-1, aka Satellite View of America
Starcade
Star Tours
Submarine Voyage, aka Finding Nemo Submarine Voyage
Tomorrowland Stage, aka Space Stage
Tomorrowland Terrace
Toy Story Funhouse
20,000 Leagues Under the Sea Exhibit
Viewliner
World Beneath Us Exhibit

Restaurants
Lunching Pad
Redd Rockett's Pizza Port
Space Bar
Space Place
Spirit of Refreshment
Yacht Club, aka Yacht Bar

Stores
Art Corner
Autopia Winner's Circle
Character Shop
Fun Fotos
Hobbyland
Little Green Men Store Command
Premiere Shop
Star Trader
Tomorrowlanding

Town Square

Attractions
Apartments
Babes in Toyland Exhibit

Bank of America, aka Bank of Main Street, aka Annual Pass Center,
   aka Annual Passport Processing Center
City Hall
Dalmatian Celebration
Fire Department, aka Fire Station
Flagpole
Great Moments with Mr. Lincoln
Guest Relations
Lost and Found
Opera House
Police Station
Santa Fe & Disneyland Railroad, aka Disneyland Railroad
Tour Guides
The Walt Disney Story, aka The Walt Disney Story, Featuring Great Moments
   with Mr. Lincoln

Restaurants
American Egg House
Hills Bros. Coffee House and Coffee Garden
Maxwell House Coffee Shop
Town Square Café

Stores
Jimmy Starr's Show Business Souvenirs
Mad Hatter of Main Street
Mickey Mouse Club Headquarters, aka Mickey Mouse Club Shop
Town Square Realty
Wonderland Music, aka Main Street Music

Other Park Locations
Berm
Entrance, aka Main Gate
Holidayland
Ken-L Land Pet Motel, aka Kennel Club, aka Pet Care Kennel
Marquee
Newsstand
Parking Lot
Pony Farm, aka Circle D Corral
Stroller Shop

Park Areas and Attractions Never Built
Discovery Bay
Duck Bumps
Edison Square

Garden of the Gods
International Street
Liberty Street
Lilliputian Land
Peter Pan Crocodile Aquarium
Reel-Ride
Rock Candy Mountain, aka Candy Mountain

Profiles of Disneyland Pioneers

Albright, Milt
Anderson, Ken
Aramaki, Hideo
Atencio, Francis Xavier
Baker, Buddy
Blair, Mary
Boyajian, Chuck
Broggie, Roger
Bruns, George
Burns, Harriet
Coats, Claude
Cottrell, Bill
Crump, Rolly
Davis, Alice
Davis, Marc
Davis, Marvin
Disney, Roy O.
Disney, Walt
Edgren, Don
Ellenshaw, Peter
Evans Brothers (Jack and Morgan)
Fowler, Joe
France, Van Arsdale
Gibson, Blaine
Goff, Harper
Gracey, Yale
Gurr, Bob
Hench, John
Irvine, Richard
Iwerks, Ub
Jani, Robert
Joerger, Fred
Jones, Mary
Justice, Bill
Kuri, Emile

Lindquist, Jack
Martin, Bill
McGinnis, George
McKim, Sam
Meck, Edward
Nunis, Dick
Olsen, Jack
Price, Harrison
Rigdon, Cicely
Rogers, Wathel
Ryman, Herb
Sherman Brothers (Robert and Richard)
Sklar, Martin
Walker, Tommy
Wood, C. V.

Profiles of Disneyland Performers
All-American College Band
Billy Hill and the Hillbillies
Boag, Wally
Burley, Fulton
Charles Dickens Carolers
Dapper Dans
Disneyland Band
Firehouse Five Plus Two
Frees, Paul
Kids of the Kingdom
Ravenscroft, Thurl
Royal Street Bachelors
Strawhatters
Taylor, Betty
Tinker Bell
Wagner, Jack
Walker, Vesey

Events and Celebrations
America on Parade
Blast to the Past Celebration
Circus Fantasy
Date Nite
Disneyland After Dark
Dixieland at Disneyland
Dream Machine

Family Fun Weekends
Family Reunion
Fireworks
40 Years of Adventure
Gift-Giver Extraordinaire Machine
Give a Day, Get a Disney Day
Grad Nite
Halloween Time
Happiest Homecoming on Earth
Holiday Season
Let the Memories Begin
Light Magic
Love Bug Day
The Magic, the Memories, and You!
Main Street Electrical Parade
New Year's Eve Party
Opening Day
Parades
Skyfest
Spring Fling
State Fair
Tencennial
What Will You Celebrate?
Year of a Million Dreams
Yippie Day
Zorro Days

Films and Television
A Day at Disneyland
Disneyland: The First 50 Magical Years
Disneyland Fun: It's a Small World
Disneyland TV Series
Disneyland, U.S.A.
40 Pounds of Trouble
Gala Day at Disneyland
Khrushchev in Disneyland
The Magic of Disneyland
Meet Me at Disneyland

Miscellaneous
Attraction Posters
Audio-Animatronics
Cast Members

Disney Dollars
Disney Vacation Club Information Desks
FASTPASS
Fun Maps
Hidden Mickeys
Magic Kingdom Club
Miss Disneyland, aka Disneyland Ambassador to the World
Omnimover
Passports
Photo Collages
Pin Trading Stations
Popcorn Carts
Queues
Restrooms
Souvenir Books, aka Souvenir Guide Books, aka Pictorial Souvenir Books
Ticket Books
Trash Cans

Notes on the Photographs

(all photographs by Chris Strodder except where noted;
dates in parentheses indicate the year each photograph was taken)

116 *Top:* Bill Cottrell's Main Street window at the Market House (2007).
     Bottom: The heads of three Jamboree characters, still mounted inside today's Many Adventures of Winnie the Pooh (2007).

119 *Top:* Cristal d'Orleans exterior (2007).
     Bottom: Critter Country statue near Splash Mountain (2010).

120 Critter Country Fruit Cart near the Rivers of America (2011).

121 *Top:* Rolly Crump's Main Street window near the Silhouette Studio (2010).
     Bottom: Crystal Arcade exterior at night (2007).

122 Daisy's Diner exterior (2010).

124 The Dapper Dans outside City Hall (2010).

125 Marc Davis's Main Street window at the Disneyana shop (2008).

128 Themed signage outside Pioneer Mercantile (2011).

130 Disneyana exterior (2007).

131 *Top:* Disney Clothiers, Ltd. exterior (2009).
     Bottom: The front of a Disney Dollars bill (2011).

132 View from the Disney Gallery when it was in New Orleans Square (2007).

133 Disneyland After Dark brochure, ca. 1964 (2011).

134 A Main Street store display with Disneyland Band themes (2011).

136 Themed signage outside the Opera House (2007).

139 Roy Disney's initials in a New Orleans Square railing (2010).

140 *Top:* Disney Showcase exterior (2007).
     Bottom: Disney Vacation Club Information Desk, themed for Tomorrowland (2011).

141 Walt Disney's bust at the Academy of Television Arts and Sciences in North Hollywood, California (2011).

142 Walt Disney's final resting place at Forest Lawn Memorial Park in Glendale, California (2011).

143 Displayed in the Opera House, this is "the actual park bench from the Griffith Park Merry-Go-Round in Los Angeles, where Walt Disney first dreamed of Disneyland," according to the plaque (2010).

145 *Top:* Walt Disney's window at Toontown's library (2007).
     Bottom: Walt Disney's initials in a New Orleans Square railing (2010).

147 Walt Disney's star on the Harbor Boulevard walkway into Disneyland (2007).

148 Daisy Duck on the prow of Donald's Boat (2010).

149 Don DeFore's star on the Hollywood Walk of Fame (2011).

150 Timothy Q. Mouse conducting Dumbo the Flying Elephant (2007).

151 *Top:* Elephants waiting to take off at Dumbo the Flying Elephant (2010).
     Bottom: Edelweiss Snacks exterior (2010).

152 Don Edgren's Main Street window at the Silhouette Studio (2010).

153 Peter Ellenshaw's 1954 painting on view in the Opera House (2010).

154 El Zocalo at Halloween (2010).

155 *Top:* Emporium exterior at night (2007).
     Bottom: One of the Emporium's interior displays near the ceiling (2010).

156 *Top:* Enchanted Chamber exterior (2010).
     Bottom: Enchanted Cottage exterior (2008).

157 *Top:* Enchanted Tiki Room statue (2011).
     Bottom: Display outside the Enchanted Tiki Room (2011).

158 Plaque above the tunnel entrance into Town Square (2008).

209 *Top:* Heraldry Shoppe exterior (2011).
Bottom (left to right): Hidden Mickeys at the King Arthur Carrousel and at a ticket booth (2007).

210 *Clockwise from top left:* Hidden Mickeys on a Toontown tire; on a Hub lamppost; inside Pirates of the Caribbean; in a Tomorrowland window; on a bench near the main entrance; on a vent inside the Golden Horseshoe (easy to miss in the vent's lower right-hand corner); and on a post outside Splash Mountain (2007–2010).

212 Main Street lamppost during the winter holidays (2010).

213 It's a Small World exterior during the winter holidays (2010).

214 Themed signage at *Honey, I Shrunk the Audience* (2007).

215 House of the Future banner hanging outside the Innoventions building (2008).

216 *Top:* The circular Hub, depicted on the large Disneyland model inside the Opera House, with Sleeping Beauty Castle at the top (2010).
Bottom: One of the many character statues at the Hub (2009).

217 Indiana Jones Adventure exterior (2010).

219 A welcoming figure just outside today's Indian Village display at the north end of Frontierland, as viewed from the Rivers of America (2010).

220 Canoe on the Rivers of America, Tom Sawyer Island on the right (2007).

221 Innoventions exterior (2010).

223 The porch outside the Silhouette Studio (formerly Intimate Apparel) (2007).

224 Jessie, the cowgirl from the *Toy Story* movies, inside It's a Small World (2010).

226 It's a Small World Toy Shop exterior (2010).

228 Themed signage outside Jewel of Orléans (2010).

230 Jolly Trolley parked in Mickey's Toontown (2007).

231 Jungle Cruise tiger (2009).

232 The Jungle Cruise's legendary "back side of water" (2010).

234 Bill Justice's Main Street window by the Main Street Cone Shop (2007).

235 Kennel Club exterior (2010).

237 Carrousel steeds (2008).

238 Ariel's statue in King Triton Gardens (2007).

240 Emile Kuri's Main Street window at the Market House (2011).

241 In today's New Orleans Square, themed signage mentions an extinct shop (2010).

242 Le Bat en Rouge exterior (2010).

244 Le Petit Chalet exterior (2007).

245 Themed signage outside the main entrance (2011).

247 The Jack Lindquist pumpkin in Mickey's Toontown (2010).

248 *Top:* Mural inside Little Green Men Store Command (2007)
Bottom: Little Red Wagon parked next to the Plaza Inn (2008).

249 *Top:* Main Street Lockers & Storage exterior (2011).
Bottom: L'Ornement Magique exterior (2011).

251 Mad Hatter of Fantasyland exterior (2011).

252 Mad Hatter of Main Street exterior (2010).

253 Teacups and Tudor at the Mad Hatter's Mad Tea Party (2010).

257 Tilly, the ticket taker from Marceline, outside the Main Street Cinema (2010).

258 Themed signage above the Main Street Cone Shop (2008).

259 *Top:* Main Street Fruit Cart parked at East Center Street (2007).
Bottom: Main Street Magic Shop exterior (2010).

260 Main Street Photo Supply Co. exterior (2007).

262 Hotel Marceline on East Center Street (2010).

264 The western side of Main Street at night (2011).

265 Double-decker omnibus parked at the Main Street Depot (2010).

268 Elias Disney's Main Street window at the Emporium (2009).

269 The Many Adventures of Winnie the Pooh interior (2010).

270 *Top:* Market House exterior (2011).
Bottom: Mural near the *Mark Twain* dock (2010).

271 *Mark Twain* dockside, with Big Thunder Mountain in background (2007).

272 A reminder of the old Disneyland marquee can be found nearby, at the Disneyland Hotel's pool (2011).

273 Marquee at Harbor Boulevard's pedestrian entrance into Disneyland (2010).

275 Matterhorn waterfalls and bobsleds (2008).

276 The Matterhorn and a submarine, viewed from the Monorail platform; (2010).

277 At the Matterhorn site, a cast of a footprint discovered on the "south slope" (2007).

279 Sam McKim's Main Street window at the Main Street Photo Supply Co. (2008).

284 Mickey's House exterior (2011).

285 *Top:* Fountain in Mickey's Toontown (2008).
Bottom: The top of City Hall in Mickey's Toontown (2009).

286 Midget Autopia car displayed along today's Autopia roadway (2009).

287 *Left:* A crate next to the Rivers of America (2010).
Right: Keel boat tied up on the Rivers of America (2008).

289 The Mineral Hall window at Rancho del Zocalo (2010).

290 Mine Train at the base of Big Thunder Mountain, as viewed from the Rivers of America (2007).

291 *Top:* Minnie's House exterior (2008).
Bottom: Themed signage outside the Mint Julep Bar (2010).

294 Mlle. Antoinette's Parfumerie exterior (2011).

295 The Monorail above the Tomorrowland lagoon (2010).

296 The Monorail under the PeopleMover track (2007).

297 The *Moonliner* viewed from Space Mountain's upper walkway (2010).

300 Painting inside Mr. Toad's Wild Ride (2009).

303 Nature's Wonderland, 1962. Fantasyland can be seen at the top, the Golden Horseshoe and the *Columbia* are to the upper right, and Cascade Peak and Tom Sawyer Island are to the lower right. Courtesy of Orange County Archives.

304 New Century Watches & Clocks exterior (2007).

305 *Top:* Stairway in New Orleans Square's Court des Anges (2010).
Bottom: Court des Anges sign in New Orleans Square (2011).

307 *Top:* New Orleans Square metalwork (2010).
Bottom: New Orleans Square Lemonade Stand (2011).

308 Newsstand at the main entrance (2008).

310 The Observatron at rest (2008).

311 Omnimover vehicle—a "Doom Buggy"—inside the Haunted Mansion (2011).

314 Walt Disney's Opening Day speech, memorialized on a Town Square plaque (2010).

315 The sign at the Main Street depot, declaring a population of 5,000,000 in 1955 (2010).

317 Top of the Opera House (2010).

319 *The Lion King* float in Walt Disney's Parade of Dreams (2007).

320 *The Princess and the Frog* float in Mickey's Soundsational Parade (2011). Photo by Sarah Guenther Ross of Cotati, CA.

321 Parasol Cart near the French Market (2011).

322 Approaching Disneyland's parking lot entrance from Harbor Boulevard in the 1970s. Courtesy of the Anaheim Public Library.

323 *Partners* statue in the Hub, with Sleeping Beauty Castle in the background (2008).

324 Annual Passport (2010).

326 Penny Arcade exterior at night (2006).

327 PeopleMover track at the Tomorrowland entrance (2007).

329 Mural inside Peter Pan's Flight (2010).

330 Petrified Tree in Frontierland (2007).

331 Photo collage displayed inside the Opera House (2007).

332 Pieces of Eight exterior (2011).

333 *Top:* Mural inside Pinocchio's Daring Journey (2008).
Bottom: Pinocchio's Daring Journey exterior (2007).

334 *Top:* Pin Trading Station formerly outside the Plaza Pavilion (2007).
Bottom: Fortune Red, the fortune-telling pirate (2010).

337 The famous jail scene inside Pirates of the Caribbean (2010).

338 Oversized objects at Pixie Hollow (2010).

339 Exiting the realm of Pixie Hollow and entering the realm of the Pixie Hollow Gift Cart (2011).

340 Carnation Plaza Gardens entrance (2010).

341 *Top:* The double roof above the Plaza Pavilion (2010).
Bottom: Plaza Pavilion exterior at twilight (2011).

342 Pluto's Dog House exterior (2011).

343 *Top:* Police Department exterior at dusk (2011).
Bottom: Free coloring paper themed to the Circle D Corral, available at Big Thunder Ranch (2011).

344 Themed signage at Pooh Corner (2011).

345 *Top:* Abominable Snowman inside the Popcorn Cart near the Matterhorn (2011).
Bottom: Portrait Artist easel, New Orleans Square (2008).

346 Port Royal exterior (2011).

348 Primeval World Diorama interior (2010).

349 Princess Fantasy Faire entrance (2009).

350 *Left:* Prof. Barnaby Owl, star of *Disneyland Fun*, as shown on themed signage in Critter Country (2010).
Right: Professor Barnaby Owl's Photographic Art Studio exterior (2009).

351 Bird in the Jungle Cruise queue (2010).

352 Winding queue outside the Mad Hatter's Mad Tea Party (2010).

353 Raft on the Rivers of America (2007).

354 Zorro-themed metalwork above the Rancho del Zocalo entrance (2008).

355 Themed signage outside Redd Rockett's Pizza Port, with the *Moonliner* at left (2008).

356 Plaza Inn interior (2010).

357 *Top:* Refreshment Corner exterior (2007).
Bottom (left to right): Three restroom signs in Fantasyland and one in Frontierland (2007–2010).

358 *Top row (left to right):* Restrooms signs in Frontierland, Critter Country, and Tomorrowland.
Middle row (left to right): In Town Square, Fantasyland, and Adventureland.
Bottom row (left to right): In Mickey's Toontown, New Orleans Square, and Critter Country (2007–2011).

359 River Belle Terrace exterior in Frontierland (2011).

360 "Wildlife" along the Rivers of America (2010).

362 A Rocket Jets vehicle as a display case inside Little Green Men Store Command (2009).

363 A modern Rocket Man display inside Innoventions (2011).

364 Rocket to the Moon attraction poster (2011).

365 Roger Rabbit's Car Toon Spin interior (2010).

366 Roger Rabbit's fountain near his Car Toon Spin (2010).

367 The Royal Street Bachelors at the French Market (2007).

369 Herb Ryman's landmark 1953 drawing, displayed in the Opera House (2007).

370 Sailing Ship *Columbia* on the Rivers of America, with Tom Sawyer Island in the background (2007).

372 The *Ward Kimball* pulling into the New Orleans Square/Frontierland station (2009).

373 Main Street station (2010).

374 Live reindeer at Big Thunder Ranch (2010).

375 The Sherman Brothers' Main Street window at the 20th Century Music Company (2010).

376 *Top:* Ship to Shore Marketplace exterior, with the *Mark Twain* in the background (2011).
Bottom: Silhouette Studio exterior (2009).

377 Silver Spur Supplies exterior (2011).

378 Martin Sklar's Town Square window at City Hall (2011).

379 Skull Rock as depicted in a Peter Pan Flight mural (2011).

380 Fantasyland's Skyway terminal, intact but unused (2009).

381 Bridge leading into Sleeping Beauty Castle (2009).

382 Sleeping Beauty Castle exterior (2011).

383 *Top:* Spouts on the front of Sleeping Beauty Castle (2009).
Bottom: Statue in front of Sleeping Beauty Castle (2011).

384 *Top:* Moat in front of Sleeping Beauty Castle (2008).
Bottom: Sleeping Beauty Castle Walk-Through interior (2011).

385 Snow White's Scary Adventures interior (2011).

386 Uppermost area of the Snow White Wishing Well and Grotto (2011).

387 *Top:* Shrunken Ned inside South Seas Traders (2011).
Bottom: Souvenir book from 1957 (2007).

388 *Top to Bottom:* Souvenir books from 1955, 1960, 1961, and 1964 (2008–2011).

389 *Top to Bottom:* Souvenir books from 1965, 1968, and 1989 (2009–2011).

390 *Top to Bottom:* Souvenir books from 1992 and 2000 (2010–2011).

392 Space Mountain exterior (2010).

393 A 1977 poster for Space Mountain, displayed inside the Star Trader (2010).

395 *Top:* Space Station X-1 attraction poster (2008).
Bottom: Spirit of Refreshment below the *Moonliner* (2009).

396 Splash Mountain attraction poster (2008).

397 Splash Mountain's Chickapin Hill (2010).

399 *Top:* Walt Disney with Orange County supervisors and other officials, seven months before Disneyland opened. Photo from the Willard Smith Collection, courtesy of Orange County Archives.
Bottom: Stage Door Café exterior (2010).

400 The *Star Wars* X-Wing fighter that used to hang above the ramp to the Starcade (2007).

401 Star Tours interior (2011).

402 Star Trader exterior (2011).

403 Cinderella's castle in Storybook Land (2010).

404 Part of Alice's Village in Storybook Land (2010).

406 *Top:* Stromboli's Wagon parked near the Casey Jr. Circus Train (2008).
Bottom: Submarine Voyage attraction poster (2009).

407 Submarine Voyage view below the lagoon surface (2009).

409 Swiss Family Treehouse attraction poster (2008).

410 Site for the Sword in the Stone Ceremony, with King Arthur Carrousel in the background (2009).

412 *Top:* Tangled exterior (2010).
Bottom: Tarzan's Treehouse interior (2010).

414 *Top:* Themed signage for Teddi Barra outside Pooh Corner (2011).
Bottom: Themed signage outside Three Fairies Magic Crystals (2007).

416 *Top:* A former ticket booth still on view outside of Alice in Wonderland (2010).
Bottom: An A ticket, ca. 1975 (2010).

417 Themed signage outside the Tiki Juice Bar (2011).

418 *Top:* Tropical Imports exterior (2010).
Bottom: Tinker Bell in Mickey's Soundsational Parade (2011). Photo by Sarah Guenther Ross of Cotati, CA.

419 Themed signage inside Tinker Bell & Friends (2008).

420 Once Upon a Time exterior (2008).

421 The Monorail and a submarine circling Tomorrowland's lagoon (2007).

423 Tomorrowlanding exterior (2010).

424 Themed signage at Tomorrowland Terrace (2009).

425 Pontoon bridge at Tom Sawyer Island (2010).

426 Sam McKim's 1957 map, handed out free at Tom Sawyer Island (2008).

427 Dead Man's Grotto, formerly Injun Joe's Cave (2010).

429 *Top:* Toontown Five & Dime exterior (2008).
Bottom: Toon Up Treats exterior (2009).

430 Topiary dolphin outside It's a Small World (2010).

431 Guided Tours exterior (2010).

432 *Top:* One of the two historic cannons in Town Square (2011).
Bottom: Town Square, depicted in the large Disneyland model inside the Opera House (2010).

433 Today's site of yesterday's Town Square Café (2009).

434 A trash can in Adventureland (2010).

435 *Top row (left to right):* Trash cans at the main entrance, in Fantasyland, in New Orleans Square, and in Tomorrowland.
Lower row (left to right): On Main Street, in Frontierland, at the Hub, and at Haunted Mansion; 2010-2011 photos.
Bottom: Trash can outside It's a Small World (2011).

436 Troubadour Tavern exterior (2011).

437 20,000 Leagues Under the Sea attraction poster (2010).

438 Two Upjohn executives on a Main Street window at the Fortuosity Shop (2011).

441 Village Haus exterior (2010).

443 Magical Fireworks attraction poster (2010).

444 Free pamphlet handed out at Great Moments with Mr. Lincoln (2007).

446 *Top:* Westward Ho Conestoga Wagon Fries exterior (2007).
Bottom: Westward Ho Trading Co. exterior (2009).

447 What Will You Celebrate? button, distributed at City Hall (2010).

451 Year of a Million Dreams banner (2007).

453 *Top:* Zorro imagery on a mural outside Rancho del Zocalo Restaurante (2010).
Bottom: Exit sign at Harbor Boulevard (2011).

454 *Top:* Display along the Jungle Cruise (2008).
Bottom: Mural at Peter Pan's Flight (2008).

455 *Top:* Alice in Wonderland interior (2010).
Middle: Autopia car and submarine (2011).

456 *Top:* The scary witch inside Snow White's Scary Adventures (2011).
Middle: Looking through Monstro toward the buildings of the Storybook Land Canal Boats (2008).

457 *Top:* Live animals at Big Thunder Ranch (2008).
Bottom: Quiet areas are scattered throughout Disneyland; this serene walkway is near Fowler's Harbor in Frontierland (2010).

458 Topiary serpent outside It's a Small World (2007).

459 Horse-drawn trolley on Main Street (2007).

460 *Top:* Themed signage in Mickey's Toontown (2009).
Middle: Books on the shelves inside Minnie's House (2007).
Bottom: Entrance into Toon Park in Mickey's Toontown (2009).

461 Haunted Mansion gargoyle (2011).

462 *Top:* Astro-Orbitor at night (2008).
Bottom: The Monorail crossing Disneyland's main entrance (2011).

463 *Top:* Themed signage at the Hub (2011).
Bottom: A mailbox in Frontierland (2011).

464 *Top:* Mural outside the Bank of Main Street, reminding guests that "a penny saved is a penny earned" (2008).
Bottom: The Disneyland Railroad's *Lilly Belle* observation car (2008).

465 Doll inside It's a Small World (2008).

466 *Top:* Fowler's Inn Exterior (2011).
Bottom: The Matterhorn looms behind Fantasyland architecture (2006).

467 *Top:* Halloween pumpkins on Main Street (2010).
Bottom: Balloons at the Hub, with Sleeping Beauty Castle in the background (2007).

468 Early morning on Main Street in 1959. Courtesy of the Anaheim Public Library.

488 Minnie heading backstage (2011).

Bibliography

Adams, Judith A. *The American Amusement Park Industry: A History of Technology and Thrills*. Boston, MA: Twayne Publishers, 1991.

Anonymous. *Disneyland: The First Quarter Century*. Burbank, CA: Walt Disney Productions, 1979.

———. *Disneyland: The First Thirty Years*. Burbank, CA: Walt Disney Productions, 1985.

Bailey, Adrian. *Walt Disney's World of Fantasy*. New York: Everest House, 1982.

Bakshi, Shahnaaz, ed. *Eyewitness Travel: Walt Disney World Resort & Orlando*. New York: DK Publishing, Inc., 2007.

Benham, Reyner. *Los Angeles: The Architecture of Four Ecologies*. New York: Harper & Row, Publishers, Inc., 1971.

Bright, Randy. *Disneyland Inside Story*. New York: Harry N. Abrams, Inc., 1987.

Britten, Loretta, and Sarah Brash, eds. *The American Dream: The 50s*. Alexandria, VA: Time-Life Books, 1998.

Broggie, Michael. *Walt Disney's Railroad Story*. Pasadena, CA: Pentrex Media Group, 1997.

Canemaker, John. *Paper Dreams: The Art & Artists of Disney Storyboards*. New York: Hyperion, 1999.

Carlson, Peter. *K Blows Top*. New York: PublicAffairs, 2009.

Childs, Valerie. *The Magic of Disneyland and Walt Disney World*. New York: Mayflower Books, Inc., 1979.

De Roos, Robert. "The Magic Worlds of Walt Disney." *National Geographic*. August 1963.

Dunlop, Beth. *Building a Dream: The Art of Disney Architecture*. New York: Harry N. Abrams, Inc., 1996.

Eco, Umberto. *Travels in Hyperreality*. New York: Harcourt Brace Jovanovich, Publishers, 1986.

Eisen, Jonathan, David Fine, and Kim Eisen, eds. *Unknown California*. New York: Macmillan Publishing Company, 1985.

Eliot, Marc. *Walt Disney: Hollywood's Dark Prince*. New York: Carol Publishing Group, 1993.

Evans, Morgan. *Walt Disney Disneyland World of Flowers*. Burbank, CA: Walt Disney Productions, 1965.

Finch, Christopher. *The Art of Walt Disney*. New York: Harry N. Abrams, Inc., 1975.

———. *Walt Disney's America*. New York: Abbeville Press, Inc., Publishers, 1978.

France, Van Arsdale. *Window on Main Street*. Nashua, NH: Laughter Publications Inc., 1991.

Gabler, Neal. *Walt Disney: The Triumph of the American Imagination*. New York: Alfred A. Knopf, 2006.

Geissman, Grant, ed. *MAD About the Fifties*. NY: E. C. Publications, 2005.

———, ed. *MAD About the Eighties*. Nashville, TN: Rutledge Hill Press, Inc., 1999.

Giroux, Henry A., and Grace Pollock. *The Mouse That Roared: Disney and the End of Innocence*. Lanham, MD: Rowman & Littlefield Publisher, Inc., 2010.

Gordon, Bruce, and David Mumford. *Disneyland: The Nickel Tour*. Santa Clarita, CA: Camphor Tree Publishers, 2000.

Gordon, Bruce, and Tim O'Day. *Disneyland: Then, Now, and Forever*. Santa Clarita, CA: Camphor Tree/Disney Editions, 2005.

Graebner, William, ed. *True Stories from the American Past*. New York: McGraw-Hill, Inc., 1993.

Grant, John. *Encyclopedia of Walt Disney's Animated Characters*. New York: Harper & Row, Publishers, 1987.

Green, Amy Boothe, and Howard E. Green. *Remembering Walt: Favorite Memories of Walt Disney*. New York: Hyperion, 1999.

Greene, Richard and Katherine. *The Man Behind the Magic*. New York: Viking, 1998.

Hagerty, Jack, and Jon Rogers. *The Saucer Fleet*. Ontario, Canada: Apogee Books, 2008.

Harasberger, Caroline Thomas, ed. *Everyone's Mark Twain*. Cranbury, NJ: A.S. Barnes and Co., Inc., 1972.

Harris, Richard. *Early Amusement Parks of Orange County*. Mount Pleasant, SC: Arcadia Publishing, 2008.

Hart, James D. *A Companion to California*. Berkeley, CA: University of California Press, 1987.

Hemingway, Ernest. *A Moveable Feast*. New York: Charles Scribner's Sons, Ltd., 1964.

Hench, John, and Peggy Van Pelt. *Designing Disney: Imagineering and the Art of the Show*. New York: Disney Editions, 2003.

Hulse, Jerry. "Dream Realized—Disneyland Opens." *Los Angeles Times*, July 18, 1955, B1.

The Imagineers (text by Kevin Rafferty, and Bruce Gordon). *Walt Disney Imagineering: A Behind the Dreams Look at Making the Magic Real*. New York: Hyperion, 1996.

The Imagineers (text by Alex Wright). *The Imagineering Field Guide to Disneyland*. New York: Disney Editions, 2008.

Jackson, Kathy Merlock, ed. *Walt Disney Conversations*. Jackson, MS: University Press of Mississippi, 2006.

Kaplan, Sam Hall. *L.A. Lost & Found*. New York: Crown Publishers, Inc., 1987.

Kaufman, J.B. *The Walt Disney Family Museum: The Man, The Magic, The Memories*. New York: Disney Editions, 2009.

Koenig, David. *More Mouse Tales: A Closer Peek Backstage at Disneyland*. Irvine, CA: Bonaventure Press, 2002.

———. *Mouse Tales: A Behind-the-Ears Look at Disneyland*. Irvine, CA: Bonaventure Press, 1995.

———. *Mouse Under Glass: Secrets of Disney Animation and Theme Parks*. Irvine, CA: Bonaventure Press, 1997.

Korkis, Jim. *The Vault of Walt*. USA: Ayefour Publishing, 2010.

Kurtti, Jeff, and Bruce Gordon. *The Art of Disneyland*. New York: Disney Editions, 2006.

Kurtti, Jeff. *Disneyland: From Once Upon a Time to Happily Ever After*. New York: Disney Editions, 2010.

———. *Disneyland Through the Decades: A Photographic Celebration*. New York: Disney Editions, 2010.

———. *Walt Disney's Imagineering Legends and the Genesis of the Disney Theme Park*. New York: Disney Editions, 2008.

Lawson, Kristan, and Anneli Rufus. *California Babylon*. New York: St. Martin's Griffin, 2000.

Lefkon, Wendy, ed. *Disney Insider Yearbook 2005*. New York: Disney Editions, 2006.

Lindquist, Jack. *In Service to the Mouse*. Orange, CA: Chapman University Press, 2010.

Maltin, Leonard. *The Disney Films*. New York: Popular Library, 1978.

Marlin, Karal Ann. *As Seen on TV*. Cambridge, MA: Harvard University Press, 1994.

Marling, Karal Ann, ed. *Designing Disney's Theme Parks: The Architecture of Reassurance*. New York: Flammarion, 1998.

Marling, Karal Ann, and Donna R. Braden. *Behind the Magic: 50 Years of Disneyland*. Oakland, CA: The Henry Ford, 2005.

Martin, Steve. *Born Standing Up*. New York: Scribner, 2007.

May, Kirse Granat. *Golden State, Golden Youth*. Chapel Hill, NC: University of North Carolina Press, 2002.

Miller, Diane Disney. *The Story of Walt Disney*. New York: Henry Holt and Company, 1957.

Moore, Charles, Peter Becker, and Regula Campbell. *The City Observed: Los Angeles*. Santa Monica, CA: Hennessey + Ingalls, 1998.

Mosley, Leonard. *Disney's World: A Biography*. New York: Stein and Day/Publishers, 1985.

O'Rourke, P. J. *Holidays in Heck*. New York: Atlantic Monthly Press, 2011.

Palm, Carl. *The Great California Story*. Austin, TX: Northcross Books, 2004.

Price, Harrison. *Walt's Revolution! By the Numbers*. Orlando, FL: Ripley Entertainment Inc., 2003.

Ridgway, Charles. *Spinning Disney's World*. Branford, CT: The Intrepid Traveler, 2007.

Rolle, Andrew. *California: A History*, 5th Edition. Wheeling, IL: Harlan Davidson, Inc., 1998.

Samuelson, Dale. *The American Amusement Park*. St. Paul, MN: MBI Publishing Company, 2001.

Schickel, Richard. *The Disney Version: The Life, Times, Art and Commerce of Walt Disney*, 3rd edition. Chicago, IL: Ivan R. Dee, Publishers, 1997.

Schroeder, Russell, ed. *Walt Disney: His Life in Pictures*. New York: Disney Press, 1996.

Schwartz, Richard A. *The 1950s: An Eyewitness History*. New York: Facts on File, Inc., 2003

Sehlinger, Bob, and Len Testa. *The Unofficial Guide to Disneyland 2011*. Hoboken, NJ: John Wiley & Sons, Inc., 2011.

Seidenbaum, Art. *Los Angeles 200: A Bicentennial Celebration*. New York: Harry N. Abrams, Inc., 1980.

Sklar, Martin A. *Walt Disney's Disneyland*. Anaheim, CA: Walt Disney Productions, 1964.

———. *Walt Disney's Disneyland*. Anaheim, CA: Walt Disney Productions, 1969.

Smith, Dave. *Disney A to Z: The Official Encyclopedia*. New York: Disney Editions, 1998.

———, ed. *The Quotable Walt Disney*. New York: Disney Editions, 2001.

Sorkin, Michael, ed. *Variations on a Theme Park*. New York: Hill and Wang, 1992.

Starr, Kevin. *Golden Dreams: California in an Age of Abundance, 1950-1963*. New York: Oxford University Press, 2009.

———. *Over California: Photography by Reg Morrison*. San Francisco, CA: Collins Publishers, Inc., 1990.

Stewart, James B. *Disney War*. New York: Simon and Schuster, 2005.

Surrell, Jason. *The Haunted Mansion: From the Magic Kingdom to the Movies*. New York: Disney Editions, 2003.

Thie, Carlene. *Disneyland . . . The Beginning*. Riverside, CA: Ape Pen Publishing Company, 2003.

Thomas, Bob. *Walt Disney: An American Original*. New York: Simon and Schuster, 1976.

Thomas, Frank, and Ollie Johnston. *Disney Animation: The Illusion of Life*. New York: Abbeville Press, Inc., Publishers, 1981.

Trahan, Kendra. *Disneyland Detective*. Mission Viejo, CA: PermaGrin Publishing, 2005.

Travaglini, Alexia, ed. *Frommer's California 2010*. Hoboken, New Jersey: Wiley Publishing, Inc., 2010.

Twain, Mark. *The Complete Tom Sawyer*. New York: Gramercy Books, 1996.

Watkins, Gaven R., ed. *Michelin California: The Green Guide*. Greenville, SC: Michelin Maps and Guides, 2007.

Watts, Steven. *The Magic Kingdom: Walt Disney and the American Way of Life*. Boston: Houghton Mifflin Company, 1997.

Yee, Kevin, and Jason Schultz. *Magic Quizdom*. Anaheim, CA: Zauberreich Press, 2004.

———. *101 Things You Never Knew About Disneyland*. Anaheim, CA: Zauberreich Press, 2005.

Zibart, Eve. *This Day in History: Disney*. Cincinnati, OH: Emmis Books, 2006.

10 Recommended DVDs with Disneyland Footage

(release dates are for the DVDs, not the theatrical films)

The Boys (film plus special features). Walt Disney Home Entertainment, 2010.

Disneyland Fun. Walt Disney Home Entertainment, 2005.

40 Pounds of Trouble. Universal Pictures, 2010.

The Haunted Mansion (special features). Walt Disney Video, 2004.

Pirates of the Caribbean: The Curse of the Black Pearl (special features). Walt Disney Video, 2003.

Sleeping Beauty (special features). Walt Disney Home Entertainment, 2008.

Swiss Family Robinson (special features). Walt Disney Video, 2002.

The Love Bug (special features). Walt Disney Home Entertainment, 2003.

Walt Disney Treasures: Disneyland Secrets, Stories & Magic. Walt Disney Video, 2007.

Walt Disney Treasures: Disneyland U.S.A. Walt Disney Video, 2001.

12 Recommended Websites

The Disneyland Encyclopedia (contact information for this book): www.encycoolpedia.com

Disney Legends (official Disney site): www.disney.go.com/disneyinsider/history/legends/find-legends

Disneyland Resort (official Disney site): www.disneyland.com

DLDHistory (unofficial fan site): www.dldhistory.com

FindingMickey.com (unofficial fan site): www.findingmickey.com

JustDisney.com (unofficial fan site): www.justdisney.com

LaughingPlace.com (unofficial fan site): www.laughingplace.com

MiceAge (unofficial fan site): www.miceage.com

MousePlanet (unofficial fan site): www.mouseplanet.com

Orange County Register (local newspaper): www.ocregister.com

Walt's Magic Kingdom (unofficial fan site): www.waltsmagickingdom.com

Yesterland (unofficial fan site): www.yesterland.com

About the Author

This second edition of *The Disneyland® Encyclopedia* is Chris Strodder's eighth book, the seventh published since the year 2000. Among his other works are the children's book *A Sky for Henry*, an adventure story for young adults called *Lockerboy*, the comic novel *The Wish Book*, the *Stories Light and Dark* collection of short fiction, a pop culture compendium entitled *The Encyclopedia of Sixties Cool*, and *Swingin' Chicks of the '60s*, a popular nonfiction volume of profiles that garnered international attention, coverage in dozens of magazines ranging from the *National Enquirer* to *Playboy*, and exposure on national TV and radio shows. The previous edition of *The Disneyland® Encyclopedia* was widely praised and named a "Best Reference Book" for 2008 by *Library Journal*. Strodder lives in the green hills of Mill Valley, California.

About the Illustrator

Coming from a family of artists and scientists, Tristan Tang enjoyed a wonderfully creative childhood in which she was encouraged to have a strong sense of curiosity and to fully develop her artistic self. She was able to combine her interests in mixed media art forms with cultural anthropology while completing her Fine Art degree. After enjoying rewarding work experiences in photography and scientific illustration, Tang discovered a love for visual effects and has worked as an artist on many films, commercials, and games. Some of her past Disney projects include the film *Pirates of the Caribbean: The Curse of the Black Pearl* and commercials for Disney's Animal Kingdom and Cruise Line. Tristan dedicates the illustrations in *The Disneyland® Encyclopedia* to her children, Trey and Anya. She thanks her husband, Alex, for his artistic contributions and inspiration on this project and her extended family for their infinite support.

Index